The series Lecture Notes in Computer Science (LNCS), including its subseries Lecture Notes in Artificial Intelligence (LNAI) and Lecture Notes in Bioinformatics (LNBI), has established itself as a medium for the publication of new developments in computer science and information technology research, teaching, and education.

LNCS enjoys close cooperation with the computer science R & D community, the series counts many renowned academics among its volume editors and paper authors, and collaborates with prestigious societies. Its mission is to serve this international community by providing an invaluable service, mainly focused on the publication of conference and workshop proceedings and postproceedings. LNCS commenced publication in 1973.

Lecture Notes in Computer Science   13765

Founding Editors

Gerhard Goos
Juris Hartmanis

Editorial Board Members

Paolo Masci · Cinzia Bernardeschi ·
Pierluigi Graziani · Mario Koddenbrock ·
Maurizio Palmieri

Editors

Software Engineering and Formal Methods

SEFM 2022 Collocated Workshops

AI4EA, F-IDE, CoSim-CPS, CIFMA
Berlin, Germany, September 26–30, 2022
Revised Selected Papers

Springer

Editors
Paolo Masci ⓘ
National Institute of Aerospace
Hampton, VA, USA

Cinzia Bernardeschi ⓘ
University of Pisa
Pisa, Italy

Pierluigi Graziani ⓘ
University of Urbino
Urbino, Pesaro-Urbino, Italy

Mario Koddenbrock ⓘ
Gesellschaft zur Förderung angewandter
Berlin, Germany

Maurizio Palmieri ⓘ
University of Pisa
Pisa, Italy

ISSN 0302-9743   ISSN 1611-3349 (electronic)
Lecture Notes in Computer Science
ISBN 978-3-031-26235-7   ISBN 978-3-031-26236-4 (eBook)
https://doi.org/10.1007/978-3-031-26236-4

Preface

The 20th International Conference on Software Engineering and Formal Methods (SEFM'22) was jointly organized in Berlin on September 28–30, 2022, by the Institute of Computer Science of Humboldt University Berlin (DE) and the School of Electronic and Information Engineering of Beijing Jiaotong University (CN). The main conference was held on September 28–30, 2022, and the collocated workshops were held on September 26–27. A Summer School was also organized as part of the event, on September 21–24.

This volume collects the proceedings of four collocated SEFM workshops:

- **AI4EA'22**: 1st Workshop on Artificial Intelligence for Engineering Applications
- **F-IDE'22**: 7th Workshop on Formal Integrated Development Environment
- **CoSim-CPS'22**: 6th Workshop on Formal Co-Simulation of Cyber-Physical Systems
- **CIFMA'22**: 4th International Workshop on Cognition: Interdisciplinary Foundations, Models and Applications

The workshop organizers ensured the quality of the papers by implementing a rigorous peer-review process. Two additional collocated workshops, the 4th International Workshop on Automated and Verifiable Software System Development (*ASYDE'22*) and the 4th Workshop on Formal Methods for Autonomous Systems (*FMAS'22*), had their proceedings published as a separate volume in the Electronic Proceedings in Theoretical Computer Science (EPTCS).

The themes and application domains covered by the SEFM collocated workshops enriched the SEFM programme. They provided a vibrant stage for discussing recent and novel methods, tools, and case studies at the intersection between the software engineering and formal methods communities.

We would like to thank the workshop organizers, program chairs, keynote speakers and authors for their effort in contributing to a rich and interesting programme. We also thank the SEFM programme committee chairs, Bernd-Holger Schlingloff and Ming Chai, for taking care of the logistics and registration process of the collocated workshops.

December 2022

Paolo Masci
Cinzia Bernardeschi
Pierluigi Graziani
Mario Koddenbrock
Maurizio Palmieri

Contents

F-IDE 2022 - 7th Workshop on Formal Integrated Development Environment

CoSim-CPS 2022 - 6th Workshop on Formal Co-Simulation of Cyber-Physical Systems

CIFMA 2022 - 4th International Workshop on Cognition: Interdisciplinary Foundations, Models and Applications

AI4EA 2022 - 1st Berlin Workshop on Artificial Intelligence for Engineering Applications

AI4EA 2022 Organizers' Message

Artificial Intelligence dominates science, industry and engineering when it comes to cutting-edge technologies. From product development, to production, to maintenance and condition monitoring, Artificial Intelligence is creating solutions that seemed unattainable just a few years ago.

It is the objective of the first Berlin Workshop on Artificial Intelligence for Engineering Applications (AI4EA) to present AI-based solutions to industrial problems. Furthermore, the workshop explicitly focuses on the knowledge exchange from research to industry. AI4EA offers a platform for scientists as well as industry professionals to discuss and publish their ideas, results and problems.

In its first year, AI4EA focused on the following application areas:

- Quality assurance in production
- Predictive maintenance
- Process control/optimization
- Product development
- Medical engineering

The first day was an international day with talks in English, while the second day was primarily contributions in German from members of the German industrial research alliance ZUSE.

We received a total of 15 submissions, 13 of which were accepted for presentation. Since the authors had the option to only give a talk or present a poster, the number of publications is slightly lower at nine. Each manuscript received three anonymous reviews, after a five-day bidding period and before a final four-day consensus discussion period.

We are grateful to the Program Committee for the dedication to the critical tasks of reviewing the submissions. We are also grateful to members of the Organizing Committee of SEFM for making the necessary arrangements and helping to publicize the workshop and prepare the proceedings. Finally, we thank the authors for their efforts in writing their papers and for the excellent presentations.

December 2022

Gregor Wrobel
Daniel Herfert
Miriam Schneider
Benny Botsch
Mario Koddenbrock

Organization

Program Committee Chairs

Gregor Wrobel — GFaI e.V., Germany
Daniel Herfert — GFaI e.V., Germany
Miriam Schneider — GFaI e.V., Germany
Benny Botsch — GFaI e.V., Germany
Mario Koddenbrock — GFaI e.V., Germany

Program Committee

Alan Akbik — Humboldt-Universität zu Berlin, Germany
Wolfgang A. Halang — FernUniversität Hagen, Germany
Steffen Ihlenfeldt — Technische Universität Dresden, Germany
Alfred Iwainsky — GFaI e.V., Germany
Jürgen Jakumeit — ACCESS e.V. , Germany
Benjamin Küster — Institut für Integrierte Produktion Hannover, Germany
Benjamin Noack — Karlsruher Institut für Technologie, Germany
Christof Puhle — GFaI e.V., Germany
Joachim Rauchfuß — Berliner Hochschule für Technik, Germany
Jörg Reiff-Stephan — Technische Hochschule Wildau, Germany
Erik Rodner — Hochschule für Technik und Wirtschaft Berlin, Germany
Adrian Schischmanow — Deutsches Zentrum für Luft- und Raumfahrt, Germany
Holger Schlingloff — Humboldt-Universität zu Berlin, Germany
Gerd Stanke — GFaI e.V., Germany

Test and Training Data Generation for Object Recognition in the Railway Domain

Jürgen Grossmann[1] , Nicolas Grube[2] , Sami Kharma[1] , Dorian Knoblauch[1] ,
Roman Krajewski[2] , Mariia Kucheiko[1], and Hans-Werner Wiesbrock[2(✉)]

[1] SQC - System Quality Center, Fraunhofer-Institut für Offene Kommunikationssysteme
FOKUS, Berlin, Germany
{juergen.grossmann,sami.kharma,dorian.knoblauch,
mariia.kucheiko}@fokus.fraunhofer.de
[2] ITPower Solutions GmbH, Berlin, Germany
{nicolas.grube,roman.krajewski,
hans-werner.wiesbrock}@www.itpower.de
http://www.fokus.fraunhofer.de/sqc/,http://www.itpower.de

Abstract. AI development and test is a data driven endeavor. To date it is magnitudes more laborious to collect and annotate training and test data, than to provide a problem matching architecture and train it. In the *KI-LOK* project, a case study seeks to validate an object recognition system to prevent potentially fatal behavior of autonomous train operations. To accommodate for the vast amount of possible scenarios a train could encounter during operation, we propose a tool chain to automatically generate labeled synthetic images and videos. We start from an ontology of elements such as: Tracks, houses, vehicles or signals, these elements are then sampled and modeled in 3D to represent a scenario. Since the objects and locations of the elements in a scenario are known, no manual annotation or labeling of the data is required. By sampling from an ontology it will be possible to build comprehensive and balanced datasets of scenarios to train and test AI, while adding the benefit of corner case generation by reducing to certain elements in the ontology. This article reports on the current status of the project and the goals it tries to achieve.

Keywords: Testing AI systems · Scenery generation for AI systems · Object recognition systems · Railway domain

1 Introduction

A major and laborious problem in the development of valid AI systems is the provision of suitable test and training data. The case study of the *KI-LOK* project deals with the recognition of objects and their localization for autonomous train driving. Thus, extensive video and image representations of a wide variety of objects such as: Tracks, vehicles, people, trees, ... are needed, with indication of the types to be recognized and

---

Supported by the German Federal Ministry for Economic Affairs and Climate Action.

P. Masci et al. (Eds.): SEFM 2022 Collocated Workshops, LNCS 13765, pp. 5–16, 2023.
https://doi.org/10.1007/978-3-031-26236-4_1

where they are located. The training data must be comprehensive and balanced to mitigate later erroneous conclusions of the AI. These requirements can hardly be met with driving records and subsequent, manual classification and segmentation. However, if the required training data can be generated and the object types used with their location are known when they are produced, the very tedious labeling of the data will no longer be necessary. The effort then shifts to generating realistic training data. In the first step, we introduce an ontology that captures the elementary properties and relationships of the various objects to be represented in the data. In the second step, we stochastically generate, using the ontology, conceptual simulations, 2-dimensional scenarios for the training and test data (TrackGenerator). In the last step, 3-dim dynamic environments are generated from them, running on Epic -Games' Unreal Engine, widely used in the gaming and movie industry, and Microsoft's AirSim extension. This paper describes the approaches and concepts as well as the current state will be reported. Specifically, this paper presents the following contributions. Section 3 introduces an information model that describes the basic concepts needed to model scenarios for testing perceptual models. The information model describes the concepts we use and serves to better understand our approach. Section 4 describes an ontology aligned with the information model, which can then be used to model specific scenarios for perceptual systems in the rail domain. The ontology is specified with OWL and introduces the domain specific concepts such as rail tracks, perimeter buildings, people on the track, etc. including their relationships and properties. Section 5 describes the Track generator, a test generator that derives concrete test scenarios based on the ontology. The track generator is designed to generate realistic railroad tracks and their surroundings. Probabilistic dependencies between the individual elements of a scenario are used for the generation in order to be able to reasonably limit the range of possibilities for test scenarios. Finally, Sect. 6 describes the generation of the visual representation of the test scenarios specified by the track generator. For this purpose, the Unreal Engine, a game engine, is used to generate high quality 3D representations, which, in addition to the visual test data, also provide information about the position of the objects and the necessary segmentation maps (Fig. 1).

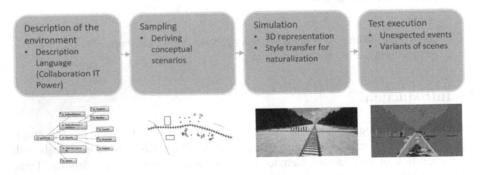

Fig. 1. Test generation chain

2 Related Work

For approval of ML-based safety critical systems the authors of [19] distinguish between two main approaches. The first deals with requirements that must be fulfilled for an approval: robustness, appropriate tackling of uncertainty, explainability, formal and empirical verification (a.k.a. testing). The other represents higher-level considerations on how to combine the above-mentioned methods in order to obtain a viable certification process. This work focuses on scenario-based testing of ML components of autonomous train's perception system as an essential part of their approval process.

2.1 Modeling the ODD

Scenario-based testing of autonomous vehicles relies on a machine readable description of their operational design domain (ODD), i.e. the conditions under which they are supposed to operate.

According to [8] ODDs are being described by means of taxonomies, as BSI PAS 1883 [10], the NHTSA framework [20], machine-readable ODD format ASAM Open-ODD[1]. Furthermore, ontologies are widely used, e.g. in [2] and [3], with an ongoing effort to standardize the vocabulary, e.g. in [21] and in project ASAM OpenXOntology[2].

In order to systematize ODD modeling, it is commonly divided into levels of abstraction. One widely adopted layered model was proposed in [16] and contains 1) road geometry and topology; 2) traffic infrastructure; 3) temporary modifications of 1) and 2); 4) actors and 5) environmental conditions.

2.2 Test Generation Approaches

One method for deriving scenarios from environmental models is suggested in [5]. The authors assign statistical distributions to parameters of the ODD and design a probabilistic programming language Scenic which samples from these distributions. Resulting scenario descriptions are then rendered using GTAV.

In [13] a matrix-based language is used to generate scenes and populate them by actors with specified positions and maneuvers. Random road networks are created consisting of curved or straight road pieces connected by clothoids, and their junctions. The scenarios are then schematically visualized in MATLAB.

Authors of [1] use an ontology to construct all possible initial scenes of a scenario and infer feasible manoeuvres from positions of traffic participants. The result is abstract scenario descriptions in natural language, which in the authors' later publication [14] are used to for deriving logical scenarios. Based on those the authors exemplarily implemented several concrete scenarios in data formats OpenDRIVE and OpenSCENARIO and executed them in the simulation environment Virtual Test Drive.

Generally, the review [8] showed that the focus of scenario-based testing has so far been on the plan and act subsystems instead of on the perception subsystem of the autonomous vehicles.

---

[1] https://www.asam.net/project-detail/asam-openodd/.
[2] https://www.asam.net/project-detail/asam-openxontology/.

In contrast, the authors of [7] use an ontology to generate synthetic image data for testing autonomous car's perception system. They also extend the layered model proposed in [16] by two layers specific for perception: "Materials" and "Sensors characteristics".

The majority of works in scenario-based testing of autonomous vehicles, including all above mentioned ones, are focusing on the automotive domain. Though certain similarities exist, the distinguishing characteristics of railway domain are higher speeds and weights, longer breaking distances, higher variability of signals and signs, potentially larger damage in case of erroneous system behavior, etc. These need to be taken into consideration while both design and testing of autonomous railway vehicles.

2.3   3D Modeling of Test Scenarios

Overcoming the obstacle of insufficient data for training and verifying of ML models with simulated data has been done by various authors. The most popular Simulator is Carla by Dosovitskiy et al. [4] it allows to control an urban driving environment and extract annotated images. Shah et al. introduced AirSim a simulator [18] for collecting large amount of labeled training data in a variety of conditions and environments. We are extending this simulator for railway specific functionalities as the original were intended for autonomous drones and cars. Automated generation tries to ease the creation of the 3D environments and also introduce automated permutations for more image material like done by Schultz with the AWS-Amit designer [17]. This approach utilizes open-street-map information to create city environments. Our approach uses generated railway centered scene decryptions for creating a 3D environment.

2.4   Generative Networks

Another feasable approach to generating test data one might think of is using generative networks like Generative Adversarial Networks (GANs) [6] or Variational Autoencoder. [11] Recent advances in the development of these networks made it possible to generate realistic looking images that resemble images from a training set [9]. The problem with those approches for generating test data is that no labels are being generated, so the images would have to be annotated, which is a costly process. Using a 3D-Simulation has the advantage, that labels to the generated images can be extracted from the engine.

Generative Networks can also be used for style transfer. Approaches like CycleGan [22] or Dall E [15] could be used to transfer labeled summer pictures into winter pictures or sunny pictures into rainy pictures. The problem with those approaches is once again the labeling. Since those methods are statistical methods, it cannot be assured, that the transfered image fits to the existing label perfectly. There most likely will be some content changes as well, even though only the style should be changed. For this reason, we are using traditional computer graphic methods for inserting wheather or other environmental conditions instead.

3 Information Model

The information model explains the basic concepts for modeling the scenarios we need for testing a perceptual system for ATO. They are adapted from work in the automotive industry, which deals with similar tasks for testing autonomous vehicles [7]. Figure 2 shows the basic concepts and their realtions.

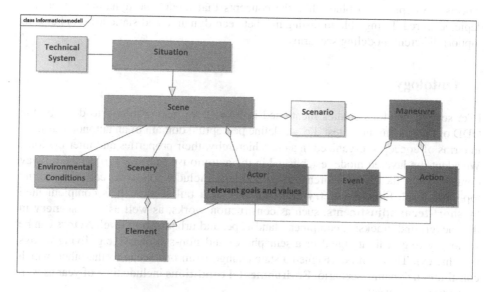

Fig. 2. Information model (UML class model)

- *Scenario:* describes the behavior of Actors over time in a given environment
- *Scene:* describes a snapshot of the environment, which includes the moving and immovable elements of the environment, the self-representation of all actors and observers, and the interconnection of these entities
- *Scenery:* assembles the static elements of a scene
- *Environmental Conditions:* describes the Environmental conditions of a scene that can not be modelled as elements. These are for example wheather and lightning conditions.
- *Element:* represents static elements of a scene including streets, tracks, trees and buildings
- *Situation:* acts as a filter on a scene that reduces a scene to relevant aspects
- *Actor:* is a dynamic element that changes position or appearance over time. These changes are triggerd by events and modelled as actions.
- *Event:* is timeless incidents that may be orderd in a certain way so that they can be used to describe progress in time.

- *Actions:* are the abstract definitions of behaviour (e.g. movement) of a specific actor that are triggerd by events and are able to cause other events.
- *Maneuvre:* is a collectino of actions and events that describe the actions of one or multiple actors.

Basically, we distinguish between the static set-up of a scenario (blue colored) and its dynamic part (green resp. red colored). The concept that mainly model the static aspects are depicted in blue while the concepts that model the dynamic aspects are depicted in red. Being able to distinguish between dynamic and static aspects helps to support different modeling scenarios.

4   Ontology

Like several previous studies mentioned in Sect. 2, we use ontology to describe the ODD of the system under test. I.e. we define perceptual domain of an autonomous train in terms of concepts, organized in a class hierarchy, their properties and interrelations. We adapt the layered model established in the automotive industry [16] to the railway domain. Thus, the class hierarchy of our ontology includes following categories at the top class level. First, **geometry and topology** of a rail section. It is complemented by **short-term adjustments**, such as construction works, as well as with **scenery** in the background: trackside equipment, landscape, and urbanization level. **Actors** can be stationary (e.g. a light signal or a semaphore) and non-stationary (e.g. living beings or vehicles). They can be assigned a state change from one scene to the other, which constitutes a dynamic scenario. **Environmental conditions** include time of year as well as daytime and weather.

Due to the fact that our ontology is machine-readable, we can programmatically select any number of objects with desired properties depending on the selected scenario. As an example, let's take the following basic scenario: "The ego locomotive is moving towards an unsecured level crossing. There is a vehicle on the level crossing and a person standing next to the track".

Here, the rail track and the level crossing are topology elements. The rail track is composed of pieces with specified curvature and length, connected to each other by clothoids if necessary (see Sect. 5).

The vehicle and the person are actors, so they have a position, orientation and speed. The appearance of the two is selectable. The vehicle can be a truck or car of different models. The person's clothing or the vehicle's body can have a plain color or a pattern (floral, checkered, camouflage, etc.); or they can belong to special services (e.g. police or railway maintenance), which would predetermine their color schemes. Advertising posters may be applied to the sides of the vehicle. Additional characteristics of a person are represented in Fig. 3.

The scenery, short-term adjustments of the railroad network and environmental conditions are not further determined in the scenario description, so they are freely selectable.

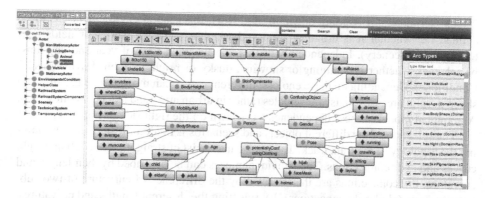

Fig. 3. Variability of a person's appearance depicted in the ontology

By combining characteristics of generated objects arbitrarily, the effect of different parameter combinations on the perceptual system can be tested.

5   Conceptual Simulation and Track Generator

Starting from a formal description of the various possible objects in a scenario, images and videos are to be generated in which trains, vehicles and people move realistically between houses and trees and which can be used for training and testing an AI. For this purpose a conceptual simulation of the scene, meaning a two-dimensional representation of its objects, is generated in a first step, with their positions and relative movements to each other, from which a realistic image of the scene is then generated in a second step by rendering and adding further details.

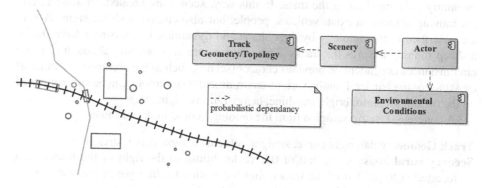

Fig. 4. Left: conceptual simulation, right: graphical model of probability distributions of different object classes. (Color figure online)

Railroad travel is the basic scenario in this project. Thus, the images to be generated center around the railroad track topology, i.e. whether it is a straight or curved track

(Track Geometry), it is going downhill, etc. Next, the general environment has to be defined i.e. whether it is urban or rural and whether there are woods or fields next to the track (Scenery). Independently of this, the weather, time of year and day must be selected, whether it is raining or snowing, dusky or bright at noon (Environmental Conditions). Depending on these choices, different actors can move in it, e.g. cattle and sheep in rural areas, cyclists and vehicles rather in urban areas and skiers only in winter. A graphical model of these dependencies is shown on the right side of Fig. 4.

The selection of the different objects and scenarios is random. It starts by determining the topology of the train track. The track can consist of straight pieces, left and right curves and their connections. The individual pieces can be described by their length and curvature, the connections are then derived by the difference of curvature of two subsequent parts (clothoid connections). By selecting the different lengths and curvatures, the pieces and their realistic connections, realistic train routes are created. Then a landscape is selected for the background. Relevant for the object recognition of the AI is the clearance profile, a narrow space around the rail track. Thus, the other elements are to be positioned primarily near the track. Different objects are detected: Railroad crossings, traffic signs, houses, individual trees and bushes are selected and placed stochastically along the track. Actors are special objects that move in the scenario, e.g. the train, other vehicles, but also railroad gates and signal signs. They are characterized by an outline that moves along specific dynamics in space, turns, falls or changes its color. They too are modeled in an ontology and with their selection, location and dynamics become co-players in the generated scenarios. Depending on the richness of the ontology, the completeness of the different object classes and their potential dynamics, this approach can be continuously extended. This approach is illustrated by a simple example. Train tracks are composed of parts strung together, track segments of certain length and curvature and their connections (track ontology). A randomly chosen number of parts, combined with their lengths and curvatures uniquely define a train track. Various objects (houses, trees, railroad crossings etc.) are then drawn from a rich pool and also randomly positioned along the track. In this way, scenes are created. In those different moving actors can exist, vehicles, people, but also changing signal signs. Actors are described in the ontology by their shape and dynamics, e.g. a barrier lowering or a sheep running towards the tracks. Their choices are also random, although in some circumstances dependent on previous choices (scene), such as the presence of a railroad crossing for the barrier. Finally, various environmental conditions can be superimposed on the overall scenario, bright sunshine, heavy rain, twilight etc.

A concrete scenario sampled from the ontology could look as follows:

Track Geometry flat, right curve, straight, left curve, right curve, straight
Scenery rural house to the left of the tracks, house to the right of the tracks, thin forestation to the left of the tracks, thin forestation to the right of the tracks, road crosses tracks, ungated level crossing
Actors vehicle on tracks and vehicle on road, person left of tracks
Environmental Conditions spring, day, sunny.

The generated scenario can be simulated in a two-dimensional representation (conceptual simulation). A snapshot of a generated scenario is shown in Fig. 4. Purple boxes represent houses, green circles represent trees and a dark green colored rectangle represents a vehicle on the tracks. For the realistic design of the scenarios, they are passed on through coordinated interfaces (image data and dynamics) for the three-dimensional simulation. Selected situations or corner cases for training and testing can also be generated by focusing on routes, objects and actors from the ontology, e.g. rural area, dusky, foggy autumn and unrestricted level crossing with different vehicles, based on a risk analysis.

6   3D Simluation

Based on the conceptual 2-dimensional representation, a 3-dimensional dynamic environment is generated. The actors can move in this environment, first and foremost the train, which travels along the track in the light space view (see Fig. 5).

Fig. 5. 3D representation of a scene. At the bottom of the image are the possible exportable representations. Among others the semantic segmentation.

On a technical level, the 3D simulation is based on Unreal Engine 4 developed by Epic-Games, which is used in the games and film industry. By default this provides a near photorealistic rendering of a scene. Howver, ground truth, which are annotations for each relevant object in the scene, is still lacking. Hence, we are using the Air-Sim extension from Microsoft, a Simulator for controling a 3D environment through a Python API [18]. Compared to alternative simulators such as CARLA [4], it allows simple extension of the tool to access arbitrary engine functionality through the Python API. It, amongst other things, allows extracting image material with semantic labels from the scene in the form of a segementation map which contains semantic information of the scene for each pixel. In order to create large number of varying images and

videos, we need various 3D enviorments. The 3D Simulation takes the scene description as an input, constructs a corresponding world and then renders it. For this, a special interface was introduced, with which the positioning and movement of objects in
the scenery is possible. This eliminates the typical manual creation of such 3D environments. One such example is a function which allows placement of rails in the 3D
environment along a spline. Another requirement for being able to position the objects
of the conceptual representation in the 3D environment is the existence of the respective
3D counterpart in the form of a 3D asset. This is a mesh representing the 3-dimensional
object, including the appropriate textures and lighting information. Detailed and high-
resolution assets are essential for rendering photorealistic scenes. In the context of the
project, such assets were created sporadically, as for example the rails. Other assets were
taken from collections that specifically provide assets for photorealistic environments.
By composition of assets, certain concepts of a scenery can be realized. For example the
concept "wooded" may be realized through a group of trees. Here, the simulator takes
the liberty to place the assets freely in a defined area. This in turn creates new types of
visual material.

Once a scenario is implemented in the 3D environment, certain factors such as time
of day, weather conditions, positions of objects and number and density of objects can
be adjusted as needed. Through slight adjustments, a variety of image and video material can be generated. It is worth mentioning that certain changes also require changes
of assets. For example, changing the scenery from a summer to a winter landscape may
require swapping out assets for trees.

7 Conclusion and Outlook

In this work it was sketched how simple scenarios for testing and training object recognition systems can be rendered. Starting with a static description of possible elements
and their properties, the ontology, it was shown how simple 2-dim. scenarios can be
generated conceptually with its help. These in turn form the basis for further enrich-
ment to 3-dim. simulations in Epic Games' Unreal Engines, and the tool chain then
used for the training and test of object recognition systems.

Not considered were the complex dependencies between the different elements to
be represented. For example, for a realistic simulation it has to be chosen in advance
whether a fast track or regional line is considered, i.e. sharp or flat curved sections in
the track geometry. This choice, however, also depends on the landscape, whether flat
or mountainous and rural or urban. Similarly, there are dependencies when people enter
the scene. A skier might be expected in winter, but not in summer, and rarely in a rainy
city. These constraints must be considered in the design of the scenario. Checking them
after generated a scenario is not feasible and so a refined graphical probabilistic model
is developed that describes these dependencies, see [12]. This work is still in its early
stages and will continue in the coming weeks.

Furthermore the complex interactions and dependencies between environment, elements and actors in the real world are the most critical limitation of this approach. A
realistic simulation of the entire world is not feasable, so the generated scenarios can
only use an approximation of the parts of the world that are the most relevant to the

system under test. It remains to be shown, that the simulation approximates the real world well enough to validate a safety critical system with it.

In the medium term, the following problem also needs to be solved. To validate the object recognition system one must prove the reliability in critical situations. The residual risk must be assessed and situations with increased hazard potential must be considered for this purpose. A ball on the rails is negligible, so is a person 20 m away from the rail track, but not in close proximity. Thus, one goal of this project is also to generate test scenarios that represent situations with high hazard potential. For this purpose, in addition to the occurrence probabilities of the entities with their properties, the graphical probabilistic model, an associated hazard potential should also be annotated to the element properties. However, this paper will not discuss these refinements further.

While great care can be taken to produce photorealistic images directly through simulation, there may be merit in utilizing machine-learning based style-transfer approaches to efficiently generated photorealistic scenes from more basic renderings of the scene. For video sequences, this will however require the usage of temporally stable style-transfer methods.

Acknowledgement. We would like to thank Daniel Gottlob for his help in preparing this work. The research project "KI-Lokomotivesysteme - Prüfverfahren für KI-basierte Komponenten im Eisenbahnbetrieb" (abbreviated KI-LOK, project website: https://ki-lok.itpower.de/) is funded by the German Federal Ministry for Economic Affairs and Climate Action and managed by TÜV Rheinland (project no.: 19121007A).

References

1. Bagschik, G., Menzel, T., Maurer, M.: Ontology based scene creation for the development of automated vehicles. In: 2018 IEEE Intelligent Vehicles Symposium (IV), pp. 1813–1820 (2018). https://doi.org/10.1109/IVS.2018.8500632
2. Czarnecki, K.: Operational world model ontology for automated driving systems - part 1: road structure. Technical report, Waterloo Intelligent Systems Engineering (WISE) Lab, University of Waterloo (2018). https://doi.org/10.13140/RG.2.2.15521.30568
3. Czarnecki, K.: Operational world model ontology for automated driving systems - part 2: road users, animals, other obstacles, and environmental conditions. Technical report, Waterloo Intelligent Systems Engineering (WISE) Lab, University of Waterloo (2018). https://doi.org/10.13140/RG.2.2.11327.00165
4. Dosovitskiy, A., Ros, G., Codevilla, F., Lopez, A., Koltun, V.: CARLA: an open urban driving simulator. In: Proceedings of the 1st Annual Conference on Robot Learning, pp. 1–16 (2017)
5. Fremont, D.J., et al.: Scenic: a language for scenario specification and data generation (2020). https://doi.org/10.48550/ARXIV.2010.06580
6. Goodfellow, I., et al.: Generative adversarial networks. Adv. Neural Inf. Process. Syst. **3** (2014). https://doi.org/10.1145/3422622
7. Herrmann, M., et al.: Using ontologies for dataset engineering in automotive AI applications. In: 2022 Design, Automation & Test in Europe Conference & Exhibition (DATE), pp. 526–531 (2022). https://doi.org/10.23919/DATE54114.2022.9774675

8. Hoss, M., Scholtes, M., Eckstein, L.: A review of testing object-based environment perception for safe automated driving. Autom. Innov. (2022). https://doi.org/10.1007/s42154-021-00172-y
9. Karras, T., Aila, T., Laine, S., Lehtinen, J.: Progressive growing of GANs for improved quality, stability, and variation (2017). https://doi.org/10.48550/ARXIV.1710.10196
10. Khastgir, S.: Operational design domain (ODD) taxonomy for an automated driving system (ADS) - specification (2020)
11. Kingma, D.P., Welling, M.: Auto-encoding variational bayes (2013). https://doi.org/10.48550/ARXIV.1312.6114
12. Koller, D., Friedman, N.: Probabilistic Graphical Models: Principles and Techniques. Adaptive Computation and Machine Learning. MIT Press, Cambridge (2009)
13. Medrano-Berumen, C., Akbaş, M.İ: Scenario generation for validating artificial intelligence based autonomous vehicles. In: Nguyen, N.T., Jearanaitanakij, K., Selamat, A., Trawiński, B., Chittayasothorn, S. (eds.) ACIIDS 2020. LNCS (LNAI), vol. 12034, pp. 481–492. Springer, Cham (2020). https://doi.org/10.1007/978-3-030-42058-1_40
14. Menzel, T., Bagschik, G., Isensee, L., Schomburg, A., Maurer, M.: From functional to logical scenarios: detailing a keyword-based scenario description for execution in a simulation environment (2019). https://doi.org/10.48550/ARXIV.1905.03989
15. Ramesh, A., Dhariwal, P., Nichol, A., Chu, C., Chen, M.: Hierarchical text-conditional image generation with clip latents (2022). https://doi.org/10.48550/ARXIV.2204.06125
16. Schuldt, F.: Ein Beitrag für den methodischen test von automatisierten Fahrfunktionen mit Hilfe von virtuellen Umgebungen. Ph.D. thesis, TU Braunschweig (2017). https://doi.org/10.24355/dbbs.084-201704241210
17. Schultz, K.: Create 3D content for simulation using Ambit (2022). https://aws.amazon.com/blogs/industries/create-3d-content-for-simulation-using-ambit/
18. Shah, S., Dey, D., Lovett, C., Kapoor, A.: AirSim: high-fidelity visual and physical simulation for autonomous vehicles. In: Hutter, M., Siegwart, R. (eds.) Field and Service Robotics. SPAR, vol. 5, pp. 621–635. Springer, Cham (2018). https://doi.org/10.1007/978-3-319-67361-5_40
19. Tambon, F., et al.: How to certify machine learning based safety-critical systems? A systematic literature review. Autom. Softw. Eng. **29**(2), 1–74 (2022). https://doi.org/10.1007/s10515-022-00337-x
20. Thorn, E., Kimmel, S., Chaka, M.: A framework for automated driving system testable cases and scenarios. Technical report, National Highway Traffic Safety Administration (2018)
21. Urbieta, I., Nieto, M., García, M., Otaegui, O.: Design and implementation of an ontology for semantic labeling and testing: automotive global ontology (AGO). Appl. Sci. **11**, 7782 (2021). https://doi.org/10.3390/app11177782
22. Zhu, J.Y., Park, T., Isola, P., Efros, A.A.: Unpaired image-to-image translation using cycle-consistent adversarial networks. In: 2017 IEEE International Conference on Computer Vision (ICCV) (2017)

A Conceptual Framework for Production Process Parameter Optimization with Modular Hybrid Simulations

Sylwia Olbrych[✉][ID], Marco Kemmerling[ID], Hans Aoyang Zhou[ID], Daniel Lütticke[ID], and Robert H. Schmitt[ID]

Institute of Information Management in Mechanical Engineering (WZL-MQ/IMA), RWTH Aachen University, Aachen, Germany
sylwia.olbrych@ima.rwth-aachen.de

Abstract. Optimizing the parameters of a manufacturing process is a time-consuming task requiring a series of experiments involving different parameter combinations. To alleviate this difficulty, we propose a conceptual framework for data-driven parameter optimization in production processes, which allows for virtual parameter tuning. To provide an insight into the practical application of our general method, we additionally explore its use on the example of lithium-ion battery (LIB) production. Our framework consists of two components: a modular hybrid simulation and an optimization tool. In the first component, the place of traditional process models is taken by a set of machine learning (ML) models which aim to imitate the behaviour of each process step. These individual models are trained on collected process data and connected in a modular simulation framework. While the resulting system already allows for manual exploration of parameter combinations, the introduction of an optimization tool unlocks further benefits. The proposed modular approach is independent of the production process type, therefore it can be applied to various manufacturing fields.

Keywords: Hybrid simulation · Process optimization · Manufacturing · Lithium-ion battery production

1 Introduction

The key contribution of this work addresses the challenges of today's complex and rapidly changing manufacturing processes. High complexity is usually associated with the numerous production steps involved in the entire manufacturing chain as well as with dependencies between process parameters, intermediate product and final product properties [8]. Due to the fast-moving and demanding market, modern manufacturing requires generic and re-adjustable solutions for optimization and performance improvement.

One approach to meet these expectations involves using simulation or artificial intelligence methods. The traditional simulation is usually a stand-alone

P. Masci et al. (Eds.): SEFM 2022 Collocated Workshops, LNCS 13765, pp. 17–25, 2023.
https://doi.org/10.1007/978-3-031-26236-4_2

application, which is designed and applied for a specific use case. Moreover, such a simulation comes at a significant cost due to the time required to develop and maintain the relevance of such a model [6]. Machine learning (ML) methods can mimic specific process steps based on real process data without the need to build up human expertise, as is required in traditional simulations. Therefore, ML algorithms are expected to accelerate the design and reconfiguration as well as shorten the time required for a new manufacturing chain to be modelled. Moreover, while the process behaviour is imitated with the use of ML models or simulated in a traditional way, the process parameters can be adjusted in a virtual manner.

In order to identify optimal process parameters we propose our conceptual framework, which consists of a modular hybrid simulation and an optimization tool. Additionally, we illustrate the applicability of our concept in the scope of currently highly relevant lithium-ion battery (LIB) manufacturing process.

The remainder of this paper is structured as follows. In the Sect. 2, research related to our conceptual framework is summarised. In Sect. 3, our concept of modelling individual process steps as well as a complete production chain is introduced. Additionally, the optimization approach is outlined. In Sect. 4, the challenges and limitations of the proposed framework are discussed. Finally, in Sect. 5, the main conclusions are presented.

2   Related Work

Over the years, a great deal of research has been conducted in simulation and ML methodologies to predict the behaviour of manufacturing processes and hence be able to improve their performance [4]. Both approaches, although significantly different, are widely applied with the aim of optimizing production processes on all levels.

The simulation design, however, is often limited to one specific application and the development of a new framework is time-consuming. Therefore the attention has been directed, not only toward the data-driven simulation approach [6,7,16], but also toward applying modular templates of simulations, which reduce simulation design time [5,12].

Some other challenges of using traditional physics-based simulation are closely related to their high complexity and expensive processing. In addition, they also require consultation with experts who are not always available at the time. To address these challenges, in parallel to physics-based models that describe processes mathematically, various ML algorithms are being tested and deployed in manufacturing processes [17]. Such models can learn the process behaviour from given data with limited involvement of process experts and further predict its response to different manufacturing parameters. In the example of LIB production, ML models have already been successfully applied in the materials science domain [11], development of battery management systems [15] as well as to improve the final performance of the battery [3,9].

It is also known, that the final analysis of the simulation output does not come effortlessly and is often focused on a specific task. Further, the conventional methods of statistical analysis could overlook hidden dependencies between operational parameters, and product and process performance. Consequently, there has been an increased interest in combining data-based ML methods with knowledge-based simulations [13]. With this approach, the ML models can automatically detect parameter dependencies [1] as well as be applied to bridge the gap in-between two simulations [14].

Although modular templates of simulation have been already built and applied, our review shows that due to a large number of process characteristics and unknown parameters' importance, the deployment and adaptability of such a simulation are still limited. Our framework overcomes this challenge by applying ML models to learn the process in a modular and data-driven manner. While knowledge-based simulation is only applicable to a specific sector, the presented concept enables the flexible design of the manufacturing process chain and thus provides a high degree of adaptability to different processes. Furthermore, we can extract the available knowledge of ML models researched in the sector of interest and embed it into the framework. Ultimately, our concept is combined with an optimization tool, which allows for virtual process parameter optimization.

3   Framework for Production Process Optimization

3.1   Modelling of Individual Process Step

The final goal of any production process is to transform raw materials into a final product. From a system perspective, materials enter the production system in a pre-processed state and leave it in a finished or post-processed state. Due to the digital transformation of production systems and advances in sensor technology, the information available about the state of the production system and the condition of materials is greater than ever. Therefore, along the material flow in the process, we can also consider the presence of an information flow. Process control parameters are treated as input information to the production system, while measurements of the production system itself and individual material states are treated as output information (see Fig. 1). We define control parameters as input values of process steps that are actively configurable and measurements as values that are collected via sensors. Each separated module has a built-in ML or traditional simulation model in order to imitate the sensors' responses.

Given the diversity of production processes and the recorded data, different ML algorithms can be used to explore the relationships between each processing step. In the case of time-dependent measurements (e.g. temperature or voltage), time-series models are suitable for learning time-dependent relationships within historic data [2]. They are capable of capturing trends, repeating patterns and seasonality. In contrast, for tabular data where each measurement is independent of the previous one traditional ML models like tree-based, Bayesian or kernel-based models can be applied. Compared to time-series approaches, these models

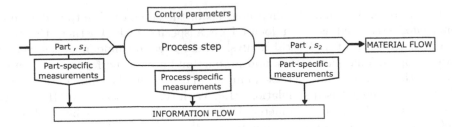

Fig. 1. In our framework, a process contains material and information flow. The material flow describes how parts are being transformed from the pre-processed state (s_1) into the post-processed state (s_2). The information layer describes the flow of information from the input in the form of control parameters to the output in the form of measurements.

treat each data instance independently, where usually one processed part depicts one data instance. Within our framework, selected ML models aim to replicate the behaviour of the process step based on the available real manufacturing data.

3.2 Modelling of Manufacturing Chain

The modelled individual process steps are further connected to the manufacturing process chain, where the module's output serves as an input to the following one. Such a generic modular approach allows for easy replacement or addition of individual process step models. Where suitable, already existing explicit knowledge-based models of individual process steps may be used for some parts of the process, while the remaining ones can be modelled in a data-driven fashion, arriving at a hybrid solution. Moreover, it enables us to validate each process step model separately and thereby locate any potential problems in the chain much more easily. Ideally, each process step is simulated using data that relates to a single end product, for example, a LIB electrode.

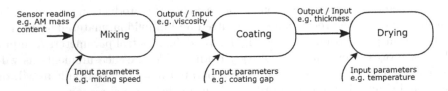

Fig. 2. The example of modular simulation chain based on selected LIB electrode manufacturing process stages.

To illustrate the aforementioned modular structure, we use selected LIB electrode manufacturing process steps of mixing, coating and drying (see Fig. 2) [10]. Throughout the mixing stage the active material (AM), conductive additives and binders are combined with the solvent to form a slurry for further processing. This step takes place at a fixed time for which the parameters like mixing sequence, temperature and speed could be altered. In this case, time-series models can be used to learn the relationship between dependent features like temperature readings and the final state of the slurry, e.g., viscosity or particle surface energy. During the coating, the slurry is applied on both sides of a copper or aluminium foil at a chosen coating gap. Since the foil moves during the slurry application at a given line speed, integrated stationary tests such as coating thickness measurement only capture a partial area of the entire foil. This ultimately leads to a limited amount of measurements per produced electrode, where each measurement of one electrode is independent of another. Consequently, traditional ML models are suitable for modelling the coating process step. In the third step, the solvent is evaporated from the slurry by passing the coated foil through the drying equipment. Similar to the coating process, the foil is in constant movement at a certain line speed and stationary measurements, like coating thickness and humidity, capture a discrete subsection of the foil. Hence, traditional ML models may be also used to learn the relationship between the pre-processed state of the coated foil to the post-processed state as the remaining humidity of the coating.

3.3   Optimization

Based on the approach described in previous sections, the modular hybrid simulation of the production chain is developed to be further connected with the optimization tool. Such a framework offers the possibility of testing different parameter combinations and finding the optimum one. To make this possible, the simulation must be able to interact with optimization algorithms. These algorithms can then iteratively optimize the parameters by alternatingly selecting parameter combinations x and observing their effect as computed by the simulation (see Fig. 3). This effect will have to be specified as some performance measure $f(x)$ of the simulated process which serves as the optimization objective. The choice of control parameters will additionally have to be constrained to some set Ω, in order to avoid physically impossible values. Given that at least one of the simulated modules does not provide gradients as output information, the employed algorithms will have to be selected from the family of black-box optimization algorithms.

Selecting the performance measure depends on the factor that should be optimized. Such a factor may be the quality of the final product, the cost of production, energy consumption, or a combination of individual factors. Once this has been identified, it is further necessary to define a way to measure the chosen optimization target in the real process and the simulation. Considering continuous production, we expect a time series of our target with variable measurements and hence the need to convert this time series into a single value that could serve as a performance measure. If the aim of optimization is to reduce energy consumption, calculating an average over a given time series may be sufficient for the proposed framework. However, if the objective is product quality, the average alone may not be adequate. While a good average quality is desirable, we may also want to avoid huge fluctuations in quality. In some cases, it might be preferable to have a lower average quality with low variance than a slightly higher average quality with high variance. In such cases, the variance of the optimization target may be introduced as a second penalty term.

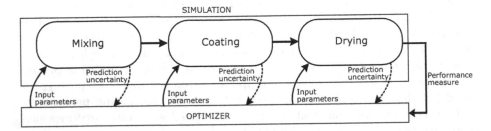

Fig. 3. The overall framework consists of two components, the simulation and the optimizer, which interface with each other by exchanging input parameters and performance measures.

Optimizing control parameters based on learned models risks making suboptimal choices due to inaccuracies of the models. Especially when multiple models are configured in a chain, inaccuracies will propagate through the chain and potentially lead to significantly misleading predictions of the overall system. If we select types of models that provide uncertainty estimates u about their predictions, we can use the uncertainty u_s of every process step s to inform the selected optimization algorithm in its decision process. Since regions with high model uncertainty lead to predictions that cannot be trusted, we want to avoid them and therefore incentivize the optimization algorithm to do so. This can be accomplished by introducing another term into the objective function which decreases the objective function value proportional to the observed model uncertainty. It may be advantageous to weigh w_s the uncertainty of each model separately (see Eq. 1), as models earlier in the process chain will contribute more to the overall simulation inaccuracy, meaning that uncertainty should be avoided among those models in particular.

$$\max_{x} \quad f(x) - \sum_{s}^{n} w_s \, u_s \tag{1}$$

$$\text{s.t.} \quad x \in \Omega$$

4   Discussion and Limitations

The idea of introducing a model uncertainty penalty to the objective function as described in the previous section can be implemented in various ways. Ideally, such a penalty term leads to objective values near zero when model uncertainty

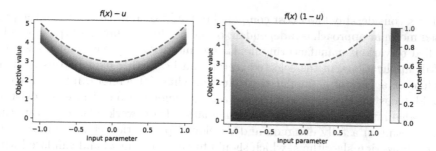

Fig. 4. Illustrative example of objective functions with different uncertainty penalty terms. The performance measure is an arbitrarily chosen function of the input parameters x such that $f(x) = 2x^2 + 3$. The uncertainty u is a real number in $(0, 1)$, where 0 represents no uncertainty and 1 maximum uncertainty. The dashed red line represents the objective value without any model uncertainty penalty. (Color figure online)

is at the theoretical maximum $(u = 1)$, since no trust can be placed in the model in this case. When model uncertainty is at the theoretical minimum $(u = 0)$, however, objective values should not be affected by the penalty at all. In between these two extrema, the effect of uncertainty should be increasing in a gradual manner. Equation 1 shows an obvious possibility of incorporating such a penalty, although it does not match the ideal profile just described, since maximum uncertainty has a fairly minor effect. This is illustrated in Fig. 4 on the left, where values of a simplified objective function $f(x) - u$ with a single uncertainty term are visualized for different uncertainty levels. Continuing with the simplified scenario of a single uncertainty term, an objective function that was found to be more suitable may be $f(x) (1 - u)$ (see Fig. 4 on the right). This objective function punishes high uncertainty parameters more heavily. Generalizing the case with multiple, weighted uncertainty terms leads to the following optimization problem:

$$\max_{x} \quad f(x) \frac{\sum_s^n 1 - w_s \, u_s}{\sum_s^n w_s} \tag{2}$$
$$\text{s.t.} \quad x \in \Omega$$

Apart from punishing the selection of parameters which lead to results with high uncertainty, it may also be advantageous to improve the models exactly where high uncertainty occurs. If the optimizer identifies such parameters, they could be saved for later investigation. Once a sizable set of these parameters has been collected, additional experiments on the real process could be carried out to collect further data to improve the models in our framework.

5 Conclusion

The successful implementation of our concept can enable the optimization of process parameters for desired system performance in a time-efficient manner and at a considerably lower cost compared to traditional methods. Since the proposed modular approach is independent of the production process type, it can be applied to various manufacturing fields. The maturity of the current knowledge of ML applications, in the selected sector, can be further exploited as a single module or a part of a simulated production chain. Therefore, future research should focus on the precise selection and implementation of already existing knowledge into the introduced by us simulation framework. Consequently, this would result in a fully designed and developed production chain connected to the optimization algorithms, which should further be trained and validated with real process data.

References

1. Bohn, B., et al.: Analysis of car crash simulation data with nonlinear machine learning methods. Procedia Comput. Sci. **18**, 621–630 (2013)
2. Bontempi, G., Ben Taieb, S., Le Borgne, Y.-A.: Machine learning strategies for time series forecasting. In: Aufaure, M.-A., Zimányi, E. (eds.) eBISS 2012. LNBIP, vol. 138, pp. 62–77. Springer, Heidelberg (2013). https://doi.org/10.1007/978-3-642-36318-4_3
3. Cunha, R.P., Lombardo, T., Primo, E.N., Franco, A.A.: Artificial intelligence investigation of NMC cathode manufacturing parameters interdependencies. Batteries Supercaps **3**(1), 60–67 (2020)
4. Fuchs, T., Enslin, C., Samsonov, V., Lütticke, D., Schmitt, R.H.: ProdSim: an open-source python package for generating high-resolution synthetic manufacturing data on product, machine and shop-floor levels. Procedia CIRP **107**, 1343–1348 (2022)
5. Gaspari, L., Colucci, L., Butzer, S., Colledani, M., Steinhilper, R.: Modularization in material flow simulation for managing production releases in remanufacturing. J. Remanuf. **7**(2–3), 139–157 (2017)
6. Goodall, P., Sharpe, R., West, A.: A data-driven simulation to support remanufacturing operations. Comput. Ind. **105**, 48–60 (2019)
7. Krenczyk, D.: Automatic generation method of simulation model for production planning and simulation systems integration. Adv. Mater. Res. **1036**, 825–829 (2014)
8. Kwade, A., Haselrieder, W., Leithoff, R., Modlinger, A., Dietrich, F., Droeder, K.: Current status and challenges for automotive battery production technologies. Nat. Energy **3**(4), 290–300 (2018)
9. Liu, K., Hu, X., Zhou, H., Tong, L., Widanage, W.D., Marco, J.: Feature analyses and modeling of lithium-ion battery manufacturing based on random forest classification. IEEE/ASME Trans. Mechatron. **26**(6), 2944–2955 (2021)
10. Liu, Y., Zhang, R., Wang, J., Wang, Y.: Current and future lithium-ion battery manufacturing. iScience **24**(4), 102332 (2021)
11. Lv, C., et al.: Machine learning: an advanced platform for materials development and state prediction in lithium-ion batteries. Adv. Mater. (Deerfield Beach Fla.) **34**, e2101474 (2021)
12. Mukkamala, P.S., Smith, J.S., Valenzuela, J.F.: Designing reusable simulation modules for electronics manufacturing systems. In: 2003 Proceedings of the 2003 Winter Simulation Conference, vol. 2, pp. 1281–1289 (2003)

13. von Rueden, L., Mayer, S., Sifa, R., Bauckhage, C., Garcke, J.: Combining machine learning and simulation to a hybrid modelling approach: current and future directions. In: Berthold, M.R., Feelders, A., Krempl, G. (eds.) IDA 2020. LNCS, vol. 12080, pp. 548–560. Springer, Cham (2020). https://doi.org/10.1007/978-3-030-44584-3_43

14. Teichert, G.H., Das, S., Aykol, M., Gopal, C.B., Gavini, V., Garikipati, K.C.: Lix-CoO2 phase stability studied by machine learning-enabled scale bridging between electronic structure, statistical mechanics and phase field theories. ArXiv (2021)

15. Vidal, C., Malysz, P., Kollmeyer, P., Emadi, A.: Machine learning applied to electrified vehicle battery state of charge and state of health estimation: State-of-the-art. IEEE Access 8, 52796–52814 (2020)

16. Wang, J., Chang, Q., Xiao, G., Wang, N., Li, S.: Data driven production modeling and simulation of complex automobile general assembly plant. Comput. Ind. 62(7), 765–775 (2011)

17. Wuest, T., Weimer, D., Irgens, C., Thoben, K.D.: Machine learning in manufacturing: advantages, challenges, and applications. Prod. Manuf. Res. 4(1), 23–45 (2016)

Forecasting Algae Growth in Photo-Bioreactors Using Attention LSTMs

Daniel Boiar[1]([⊠])(iD), Nils Killich[2]([⊠])(iD), Lukas Schulte[2](iD),
Victor Hernandez Moreno[3](iD), Jochen Deuse[2](iD), and Thomas Liebig[1](iD)

[1] TU Dortmund University, Otto-Hahn-Straße 12, 44227 Dortmund, Germany
{daniel.boiar,thomas.liebig}@cs.tu-dortmund.de
[2] TU Dortmund University, Leonhard-Euler-Straße 5, 44227 Dortmund, Germany
{nils.killich,lukas.schulte,jochen.deuse}@ips.tu-dortmund.de
[3] University of Technology Sydney, 15 Broadway, Ultimo, NSW 2007, Australia
victor.hernandezmoreno@student.uts.edu.au

Abstract. Sustainability is the current global challenge. This is reflected in the demand for healthy food and CO_2 neutrality. These challenges can be met with the industrial cultivation of algae: Algae can be used as food supplements, nutraceuticals, pharmaceuticals, fuel, CO_2 sinks, and obtain high relative yield density per area. Current limitations in their large-scale use exists, as scaling up from laboratory environments to pilot applications typically requires more than 5 years, because of highly complex interactions in the growth behavior: They are influenced by current and past environmental conditions. These interactions make current pilot applications inefficient due to insufficient control and monitoring techniques. This limitation can be countered: By using modern communication and evaluation technologies, a "smart" bioreactor can be developed, which evaluates algae growth in real-time, performs process adaptations and thus significantly accelerates algae growth and scale-up. Therefore, an algae bioreactor was established at the University of Technology Sydney. The subject of this paper is the study of algae growth using Long Short-Term Memory Neural Networks (LSTMs). In order to learn the behavior of algae in the shortest possible series of experiments, repetitive change intervals were run by systematically varying the environmental parameters. LSTMs were trained to model algae growth. Attention mechanism is used on variable and temporal direction for importance. The LSTM is compared to a Transformer and an ARIMA. Based on the trained models, the behavior of algae growth is interpreted.

Keywords: Algae growth · LSTM · Attention · Multivariate time series · Forecasting · Industry 4.0 · Photo-bioreactor · XAI

The infrastructure used for this work was funded by the Australian Government, Department of Industry, Innovation and Science as part of the Industry 4.0 Testlabs for Australia pilot program. This research has been funded by the Federal Ministry of Education and Research of Germany and the state of North-Rhine Westphalia as part of the Lamarr-Institute for Machine Learning and Artificial Intelligence, LAMARR22B.

P. Masci et al. (Eds.): SEFM 2022 Collocated Workshops, LNCS 13765, pp. 26–37, 2023.
https://doi.org/10.1007/978-3-031-26236-4_3

1   Introduction

With the increase in new market applications for biologics productions, microalgae are considered a promising new platform [22]. Besides being processed for biofuels, microalgae show great potential for the production of food dyes, animal feed, bioplastic synthesis, recombinant antibodies for medical use and many more. An important side effect of the production of microalgae is linked to their continuous consumption of CO_2 for life-essential photosynthesis. The production of microalgae for end products that involve the permanent binding of CO_2 in their biomass, such as construction materials [20], is seen as a CO_2 sink and can directly contribute to the current global sustainability challenge.

To meet the growing demand for microalgae biomass, the industry is compelled to efficiently upscale from laboratory-scale to commercial production. However, this process is considered hindered [18], as microalgae's behaviour and lifecycles are highly complex due to great biological and physiological diversity [9] and difficulties in modelling light as a nutrient [4]. Furthermore, the product yield is highly sensitive to changes in environmental conditions [17] which have a time-delayed effect on algae growth, and the magnitude of their influence depends on their timing and different input variables. The influence can increase and decrease over the course of a day [15]. Gao et al. identified main dependency groups, including light distribution, nutrition concentration, biomass distribution, algae growth rate, and fluid dynamics [8].

In conventional semi-mechanistic models, the algae growth is biased with simplified assumptions as in hyperbolic tangent models [5] or the Beer-Lamber law for modeling light distribution [4] which captures the algae life cycle inaccurately and does not scale with the tank volume or other parameters. Therefore, the optimal conditions for cultivation in commercial production photo-bioreactors are not yet known, making optimization of process parameters difficult.

Furthermore, current methods for operating microalgae production plants require a significant reduction in operating costs to become competitive [2]. One of the influencing factors is the need for trained personnel to monitor and control the equipment during the whole production cycle.

In this paper, we explore the applicability of Neural Networks to predict algae growth within an industrial photo-bioreactor. Neural Networks provide the potential to build accurate models without much expertise regarding algal characteristics and don't introduce large biases. Thus, neural networks are chosen to model the growth. While most approaches are made for outdoor cultivation, indoor cultivation machine learning was not applied much. The key contributions in this paper are as follows: (1) A practical application of state-of-the-art machine learning methods to an industry-relevant use case. (2) Using attention for importance measure to identify important features across two dimensions: time and variable-wise in order to see what is important and what should be changed. For reproducibility, the code is available at https://github.com/KhakiSalad/ma_pbr_rnn.

The remainder of this paper is structured as follows: Sect. 2 provides an overview of related work. In Sect. 3, we formulate the encountered forecasting problem and our method, which achieves an accurate prediction model under the given circumstances. Section 4 is dedicated to an experimental evaluation, before we conclude our contribution in Sect. 5.

2   Related Work

This section first provides an overview of current approaches to the growth model. Subsequently, other models of the state-of-the-art on non-recurrent and recurrent interpretable models are described.

2.1   Algae Models

Biologists' models are based on bio-physical laws and numbers of experiments, e.g. the light oxygen production can be modeled by the light intensity. Hyperbolic tangent [5] models oxygen production P, based on the light intensity I, by $P(I) = P_m \cdot tanh(\alpha I)$, where P_m is the maximum oxygen production, and α constant.

Neural networks, on the other hand, involve less assumptions and are therefore more flexible. They are used for outdoor prediction of algal blooms in rivers [12–14].

Semi-indoor cultivation is approached by LSTM reinforcement learning [6] with a different setup: In their setup real sunlight is used and controlled with a folding top. The liquid algae mass is pumped from a small tank through tubes to receive sunlight. The lights are varied only such that an univariate problem is addressed and scaling issues do not occur due to a small setup. It was possible to develop a blackbox model that improves yields.

The integration of commercial flow simulation software into a convolutional neural network was performed via learning from the label that come from the simulation to model the turbulences in the reactor [19].

2.2   Non-recurrent Interpretable Models

Transformers with attention [23] have been introduced in natural language processing and approach the shortcomings of LSTMs to process the input sequentially by building an attention connectivity mapping to handle the importance between all inputs and by using a positional encoding to model time dependence. Processing all data simultaneously allows for a runtime advantage that makes the Transformer learn from more data with equal training time in comparison to the LSTM. On the other hand, processing sequentially with memory cells in a more natural way using the stronger markovian assumption can help in this context of algae growth. Additionally, faster learning is not needed when dealing with little data. A comparison with LSTMs is shown in the experiments.

AutoRegressive Integrated Moving Average with Exogenous Variables (ARI-MAX) [3] is a classical statistical model which is composed of interpretable linear terms: autoregression, moving average, and a term to model K exogenous variables X. With autoregressive lags p, the differencing degree d, and the moving average lags q, the ARIMAX model is given by:

$$\left(1 - \sum_{i=1}^{p} \phi_i B^k\right)(1 - B)^d y_t = \left(1 + \sum_{j=1}^{q} \theta_j B^k\right)\varepsilon_t + \sum_{k=1}^{K} \psi_k X_{kt} + \varepsilon_t,$$

where B is the backward-shift operator $By_t = y_{t-1}$. The weights ϕ_i, θ_j, ψ_k are learnable, and $\varepsilon_t \sim N(0, \sigma^2)$ is a white noise process. The autoregressive part describes the modelling of future series values by its history. The differencing operator takes care of using the discrete derivative. The moving average models the mean based on the current history, and the exogenous variables model dependent variables. In comparison to LSTM the ARIMAX describes a combined stochastical process and can not model non-linearities nor memory.

2.3 Recurrent Interpretable Models

The Interpretable Multi-Variable LSTM (IMV-LSTM) approach [10] uses an LSTM per variable and selects the variable with an attention mechanism. Additionally, the attention mechanism gives the importance measure for the time dimension. More complex architectures as [16] build up on top of [10] and extend the idea with multiple layers and introduce with the composed architecture more parameters and complexity. Because we deal with small amount of data, we stick to the basic variant [10] for getting a simpler and thus a more interpretable model. This method is now described in more detail.

3 Approach

The following time series forecasting problem is considered: We are given measurements and target $\underbrace{x^1, ..., x^{N-1}}_{x}, y$, where $x^i = (x_1^i, \ldots, x_T^i) \in \mathbb{R}^T, i = 1..N-1$,

$y = (y_1, \ldots, y_T) \in \mathbb{R}^T$. The goal is to find a model f on $x_t, y_t \ \forall \ t \in \{1, \ldots, T\}$, such that a loss function $L\big(f(x_{t+1}), y_{t+1}\big)$ is minimized.

The Long Short-Term Memory (LSTM) [11] has been successfully applied to time series analysis and is a promising architecture for algae forecasting (e.g. [14]). The idea derives from the recurrent neural network (RNN) [7]. While the input of the RNN is slided over time series, the output is fed again as a second input into the next state at the next time stamp $t + 1$, as seen in Fig. 1. Remembering the prediction of the last state and interconnecting with the current input, yields a model that catches sequence pattern. Trainable weights guide the two inputs, and an activation function contribute non-linearity following the merging, result in the equation for hidden state h_t and output y_t at time t:

$$h_t := \sigma_h(W_h x_t + U_h h_{t-1} + b_h)$$
$$y_t := \sigma_y(W_y h_t + b_y)$$

where W_h, U_h, W_y are weight matrices and b_h, b_y bias weights. The RNN is visualized in Fig. 1.

After comparing the prediction with the actual value, the gradient flows back through the hidden states, such that a time dependence is created, enables the RNN to decide based on multiple time stamps back in the history. One drawback of this method is the vanishing gradient when going more steps back in the history. The LSTM provides a solution for this, by inserting a memory cell that can let the memory state flow into the decision process where the trainable weights together with the input and the memory state decide if the input or the memory state is used, or if the memory state is forgotten. The LSTM with the forget, input and output gate is visualized in Fig. 1 and given by

$$
\begin{aligned}
\text{forget activation} \quad & f_t := \sigma_{sig}(W_f\, x_t + U_f\, h_{t-1} + b_f) \\
\text{input activation} \quad & i_t := \sigma_{sig}(W_i\, x_t + U_i\, h_{t-1} + b_i) \\
\text{output activation} \quad & o_t := \sigma_{sig}(W_o\, x_t + U_o\, h_{t-1} + b_o) \\
\text{cell activation} \quad & \tilde{c}_t := \sigma_{tanh}(W_c\, x_t + U_c\, h_{t-1} + b_c) \\
\text{cell state} \quad & c_t := f_t \odot c_{t-1} + i_t \odot \tilde{c}_t \\
\text{hidden state} \quad & h_t := o_t \odot \sigma_{tanh}(c_t)
\end{aligned}
$$

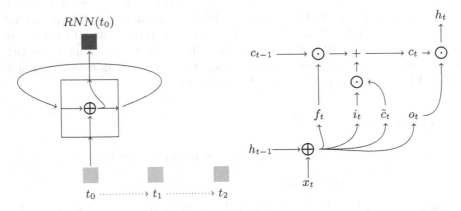

Fig. 1. RNN is slid over a time series (left) and LSTM cell structure (right).

where W_j, U_j, b_j are trainable weights $j \in \{f, i, o, c\}$ and $\sigma_{sig}, \sigma_{tanh}$ are the sigmoid and tanh activation function. In the cell state equation, it can be seen that forgetting activation decides whether the cell state is forgotten by scaling the last cell state. Thereby input activation scales the cell activation, which together with the (possibly) partial forgotten results in the cell state. Equally, the output activation acts similar to the cell state, resulting in the hidden state. The gradient can pass without vanishing the cell states connection in time because no activation function is interposed between the cell states. Only the forget gate and second product influence the gradient flow indirectly by splitting the gradient.

In stacked LSTMs with multiple layers the hidden states h_t^l are used as new inputs x_t^{l+1} on the next layer $l+1$.

Interpretable LSTM with attention (IMV-LSTM) [10] consists of one LSTM per variable. These LSTMs are connected through an attention layer. The attention weights can select from the incoming signals. Additionally, the attention layer can choose in the time dimension the important time stamps for each variable. The attention layer for time is calculated by summing up all variable hidden states per time stamp, and the attention layer for a variable is calculated by summing up all time stamps per variable.

4   Experimental Evaluation

Before the experiments are described, the setup consisting of the algae photo-bioreactor and data generation is specified. The photo-bioreactor is not cylindrically shaped but has a rather specific shape. The sensors and actuators are placed around the reactor: The LEDs shine on the reactor all around and from above. The sensors for pH and relative density, however, are placed at the bottom, where the reactor changes into a funnel shape.

We provide a real dataset for the algae species Chlorella Vulgaris that consists of two batches, that are shown in Fig. 2 and Fig. 3. Chlorella Vulgaris is a popular species with great commercial potential and to use this species is intended to create comparability. The first batch includes 24 days in which the parameter follow a controlled experimental design protocol. The lights and pH value are set periodically approx. every 10 h according to the following lists starting at day 8 of the experiment:

- pH series: [7.5, 6.5, 8.5, repeat]
- light series: [40%, 60%, 80%, 100%, repeat]

The amount of CO_2 injected is automatically controlled by the reactor until the defined pH value is reached. This variation, due to periodically setted lights and pH values, in the data is not the way a biologist would manipulate the algae growth. Instead it is based on concepts of Six Sigma experimental design: In the concepts of design of experiments (DoE), the aim is to achieve the best possible understanding of the entire experimental space with the smallest possible scope of experiments. For this purpose, the parameter space to be investigated is divided into different areas according to the selected experimental plan. In the given application, the parameter values for the pH value and the PBR light intensity were successively changed. In particular, the control limits for the pH value between 6.5–8.5 were selected, as this range proved to be non-lethal for the algae cultures in preliminary experiments. Due to the parameter settings over an experimental period of 16 experimental days, a high variation of the experimental environment could be realized. The generated batch is used as train (60%) and validation (40%) data. The second batch is recorded at a later time point and is recorded with small variance in usual way a biologist grow algae and record the data. This batch is put aside and serves as test data.

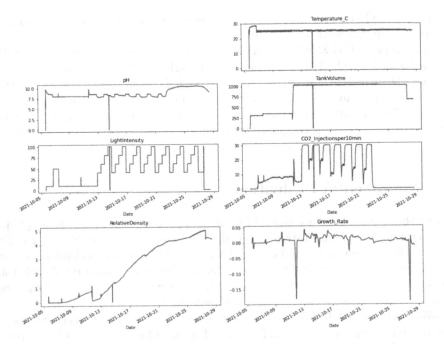

Fig. 2. First batch: train data.

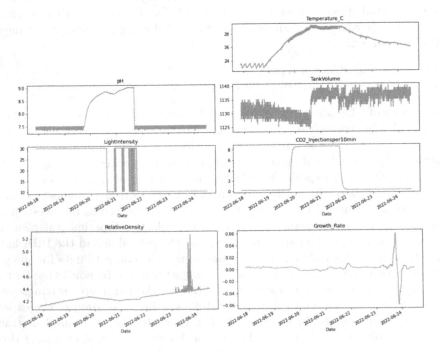

Fig. 3. Second batch: test data.

Fig. 4. Sliding window extraction of fixed length windows from a time series.

The data is preprocessed with removing conspicuities, which contains removing start, end points and shut downs of the reactor. Further applied preprocessing is standardizing the data to get a zero mean and standard deviation of one. Each 30 min are averaged to their mean value. Moreover the resulting time series slices are extracted. This is shown in Fig. 4.

The experiments to model the growth on the data is divided in two experiments. The first compares the machine learning algorithms with the label is chosen from the next time stamp. The second experiment shifts the prediction horizon to 24 h, 48 h and 96 h. The error loss compares the error between the next true value and the prediction for each time stamp t with the mean absolute error $mae = \frac{1}{T} \sum_{i=t}^{T} |f(x_t) - y_t|$ and mean square error $mse = \frac{1}{T} \sum_{i=t}^{T} (f(x_t) - y_t)^2$ where f is the model, and x_t the time window and y_t the true relative density.

The hyperparameter optimization is executed five times on the training set and validation set. The IMV-LSTM is compared to LSTM, ARIMAX, Transformer and RF on the test set. The results are shown in Table 1 with the parameter search configuration in Table 2 using the architectures of [10] for IMV-LSTM and [24] for the Transformer. The Transformer model performed best when all variables are included. The predictions and true values can be seen in Fig. 5. The performance of the IMV-LSTM is increased when considering the three best variables, and also reaches the Transformer performance.

IMV-LSTM allocates the highest variable importance to the relative density. Other importance values are close to each other and distinctly lower. While the exact values vary between executions, temperature, light intensity and pH are next most important. Variable-wise temporal importance for IMV-LSTM is shown in Fig. 6. Distinct differences can be observed only for the CO_2 injection rate. For the injection rate, time points at the end of the window are most important. The importance decreases with increasing distance.

The predictions for varying prediction horizons are worse than the prediction for the next measured value in each case. They become worse for increasing horizons, with the greatest increase between distance 1 and 48. The variance of the prediction error also increases noticeably.

4.1   Findings

Against the expectation, the actual value of the bio mass shown in Fig. 5 is not steadily increasing, we find an explanation for this when we assign the event log to the data: One event is the injection of CO_2. The CO_2 is injected with

Table 1. Performance evaluation on the test set for the next step prediction.

Model	mae	mse
IMV-LSTM (all variables)	0.22 ± 0.02	0.19 ± 0.02
IMV-LSTM (3 best variables)	$\mathbf{0.16 \pm 0.02}$	$\mathbf{0.10 \pm 0.01}$
LSTM	0.63 ± 0.12	0.70 ± 0.25
ARIMAX	0.45 ± 0.01	0.56 ± 0.04
Transformer	$\mathbf{0.17 \pm 0.05}$	$\mathbf{0.12 \pm 0.03}$
Random Forest	0.33 ± 0.00	0.36 ± 0.00

Table 2. Parameter search for IMV-LSTM and Transformer optimized by Optuna [1].

Model	Parameter	Search values	Best value
IMV-LSTM	Channels	$\{32, 64, 128, 256, 512, 1024\}$	32
	Learning rate	$[0.0001, 0.01]$	0.005
	Window size	$\{12, 24, 48, 96\}$	12
Transformer	# decoder layer	$[2,6]$	2
	# encoder layer	$[2,6]$	4
	Decoder input size	$[29,100]$	31
	Window size	$\{12, 24, 48, 96\}$	96
	# attention heads	$\{8, 16\}$	16
	Channels	$\{32, 64, 128, 256, 512, 1024\}$	64

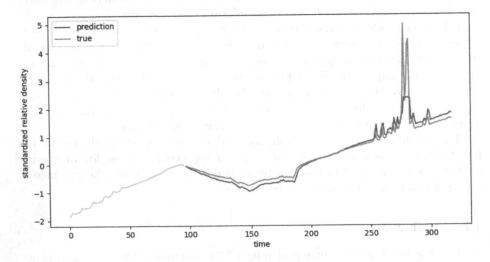

Fig. 5. Algae growth modeled by Transformer in one step horizon.

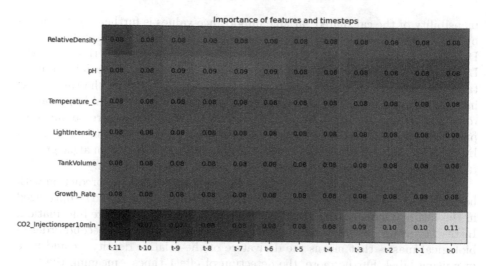

Fig. 6. IMV-LSTM importance scores across time and variable.

bubbles and creates motion of the particles. This motion leads to an intermixing of the algae mass within the water such that some particles receive more light and at the same time, the relative density is getting lower because more light can shine through the reactor. This is what we see in Fig. 5 when the bio mass is decreasing. On the other hand, these fluid dynamics have influence of the growth, because more particles will get more light. This makes it difficult to detect, how much influence came from the fluid dynamics and how much CO_2 does the algae need and which particles receive the CO_2. To get a distinction between these two factors the fluid dynamics can be modeled, in order to make the algae growth model the only unknown system.

5   Conclusion

Algae are important in a variety of applications for humans. Due to a lack of understanding about the growth of algae, experiments were set up in a controlled photo-bioreactor to predict algae growth with interpretable LSTMs. The LSTMs were compared to different state-of-the-art models. In our experiments IMV-LSTM delivers the second best prediction results after Transformer with both having comparable results when only using the three most important features for IMV-LSTM. Even when the model is applied to the test data set, predictions can be made reliably. It is shown that after training with the data set of a growth experiment, the model can be transferred to future algae batches and still provides good predictions.

The calculated values for variable importance can be supported by the use case. The change in biomass concentration depends on the algal biomass present and the relative density changes slowly compared to the frequency of measurements, so that the relative density is the most important input variable. The plausibility of the calculated variable importance values is further substantiated by the performance increase achieved by selecting the most important features. Despite the plausibility of the variable importance, in our experiments IMV-LSTM failed to deliver satisfying importance metrics. While variable importance was used to increase prediction performance by selecting the three most important features for the prediction task, variable-wise temporal importances remained opaque. Although additional experiments might help increase the interpretability the inherent non-linearity of algal growth, the importance metrics of IMV-LSTM may be unable to capture the non-linearity inherent in algae growth to the extend of extracting new knowledge about this mechanism.

For future work we intend to do the following: The multi step prediction with horizons 24 h, 48 h, 96 h didn't show convincing results, which has to be optimized in the future. One approach could be to enrich the label with more information. Instead of using the first order derivative of the algae mass, the second order of biological mass - that means the derivative of the relative density - could be a promising label. Furthermore, the detection of effect times - meaning the time horizon until an affect can be measured after an event (e.g. a control parameter changed) - is a next step. A further direction is to determine the optimal harvest time point. This can gives a trade-off between light transmittance and yield.

In the future we plan to let the algorithm control the hyperparameter of the photobioreactor. Optimizing the control parameter can be done using e.g. back-propagation on the input parameters with frozen network weights optimizing the loss function. When applying the model in the live production the model can be used for getting suggestions for changes, and the model can be adapted and reinforce itself. Additionally uncertainties for the parameter can be modeled by using Bayesian Optimization [21].

References

1. Akiba, T., Sano, S., Yanase, T., Ohta, T., Koyama, M.: Optuna: a next-generation hyperparameter optimization framework. In: Proceedings of the 25rd ACM SIGKDD International Conference on Knowledge Discovery and Data Mining (2019)
2. Benedetti, M., Vecchi, V., Barera, S., Dall'Osto, L.: Biomass from microalgae: the potential of domestication towards sustainable biofactories. Microb. Cell Fact. **17**(1), 1–18 (2018)
3. Box, G.E., Jenkins, G.M., Reinsel, G.C., Ljung, G.M.: Time series analysis: forecasting and control. Wiley, Hoboken (2015)
4. Béchet, Q., Shilton, A., Guieysse, B.: Modeling the effects of light and temperature on algae growth: state of the art and critical assessment for productivity prediction during outdoor cultivation. Biotechnol. Adv. **31**(8), 1648–1663 (2013)
5. Chalker, B.E.: Modeling light saturation curves for photosynthesis: an exponential function. J. Theor. Biol. **84**(2), 205–215 (1980)
6. Doan, Y.T.T., Ho, M.T., Nguyen, H.K., Han, H.D.: Optimization of spirulina sp. cultivation using reinforcement learning with state prediction based on LSTM neural network. J. Appl. Phycol. **33**(5), 2733–2744 (2021)
7. Elman, J.L.: Finding structure in time. Cogn. Sci. **14**(2), 179–211 (1990)

8. Gao, X., Kong, B., Vigil, R.D.: Simulation of algal photobioreactors: recent developments and challenges. Biotechnol. Lett. **40**(9), 1311–1327 (2018)
9. Graham, L.E., Graham, J.M., Wilcox, L.W.: Algae, 2nd edn. Pearson Benjamin Cummings, San Francisco (2009)
10. Guo, T., Lin, T., Antulov-Fantulin, N.: Exploring interpretable LSTM neural networks over multi-variable data. In: Chaudhuri, K., Salakhutdinov, R. (eds.) Proceedings of the 36th International Conference on Machine Learning, ICML 2019, 9–15 June 2019, Long Beach, California, USA. Proceedings of Machine Learning Research, vol. 97, pp. 2494–2504. PMLR (2019)
11. Hochreiter, S., Schmidhuber, J.: Long short-term memory. Neural Comput. **9**(8), 1735–1780 (1997)
12. Jeong, K.S., Recknagel, F., Joo, G.J.: Prediction and elucidation of population dynamics of the blue-green algae *microcystis aeruginosa* and the diatom *stephanodiscus hantzschii* in the nakdong river-reservoir system (south korea) by a recurrent artificial neural network. In: Recknagel, F. (ed.) Ecological Informatics, pp. 255–273. Springer, Heidelberg (2006). https://doi.org/10.1007/3-540-28426-5_12
13. Jeong, K.S., Kim, D.K., Joo, G.J.: River phytoplankton prediction model by artificial neural network: model performance and selection of input variables to predict time-series phytoplankton proliferations in a regulated river system. Eco. Inform. **1**(3), 235–245 (2006)
14. Lee, S., Lee, D.: Improved prediction of harmful algal blooms in four major south Korea's rivers using deep learning models. Int. J. Environ. Res. Public Health **15**(7), 1322 (2018)
15. Levy, O., Dubinsky, Z., Schneider, K., Achituv, Y., Zakai, D., Gorbunov, M.Y.: Diurnal hysteresis in coral photosynthesis. Mar. Ecol. Prog. Ser. **268**, 105–117 (2004)
16. Lim, B., Arik, S.Ö., Loeff, N., Pfister, T.: Temporal fusion transformers for interpretable multi-horizon time series forecasting. CoRR abs/1912.09363 (2019)
17. Lucker, B.F., Hall, C.C., Zegarac, R., Kramer, D.M.: The environmental photobioreactor (ePBR): an algal culturing platform for simulating dynamic natural environments. Algal Res. **6**(Part B), 242–249 (2014)
18. Rawat, I., Kumar, R.R., Mutanda, T., Bux, F.: Biodiesel from microalgae: a critical evaluation from laboratory to large scale production. Appl. Energy **103**, 444–467 (2013)
19. del Rio-Chanona, E.A., Wagner, J.L., Ali, H., Fiorelli, F., Zhang, D., Hellgardt, K.: Deep learning-based surrogate modeling and optimization for microalgal biofuel production and photobioreactor design. AIChE J. **65**(3), 915–923 (2019)
20. Rossignolo, J.A., Felicio Peres Duran, A.J., Bueno, C., Martinelli Filho, J.E., Savastano Junior, H., Tonin, F.G.: Algae application in civil construction: a review with focus on the potential uses of the pelagic Sargassum spp. biomass. J. Environ. Manag. **303**(December 2021), 114258 (2022)
21. Shahriari, B., Swersky, K., Wang, Z., Adams, R.P., de Freitas, N.: Taking the human out of the loop: a review of Bayesian optimization. Proc. IEEE **104**(1), 148–175 (2016)
22. Taunt, H.N., Stoffels, L., Purton, S.: Green biologics: the algal chloroplast as a platform for making biopharmaceuticals. Bioengineered **9**(1), 48–54 (2018)
23. Vaswani, A., et al.: Attention is all you need. Adv. Neural Inf. Process. Syst. **30**, 6000–6010 (2017)
24. Wu, N., Green, B., Ben, X., O'Banion, S.: Deep transformer models for time series forecasting: the influenza prevalence case. CoRR abs/2001.08317 (2020)

Evaluating Zero-Cost Active Learning for Object Detection

Dominik Probst[1], Hasnain Raza[2], and Erik Rodner[1]($\boxtimes$) (iD)

[1] KI-Werkstatt/Ingenieurinformatik, Fachbereich 2, University of Applied Sciences Berlin, Berlin, Germany
erik.rodner@htw-berlin.de
[2] Hasty GmbH, Berlin, Germany

Abstract. Object detection requires substantial labeling effort for learning robust models. Active learning can reduce this effort by intelligently selecting relevant examples to be annotated. However, selecting these examples properly without introducing a sampling bias with a negative impact on the generalization performance is not straightforward and most active learning techniques can not hold their promises on real-world benchmarks. In our evaluation paper, we focus on active learning techniques without a computational overhead besides inference, something we refer to as zero-cost active learning. In particular, we show that a key ingredient is not only the score on a bounding box level but also the technique used for aggregating the scores for ranking images. We outline our experimental setup and also discuss practical considerations when using active learning for object detection.

Keywords: Active learning · Object detection · Evaluation paper

1 Introduction

When creating machine learning models, one is often faced with the problem that although enough data is available, a large part of it is not annotated. To reduce the amount of annotated data required, various types of methods can be used: semi-supervised learning [28] for integrating unlabeled examples, weakly-supervised learning [17] for using cheap annotation types, transfer learning [19], or domain adaptation [20] to exploit information from related tasks and data distributions. However, we focus on an orthogonal technique called active learning (AL), where an algorithm suggests informative samples to be labeled by an oracle (*e.g.*, a human) which will likely yield the highest gain in model quality once being annotated and used for training.

In contrast to a majority of AL literature that focuses on classification tasks [10,12,14,15], our application scenario is object detection, where annotation is even more costly. In addition, object detection is highly relevant for

Supported by Investitionsbank Berlin, Germany and computational resources of the BMBF grant programme "KI-Nachwuchs@FH".

P. Masci et al. (Eds.): SEFM 2022 Collocated Workshops, LNCS 13765, pp. 38–47, 2023.
https://doi.org/10.1007/978-3-031-26236-4_4

industrial visual inspection or autonomous mobility. In our work, we concentrate on AL methods that do not require changing the model architecture and where scores can be calculated with a low computational overhead, something we define as *zero-cost active learning* in this paper. With these practical constraints, a large number of active learning approaches are simply impossible to apply, since they require either an architectural change or a large additional computational overhead [25].

2 Related Work

While a lot of the literature focuses on active learning for image classification, it is difficult to find previous research that explore how these simple methods for uncertainty sampling perform on more complicated tasks like object detection, let alone their aggregation strategy. Furthermore, due to the rather low annotation cost of most classification tasks, active learning often does not yield performance benefits in practise. The publications of [15] and [14] introduce uncertainty sampling. Joshi *et al.* [12] explore uncertainty sampling for active learning by using the entropy as an uncertainty measure. Further works have extended these ideas to utilize other uncertainty measures such as variation ratios [9], mean standard deviation [3], margin [21], and variance of the class probability distributions. The paper of Sener and Savarese [23] is interesting as it specifically tackles the active learning problem for convolutional neural networks [13] (relevant for object detection) and formulates it as a core set selection problem.

A lot of these ideas have similarly been combined with Bayesian neural networks (*cf.* [11] for a primer). Since Bayesian statistics are often approximated with multiple forward passes, using them in AL is often too time-consuming. For object detection, using the scores of all object instances in the image can be used as a surrogate statistic. This is precisely the setting we explore. Choi *et al.* [5] presents active learning specifically for object detection, but their method involves modifying the detector network with mixture density networks for the localization and classification heads. Agarwal *et al.* [2] explores a distance measurement based "contextual diversity". The work of Yuan *et al.* [26] is similar to our approach since images are considered as "bags of instances". However, their method makes modifications to the detector model, impractical for several applications. The same holds for [22], although their setup is similar to ours except for the white boxing approach. Brust *et al.* [4] is comparable to the methodology and idea of our work, the only difference being that we benchmark more active learning scoring functions. The paper of [8] presents a framework for benchmarking active learning algorithms. Our underlying software design is similar, but it's presentation is not in the scope of this paper.

3 Zero-Cost Active Learning for Object Detection

Our setup for active learning is as follows: first, we assume an initial annotated training set of minimal size or directly a pre-trained detector model (already on the target task) to be given. Furthermore, we assume to have access to a large unlabeled dataset $\mathcal{D}_u = \{I_k\}_k$. The detector is applied to all images of this dataset. However, if this is computational infeasible a random sampling could be applied to reduce the set, although we do not investigate this possibility here.

After applying the detector, we get multiple bounding boxes $B_{k,i}$ with $1 \leq i \leq M_k$ for every image I_k, with each having class probabilities $p_{k,i,d}$, for all classes $1 \leq d \leq D$. Selecting the most relevant examples to be labeled is then done by scoring each image I_k with a function s and finally providing the L images with the highest score to the oracle. In a real-world scenario, the oracle would be a human annotator, while in our experimental setup we directly use the ground-truth of the benchmark dataset to automate the evaluation process.

In the following, we outline the different options for the scoring function s, which is calculated by first scoring bounding boxes and accumulating these individual scores for each image.

3.1   Scoring Bounding Boxes

The majority of the research done for active learning focuses on image classification. Therefore, there are multiple established methods directly using inferred class probabilities p and are thus suitable to define a scoring function $x(k,i)$ for a bounding box i in image k.

In the following, we skip the index k of the image for notational brevity.

Margin Score for Active Learning. The margin method of [21], in other literature sometimes referred to as 1-vs-2 method, is a measure for the uncertainty of the predicted probabilities. For a bounding box B_i it is defined by:

$$x_{ms}(i) = 1 - (p_{i,d_1} - p_{i,d_2}) \tag{1}$$

with d_1 being the class with the highest and d_2 being the class with the second highest predicted probability, respectively. If the detector is uncertain, at least two classes will be likely predicted with a similar probability. This results in a high value of x_{ms} close to 1. In rather certain cases, we will observe lower values of the score.

Variance Score for Active Learning. An alternative for the margin score, is to measure the variance of the predicted probabilities directly:

$$x_{vs}(i) = 1 - \frac{1}{D-1} \sum_{d=1}^{D} \left(p_{i,d} - \frac{1}{D} \sum_{j=1}^{D} p_{i,j} \right)^2. \tag{2}$$

The reasoning for this measure is the same as the one for the margin score with the difference being that it does not only focus on the two most likely classes being predicted.

Entropy Score for Active Learning. Since the output of the detector is a probability vector, we should more consequently use entropy as a measure of uncertainty:

$$x_{\text{ent}}(i) = -\left(\sum_{d=1}^{D} p_{i,d} \cdot \log_2 p_{i,d}\right) / \log_2(D) \ . \tag{3}$$

Similarily to both previous scores, this score has its maximum at 1 and we are interested in the examples with the highest score.

Random. To compare with an iterative annotation cycle that does not use active learning at all (passive learning), all images for the next learning process can also be selected with a random scoring function. This baseline has to be evaluated in any active learning benchmark, because none of the state-of-the-art active learning methods can guarantee any benefit at all compared to classical passive learning without an intelligent selection of examples during annotation.

3.2   Scoring Images by Accumulating Bounding Box Scores

Since several objects can be detected for one image, the values x of the individual detections must be accumulated to result in a score s for the whole image instead of a single bounding box. Please note that in the following, $x(k,i)$ denotes an arbitrary active learning score (margin, variance, entropy, or random) of a bounding box $B(k,i)$. In our work, we use one of the following accumulation functions:

Mean Accumulation. A straightforward way to accumulate bounding box active learning scores is to calculate the mean of all the scores for an image I_k:

$$s_{\text{mean}}(k) = \frac{1}{M_k} \sum_{i=1}^{M_k} x(k,i). \tag{4}$$

Therefore, all bounding boxes affect the resulting score, also the ones that were detected with high confidence. This might be disadvantageous in the following scenario: let's assume that one of the existing object categories of the task is rather easy to detect with multiple instances in nearly every image, e.g., a face category. A detector that has very well learned to detect faces but confuses and misses all other categories, would still lead to a low active learning score for nearly all unlabeled images, despite the fact that they contain relevant instances of other object categories that should be annotated.

Sum Accumulation. An alternative is to compute the sum of all bounding box active learning scores:

$$s_{\text{sum}}(k) = \sum_{i=1}^{M_k} x(k,i). \tag{5}$$

The result does strongly depend on the number of objects in an image. This can have the effect that images with many objects achieve a higher score than images with fewer objects. For active learning, this can be reasonable, since the annotator automatically focuses on images with many objects in scenarios that are likely more challenging (due to overlaps, different sizes, etc.). However, it would also prevent the annotator from seeing images with object categories that usually appear in isolated environments.

Maximum Accumulation. Given the obvious caveats of the previous methods, we can also compute the maximum bounding box active learning score of the whole image:

$$s_{\max}(k) = \max_{1 \le i \le M_k} x(k, i). \tag{6}$$

Consequently, the active learning score of an image only depends on a single most uncertain object detection.

4   Experiments and Evaluation

In the following, we evaluate all resulting active learning approaches, *i.e.* all combinations of bounding box scores x and accumulation functions s.

4.1   Design of the Experiments

First, we elaborate on our experimental setup including data, detector, and evaluation criterion used.

Dataset. Running active learning experiments requires hundreds of training runs to be performed. We therefore choose the Pascal VOC 2012 [7] dataset with the usual splits for experiments, since it has a medium size allowing several experiments on a standard GPU workstation (with two NVIDIA RTX 3090) and is non-trivial for object detection. The dataset contains several thousand images with overall twenty object categories. We use the validation dataset of Pascal VOC 2012 for evaluating the models. The Pascal VOC 2012 training set is used for the initial random training set as well as for the images the active learning techniques can select from.

Detector. As a detector, we use a Faster R-CNN model [18] (ResNet-50, FPN) since it is prevalent in many standard object detection implementations in industry. In particular, we used the implementation of detectron2 [24] and the standard training scheme implemented therein. All of our training runs had a length of 100 epochs with early stopping.

Evaluation Criteria. To compensate for deviations, the active learning process (all cycles) was repeated five times and the performance was determined using the mean average precision (mAP) of all categories with an intersection over union (IoU) threshold of 0.5 following the standard evaluation procedure for Pascal VOC 2012. Our oracle always annotated the given images with all ground-truth bounding boxes (see below for an discussion on oracle assumptions).

Experimental Setup. The model was initially trained with 10 fully annotated images. Afterwards, an active learning technique was used to score each image.

In active learning cycle ℓ, the $L = 10\ell + 10$ images with the largest score were then given to the oracle to be labeled and used in the next cycle for training. Note that the number of training examples annotated increases over time.

The training data set was initially started with randomly selected labelled images and then steadily increased.

Oracle Design. It is important to note that we use a specific design of the oracle in our experiments. The oracle simulates a human annotator and should be adapted to the application under consideration. In our case, we make the following assumptions:

1. Given an image, the annotator annotates all ground-truth object instances present in the given images.
2. The annotator annotates perfect bounding boxes.
3. An annotator is provided with several images at once and all images are annotated before the next active learning cycle ℓ continues.

Assumption 1 and 2 definitely do not hold in practice. However, breaking these assumptions results in label noise for object detection as already studied in several works, such as [1]. We therefore assume perfect annotations to reduce the complexity of the experiments and since we did not see any surprising insights under noise influence in preliminary experiments. Selecting and annotating multiple images at once (assumption 3) is a batch active learning setting [6]. There are multiple approaches tackling this scenario [27] for classification tasks, since the relevance of the examples in a batch is not independent from each other. All images in a batch might be individually relevant to be labeled but might be highly redundant when all of them are similar in the batch. In our evaluation, batch active learning is not considered, since it would involve an additional computational cost currently not feasible in practice.

4.2 Evaluation

Quantitative Evaluation. Our main results are given in Fig. 1, where we plot mAP performance of the resulting detector with respect to the number of training examples used. This plot shows the results for all method combinations (selection of a bounding box score method and accumulation technique).

It can be seen that the margin criterion performs best in combination with a maximum accumulation. The choice of accumulation is indeed relevant, since mean accumulation of the margin scores results in significantly worse models with respect to mAP performance. Furthermore, the margin criterion is, irrespective of the accumulation method, the scoring technique of choice, since all studied alternatives (entropy and variance) are often even worse than classical passive learning (denoted as random in the plot). The results shown in Fig. 1 hide the variation of the model performance, *i.e.* the standard deviation of the mAP values. Therefore, Fig. 2 shows three points in time (related to the number of training examples used) in detail with error bars.

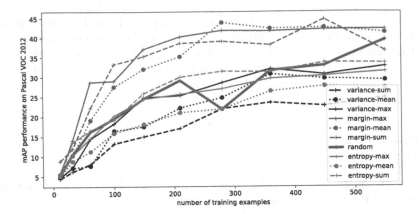

Fig. 1. Performance of the different AL models with an increasing number of training examples.

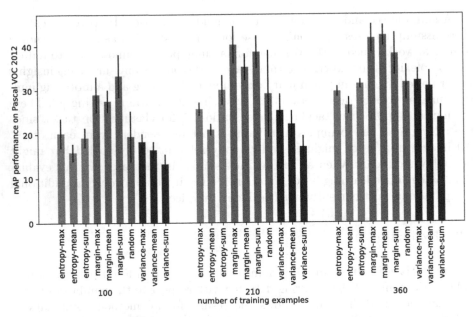

Fig. 2. Performance of the different AL models for different numbers of training examples. The standard deviation resulted from different data splits.

Qualitative Evaluation. To understand the method's behaviour, we show some examples selected by our margin technique in Fig. 3. The sum accumulation method clearly results in images being selected that contain a large number of objects. Therefore, we observe empirical evidence for our reasoning in Sect. 3.2.

Comparison with Non-zero-cost Methods. We also compare the best zero-cost active learning technique "margin-max" with CALD [25], a recently pub-

Fig. 3. Qualitative results of models trained at different active learning cycles for two method combinations of our active learnign schemes. Bounding boxes are shown with red color irrespective of their category for simplicity. (Color figure online)

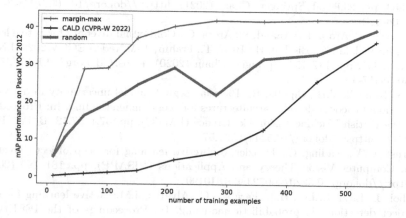

Fig. 4. Comparison of our best zero-cost active learning method, the random baseline and the active learning method of [25].

lished active learning method that measures the relevance of an unlabeled image by augmenting the image and evaluating the stability of the detector results. A technique that involves a significant computational overhead. The results are depicted in Fig. 4. At first sight, the state-of-the-art method of [25] results in inferior performance even compared to standard passive learning (random). However, this is most likely due to the different pretrained weights being used. In our case, we make use of models pretrained on the MS-COCO dataset [16]. In contrast, our results of [25] only use ImageNet classification weights. Furthermore, the results shown in the original work of [25] are based on models with a larger initial set of annotated examples. Further evaluation is necessary to allow for full comparision with [25].

5 Conclusion and Future Work

In our paper, we evaluated active learning techniques that are easy to implement and do not involve a significant computational overhead besides model inference. In total, nine method combinations have been evaluated and compared. Our best method achieved a significant performance gain compared to passive learning (no intelligent selection of unlabeled examples for annotation) and comes without additional cost.

Future work will concentrate on batch active learning with minimal computational overhead as well as integrating location uncertainty into the scoring functions.

References

1. Adhikari, B., Peltomäki, J., Germi, S.B., Rahtu, E., Huttunen, H.: Effect of label noise on robustness of deep neural network object detectors. In: Habli, I., Sujan, M., Gerasimou, S., Schoitsch, E., Bitsch, F. (eds.) SAFECOMP 2021. LNCS, vol. 12853, pp. 239–250. Springer, Cham (2021). https://doi.org/10.1007/978-3-030-83906-2_19

2. Agarwal, S., Arora, H., Anand, S., Arora, C.: Contextual diversity for active learning. In: Vedaldi, A., Bischof, H., Brox, T., Frahm, J.-M. (eds.) ECCV 2020. LNCS, vol. 12361, pp. 137–153. Springer, Cham (2020). https://doi.org/10.1007/978-3-030-58517-4_9

3. Alex Kendall, V.B., Cipolla, R.: Bayesian segnet: model uncertainty in deep convolutional encoder-decoder architectures for scene understanding. In: Proceedings of the British Machine Vision Conference (BMVC), pp. 57.1–57.12. BMVA Press (2017). https://doi.org/10.5244/C.31.57

4. Brust, C.A., Käding, C., Denzler, J.: Active learning for deep object detection. In: Computer Vision Theory and Applications (VISAPP), pp. 181–190 (2019). https://doi.org/10.5220/0007248601810190

5. Choi, J., Elezi, I., Lee, H.J., Farabet, C., Alvarez, J.M.: Active learning for deep object detection via probabilistic modeling. In: Proceedings of the IEEE/CVF International Conference on Computer Vision (ICCV), pp. 10264–10273 (2021)

6. Citovsky, G., et al.: Batch active learning at scale. Adv. Neural. Inf. Process. Syst. **34**, 11933–11944 (2021)

7. Everingham, M., Eslami, S., Van Gool, L., Williams, C.K., Winn, J., Zisserman, A.: The pascal visual object classes challenge: a retrospective. Int. J. Comput. Vision **111**(1), 98–136 (2015)

8. Feng, Z., et al.: ALBench: a framework for evaluating active learning in object detection. arXiv preprint arXiv:2207.13339 (2022)

9. Freeman, L.C.: Elementary Applied Statistics: For Students in Behavioral Science. Wiley, New York (1965)

10. Freytag, A., Rodner, E., Denzler, J.: Selecting influential examples: active learning with expected model output changes. In: Fleet, D., Pajdla, T., Schiele, B., Tuytelaars, T. (eds.) ECCV 2014. LNCS, vol. 8692, pp. 562–577. Springer, Cham (2014). https://doi.org/10.1007/978-3-319-10593-2_37

11. Gal, Y.: Uncertainty in deep learning. Ph.D. thesis, University of Cambridge (2016)

12. Joshi, A.J., Porikli, F., Papanikolopoulos, N.: Multi-class active learning for image classification. In: 2009 IEEE Conference on Computer Vision and Pattern Recognition, pp. 2372–2379. IEEE (2009)
13. LeCun, Y., Bengio, Y., et al.: Convolutional networks for images, speech, and time series. Handb. Brain Theory Neural Netw. **3361**(10), 1995 (1995)
14. Lewis, D.D., Catlett, J.: Heterogeneous uncertainty sampling for supervised learning. In: Machine Learning Proceedings 1994, pp. 148–156. Elsevier (1994)
15. Lewis, D.D., Gale, W.A.: A sequential algorithm for training text classifiers. In: Croft, B.W., van Rijsbergen, C.J. (eds.) SIGIR 1994, pp. 3–12. Springer, London (1994). https://doi.org/10.1007/978-1-4471-2099-5_1
16. Lin, T.-Y., et al.: Microsoft COCO: common objects in context. In: Fleet, D., Pajdla, T., Schiele, B., Tuytelaars, T. (eds.) ECCV 2014. LNCS, vol. 8693, pp. 740–755. Springer, Cham (2014). https://doi.org/10.1007/978-3-319-10602-1_48
17. Reiß, S., Seibold, C., Freytag, A., Rodner, E., Stiefelhagen, R.: Every annotation counts: multi-label deep supervision for medical image segmentation. In: Proceedings of the IEEE/CVF Conference on Computer Vision and Pattern Recognition, pp. 9532–9542 (2021)
18. Ren, S., He, K., Girshick, R., Sun, J.: Faster R-CNN: towards real-time object detection with region proposal networks. Adv. Neural Inf. Process. Syst. **28** (2015)
19. Rodner, E., Denzler, J.: One-shot learning of object categories using dependent Gaussian processes. In: Goesele, M., Roth, S., Kuijper, A., Schiele, B., Schindler, K. (eds.) DAGM 2010. LNCS, vol. 6376, pp. 232–241. Springer, Heidelberg (2010). https://doi.org/10.1007/978-3-642-15986-2_24
20. Rodner, E., Hoffman, J., Donahue, J., Darrell, T., Saenko, K.: Towards adapting imagenet to reality: scalable domain adaptation with implicit low-rank transformations. arXiv preprint arXiv:1308.4200 (2013)
21. Roth, D., Small, K.: Margin-based active learning for structured output spaces. In: Fürnkranz, J., Scheffer, T., Spiliopoulou, M. (eds.) ECML 2006. LNCS (LNAI), vol. 4212, pp. 413–424. Springer, Heidelberg (2006). https://doi.org/10.1007/11871842_40
22. Roy, S., Unmesh, A., Namboodiri, V.P.: Deep active learning for object detection. In: Proceedings of the British Machine Vision Conference (BMVC), p. 91 (2018)
23. Sener, O., Savarese, S.: Active learning for convolutional neural networks: a coreset approach. In: International Conference on Learning Representations (ICLR) (2017)
24. Wu, Y., Kirillov, A., Massa, F., Lo, W.Y., Girshick, R.: Detectron2 (2019). https://github.com/facebookresearch/detectron2
25. Yu, W., Zhu, S., Yang, T., Chen, C.: Consistency-based active learning for object detection. In: Proceedings of the IEEE/CVF Conference on Computer Vision and Pattern Recognition, pp. 3951–3960 (2022)
26. Yuan, T., et al.: Multiple instance active learning for object detection. In: Proceedings of the IEEE/CVF Conference on Computer Vision and Pattern Recognition (CVPR), pp. 5330–5339 (2021)
27. Zhdanov, F.: Diverse mini-batch active learning. arXiv preprint arXiv:1901.05954 (2019)
28. Zheng, M., You, S., Huang, L., Wang, F., Qian, C., Xu, C.: SimMatch: semi-supervised learning with similarity matching. In: Proceedings of the IEEE/CVF Conference on Computer Vision and Pattern Recognition, pp. 14471–14481 (2022)

Fast Simulation Response by a Simulation Based Machine Learning (SMiLe) Approach

Youness Bami, Yannik Luysberg, and Juergen Jakumeit[✉]

Access e.V., Intzestr. 5, 52072 Aachen, Germany
j.jakumeit@access-technology.de

Abstract. Process simulation is an important tool for designing manufacturing processes before manufacturing a part, optimizing the process, and later identifying the causes of problems and failures during manufacture. Calculation times for complex manufacturing processes can be several hours to days. This prevents rapid response through simulation in the event of a failure during production and integration of process simulation into design optimization loops.

Simulation-based Machine Learning (SMiLe) can be an approach to achieve fast response times using simulations: Many simulations of process and material parameter variations and different designs are used to create a database for training machine learning algorithms that predict the key results of the process simulation. The machine learning algorithms can then be integrated into a design optimization loop or provide quick hints for avoiding failures in a production process. The basis for this approach is a simulation that is well calibrated by experimental data for the manufacturing process and the materials involved. If computing resources and software licenses are available, the simulation can be used continuously to improve the simulation database by adding simulation results, thereby increasing the quality of the machine learning algorithm's prediction. This is a paradigm shift from running simulations when results are needed, to running simulations before results are needed, to getting quick solution hints through simulation when needed.

The SMiLe method and workflow are presented and machine learning algorithms are discussed. The method is demonstrated on an industrial manufacturing process, the prediction of cast iron microstructural properties for wind turbine applications.

Keywords: Process simulation · Machine learning · Process optimization

1 Introduction

Process simulation is an important tool for designing manufacturing processes before a part is produced, for optimizing the process, and later identifying the causes of problems and failures during manufacture. In small and medium-sized companies, the need for a specialized simulation program with expensive licenses running on a high-performance computer and an expert running the simulation can represent a high barrier to using simulation. This is especially true when simulation is not used as a standard tool, but

P. Masci et al. (Eds.): SEFM 2022 Collocated Workshops, LNCS 13765, pp. 48–58, 2023.
https://doi.org/10.1007/978-3-031-26236-4_5

only in the case of a manufacturing problem to analyze the problem and develop proposed solutions. Cloud computing is a way to lower this threshold by providing licenses and software on-demand with a flexible amount of computing power. Simulation platforms such as AixViPMaP [1] can add a user-friendly interface that allows process engineers to run the simulation and prepare the results without special simulation knowledge.

Although platform computing can reduce computing times by using a large number of processes, it does not fundamentally change the problem that computing times for complex manufacturing processes can be several hours to days. This prevents rapid reaction through simulation in the event of an error during production and the integration of process simulation into design optimization loops.

Simulation-based machine learning (SMiLe) can be an approach to achieve fast response times using simulations: Many simulations of process and material parameter variations and different designs are used to create a database for training machine learning algorithms that predict the key process simulation results. The machine learning algorithms can then be integrated into a design optimization loop or provide quick hints to avoid errors in a production process. The basis for this approach is a simulation that is well calibrated by experimental data for the manufacturing process and the materials involved.

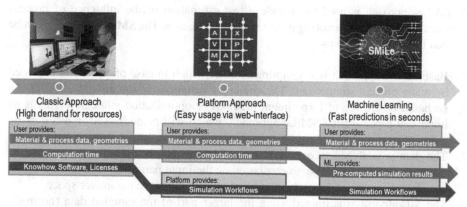

Fig. 1. Reducing the effort for process simulation by platform computing (middle) and a Simulation based Machine Learning approach (SMiLe, right)

Figure 1 illustrates the new simulation approaches using a simulation platform and machine learning. Starting from a classic approach (left), in which knowledge, software, licenses, computing power and computing time have to be provided by the user, cloud computing with a simulation platform (middle) reduces the need for knowledge, software with licenses and computing power, but only the use of machine learning with a SMiLe approach (right) addresses the problem of high computing times.

In a classic or platform-based simulation approach, the simulations are performed when problems arise in the manufacturing process. The long computing times often impede a quick reaction through simulation and reduce the use of simulation to support problem solving. In contrast, the SMiLe approach enables the simulation of many parameter variations before an error occurs in the manufacturing process, to ensure that in case of a manufacturing error, a well-trained ML algorithm is available and a fast simulation response can guide the process engineers to solve the manufacturing problem. This is a paradigm shift from running simulations when results are needed, to running simulations before results are needed, to getting quick solution hints through simulation when needed.

The continuous use of available computing resources and software licenses to improve the simulation database and thus the quality of the ML algorithm's prediction is an important and powerful feature of the SMiLe approach. The data analysis of the simulated database can be used to identify parameter combinations for which a simulation result significantly improves the quality of the prediction.

Machine learning algorithms used in the SMiLe-approach are discussed in the next chapter and the method is demonstrated on an industrial manufacturing process in the following chapters: The estimation of microstructure parameters of components for wind turbines casted from nodular cast iron alloys. Finally, the results are summarized and an outlook is given.

2 The SMiLe Approach

A SMiLe-approach is used to provide a fast estimation of the influence of process parameters on the manufacturing process using simulation. The SMiLe-approach can be divided into four basic steps:

1. Basis of the approach is a sampling of data, which in case of SMiLe is provided by many process simulations. The choice of variations of the input parameter can be based on Design of Experiment methods or optimization strategies. This is an important aspect of the SMiLe-approach, which will be addressed in a follow up publication.
2. The data is analyzed to ensure, that correlations can be found which enable an estimation of the output parameter based on the input parameter. In addition strong correlations are identified, which can be used to reduce the parameter space.
3. The ML-algorithm is trained using the larger part of the sampled data (normally 80%) and the remaining data is used to test the quality of the estimation.
4. The ML-algorithm is used to predict the influence of material and process parameter on the manufacturing process outcome described by several output parameters.

In step 2, in order to avoid a poor performance of the ML-algorithm due to a poor quality of the data, the data is checked in advance with statistical methods and visualizations. Missing values and outliers are identified and the range and distribution of data is checked. For the data analysis a correlation matrix is used to show strong and week correlations between input and output parameters. Strong correlations between input parameters are used to reduce the parameter space by replacing one input parameter by the strong correlation to the other input parameter. Correlations between input and output parameters are important to ensure a predictive quality of the ML-approach.

A Principal Component Analysis (PCA) of the input data can be applied to reduce the dimension of the parameter space. The PCA structures large datasets by using the eigenvectors of the covariance matrix. This allows data sets to be simplified and illustrated by approximating a large number of statistical variables using a smaller number of linear combinations (the principal components) that are as meaningful as possible.

In step 3, 80% of the database is used to train a ML-algorithm. Since the output value for a specific input parameter variation is given by the simulation output, methods from supervised learning are used to analyze the training data and produce an inferred function, which can be used for mapping new examples. Supervised learning maps an input to an output based on example input-output pairs [2]. Each example is a pair consisting of an input object and a desired output value.

In this work linear regression methods are used as ML-algorithm. The regression methods are taken from the ML toolbox Scikit-learn [3]. In linear regression, an attempt is made to set up a linear relation between n input parameters X to one or more output parameters y using weights w in order to approximate y with the smallest possible error.

$$\|Xw - y\|_2^2 \to min_w \tag{1}$$

In Scikit-learn, the error is calculated using the least squares method, which is based on the singular value decomposition [3].

Regression problems are often ill-posed, the solution does not depend continuously on the data. Collinearity in data increases the number of degrees of freedom without introducing new information. Regularization techniques helps to handle this problem. The most common method is Tikhonov regularization, which is a compromise between fitting the data and a reduction of the norm. Regularization reduces the influence of collinearity and limits the degrees of freedom in a meaningful way [4, 5].

Ridge Regression (Weight Decay) is a least squares model with L2 regularization. The loss function

$$\|Xw - y\|_2^2 + \lambda \|w\|_2^2 \tag{2}$$

is minimized. By the regularization term, the loss function becomes larger when the weight is large. Since large values of the loss function are attempted to be optimized, the weights are kept small in order to avoid overfitting.

With the Polynomial Features module of Scikit-learn, the input features are converted to a polynomial of a higher order. In addition, the products of the individual features are included. For the input set [a, b], the polynomial-features with order two is:

$$[a, b] \to [1, a, b, a, ab, b] \tag{3}$$

In this way, even with linear regression models, a nonlinear function can be approximated. However, the number of elements increases exponentially, which increases the effort for fitting the model and may lead to overfitting.

Training a ML-model means searching for the weights w, which minimize the loss-function. Scikit-learn uses the Grid Search Method, which considers several parameter combinations and chooses the one that returns a lower error score. A part of the input and output sets is passed as a calibration set. This is divided into folds to train and validate the model with the parameters. Scikit-learn uses the coefficient of determination R^2 to find the best parameter combinations. The coefficient of determination R^2 of the regression indicates the proportion of the variability of y which is explained by the independent variables in the model. The best possible result for the coefficient of determination is 1, but can also be negative, since a model can be arbitrarily worse. R^2 is given by:

$$R^2 = 1 - \frac{\sum_{i=1}^{n} (y_i - \hat{y}_i)^2}{\sum_{i=1}^{n} (y_i - \bar{y})^2},$$ (5)

where $\hat{y}_i$ is the estimated value and $\bar{y}$ the mean value. Besides R^2, the mean square error (MSE) and the time needed to train the model are used to evaluate the quality of the prediction of a ML-model. MSE is calculated using:

$$\frac{1}{n} \sum_{i=1}^{n} (y_i - \hat{y}_i)^2$$ (5)

Once the model is fixed, a principal component regression (PCR) is applied to test whether the number of coefficients to be estimated can be reduced in the regression modeling [6].

PCR is a regression analysis technique based on principal component analysis (PCA). More specifically, PCR is used to estimate the unknown regression coefficients in a standard linear regression model. PCR uses PCA in combination with a regressor trained on the transformed data [7].

3 Application: Wind Turbine Components from Cast Iron

The SMiLe-approach is applied for the estimation of microstructure properties of nodular cast iron, used to manufacture modern wind turbine parts as slow speed shaft, torque arm and blade pitch control. Microstructure determines the mechanical properties that affect the size and weight of parts required to meet part specifications. Multiphase casting simulation is combined with a microscopic diffusion-driven growth model for eutectic grains in nodular cast iron to calculate microstructure parameters and estimate local material properties of wind turbine components. The flow of multiple phases is described using the volume of fluid (VoF) approach [8, 9]. Mass conservation equations are solved separately for both the liquid and solid phase. At the micro-level the diffusion-controlled growth model for grey iron eutectic grains by Wetterfall et al. [10] is combined with a growth model for white iron eutectic grains by Nastac and Stefanescu [11]. The micro-solidification model is coupled with macro-transport equations via source terms in the energy and continuity equation. Details of the simulation approach and validation results are reported in [12, 13].

The test geometry (Fig. 2) used consists of cubes of different sizes, each of which has a connection to a feeder through which the melt is filled. The geometry consists of 10 cubes with edge length 200 mm, 300 mm and 500 mm. The casting module of the three squares is representative for the casting modules found in wind turbine parts. The casting modulus is the relation between volume and surface of a geometry and is related to the cooling rate and solidification conditions. Therefore, solidification conditions in the test geometry are in the range found in wind turbine components. In order to have enough material to fabricate test samples for mechanical analysis, several squares of the smaller edge length were part of the test geometry.

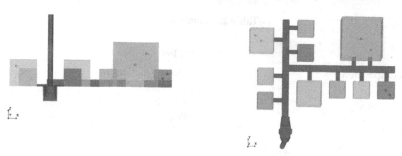

Fig. 2. Test geometry with cubes of edge length 200 mm, 300 mm and 500 mm. 6 positions of selected points for post-processing are marked.

Table 1. The variation of the input variables with which different simulations were set up. The values for these are all within the min-/max- specification of the alloy.

Parameter	Start	End	Step
Temperature (°C)	1290	1330	10
C (%)	3.5	3.7	0.1
Si (%)	2.3	2.6	0.1
Mn (%)	0.2	0.25	0.05

The pouring temperature and the composition of the melt were varied to generate parameter variations (Table 1). The casting temperature is changed in a range from the 1290 °C to 1330 °C. For the melt itself, the proportion of the alloying elements carbon (C), silicon (Si) and manganese (Mn) were varied within the specification range. In addition the edge length of the cube, the position of the test probes and the casting modulus are used as input parameters. Output parameters of the simulation are the distribution of graphite balls called nodular count in 2D, the solidification time, the critical cooling rate at liquidus temperature and the volume fraction of Graphite, Ferrite and Perlite. Table 2 lists the input and output parameters.

Table 2. Input and output parameters used in the ML-approach

Input	Output
Edge length of the box	NodularCount2D
Position within the box	Solidification time
Casting modulus	Critical cooling rate
Casting temperature	Max. Temperature

(continued)

Table 2. (*continued*)

Input	Output
Alloy composition - C - Si - Mn	Volume fractions of - Graphite - Ferrite - Pearlite

For step 1 of the SMiLe-approach 120 combinations of the input parameters casting temperature and the composition of the melt were simulated and the output values for the six test probes in the middle and on the diagonal of a 200 mm, 300 mm and 500 mm cube collected giving a data set of a total of 720 data sets.

In the second step the 720 data sets were analyzed and a correlation matrix calculated (see Fig. 3).

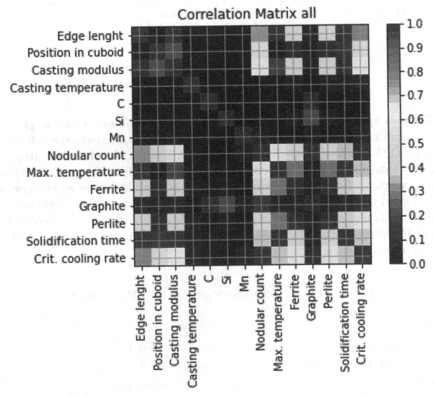

Fig. 3. Correlation matrix of the 7 input and 7 output parameters.

For step 3, the data sets are divided into training and test sets, with the training set containing 80% and the test set containing 20% of the data. Figure 4 gives the workflow of the ML-training approach.

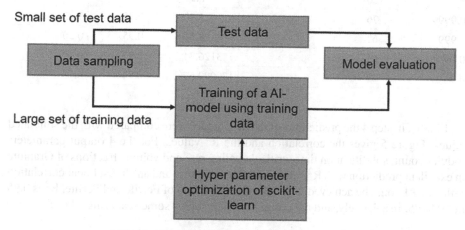

Fig. 4. Workflow of the ML-training approach.

The input features X were transformed into the dimensions up to five using polynomial features and results of the trained ridge models were compared. The model with polynomials of order 3 already provides solid predictions for the MSE and R2 score (see Table 3). Models with polynomials of order 4 and 5 have similarly good predictions, but training takes longer and overfitting is more likely due to the large number of input values.

Table 3. Comparison of Ridge model results using polynomial features from 1 to 5.

Order	Input	MSE	R^2	Time [s]
1	8	81466	0.76	1.08
2	36	61	0.95	0.07
3	120	0.29	0.95	0.34
4	330	0.23	0.96	3.05
5	792	0.15	0.96	16.6

The model with order 3 polynomial features was then used to reduce parameter space and training times through a PCR. Table 4 gives the results of the PCR. With decreasing variance and number of parameters, the training time can be reduced from 1.4 s to 0.1s. However, this is accompanied by a significant reduction in the prediction quality of the ML algorithm. Since the training time is not critical, the PCR was not used in the application to get the maximum prediction quality.

Table 4. Principal component regression on the transformed input data

Variance	Number of components	MSE	R^2	Time [s]
1	120	0.29	0.95	1.40
0.9999	76	5.49	0.95	1.22
0.999	67	8.56	0.95	0.20
0.99	62	3126.31	0.93	0.10
0.9	42	179999.57	0.74	0.18

Finally, in step 4 the predictions of the ML-model were compared with the simulated values. Figure 5 gives the correlation and the R^2 values. For the 4 output parameters nodular count, solidification time, critical cooling rate and volume fractions of Graphite an excellent prediction with R^2 values of 0.99 and higher and an almost linear correlation with slope 1 could be achieved. For the volume fraction of Ferrite and Perlite, R^2 is 0.95 and 0.9475, respectively, and the correlation plot shows some scattering.

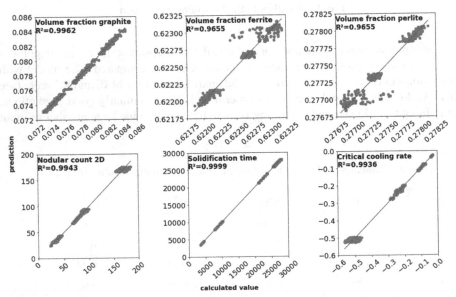

Fig. 5. Correlation between the calculated and predicted values of the test data sets for the volume fraction of Graphite, Ferrite and Perlite as well as nodular count, solidification time and critical cooling rate. The R^2 values are given.

As a first application the nodular count distribution in the cube of edge length 500 mm was predicted using the SMiLe-approach. Results for data points along the diagonal of the large cube were analyzed and the Ridge model with polynomial features of order 3 trained as described above. Figure 6 shows the data points and compares simulated and ML-predicted nodular count distribution. The general distribution of graphite balls is well predicted by the ML-algorithm, details at the center of cube differ slightly. A more detailed description of these calculation can be found in [13].

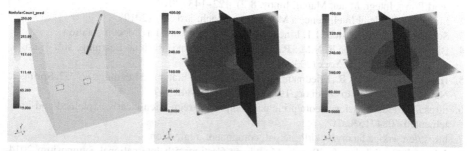

Fig. 6. Data points along the diagonal of the large cube (left) and a comparison of simulated (middle) and ML-predicted (right) nodular count distributions.

4 Summary and Outlook

A new simulation-based machine learning (SMiLe) approach was presented and applied to the industrial application of microstructure prediction for wind turbine parts cast from nodular cast iron. In the SMiLe approach, many simulations of process and material parameter variations and different designs are used to create a database for training machine learning algorithms that predict the key results of the process simulation. For the application in the field of casting wind turbine parts, a validated simulation model was used to run 120 simulations and create 720 datasets to train the ML algorithm. Linear ridge regression with polynomial features of the order 3 was found to give good results in terms of the R^2 value and the calculated correlations to the predicted results for the important result of the nodular count 2D. This shows that machine learning based on simulation results can be used to predict the outcome of otherwise time-consuming process simulations.

Next steps will be a validation of the SMiLe-predictions by a comparison with experimental data and the extension of the SMiLe approach to more complex geometries. To complete the SMiLe idea, an important development will be the use of design-of-experiment and optimization techniques to continuously determine new parameter settings that improve the completeness of the database and the prediction quality of the ML algorithms as simulation results for these parameter settings are added to the database.

Acknowledgements. Research work presented in this paper is a part of the research project "Numerical and experimental investigation of the solidification process in thick-walled castings made of nodular cast iron for wind power plants – LeKoGuss-WEA". Authors would like to thank the German Federal Ministry for Economic Affairs and climate Action for its financial support of this work. The authors acknowledge the support by Siemens PLM, agreement 60068580, for providing STAR-CCM+ licenses.

References

1. Koschmieder, L., et al.: AixViPMaP®—an operational platform for microstructure modeling workflows. Integr. Mater. Manuf. Innov. **8**(2), 122–143 (2019)
2. Stuart, J.: Artificial Intelligence a Modern Approach. 3rd edn. (2010)
3. Scikit Lineare Regression, 1.1. Linear Models—scikit-learn 1.1.2 documentation
4. Bishop, C.M., Nasrabadi, N.M.: Pattern Recognition and Machine Learning, vol. 4, no. 4, p. 738. Springer, New York (2006)
5. Hastie, T., Tibshirani, R., Friedman, J.: The Elements of Statistical Learning, vol. 52. Springer, New York (2001). https://doi.org/10.1007/978-0-387-84858-7
6. https://towardsdatascience.com/principal-component-regression-clearly-explained-and-implemented-608471530a2f
7. https://en.wikipedia.org/wiki/Principal_component_regression
8. Jakumeit, J., Subasic, E., Bünck, M.: Shape Casting: 5th International Symposium 2014 (2014)
9. Jakumeit, J., Laqua, R., Peric, M., Schreck, E.: Proceedings of Modeling of Casting, Welding and Advanced Solidification Processes XI (2006)
10. Wetterfall, S.E., Fredriksson, H., Hillert, M.: Solidification process of nodular cast iron. J. Iron Steel Inst. **210**(5), 323–333 (1972)
11. Nastac, L., Ştefănescu, D.M.: Modeling of the stable-to-metastable structural transition in cast iron. In: Advanced Materials Research, vol. 4, pp. 469–478. Trans Tech Publications Ltd. (1997)
12. Subasic, E., Huang, C., Jakumeit, J., Hediger, F.: Combination of microscopic model and VoF-multiphase approach for numerical simulation of nodular cast iron solidification. In: IOP Conference Series: Materials Science and Engineering, vol. 84, no. 1, p. 012024. IOP Publishing (2015)
13. Bami, Y., et al.: Design of light wind turbine parts by Simulation based machine learning. In: proceedings of TMS (2023, accepted)

Condition Monitoring of a Mechanical Pulsatile Heart Support System via Support-Vector Machine

Mario Koddenbrock[1]([✉]) [iD] and Hendrik Heinze[2]

[1] Gesellschaft zur Förderung angewandter Informatik e.V., Volmerstraße 3, 12489 Berlin, Germany
koddenbrock@gfai.de
[2] Berlin Heart GmbH, Wiesenweg 10, 12247 Berlin, Germany
heinze@berlinheart.de

Abstract. Patients with life-threatening heart failure where all conservative therapeutic options have been exhausted may be indicated for mechanical pulsatile ventricular assist devices. These paracorporeal VADs are used for short- and long-term support of left and/or right ventricular pumping function (see [1]). Currently, these systems require short monitoring cycles by clinical professionals and allow little mobility for the patient. To extend these cycles and improve mobility, this paper presents a method to detect increased risk of complications during the use of a VAD.

The VADs membrane is monitored using acoustic measurements, where ultrasonic pulses are emitted and the corresponding echo is measured. The main challenge is that a change in the essential performance characteristics of the blood pump would threaten the already granted approval as a medical device. Furthermore, there is the problem that the ultrasonic pulse has to pass through a two-meter long tube and that the motion behavior of the membrane is not symmetrical, but rather resembles the inflation and deflation of a plastic bag.

A supervised classification using support vector machine (SVM) has proven to be a sufficiently accurate method for this problem and this type of data. The SVM operates on the frequency spectra of the impulse responses and classifies three trained states that must occur during a single pump cycle if the system is fully functional. A faulty state of the system is detected by the absence of certain states within a pumping cycle.

Keywords: Condition monitoring · Medical engineering · Supervised learning · Support vector machines

1 Introduction

EXCOR® Pediatric by Berlin Heart GmbH (see [1]) is the only mechanical pulsatile heart support system (Ventricular Assist Device, VAD) that has regulatory approval to treat patients in the United States, Canada, the European Union and many other countries worldwide. The paracorporeal VAD can assist pediatric patients of all ages,

P. Masci et al. (Eds.): SEFM 2022 Collocated Workshops, LNCS 13765, pp. 59–70, 2023.
https://doi.org/10.1007/978-3-031-26236-4_6

from newborns to adolescents, and is used for short- to long-term support of left and/or right ventricular pump. It is indicated for children with life-threatening heart failure after all conservative treatment options have been exhausted.

Current safety mechanisms are:

- The driving unit alerts if there is a change in pumping capacity
- The membrane of the pump consists of three layers instead of only one. If one of the layers has a defect, the membrane remains fully functional
- The clinical staff is trained to visually check the condition of the pumps. Currently, however, this system requires short monitoring cycles, allowing patients little mobility.

2 Requirements

EXCOR® Pediatric had to go through an extensive regulatory process before being approved as a medical device. A change in the system would put this approval in risk. Therefore, if possible, a condition monitoring system should not make any changes to the mechanical pump itself. This includes not connecting any sensors to the pump. Sensors may only be attached on the side of the driving unit and only in such a way that the airflow, which operates the pump through the tube, is not influenced significantly. After all, approval always depends on the test system not having any effects on the essential performance characteristics of the blood pump.

To summarize briefly, the following requirements apply to the sensor technology:

1. No sensors are allowed to be placed anywhere near the pump itself
2. Sensors used at the driving unit must not affect the air flow in the tube and thus the pumps performance

This implies that the sensors must be able to detect the condition of the membrane over the 2-m long tube.

General requirements for the system are:

3. Detection of the membrane position
4. Detection of the membrane condition (OK or not OK)

3 Technical Implementation

In order to comply with the demanding sensor requirements, an acoustic measurement method by means of ultrasound is used in the presented procedure. The position of the pumps membrane is determined by means of emitted sound pulses and the evaluation of the corresponding echo. One challenge that arises from this is the need for this ultrasonic pulse to pass through a two-meter-long tube.

Due to the expected significance of wave propagation in the direction of the tube, a shock wave was transmitted in the axial direction of the tube and its echo was analyzed. The ultrasonic sensor was mounted at the end of the tube leading to the blood pump in a

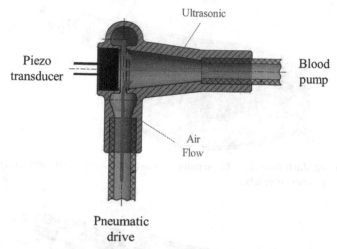

Fig. 1. Ultrasonic coupling into the airflow. To minimize the ultrasound insertion loss, a customized ultrasound coupler was developed, which is placed in the air stream between the pneumatic drive and the blood pump.

special coupling module. This was designed to ensure that the ultrasound signal reaches the blood pump with minimal loss and without disturbing the airflow (see Fig. 1).

The ultrasonic sensor has been configured to transmit and receive Barker codes (see [2]) in the range around 40 kHz. The transmitted signal (burst) has a duration of about 700 microseconds and varies in phase. This turned out to be best for covering the length of the tube while ensuring that the echo arrives before the next pulse is transmitted.

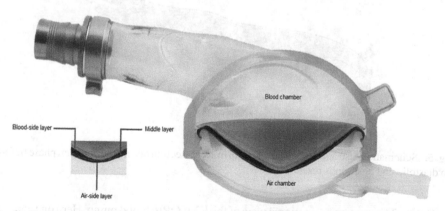

Fig. 2. Design of the EXCOR® blood pump in cross-section and a detailed view of the three-layer membrane

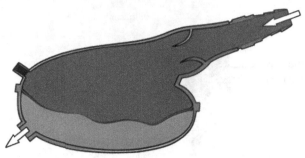

Fig. 3. Schematic illustration of the blood pump in cross-section during the inflation phase before the systolic end position is reached

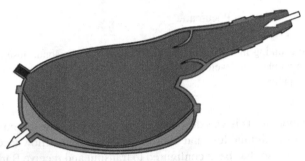

Fig. 4. Schematic illustration of the blood pump in cross-section when the systolic end position is reached

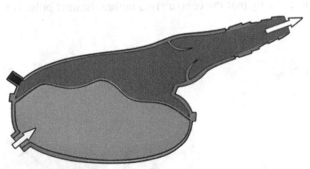

Fig. 5. Schematic illustration of the blood pump in cross-section during the deflation phase before the diastolic end position is reached

Figure 2 shows a cross-sectional view of the EXCOR® blood pump. Here one can see the blood chamber and the air chamber, which are separated by a three-layer membrane. The tube from the driving unit leads to the air chamber and the cannulas connected to the heart respectively the patient's blood circulation lead to the blood chamber.

Figures 3, 4, 5 and 6 shows schematically the different membrane positions during a single pump cycle.

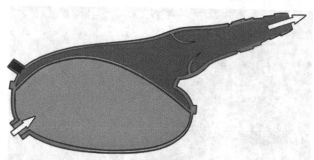

Fig. 6. Schematic illustration of the blood pump in cross-section when the diastolic end position is reached

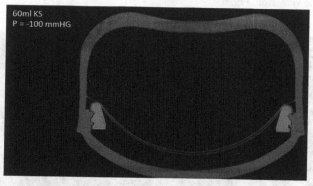

Fig. 7. X-ray scan of the blood pump when the systolic end position is reached. The scan corresponds to the view from Fig. 4

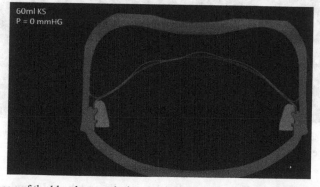

Fig. 8. X-ray scan of the blood pump during the deflation phase, before the diastolic end position is reached. The scan corresponds to the view from Fig. 5

To validate the behavior of the membrane during a pumping cycle, X-ray scans were done (see Figs. 2, 3, 4, 5, 6, 7, 8 and 9.). These clearly showed the same behavior of the membrane, as well as its three layers, as assumed in Figs. 3, 4, 5 and 6.

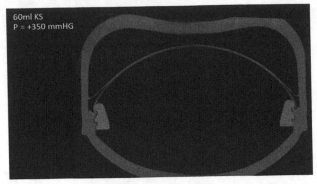

Fig. 9. X-ray scan of the blood pump when the diastolic end position is reached. The scan corresponds to the view from Fig. 6

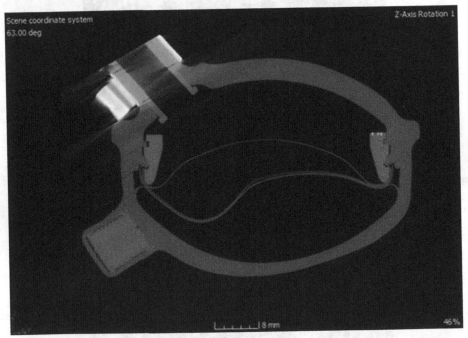

Fig. 10. X-ray scan of the blood pump with simulated defect. Air is pumped between two layers of the membrane

It can be seen from the X-ray scans that the systolic and diastolic end positions have a smooth defined surface, whereas the membrane takes on a more random shape during the intermediate states. The three layers of the membrane are close together in the two end positions, so they all share a common shape.

In the case of a membrane defect, two types of defect can be assumed. A damage of the blood chamber side layer and a damage of the air chamber side layer (See Fig. 11 and Fig. 12). In the first case, blood will leak between two layers of the membrane. In the second case, air will get between two layers of the membrane. These defects were reproduced and analyzed in an X-ray scan (See Fig. 10).

Figure 10 shows how the air that has entered between two layers of the membrane causes a large bubble. Therefore, at least in one of the two end positions, during a pumping process, the membrane does not reach the smooth shape.

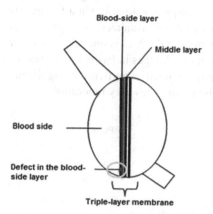

Fig. 11. Schematic view of the blood pump in cross-section. The blood chamber side layer of the membrane is defective and blood gets between the first and second layer

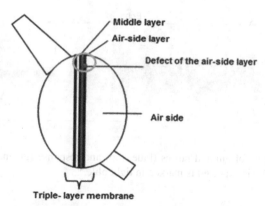

Fig. 12. Schematic view of the blood pump in cross-section. The air chamber side layer of the membrane is defective and blood gets between the second and third layer

4 Algorithmic Approach

To evaluate the ultrasonic echo, we first isolated the time range within which it is expected to return after passing through the two-meter-long tube. The speed of sound is independent of the frequency and amplitude of the sound, only the temperature of the medium (in our case air) matters. A change in temperature of ±5 °C means a change in the propagation speed of the sound of about ±3 m/s. This influence of the temperature is taken into account by a formula for the variation of sound velocity.

Figure 13 shows an example of the emitted pulses (top in blue) and the echo (bottom in green). The time range in which the transmitted echo is expected to return is marked in light blue and shown enlarged in Fig. 14. For further analysis, the signal response is moved into the frequency domain via a Fourier transformation. In Fig. 15, the resulting frequency spectra are visualized as a spectrogram. Here, each individual frequency spectrum is plotted on the Y-axis one after the other. The resulting heat map provides information about the changes in frequencies over time. Here, the emitted frequency of 40 kHz can be recognized as particularly significant in the response. During the intermediate states, the frequencies vary randomly.

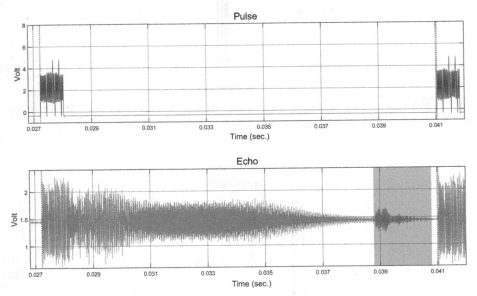

Fig. 13. Exemplary plot of emitted pulses (blue, top) and response (green, bottom). The time range in which the echo is expected is marked in light blue.

4.1 Feature Selection

Therefore, three states of the membrane were considered distinctive enough to be trained and detected by a machine learning approach. The systolic and diastolic end positions and all intermediate states. The entire frequency band was chosen as features, and a principal component analysis (PCA) (see [3]) for dimensionality reduction was applied in a preprocessing step. The PCA was set to retain 95% of the variability in the data. This resulted in a reduction of the frequency band from 700 frequency lines to five principal components.

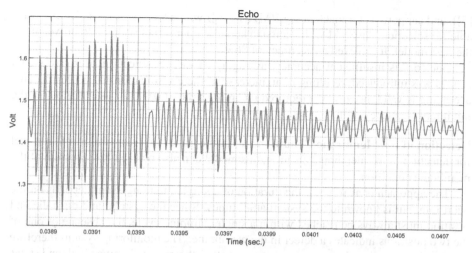

Fig. 14. Time snippet of the response signal in which the echo is expected to return. The waveform was recorded at a total reflection at the closed end of the tube

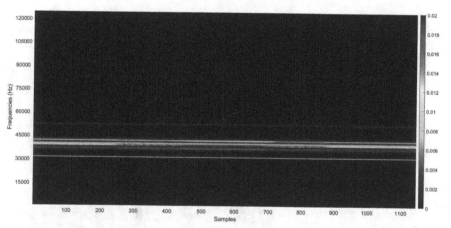

Fig. 15. Spectrogram over 1150 samples during a single pumping cycle. The transmitted signal is at 40 kHz. In the same frequency range, the response is highly significant as well

4.2 Data Basis

The data consisted of 2903 samples of 700 frequencies. The data was divided into training and test data with a 25% split.

4.3 Model Selection

Detection of the Membrane Position. To select a suitable 3-class classifier, an extensive hyperparameter optimization was performed using grid search. Validation of the search was done via 5-fold cross-validation. Linear models (see [4]), decision trees (see

[5]), and support vector machines (SVM) (see [6]) with a variety of kernels were available for selection. An SVM with Gaussian kernel with a kernel scale of 26 proved to be the best model. It achieved an accuracy of 86%.

Due to this insufficient accuracy, averaging of the classification over five signal echoes was introduced, resulting in an increase of the classification rate to 100%. This averaging is valid, because the required recording time of 0.015 s is still far below the minimum frequency of the pump.

Detection of the Membrane Condition. With the successful generation of a model for detection of the membrane position, this model can also be used for detection of the membrane condition.

The approach is as follows: the duration of a single pumping event depends on the heart rate, but is known to the system at all times. Since the systolic and diastolic end position must always be reached within a single pumping cycle, the absence of one of the two positions indicates a defect in the membrane. The monitoring system therefore checks, depending on the pump frequency, whether the model classifies both end states of the membrane at least once.

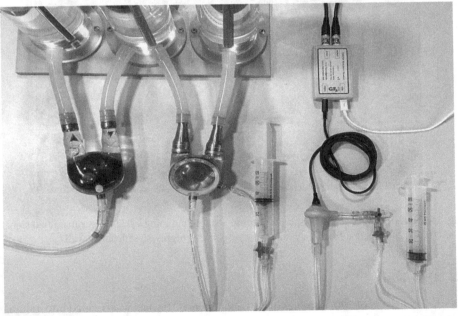

Fig. 16. Simulative experimental setup with blood circuit and two connected heart pumps. The right pump is prepared to simulate defects via air injection between two layers. This air bubble is controlled by a syringe. The membrane position can be controlled very precisely via another syringe. This means that static membrane positions can be set as well. In addition, the ultrasonic module including control is connected for condition monitoring

5 Validation and Results

The model for detecting the membrane position was validated on the data set and achieved a classification rate of 100% based on the averaging described above. The monitoring system based on this model reliably evaluated each pumping operation correctly in the endurance test of 24 h. However, the endurance test ran exclusively without any membrane faults. Thus, only the good condition was validated in the endurance test. In order to also validate the faulty condition, air was pumped between two layers of the membrane as shown in Fig. 10. This defect simulation was reliably and immediately detected in all performed tests. The simulative experimental setup can be seen in Fig. 16.

The complete experimental setup including control and coupling for the ultrasonic transmitter and receiver can be seen in Fig. 17.

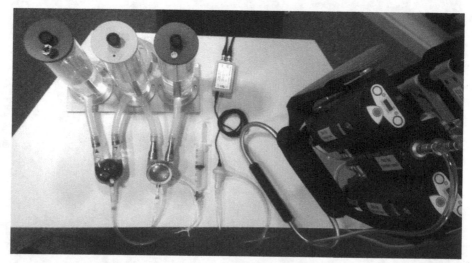

Fig. 17. Final view of the setup with the pneumatic driving unit of the VAD system, the ultrasound controller, and coupling. The heart pump is modified so that defects in the membrane can be simulated via the syringe in the center of the image. It can pump air between the layers of the membrane

6 Conclusions and Future Work

In real applications, both the tube between driving unit and pump and the pump itself are in motion a lot. In addition, the environmental conditions of the system may vary in many ways. It remains to be validated whether the trained model can be used in these changing conditions.

If the transfer from the laboratory to real operation is successful, the development can contribute to further increase the safety of the heart support system. It would enable fully automated monitoring of the membrane condition and thus more mobility for patients. After all, extended monitoring cycles mean that patients can move around for longer periods without medical professionals.

References

1. Almond, C.S., et al.: Berlin Heart EXCOR pediatric ventricular assist device for bridge to heart transplantation in US children. Circulation **127**(16), 1702–1711 (2013)
2. Barker, R.H.: Group synchronizing of binary digital sequences. In: Communication Theory, pp. 273–287, London (1953)
3. Jolliffe, I.T., Cadima, J.: Principal component analysis: a review and recent developments. Philos. Trans. R. Soc. A **374**, 2015020220150202. The Royal Society Publishing (2016)
4. Yuan, G.-X., Ho, C.-H., Lin, C.-J.: Recent advances of large-scale linear classification. Proc. IEEE **100**, 2584–2603 (2012). 10.1109 JPROC.2012 2188013
5. Breiman, L., Friedman, J., Olshen, R., Stone, C.: Classification and Regression Trees. Wadsworth, Belmont, CA (1984)
6. Schölkopf, S.: Learning with Kernels. MIT Press, Cambridge (2001)

Siamese Basis Function Networks for Data-Efficient Defect Classification in Technical Domains

Tobias Schlagenhauf[1]([⊠]) [iD], Faruk Yildirim[1], and Benedikt Brückner[2]

[1] Karlsruhe Institute of Technology, Wbk Institute of Production Science, Karlsruhe, Germany
tobias.schlagenhauf@kit.edu
[2] Imperial College London, London, UK

Abstract. Training deep learning models in technical domains is often accompanied by the challenge that although the task is clear, insufficient data for training is available. Additional to that, often also no similar source-datasets are available which can be used for transfer-learning to reduce the need for data in the target-domain. In this work, a novel approach based on the combination of siamese networks and radial basis function networks is proposed where the siamese networks serve as effective feature extractors. The architecture performs data-efficient classification without pretraining by measuring the distance between images in the semantic space in a data- efficient manner. The so called SBF-Net structure is developed and tested on three technical as well as two non-technical datasets. The architecture shows superior performance for all data sets, especially when only small data is available for training. The approach significantly outperforms existing ResNet50 and ResNet100 architectures when only 3, 5, 10 and 20 data points per class are available. Also, in data-setups where 75% of the data is used for training, the model yields the same performance as state-of-the-art-models. The main contribution of this work is a model that works particularly data efficient with small amounts of data without making prior constraints.

Keywords: Condition monitoring · Deep learning · Data efficiency · Predictive maintenance · Siamese networks

1 Introduction

The classification of objects in various domains has been gaining attention since the development of modern and powerful deep learning techniques [1]. Until recently, the human visual system had been unreached by computer algorithms. This has changed with the development of deep learning architectures [5]. Substantial successes could, for example, be achieved in the ILSVRC-ImageNet contest [2] using deep learning architectures. But deep learning architectures have also been gaining considerable success in the technical domain [3]. To make progress on the way towards autonomous systems, tools, and machines in the industrial context – but also in all other domains –, it is important to have accurate models for the classification of objects and the quality assessment of products. Additionally, to realize autonomous systems, it is important to enable them to self-describe their condition to prevent breakdowns. This is called predictive maintenance [48]. Especially in the technical domain, one is confronted with the fact that data is rare in a sense that it is either not available in large quantities or must be generated, which in turn is very costly [48]. An example is the automatic vision-based quality inspection of products, which is often difficult since examples of rejects are rare. The same holds for the detection of failures in the context of condition monitoring. Another challenge in the technical domain is the long tail of possible classes. Firstly, the objects which are of interest in the technical domains are numerous, like for instance failures on rails [7], failures in concrete [6], failures in wood [8], failures on metallic surfaces [4], and failures on machine tools [9], to name only a few examples. Secondly, each possible and produced product could, in principle, be a possible class. The numerous possible cases make it difficult to generate large datasets by combining datasets of the same objects as can be done in "pie, house, cat, mouse, car" cases. In addition to that, the classes rarely have counterparts in the real world, which amplifies the latter argument. Hence the classical One-Shot and Few-Shot learning approaches named in the literature are not directly applicable in these cases since they mostly require a source-dataset which is similar to the target-dataset. Since these data sets are often not available for very specialized (technical) applications, the approach presented here is based on the assumption that no prior transfer-learning can be performed and the model must work "out-of-the-box".

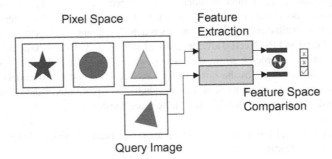

Fig. 1. Image comparison in feature space

The presented approach is based on the idea of comparing images in the feature domain and assigning the class of the image most similar to the questioned image. This is depicted in Fig. 1. The main idea of this paper is based on the concept of a nearest-neighbor-classifier used in a radial basis function network (RBF network) calculating a similarity measure between an input image and a query image. A drawback of the classical RBF network is its limited size [10] together with the limitation of the L2 norm in terms of describing a semantically useful similarity measure on raw image pixel data [43]. The authors implemented the basis function kernels as so-called Siamese-Kernels where a Siamese network was implemented for each kernel in the (R)BF network. By using these kernels as feature extractors, this allows for more meaningful comparisons to be made in the feature space.

The here presented approach is different from a classical CNN-based instance classification in that the authors perform an instance filtering using a Siamese network architecture by comparing the extracted feature vector of the query image to the extracted feature vectors of eligible images. The resulting distance is then processed in a RBF nearest-neighbor approach.

The main achievements of the paper are:

1. The authors provide a novel deep learning architecture (SBF-Net) for the data efficient "out-of-the-box" classification of images based on the comparison of their semantic representations. Using this method the authors demonstrate that it is possible to classify data-efficiently without relying on prior transfer learning.
2. The authors show a novel approach to train a Siamese-Kernel-Feature-Extractor with one single center per Kernel to generate, cum grano salis, an ensemble of experts which make a common decision but are experts for one image each.
3. The authors show the superior data efficiency, defined as validation accuracy given a specific number of training points, of the SBF-Net in comparison with state-of-the-art models.

The remainder of the paper is structured as follows. Section 2 reviews the related work in the field of RBF networks and Siamese networks for failure classification together with the general approach of failure classification on metallic surfaces. Section 3 presents the own approach and discusses the approach of using Siamese networks as kernels in an RBF network. Section 4 briefly describes the representatives of the technical datasets: The Northeastern University (NEU) surface defect database [11] showing six different kinds of defects on metallic surfaces, the ball screw drive (BSD) dataset [46] of defective machine tool elements, and the fabric (TEX) dataset [47] of failures on woven textiles. The well-known MNIST and cifar10 datasets are not described further. Section 5 presents the results of the SBF-Net by first investigating the basic effect of the number of Siamese-Kernels per class as well as the effect of data on the performance of the SBF-Net using the NEU dataset. Based on these findings, the data efficiency on the NEU, BSD, TEX, MNIST, and cifar10 datasets in comparison to the classical ResNet50 and ResNet101 models is investigated by using 3, 5, 10, 20, 50, and 100 data points per class. The results are followed by a discussion. Section 6 concludes the work and states open research questions.

2 Related Work

According to [10, 20], RBF networks nowadays are kind of forgotten neural network structures. Indeed, in comparison to classical CNN based approaches, there is only a limited number of RBF based image classification approaches such as those described, for instance, by [12] and [13]. This is likely due to the fact that the classical L2 norm is not a proper distance function to be used when dealing with raw image values in high-dimensional pixel space. Further, the classical RBF approach can be described as a version of a k-nearest-neighbor classification algorithm [10] which, for instance, [14] has proven to be underperforming in comparison to other classical machine learning algorithms like support vector machines. Nevertheless, one outstanding architecture implementing RBF elements is the well-known LeNet5 [15] architecture which uses Gaussian kernels in one of its last layers. Besides that, another recent approach described in [16] presents a deep RBF learning algorithm based on the well-known LeNet5 architecture for classification of the MNIST dataset. In [17], for instance, a somewhat earlier application of RBF networks is depicted which uses an RBF network for the classification of texture images. There, the authors emphasize the relevance of correctly choosing the prototype centers. Another contemporary application of RBF networks presented in [18] is the use of an RBF module as part of a pipeline for breast cancer detection in medical images. The images, though, are not processed in their raw formats. Yet another application of RBF networks in the medical image classification sector can be found in [19], where the authors used an RBF network for the classification of brain diseases by extracting classification features in advance. An interesting application is the use of RBF networks in the work by [20]. Here, the ReLu activation function in classical convolutional neural networks is replaced by RBF kernels to classify the MNIST, cifar10, and cifar100 datasets. It was found that using RBF activation functions is difficult since the network easily gets stuck in local minima during training.

Siamese networks have recently experienced significant attention due to their successful application in numerous domains. Substantial progress, enabled by their use, was made in the field of computer vision, especially in face recognition applications [21]. Nevertheless, their potential extends to other fields of research as well, e.g., to natural language processing [22] and object tracking [23].

The use of Siamese architectures for the purpose of defect detection, as showcased in this work, is an area of research that has been studied only insufficiently. Few works explore the potential of these approaches, but the results obtained are generally promising. [24] demonstrates that once trained on a specific task, such network may easily be reused for different purposes. Particular cases of application are presented in [25], where defective buttons are identified using Siamese networks, and [26], where the quality of a steel is assessed based on the appearance of its surface.

On the contrary, defect classification approaches leveraging different architectures are considered more frequently. They are mostly used to detect faults appearing on the surface of steel, and there is a broad variety of models for this purpose. [27] presents a detector using shearlet encoding and linear regression, while [28] models defect classes using hyperspheres in order to recognize potential surface anomalies. Further approaches include [29], employing kernel classifiers for detection, and [30], where a CNN network is used. Use of convolutional networks for this application is quite common. Another example may be found in [31] for more general applications beyond steel inspection. Lastly, [32] describes a system that learns through inputs provided by an expert. Various works demonstrate that these techniques can be used for other materials, too. Cracks in electrical components are detected in [33] through image segmentation performed by CNNs. A problem that appears more difficult to the human eye is the treatment of fabric due to its irregular surface. However, even such difficult problems may be solved as is demonstrated in [34] using autoencoders.

One will easily notice that most of the aforementioned approaches employ deep learning techniques in order to outperform earlier models. This is part of a greater trend that may be observed in various fields of research [35]. Besides the works addressing the topic of defect classification in general, many research projects have specifically investigated the NEU dataset which is used in this work as one technical dataset to demonstrate the advantage of our approach. [36] generates features using a CNN variant and then classifies the NEU images using a heuristic. Convolutional networks are equally employed in [37], the features generated are then fed into a fusion and a region proposal network before classification takes place. A major drawback of CNN approaches is the fact that training the network is usually expensive in terms of time and resources. To tackle this issue, [38] implements a transfer learning approach using pretrained networks and obtains promising results. [39] proposes a classifier which, once trained, may easily be adapted to changing conditions, such as an alteration of the production process supervised by the model. An approach particularly robust to noisy inputs, which are likely to occur in a real-world setting, is presented in [40].

Summa summarum, the literature shows that Siamese networks can serve as powerful feature extractors. Further RBF nets perform a distance-based classification but lack the fact that the pixel space is too high dimensional to achieve good results.

The here presented approach picks up the fact that the need for large datasets in the technical domain is often described in the literature but to the best of our knowledge, no investigations in terms of data efficiency in comparison to state-of-the-art models in the technical domain have been undertaken under the assumption that no transfer-learning is feasible.

The findings provide a novel method for both researchers and practitioners to further develop data-efficient classification algorithms in the technical domain.

3 Own Approach

The proposed architecture is based on three main components which are depicted, combined as a Siamese basis function network (SBF-Net), in Fig. 2.

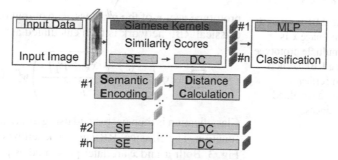

Fig. 2. Qualitative architecture of the SBF-Net

The first component is the architecture of a radial basis function network as a method of performing a classification based on the comparison of samples through a similarity measure like in nearest-neighbor classification. In these networks, the distance metrics to calculate the similarity score are classical distance metrics like the Euclidean distance or the cosine similarity which are, as described by e.g. [43], an insufficient way to compute a similarity measure in high-dimensional data like image data. During classification, normally statements such as: "Are the objects shown in the image the same as those in an image of a certain class, respectively is the underlying semantics in the images the same?" are derived. Our approach is less interested in the rare differences of pixel values but in encoding the semantics in images and in obtaining similarity scores between the encoded semantics. To achieve this behavior, the authors build upon Siamese networks and use them as effective semantic-feature extractors for classification. The authors name these feature extraction units Siamese-Kernels and implement them instead of the classical radial basis function kernels in the RBF network as the first part of the SBF-Net. To reinforce the classification ability, the authors additionally equip the network with a multilayer perceptron (MLP) instead of the single-layer neural network used in classical RBF networks. In the following paragraphs, the authors will explain in detail the single components together with the training setup.

3.1 Basis Function Network

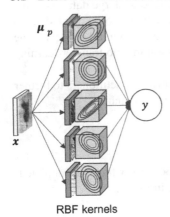

RBF kernels

Fig. 3. Classical RBF network setup where an image x is compared to multiple prototype vectors μ using RBF kernels which are then further processed using a weighted sum of the distances.

The idea of a radial basis function network as proposed by [41] is to use prototype vectors to realize a weighted comparison to an input vector. In contrast to a classical neural network in which the output per node is calculated as $o_p = \sigma(\sum_k x_k w_p^k)$, a radial basis function network implements so-called RBF kernels, where the input x is compared to a prototype vector μ which can be viewed as a class center in a nearest-neighbor approach. A distance score like the Euclidean distance is calculated on x and μ followed by a Gaussian mapping. The output may be calculated as $o_p = exp\left(-\dfrac{\sqrt{\sum_k (x_k - \mu_k^p)^2}}{2\sigma_p^2}\right)$ with μ_k^p the kth prototype vector of the pth class. The output of the whole classical RBF network is then calculated as follows:

$$y = \sum_p \left(exp\left(-\frac{\sqrt{\sum_k (x_k - \mu_k^p)^2}}{2\sigma_p^2}\right) w_{out}^p\right) = ow_{out}^T.$$

Classification is then performed using a classical sigmoid function. The classical RBF network setup is depicted in Fig. 3. Both μ and x are later presented as preprocessed feature vectors.

Due to the idea of calculating a weighted sum of multiple similarity scores to classify an input image, the RBF network is designated by e.g. [12] as an expansion of a k-nearest- neighbor classifier. The presented approach emphasizes the elimination of the well-known disadvantages of using classical distance metrics to calculate distances directly in high-dimensional space, such as pixel space in image data. To further increase the classification ability of a classical RBF network, the authors reinforced the structure by an MLP instead of a classical one-layer neural net as depicted in Fig. 3. The setup is explained later on. Unlike in the case of the classical setup, the authors use the cosine distance instead of the Euclidean distance in their calculations. The nodes in the radial basis function network are replaced by so-called Siamese-Kernels to build the architecture of the SBF-Net. These kernels are explained in the next section.

3.2 Siamese Kernels

The basis for the Siamese-Kernels is the architecture of a Siamese network. A Siamese network, as proposed by [42], is a convolutional neural network (CNN) architecture consisting of two identical convolutional neural networks sharing weights. Using the triplet loss function, which we will explain later on, the Siamese network is trained in such a way that the distances between generated vectors are small for instances with the same class and large for instances with different classes. *Cum grano salis*, the triplet loss function is the main difference in comparison to a classical CNN architecture and led the Siamese network to produce semantically useful feature embeddings of the input instances. Since the network computes feature vectors to classify instances, these feature vectors must encode the useful semantic information needed for classification. Finally, after training, a Siamese network has learned to distinguish images based on a distance metric computed on the semantic encodings. The architecture of a Siamese neural network implementing the VGG16 CNN [44] is depicted in Fig. 4. A version of this architecture is used as basis for the Siamese-Kernels in the SBF-Net to map x and μ from pixel space to semantic space. The single components of the Siamese-Kernels are explained together with the training setup in the following.

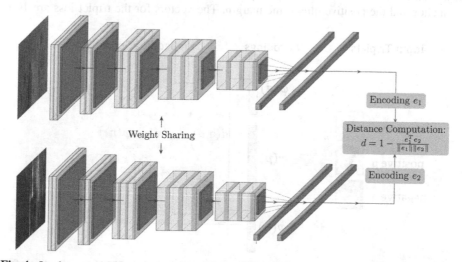

Fig. 4. Implemented Siamese network architecture based on the VGG16 backbone which shares weights (identical VGG16 models) between the branches of the Siamese network [45]

Convolutional Neural Network: The authors implemented a CNN based on the VGG16 architecture with the difference that the authors use 100 instead of 4096 neurons in the fully connected layers to make the feature representation more dense. Hence the dimension of the vector representing the feature embedding is chosen with 100. Additional experiments regarding the effect of the dimensionality of the embedding vector can be found in the experiments chapter. The network starts in the first layer with a feature map of size $200 \times 200 \times 64$ and ends with size $6 \times 6 \times 512$ in the last convolutional layer. The feature matrix is flattened and fed into two fully connected layers with 100 neurons each. ReLu is used as activation function in all models in all layers.

The output of the second fully connected layer is used as a feature vector for the following distance computations. A single Siamese network is trained with the Adam optimizer and triplet loss as loss function [45]. The triplet loss forms a core element of the Siamese network architecture and can be formalized as:

$$TripletLoss = \max(0, g(\varphi(a), \varphi(p)) + \alpha - g(\varphi(a), \varphi(n)))$$

Here, a is called an anchor, which in this case is an image of a specific class. p is called positive, which is an image of the same class as the anchor, and n is called negative, which is an image of a different class. $\varphi(.)$ represents the feature extractor in the form of the Siamese-Kernel. As distance function g, the authors implemented the cosine distance. The distance is calculated with: $Distance = 1 - \frac{x^T y}{\|x\| \times \|y\|}$, where the latter part of the equation is the classical cosine similarity. Since the model only forwards positive values, the cosine similarity takes values between 0 and 1, where 1 means that the vectors coincide. Therefore, the cosine distances take only positive numbers between 0 and 1, where values closer to 0 indicate larger similarity (or lower distance) and values closer to 1 indicate smaller similarity (or larger distance). α is a so-called margin parameter to ensure encodings where the distance between the anchor and the negative is larger than the distance between the anchor and the positive but smaller than the distance between the anchor and the positive plus some margin. The vectors for the triplet loss are 100

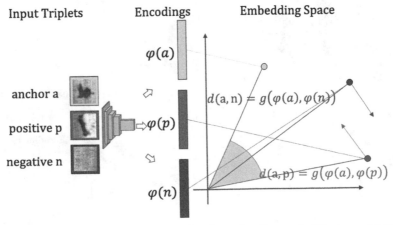

Fig. 5. Triplet loss implementing and visualizing the cosine distance in 2D where $\varphi(.)$ stands for the encoding Siamese network.

dimensional vectors. The idea of the triplet loss together with the cosine distance is presented in Fig. 5.

Using this setup, the Siamese-Kernels learn to distinguish between images of the same class and images of different classes by pushing away images from different classes and pulling images which share classes. After training, the Siamese-Kernels return small values for images which belong to the same class and large values for images which belong to different classes. In the presented approach, the kernels are trained with a learning rate of 0.00001, for 5000 iterations using semi-hard triplet loss with margin α of 0.3.

Siamese Network Implementation: A key aspect of the approach is the specific implementation of the Siamese-Kernels and their subsequent combination. The kernel networks are trained with one constant anchor per network. In this setup, the authors pick one image to be used as anchor of the Siamese network in advance and train the network randomly drawing positives and negatives from the training set using the triplet loss function. The anchor remains constant during training. Therewith, the center image is compared to different setups of positive and negative images and learns to accurately classify the center image as belonging to one specific class. If an image of the same class is presented after training, the network ideally returns a feature vector which results in a small distance value, whilst it returns a large distance value for images of other classes. Prior to the training, k center images are selected randomly for each class c in the dataset D which leads to a total number of $|C|*k$ kernel networks, each one specialized on distinguishing the class of its anchor. This aspect is important because it prevents the model from overfitting to the specific center images but creating a kind of class awareness over the ensemble of kernels. This approach could be considered as an association of individual experts who make a joint decision.

Using a fixed center per kernel, the classical classification task is kind of reversed since it is not the image which is assigned a class label, but it is rather the network that tells if the center (prototype) belongs to the same class as the input image. Since each Siamese-Kernel distinguishes all classes from the respective prototype class by comparing input encodings to prototype encodings, the prototypes are by design the ideal centers for the radial basis function computation. To yield a Siamese-Kernel, a Siamese net is implemented together with a Gaussian mapping in feature space.

3.3 Siamese Basis Function Network (SBF-Net)

Using the described approach, the Siamese networks allow effective encoding of the image information for classification. The architecture of the SBF-Net is now built by combining the single Siamese networks with the RBF structure by replacing Fig. 3. With Siamese-Kernels which then preprocess the x from pixel to feature space. The μ are chosen as center images from specific classes. The whole structure is depicted in Fig. 6.

Each of the Siamese kernels returns a similarity value measuring the semantic distance between the center image and the image presented as the input. Note that each input image is compared to each Siamese node, hence the respective Siamese network in the kernels returns feature vectors which encode the affiliation between the input image and the images used as centers. Since different images are used as centers, it is more likely that similarities between images are discovered. For each image at the input, a $|C|*k$ -dimensional feature similarity vector is output. This vector encodes the similarity information between the input image and the centers, which is then passed into an MLP for classification (Fig. 7). To increase the classification ability, the authors implemented a four-layer neural network with 50 neurons per layer implementing ReLU activations. The authors implemented dropouts with a value of 0.1 after each layer. The network is appended an output layer with softmax activations for multiclass classification and is trained with categorical cross entropy loss for 1000 iterations with a learning rate of 10^{-6}.

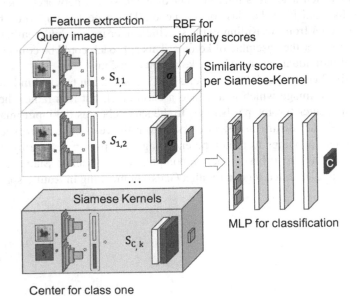

Fig. 6. SBF-Net architecture which extracts features from multiple centers per class and a query image and compares them using a RBF function before MLP classification

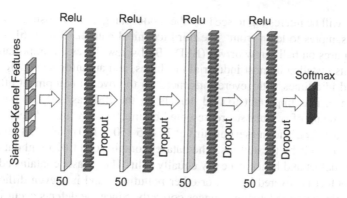

Fig. 7. MLP classifier for the Siamese-Kernel features processed by a RBF function

4 Datasets

As datasets of interest, the authors chose three technical and two non-technical datasets. As representatives of the non-technical datasets, the authors chose the well-known MNIST and cifar10 datasets which will not be further described here. As first representative of the technical datasets, the authors used the Northeastern University (NEU) surface defect database [11]. The NEU dataset is a state-of-the-art dataset for defect classification and detection on metallic surfaces. It depicts six kinds of common defects on metallic surfaces of hot-rolled steel strips: rolled-in scale, patches, crazing, pitted surface, inclusion, and scratches. The dataset consists of 1800 grayscale images, where each image is 200×200 pixels. The images are equally split by categories (300 each). The classes have a low inter-class variance while the intra-class variance is high. Additionally, there are different lighting conditions, which altogether leads to situations of similar-looking images between classes, which complicates the classification. Examples of the technical datasets are shown in Fig. 8. For training, we split the images randomly in 80% for training and 20% for testing.

The second representative of the technical datasets is the TEX dataset [47] (originally called fabric dataset) which shows five different types of failures in textiles together with one "good" class. The failures are color, cut, hole, thread, and metallic contamination. The dataset contains of 108.000 64×64 pixel grayscale images where the classes are equally represented. As can be seen in the example images in Fig. 8, the defects are neither easy to distinguish nor is it trivial to specify a failure at all – at least for the human

Fig. 8. NEU surface defect, TEX and BSD datasets

inspector. It will be interesting to see how the model can generalize using only a limited number of samples to learn from. The third technical dataset (BSD [46]) is a dataset showing failures on ball screw drives (BSD). Ball screw drives are important machine tool elements installed in most industrial machines, and an unforeseen defect can lead to unwanted idle times with severe influences on the overall equipment effectiveness (OEE). Hence, it is important to find defects on the BSD as early as possible. The dataset is made up of two classes represented by images showing a defect and images not showing a defect. The dataset contains of 21.835 150 × 150 pixel RGB images scaled to 100 × 100 pixels by the authors. The dataset contains of 11.075 without defect and 10.760 with defect and hence is nearly equally split. The dataset contains edge images where the defect is covered by soil or other pollutions, and it is even difficult for the human domain expert to label the images correctly. Since the defects occur in different sizes, the transition from images with no defect to images showing a defect is continuous especially when pollution comes into play.

Each image in the training datasets is used in its original form together with a four times random augmentation with the following imgaug classes: All channels contrast limited histogram equalization (CLAHE) with clip limit of (1, 10), random rotation between ±5°, 30% chance of horizontal and vertical flipping, Laplace noise with a per-channel scale of 0.03*255, Random multiplication of the channel values with a value between 0.7 and 1.3 as well as a perspective transformation within a scale of (0, 0.15). All images are normalized to values between 0 and 1. The validation images are not augmented.

5   Experiments and Results

In the section below, the experiments are described followed by the associated results as well as the discussion of the results. The focus of the experiments is on the classification of technical datasets (NEU, BSD, TEX). The experiments on the cifar10 and MNIST datasets can be viewed as an ablation study which should show the performance and transferability of the approach to non-technical domains.

The results are structured in three main research blocks. 1. The development of the SBF-Net architecture which has been shown above. 2. The effect of the number of kernels per class together with the amount of data available for model training and the sizes of the embedding vectors. 3. The performance and data efficiency of the SBF-Net in comparison with state-of-the-art models.

A critical aspect of the SBF-Net is the number of kernels used per class. The hypothesis is that the performance of the model increases with an increasing number of kernels per class. Figure 9 depicts the validation accuracy on the BSD dataset when training the SBF-Net with altering training data sizes of 0.1%, 1%, 10%, 30%, and 75% and an altering number of kernels per class (1, 3, 5, 7). In the experiments, always 25% of the BSD dataset was set aside as test set.

The performance of the model increases with increasing size of the dataset. However, the results flatten out towards larger datasets which is a well-known effect in training deep learning models. Considering the accuracy with altering numbers of centers, the hypothesis was that the performance of the model increases with an increasing number of

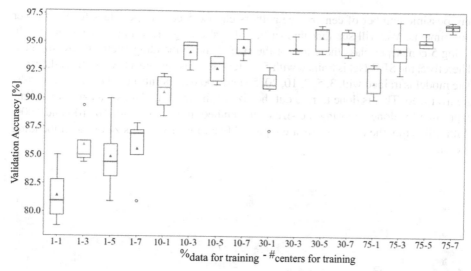

Fig. 9. Effect of training samples and number of centers on the model performance. First number of the x-axis labeling describes the percentage of data used for training. Second number describes the number of centers used for training.

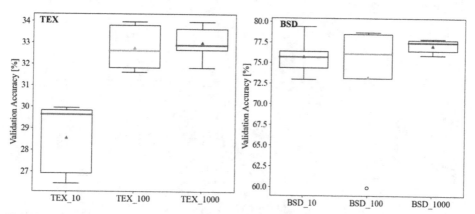

Fig. 10. Effect of the embedding vector size on the model performance. BSD and TEX describe the datasets used. _10, _100, _1000 represent the embedding vector size for the respective dataset.

centers per class. Overall, this effect can be confirmed but there is a large variation over the number of centers. This effect can be explained by the fact that the center-images for the single kernels are randomly chosen from the dataset. This results in selections which are more representative for the given task and selections which are less appropriate. Hence, the choice of the centers seems to have a significant effect on the performance of the model which can lead to situations in which 3 centers perform better than 5 or 7 centers per class. Given a large enough dataset, an open research question which could be possibly addressed by active learning strategies like [49] is how to choose centers which are optimal. Given the fact that, given enough data, this selection can be done for any possible number of centers, the authors choose 5 centers per class for the further experiments. We will see that this suffices for showing the validity of the approach. Using 5 center per class the effect of the size of the embedding vector is investigated. Therefore, the SBF-Net is trained with 5 centers per class on the TEX and BSD datasets. The model is trained with 3, 5, 7, 10, 20, 50 and 100 data points per class and the results are averaged. This is done to rule out the size of the training data set as an effect. This experiment is done choosing the size of the embedding vector with 10, 100 and 1000. With this setup, the experiments are repeated five times for each size of the embedding vector.

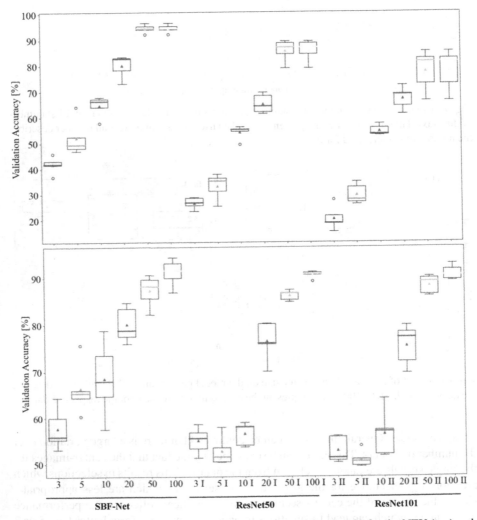

Fig. 11. Data efficiency of the SBF-Net against ReNet50 and ResNet101 for the NEU (top) and BSD (bottom) datasets

The results are shown in Fig. 10. It is visible that increasing the dimensionality of the feature vector from 10 to 100 aids the performance for the TEX-dataset while the effect is not clear for the BSD-dataset. The choice of the dimensions of the embedding vectors with 100 or 1000 has a small influence for both data sets. Although the variance in the results decreases slightly with 1000 dimensions, slightly better results can be achieved for both data sets with the choice of 100 dimensions. Furthermore, the density of the vectors is higher with 100 dimensions, which is why the size of the embedding vectors is chosen with 100 for the further experiments.

Using 5 centers per class and an embedding size of 100, the authors trained the SBF-Net on the BSD, NEU, TEX, cifar10, and MNIST datasets with an increasing number of data points (3, 5, 10, 20, 50, 100) using 25% of the data as hold out test set. The results for the NEU and BSD datasets are shown in Fig. 11 while the results for the TEX, MNIST, and cifar10 datasets are shown in Table 1. Considering the results for the classification of the NEU and BSD data, the SBF-Net performs about 10% better than the ResNet50 and ResNet101 for 3, 5, and 10 images per class. Using 20 data points per class, the advance of the SBF-Net decreases for the BSD data and stays constant for the NEU data. For 50 and 100 data points per class, the SBF-Net is on a par or slightly better than the state-of-the-art models. This picture is also reflected in Table 1.

For 3, 5, and 10 data points, the SBF-Net is leading. Whereas for 20 TEX images the performance drops, the difference in the accuracy is in principle neglectable. In the MNIST case, the model is leading for all data set sizes. The picture is a little bit more diverse in the CIFAR10 case. Here, the model is still the best for 3 and 5 data points but then gets passed by the other models. This could be explained by the fact that

Table 1. Data efficiency of the SBF-Net against ReNet50 and ResNet101 for the TEX, MNIST, and CIFAR10 Datasets

SBF-NET						ResNet50						ResNet101					
3	5	10	20	50	100	3	5	10	20	50	100	3	5	10	20	50	100
TEX																	
0.209	0.269	0.334	0.294	0.466	0.491	0.249	0.210	0.259	0.321	0.357	0.490	0.177	0.198	0.276	0.305	0.346	0.487
0.191	0.247	0.231	0.275	0.387	0.512	0.233	0.234	0.257	0.293	0.368	0.451	0.235	0.176	0.263	0.320	0.378	0.470
0.275	0.269	0.319	0.316	0.416	0.469	0.177	0.236	0.276	0.318	0.361	0.464	0.234	0.233	0.291	0.311	0.361	0.443
0.262	0.237	0.278	0.303	0.369	0.484	0.247	0.216	0.270	0.303	0.368	0.440	0.178	0.203	0.279	0.295	0.371	0.417
0.247	0.284	0.319	0.303	0.434	0.509	0.191	0.252	0.251	0.281	0.400	0.477	0.180	0.207	0.310	0.287	0.368	0.447
0.237	0.261	0.296	0.298	0.414	0.493	0.219	0.230	0.263	0.303	0.371	0.464	0.201	0.204	0.284	0.304	0.365	0.453
MNIST																	
0.691	0.775	0.881	0.950	0.959	0.981	0.172	0.486	0.766	0.872	0.926	0.954	0.112	0.272	0.507	0.782	0.876	0.936
0.753	0.791	0.903	0.913	0.959	0.972	0.252	0.307	0.832	0.880	0.916	0.954	0.198	0.499	0.675	0.824	0.879	0.900
0.806	0.719	0.875	0.934	0.956	0.981	0.176	0.466	0.744	0.859	0.933	0.952	0.160	0.382	0.642	0.850	0.916	0.943
0.688	0.806	0.894	0.928	0.966	0.969	0.190	0.475	0.735	0.898	0.930	0.958	0.190	0.276	0.690	0.853	0.885	0.916
0.625	0.747	0.875	0.922	0.950	0.972	0.175	0.448	0.718	0.887	0.929	0.959	0.121	0.286	0.673	0.831	0.893	0.908
0.713	0.767	0.886	0.929	0.958	0.975	0.193	0.436	0.759	0.879	0.927	0.955	0.156	0.343	0.637	0.828	0.890	0.921
CIFAR10																	
0.206	0.219	0.206	0.213	0.356	0.259	0.146	0.188	0.263	0.269	0.328	0.398	0.134	0.197	0.235	0.253	0.281	0.275
0.169	0.200	0.259	0.259	0.297	0.131	0.138	0.170	0.254	0.270	0.329	0.360	0.114	0.150	0.215	0.221	0.313	0.318
0.216	0.203	0.262	0.269	0.281	0.259	0.132	0.173	0.238	0.277	0.355	0.385	0.118	0.152	0.233	0.262	0.331	0.243
0.188	0.206	0.253	0.228	0.275	0.309	0.162	0.180	0.274	0.269	0.339	0.394	0.132	0.162	0.222	0.271	0.316	0.262
0.178	0.172	0.219	0.247	0.188	0.228	0.121	0.189	0.243	0.281	0.315	0.335	0.122	0.170	0.220	0.267	0.287	0.297
0.191	0.200	0.240	0.243	0.279	0.238	0.140	0.180	0.254	0.273	0.333	0.375	0.124	0.166	0.225	0.255	0.306	0.279

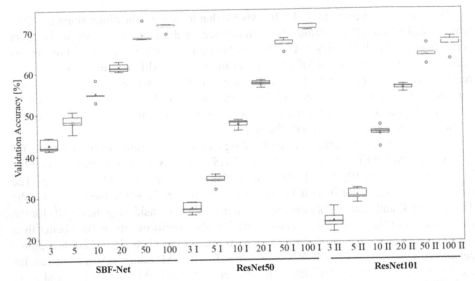

Fig. 12. Average performance of the models over all datasets given 3, 5, 10, 20, 50, and 100 data points per class

the CIFAR10 dataset is structurally different from the TEX, MNIST, BSD, and NEU datasets. These datasets could be described as sharing some prominent features like lines, edges, and other regular basic structures whereas the cifar10 dataset is very diverse. Since the ResNet50 and ResNet101 models have more learning capacity because of their size, they may be better suited to fit the diverse data. The single kernels in the SBF-Net may not have the performance to encode the differences or similarities between the images given as centers and all other images in the dataset. In the case of the TEX-dataset, the gap for the SBF-Net is small compared to the gap on the MNIST-dataset. This could be explained by the much higher inter-class-variance of the TEX-dataset which makes it harder to learn the class specific features only from a few samples. The assumption is, that the larger the inter-class-variance, the harder it is to learn distinguishing features from only a few samples. Though, further research is necessary to understand the reasons for the differences in the classification performance.

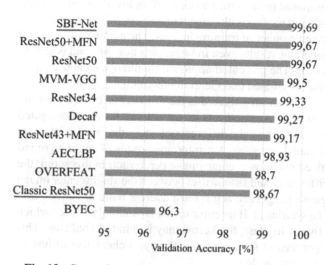

Fig. 13. Comparison of classification results based on [4]

To get a better picture of the overall performance, Fig. 12 shows the average validation accuracy over all datasets. The large advantage of the SBF-Net especially in the low data regime is obvious. But also for the larger data setups, the model performs on par with the state-of- the-art models. *Summa summarum*, it can be concluded that the SBF-Net architecture has an advantage when it comes to low data sizes and can even be as accurate as the state-of-the-art models for larger datasets.

In an additional ablation study, the authors pre-trained the base CNN of the Siamese-Kernels on the ImageNet-dataset to investigate the effect of classical transfer learning. With the exception of the cifar10 dataset, the results could only be marginally improved. This underlines the here presented approach where it is assumed that no similar dataset is available for transfer learning. The improvement in the case of the cifar10-dataset can be explained by the similarity of the datasets.

A remarkable result is achieved when training the model on 75% of the NEU data as shown in Fig. 13. The achieved 99.69% are above the current state of the art. As supporting argument, the benchmark in [4] contains several versions of the ResNet architecture. The performance of the classic ResNet-50 architecture used by the authors is highlighted as well.

6 Conclusion

The motivation of the work was to provide a novel data-efficient method which can classify images from the technical domain (BSD, NEU, TEX) using small amounts of training data without transfer knowledge ("out-of-the-box") from other datasets. In addition, the generality of the approach should be shown on non-technical datasets (MNIST, cifar10) as well. To achieve this goal, the authors proposed a novel so-called SBF-Net model which is based on a combination of multiple Siamese networks and a radial basis function network in which the Siamese nets are used as so-called Siamese-Kernels for effective feature extraction. The model then computes semantically relevant feature vectors and performs a distance-based classification. An important aspect is the training of the Siemese-Kernels with one specific center image per kernel. The single kernels learned the semantic representations of the center images in comparison to all other images. This approach led the whole SBF-Net to some kind of class awareness.

The authors showed that the proposed architecture works well in low data regimes and outperforms classical state-of-the-art models with respect to data efficiency measured by the validation accuracy for a given number of training images. The authors also showed that the SBF-Net achieves comparable results even in larger data domains and is able to outperform state-of-the-art models. The presented approach should open a new chapter in the field of data-efficient similarity-based deep learning research.

A limitation which has to be further investigated is the drop in performance for the cifar10 dataset for larger data set sizes. A hypothesis which must be further investigated is that the variation in the vectors describing the different objects in the cifar10 dataset is too large to be mapped by the model structure. A reinforcing argument could be found in the way the SBF-Net is trained using one center image per kernel. In this setup, the model must learn to find the differences and similarities between the single center image and all other positive and negative images. Hence it must address both, the inter-class-variance as well as the intra-class-variance. If a center image is randomly chosen which is not a distinctive representative of its class, the kernel may be kind of confused. This effect could increase with larger dataset size. A practical way to check this in further experiments is the use of much larger models.

In addition to that, comparing the performance of all three models on the cifar10 dataset in comparison to e.g., [50] who also checked the performance of a ResNet20 on 10 data points per class, it is notable that the performance is lower even though the architectures are quite similar. This could most likely be reduced to the fact that the authors of [50] designed their data augmentation strategy for the cifar10 dataset while here, the data augmentations are designed to aid a model trained on technical dataset. This could lead to insufficient augmentations in the cifar10 case which do not help but even harm the model performance. This should be checked in further experiments.

Another interesting aspect already mentioned above is the choice of the center images for the Siamese-Kernels. It has been shown that the proposed architecture can serve as a very strong classifier even in larger data domains. Hence, it is interesting what performance the model can achieve if perfect center images are chosen, and the number of kernels is increased at the same time. The optimal choice of most valuable (representable) center-images per class is an open research question and should be investigated in further work.

Since for each kernel, a Siamese network is trained, the needed computation increases linearly with the number of kernels. Hence, there should be developed ways to increase the number of kernels and at the same time reduce the model complexity of the single kernels such that the overall needed computation remains. A promising direction could be the use of knowledge distillation as described by e.g., [51].

Another question that directly emerges from the research results and needs to be further investigated is how to further increase the performance of the model even with small data sets and close the gap to the performance achieved with large data sets. Thinkable approaches are general transfer-learning approaches which does not only work for one limited domain but for a large number of domains by extracting generally applicable features which are not only located in the lower layers but are also located in deeper layers. Some kind of learnable drop-out or selection mechanism/strategy could be implemented to only use specific features when needed for a specific task. Therewith the "out-of-the-box" assumption of the presented approach remains.

7 Declarations

7.1 Funding

There is no funding available for this work.

7.2 Conflicts of Interest/Competing Interests

There are no competing interests.

7.3 Author Contributions

All authors contributed to the study conception and design. Material preparation, data collection and analysis were performed by Tobias Schlagenhauf, and Faruk Yildirim. The first draft of the manuscript was written by Benedikt Brückner and all authors commented on previous versions of the manuscript. All authors read and approved the final manuscript.

7.4 Data Availability

See Sect. 4. Datasets.

References

1. LeCun, Y., Bengio, Y., Hinton, G.: Deep learning. Nature **521**(7553), 436–444 (2015). [10.11.2020]
2. Krizhevsky, A., Sutskever, I., Hinton, G.E.: ImageNet classification with deep convolutional neural networks. In: Pereira, F., Burges, C.J.C., Bottou, L., Weinberger, K.Q. (eds.), Advances in Neural Information Processing Systems, vol. 25, pp. 1097–1105. Curran Associates, Inc. (2012). http://papers.nips.cc/paper/4824-imagenet-classification-with-deep-con volutional-neural-networks.pdf
3. Nash, W., Drummond, T., Birbilis, N.: A review of deep learning in the study of materials degradation. NPJ Mater. Degrad. **2**(1), 85 (2018). https://www.nature.com/articles/s41529-018-0058-x.pdf [22.04.2019]
4. Song, K., Yunhui, Y.: NEU_surface_defect_database (2019). http://faculty.neu.edu.cn/yun hyan/NEU_surface_defect_database.html. Accessed 08 Oct 2019
5. Geirhos, R., Janssen, D.H.J., Schütt, H.H., Rauber, J., Bethge, M., Wichmann, F.A.: Comparing deep neural networks against humans: object recognition when the signal gets weaker (2017). https://arxiv.org/pdf/1706.06969
6. Koch, C., Georgieva, K., Kasireddy, V., Akinci, B., Fieguth, P.: A review on computer vision based defect detection and condition assessment of concrete and asphalt civil infrastructure. Adv. Eng. Inform. **29**(2), 196–210 (2015)

7. Faghih-Roohi, S., Hajizadeh, S., Nunez, A., Babuska, R., Schutter, B.D.: Deep convolutional neural networks for detection of rail surface defects, pp. 2584–2589 (2016)

8. He, T., Liu, Y., Xu, C., Zhou, X., Hu, Z., Fan, J.: A fully convolutional neural network for wood defect location and identification. IEEE Access **7**, 123453–123462 (2019)

9. Schlagenhauf, T., Ruppelt, P., Fleischer, J.: Detektion von frühzeitigen Oberflächenzerrüttungen, wt Werkstattstechnik online **110**(7/8), 501–506 (2020). https://e-paper.vdi-fachmedien.de/webreader-v3/index.html#/2657/50

10. Aggarwal, C.C.: Neural Networks and Deep Learning. Springer, Cham (2019). https://doi.org/10.1007/978-3-031-03758-0_5. http://www.springer.com. ISBN: 978-3-319-94462-3

11. Zadeh, P.H., Hosseini, R., Sra, S.: Deep-RBF Networks revisited: robust classification with rejection (2018). https://arxiv.org/pdf/1812.03190

12. Buhmann, M.D.: Radial Basis Functions. Theory and Implementations, Cambridge Univ. Press, Cambridge (2006). ISBN: 0521633389

13. Xiao, M., Jiang, M., Li, G., Xie, L., Yi, L.: An evolutionary classifier for steel surface defects with small sample set. EURASIP J. Image Video Process. **2017**(1), 1–13 (2017). https://doi.org/10.1186/s13640-017-0197-y

14. Lecun, Y., Bottou, L., Bengio, Y., Haffner, P.: Gradient-based learning applied to document recognition. Proc. IEEE **86**(11), 2278–2324 (1998). [11.11.2020]

15. Chang, C.-Y., Fu, S.-Y.: Image classification using a module RBF neural network. In: Pan, J.-S., Shi, P., Zhao, Y. (eds.) First International Conference on Innovative Computing, Information and Control, 2006. ICICIC 2006; [August 30–1 September] 2006, [Beijing, China; Proceedings, IEEE Computer Society, Los Alamitos, Calif., pp. 270–273 (2006). ISBN: 0-7695-2616-0. [19.11.2020]

16. Beltran-Perez, C., Wei, H.-L., Rubio-Solis, A.: Generalized multiscale RBF networks and the DCT for breast cancer detection. Int. J. Autom. Comput. **17**(1), 55–70 (2020) [11.11.2020]

17. Lu, Z., Lu, S., Liu, G., Zhang, Y., Yang, J., Phillips, P.: A Pathological brain detection system based on radial basis function neural network. J. Med. Imaging Health Inform. **6**(5), 1218–1222 (2016)

18. Hryniowski, A., Wong, A.: DeepLABNet: end-to-end learning of deep radial basis networks with fully learnable basis functions (2019). https://arxiv.org/pdf/1911.09257

19. Taigman, Y., Yang, M., Ranzato, M., Wolf, L.: DeepFace: closing the gap to human-level performance in face verification. In: 2014 IEEE Conference on Computer Vision and Pattern Recognition, pp. 1701–1708. IEEE (2014). ISBN: 978-1-4799-5118-5

20. Deudon, M.: Learning semantic similarity in a continuous space. In: Proceedings of the 32nd International Conference on Neural Information Processing Systems, Curran Associates Inc., pp. 994–1005 (2018)

21. Bertinetto, L., Valmadre, J., Henriques, J.F., Vedaldi, A., Torr, P.H.S.: Fully-convolutional Siamese networks for object tracking (2016). https://arxiv.org/pdf/1606.09549

22. Luan, C., Cui, R., Sun, L., Lin, Z.: A Siamese network utilizing image structural differences for cross-category defect detection. In: 2020 IEEE International Conference on Image Processing (ICIP), pp. 778–782. IEEE (2020). ISBN: 978-1-7281-6395-6

23. Wu, S., Wu, Y., Cao, D., Zheng, C.: A fast button surface defect detection method based on Siamese network with imbalanced samples. Multimed. Tools Appl. **78**(24), 34627–34648 (2019). https://doi.org/10.1007/s11042-019-08042-w

24. Deshpande, A., Minai, A., Kumar, M.: One-shot recognition of manufacturing defects in steel surfaces. Procedia Manuf. **48**, 1064–1071 (2020). https://doi.org/10.1016/j.promfg.2020.05.146

25. Dong, Y., Tao, D., Li, X., Ma, J., Pu, J.: Texture classification and retrieval using shearlets and linear regression. IEEE Trans. Cybern. **45**(3), 358–369 (2015) [10.11.2020]

26. Chu, M., Zhao, J., Liu, X., Gong, R.: Multi-class classification for steel surface defects based on machine learning with quantile hyper-spheres. Chemom. Intell. Lab. Syst. **168**, 15–27 (2017)
27. Ghorai, S., Mukherjee, A., Gangadaran, M., Dutta, P.K.: Automatic defect detection on hot-rolled flat steel products. IEEE Trans. Instrum. Meas. **62**(3), 612–621 (2013)
28. Lv, X., Duan, F., Jiang, J.-J., Fu, X., Gan, L.: Deep metallic surface defect detection: the new benchmark and detection network. Sensors (Basel, Switzerland) **20**(6) (2020)
29. Kotyuzanskiy, L.A., Ryzhkova, N.G., Chetverkin, N.V.: Semantic segmentation in flaw detection. In: IOP Conference Series: Materials Science and Engineering, vol. 862 (2020)
30. Caleb-Solly, P., Smith, J.E.: Adaptive surface inspection via interactive evolution. Image Vis. Comput. **25**(7), 1058–1072 (2007)
31. Tabernik, D., Šela, S., Skvarč, J., Skočaj, D.: 'Segmentation-based deep-learning approach for surface-defect detection. J. Intell. Manuf. **31**(3), 759–776 (2020). [11.11.2020]
32. Bergmann, P., Löwe, S., Fauser, M., Sattlegger, D., Steger, C.: Improving unsupervised defect segmentation by applying structural similarity to autoencoders. In: Proceedings of the 14th International Joint Conference on Computer Vision, Imaging and Computer Graphics Theory and Applications, SCITEPRESS - Science and Technology Publications, pp. 372–380 (2019). ISBN: 978-989-758-354-4
33. Chen, P.-H., Ho, S.-S.: Is overfeat useful for image-based surface defect classification tasks? In: 2016 IEEE International Conference on Image Processing. Proceedings, 25–28 September 2016, Phoenix Convention Center, Phoenix, Arizona, USA, IEEE, Piscataway, NJ, pp. 749–753 (2016). ISBN: 978-1-4673-9961-6 [10.11.2020]
34. Ren, R., Hung, T., Tan, K.C.: A generic deep-learning-based approach for automated surface inspection. IEEE Trans. Cybern. **48**(3), 929–940 (2018). [31.10.2020]
35. He, Y., Song, K., Meng, Q., Yan, Y.: An End-to-end Steel Surface Defect Detection Approach via Fusing Multiple Hierarchical Features', IEEE Transactions on Instrumentation and Measurement, p. 1 [09.10.2019]
36. Song, K., Yan, Y.: A noise robust method based on completed local binary patterns for hot-rolled steel strip surface defects. Appl. Surface Sci. **285**, 858–864 (2013) [08.10.2019]
37. Broomhead, D., Lowe, D.: Radial basis functions, multi-variable functional interpolation and adaptive networks, Royal Signals and Radar Establishment Malvern (United Kingdom), RSRE-MEMO-4148 (1988)
38. Koch, G., Zemel, R., Salakhutdinov, R.: Siamese neural networks for one-shot image recognition. In: Proceedings of the 32nd International Conference on Machine Learning (2015). Journal of Machine Learning Research [02.11.2020]
39. Chicco, D.: Siamese Neural Networks: An Overview. In: Cartwright, H. (eds.) Artificial Neural Networks. Methods in Molecular Biology, vol. 2190, pp. 73–94. Humana, New York, NY (2021). https://doi.org/10.1007/978-1-0716-0826-5_3. ISBN: 978-1-0716-0825-8
40. Simonyan, K., Zisserman, A.: Very deep convolutional networks for large-scale image recognition (2015). https://arxiv.org/pdf/1409.1556
41. Schroff, F., Kalenichenko, D., Philbin, J.: FaceNet: a unified embedding for face recognition and clustering. Computer Vision and Pattern Recognition (CVPR). In: 2015 IEEE Conference on. Date, 7–12 June 2015, [EEE], [Piscataway, New Jersey], pp. 815–823 (2015). ISBN: 978-1-4673-6964-0
42. Gong, D., Chang, J., Wei, C.: An adaptive method for choosing center sets of RBF interpolation. JCP **6**, 2112–2119 (2011). https://doi.org/10.4304/jcp.6.10.2112-2119
43. Gomm, J.B., Yu, D.L.: Selecting radial basis function network centers with recursive orthogonal least squares training. IEEE Trans. Neural Netw. **11**(2), 306–314 (2000). https://doi.org/10.1109/72.839002

44. Deloitte (2017). DeloittePredictive-MaintenancePositionPaperpdf. https://www2.deloitte. com/content/dam/Deloitte/de/Documents/deloitte-analytics/Deloitte_Predictive-Mainte nance_PositionPaper.pdf
45. https://github.com/HarisIqbal88/PlotNeuralNet
46. Schlagenhauf, T.: Ball screw drive surface defect dataset for classification. Hg. v. Karlsruher Institut für Technologie (KIT). Karlsruher Institut für Technologie (KIT) wbk Institute of Production Science. Online verfügbar unter (2021). https://publikationen.bibliothek.kit.edu/ 1000133819
47. https://www.kaggle.com/belkhirnacim/textiledefectdetection
48. Fink, O., Wang, Q., Svensén, M., Dersin, P., Lee, W.-J., Ducoffe, M.: Potential, challenges and future directions for deep learning in prognostics and health management applications (2020). https://arxiv.org/pdf/2005.02144
49. Konyushkova, K., Sznitman, R., Fua, P.: Learning active learning from data. Online verfügbar unter (2017). https://arxiv.org/pdf/1703.03365
50. Brigato, L., Iocchi, L.: A Close Look at Deep Learning with Small Data. Online verfügbar unter (2020). https://arxiv.org/pdf/2003.12843
51. Rajasegaran, J., Khan, S., Hayat, M., Khan, F.S., Shah, M.: Self-supervised Knowledge Distillation for Few-shot Learning. Online verfügbar unter (2020). https://arxiv.org/pdf/2006. 09785

Quality Monitoring Procedure in Additive Material Extrusion Using Machine Learning

Anne Rathje[1]([⊠]), Ronja Witt[2], Anna Lena Knott[2], Benjamin Küster[1], Malte Stonis[1], Ludger Overmeyer[1,3], and Robert H. Schmitt[2,4]

[1] IPH – Institut für Integrierte Produktion Hannover gGmbH, Hollerithallee 6, 30419 Hannover, Germany
rathje@iph-hannover.de
[2] WZL der RWTH Aachen – Lehrstuhl für Fertigungsmesstechnik und Qualitätsmanagement, Campus-Boulevard 30, 52074 Aachen, Germany
[3] Leibniz Universität Hannover, Institut für Transport- und Automatisierungstechnik, An der Universität 2, 30823 Garbsen, Germany
[4] Fraunhofer Institute for Production Technology IPT, Steinbachstr. 17, 52074 Aachen, Germany

Abstract. Additive manufacturing enables the economical production of complex components with a high degree of customization. Therefore, the medical industry is using the advantages of additive manufacturing to produce individualized medical devices. Medical devices are subject to special quality control requirements that additive manufacturing processes do not meet yet. This article deals with the introduction of an in situ process monitoring concept using the example of fused deposition modeling. The process monitoring is carried out by a quality model, which accesses the data of a self-developed sensor concept integrated in the printer. This data is analyzed using a machine learning pipeline to predict process and product quality. Thereby, the machine learning pipeline consist of several sequential steps, ranging from data extraction and preprocessing to model training and deployment. The procedure presented for ensuring print quality forms a basis for the production of safety-relevant components in batch size one and extends conventional quality assurance methods in additive manufacturing.

Keywords: Additive manufacturing · Quality control · Machine learning

1 Introduction

Additive manufacturing (AM) offers new and innovative possibilities compared to conventional manufacturing processes such as turning and milling. AM includes all manufacturing processes in which material is applied layer by layer [1]. The layer-by-layer assembly of volume elements within the manufacturing process offers a very large freedom of design and allows the production of complex and filigree components. Since each component can be individually changed and adjusted by the modification of the design data (CAD), a production with variable batch size, especially single parts and small series, is possible [2].

P. Masci et al. (Eds.): SEFM 2022 Collocated Workshops, LNCS 13765, pp. 93–102, 2023.
https://doi.org/10.1007/978-3-031-26236-4_8

This advantage of AM, the easy individualization of components, is used by the medical industry to address specific product requirements for each individual patient. This has revolutionized large parts of the medicine field, such as the fields of ortheses, protheses, and implants [3]. One in three companies in the medical technology and the pharmaceutical sectors already reported using the AM process in 2016 [4].

There are very high requirements for quality management of medical devices to protect the patients. In 2020, a new European medical device regulation has been adopted, which requires a full traceability of product manufacturing and supply chain. This leads to complicated approval procedures for patient-specific medical devices [5]. Because of the high demands there is still a great need for research and development in quality monitoring of AM for the implementation of these regulations. There are many influencing factors, like the material flow, which have an impact on part quality and which condition often cannot be continuously controlled by the operator. Due to the lack of a monitoring systems within the additive manufacturing processes, quality monitoring currently takes place only with great effort and high costs. This results in major challenges for the manufacturing of personalized devices.

This paper presents a new approach for in situ quality monitoring for the Fused Deposition Modeling (FDM) process. For this purpose, the process is monitored with a sensor concept that records the most important influencing parameters during production. Additionally, quality characteristics are to be investigated on the basis of printed specimens: Geometric accuracy, material strength, elongation at break, and impact strength. This data is then used to create a quality model based on machine learning approaches. The model maps the production process of additive manufacturing with regard to the recorded influencing parameters and thus enables conclusions to be drawn about the quality of the end product during production. Hence, a machine learning model for predictive quality is presented that evaluates process data to determine process quality and predict part quality and use the knowledge gained to improve the process.

2   Quality Assurance in Fused Deposition Modeling

Among the different additive manufacturing processes, the FDM process is one of the most common used methods. For this reason, the focus of the research project is on this technology. In the FDM process, a thermoplastic filament is melted within a heating element and extruded trough a nozzle. Figure 1 shows a schematic of an FDM printer in which a component is built up layer by layer. Due to the layer-wise, local extrusion and solidification of the material, the final part is manufactured [6]. Ensuring quality is one of the major future challenges in industrial additive manufacturing. Several studies have investigated the influence of different parameters on FDM. The temperature is one of the most important influencing variables, regarding the part quality in the FDM process [7]. The thermoplastic FDM materials are very sensitive to temperature fluctuations. The processing temperature has a strong influence on the strength [8, 9] as well as the geometric accuracy [10] of the printed part. The most commonly used temperature controls in the FDM process are the extruder temperature, build plate temperature, build chamber temperature and the cooling fan. Another parameter with great influence is the printing speed, where the print speed also has an influence on the mechanical properties and the geometric accuracy of the part [9, 11]. In addition, the vibrations that occur at the printer can have an influence, in a positive sense, as intentionally induced vibrations can improve the connection of the filament strands [9], but also in negative sense, as unwanted vibrations have a negative influence on the print accuracy. Another factor that has yet received little attention is the quality of the used filament material. The part quality is strongly dependent on the quality of the material used. If the material has absorbed humidity during storage, the absorbed water vaporizes during heating in the nozzle and decreases the mechanical properties of the part [12]. There are many more significant influencing factors, such as layer thickness [13, 14], gap between filament strands (air gap) [15, 16], and raster angle [17, 18]. Some parameters, such as the layer thickness, can be ensured by qualifying the parameter set and the printer after printer calibration.

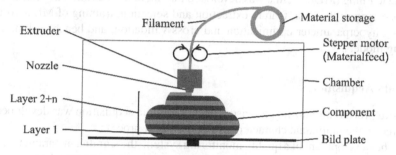

Fig. 1. Schematic representation of the FDM process

Due to the high number of influencing parameters, different filament materials, and printer types, it is necessary to qualify every combination of printer, material, and parameter set, if safety-relevant parts, like medical components, are produced. The qualification is used to identify the expected properties of the parts if there are no disturbances and deviations within the process. In addition, the qualification should be repeated at certain intervals to ensure the performance of the printers. For the case of disturbances in the process flow, an in situ monitoring of the printing process is mandatory. For this reason, there has already been an increase in research activities on process monitoring in recent years [19]. For example, 2D and 3D vision sensors are used to capture images, which are mostly used to monitor individual layers and identify defects within the component [20–24]. Acoustic sensors are used to analyze the noise of the different printer components. Anomalies in the actuators and mechanical components cause changes in the acoustic emissions. Whereby the filtering of interfering noise is a challenge [25, 26]. Another example are vibration sensors attached to various mechanical components of the printer to detect, for example, nozzle clogging [27, 28] and part deformations [29]. Nevertheless, there is a lack of an overall concept for the comprehensive monitoring of process quality. This project aims to close this gap and provides a general monitoring system which learns relations between parameter and quality and detects deviations within the process.

To determine the quality of the product, predictive quality is used. Predictive quality describes the ability to make data-based predictions about product and process quality already during the manufacturing process [30]. It is already applied in other areas of production (e.g. automotive industry) [31]. Now predictive quality is to be expanded to the field of medical additive manufacturing.

3   Implementation of a Quality Monitoring System

The quality monitoring system consists of two components: Data acquisition and quality model. The data acquisition includes a sensor concept that records the data during the FDM process, while the quality model handles data preparation and analysis. The quality model was then adapted to the recorded data sets. For this purpose, a machine learning (ML) pipeline was developed that includes the following components: Pre-processing of the data, feature extraction and selection, training of ML algorithms including hyperparameter optimization and cross-validation, and benchmarking of the resulting models.

3.1   Data Acquisition

For in situ process monitoring, a sensor concept for data acquisition was developed that is tailored to the individual characteristics of the FDM process.

For the development of a quality monitoring system, the significant parameters in the FDM process were identified and divided into two categories: Sensor data (conditions that can be monitored with sensors) and operator input (parameters that need to be specified by the operator). Table 1 lists all monitored parameters, divided into both categories. The operator input is entered via an app developed for this purpose. The ID designation is used to guarantee a subsequent traceability, due to the connection of part, parameter, and quality. The sensor data is divided into sensors which are already installed in the printers by the manufacturer and sensors that were added to the printer afterwards. Most printers already come with sensors for extruder temperature, chamber temperature, build plate temperature, and track fan speed. To ensure that the filament has not absorbed any moisture, the filament is stored and printed directly out of a drying chamber.

The sensors added to the printer consist of accelerometers, sensors to monitor environmental conditions near the extruder, a filament tracking unit consisting of multiple sensors, and a door sensor. The accelerometers are connected to extruder and build plate to measure the occurring vibrations. Vibration can cause inaccuracies in the print and is supposed to indicate process defects such as a clogged nozzle, warpage in the component, or problems with the mechanics of the printer. Close to the extruder, the temperature of the ambient air at the nozzle and the humidity are measured in addition to the existing printer data. The filament tracking unit consists of two specially developed diameter sensors mounted with 90° tilt after the other to additionally monitor the shape of the filament. Together with an installed encoder that monitors the feed of the filament, the filament tracking unit determines the exact amount of material extruded and additionally monitors clogging or partial clogging of the nozzle [32].

Table 1. List of parameters to be monitored

Operator input	Sensor Data
Part-ID	Extruder temperature
Build-job-ID	Build plate temperature
Material batch	Chamber temperature
Date of opening (Material related)	Fan speed
Parameter settings	Ambient temperature near nozzle
	Humidity in the chamber
	Acceleration of the extruder
	Acceleration of the build plate
	Filament cross section
	Filament feed
	Door sensor

The basic data set used for training the ML-models is stored in a database for further use and is continuously extended by the inclusion of new data. The database structure and the underlying metamodel allow for consistent data storage, which enables the data to be traced back to individual products.

3.2   Quality Model

The quality model describes the additive manufacturing process in terms of the quality of the final product. The previously recorded data, which will be referred to as the basic data set in the following, provides the fundamental foundation for the quality model. This quality model serves to predict the quality of a newly printed part already during production.

Describing the quality of products during production poses a problem, since the quality parameters of the printed parts, like tensile strength and elongation at break, are determined only after production. Consequently, we do not have a data base describing the quality of the products during production. To solve this problem, a quality model is developed, which is based on several machine learning (ML) models that describe the process in its entirety. For this purpose, the production process is divided into several stages. For each of these time segments, a ML-model is formed that describes these segments in terms of the final product quality. To illustrate this procedure, the quality model consisting of the individual ML-models is shown in Fig. 2. An exemplary data set of a sensor is shown here, which is representative of the entire data set of a production process. The individual ML-models describe the quality of the final product in the various stages of production.

To be able to use the data for a ML-model, the data must first be prepared. To automate the workflow for creating a ML-model, a ML-pipeline was developed. This ML-pipeline consists of several sequential steps ranging from data extraction and preprocessing to model training and deployment. The structure of the ML-pipeline is shown in Fig. 3.

During **pre-processing** of the data, null-values are first identified and removed. To better handle categorial data, one hot encoding is applied in the next step to convert the data into numerical data. The third step is to tailor the length of the training data for the particular ML-model in order to train the ML-models for the different stages of production (see Fig. 2). For example, if a model is created that describes the product quality in the first 15% of the production progress, only the first 15% of all data is used for training.

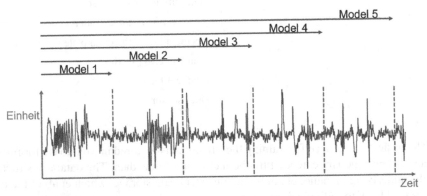

Fig. 2. The quality model consists of several ML-models that describe the printing process in terms of quality at different stages of production.

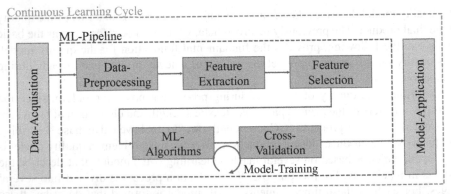

Fig. 3. The ML pipeline automates data preparation, feature extraction and selection, and the training and deployment of ML models.

Feature extraction is one of the most important steps in the ML-pipeline, as it determines which features are considered for the feature selection. If the most important features are not mapped, the model will not be able to represent the process appropriately. To use both time series data and static data for building the models, time series data is first transferred from the time domain to the feature domain. This means that they lose their temporal character and individual features are extracted from the time series. There are several libraries that support feature extraction from the time domain into the feature domain. For the present quality model, tsfresh [33] is used since they support a broad range of features.

Feature selection is used to reduce the number of input variables for the development of the predictive model. This decreases the computational costs and, in some cases, can improve the performance of the ML-model. To evaluate the relationship between each input variable and the target variable, a filter method, which uses statistical techniques, is applied to the extracted features. In this case the feature selection from sklearn is used to calculate an ANOVA F-value. It evaluates the relevance of features outside the predictive models and has relatively low computational costs compared to wrapper methods.

Model training and benchmarking include the following steps: Splitting the dataset, cross-validation (CV), hyperparameter optimization, and evaluation. A listing of the algorithms considered and the parameters to be optimized is given in Table 2. A total of five algorithms are studied, including support vector, K-nearest neighbors, random forest, naive bayes and gaussian progress. Different parameters were optimized for the different classifiers. The base data set is first divided into training data, validation data and test data. The training data and validation data is used in the CV for the training of the models and the hyperparameter optimization, while the test data is utilized to evaluate the models. For training the models and hyperparameter optimization, a 10 fold-CV is performed. For hyperparameter optimization, a grid search is used and as a metric the area under the receiver operating characteristics curve (AUC) value is chosen to compare the models with each other. The best ML model for the particular production stage is selected based on the AUC value. Through the different parameter combinations of the grid search, 125 models are created. Since a 10 fold-CV is performed, a total of 1250 models are compared with each other.

Table 2. Algorithms used for model training and parameters used for hyperparameter optimization.

Algorithms	Parameters to be optimized	Grid-Search
Support vector classifier	C Kernel gamma	[0.01, 0.1, 1] ['rbf', 'poly'] [0.01, 0.1, 1.0]
K-nearest neighbors classifier	n-neighbors	[3, 7, 10, 12, 14]
Random forest classifier	n-estimators criterion max-features min-samples-leaf	[10, 20, 30] ['gini', 'entropy'] [3, 4, 5, 6] [3, 4, 5, 6]
Naive bayes classifier	alpha	[0.01, 0.1, 1.0]
Gaussian process classifier	kernel	[RBF(l) for l in np.logspace(−1, 1, 2)]

The next step of the ML-Pipeline is the **application of the ML-models** during the production process. The trained ML-models describing the individual stages of the production process are provided during production. The duration of the new production process is known before production begins, which means that during production the process can be divided into the various stages of production. At certain stages of the production process, the data is processed using the ML-pipeline, features are extracted and selected. Finally, the quality features of the current product can be predicted during production.

The quality model is able to determine the quality of the final product during the production process. The ML pipeline enables automatic processing of data and training and deployment of ML models.

4 Conclusion

In this paper the procedure for implementing an in situ FDM process monitoring is described. A concept was elaborated to monitor the parameters with significant influence on the printing process. The developed ML-pipeline accesses data directly from the printing process to predict process and part quality. For ML-model training, the mechanical material properties and geometric accuracy are used as measures of part quality.

In a next step, the database is to be extended to train the quality model on its basis. The accuracy and the AUC value of the resulting model can then be determined for the respective process.

It is important to note that the machine learning models describing the individual process stages are based on supervised learning, whereby the Quality of the product can only be evaluated at the end of each process. This means that process stages are assigned to a final product quality that may not yet have an impact on the quality of the final product, and only at later times does an event occur that leads to a change in the quality of the final product. In order to improve the assignment of product quality to a specific event, the algorithm should recognize in the future at which stage of production an event occurred that led to a deterioration in quality.

Acknowledgement. This research is funded by the Deutsche Forschungsgemeinschaft (DFG, German Research Foundation) under Germany's Excellence Strategy—EXC-2023 Internet of Production—390621612.

The IGF-promotion plan 21610 N (saviour) of the Research Community for Quality (FQS), August-Schanz-Straße 21A, 60433 Frankfurt/Main has been funded by the AiF within the program for sponsorship by Industrial Joint Research (IGF) of the German Federal Ministry of Economic Affairs and Energy based on an enactment of the German Parliament.

References

1. Lachmayer, R. Lippert, R. B.: Development methodology for additive manufacturing (in German). Springer, Berlin, Heidelberg (2020). https://doi.org/10.1007/978-3-662-59789-7

2. Richard, H.A., Schramm, B., Zipsner, T.: Hrsg., *Additive manufacturing of components and structures: new insights and practical examples* (in German). Wiesbaden: Springer Fachmedien, Wiesbaden (2019). https://doi.org/10.1007/978-3-658-27412-2
3. Schramm, B., *et al:* Medizintechnische Anwendungen der additiven Fertigung. In: Richard, H., Schramm, B., Zipsner, T. (eds.) Additive Fertigung von Bauteilen und Strukturen, pp. 21–40. Springer Vieweg, Wiesbaden (2017). https://doi.org/10.1007/978-3-658-17780-5_2
4. Anwendung von 3D-Druck weltweit nach Branchen 2016. *Statista.* https://de.statista.com/statistik/daten/studie/581453/umfrage/anwendung-von-3d-druck-weltweit-nach-branchen/. Accessed 18 Aug 2022
5. Menean, F., Menean, N., Rometsch, F., Großmann, M., Becker, T.: Maßnahmen zur umsetzung der europäischen medical device regulation bei klein- und mittelständischen herstellern von medizinprodukten. In: Pfannstiel, M.A., Rasche, C., Braun von Reinersdorff, A., Knoblach, B., Fink, D. (eds.) Consulting im Gesundheitswesen, pp. 179–200. Springer, Wiesbaden (2020). https://doi.org/10.1007/978-3-658-25479-7_10
6. Oleff, A., Küster, B., Stonis, M., Overmeyer, L.: Optical quality inspection for additive material extrusion (in German). ZWF Z. Für Wirtsch. Fabr. **115**, 52–56 (2020). https://doi.org/10.3139/104.112228
7. Bähr, F., Westkämper, E.: Correlations between influencing parameters and quality properties of components produced by fused deposition modeling. Procedia CIRP **72**, 1214–1219 (2018). https://doi.org/10.1016/j.procir.2018.03.048
8. Zekavat, A.R., Jansson, A., Larsson, J., Pejryd, L.: Investigating the effect of fabrication temperature on mechanical properties of fused deposition modeling parts using X-ray computed tomography. Int. J. Adv. Manuf. Technol. **100**(1–4), 287–296 (2018). https://doi.org/10.1007/s00170-018-2664-8
9. Coogan, T., Kazmer, D.: Bond and part strength in fused deposition modeling. Rapid Prototyp. J. **23**, 414–422 (2017). https://doi.org/10.1108/RPJ-03-2016-0050
10. Vanaei, H.R., et al.: Toward the understanding of temperature effect on bonding strength, dimensions and geometry of 3D-printed parts. J. Mater. Sci. **55**(29), 14677–14689 (2020). https://doi.org/10.1007/s10853-020-05057-9
11. Ansari, A.A., Kamil, M.: Effect of print speed and extrusion temperature on properties of 3D printed PLA using fused deposition modeling process. Mater. Today Proc. **45**, 5462–5468 (2021). https://doi.org/10.1016/j.matpr.2021.02.137
12. Kim, E., Shin, Y.-J., Ahn, S.-H.: The effects of moisture and temperature on the mechanical properties of additive manufacturing components: fused deposition modeling. Rapid Prototyp. J. **22**(6), 887–894 (2016). https://doi.org/10.1108/RPJ-08-2015-0095
13. Shubham, P., Sikidar, A., Chand, T.: The influence of layer thickness on mechanical properties of the 3D printed ABS polymer by fused deposition modeling. Key Eng. Mater. **706**, 63–67 (2016). https://doi.org/10.4028/www.scientific.net/KEM.706.63
14. Milde, J., Morovič, L., Blaha, J.: Influence of the layer thickness in the fused deposition modeling process on the dimensional and shape accuracy of the upper teeth model. In: *MATEC Web Conference,* vol. 137, pp. 02006 (2017). https://doi.org/10.1051/matecconf/201713702006
15. Somireddy, M., de Moraes, D., Czekanski, A.: *Flexural behavior of FDM Parts: experimental, analytical and numerical study* (2017)
16. Rodriguez, J., Thomas, J., Renaud, J.: Mechanical behavior of acrylonitrile butadiene styrene (ABS) fused deposition materials. experimental investigation. Rapid Prototyp. J. **7**, 148–158 (2001). https://doi.org/10.1108/13552540110395547
17. Ahn, S., Montero, M., Odell, D., Roundy, S., Wright, P.K.: Anisotropic material properties of fused deposition modeling ABS. Rapid Prototyp. J. **8**(4), 248–257 (2002). https://doi.org/10.1108/13552540210441166

18. Magalhães, L.C., Volpato, N., Luersen, M.A.: Evaluation of stiffness and strength in fused deposition sandwich specimens. J. Braz. Soc. Mech. Sci. Eng. **36**(3), 449–459 (2013). https://doi.org/10.1007/s40430-013-0111-1

19. Oleff, A., Küster, B., Stonis, M., Overmeyer, L.: Process monitoring for material extrusion additive manufacturing: a state-of-the-art review. Prog. Addit. Manuf. **6**(4), 705–730 (2021). https://doi.org/10.1007/s40964-021-00192-4

20. Liu, C., Law, A.C.C., Roberson, D., Kong, Z.J.: Image analysis-based closed loop quality control for additive manufacturing with fused filament fabrication. J. Manuf. Syst. **51**, 75–86 (2019). https://doi.org/10.1016/j.jmsy.2019.04.002

21. Liu, C., Roberson, D., Kong, Z.: *Textural analysis-based online closed-loop quality control for additive manufacturing processes* (2017)

22. Borish, M., Post, B.K., Roschli, A., Chesser, P.C., Love, L.J., Gaul, K.T.: Defect identification and mitigation via visual inspection in large-scale additive manufacturing. JOM **71**, 893–899 (2018). https://doi.org/10.1007/s11837-018-3220-6

23. Borish, M., Post, B.K., Roschli, A., Chesser, P.C., Love, L.J.: Real-time defect correction in large-scale polymer additive manufacturing via thermal imaging and laser profilometer. Procedia Manuf. **48**, 625–633 (2020). https://doi.org/10.1016/j.promfg.2020.05.091

24. Holzmond, O., Li, X.: In situ real time defect detection of 3D printed parts. Addi. Manuf. **17**, 135–142 (2017). https://doi.org/10.1016/j.addma.2017.08.003

25. Wu, H., Yu, Z., Wang, Y.: Real-time FDM machine condition monitoring and diagnosis based on acoustic emission and hidden semi-Markov model. Int. J. Adv. Manuf. Technol. **90**(5–8), 2027–2036 (2016). https://doi.org/10.1007/s00170-016-9548-6

26. Li, F., Yu, Z., Yang, Z., Shen, X.: Real-time distortion monitoring during fused deposition modeling via acoustic emission. Struct. Health Monit. **19**, 412–423 (2019). https://doi.org/10.1177/1475921719849700

27. Tlegenov, Y., Hong, G.S., Lu, W.F.: Nozzle condition monitoring in 3D printing. Robo. Comput. –Integr. Manuf. **54**, 45–55 (2018). https://doi.org/10.1016/j.rcim.2018.05.010

28. Tlegenov, Y., Wong, Y., Hong, G.-S.: A dynamic model for nozzle clog monitoring in fused deposition modelling. Rapid Prototyp. J. **23**, 391–400 (2017). https://doi.org/10.1108/RPJ-04-2016-0054

29. Li, Y., Zhao, W., Li, Q., Wang, T., Wang, G.: In-situ monitoring and diagnosing for fused filament fabrication process based on vibration sensors. Sensors **19**, 2589 (2019). https://doi.org/10.3390/s19112589

30. Brecher, C., Schmitt, R.H., Klocke, F.: Internet of production for agile companies: awk aachen machine tool colloquium 2017 (in German), apprimus verlag, 18. bis 19. Mai, 1. Auflage. Aachen: Apprimus Verlag (2017)

31. Liang, J.: Towards predictive quality in production by applying a flexible process-independent meta-model. Procedia CIRP **104**, 1251–1256 (2021). https://doi.org/10.1016/j.procir.2021.11.210

32. Rathje, A., Knott, A.-L., Küster, B., Stonis, M., Overmeyer, L.: Introduction of in-situ process monitoring in additive material extrusion(in German). Z. Für Wirtsch. Fabr **116**, 707–710 (2021). https://doi.org/10.1515/zwf-2021-0156

33. Christ, M., Braun, N., Neuffer, J., Kempa-Liehr, A.W.: Time series FeatuRe extraction on basis of scalable hypothesis tests (tsfresh – a python package). Neurocomputing **307**, 72–77 (2018). https://doi.org/10.1016/j.neucom.2018.03.067

F-IDE 2022 - 7th Workshop on Formal Integrated Development Environment

F-IDE 2022 Organizers' Message

The Formal Integrated Development Environment (F-IDE) Workshop aims at bringing together researchers and practitioners from academia and industry who are interested in applying formal methods to specify and develop standard-compliant software for highly dependable systems. The assessment process (accompanying safety, security and also privacy standards) benefits from documentation of the application of formal methods to justify the design choices and the review of code and proofs.

An F-IDE dedicated to such developments should associate sound semantics (in the form of some logical theory) with a programming/modelling language, in a way that facilitates the tightly coupled handling of specification properties and system constructs; offer a language/environment simple enough to be usable by most developers, in particular by making the development of proofs as easy as possible; and offer automated management of application documentation. It may also be expected that developments done with such an F-IDE are reusable and modular. Tools for testing and static analysis may be embedded within F-IDEs to support the assessment process.

The 7th Formal Integrated Development Environment Workshop focussed on the development and usage of F-IDEs. We had the privilege of welcoming Alessandro Cimatti as the keynote speaker, giving a talk titled "A Formal IDE for Railways Applications". The contribution of the keynote speaker as a short paper is also included in this volume. The workshop received eight paper submissions, seven of which were accepted for presentation and publication. Each submission was reviewed by at least three Program Committee members. The workshop was held in three sessions. In the first session, the topic of building better interfaces to improve the user experience with F-IDEs was discussed; the second session focused on the usage of formal methods at different stages of the software development process. The final session continued with the theme of debugging formal models and with the lessons learnt from building a diagrammatic front end for a formal modelling language.

We are grateful to the Steering Committee and to the local organisers for their constant support during the preparation and running of the workshop. We are in debt to Franco Mazzanti, Colin Snook, and Alessandro Cimatti for chairing the presentation and discussion sessions at the workshop. A special thank to the Programme Committee members for their time to review the submissions. Finally, we would like to thank the contributors and participants for their valuable participation in discussions, the most important part of the workshop.

December 2022

Cinzia Bernardeschi
Thai Son Hoang

Organization

Program Committee Chairs

Cinzia Bernardeschi   University of Pisa, Italy
Thai Son Hoang   University of Southampton, UK

Steering Committee

Catherine Dubois   Samovar/ENSIIE, France
Paolo Masci   National Institute of Aerospace (NIA), USA
Dominique Méry   LORIA/Université de Lorraine, France

Program Committee

Aaron Dutle   NASA LaRC, USA
Andrea Domenici   University of Pisa, Italy
Bernhard Rumpe   RWTH Aachen University, Germany
Carlo A. Furia   Università della Svizzera Italiana, Switzerland
Enrico Tassi   Inria, France
Franco Mazzanti   ISTI/CNR, Italy
François Pessaux   ENSTA ParisTech, France
José Proença   CISTER/ISEP, Portugal
Laurent Voisin   Systerel, France
Makarius Wenzel   Sketis.net, Germany
Markus A. Kuppe   Microsoft Research, USA
Mattias Ulbrich   Karlsruhe Institute of Technology, Germany
Rosemary Monahan   Maynooth University, Ireland
Simão Melo de Sousa   University of Beira Interior, Portugal
Stefan Mitsch   Carnegie Mellon University, USA
Stephan Merz   Inria Nancy, France
Virgile Prevosto   Université Paris-Saclay, CEA, List, France
Yannick Moy   AdaCore, France
Yi Zhang   Massachusetts General Hospital, USA

A Formal IDE for Railways: Research Challenges

Roberto Cavada, Alessandro Cimatti$^{(\boxtimes)}$, Alberto Griggio, and Angelo Susi

Fondazione Bruno Kessler, Trento, Italy
{cavada,cimatti,griggio,susi}@fbk.eu

Abstract. The development of modern railways applications must be supported by trusted tools, able to cover the whole development process. In this paper we report on the research challenges underlying a comprehensive toolset for the design of computer-based interlocking systems. Following a VV development process, the framework adopts a clear separation between the abstract interlocking logic and the instantiations characterizing the single stations. The challenges include the definition of adequate specification languages, the generation of executable code and simulation infrastructure, traceability, test case generation, and formal verification.

Keywords: Railways interlocking systems · Model-based design · Formal verification · Automated test case generation · Reverse engineering

1 Introduction

The development of modern railways applications must be supported by trusted tools, able to cover the whole development process. In this paper, we describe the research challenges underlying an important effort aiming at the definition of a comprehensive design methodology for the design of computer-based interlocking systems for the Italian railways network [3]. The framework is intended to provide great usability to signaling engineers and it is based on advanced formal techniques to ensure adequate verification and validation capabilities.

The framework adopts a VV development process, clearly separating the abstract interlocking logic (corresponding to the first V, for domain-specific design aspects) and the various instantiations characterizing the single stations (corresponding to the second V, for product specific design aspects). The framework is supported by three tools, tightly integrated together, covering different aspects of the design flow. The AIDA tool [2] allows to represent the generic interlocking logic, providing various validation steps and supporting the compilation to executable code. The TOSCA tool supports the specification, generation and execution of test cases. The NORMA tool deals with the legacy interlocking solution, based on electromechanical, relay-based technology.

This invited contribution is based on the keynote presentation given by Alessandro Cimatti at the 2022 F-IDE workshop, affiliated with SEFM'22, Berlin (DE).

© The Author(s) 2023
P. Masci et al. (Eds.): SEFM 2022 Collocated Workshops, LNCS 13765, pp. 107–115, 2023.
https://doi.org/10.1007/978-3-031-26236-4_9

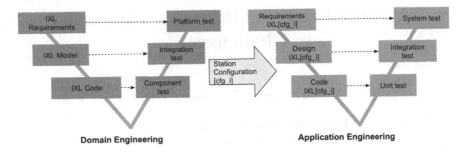

Fig. 1. The VV model in the interlocking logic development and testing.

The challenges include leveraging the domain-product separation (Sect. 2), the definition of adequate specification languages and the traceability across levels of abstraction (Sect. 3), automated test case generation (Sect. 4), formal verification (Sect. 5), trusted compilation and tool qualification (Sect. 6), and reconciliation between computer-based and relay-based interlocking (Sect. 7).

2   General VV Flow

The approach to the design, development and verification of the interlocking system relies on the fact that it is a parameterized system that is instantiated for each railway station. It can be seen as a software product line (PL). In particular, a generic Interlocking logic (IXL) is instantiated by specifying different station configurations $\{cfg_1, \ldots, cfg_i, \ldots, cfg_n\}$ in different specific IXLs for each of the different stations $\{\text{IXL}[cfg_1], \ldots, \text{IXL}[cfg_i], \ldots, \text{IXL}[cfg_n]\}$. The development and testing methodologies typical of PL systems can be applied to these configurations. A product line (PL) is a family of products with common core features and other alternative features. The focus is on optimally managing product variability. The PL is instantiated in a specific product by putting together the features in common and the specific features for that product. One of the methodologies implemented for testing PL systems is the VV model [11] (see Fig. 1) that groups the design implementation and testing activities of PL-type systems into two parts: domain engineering and application engineering.

During the domain engineering phase, the analysis of the requirements and models in the domain is carried out in order to then be able to design the product line by identifying the points of variability. Once the features in common and the variants have been identified, the implementation of the features in common and some of the variants can be performed, thus producing reusable artifacts during the development phase of specific applications. The testing activities during domain engineering are carried out by applying component testing to each of the developed components, their integration and finally testing the functioning of the platform in general. Since a specific product does not yet exist during domain engineering, an exemplary product is used to carry out the test activities. During the application engineering phase, the specific product that is about to be built and deployed is analysed using all the artifacts already developed and tested during the domain engineering phase. In this phase, therefore, all the components that are necessary to build the specific desired product are implemented. The testing activities in this phase are similar to those of a traditional application in which typical testing methods are applied; in this case all the artifacts developed and tested during the domain engineering phase are reused. Therefore, during the application engineering phase, attention is focused on the development and testing of new components, taking into account the test cases already produced by the testing activities during the domain engineering phase.

3   Modeling Layers

The development process described above takes as its informal starting point the domain knowledge and the railway documents (national provisions, regulations and legacy relay circuits diagrams). These documents are formalized in three, tightly related levels of abstraction [2]: requirements level, models level and code level (Fig. 2):

- At the requirements level, national provisions, regulations, and relay-circuit diagrams are manually translated by domain experts into *Functional Requirements Specifications (FRS)*, a formalism for expressing railway-specific requirements via the use of *Controlled Natural Language (CNL)*, a programming language designed to resemble the technical Italian language used in regulations and provisions;
- At the models level, a representation in SysML is automatically derived from the FRS. The SysML level contains structural (e.g. dependencies between classes) and behavioral aspects (transitions of state machines, communication between state machines) of the IXL system;
- Finally, at the code level (multiple variants of) the actual IXL C code are automatically derived from the SysML models.

The approach ensures the full traceability between the three development levels. The overall development process is supported by the tool AIDA, implemented as an Eclipse plug-in on top of CHESS platform [8].

The same levels of abstraction are retained for the testing framework. Depending on the level of abstraction, test cases can be specified/represented at the FRS level, at the model level, and at the code level. The execution of these test cases can take place as a simulation on the model or as a concrete execution on the code. The traceability between the different levels of abstraction allows the tool to map the execution of one level to the other levels. Similarly, coverage information can be related across abstraction levels.

The main challenge is to define a suitable trade-off between the usability of the language and its level of formality. This was achieved by designing domain-specific, controlled natural languages, both for control procedures and for test scenarios, that are very close to the style of the informal documents typically adopted in this domain. Despite their natural language flavor, the controlled

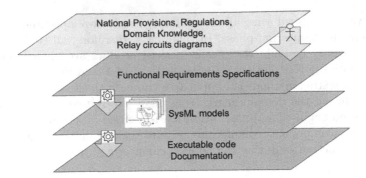

Fig. 2. The modelling and implementation layers.

natural languages have a clear execution semantics that is exploited in the compilation to SysML and to code.

Another important challenge is achieving high-quality requirements. This is supported by providing extensive checking on the controlled natural language, both at the syntactic and at the sematic level. Furthermore, the automated extraction of documentation (class diagrams, finite-state machines) provides support for manual inspection and immediate validation. Finally, the toolset provides the possibility to animate the specifications, to run them in closed loop with a station simulator, and to inspect the various phases by means of a dedicated debugger.

Further research efforts will address the problem of supporting the experts in the automated or semi-automated derivation of the specification of the procedures and test cases directly from railway regulations and technical specifications. These are usually written in uncontrolled natural language, following a domain jargon, and pose substantial challenges for current state-of-the-art natural language processing techniques.

4   Testing

The approach proposes a testing process that goes from the test cases specification, to their execution, to the collection of testing results in terms, for example, of code or SysML model entities coverage. The process also distinguishes between the abstract test cases, specified in the domain engineering phase, and those that are configuration specific defined in the application engineering phase, namely concrete test cases. The methodology is supported by the tool TOSCA, implemented as an Eclipse plug-in.

The testing methodology allows the tester, in general a railway expert, to prepare test suites containing abstract test cases for the interlocking system using a specific Controlled Natural Language that represents assumption, assertion, and verification statements in a test case using the railway jargon. Abstract test cases do not refer to the entities of a specific station configuration, so they are generic with respect to specific railway plant. The tester can write the test suites using the frontend of TOSCA that supports the expert providing editing services such as autocompletion and syntax check of the test statements, in order to continuously guide the expert in the specification of well-formed test cases.

Abstract test cases can be directly instantiated for a specific railway plant configuration cfg_i, obtaining concrete test cases that explicitly refer to the entities of the specific railway interlocking system for that plant (IXL[cfg_i]). Specifically, for each abstract test case it is possible to either instantiate it on a specific route, signal, track circuit, producing a single concrete test case or to generate all possible concrete test cases to be instantiated for the station under test.

Concrete tests can then be automatically transformed into executable tests to be run on the interlocking system of the plant under test. The results of the test cases execution can be analyzed having different objectives in mind. On the one hand it is possible to perform functional system testing with the objective of identifying test cases able to detect system failures. On the other hand the objective could be that of maximizing the coverage of the system code, in terms of lines or branches that are executed, or of the SysML model entities, in terms of states and transitions that are traversed during the execution.

The approach also allows to automatically generate Test cases with the main objective of producing tests able to cover portions of code or SysML models that are difficult to be covered using manually specified test cases. The approach relies on search-based techniques, specifically genetic algorithms, that use the SysML model to drive the test case generation.

Research challenges in the testing area are twofold. On the one hand we aim at supporting the experts in translating railway regulations expressed in natural language into abstract or concrete test cases in controlled natural language. This aspect is an important step to be sure that, for example, all the regulations have been translated into a comprehensive set of test suites. On the other hand, concerning the automated generation of test cases, we aim at investigating the possibility of mixing search-based approaches with formal techniques, such as model checking, in order to exploit the power of the two techniques to overcome limitations related to the accuracy of cases in the current search approach.

5   Formal Verification

Complementary to testing, which focuses on producing execution traces witnessing existential properties (i.e. "scenarios") and on providing coverage of the system at the various levels of abstraction discussed above, formal verification aims at proving universal properties of the IXL system, i.e. properties that must hold in all executions. More specifically, we focus mainly on railway safety requirements of the system, which ensure that no harmful situation can occur in operation, and which from the formal point of view can be characterised as invariant properties.

Similarly to the case of testing, we distinguish two main verification activities: (i) verification of the *generic, uninstantiated* IXL logic, independently from the specific configuration, and (ii) verification of a specific instantiation IXL[cfg_i] of the logic for a given station/application. Although ideally the ultimate goal is being able to verify the IXL logic at the generic level, it is important to highlight that the two approaches provide different trade-offs and strengths. Verification of a specific instantiation of the logic is a conceptually simpler problem, which can in principle be reduced to standard model checking and/or program analysis amenable to a high degree of automation. On the other hand, the obtained verification results might not be easily reusable across different configurations; moreover, the large size of the configurations corresponding to realistic stations might be a significant hurdle for scalability in practice. In order to tackle such challenges, we are investigating domain-specific abstraction techniques for reducing the complexity induced by the IXL instantiation on specific configurations, and for reusing verification results across similar instantiations (such as property decomposition, symmetry detection, and domain-specific slicing/cone of influence reduction methods).

One obvious advantage of performing verification at the generic level is the fact that the results do not depend on any specific configuration. However, generic verification is significantly more challenging than verification of specific configurations already from the conceptual point of view. Formally, the problem can be formulated as verification of parameterized systems. Differently from most settings considered in the literature though, in which typically the focus is on communication protocols and/or distributed systems consisting of processes arranged in a fixed and known topology, in this case the topology is not known a priori, but part of the configuration space. Moreover, the size of the (parametric) system to analyse is significantly larger than what normally considered by automatic approaches. Therefore, in practice rather than a fully automatic solution, we aim to investigate hybrid approaches, combining the use of interactive theorem provers, code annotations and contract-based decompositions for defining the overall verification strategy, coupled with automatic model checkers for parameterized systems (such as e.g. [9,10]) for discharging individual verification conditions.

6   Tool Qualification and Certification

Ensuring the correctness of the sequence of transformations that produce the IXL code from the FRS requirements is critical for the trustworthiness of the whole toolchain. In fact, the regulations for safety-critical systems such as railway interlockings mandate the use of qualified toolchains, whose correctness has been certified/validated according to some procedures established by law. In our context, this can be achieved via several different approaches: (i) formal verification of the translator itself, (ii) formal verification of the correctness of the translations, or (iii) validation of the translations by comparing independent implementations of the toolchains. While in principle more appealing, approaches (i) and (ii) would require a significant effort of several man-years, making their cost prohibitive. Moreover, they would require a full formal specification of the translation procedures and the CNL semantics, which do not currently exist, and which would be far from trivial to produce. Therefore, we are currently working towards option (iii), by developing a methodology to allow to perform formal proofs of equivalence of two independent translations using automated program analysis techniques, leveraging domain knowledge on the specific syntactic structure of the inputs and outputs of the translation steps in order to aid the semantic analysis of the equivalence of the two independent translation results.

7 Dealing with Legacy

The need to relate the current, relay-based interlocking technology and the new, computer based interlocking solution, poses several challenges.

The first one is the digitalization of legacy relay circuit diagrams, that is supported by the tool NORMA [1]. NORMA provides the user with the ability to create a digital model, covering the whole space of electrical components adopted in relay-based interlocking systems. The schematics are then converted into a format that is amenable for the simulation and formal verification using the underlying nuXmv [7] model checker. The resulting models are extremely large and need an expressive representation, and compositional methods will be investigated to increase the capacity of the formal verification even further.

Another important challenge is to provide automated support for the extraction of models from design documents and schematics. This informal-to-formal conversion is currently being investigated with the integration of image recognition based on deep learning and background knowledge at the symbolic level.

Once a formal representation is available, and its properties have been validated, the analyst needs to be supported in the comparison of the behavior of the legacy relay-based system with that of the new digitalized IXL system. On the one side, it is possible to generate test suites that are covering for the relay-based system and that can be expected to properly stimulate the computer-based design. More interestingly, the relay-circuit model is expected to provide the reference behavior for the computer-based solution. However, the two semantics are hard to harmonize: while the computer-based solution has a cycle-based semantic, the relay-circuit model implements a run-to-completion semantics. For this reason, we are actively investigating the problem of extracting from the relay circuits an abstract view that "absorbs" the unstable states and provides for properties to be satisfied by the computer-based solution [1, 4–6].

8 Conclusions

In this paper we described the challenges deriving from the development of a formal framework for the design of interlocking systems. These include: the ability to support the signaling engineers with a structured natural language, that combines high usability and a well-defined execution semantic; the traceability between levels of abstraction, and the reconciliation of the exectutions for the legacy and new technology; the definition of suitable testing techniques, and the effective integration of formal verification methods and tools; the qualification of the tools, with particular reference to the correctness of the compiled code.

References

1. Amendola, A., et al.: NORMA: a tool for the analysis of relay-based railway interlocking systems. In: TACAS 2022. LNCS, vol. 13243, pp. 125–142. Springer, Cham (2022). https://doi.org/10.1007/978-3-030-99524-9_7
2. Amendola, A., et al.: A model-based approach to the design, verification and deployment of railway interlocking system. In: Margaria, T., Steffen, B. (eds.) ISoLA 2020. LNCS, vol. 12478, pp. 240–254. Springer, Cham (2020). https://doi.org/10.1007/978-3-030-61467-6_16
3. Arenella, A., et al.: Model-driven design and validation of CBI applications. In: Proceedings of the World Congress on Railways Research, pp. 702–705 (2022)
4. Becchi, A., Cimatti, A.: Abstraction modulo stability for reverse engineering. In: Shoham, S., Vizel, Y. (eds.) Computer Aided Verification. CAV 2022. LNCS, vol. 13371, pp. 469–489. Springer, Cham (2022). https://doi.org/10.1007/978-3-031-13185-1_23
5. Becchi, A., Cimatti, A., Zaffanella, E.: Synthesis of P-stable abstractions. In: de Boer, F., Cerone, A. (eds.) Software Engineering and Formal Methods. SEFM 2020. LNCS, vol. 12310, pp. 214–230. Springer, Cham (2020). https://doi.org/10.1007/978-3-030-58768-0_12
6. Becchi, A., Cimatti, A., Zaffanella, E.: Reverse engineering with p-stable abstractions. In: OVERLAY@GandALF, volume 2987 of CEUR Workshop Proceedings, pp. 91–95. CEUR-WS.org (2021)
7. Cavada, R., et al.: The NUXMV symbolic model checker. In: Biere, A., Bloem, R. (eds.) CAV 2014. LNCS, vol. 8559, pp. 334–342. Springer, Cham (2014). https://doi.org/10.1007/978-3-319-08867-9_22
8. Cicchetti, A., et al.: CHESS: a model-driven engineering tool environment for aiding the development of complex industrial systems. In: ASE, pp. 362–365. ACM (2012)
9. Cimatti, A., Griggio, A., Redondi, G.: Universal invariant checking of parametric systems with quantifier-free SMT reasoning. In: Platzer, A., Sutcliffe, G. (eds.) CADE 2021. LNCS (LNAI), vol. 12699, pp. 131–147. Springer, Cham (2021). https://doi.org/10.1007/978-3-030-79876-5_8
10. Cimatti, A., Griggio, A., Redondi, G.: Verification of SMT systems with quantifiers. In: Bouajjani, A., Holik, L., Wu, Z. (eds.) Automated Technology for Verification and Analysis. ATVA 2022. LNCS, vol. 13505, pp. 154–170. Springer, Cham (2022). https://doi.org/10.1007/978-3-031-19992-9_10
11. Jin-Hua, L., Qiong, L., Jing, L.: The w-model for testing software product lines. In: ISCSCT, vol. 1, pp. 690–693. IEEE Computer Society (2008)

Ivette: A Modern GUI for **Frama-C**

Loïc Correnson[✉]

CEA, LIST, Software Safety Laboratory, PC 174, 91191 Gif-sur-Yvette, France
loic.correnson@cea.fr

Abstract. Using a static analyzer such as Frama-C is known to be difficult, even for experienced users. Building a comfortable user interface to alleviate those difficulties is however a complex task that requires many technical issues to be handled that are outside the scope of static analyzers techniques. In this paper, we present the design directions that we have chosen for completely refactoring the old Graphical User Interface of Frama-C within the ReactJS framework. In particular, we discuss middleware and language issues, multithreaded client *vs.* batch analyzer design, synchronization issues, multiple protocol support, plug-in integration, graphical and user-interaction techniques and how various programming language traits scale (or not) for such a development project.

Keywords: Frama-C · ReactJS · Reactive programming · Static analysis server

1 Introduction

Frama-C [1,2] is a platform that offers mature and industrial strength static analyzers for C/C++ programs. Built around a kernel responsible for parsing, type-checking and analysis-results consolidation, the platform is extensible *via* plug-ins that can offer new analyzers, new frontends or combine existing ones in various ways. Frama-C is known to be used in education for teaching formal methods [3–5], in research projects for prototyping new static analyzers [6–8] and in industrial settings with the highest-level of certification constraints [9,10].

Like any other state-of-the-art static analyzer, Frama-C is generally easy to use at a first glance. However, for programs of increasing complexity, it becomes difficult, even for expert and experienced users, to tune the analyzers and to understand and fix issues. Actually, Frama-C static analyzers like the EVA Abstract Interpretation Analyzer and the WP Deductive Verification Engine, produce huge sets of complex data during their computations. Sometimes, the end-user will have to dive into those complex data for investigating the source of a possible bug or an over-approximation of the analyzer, then re-start the analyzer until all problems are fixed.

To make such a development cycle practicable, Frama-C was designed from its very beginning to be accompanied by a Graphical User Interface (GUI). Instead of running the `frama-c` command line, one can run the `frama-c-gui` command

© The Author(s), under exclusive license to Springer Nature Switzerland AG 2023
P. Masci et al. (Eds.): SEFM 2022 Collocated Workshops, LNCS 13765, pp. 116–131, 2023.
https://doi.org/10.1007/978-3-031-26236-4_10

with exactly the same arguments: this will perform exactly the same computations and open the GUI in order for the user to dive into the obtained results and launch other computations interactively. Like the command-line interface, frama-c-gui supports extension by plug-ins, such that any Frama-C plug-in may extend the GUI with dedicated components.

Pitfalls of Frama-C's Mainstream GUI

Despite the many success stories we have encountered with frama-c-gui, we also acknowledge many design, usability and deprecation issues. From a technical point of view, frama-c-gui is written in OCaml with the LablGTK bindings to the GTK graphical environment. See Fig. 1 for an illustration of this GUI.

Fig. 1. The mainstream Frama-C GUI based on GTK

Although the choice of LablGTK had some advantages in the past, we have experienced many pitfalls over the years with such a design:

- Experienced developers fluent in both GTK and OCaml are extremely rare; more generally, experts in both *Static Analyzers* and *User Interfaces* are also extremely rare, despite any personal affinities in both fields.
- Developing a new graphical component in LablGTL/GTK is very difficult (*e.g.* to visualize graphs or diagrams).
- The GUI code is strongly coupled with the static analyzer. However, the GUI code is necessarily interactive (asynchronous) from a user point of view, whereas analyzer runs are definitely in batch mode (synchronous). Interleaving the two approaches inevitably produces reliability issues that are difficult to debug and fix.
- The GUI code is actually *part* of the static analyzers, which prevents Frama-C from being integrated with other user environments (*e.g.* code editors) without duplicating a lot of already existing code dedicated to the GUI.
- Last, but not least, after more than 12 years of uncontrolled hacking, the GUI code base has become completely unmaintainable.

In addition to technical problems cited above, the mainstream Frama-C GUI also has many issues from an end-user point of view:

- The user must wait before static analyzers finish their jobs *before* the GUI becomes visible.
- In case the analyzers raise errors, it is difficult to restore a safe state without exiting the GUI and restarting the entire process.
- The current implementation is cluttered by so many little bugs that using the GUI on a regular basis can be tedious.
- The existing components are not completely satisfactory, but because of the technical issues listed above, hardly nobody is akin to implement any new features in this GUI.
- The organization of the main GUI window is far too rigid, and GUI plug-ins have a very limited area available to interact with the user. This prevents designing new components and new user interactions with the static analyzers.
- With GTK, we have experienced some cross-platform differences and some difficulties with system integration: they are difficult to predict, document or even fix (*e.g.* on non-Linux platforms).

To finish on a more humorous note, we also acknowledge that using GTK has become totally old-fashioned, just have a look to Fig. 1! How to hype Formal Methods, then?

Contributions

In response to the many pitfalls mentioned above, we decided to completely redesign a new user interface for Frama-C. This led to a long-term engineering effort, supported by many projects over the last 6 years. We started with a deep survey of existing frameworks, experimenting with different platforms and prototypes.

In this article, we overview in Sect. 2 our search for new design guidelines and the final technical stack we ended up with. We then expose implementation details of the fundamental building blocks of our new Ivette graphical user interface for Frama-C: in Sect. 3 we will discuss middleware and the Frama-C/Server plug-in; Sect. 4 will present how *React Programming* dramatically reduced the complexity of GUI code; in Sect. 5 we will briefly present our Dome framework of front-end components; finally we will present in Sect. 6 some specific features of Ivette as a *Static Analyzer* user interface. Finally, we will briefly mention future work directions in Sect. 7.

2   Towards a New GUI for Frama-C

Modern engines for HTML5, CSS and JavaScript are currently the most powerful means to build complex graphical user interfaces, especially for scientists: no research team will have enough manpower to re-create all the flexibility in layouts, theming, system and GPU integration, that those technologies are offering.

However, there was still an open question for the Frama-C new user interface: should it be a *web* application, a *desktop* one or an extension of some existing Code Editor ? The last option would make Frama-C bound to a particular IDE, although it is still an interesting option. However, we want to open the route to like to radically different user interactions and more *graphical* data presentations. Hence, since code editors remains intrinsically text-code oriented, we leave this option for future work and keep on an HTML-based solution.

The common idea that both *web* and *desktop* applications are the same is *wrong*! Although they can share a lot of common code, *web* and *desktop* apps do not share the same design principles and are very different from a user perspective: for instance, in *web* applications, the data the user works with must be centralized in a distant server, whereas in a *desktop* app, the user works with its own file system.

As many Frama-C developers and users, we really want a *desktop* application: we are running *possibly under development* Frama-C plug-ins on *mostly under development* source files. The co-development cycle of analyzers and analyses would be too slow if one had to connect-push-compile-and-run any modification on-the-fly. We finally ended-up with the following strong design directions:

- The GUI shall be a *desktop* application based on an HTML/CSS engine.
- The GUI shall be coded in a language that *User Interface* experts know about, with very good community support and open-source tools. This allows for taking advantage of state-of-the art human-computer interaction techniques.
- The GUI and the Static Analyzer shall live in independent processes, with middlewares and protocols to connect them with each other; this will open the route towards integration with different user environments and solve many reliability issues.
- GUI components shall be as much as possible agnostic to the precise *meaning* of static analyzer data; no complex semantic treatment over data shall be performed on the GUI side, just like Excel doesn't know what kind of data a sheet deals with, but just organizes computations over strings and numbers into cells.
- Static Analyzer plug-ins shall be ready to interact with some external User Environment, but without any dependency on the middleware that will be actually responsible for the connection. This interaction shall be coded into the Frama-C code base with some dedicated support, hence in OCaml.

Ivette Overview

Of course, there is a choice of technical platforms that are suitable for implementing such a plan. Note also that in this domain, libraries and tools are in constant evolution. The technical stack we have chosen so far consists of the following frameworks, also illustrated in Fig. 2:

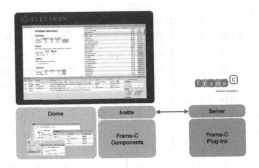

Fig. 2. Technical organization of Ivette

- A GUI desktop application using the HTML5 and NodeJS engine of the Electron [11] framework.
- A GUI code base written in TypeScript with the *Reactive Programming* framework ReactJS [12].
- A Frama-C/Server plug-in written in OCaml, that provides an asynchronous, JSON-based, strongly typed *Request System*.
- Each Frama-C plug-in will then register new requests in the Server plug-in, independently of any communication protocol with any external User Environment.
- A collection of middlewares and protocols written in different languages to specifically connect the Frama-C/Server plug-in and the ReactJS code with each other.

The GUI code itself is entirely written in TypeScript and is split into three parts:

- The Dome framework, which is a collection of carefully designed and themed high-level components, offering a predefined choice of features, but that are robust and well adapted to end-user needs (*e.g.* tables with built-in sizing, sorting and filtering, text-editors with dynamic tag highlighting, *etc.*).
- The Ivette framework, which is an application built with Electron and Dome featuring the main Frama-C GUI graphical environment and managing the connection with Frama-C *via* the Server plug-in.
- The Frama-C plug-in components for Ivette are build from Dome components and interact with the Frama-C static analyzer plug-ins *via* registered Server requests.

Notice that since the very beginning of the project 6 years ago, some design choices have evolved, because of the technical evolutions of the frameworks over the years; and also to fix some wrong early design choices.

3   The **Frama-C** Server Plug-in

The Server plug-in extends the Frama-C platform by providing to every other plug-in a central way to register *Asynchronous Typed Requests*, without any knowledge on how the server will be actually connected to external clients. The requests are entirely written in OCaml, in the same programming environment than any other Frama-C plug-in.

The Server API offers two different kinds of services: (1) a library for Frama-C plug-ins for writing and registering typed and documented requests; (2) a library for writing protocols for connecting the server to external clients. Several issues are addressed and solved by the architecture and design of the Server plug-in, notably:

- how to reconcile the sequential implementation of most Frama-C analyzers with the asynchronous requirements of a server connected to an external GUI environment;
- how to document the collection of requests registered by all Frama-C plug-ins in a consistent and maintainable way;
- how to ensure that data exchanges between the Server and the Client are well-typed, despite the fact that both programs might be developed in different programming languages;
- how to extend the server capabilities by implementing new communication protocols via external plug-ins of Frama-C.

We will present in this section the design of the Frama-C/Server plug-in and how it provides a solution to those issues. This plug-in has been open-sourced since the Frama-C v20.0 (Calcium, Dec. 2019) official release and is still in active development, although its API is quite stable.

3.1 The Request System

A discipline existing since the beginning of Frama-C is that any static analyzer shall regularly invoke a specific function, now called Db.yield(). In the mainstream Frama-C GUI, this function is used to periodically give an opportunity for GTK to handle user events. This is a well-known technique for implementing *Cooperative Threads* without writing the entire code of a static analyzer in any lightweight thread framework such as OCaml/Lwt.

The Server takes benefit from this old discipline to offer a similar mechanism to connected clients: each time the Db.yield function is invoked by a static analyzer, the server will give a chance to requests to be answered. However, the difficulty is to not interleave requests that might modify a static analyzer semantics *while* it is running.

To this end, the Server plug-in offers different kinds of requests in order to reconcile the synchronous behavior of static analyzers with asynchronous requests from external clients. Notice that all requests are initiated by the Client, whatever their kind:

- GET requests are meant to be very quick to compute; they can be answered at any time, even when a static analyzer is running, typically on Db.yield calls; they shall *not* modify the semantics of the static analyzer computations.

- **SET** requests are meant to perform analyzer configuration; they will be treated *between* static analyzer runs, hence not by `Db.yield` calls.
- **EXEC** requests are reserved for launching computations of static analyzers, which cannot be interleaved with each other and must be run in sequence. Handlers of **EXEC** requests are responsible for calling `Db.yield` periodically.

When registering a new request of some kind in the server, each plug-in is responsible for obeying the associated constraints listed above. A request actually consists of the following elements:

- the request package and name;
- a markdown documentation snippet;
- the request kind: GET, SET or EXEC;
- a module with signature `Input` for decoding the input parameters;
- a module with signature `Output` for encoding the output responses;
- the function, with type `Input.t -> Output.t`, responsible for answering the request.

The parameter and returned module signatures are two variants of a more general `Value` signature illustrated below:

```
module type Value =
sig
  type t
  val jtype : jtype
  val of_json : json -> t (* only for Input *)
  val to_json : t -> json (* only for Output *)
end
```

The OCaml type `jtype` encodes JSON types, which are a simplified version of *JSON Schemas*. Here is an illustrative extract from its definition:

```
type jtype =
  Jnull | Jnumber | Jstring | Jlist of jtype | ...
```

The `Server` plug-in offers a rich library for building and combining `Input` and `Output` modules. One can also declare *named* types whose documentation will be added to the request documentation.

3.2   Generic Server and Protocols

The `Server` plug-in provides a generic function to create a server. This function must be instantiated with a fetching function having the following (simplified) signature:

```
type 'a message = {
  requests : 'a request list ;
  callback : 'a response list -> unit ;
}
val Server.Main.create :
  fetch:(unit -> 'a message option) -> server
```

The `fetch` function is responsible for interacting with the external Client; it decodes its data into some optional `message`. A message consists of a list of input requests, together with a callback to send responses back to the client.

A very important difference between the protocol function and the plug-in request interface is that requests and responses are *not* associated in the same way. From the protocol point of view, each message consists of a list of request inputs (n, f, x) where n is some request identifier (of type `'a`), f the request name and x its JSON parameter; response messages will consist of pairs (n, y) where n is the identifier of some request from *any* of the previously received messages, and $y = f(x)$ the output JSON value resulting from processing the request (n, f, x) identified by n.

Hence, from the Client perspective, the Server is fed with requests and replies with (some of) the available responses of past requests. It is the responsibility of the Client to re-associate responses to requests pairwise and to poll the server by (possibly empty) messages until all responses are fetched back.

The current release of the Frama-C/Server plug-in comes with three server protocol implementations usable out-of-the box:

- `SocketServer`: based on UNIX system sockets;
- `ZmqServer`: based on the ZeroMQ [13] well-known library[1];
- `BatchServer`: this server reads static requests from JSON files and prints the responses to the terminal; this server is used for implementing unit tests for requests registered by Frama-C plug-ins. This protocol can also be used as it is for just scripting Frama-C plug-ins.

3.3 Extended Requests Features

In addition to the low-level GET, SET and EXEC requests depicted so far, the Server plug-in also offers more elaborated features that reveal to be very useful and intensively used in practice.

First, the Server implements *Signals* that can be used to tell the Client that something happened during a static analyzer computation. In order to save data in message exchanges, signals are only sent when the Client explicitly asks to receive them (by message type). Hence, protocol messages are extended with signal-specific requests and responses. Optionally, it is possible to associate signals to requests: hence the Client can be informed to re-issue requests when their associated signals are emitted.

Second, the Server plug-in provides so-called *Synchronized Values* which are used to automatically mirror any Frama-C internal state to the Client. Synchronized values simply consist of a combination of three basic ingredients: a GET request for reading the current value of the state, a SET request for updating the state, and a dedicated SIGNAL for signaling state updates to the Client.

Finally, the Server plug-in provides so-called *Synchronized Arrays* which are used to automatically mirror large *collections* of values between the Server and

---

[1] ZeroMQ has been notoriously used for the CERN Large Hadron Collider.

the Client. This is a generalization of synchronized values, with optimizations in order to scale for huge collections: the Client is able to ask only for a limited range of records in the collection, and the Server will only send *updates* of the collection from what has already been sent in the past.

3.4   Client Side Facilities

The Server plug-in provides also facilities for building Clients.

First, the Server plug-in is capable of generating an HTML documentation of all the registered requests, with their kind, input and output JSON types and general documentation, from all the data provided programmatically by plug-ins when registering their requests into the server.

Second, the Server plug-in offers an API to programmatically browse the available requests with their type. This can be used to automatically generate well-typed JSON decoders and encoders for all requests. Typically, for the purpose of the Ivette GUI for Frama-C, we have developed a Frama-C plug-in that generates a strongly typed TypeScript module for each request registered in the Server plug-in. This way, Ivette GUI code can be type-checked with respect to the actual type of each request parameter and returned value, despite their low-level encoding into raw JSON data.

4   Reactive Programming with ReactJS

Although HTML5 engines are extremely powerful for their graphical rendering capabilities, developing in JavaScript and hacking the DOM object model is definitely unmaintainable for a large project.

4.1   The Language Perspective

From the language perspective itself, we decided to migrate from JavaScript to TypeScript in the middle of the project, just because non-typed languages can *not* resist refactoring: even minor API changes can simply *not* be tracked over any code base, even small ones! However, we must also mention that TypeScript comes with its own pitfalls. Namely, we have often and painfully experienced that open record typing is indeed a terrible mistake: despite being an appealing feature to deal with optional record fields, it hides all bugs caused by misspelled or renamed fields! Combined with polymorphic type inference, this makes such bugs *very* difficult to investigate and fix.

Despite those difficulties, the TypeScript ecosystem is very mature, with a lot of existing type-annotation bindings available for many popular JavaScript libraries. This is a very important requirement since we need to build upon powerful existing libraries with relatively large APIs.

The lack of available bindings for state-of-the-art JavaScript libraries is one reason for not choosing another language with a better type system than Type-Script, *e.g.* the promising ReScript [14] project. However, we still envision to change the base language of our GUI in the future when bindings will not be a pain: even if it is a large amount of work, type safety will always make the difference.

4.2 Beyond the Model-View-Controller Paradigm

At the beginning of the Ivette project, the ReactJS [12] framework was becoming very popular for building HTML5 applications. This framework actually induced disruptive directions for *thinking* the architecture of applications, which makes GUI development *just scale* far beyond the traditional *Model-View-Controller* architectural pattern.

The following code snippet is an idiomatic example of ReactJS usage:

```
function Dlist(props) {
  const [N,setN] = React.useState(props.size);
  return (
    <div>
      <button label="+" onClick={() => setN(N+1)}/>;
      <button label="-" onClick={() => setN(N-1)}/>;
      {(new Array(N)).map((_,k) => <div>Item #{k}</div>)}
    </div>
  );
}
```

In this very simplified example, we define a new component named Dlist. The component defines a local state and, from its current value, it builds a non-trivial subtree of components, namely two buttons for updating the state and a number of items depending on the current state. Once defined, this new component can be mixed with any other standard HTML5 markup, *e.g.* <Dlist size={4} />; the entire application window is built in this way.

This toy example illustrates the fundamental concept of React: the entire application window is a *purely functional* projection of the application's *internal states*, organized into components that are *function closures* that recursively build *entire subtrees* of the graphical DOM model. We now briefly comment the important terms of this statement.

Purely Functional: any React component, like the toy component <Dlist/> above, are *functions* that take HTML5 markup properties and render a subtree of HTML5 or Component markups. Hence, components become *first-order* citizens of the host language, like any other function closure. As such, they can be computed, stored, duplicated, partially applied and passed to other functions or components as arguments. This allows for, typically, dynamically generating entire parts of an application from both data *and* events.

Internal States: ReactJS comes with so-called Hooks [15], like the useState() function in the previous example. This standard hook provides the simplest possible internal state: a variable N initialized with the property size of the Dlist component; this state comes with an update function setN() for updating the state in response to any HTML5 or programmatic events via callbacks. The developer can also create its own hooks by combining existing ones.

Components Subtree Updates: each time an application internal state is modified *via* hooks, React knows that the associated component has to be updated; this is eventually done by running again the rendering functions of each of the impacted components, and updating the concrete DOM accordingly. The magic and power of ReactJS actually lies in the amazing diffing algorithms involved in this dynamically updating process.

Compared to the classical *Model-View-Controller* paradigm, we have experienced that the main disruptive innovations that make the difference are the following ones:

- The *Model* concept is simplified by user-defined internal states powered by hooks, which are actually *part of* and *local to* each component, *together* with their associated callbacks.
- The *View* part of the paradigm has been extended to recomputing *entire subtrees* of the application graphical components, not only individual components.
- Finally, the *Controller* part of the paradigm comes almost for free: the management of component creation, deletion and layout are left to the underlying frameworks. Thanks to HTML5 and CSS layout capabilities this saves a huge amount of code compared to classical frameworks such as GTK.

Combined all-together, those major innovations allow GUI development to *just scale* for large projects. We have experienced roughly an order of magnitude reduction of the code complexity: for n components connected with each other in the GUI, the code grows in $O(n)$ complexity within ReactJS-like frameworks, whereas it reaches $O(n^2)$ complexity within GTK-like frameworks.

Last but not least, we shall also mention two *really amazing* features powered by the JavaScript environment: the first one comes from the Chromium engine embedded inside Electron, which offers a rich collection of debugging facilities for HTML5, and also direct support for ReactJS components and hooks; the second one comes from the JavaScript hot-loading features with ReactJS support, which actually allows developers to *live edit* their code: you see what you code in real time, with live interactions on your data! Compared to a traditional *compile-link-and-restart-your-analysis-to-fix-your-app* cycle of development, live-code editing provides incredibly faster development cycles.

4.3 A Quick Overview of Ivette's Hooks

For the purpose of the Ivette graphical user interface, we have typically implemented a collection of hooks dedicated to data exchanges with the Frama-C/Server presented in Sect. 3. For instance, given a request rq, one simply uses the following Hook for interacting with Frama-C:

```
const result = FramaC.Server.useRequest(rq, params);
```

The hook then automatically re-emits the request `rq` to the server each time the parameters `params` are modified or associated signals are emitted, including server shutdowns and restarts; server responses are then automatically collected and push to the `useRequest()` internal state, which will eventually make the associated components to be automatically updated.

Frama-C states and arrays (Cf. Sect. 3.3) also benefit from dedicated React hooks that make them automatically mirrored on demand inside the code of GUI components. The Ivette middleware actually uses internal sophisticated cache mechanisms to make all this machinery very efficient: communication between the GUI part and the Server part is super simple and smooth.

5   The Dome GUI Framework

The Electron [11] framework handles a lot of features regarding system integration and cross-platform deployment of a desktop application. However, its Chromium engine is a generic HTML5 engine agnostic *w.r.t* the *web* or *desktop* application it is actually running. It is entirely the responsibility of the developers to confer an appealing and consistent look & feel to their applications.

On another hand, there exists a huge amount of libraries available in the JavaScript community that provide interesting CSS style sheets and collections of basic components. However, they are often incomplete and complementary with each other. What is absolutely missing is a collection of all-in-one *desktop app* components designed for large real projects. This contrasts with "old-fashioned" frameworks like GTK, where you only have components consistent with each other, but it is hardly possible to create new graphical components with complex behavior, compared to the flexibility of HTML5.

Hence, we started to develop a library named Dome that consists of carefully designed and themed React components for building great *desktop* applications.

This Dome library has been designed to be re-used for User Interface projects outside Ivette/Frama-C. It is meant to be developed and maintained by GUI experts that might have zero knowledge about static analyzers and formal methods. Currently, it is still under active development driven by the Ivette needs, although we envision to open-source Dome as an independent project on a midterm basis. Here follows an overview of the already useful features currently available in Dome:

Command Line Integration: The desktop application is ready to also support command-line invocations.

User Settings: The application has built-in support for user preferences, with per-user scope and/or project scopes. Most Dome widgets have built-in support for storing their state in user settings.

Dark & Bright Themes: The desktop application supports theming *w.r.t* to system user settings.

Themed Widgets: Basic components (buttons, labels, checkboxes, icons, *etc.*) come with a consistent look & feel and consistent API.

Layout Widgets: Flexible layout containers, such as boxes, draggable splitters, grids, toolbars, sidebars, foldable panels, *etc.* with user settings support when relevant.

Icon Library: A consistent, extensible, collection of open-sourced SVG icons that do not depend on the underlying platform (necessary for documenting cross-platform apps).

Forms Widgets: A library for building hierarchical forms with support for dynamic form validation.

Hooks Library: A collection of useful React hooks to deal with events, timers, promises, etc.

JSON Library: A set of parsing operators for safely decoding JSON data in a typed way. This is typically used for User Settings, but revealed to be also useful type-safe protocol implementation such as the one of Frama-C/Server.

Drag & Drop Facilities: A library based on `react-draggable` [16] components, which offers ready-to-use Drag Source and Drop Target containers and the necessary controllers that ease the development of Drag & Drop features, which are well known to be difficult to implement. The underlying `react-draggable` library is also widely used throughout Dome.

Text & Code Editors: A library for working with large text data with arbitrarily nested semantic tags and dynamic tag highlighting. Largely based on the awesome CodeMirror [17] (v5) library, we still had to package it specifically to scale for very large texts within the ReactJS framework. Managing nested semantic tags and efficient dynamic tag highlighting typically required to hack directly with the DOM in cooperation with low-level features of the CodeMirror API.

Dynamic Tables: A library to efficiently deal with huge, filtered, sorted, dynamically loaded and updated tables. The library offers rich classes for managing the table model and customizable table views with smooth user interaction. The table views is built upon the `react-virtualized` [18] library, which offers efficient rendering of virtually infinite data sets with shadowing techniques.

6   Ivette: A Static Analyzer Oriented Interface

As a graphical user interface for the Frama-C static analyzers, Ivette has some specific design orientations that, in our opinion, can be transposed to other static analyzers. The main Ivette window is organized around into a central mosaic of components the user can rearrange, picking available components from a library panel. Predefined views are also made available by Frama-C developers, and the user can also create and register their own ones.

However, all these components are *not* independent of each other. Consider for instance the AST component, which is responsible for rendering the abstract syntax tree of a C function after typing and normalization by the Frama-C kernel.

Each node of the syntax tree (variable, expression, statement, *etc.*) is associated to unique tags. The user intuitively expects that all other Ivette components will synchronize with the currently selected tag from the AST. Conversely, the user selecting an alarm emitted from the Property panel wants the AST to scroll to the origin of the alarm.

Hence, Ivette not only consists of independent components, but also consists of shared selection states. Currently, we have: (1) a shared (multiple) semantic tag selection state, with saved and navigable history; (2) a volatile shared semantic selection associated with mouse hover moves: each time the mouse is hovering something associated with a semantic tag, all other components can dynamically adjust their rendering.

Such a simple feature can be seen as anecdotal at first sight. However, it ends up greatly contributing towards a smooth user experience. Actually, there is always a tension when providing complex data to the user: if you provide all the available data regarding the current selection, it might clutter the limited area available to each component inside the user window. Instead, you can display a short summarized portion of the data and let the user hover this summary with the mouse, then display more detailed information for each hovered part, typically inside another dedicated component. An example of such a behavior is the Inspector component, which always displays a brief collection of information (that every Frama-C plug-in can extend directly *via* the Server services) related to all currently selected tags, but also for the *currently hovered* tag. This turns out to be much more comfortable for the user than, say, pop-up windows. And ReactJS is fast enough to make such a dynamic behavior very smooth.

We currently have a few basic components available for Ivette, mainly dedicated to the Frama-C/EVA abstract interpretation analyzer, that reproduce and enhance the features that were available for this plug-in from the mainstream frama-c-gui. We intend to add more components in a near future, namely for the Frama-C/WP deductive verification analyzer.

Some very new experimental components are also available that we could not have implemented easily inside the mainstream GTK interface: (1) an interactive exploration of the graph of EVA imprecision sources, namely the Frama-C/Dive plug-in; and (2) a dynamic pivot table data extraction of kernel and EVA results. Ivette has been open-sourced with the Frama-C v25 (Vanadium, June 2022) release.

As a general feedback from developers that contributed to the work described above, it seems that our Dome and the Ivette environments allows, even for non-GUI experts, to quickly experiment with new interaction techniques and complex data raveling.

7 Feedback and Future Work

We started to deploy experimental versions of Ivette with a few industrial and institutional partners. Initial feedback is very encouraging despite the few Frama-C components currently available. From a developer point of view, the Ivette platform offers a very exciting and efficient environment for developing static analyzer components.

Future work will mainly focus on the development of new Frama-C components inside Ivette. We are also preparing the Dome framework for open sourcing. We want to extend the Dome framework with 2D and 3D graph capabilities, and to design components for authoring *User Documentation* directly from the GUI. There is also a need for Dome applications to support external plug-ins, in order to have dynamically installed Ivette extensions.

Another interesting direction to explore is to design Frama-C/Server protocols for other external User Environments, for instance a *Language Server Protocol* implementation.

8   Conclusion

To overcome the technical and design limitations of the mainstream graphical user interface of Frama-C, we have designed a radically different platform named Ivette. Thanks to modern technologies, namely HTML5 and CSS engines, and with the support of the disruptive *Reactive Programming* framework provided by ReactJS, we have successively reached most of our objectives.

Moreover, we managed to dispatch the necessary expertise in *User Interfaces* and *Static Analyzers* among different people: developers with strong GUI skills are dedicated to the development of Dome rich components; Frama-C developers with basically no GUI skills can still perform the hard work of implementing all necessary semantic data processing *via* Frama-C/Server requests without leaving the standard Frama-C environment; finally, those who are interested in developing new Static Analyzer GUI components can play with the Dome and Ivette environments without being GUI experts, while still producing in the end professional user interfaces for their favorite static analyzers.

The architectural design we have introduced is totally general and not dependent on Frama-C internals. The design of the Server component can be transposed to any other static analysis tool and the Dome framework can be re-used for the development of any other scientific Desktop application.

Interestingly enough, some considerations on programming language traits have been exposed and compared with each other. It is also noticeable that such a large project can not be conducted without the support of communities and open-source tools that are far beyond the capabilities of isolated research teams. We sincerely hope that this experience and feedback report will help people in the community of Formal Methods to design and build a new (hyping!) generation of Static Analyzer Graphical User Interfaces.

Acknowledgements. My very special thanks to Michele Alberti, Allan Blanchard, François Bobot, David Bühler, Maxime Jacquemin, André Maroneze, Valentin Perrelle and Virgile Prevosto for their support, valuable insights and direct contributions to this project.

References

1. Baudin, P., et al.: The dogged pursuit of bug-free C programs: the Frama-C software analysis platform. Commun. ACM **64**(8), 56–68 (2021)
2. Cuoq, P., Kirchner, F., Kosmatov, N., Prevosto, V., Signoles, J., Yakobowski, B.: Frama-C: a software analysis perspective. In: Eleftherakis, G., Hinchey, M., Holcombe, M. (eds.) SEFM 2012. LNCS, vol. 7504, pp. 233–247. Springer, Heidelberg (2012). https://doi.org/10.1007/978-3-642-33826-7_16
3. Creuse, L., Dross, C., Garion, C., Hugues, J., Huguet, J.: Teaching deductive verification through Frama-C and SPARK for non computer scientists. In: Dongol, B., Petre, L., Smith, G. (eds.) FMTea 2019. LNCS, vol. 11758, pp. 23–36. Springer, Cham (2019). https://doi.org/10.1007/978-3-030-32441-4_2
4. Souaf, S., Loulergue, F.: Experience report: teaching code analysis and verification using Frama-C. Electron. Proc. Theor. Comput. Sci. **349**, 69–75 (2021)
5. Dubois, C., Prevosto, V., Burel, G.: Teaching formal methods to future engineers. In: Dongol, B., Petre, L., Smith, G. (eds.) FMTea 2019. LNCS, vol. 11758, pp. 69–80. Springer, Cham (2019). https://doi.org/10.1007/978-3-030-32441-4_5
6. Many contributors: Frama-C publications on external plug-ins. https://frama-c.com/html/publications.html#external
7. Shankar, S., Pajela, G.: A tool integrating model checking into a C verification toolset. In: Bošnački, D., Wijs, A. (eds.) SPIN 2016. LNCS, vol. 9641, pp. 214–224. Springer, Cham (2016). https://doi.org/10.1007/978-3-319-32582-8_15
8. Karpman, P.: Building up on SIDAN: improved and new invariants for a software hardening Frama-C plugin. Master's thesis, Supélec, équipe Cidre (2012)
9. Brahmi, A., et al.: Industrial use of a safe and efficient formal method based software engineering process in avionics. In: Embedded Real Time Software and Systems (ERTS 2020) (2020)
10. Djoudi, A., Hána, M., Kosmatov, N.: Formal verification of a JavaCard virtual machine with Frama-C. In: Huisman, M., Păsăreanu, C., Zhan, N. (eds.) FM 2021. LNCS, vol. 13047, pp. 427–444. Springer, Cham (2021). https://doi.org/10.1007/978-3-030-90870-6_23
11. The OpenJS Foundation: Electron, building desktop applications with HTML, JavaScript and CSS. https://www.electronjs.org
12. Facebook: React, a JavaScript library for building user interfaces. https://reactjs.org
13. The ZeroMQ Authors: ZeroMQ, an open-source universal messaging library. https://zeromq.org
14. Project, T.R.: Fast, simple, fully typed javascript from the future. https://rescript-lang.org
15. Facebook: React Hooks at a glance. https://reactjs.org/docs/hooks-intro.html
16. Zabriskie, M., et al.: React-Draggable, a simple component for making elements draggable. https://github.com/react-grid-layout/react-draggable
17. Haverbeke, M., et al.: CodeMirror, an extensible code editor. https://codemirror.net/5/
18. Vaughn, B., et al.: React-Virtualized, react components for efficiently rendering large lists and tabular data. https://github.com/bvaughn/react-virtualized

Building an Extensible Textual Framework for the Rodin Platform

Thai Son Hoang[✉][ID], Colin Snook[ID], Dana Dghaym[ID],
Asieh Salehi Fathabadi[ID], and Michael Butler[ID]

ECS, University of Southampton, Southampton, UK
{t.s.hoang,cfs,d.dghaym,a.salehi-fathabadi,m.j.butler}@soton.ac.uk

Abstract. We present the CamilleX framework for the Rodin platform in this paper. The framework provides a textual representation and persistence for the Event-B modelling constructs. It supports direct extensions to the Event-B syntax, such as machine inclusion and record structures, and indirect extensions provided by other plugins, such as UML-B diagrams. We discuss CamilleX's design, its extension mechanisms, and examples of their use.

Keywords: Event-B · Rodin platform · CamilleX · XText

1 Introduction and Motivation

The Event-B modelling method [1] is a discrete state-transition formal modelling language. The main supporting tool for Event-B is the Rodin Platform (Rodin) [2], which facilitates the editing of Event-B models and reasoning about them. Rodin is based on Eclipse and provides an extensible platform via Eclipse's plug-in mechanism. This is very important for the openness to extensibility of both Event-B as the modelling method and to the supporting Rodin [15].

One of the main functions of Rodin is to provide a database of modelling elements. Essentially, an Event-B model in Rodin is a collection of modelling elements. The "syntax" using keywords that users see in the GUI is provided by the corresponding editors and does not exist in the serialised model. The internal structure of the model repository (called the 'Rodin database') was motivated by the choice design decision to have an extensible Event-B modelling language for Rodin [15]. In particular, Event-B models are serialised in XML Metadata Interchange format.

While this makes tooling extensions to Event-B and Rodin easy, team-based development of models is challenging because model changes (e.g. differences in compare viewing tools) are difficult to comprehend with XML-based files. Hence, our work starts with the motivation to have a true user-readable textual input for Rodin and for the serialised models to be in this same format. This paper is an extended version of [9] with more details on our motivation and some lessons learnt in designing CamilleX.

© The Author(s), under exclusive license to Springer Nature Switzerland AG 2023
P. Masci et al. (Eds.): SEFM 2022 Collocated Workshops, LNCS 13765, pp. 132–147, 2023.
https://doi.org/10.1007/978-3-031-26236-4_11

The paper is structured as follows. Section 2 gives an overview of Rodin, the Event-B EMF framework and XText technology. Section 3 presents the basic design of the CamilleX framework. We discuss direct extensions to the CamilleX syntax using examples of machine inclusion and record structures in Sect. 4. Section 5 provides a framework for contributing to the CamilleX models by plug-ins. We elaborate on the future work for CamilleX in Sect. 6 and conclude in Sect. 7.

2 Background

2.1 The Rodin Platform

Rodin [2] is the supporting platform for Event-B and is developed on top of Eclipse. The architectural overview of the Event-B tool can be seen in Fig. 1. The core Rodin platform is built on top of the Eclipse platform. The Event-B library bundles include the Abstract Syntax Tree (AST) and the sequence prover (SEQP). The next layer contains the core supporting tools for Event-B, namely, the static checker (SC), the proof obligation generator (POG) and the proof obligation manager (POM). The Event-B user interfaces are the top layer, including the modelling UI (MUI) and the proving UI (PUI).

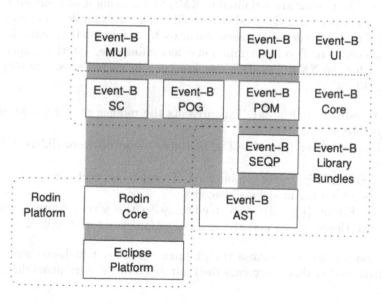

Fig. 1. Architectural overview of the Event-B Tools [2]

One of the main components of the Rodin Core is the Rodin database which stores the modelling elements in a tree-shaped structured database. Since Rodin 3.0, the database elements must obey the constraints defined by the plugins.

However, these constraints can be extended by contributing to an extension point. As the structure is independent of the Event-B modelling language, it makes extending Event-B straight-forward by adding new elements and declare their relationships with existing elements as constraints. Another essential component of Rodin is the Rodin builder that automatically runs the Event-B core tools. The tool-chains can be seen in Fig. 2.

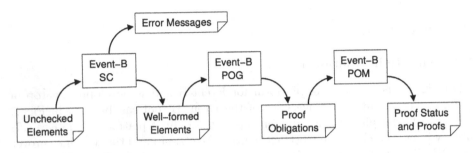

Fig. 2. The Tool-Chain in the Rodin builder [2]

While the design of the Rodin database aids extensibility, it has other consequences. The models are serialised in XML files making it difficult for humans to read and understand the model. It is difficult, for example, to compare two versions of a model when using version control tools for collaboration. Moreover, it is challenging to develop a functional modelling user interface, specifically the editor for the XML files. Different kind of editors have been developed for Event-B (Fig. 3).

- Tree-based editor (Fig. 3a): This presents the models as a tree with overlay widgets for editing.
- Form-based editor (Fig. 3b): The editor is made up from different Eclipse forms.
- Rodin Editor (Fig. 3c): A combination of a read-only text editor with overlay widgets for editing modelling elements.
- Camille Editor (Fig. 3d): A text editor with the actual "outer" syntax of Event-B. However, the underlying serialisation structure is still XML-based.

Our motivation is to have a true, human readable, text-based serialisation of Event-B models that overcomes the limitations of the current modelling user interface.

2.2 EMF and Event-B EMF

The Eclipse Modelling Framework (EMF) framework [14] is an Eclipse-based framework for implementing modelling languages. An abstract syntax is defined by a meta-model and code is then generated to provide a repository for instances

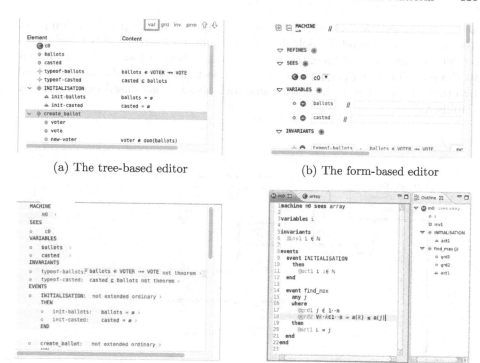

(a) The tree-based editor

(b) The form-based editor

(c) The Rodin Editor

(d) The Camille Editor

Fig. 3. Different editors for Rodin

of the model. In previous work [13], we have implemented the EMF tooling for Event-B models with serialisation into the Rodin database. Many of our plug-ins, including UML-B, are based on this Event-B EMF framework and utilise the extension mechanism that we built in. The meta-model of the Event-B EMF framework is shown (in part) in Fig. 4. The meta-classes, **Machine**, **Event** and **Context** define some of the concrete modelling elements needed for Event-B with relationships (e.g. **refines**, **sees** and **extends**) and containment (e.g. **variables**, **invariants**, **variants**, **events** etc.). The meta-model makes extensive use of inheritance from abstract meta-classes (most of which are omitted in Fig. 4). The basis of this inheritance structure is the generic meta-class, *EventBElement* which provides facilities for extending the meta-model with new features. The most important of these are the *extensions* containment of *AbstractExtension*. Since this is inherited by all other model element classes, an extension containment can be defined for any concrete model element kind by sub-classing *AbstractExtension* and providing support for serialisation, processing and translation as required. To support the various model-to-model translations that arise from using the extension mechanism, we have developed a generic EMF-to-EMF translation framework plugin with specialised support when targeting Event-B. This plugin provides the basic infrastructure to make it relatively easy to define an efficient translation as a set of Java-based rules via the Eclipse extension point mechanism. The CamilleX tools described herein are based on this EMF meta-model and make use of its extension mechanism, both for syntactic extensions to the modelling language as well as to support model contributions provided by other plugins. The translation framework plugin is also used extensively by CamilleX.

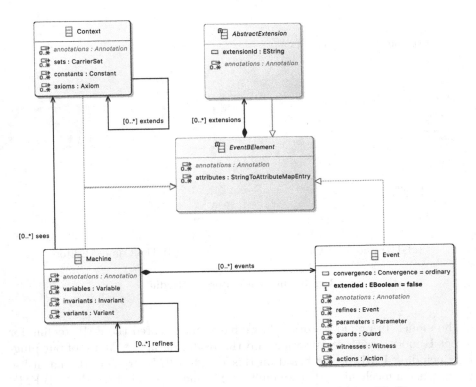

Fig. 4. The Event-B EMF framework meta-model (simplified)

2.3   XText

XText [4] is a powerful framework for developing programming languages and domain-specific languages. The input to the framework is a grammar describing the input language and the result of the framework tooling is "a full infrastruc-ture, including parser, linker, type-checker, compiler as well as editing support for Eclipse" [12]. In particular, the editing support generated from XText includes features such as content assist and a customisable framework for validation and code generation. Internally XText relies on EMF, e.g., for loading the in-memory representation of any parsed text files. This enables XText models to be used by any other EMF-based tools since the XText grammar can be seen as 'just' an alternative serialisation for EMF models.

3   CamilleX

The main aim of the CamilleX Framework is to provide a text-based serialisation of Event-B models. Furthermore, given the existing facilities for Event-B in Rodin, we have the following design principles for CamilleX.

– Reuse the existing Event-B tools of Rodin as much as possible.
– Support direct extension of the Event-B syntax to provide additional features.
– Provide compatibility with other kinds of 'higher-level' models that contribute to the overall model, e.g., UML-B diagrams.

The rest of this section gives an overview of the basic design for the CamilleX framework and the syntax of CamilleX components, namely XMachines and XContexts. We will discuss direct extensions to the Event-B syntax in Sect. 4 and indirect extension by plug-ins to contain other kinds of models in Sect. 5.

3.1   The Basic Design

CamilleX provides a textual representation of Event-B models, as opposed to the XML Rodin files. CamilleX supports two types of textual files XMachine and XContext, which in turn will be automatically translated to the corresponding Rodin Event-B components (machine and context). The reverse transformation from Event-B to CamilleX is also supported and can be manually invoked, as shown in Fig. 5. Note that the representation of CamilleX constructs (XMachines and XContexts), uses an extended Event-B EMF to accommodate Event-B syntax extensions (e.g., machine inclusion and records structure) which is 'flattened' into the (core) Event-B EMF during the automatic translation.

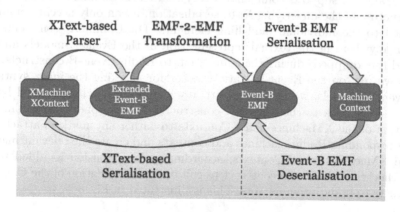

Fig. 5. Overview of CamilleX and Rodin Event-B Constructs

3.2 XContexts and XMachines

The syntax of CamilleX constructs is similar to that of Camille (see Fig. 6 for XContexts and Fig. 7 for XMachines). The description of the different syntactic tokens is as follows:

- ID denotes an identifier.
- LABEL denotes a label.
- FORMULA denotes a sequence of one or more tokens representing:
  - Event-B mathematical symbols
  - integer literals
  - identifiers

Essentially, CamilleX provides the "outer" syntax to Event-B models while relying on the Event-B static checker to check the "inner" syntax of Event-B (i.e., Event-B mathematical formulae).

```
context ID
(extends ID+)?
(sets ID+)?
(constants ID+)?
(axioms (theorem? @LABEL: FORMULA)+ )?
end
```

Fig. 6. The basic XContext syntax

A significant difference between the syntax of CamilleX and that of Camille is that CamilleX supports comments "everywhere". As Camille relies directly on the structure of the underlying XML serialisation, it can only accept comments attached to the individual modelling elements. For CamilleX, comments can appear anywhere in the textual representation of the Event-B models and are ignored (i.e. dropped) during the translation to Rodin Event-B constructs.

As we rely on the Event-B static checker for checking the inner syntax of the Event-B models, we need to report any errors and warnings raised by the static checker back to the CamilleX constructs. This is done by extending the validation of the XMachines and XContexts to gather any markers attached to the corresponding Rodin machines and contexts and create the relevant markers on the XMachines and XContexts, accordingly. An extension is added to the static checker of the Rodin construct to call back the validation of the CamilleX constructs to update the markers. This is illustrated in Fig. 8.

```
machine ID
(refines ID)?
(sees ID+)?
(variables ID+)?
(invariants (theorem? @LABEL: FORMULA)+ )?
(variants (@LABEL: FORMULA)+)?
(events
   (event ID
     (ordinary|convergent|anticipated)?
     ( (refines ID+) | (extends ID) )?
     (any ID+)?
     ( (where|when) (theorem? @LABEL: FORMULA)+ )?
     ( (begin|then) (@LABEL: FORMULA)+ )?
     (with (@ID: FORMULA)+)?
   end)+
)?
end
```

Fig. 7. The basic XMachine syntax

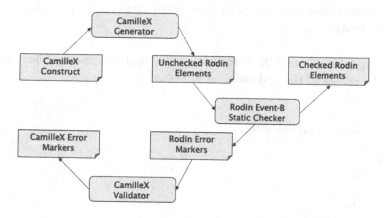

Fig. 8. CamilleX validator for creating CamilleX markers

4   Direct Extensions to the Event-B Syntax

In this section, we present two extensions of the CamilleX constructs to support machine inclusion [8] and records structure [6]. The steps for extending CamilleX are as follows.

1. Extend the Event-B EMF with new modelling elements.
2. Extend the grammar of the CamilleX construct and regenerate the supporting tools.
3. Extend the CamilleX validator to ensure the consistency of the added modelling elements.
4. Extend the CamilleX generator to translate the newly added modelling elements.

4.1 Machine Inclusion

The machine inclusion extension provides the concepts for a machine to include other machines and for an event to synchronise with one or more events from the (different) included machines. The details of the mechanism is described in [8]. We summarise the main ideas of for *machine* A *to include machine* B below:

- A inherits all variables of B.
- A inherits all invariants of B.
- B's variables can only be modified from A via synchronising with an event of B.
- Multiple instances of B can be included via *prefixing* and in that case, B's variables, events, and event parameters are renamed accordingly.

Extending the Event-B EMF. We first extend the Event-B EMF with two new classes representing the machine inclusion clause and the event synchronisation clause. The relationship of the two new modelling elements with the existing elements can be seen in Fig. 9. Both machine inclusion and event synchronisation clauses are sub-classes AbstractExtension which allows them to be added as children of machines and events to their extensions collections (inherited from EventBElement).

Extending the CamilleX Grammar. To support machine inclusion, we extend the syntax of the XMachine as follows.

```
machine ID
...
( includes ID(.ID)∗ (as ID+)? )∗
...
(events
  (event ID
    ...
    (any ID+)?
    ( synchronises (ID.)? ID )∗
    ...
  end)+
)?
end
```

The qualified name (i.e., ID(.ID)∗) allows to include the machines from a different project. If no project is specified, the machine is assumed to be in the same project as the including machine. The optional list of prefixes (specified by the keyword as) enables the renaming of the imported modelling elements (i.e., variables, events, etc.) by prefixing. Multiple instances of the same machine can also be included by providing different prefixes for the same machine.

Similarly, for the event, the synchronises clause is added (with possible instance name) to synchronise with one or more events. The optional qualifier name is to specify the prefix of the included machine from which the synchronised event comes.

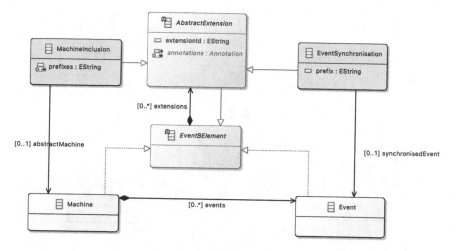

Fig. 9. Extending Event-B EMF for machine inclusion

Extending the CamilleX Generator. The CamilleX generator is extended to "flatten" the machine inclusion and event synchronisation into standard Event-B EMF before serialisation into Rodin Event-B constructs. We make use of the EMF-to-EMF framework introduced in Sect. 2.2 to implement our translation.

- For each **includes** clause of a machine, the translator copies the variables and invariants from the included machine. If there are prefixes, multiple copies of the variables and invariants are generated and renamed accordingly.
- For each **synchronises** clause of an event, the translator copies the content of the included events (i.e., the parameters, guards, actions) and renamed appropriately if the prefix is present.

4.2 Record Structures

The records structure extension provides the ability to use record structures within Event-B machines and contexts. The description of the record structures and their translation to Event-B are described in [6]. Records can be declared in both contexts and machines and will generate different Event-B modelling element depending on where records are used.

Extending the Event-B EMF. Records and fields are added to the Event-B EMF. The newly created modelling elements can be seen from the diagram in Fig. 10. Notice that **Record** is a sub-class of AbstractExtension and can be include as child of **Context** and **Machine** in the extensions collection.

Extending the CamilleX Grammar. We extend the syntax of XContexts and XMachines accordingly.

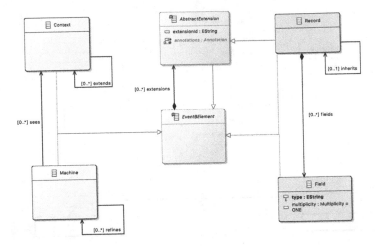

Fig. 10. Extending the Event-B EMF for records structures

```
context ID
...
/* This comes after constants */
(records
    (record ID (inherits ID)?
    ( ID : (one|many|opt)
        TYPE_FORMULA )*
    )+
)?
...
end
```

```
machine ID
...
/* This comes after variables */
(records
    (record ID inherits ID
    ( ID : (one|many|opt)
        TYPE_FORMULA )*
    )+
)?
...
end
```

Here the new syntactic token **TYPE_FORMULA** matches some expression representing Event-B types (i.e., some basic types, the power-set of some type, or the Cartesian product of two or more types).

Extending the CamilleX Generator. The CamilleX generator is extended to "flatten" the records into standard Event-B EMF before serialisation into Rodin Event-B constructs. A record in a context will generate either a carrier set or a constant (if it is an inheriting record). The fields of a record in a context will be generated as constants with the appropriate type, depending on the multiplicities, i.e., **one** (total functions), **many** (binary relations), or **opt** (partial functions). A record in a machine must inherit another record, and is generated as a variable of the machine. The fields of a record in a machine will also be generated as variables with the appropriate type in the machine (depending on the record's multiplicity).

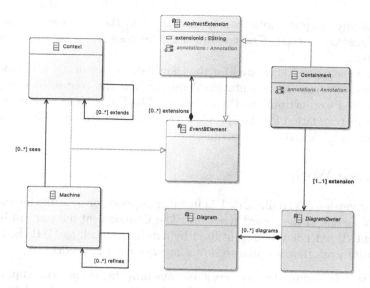

Fig. 11. Extending the Event-B EMF to support containment

5   Indirect Extensions by Plug-ins

In the previous section, we showed how to directly extend the syntax of the CamilleX constructs, i.e. XContexts and XMachines to support mechanisms such as machine inclusion and record structures. These extensions require us to extend the grammar of the CamilleX components and regenerate the CamilleX infrastructure taking into account the grammar extension. Here, we describe a generic extensible mechanism for integration with other plug-ins such as UML-B.

We introduce the notion of *containment*, to enable XContexts and XMachine to include external components such as UML-B diagrams. We introduce Containment which references a DiagramOwner. The DiagramOwner contains zero or more Diagrams which will contribute to the containing Machine or Context. The abstract meta-class, Diagram, can then be sub-classed to contribute the desired model syntax. For example, the individual UML-B diagram types all extend Diagram.

Since Containment is a sub-class of AbstractExtension, they can be included as children of Machine or Context in the extension collection (Fig. 11).

The CamilleX grammar is extended by adding a contains clause to extend context or machines so that they can contain Containment elements. At the moment, only XMachine can own Containments with the following syntax.

```
machine ID
...
/* This comes after refines/sees/includes clauses */
( contains ID+ )*
end
```

Note that any DiagramOwner can be contained in the machines, regardless of their serialisation format. The contained model does not need to be serialised using XText.

An extension point is created for the CamilleX generator, which allows plug-ins to contribute an implementation detailing how the contained components are translated to contribute to the machines. The CamilleX generator will then defer to this translation for the specific type of DiagramOwner as declared in the extension, e.g., UML-B state-machine.

6   Future Work

The latest version of CamilleX (2.1.1) includes support for machine inclusion and an initial version of the record structure. The Containment mechanism has been implemented, but not yet fully utilised by extensions such as UML-B. Below is some future work that we plan to do to improve the framework.

- *Machine Inclusion.* Future work on machine inclusion will suppress the generation of unnecessary proof obligations (e.g., those related to correct-by-construction included invariants), support importing a refinement-chain (instead of the individual machine), and integrate with context instantiation.
- *Record Structures.* Currently, CamilleX does not yet support the extension refinement of record structures as described in [6]. At the moment, properties of the record fields are translated as axioms and invariants after other "normal" axioms and invariants. Often, we need to rearrange the order, e.g., the generated elements need to go before or in between the other normal elements. This can be done with the restructuring of the Event-B EMF to have a single collection of child elements. At the moment, we are working on a prototype of CamilleX 3.0.0 (together with a new version of the Event-B EMF framework) to address this.
- *UML-B integration.* Although the CamilleX containment extension allows for integration with UML-B, the UML-B diagrams are currently serialised in EMF XML Metadata Interchange format. For similar reasons to CamilleX, it would be advantageous to have a human-readable text serialisation for UML-B diagrams. We are therefore developing XUML-B, which will provide an XText serialisation for UML-B.
- *Extending the CamilleX validator.* Currently, CamilleX error markers related to extensions such as machine inclusion and record structures are not attached to the extensions, e.g., event synchronisation or record field. We will explore the capability of the EMF-to-EMF translator to record the source (in CamilleX) of the generated elements (in the unchecked Rodin elements) to implement this feature in the future.

7   Conclusion

This paper presents the CamilleX framework which provides textual serialisation of Event-B models. In particular, we reuse the existing Event-B tool-chain of

Rodin, by providing only the "outer" syntax for the Event-B models. The design of CamilleX supports both direct extensions to the Event-B syntax and indirect extensions by plug-ins to contain other types of components such as UML-B diagrams. Our experience shows that CamilleX improves the usability of Rodin and assists users in developing Event-B models [7].

The main lessons that we have learnt and design decisions that were made from our experience of developing CamilleX are:

– It is essential to have a textual serialisation for Event-B models. The evolution of the different editors for Rodin illustrates a persistent desire to move away from the Event-B model (essentially a tree-based structure model) serialised into Rodin using a tree-based editor (directly reflecting the underlying serialisation structure) to a form-based editor (attempting to provide a looks-like-text editor) to true text-based editors. Most developers would prefer to have textual input for a language and both Camille (Fig. 3d) and the Rodin editor (Fig. 3c) partially provided that. However, in both these editors, their underlying XML Metadata Interchange serialisation format still did not provide modellers with a human usable text serialisation needed for version control and teamworking. Hence CamilleX was developed to address that.
– The main challenge in this work is to leverage the extensibility of the Rodin database (an important design decision for the Event-B modelling method itself to be extensible). XText provides a framework for building tools supporting domain-specific languages but not for language extensibility. We have carefully designed CamilleX with two different mechanisms for doing that: direct extensions and indirect extensions.
– The main difference between direct and indirect extensions is the dependency between CamilleX and the extensions.
  • Direct extensions imply that CamilleX will depend on the extended features, e.g., machine inclusion or records.
  • Indirect extensions imply that the extended features, e.g., UML-B will depend on CamilleX.
The consequences of these are as follows:
  • For developers, releasing a new version of CamilleX will potentially require upgrading the direct extension features to be compatible (mostly ensuring that they have compatible dependency), but will be independent of the indirect extensions. The maintainer of the indirect extensions will need to update their features accordingly.
  • For users, installing CamilleX will require installation of all direct extensions, but indirect extensions can be installed separately. Moreover, for the direct extensions such as machine inclusion and record structures, it is more natural to have their modelling elements (i.e., event synchronisation, records and fields etc.) together with the Event-B models. For indirect extension, at the moment, their modelling elements are kept in a separate file and integrated with the Event-B model through the Containment mechanism.

Related Work. In [3], the authors describe the architecture for Proof General in Eclipse relying on the Proof General Interaction Protocol (PGIP). In [11], the authors present a tool for the engineering of hybrid systems. The tool includes different components for graphical and textual modelling in Eclipse. In [10], the authors discuss the development of an IDE for PVS based on VSCode. In [5], the authors present a tool for developing proofs for Coq based on Eclipse. The main difference between our work and the fore-mentioned related work is that CamilleX is built to support an *extensible* modelling language.

Acknowledgement. This work is supported by the following projects:
 – HiClass project (113213), which is part of the ATI Programme, a joint Government and industry investment to maintain and grow the UK's competitive position in civil aerospace design and manufacture.
 – HD-Sec project, which was funded by the Digital Security by Design (DSbD) Programme delivered by UKRI to support the DSbD ecosystem.

References

1. Abrial, J.-R.: Modeling in Event-B: System and Software Engineering. Cambridge University Press, Cambridge (2010)
2. Abrial, J.-R., Butler, M., Hallerstede, S., Hoang, T.S., Mehta, F., Voisin, L.: Rodin: an open toolset for modelling and reasoning in Event-B. Softw. Tools Technol. Transfer **12**(6), 447–466 (2010)
3. Aspinall, D., Winterstein, D., Lüth, C., Fayyaz, A.: Proof general in eclipse: system and architecture overview. In: Burke, M.G., Orso, A., Robillard, M.P. (eds.) Proceedings of the 2006 OOPSLA Workshop on Eclipse Technology eXchange, ETX 2006, Portland, Oregon, USA, 22–23 October 2006, pp. 45–49. ACM (2006)
4. Bettini, L.: Implementing Domain-Specific Languages with Xtext and Xtend, 2nd edn. Packt Publishing, Birmingham (2016)
5. Faithfull, A.J., Bengtson, J., Tassi, E., Tankink, C.: Coqoon - an IDE for interactive proof development in Coq. Int. J. Softw. Tools Technol. Transf. **20**(2), 125–137 (2018)
6. Salehi Fathabadi, A., Snook, C., Hoang, T.S., Dghaym, D., Butler, M.: Extensible record structures in Event-B. In: Raschke, A., Méry, D. (eds.) ABZ 2021. LNCS, vol. 12709, pp. 130–136. Springer, Cham (2021). https://doi.org/10.1007/978-3-030-77543-8_12
7. Hammond, J.: Safety and security case study experiences with Event-B and Rodin. https://wiki.event-b.org/images/RodinWorkshop2021_Safety_and_Security_Case_Study_Experiences_with_Event-B_and_Rodin.pdf
8. Hoang, T.S., Dghaym, D., Snook, C.F., Butler, M.J.: A composition mechanism for refinement-based methods. In: 22nd International Conference on Engineering of Complex Computer Systems, ICECCS 2017, Fukuoka, Japan, 5–8 November 2017, pp. 100–109. IEEE Computer Society (2017)
9. Hoang, T.S., Snook, C., Dghaym, D., Salehi Fathabadi, A., Butler, M.: The CamilleX framework for the Rodin platform. In: Raschke, A., Méry, D. (eds.) ABZ 2021. LNCS, vol. 12709, pp. 124–129. Springer, Cham (2021). https://doi.org/10.1007/978-3-030-77543-8_11

10. Masci, P., Muñoz, C.A.: An integrated development environment for the prototype verification system. In: Monahan, R., Prevosto, V., Proença, J. (eds.) Proceedings Fifth Workshop on Formal Integrated Development Environment, F-IDE@FM 2019, Porto, Portugal, 7 October 2019. EPTCS, vol. 310, pp. 35–49 (2019)
11. Mitsch, S., Passmore, G.O., Platzer, A.: Collaborative verification-driven engineering of hybrid systems. Math. Comput. Sci. 8(1), 71–97 (2014)
12. The XText Project. XText website (2020). https://www.eclipse.org/Xtext/
13. Snook, C., Fritz, F., Iliasov, A.: Event-B and Rodin Documentation Wiki: EMF Framework for Event-B (2009). http://wiki.event-b.org/index.php/EMF_framework_for_Event-B. Accessed May 2020
14. Steinberg, D., Budinsky, F., Paternostro, M., Merks, E.: Eclipse Modeling Framework. The Eclipse Series, 2nd edn. Addison-Wesley Professional, Boston (2008)
15. Voisin, L., Abrial, J.-R.: The Rodin platform has turned ten. In: Aït Ameur, Y., Schewe, K.-D. (eds.) ABZ 2014. LNCS, vol. 8477, pp. 1–8. Springer, Heidelberg (2014). https://doi.org/10.1007/978-3-662-43652-3_1

Debugging Support in Atelier B

Léa Riant[✉][iD]

ClearSy System Engineering, Aix-en-Provence, France
lea.riant@clearsy.com

Abstract. Insightful error reports save precious time in the design of systems. When using the formal B method, design errors correspond to invalid proof obligations. The legacy automatic provers in Atelier B are not capable to identify if a failure to prove is due to a logical error. In contrast, SMT solvers are capable to prove a first-order logic formula but also to disprove it and to produce a counter-example. Those counter-examples can give precious indications to the user on design errors. SMT solvers have been integrated in the most recent version of Atelier B, but only to use their proving capabilities. We present here counter_example_reader, a tool to interpret a counter-example produced by an SMT solver into a B counter-example.

Keywords: Atelier B · Debugging · B method · SMT

1 Introduction

The development of critical systems requires a level of safety that can not be obtained by submitting the system to a series of tests that simply cannot be exhaustive. Thus, the use of formal method for critical safety has been democratized.

The B method [1] was defined in the late 80s. It was use industrially for the first time in the development of the automatic pilot of a metro line in Paris. The formal IDE Atelier B was developed in parallel to implement the B method. Atelier B and the B method have been used in many critical systems, mainly in the railway industry.

Atelier B historically has two internal provers. A plugin now allows the use of the ProB model checker [8] in Atelier B. Its prover can manage bigger data structures [7] and return counter-examples. The BWare project [6] develops a framework to use the Why3 [4] platform on Atelier B's projects. Why3 is a platform that allows to call different automatic theorem provers. SMT solvers are regularly used in logic-based verification task. They have already been implemented in Rodin [5], another formal IDE. Since its last release, Atelier B 4.7 include the use of SMT solvers.

The purpose of the integration of external provers in Atelier B is to facilitate the validation of user-made rules. Atelier B allows to write new logical rules for its provers but they need to be justified by hand. To accelerate this process, we

P. Masci et al. (Eds.): SEFM 2022 Collocated Workshops, LNCS 13765, pp. 148–155, 2023.
https://doi.org/10.1007/978-3-031-26236-4_12

can use external prover to determine if the new rules are correct. They also can be use in early stages of a project to distinguish incorrect parts of specifications.

We present here the continuation of the integration of automated provers in Atelier B by exploiting the possibility to return counter-examples, described in Sect. 3. It adds a counter-example translator, named counter_example_reader and described in Sect. 4, and modify the translation of B component into SMT input. The necessary setup and a brief overview of use will be presented in Sect 5. We will mention the limitations of the tools in Sect 6.

2   Presenting the B Method

A project using the B method starts with mathematical models and ends with computer implementations through refinements. Atelier B generate lemmas (called here proof obligations) to assure the coherence of a model. Then, for each refinement, proof obligations are automatically produced to ensure that the new one is consistent with the previous level. A proof obligation is an implication $H \Rightarrow G$, where H is a set of hypotheses and G is the goal. There can be a quite considerable number of consistency and refinement proof obligations. Real projects can easily have around 160.000 proof obligations. Atelier B's internal prover can prove a great part with its library of logical rules. The rest needs to be discharged through an interactive proof's interface, by adding new rules for the provers or by guiding manually the provers, which represent a considerable time. Those interactive proofs are a great part of the development cost. Atelier B offers a tool to translate user-made rules into mathematical models. Proving the rule amounts to discharging associated proof obligations.

3   SMT Solver

3.1   Reliability of Results

Unlike Atelier B's internal provers, external provers are not necessarily certified for critical use. But critical projects must prove that they respect safety requirements. Due to that, those solvers are only used as auxiliary tools to provide information but with a certified solver or redundancy, their result could be relied on.

Therefore, the result of an external prover cannot be used to discharge a proof obligation, but it provides useful information as results of an SMT prover have an high probability to be true. In the preliminary stages of a project, a lot of proof obligations cannot be discharged by Atelier B. SMT solvers tend to prove more proof obligations than Atelier B's provers [9]. So SMT provers can be used to sort provable proof obligations from false ones arising from incorrect specifications. Time is not wasted on trying to prove impossible proof obligations. And in the event that an SMT solver provides a counter-example, it can point at problematic cases and speed up the correction of the specification.

3.2 Satisfiability and Validity

An SMT solver does not prove the validity of a formula but its satisfiability. It consider a formula as a boolean instance where each atomic predicate is a boolean variable. If the instance possesses a solution, the solver check if the truth values of the predicates are consistent with its theories. If it is consistent, then the formula is satisfiable, else the solver search for another solution. In some case, particularly when quantified expressions are involved, the solver cannot prove that the theories are respected or not, and the solution is considered uncertain. The solver can also have a time limit. An SMT solver result will be either "sat", "unsat" or "unknown".

Subsequently, we can not use an SMT solver to prove or disprove the original proof obligation. To prove $H \Rightarrow G$, we need to check the satisfiability of its negation, $H \wedge \neg G$.

If the solver cannot build a valuation of the variables of $H \wedge \neg G$ that respect the formula and its theory, the formula is unsatisfiable and $H \Rightarrow G$ is valid.

Otherwise, if the solver can build a valuation within the constraints, $H \wedge \neg G$ is satisfiable, which disprove $H \Rightarrow G$ and the valuation can be return as a counter-example.

If the solver is uncertain of its valuation, the formula will be deemed "Unknown" but the valuation can still be retrieved and used as a possible counter-example.

3.3 Translating to SMT-LIB

Most SMT solvers use the standard language SMT-LIB [2]. To translate a B component into the SMT-LIB format, we adapted a tool already developed by Clearsy, ppTransSmt. The major change was not in the actual translation of a proof obligation but in the additional information that may be needed by the solver, such as an axiomatization of B operators. However, such definitions often contain quantified expressions that are not only useless for the proof of the current goal, but that can cause the solver to be inconclusive regarding the satisfiability and to produce the result "Unknown".

A database of 1.543 rules has produced 23.776 proof obligations. 19.732 were discharged by internal provers. Before the modification, 952 proof obligations were proved and 0 disproved by cvc4 and z3. But now, 968 are proved and 56 are disproved.

4 Integration of External Provers

To use SMT solver and their counter-example functionality, four processes are required. We need a sound (and efficient) translator from B to SMT-LIB, the solver itself, a reader associated to the first translator, and a translator from SMT-LIB to B models.

Driver. As we can use multiple solvers, translators or readers, we chose an approach similar to Why3 by declaring mechanisms that can contain drivers which describe how Atelier B should interact with each solver and which processes should fulfill each role.

Writer. Its role is to translate $H \wedge \neg G$ into SMT-LIB format. We already evoked ppTransSmt, the writer currently used by most drivers in Atelier B to translate proof obligation into SMT-LIB format. There also exist a simplified writer that expresses set operators as uninterpreted symbols but is less accurate as its translation is not equivalent to $H \wedge \neg G$ but a consequence of it.

Prover. An SMT solver need to process SMT-LIB and a driver specifying its parameters to allow Atelier B to launch it.

Status Reader. The reader is the most straightforward process of the four. It changes the status of the result by its interpretation, according to the accuracy of the writer. Typically, for the reader associated with ppTransSmt:

$$sat \Rightarrow Disproved$$
$$unsat \Rightarrow Proved$$
$$unknown \Rightarrow Unknown$$

Counter-Example Reader. The translator counter_example_reader can work with any SMT solver. It browses the counter-example returned by the solver line by line and stores information on variables. The information are retrieved with regular expressions and sorted. The name of the constant is deobfuscated, its value and type are translated to B models by analyzing their SMT-LIB description operator by operator. For example, in the Fig. 1:

```
(define-fun g_delta_e_c_4 () Bool
   false)
(define-fun g_set10_0 () (P Int)
   P!val!0)
(define-fun g_var_dd_2 () (P (C (C Int Int) Bool))
   P!val!1)
(define-fun g_delta_p_a_6 () Bool
   true)
(define-fun g_var_b_8 () Int
   9)
(define-fun g_var_c_9 () Int
   10)
```

Fig. 1. Extract of a counter-example returned by the solver z3 for the proof obligation in Fig. 3

The first line describes a constant function named g_delta_e_c_2 that will be stored in a Variable object as:

Variable ("delta_e_c", "BOOL", "FALSE").

For simple types, the name and value are printed. For sets and functions, the name and type are translated and printed but the value is not. The set encoding implemented in ppTransSmt results in counter-examples produced by SMT solvers difficult to interpret, and are not yet translated by counter_example_reader.

5   Uses

To use SMT-solver in Atelier B, a driver adapted to the solver and the objectives is needed. The use of external prover must be enabled, the driver must be selected in the available mechanisms list, and the path to the solver must be added to the resources of the project in its settings. The matching button can be added in the visual interface via the option "Add an external prover".

Each component will have two more categories of status: "Unreliably proved" and "Disproved", as in Fig. 2.

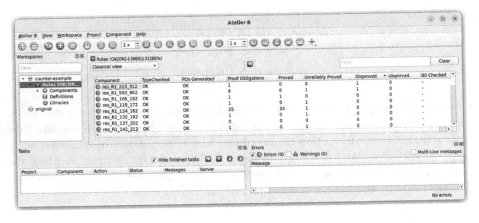

Fig. 2. Atelier B's project management window

5.1   CLI

Once the project is open with:
    open_project < name>

An external solver can be called in the command line interface:
    extprove <component> <mechanism> [option = 0 (all), 1 (fast only)]

And a counter-example can be retrieved:
    extcounter_example <component> <po> <mechanism> <driver>

5.2 GUI

When a component is selected, the external provers buttons are available. When a mechanism is chosen, Atelier B tries to prove all proof obligations yet unproven of the component with each driver.

Once a solver has tried to prove a proof obligation and failed (either Disproved or Unknown status), an option is available in the edition window, shown in Fig. 3. With a right click on the name of a proof obligation, a list of all drivers having disproved or failed to prove the proof obligation will be unrolled. They can produce counter-example and uncertain counter-example respectively, which will be printed in the "Counter-example" window.

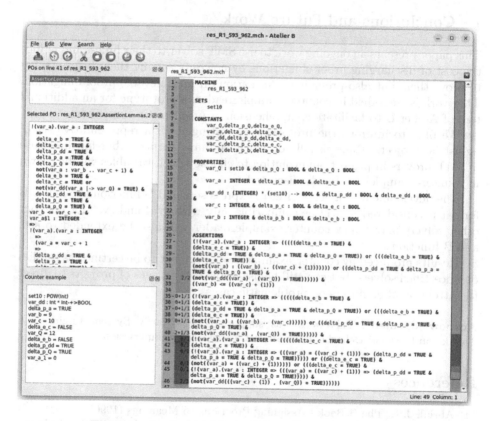

Fig. 3. A simple counter-example in the edition window

6 Limitations

Atelier B currently provides only writers from B to SMT-LIB, so it can only call solvers compatible with the SMT-LIB format.

Not all SMT solvers have the capability to return counter-examples when their result is "sat" and/or "unknown".

An SMT-solver can only process first order logic problems. Some can manage quantified expressions. SMT-LIB has evolved to express finite sets, but most solvers do not implement this logic. For now, the sets are encoded by ppTransSmt with a membership function that makes explicit the properties of sets and functions of B. Its encoding makes counter-examples difficult to translate.

Currently, the translator is only included in the mechanisms of cvc4 [3] and z3 [10] as they are the only external solvers with built-in drivers in Atelier B. Implementing a new SMT solver would be as easy as writing its driver. But each solver has its own way to describe sets, so the translator should be updated as well.

7   Conclusions and Future Work

This paper presents an ongoing work to use SMT solver to their fullest and reduce the cost of discharging proof obligations by not only sorting them before trying to prove them but also providing information on unachievable proof obligation. This work is embodied in counter_example_reader, a prototype for an additional tool of Atelier B to facilitate comprehension of problems in components.

We plan to improve the prototype by testing it on a representative set of industrial projects. Rules usually do not have many variables but for direct use of SMT provers in project, an evolution to choose which variables will be shown in counter-examples is already discussed.

The development of a new writer to express sets and B function in SMT-LIB format is considered. It will be compatible only with cvc4 and cvc5 for now but other solvers may follow counter_example_reader will also be extended to sets and B functions.

Results produced by counter_example_reader are not to be certified as it relies on uncertified solvers, but can still be use in the early stages of projects to direct the attention of engineers on problematic cases.

Acknowledgement. This work was supported by ClearSy System Engineering. Thank you to David Deharbe, engineer at Clearsy, for his supervision.

References

1. Abrial, J.R.: The B-Book - Assigning Programs to Meanings (1996)
2. Barrett, C., Fontaine, P., Tinelli, C.: The SMT-LIB standard: version 2.6. Technical report, Department of Computer Science, The University of Iowa (2017). www.SMT-LIB.org
3. Barrett, C., et al.: CVC4. In: Gopalakrishnan, G., Qadeer, S. (eds.) CAV 2011. LNCS, vol. 6806, pp. 171–177. Springer, Heidelberg (2011). https://doi.org/10.1007/978-3-642-22110-1_14
4. Bobot, F., Filliâtre, J.C., Marché, C., Paskevich, A.: Why3: shepherd your herd of provers (2011)

5. Déharbe, D., Fontaine, P., Guyot, Y., Voisin, L.: SMT solvers for Rodin. In: Derrick, J., et al. (eds.) ABZ 2012. LNCS, vol. 7316, pp. 194–207. Springer, Heidelberg (2012). https://doi.org/10.1007/978-3-642-30885-7_14
6. Delahaye, D., Dubois, C., Marché, C., Mentré, D.: The BWare project: building a proof platform for the automated verification of B proof obligations. In: Ait Ameur, Y., Schewe, K.D. (eds.) ABZ 2014. LNTCS, vol. 8477, pp. 290–293. Springer, Heidelberg (2014). https://doi.org/10.1007/978-3-662-43652-3_26
7. Falampin, J., Le-Dang, H., Leuschel, M., Mokrani, M., Plagge, D.: Improving railway data validation with ProB. In: Romanovsky, A., Thomas, M. (eds.) Industrial Deployment of System Engineering Methods, pp. 27–43. Springer, Heidelberg (2013). https://doi.org/10.1007/978-3-642-33170-1_4
8. Leuschel, M., Butler, M.: ProB: a model checker for B. In: Araki, K., Gnesi, S., Mandrioli, D. (eds.) FME 2003. LNCS, vol. 2805, pp. 855–874. Springer, Heidelberg (2003). https://doi.org/10.1007/978-3-540-45236-2_46
9. Mentré, D., Marché, C., Filliâtre, J.-C., Asuka, M.: Discharging proof obligations from atelier B using multiple automated provers. In: Derrick, J., et al. (eds.) ABZ 2012. LNCS, vol. 7316, pp. 238–251. Springer, Heidelberg (2012). https://doi.org/10.1007/978-3-642-30885-7_17 https://hal.inria.fr/hal-00681781
10. de Moura, L., Bjørner, N.: Z3: an efficient SMT solver. In: Ramakrishnan, C.R., Rehof, J. (eds.) TACAS 2008. LNCS, vol. 4963, pp. 337–340. Springer, Heidelberg (2008). https://doi.org/10.1007/978-3-540-78800-3_24 http://dblp.uni-trier.de/db/conf/tacas/tacas2008.html#MouraB08

VarCorC: Developing Object-Oriented Software Product Lines Using Correctness-by-Construction

Tabea Bordis[1]([✉]), Maximilian Kodetzki[2], Tobias Runge[1], and Ina Schaefer[1]

[1] Karlsruhe Institute of Technology (KIT), Karlsruhe, Germany
{tabea.bordis,tobias.runge,ina.schaefer}@kit.edu
[2] TU Braunschweig, Braunschweig, Germany
m.kodetzki@tu-bs.de

Abstract. Functional correctness is an important concern, especially in the field of safety-critical systems. Correctness-by-Construction (CbC) is an incremental software development technique to create functionally correct programs guided by a formal specification. The specification is defined first, and then the program is incrementally created using a small set of refinement rules that define side conditions preserving the correctness. CbC is mostly used to create small algorithms. However, software in-field is often larger and more complex to meet the requirements of today's life. Therefore, our vision is to scale the applicability of CbC to larger scale software systems, like software product lines (SPLs). SPLs are one way to implement a whole product family by managed reuse. Advanced implementation techniques for SPLs rely on object-orientation and variability realization mechanisms on the source code level.

In this tool paper, we present our tool VarCorC which supports the development of correct SPLs using CbC including object-orientation and feature-oriented programming. We describe VarCorC from user-perspective and explain how it works internally. Additionally, we provide a feasibility evaluation of VarCorC on three case studies that are used as benchmarks in the field of product line verification.

Keywords: Correctness-by-Construction · Software product lines · Object-oriented programming · Program verification

1 Introduction

The demand for software in electronic devices is rapidly increasing, also including safety-critical applications like in the automotive, medical, or avionic field [13]. Correctness-by-Construction (CbC) as proposed by Dijkstra [9], Gries [10], or Kourie and Watson [12] gives a guarantee for functionally correct software which is crucial for safety-critical applications. CbC follows an incremental approach of program construction based on a formal specification in form of pre- and post-condition pairs. The specification is refined into an implementation using a set

ⓒ The Author(s), under exclusive license to Springer Nature Switzerland AG 2023
P. Masci et al. (Eds.): SEFM 2022 Collocated Workshops, LNCS 13765, pp. 156–163, 2023.
https://doi.org/10.1007/978-3-031-26236-4_13

of refinement rules. To guarantee the correctness of these refinement steps, each rule defines specific side conditions for its applicability. In comparison to CbC, classical post-hoc verification offers an approach where a program is specified and verified *after* implementation. As a result, when using CbC errors are likely to be detected earlier in the design process [14]. CorC [18] is a tool that supports CbC to develop single algorithms. First evaluation results show decreased verification effort compared to post-hoc verification [6, 18].

Our long-term vision is to make the construction of correct software using CbC applicable for large-scale systems, such as *software product lines* (SPLs). SPLs [17] enable the implementation of product families that share a common code base by managed reuse [8], therefore lowering costs and effort in producing custom-tailored software. The common and varying parts of an SPL are called *features*. The relationship of these features are modeled in *feature models* and variability realization mechanisms are used to implement their functionality. In the end, software variants can be created according to a certain selection of features. Many implementation techniques for SPLs, such as FeatureHouse [4] or DeltaJ [11], rely on *object-oriented design* since it is well suited to model large software systems. However, object-orientation poses some challenges for verification as fields can be globally accessed and concepts like inheritance increase the complexity of dependencies between classes. The complexity even increases for SPLs since variability is added to the code by variability realization mechanisms. Besides CbC as we pursue it, there are also other tools that implement different refinement-based approaches, such as Event-B [1] and its platform Rodin [2], ArcAngel [15], and SOCOS [5]. However, Event-B works on automata-based systems rather than on code and specifications and they all do not support the development of SPLs.

In this tool paper, we present VarCorC as an extension of CorC to develop object-oriented SPLs using CbC. In previous work, VarCorC has been developed from single variational methods [6], to feature-oriented SPLs with methods as simple procedures [7]. In this tool paper, we focus on the integration of object-orientation into VarCorC to enable the development of large-scale SPLs, since object-orientation allows for more complex projects and feature interactions over fields and objects. As specification, we use pre- and postconditions for methods and class invariants. Besides technical details of VarCorC, we also provide a workflow description from user-perspective to highlight VarCorC's usability features. Lastly, we present a short feasibility evaluation on three case studies.

2 The Development Process with VarCorC

In this section, we describe the development process in VarCorC as shown in Fig. 1 from the perspective of developer Alice. Alice develops an SPL that implements a bank account system and has already created a feature model ①. A feature model defines all features and their relationships in a tree structure. For the *BankAccount* SPL, Alice defined the features *BankAccount* (provides a base implementation of an account), *DailyLimit* (adds a limit that can be withdrawn from the account per day), and *Interest* (adds an interest to the account).

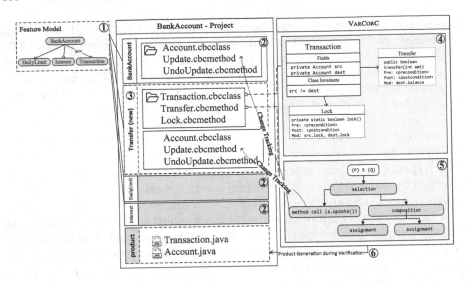

Fig. 1. Development process in VARCORC

Apart from the root feature *BankAccount*, all of the features are optional, which means that the user can select them individually. A valid selection of features is also called *feature configuration* and is used to form a software variant. Alice already implemented the features *BankAccount*, *Interest*, and *DailyLimit* in separate feature modules using feature-oriented programming (FOP) ②. A feature can add new classes or extend already existing classes by adding fields, class invariants, and methods or by refining existing methods. When a method is refined, its implementation is overridden with the option for reuse by using the FOP-specific keyword `original` to call the implementation of that method in another feature. Analogously, the specification of a method is overridden and the predicates `original_pre` and `original_post` can be used. In previous work [7], we already proposed an extension of CbC for original calls to implement methods in an SPL.

Alice now wants to add feature *Transaction* to enable a transfer of money between accounts ③. Therefore, she inserts a new class called `Transaction` which is displayed as UML-like class diagram in VARCORC ④. She defines the fields `src` and `dest` of type `Account`, a class invariant, and methods `transfer` and `lock` to transfer money between two accounts and to lock an account such that the balance is unmodifiable. She defines these two methods with a signature and a method contract consisting of a first-order logic pre- and postcondition. Afterwards, she implements method `transfer` in the corresponding cbcmethod file ⑤ starting with the defined pre- and postcondition from the method contract. For the implementation, she uses the basic set of CbC refinement rules as defined by Kourie and Watson [12] and our refinement rules for method calls and original calls [7] which we display in Fig. 2. For example, to apply the assignment refinement rule a Hoare triple of the form `{P} S {Q}` with precondition

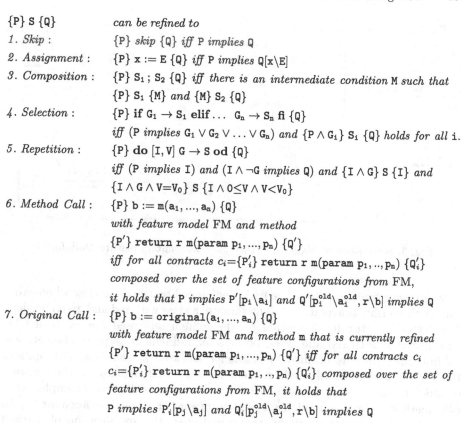

$\{P\}$ S $\{Q\}$	*can be refined to*
1. Skip :	$\{P\}$ *skip* $\{Q\}$ *iff* P *implies* Q
2. Assignment :	$\{P\}$ x := E $\{Q\}$ *iff* P *implies* $Q[x \backslash E]$
3. Composition :	$\{P\}$ S_1 ; S_2 $\{Q\}$ *iff there is an intermediate condition* M *such that* $\{P\}$ S_1 $\{M\}$ *and* $\{M\}$ S_2 $\{Q\}$
4. Selection :	$\{P\}$ **if** $G_1 \rightarrow S_1$ **elif** ... $G_n \rightarrow S_n$ **fi** $\{Q\}$ *iff* (P *implies* $G_1 \vee G_2 \vee \ldots \vee G_n$) *and* $\{P \wedge G_i\}$ S_i $\{Q\}$ *holds for all* i.
5. Repetition :	$\{P\}$ **do** $[I, V]$ $G \rightarrow S$ **od** $\{Q\}$ *iff* (P *implies* I) *and* ($I \wedge \neg G$ *implies* Q) *and* $\{I \wedge G\}$ S $\{I\}$ *and* $\{I \wedge G \wedge V=V_0\}$ S $\{I \wedge 0 \leq V \wedge V < V_0\}$
6. Method Call :	$\{P\}$ b := $m(a_1, ..., a_n)$ $\{Q\}$ *with feature model* FM *and method* $\{P'\}$ **return** r $m(\text{param } p_1, ..., p_n)$ $\{Q'\}$ *iff for all contracts* $c_i = \{P'_i\}$ **return** r $m(\text{param } p_1, .., p_n)$ $\{Q'_i\}$ *composed over the set of feature configurations from* FM, *it holds that* P *implies* $P'[p_i \backslash a_i]$ *and* $Q'[p_i^{old} \backslash a_i^{old}, r \backslash b]$ *implies* Q
7. Original Call :	$\{P\}$ b := $\text{original}(a_1, ..., a_n)$ $\{Q\}$ *with feature model* FM *and method* m *that is currently refined* $\{P'\}$ **return** r $m(\text{param } p_1, ..., p_n)$ $\{Q'\}$ *iff for all contracts* c_i $c_i = \{P'_i\}$ **return** r $m(\text{param } p_1, .., p_n)$ $\{Q'_i\}$ *composed over the set of feature configurations from* FM, *it holds that* P *implies* $P'_i[p_j \backslash a_j]$ *and* $Q'_i[p_j^{old} \backslash a_j^{old}, r \backslash b]$ *implies* Q

Fig. 2. List of refinement rules in correctness-by-construction [12] and method call and original call refinement rule [7]

P, postcondition Q and abstract statement S can be refined to an assignment x := E with x being a variable and E an expression of the same type or subtype if and only if the side condition that precondition P implies postcondition Q where variable x has been replaced by expression is fulfilled. All of the listed refinement rules are implemented in VARCORC. For each applied refinement rule, the side condition is checked in the background by generating a proof file which is (semi)-automatically proven by the program verifier KeY [3]. Therefore, the method under development is guaranteed to be correct.

During this verification process, all variants of a method according to the feature model are generated into Java classes ⑥. This has the advantage that (1) Alice can export correct code developed with VARCORC into other projects and (2) Alice can call externally implemented code in VARCORC when placed in these classes. As a result, Alice can decide about the degree of using CbC as opposed to using Java verified with a different tool or checked with testing.

One of VARCORC's main usability features provides Alice with an overview on the verification status of all methods in the SPL and the traceability of errors

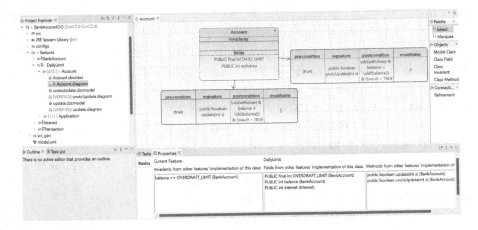

Fig. 3. Screenshot of VARCORC with class `Account` in feature *DailyLimit*

down to one refinement step. The first is enhanced by the class view where Alice can see the verification status of all methods of a class with red and green borders. The latter is naturally supported by the refinement-based approach of CbC and displayed with red and green borders for refinement steps in cbcmethods. Additionally, Alice is notified by a *change tracking mechanism* that updates the verification status of single refinement steps that depend on the contract of other methods, such as method calls and original calls. For example, Alice calls method `update` to implement method `transfer` from class `Account` ⑤. To guarantee the correctness of this refinement step, the specification of method `update` is checked to comply with the specification used in this refinement step. However, if Alice changes the specification of method `update` in another feature, the refinement step in method `transfer` has to be re-verified. VARCORC checks for these dependencies in the background and marks corresponding verification steps as "not verified" and notifies Alice about affected parts.

3 Object-Oriented Software Product Lines in VARCORC

In this section, we give implementation details for our tool VARCORC[1] which is an open-source Eclipse plug-in supporting the development of object-oriented SPLs using CbC and FOP. VARCORC captures the CbC structure of methods and classes through a meta-model modeled with Eclipse Modeling Framework.[2] The graphical editor visualizes the underlying meta-model in a tree-like structure for methods and UML-like class diagrams.

In Fig. 3, we show a screenshot of VARCORC with class `Account` in feature *DailyLimit*. The project structure consists of a feature model, feature

---

[1] VARCORC implements SPL development using CbC and is part of the tool CORC: https://github.com/TUBS-ISF/CorC.

[2] https://eclipse.org/emf/.

Table 1. Metrics of the case studies

Case study	Features	Classes	Methods	Original calls
BankAccount [21]	4	3	10	5
IntegerList [19]	5	1	5	2
Elevator [16]	5	4	35	5

modules, and class folders. The cbcclass and cbcmethod files are split into a *<methodName>\<classname>.diagram* file, which contains the graphical information, and a *<methodName>.cbcmodel\<classname>.cbcclass* file which is an instance of the corresponding meta-model. The *src-gen* folder contains generated Java classes, which store composed software variants for the proofs.

In the bottom properties view, we show SPL information, such as all valid feature configurations or accessible fields and methods. The information displayed differs for classes and methods. In this case, we provide an overview on class invariants, fields, and methods of class `Account` in other features.

In the center of Fig. 3, class `Account` in feature *DailyLimit* adds two fields (`DAILY_LIMIT` and `withdraw`) and two methods (`update` and `undoUpdate`). As displayed in the properties view, both methods have already been defined for this class in feature *BankAccount*, which means that they are refined and can use an original call to call their implementation in feature *BankAccount*.

To guarantee the correctness of a whole SPL, every variant has to be correct. In FOP, each variant can have a different set of classes, classes can have a different sets of fields, class invariants, and methods, and methods can have different implementations and specifications. We use a product-based approach [20] for showing correctness. Once the verification of a refinement step in a method is triggered, all valid feature configurations are calculated such that original calls can be resolved. For each configuration, the corresponding variant in form of Java classes is generated. At the same time, a proof file is created which contains the side condition of the CbC refinement step. If all proofs are successful, the statement is considered to be correct.

Evaluation. We evaluate VarCorC regarding feasibility by implementing three case studies, namely *BankAccount* [21], *IntegerList* [19], and *Elevator* [16]. All case studies have already been used as benchmarks in SPL verification.[3] In Table 1, we show metrics for the case studies. The *BankAccount* SPL implements basic functions of a bank account and has been used throughout this paper as an example. The *IntegerList* SPL implements a list of integers with add and sort operations. The third case study, *Elevator*, implements basic functions of an elevator, such as the movement and entering and leaving of persons. We transferred the case studies into the object-oriented structure as introduced in this paper. For every class, we created cbcclass files with fields and class invariants. All methods are verified individually for all valid feature configurations in VarCorC, therefore showing correctness of the whole SPL.

---

[3] Case studies and VarCorC: https://github.com/TUBS-ISF/CorC.

4   Conclusion

We believe that the specification-first, refinement-based approach of CbC increases the awareness of correctness when developing safety-critical software in today's engineered world. Until recently, CbC has only been used for independent algorithms. Therefore, we presented our tool VARCORC which enables program development with CbC for object-oriented SPLs. We showed, how we include object-orientation into CbC and highlighted usability features of VAR-CORC that streamline the development of SPLs. Currently, VARCORC relies on a product-based approach limiting its scalability. Therefore, in future work we want to experiment with more efficient approaches, such as family-based verification.

References

1. Abrial, J.R.: Modeling in Event-B: System and Software Engineering. Cambridge University Press, Cambridge (2010)
2. Abrial, J.R., Butler, M., Hallerstede, S., Hoang, T.S., Mehta, F., Voisin, L.: Rodin: an open toolset for modelling and reasoning in Event-B. Int. J. Softw. Tools Technol. Transfer **12**(6), 447–466 (2010). https://doi.org/10.1007/s10009-010-0145-y
3. Ahrendt, W., Beckert, B., Bubel, R., Hähnle, R., Schmitt, P.H., Ulbrich, M.: Deductive Software Verification - The KeY Book. Springer, Cham (2016). https://doi.org/10.1007/978-3-319-49812-6
4. Apel, S., Kästner, C., Lengauer, C.: Language-independent and automated software composition: the FeatureHouse experience. IEEE Trans. Softw. Eng. **39**(1), 63–79 (2013)
5. Back, R.-J., Eriksson, J., Myreen, M.: Testing and verifying invariant based programs in the SOCOS environment. In: Gurevich, Y., Meyer, B. (eds.) TAP 2007. LNCS, vol. 4454, pp. 61–78. Springer, Heidelberg (2007). https://doi.org/10.1007/978-3-540-73770-4_4
6. Bordis, T., Runge, T., Knüppel, A., Thüm, T., Schaefer, I.: Variational correctness-by-construction. In: Proceedings of the 14th International Working Conference on Variability Modelling of Software-Intensive Systems, pp. 1–9 (2020)
7. Bordis, T., Runge, T., Schaefer, I.: Correctness-by-construction for feature-oriented software product lines. In: International Conference on Generative Programming: Concepts and Experiences, pp. 22–34 (2020)
8. Czarnecki, K., Eisenecker, U.: Generative Programming: Methods, Tools, and Applications. Citeseer (2000)
9. Dijkstra, E.W.: A Discipline of Programming, 1st edn. Prentice Hall PTR (1976)
10. Gries, D.: The Science of Programming, 1st edn. Springer, New York (1981). https://doi.org/10.1007/978-1-4612-5983-1
11. Koscielny, J., Holthusen, S., Schaefer, I., Schulze, S., Bettini, L., Damiani, F.: DeltaJ 1.5: delta-oriented programming for Java 1.5. In: International Conference on Principles and Practices of Programming on the Java Platform, pp. 63–74 (2014)
12. Kourie, D.G., Watson, B.W.: The Correctness-by-Construction Approach to Programming. Springer, Heidelberg (2012). https://doi.org/10.1007/978-3-642-27919-5

13. Liu, J., Dehlinger, J., Lutz, R.: Safety analysis of software product lines using state-based modeling. J. Syst. Softw. **80**(11), 1879–1892 (2007)
14. Meyer, B.: Applying design by contract. Computer **25**(10), 40–51 (1992)
15. Oliveira, M., Cavalcanti, A., Woodcock, J.: ArcAngel: a tactic language for refinement. Formal Aspects Comput. **15**, 28–47 (2003). https://doi.org/10.1007/s00165-003-0003-8
16. Plath, M., Ryan, M.: Feature integration using a feature construct. Sci. Comput. Program. **41**(1), 53–84 (2001)
17. Pohl, K., Böckle, G., van der Linden, F.J.: Software Product Line Engineering: Foundations, Principles and Techniques. Springer, Heidelberg (2005). https://doi.org/10.1007/3-540-28901-1
18. Runge, T., Schaefer, I., Cleophas, L., Thüm, T., Kourie, D., Watson, B.W.: Tool support for correctness-by-construction. In: Hähnle, R., van der Aalst, W. (eds.) FASE 2019. LNCS, vol. 11424, pp. 25–42. Springer, Cham (2019). https://doi.org/10.1007/978-3-030-16722-6_2
19. Scholz, W., Thüm, T., Apel, S., Lengauer, C.: Automatic detection of feature interactions using the Java modeling language: an experience report. In: International Software Product Line Conference (2011)
20. Thüm, T., Apel, S., Kästner, C., Schaefer, I., Saake, G.: A classification and survey of analysis strategies for software product lines. ACM Comput. Surv. **47**(1), 1–45 (2014)
21. Thüm, T., Schaefer, I., Apel, S., Hentschel, M.: Family-based deductive verification of software product lines. In: International Conference on Generative Programming and Component Engineering (2012)

A Case Study in Formal Analysis of System Requirements

Dimitri Belli[ID] and Franco Mazzanti[✉][ID]

Istituto di Scienza e Tecnologie dell'Informazione "A. Faedo" CNR,
Via G. Moruzzi 1, 56124 Pisa, Italy
{dimitri.belli,franco.mazzanti}@isti.cnr.it

Abstract. One of the goals of the 4SECURail project has been to demonstrate the benefits, limits, and costs of introducing formal methods in the system requirements definition process. This has been done, on an experimental basis, by applying a specific set of tools and methodologies to a case study from the railway sector. The paper describes the approach adopted in the project and some considerations resulting from the experience.

Keywords: Critical systems of systems · Formal methods · Standard interfaces · Systems modeling language · Railway signaling system

1 Introduction

The railway infrastructure is constituted by a large, heterogeneous, and distributed system with components that are on board, trackside, centralized, crossing regional and national borders, managed by different authorities, and developed by different providers. Not surprisingly, the current trend is to standardize the requirements of the various system components together with their interfaces (see, e.g. EULYNX [22]). Standardization is expected to increase market competition, reduce vendor lock-in, and promote the reduction of long-term maintenance costs. However, to produce the desired outcomes, the defined standard requirements for the various system components must be precise, i.e., not suffer from ambiguous interpretation issues, and correct, i.e., not give rise to interoperability problems and not suffer of inconsistencies or missing points. The current state of the art is based on the use of natural language requirements possibly associated with SysML/UML graphical artifacts [41–45]. Such a choice is not risk-free because natural language and SysML/UML are usually not rigorous enough to allow a precise system specification [13,23]. One of the goals of the 4SECURail [3] project is to observe the impact of the integration of formal methods inside the requirements definition process. This has been achieved with the definition of a "Demonstrator", i.e., an example of requirements construction process based on formal methods, and its application to a case study selected from the railway signaling sector [1].

P. Masci et al. (Eds.): SEFM 2022 Collocated Workshops, LNCS 13765, pp. 164–173, 2023.
https://doi.org/10.1007/978-3-031-26236-4_14

2   The Case Study and Demonstration Process

The 4SECURail case study is derived from the communication layers specified by UNISIG-39 [21] and UNISIG-98 [20], describing the establishment, supervision, and management of the RBC[1]-RBC communication line used to support the RBC-Handover protocol. The full system can be modeled as a set of four UML state machines interacting with other three state machines modeling other parts of the execution environment (see Fig. 1). In our modeling, we introduced an additional abstract "Timer" component that allows the various components to proceed in parallel but in a constrained way with respect to their relative execution speed. The requirements of the Communication Supervision Layer (CSL) and Safe Application Intermediate Sub-Layer (SAI) components are defined in natural language, and their initial specification can be found in Deliverable D2.3 [3]. The 4SECURail demonstrator process (see Fig. 2) begins with the analysis of the natural language descriptions of the requirements and with the construction of an operational SysML/UML model of the system components. The UML designs are complemented by an explicit and precise set of assumptions on the characteristics of inter-state machine communications. We make a restricted use

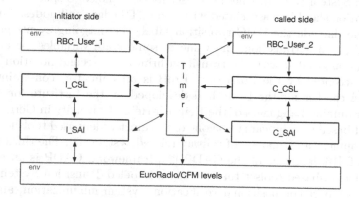

Fig. 1. The 4SECURail case study structure

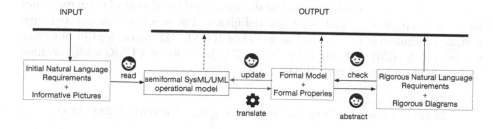

Fig. 2. The 4SECURail demonstrator process

---

[1] Radio Block Centre.

of the features provided by UML so that the design has a clear and simple semantics allowing, with a low effort, its mechanical translation into the different notations used for formal analysis. This paper focuses on the presentation of the adopted approach for the translation of the SysML/UML models into the formal notations supported by three different verification frameworks, namely UMC [8–10], ProB [28,33], and CADP [24,31]. For all the details of the formalization and analysis process, we refer to the project deliverables [3].

3   The Formal Modeling

The first notation used to model the case study is the KandISTI/UMC framework developed by the Formal Methods && Tools (FMT) Laboratory[2] at ISTI-CNR in Pisa. This notation allows us to define a system as a set of UML state machines, expressed in a simple textual form[3] to explore the possible system evolutions, and to verify branching time properties on it. Despite its still prototypical status, this framework has been chosen as the first target since it fits well the needs of fast design prototyping. The resulting graph describing the system evolutions can be analyzed or saved in the form of a Doubly Labeled Transition System (L2TS), where the user has the choice to specify which kind of information should be associated with the L2TS edges and nodes. This information may include the UMC transition label, the outgoing events generated by the effects of a transition, the value of some state variables, or any other custom flag associated with the transition firing. The second notation is the B language accepted by the ProB tool. ProB is an animator, constraint solver, and model checker for the B-Method developed by the Institute for Software and Programming Languages of the Heinrich-Heine University in Germany. The B-method-based tool appears to be one of the most widely used tools for the formal development and analysis of railway-related systems [7]. The third notation is the LNT [16] language of the CADP [24] framework. CADP is an advanced process algebra-based toolset that leverages Labeled Transition Systems (LTS) theory to support compositional verification, system minimization, animation, and testing. The LNT notation has an imperative style of process descriptions that is well-suit to the description of the behavior of UML state machines.

In UMC, a system is defined as a static instantiation of a set of state machines from their template defined as a Class definition. The event pool associated with a state machine can be qualified as FIFO or RANDOM queue, and in our case, we rely on the UML FIFO default choice. The behavior of a UMC state machine is described by a set of rules in the form:

```
Transition_Label:
SourceStates -> TargetStates {Trigger [Guard] / Effects}
```

---

[2] https://fmt.isti.cnr.it.
[3] UMC is freely accessible online at http://fmt.isti.cnr.it/umc and a detailed description of the syntax can be found in http://fmt.isti.cnr.it/umc/DOCS/sdhelp.html.

In ProB, our encoding models a system as a single B Machine that includes the local state and the behavior of all the UML state machines constituting the system. The main difference between the ProB model and the UMC/LNT models is that in ProB, the UML event pools are modeled by global variables manipulated by the (atomic) state machine operations, while in UMC and LNT the event pools are handled locally inside each state machine, and their manipulation occurs via synchronizations or message exchange. A UML transition of a state machine is mapped on a ProB *OPERATION*, appropriately conditioned with respect to the trigger and guard, and performing the specified effects. The sending of an event is explicitly modeled with the insertion of data into a FIFO buffer modeling the event pool of the target state machine.

In the LNT encoding, a state machine is represented by an LNT process, and the various LNT processes are composed in parallel, appropriately synchronizing the sending/accepting actions. Each process executes a loop inside which several alternatives are non-deterministically possible. These alternatives model either the condition and effects of the triggering of state machine transitions, or the unconditioned acceptance in the event pool of incoming events. Also in this case, the event pool of the state machine is explicitly modeled as a FIFO buffer in the local state of the process.

Figure 3 shows one of the natural language requirements for the initiator CSL subsystem, while Fig. 4 shows the graphical layout of the state machine diagram of the CSL system component on the initiator side of the communication line. We can see how the requirement $R4$ is modeled by the corresponding transition in the state machine diagram. Figure 5 shows, from left to right, the encoding of the R4 transition for UMC, ProB, and LNT. Clearly, the executable model contains more implementation details than the abstract UML design shown in Fig. 4, which just describes the system requirements in a semi-formal notation acting as a bridge between the natural language and the executable/formal notations. The colors in the figure help to see the matching of the various information present in each encoding. We can see that the transition label in UMC becomes the operation name in ProB, that the change of state is modeled in ProB and LNT by the change of the value of a variable, and that signaling-related operations are modeled in ProB and LNT as explicit operations on lists/tuples. An essential consequence of using a UML subset (e.g., no composite states, no parallel states, no deferred events, no competition between triggered and completion transitions) is that it becomes rather easy to implement a mechanical translation from the UMC encoding to the ProB and LNT notations.

Requirement R4:
When in the **NOCOMMS**connecting state a *ISAI_Connect_confirm* is received, the initiator CSL moves to **COMMS** state, sends a RBC_User_connect_indication to the RBC and starts both the send and receive timers.

Fig. 3. The R4 requirement for the initiator CSL in natural language

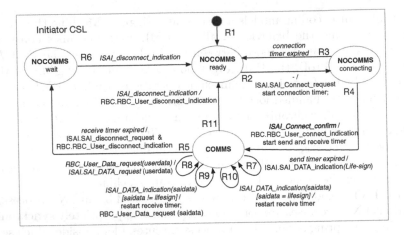

Fig. 4. The state machine diagram of the CSL component on the initiator side

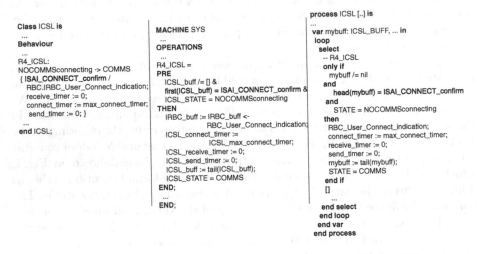

Fig. 5. UMC, ProB, and LNT encoding of the R4 ICSL transition

All these three notations, moreover, natively support data type operations on lists or tuples that can be exploited in an equivalent way to handle FIFO buffer operations. The final effect of the transformations is the generation of formal models with almost the same readability as the first UMC model; also, the original comments present in the UMC code are preserved in the generated ProB and LNT encodings. Because of the strict budget and timing constraints of the project, our goal has been limited to the translation of the set of features currently used in our models. Still, the set of supported features can surely be further extended (e.g., by allowing sequential composite states and constrained forms of parallel states).

The CADP environment allows saving the statespace of an LNT model in the simple textual *.aut* [14] format (as an LTS whose labels denote communication actions). The ProB tool saves the full statespace of a model in textual format which can be easily mechanically converted into the *.aut* format (as an LTS whose labels denote the triggered operation names). Finally, also the UMC environment allows saving the statespace of a model in the *.aut* format, permitting the user to specify which information to encode in the LTS labels (communication actions or transition labels, or both). The strong equivalence of the three models can therefore be easily checked with tools like mCRL2 *ltscompare* [38] or CADP *bcg_cmp* [15]. While defects in the code of the translators can often immediately be put in evidence by just the observation of the size of the generated state spaces, the formal LTS comparison of the *.aut* representations allows observing also one of the specific execution traces that are at the root of the dissimilarity. This proved to be very useful during the testing of our translators.

4   Hints on the Formal Analysis

The tool diversity adopted in the project allows us to analyze the system from different perspectives: e.g., state-based linear time properties with ProB, event-based branching time properties with CADP, state- and event-based properties with UMC, information hiding and model reductions with CADP. Because of the parametricity of the system and the presence of several wide-range parameters in communications, formal analysis can only be done by reasoning on selected scenarios where the system parameters are fixed and the environment components have a desired stimulating behavior. Several examples of these scenarios are shown in [37] and described in Deliverable D2.5 [3]. Linear (or lazo-shaped) counterexamples or reachability proofs from UMC and ProB can be displayed in a friendly way as sequence diagrams. Due to the complexity of the issue, for more details on the subject, we refer to the final project deliverable D2.5 [3] and the presentations in [11,35,36].

5   Related Works

The goal of the 4SECURail Demonstrator is to show a possible way to improve the quality of standard specifications by exploiting formal methods. The project Formasig [53] has a very similar goal, which is the development of a formal method allowing railway standardization projects to formally verify standardized interfaces. Also in the case of Formasig, the starting point is the EULYNX natural language specification enriched with SysML artifacts. The Formasig approach aims to translate these EULYNX SysML models, developed with the commercial PTC framework [47], into the process specification language mCRL2 [25,39] for formal analysis. Several other Shift2Rail [48] projects have investigated the use of formal methods for the analysis of signaling systems like ASTRAIL [29], which focuses on a survey of the available tools on this subject, and PERFORM-INGRAIL [30] (still in progress) more centered on ERTMS [19] moving block specifications. The impact of the adoption of formal methods during railway-related software development has been studied in Shift2Rail projects X2RAIL2 and X2RAIL5 (in progress). Unfortunately, not all the produced material in these last projects is publicly available. Many studies investigate the formal verifications of UML models (e.g. [12, 26, 27, 34, 40, 46]). Because of the ambiguity, variability, and complexity of the OMG UML documents, all these efforts appear as particular personal interpretations of specific UML subsets, without reaching the goals of providing UML with precise and widely recognized semantics. We have focused our effort on the model checking techniques provided by ProB for Event-B specifications. An alternative approach, based on theorem proving to develop formally verified refinements, is supported by Atelier-B [17] and Rodin [5]. When using Rodin the input models can also be derived by UML-B [18, 49, 51] designs. A fragment of our case study, i.e., the SAI communications levels, has also been specified and verified, as a spin-off of the project [6], using UPPAAL [54]. Hugo [32, 52] is another interesting example of formal methods diversity that still uses UML state machines as a starting point while exploiting UPPAAL and Spin [50] for formal analysis.

6   Conclusions

The effort described in this short paper is just a fragment of the overall activity performed inside the project and does not describe many other points analyzed or discussed in the project deliverables. Among these, an analysis of the cost and benefits from the point of view of Infrastructure Managers for the use of formal methods, the reasons for choosing UMC, Prob, and LNT as reference platforms, the reasons and difficulties implied by the choice of using UML as starting point of the analysis process, the relation between the natural language requirements and the semi-formal and formal artifacts, the kind of easily understandable feedback that the formal analysis can give to the initial standard interface designer. Some of these themes have also been touched in [11, 35, 36]. The experience gained in the experimentation has confirmed that a simplified version of UML is a viable choice for the modeling of requirements. A simplified UML can be the base for rigorous, clear, and easy to understand designs that can be mapped more directly with natural language requirements, and that can be translated into still understandable formal notations. A second confirmation coming from our experimentation is that the exploitation of formal methods diversity, i.e., multiple translations of the same specification into different formal notations, allows from one side to reduce and detect as early as possible the introduction of encoding errors, and from the other side the widening of the available formal analysis techniques and tools. The project deliverables, the generated models, the verified scenarios, and the source code of the translators are publicly available from Zenodo repositories [2, 4, 37].

Acknowledgements. This work has been partially funded by the 4SECURail project (Shift2Rail GA 881775). The content of this paper reflects only the author's view and the Shift2Rail Joint Undertaking is not responsible for any use that may be made of the included information.

References

1. 4SECURail: Project Deliverable D2.1 (2020). https://www.4securail.eu/Documents.html
2. 4SECURail: Deliverabled of WorkStream 1 (2022). https://zenodo.org/record/5807738
3. 4SECURail: Project Deliverables (2022). https://www.4securail.eu/Documents.html
4. 4SECURail: Translation Tools (2022). https://zenodo.org/record/5541350
5. Abrial, J., Butler, M.J., Hallerstede, S., Hoang, T.S., Mehta, F., Voisin, L.: Rodin: an open toolset for modelling and reasoning in Event-B. Int. J. Softw. Tools Technol. Transf. **12**(6), 447–466 (2010). https://doi.org/10.1007/s10009-010-0145-y
6. Basile, D., Fantechi, A., Rosadi, I.: Formal analysis of the UNISIG safety application intermediate sub-layer. In: Lluch Lafuente, A., Mavridou, A. (eds.) FMICS 2021. LNCS, vol. 12863, pp. 174–190. Springer, Cham (2021). https://doi.org/10.1007/978-3-030-85248-1_11
7. ter Beek, M.H., et al.: Adopting formal methods in an industrial setting: the railways case. In: ter Beek, M.H., McIver, A., Oliveira, J.N. (eds.) FM 2019. LNCS, vol. 11800, pp. 762–772. Springer, Cham (2019). https://doi.org/10.1007/978-3-030-30942-8_46
8. ter Beek, M.H., Fantechi, A., Gnesi, S., Mazzanti, F.: A state/event-based model-checking approach for the analysis of abstract system properties. Sci. Comput. Program. **76**(2), 119–135 (2011). https://doi.org/10.1016/j.scico.2010.07.002
9. ter Beek, M.H., Fantechi, A., Gnesi, S., Mazzanti, F.: States and events in KandISTI. In: Margaria, T., Graf, S., Larsen, K.G. (eds.) Models, Mindsets, Meta: The What, the How, and the Why Not? LNCS, vol. 11200, pp. 110–128. Springer, Cham (2019). https://doi.org/10.1007/978-3-030-22348-9_8
10. ter Beek, M.H., Gnesi, S., Mazzanti, F.: From EU projects to a family of model checkers. In: De Nicola, R., Hennicker, R. (eds.) Software, Services, and Systems. LNCS, vol. 8950, pp. 312–328. Springer, Cham (2015). https://doi.org/10.1007/978-3-319-15545-6_20
11. Belli, D., Fantechi, A., et al.: The 4SECURail approach to formalizing standard interfaces between signalling systems components (2022). Paper Accepted as Poster Presentation at Transport Research Arena Conference (TRA). https://doi.org/10.5281/zenodo.7225869
12. Bouwman, M., Luttik, B., van der Wal, D.: A formalisation of SysML state machines in mCRL2. In: Peters, K., Willemse, T.A.C. (eds.) FORTE 2021. LNCS, vol. 12719, pp. 42–59. Springer, Cham (2021). https://doi.org/10.1007/978-3-030-78089-0_3
13. Broy, M., Cengarle, M.V.: UML formal semantics: lessons learned. Softw. Syst. Model. **10**(4), 441–446 (2011). https://doi.org/10.1007/s10270-011-0207-y
14. CADP: AUT format man page. https://cadp.inria.fr/man/aut.html
15. CADP: bcgcomp format man page. https://cadp.inria.fr/man/bcg_cmp.html

16. Champelovier, D., Clerc, X., et al.: Reference Manual of the LOTOS NT to LOTOS Translator (Version 5.8) (2013). https://cadp.inria.fr/ftp/publications/cadp/Champelovier-Clerc-Garavel-et-al-10.pdf
17. Clearsy: Atelier B. https://www.clearsy.com/outils/atelier-b/
18. Dghaym, D., Dalvandi, M., Poppleton, M., Snook, C.: Formalising the hybrid ERTMS level 3 specification in iUML-B and Event-B. Int. J. Softw. Tools Technol. Transf. **22**(3), 297–313 (2019). https://doi.org/10.1007/s10009-019-00548-w
19. ERA: ERTMS Home Page. https://www.era.europa.eu/activities/european-rail-traffic-management-system-ertms
20. ERA: UNISIG SUBSET 098 RBC-RBC Safe Communication Interface (2012)
21. ERA: UNISIG SUBSET 039 FIS for the RBC/RBC Handover (2015)
22. Eulynx: The Eulynx initiative. https://eulynx.eu/
23. Fecher, H., Schönborn, J., Kyas, M., de Roever, W.-P.: 29 new unclarities in the semantics of UML 2.0 state machines. In: Lau, K.-K., Banach, R. (eds.) ICFEM 2005. LNCS, vol. 3785, pp. 52–65. Springer, Heidelberg (2005). https://doi.org/10.1007/11576280_5
24. Garavel, H., Lang, F., Mateescu, R., Serwe, W.: CADP 2011: a toolbox for the construction and analysis of distributed processes. Int. J. Softw. Tools Technol. Transf. **15**(2), 89–107 (2013). https://doi.org/10.1007/s10009-012-0244-z
25. Groote, J.F., Keiren, J.J.A., Luttik, B., de Vink, E.P., Willemse, T.A.C.: Modelling and analysing software in mCRL2. In: Arbab, F., Jongmans, S.-S. (eds.) FACS 2019. LNCS, vol. 12018, pp. 25–48. Springer, Cham (2020). https://doi.org/10.1007/978-3-030-40914-2_2
26. Grumberg, O., Meller, Y., Yorav, K.: Applying software model checking techniques for behavioral UML models. In: Giannakopoulou, D., Méry, D. (eds.) FM 2012. LNCS, vol. 7436, pp. 277–292. Springer, Heidelberg (2012). https://doi.org/10.1007/978-3-642-32759-9_25
27. Hvid Hansen, H., Ketema, J., Luttik, B., Mousavi, M.R., van de Pol, J., dos Santos, O.M.: Automated verification of executable UML models. In: Aichernig, B.K., de Boer, F.S., Bonsangue, M.M. (eds.) FMCO 2010. LNCS, vol. 6957, pp. 225–250. Springer, Heidelberg (2011). https://doi.org/10.1007/978-3-642-25271-6_12
28. Heinrich-Heine-Univ.: ProB Project Home Page. https://prob.hhu.de/
29. Horizon 2020: Project AstRail. https://cordis.europa.eu/project/id/777561
30. Horizon 2020: Project PerformingRail. https://cordis.europa.eu/project/id/101015416
31. INRIA: CADP Web site. https://cadp.inria.fr
32. Knapp, A., Merz, S., Rauh, C.: Model checking timed UML state machines and collaborations. In: Damm, W., Olderog, E.-R. (eds.) FTRTFT 2002. LNCS, vol. 2469, pp. 395–414. Springer, Heidelberg (2002). https://doi.org/10.1007/3-540-45739-9_23
33. Leuschel, M., Butler, M.J.: ProB: an automated analysis toolset for the B method. Int. J. Softw. Tools Technol. Transf. **10**(2), 185–203 (2008). https://doi.org/10.1007/s10009-007-0063-9
34. Liu, S., et al.: A formal semantics for complete UML state machines with communications. In: Johnsen, E.B., Petre, L. (eds.) IFM 2013. LNCS, vol. 7940, pp. 331–346. Springer, Heidelberg (2013). https://doi.org/10.1007/978-3-642-38613-8_23
35. Mazzanti, F., Belli, D.: The 4SECURail formal methods demonstrator. In: Collart-Dutilleul, S., Haxthausen, A.E., Lecomte, T. (eds.) RSSRail 2022. LNCS, vol. 13294, pp. 149–165. Springer, Cham (2022). https://doi.org/10.1007/978-3-031-05814-1_11

36. Mazzanti, F., Belli, D.: Formal modelling and initial analysis of the 4SECURail case study. In: Proceedings: Models for Formal Analysis of Real Systems (MARS). EPTCS 355, pp. 118–144 (2022). https://doi.org/10.4204/EPTCS.355.6
37. Mazzanti, F., Belli, D.: Formal models of the 4SECURail project (2022). https://zenodo.org/record/6322392
38. mCRL2: ltscompare man page. https://www.mcrl2.org/web/user_manual/tools/release/ltscompare.html
39. mCRl2: Project Home Page. https://www.mcrl2.org/
40. Ober, I., Graf, S., Ober, I.: Validation of UML models via a mapping to communicating extended timed automata. In: Graf, S., Mounier, L. (eds.) SPIN 2004. LNCS, vol. 2989, pp. 127–145. Springer, Heidelberg (2004). https://doi.org/10.1007/978-3-540-24732-6_9
41. OMG: Unified Modeling Language, Version 2.5.1 (2017). https://www.omg.org/spec/UML/2.5.1
42. OMG: Action Language for Foundational UML (Alf) (2018). https://www.omg.org/spec/ALF/1.1
43. OMG: Semantics of a Foundational Subset for Executable UML Models (2018). https://www.omg.org/spec/SysML/1.6
44. OMG: Precise Semantics of UML State Machines (2019). https://www.omg.org/spec/PSSM/1.0
45. OMG: System Modeling Language version 1.6 (2019). https://www.omg.org/spec/SysML/1.6
46. Pétin, J.F., Evrot, D., Morel, G., Lamy, P.: Combining SysML and formal methods for safety requirements verification. In: 22nd International Conference on Software & Systems Engineering and Their Applications, Paris, France (2010). https://hal.archives-ouvertes.fr/hal-00533311
47. PTC: Windchill Expert Packages. https://www.ptc.com/en/products/windchill/expert-packages
48. Shift2Rail: now Europe'srail. https://rail-research.europa.eu/
49. Snook, C., Savicks, V., Butler, M.: Verification of UML models by translation to UML-B. In: Aichernig, B.K., de Boer, F.S., Bonsangue, M.M. (eds.) FMCO 2010. LNCS, vol. 6957, pp. 251–266. Springer, Heidelberg (2011). https://doi.org/10.1007/978-3-642-25271-6_13
50. SPIN: Project Home Page. https://spinroot.com/spin/whatispin.html
51. UML-B: Project Home Page. https://www.uml-b.org/
52. Univ. AUgsburg: HUGO Home Page. https://www.uni-augsburg.de/en/fakultaet/fai/informatik/prof/swtsse/hugo-rt/
53. Univ. of Twente: Formasig Home Page. https://www.utwente.nl/en/eemcs/fmt//research/projects/formasig
54. UPPAAL: Project Home Page. https://uppaal.org/

The TLA$^+$ Debugger

Markus A. Kuppe$^{(\boxtimes)}$

Microsoft Research, Redmond, USA

makuppe@microsoft.com

Abstract. Formal methods have to meet developers where they are to achieve broad industrial adoption. Where is that? Today, many developers write software while debugging the program. This is the motivation for designing and developing a debugger for TLA$^+$. With it, developers can debug the formulas of a specification like the code of a program. However, the debugger can not only debug the evaluation of formulas but also has a first-class representation of the state machine; developers can inspect and explore the states and transitions of the state machine. This debug functionality is not limited to TLA$^+$ but generalizes to state-based formalisms when checked with an explicit state model-checker.

Keywords: TLA+ · Debugging · Debug adapter protocol · Specification · Model checking · Formal verification

1 Introduction

TLA$^+$ is a high-level, math-based, formal specification language to design, specify, and document systems. A specification describes a state machine and is specified by formulas expressed in the Temporal Logic of Actions [5,6], a variant of Pnueli's original linear-time temporal logic [10]. TLA$^+$ is an untyped language where data structures are represented with Zermelo-Fraenkel set theory with choice. Generating code is not in the scope of TLA$^+$. It is implementation language agnostic and meant to find bugs above the code level. Readers unfamiliar with TLA$^+$ should read [5] first.

The available tools with which users check and reason about TLA$^+$ specs are the explicit state model checker TLC, the symbolic model-checker Apalache, and the TLA$^+$ proof system (TLAPS). While TLC and Apalache are used to check a finite model of a spec, TLAPS supports deductive reasoning about a specification with infinitely many reachable states [1,3,13]. Apalache has not yet been integrated into the existing integrated development environments (IDE). On the contrary, TLC and TLAPS are integrated into the TLA$^+$ Toolbox [4]. In addition to the TLA$^+$ Toolbox, a VSCode-based TLA$^+$ extension has been developed in recent years[1]. The extension currently supports model-checking specifications with TLC.

---

[1] https://github.com/tlaplus/vscode-tlaplus.

P. Masci et al. (Eds.): SEFM 2022 Collocated Workshops, LNCS 13765, pp. 174–180, 2023.
https://doi.org/10.1007/978-3-031-26236-4_15

TLA$^+$ is used in the industry by developers at companies such as Amazon and Microsoft to, e.g., specify cloud systems [9,12]. To *meet developers where they are,* and, thus, narrow the gap between programming and (formally) specifying systems, a debugger has been added to TLC and integrated via the Debug Adapter Protocol (DAP)[2] into the TLA$^+$ VSCode extension. Additionally, a state-based formalism such as TLA$^+$ lends itself to an interactive exploration of the state-space of a specification through the lens of the debugger.

In the next section, this paper describes and highlights the TLA$^+$ debugger's features with the help of the TLA$^+$ specification of *EWD*998 [2,8]. Most of this functionality is not specific to TLA$^+$ but applies to any state-based method when checked by an explicit model-checker. Section 3 outlines the implementation of the TLA$^+$ debugger in TLC and its integration into VSCode via the DAP.

2   Debugger Features

Debugging the Evaluation of Formulas. One advantage of the mathematical foundation of TLA$^+$ is that it does not have to define operational semantics for its formulas. A formula is either true or false based on its standard logical interpretation unless it is a silly expression[3] whose meaning is left undefined [7]. On the other hand, a user of the TLC model-checker encounters TLC's left-to-right evaluator traversing the abstract semantic graph (ASG) constructed from the specification and the model. Here, a user may intercept the evaluation at each vertex of the ASG. At the level of TLA$^+$, the formulae whose evaluations may be intercepted are constant-, state-, or action-level formulae that appear in the initial predicate, the next-state relation, action- and state-constraints, invariants, or a refinement mapping. In other words, the ASG has multiple roots from which the evaluation starts; a root for the initial-state predicate and a root for each sub-action of the next-state relation. Only temporal formulae cannot be intercepted because they lack a direct representation in the ASG. Moreover, a user can advance or reverse the traversal of the ASG within the boundaries of the current formula. Contrary to debugging a single behavior, the TLA$^+$ debugger will traverse the sub-graph for an action-level formula in the ASG multiple times in succession if and only if the formula non-deterministically defines multiple successor states.

Users can pause the evaluation at any time, causing the traversal of the ASG to halt at the current vertex. Additionally, users can choose to set line-based or inline breakpoints that pause the evaluator on its next visit to the corresponding ASG vertex. If a breakpoint is also annotated with a hit count of h, the evaluator pauses after visiting a vertex h-times. Because the TLA$^+$ parser (SANY) lacks support for parsing additional formulae at runtime, the debugger does not support expression-based breakpoints that would pause the evaluation when the given expression, i.e., the TLA$^+$ formula is true. A workaround is adding the expression as an ordinary formula to the specification before starting

---

[2] https://microsoft.github.io/debug-adapter-protocol.
[3] Compare *"Silly Espressions"* in Sect. 6.2 of [6].

the debugger. Breakpoints are verified if the breakpoint source code location can be matched to a vertex in the ASG. An unverified breakpoint is marked as such in the frontend. The debugger always intercepts the evaluation at the vertex that failed to evaluate to help users diagnose silly expressions. Halting on evaluation errors may be disabled. When the evaluation is paused, the values of all constants, the (bound) variables in the current context, and any intermediate stack values are available for inspection. However, none of the values can be manipulated at debug time. Moreover, the call stack, i.e., the current path in the ASG, is shown. Navigating the call stack traverses the frames (compare Sect. 3) corresponding to the current path in the ASG up to its root.

In Fig. 1, we see a screenshot of the VSCode extension with its debugger UI open. In the specification editor on the right, an excerpt of the TLA$^+$ specification of $EWD998$ is visible[4]. The TLA$^+$ debugger halted the evaluation of the ASG because the arguments of Sum on line 120 are in the wrong order. This causes TLC to compare the values of the variables to and fun, which results in an exception. Diagnosing the cause of the exception is straightforward because the evaluation is intercepted at the vertex where it happened. A user could navigate the call stack to inspect the values of the variables at each frame. Additionally, a user may reverse the traversal of the ASG back to the root, which, in this case, would be the first conjunct of the $PassToken$ action on line 78. Subsequently, she may re-evaluate the $PassToken$ action, the invariant Inv (not seen in the editor), and the Sum operator step by step by using the debugger controls on top of the variables view on the left. The variables view shows the values of the arguments in the current context, i.e., the operator Sum. We also see the values of the specification constants $Color$, N, and $Node$, and the enabling conditions of the $PassToken$ action on lines 78 and 79.

Debugging the State-Space Exploration. Except for the brief appearance of non-determinism in the previous section, nothing we have seen thus far differs from an ordinary programming language debugger. However, because TLA$^+$ is a state-based formalism where a TLA$^+$ specification defines a state-machine, the debugger can also intercept the exploration of the possible transitions, i.e., actions of the state-machine defined by the behavior formula $Init \wedge \Box[Next]_v$. In other words, users may not only intercept and inspect the evaluation of the ASG as outlined above but also the traversal of the on-the-fly generated state graph by our explicit-state model-checker. To intercept the exploration of every step of a behavior, users may set a "Spec" -breakpoint at the source location of the behavior formula. This breakpoint pauses $s \xrightarrow{A} t$ where A is a sub-action of $Next$. If the "Spec"-breakpoint has a hit count of l, the exploration pauses every $s \xrightarrow{A} t$ where the length of the path from t to an initial state is equal to or greater than l. Additionally, a user may set (inline) breakpoints on the source location of the left-hand side of an action's definition in the specification. These breakpoints pause the state-machine after an A-action for state s, i.e., after the model-checker generates the set of A-successors of state s. Again, a user may

---

[4] https://github.com/tlaplus/Examples/tree/master/specifications/ewd998

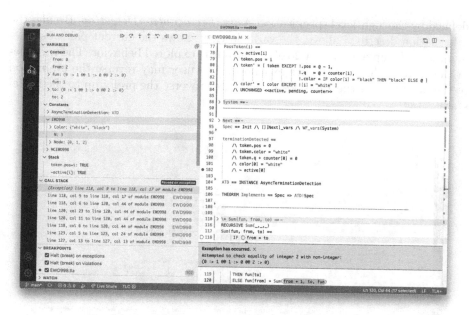

Fig. 1. Debugging an evaluation error with the TLA+ debugger in the TLA+ VSCode extension.

annotate this type of breakpoint with a hit count of c, the breakpoint will pause exploration exactly when the cardinality of the set of A-successors is equal to or greater than c. Like stopping the traversal of the ASG on evaluation errors, the model-checker will halt the exploration of th e state machine when an invariant is violated.

Whenever the exploration is paused, a user can reverse from the current breakpoint into the evaluation of the ASG at the root for the current path. In other words, the debugger allows to transparently switch between traversing the ASG and the exploration of the state machine. If TLC is configured to check the specification probabilistically (simulation mode) instead of exhaustively, a user may step over the successor state when a "Spec"-breakpoint stops the exploration. Moreover, the user can not only reverse the evaluation of the ASG, but also reverse the exploration to any predecessor state in the current prefix of a behavior. A different behavior may be explored when resuming forward exploration.

When the exploration is paused, the debugger allows users to inspect the values of the variables of all states in the prefix of the current behavior. A debugger command exists with which a user can trigger the violation of an artificial invariant. This causes TLC to write an error trace for the current prefix.

Auxiliary functionality, such as attaching to and detaching from a running model-checker, launching the model-checker in debug mode, or gracefully terminating the model-checker, are implemented but not discussed here.

In Fig. 2, the state space exploration has been halted because the *PassToken* action in *EWD*998 for a state at diameter 28 does not refine the behaviors defined by the high-level specification *AsyncTerminationDetection*. Besides the information described above, the variable view shows the current pair of states, and the prefix up to diameter 28 of the currently explored behavior. The variables of the state at diameter 25 are expanded. The user may reverse the evaluation to the beginning of the *PassToken* action, or reverse the prefix up to the initial state.

Fig. 2. Debugging an invariant violation.

3   Debugger Architecture

Architecturally, the debugger is separated into a frontend and a backend. The backend hooks into TLC's stack machine that evaluates TLA⁺ formulae, and the code that generates and checks initial- and successor states. To let users step back and forth in the ASG and see consistent information for each vertex, the debugger creates frames that capture the model-checker's state for each vertex in the ASG and state or action in the state graph. Clearly, the overhead of copying relevant internal state, such as intermediate (variable) values and states is significant. Thus, the debugger is not designed to run during ordinary model-checking of specifications. Related, the debugger does not support running TLC in parallel or distributed mode. The TLA⁺ debugger was implemented over a period of two months. Approximately one-third of the development time was spent on conceptually mapping the TLA⁺ to DAP and implementing the debugger's frontend in the VSCode extension. Two-thirds of the time went into adding the debugger capability to TLC. However, the major effort was to carefully layer the debugger on top of TLC's legacy code to avoid introducing regressions. It is likely that a more modern tool or even a greenfield development would require significantly less time. The TLC test suite proved useful to validate the absence of regression; none of the existing unit and functional tests broke when TLC ran in debug mode.

Debug Adapter Protocol. The communication between the debugger's frontend and backend uses the Debug Adapter Protocol in version 1.44. Like the popular Language Server Protocol, DAP enforces strict decoupling. This separation has the advantage that TLA$^+$ debugger support can easily be added to other IDEs. For example, adding the debugger to the Toolbox would merely be an engineering effort. For the same reason, customizations were pushed into the backend to minimize the TLA$^+$ specific implementation of the TLA$^+$ VSCode extension to less than 1k LOC of Typescript. The majority of this code implements the launching and termination of TLC. Because TLC is implemented in Java, the natural choice to build the DAP's backend was LSP4J in version 0.12[5]. The mapping from DAP to the debugger is mostly straightforward and, thus, not discussed in detail. However, the frontend implementation in VSCode occasionally lags behind the DAP's specification, such that some recent protocol additions are not yet available in the VSCode. For example, starting with version 1.41, DAP supports switching the granularity when stepping forward and backward. This protocol addition would map nicely to the debugger's stepping granularities: evaluation and exploration. Unfortunately, the TLA$^+$ debugger does not make use of step granularities.

4 Conclusion and Future Work

This paper discussed the features of the TLA$^+$ debugger, which generalizes to any state-based formalism when verified by an explicit state model-checker. The TLA$^+$ debugger is comparable with what are typically described as time-traveling debuggers[6] of ordinary programming languages.

While the TLA$^+$ debugger has not yet been officially released, it has been part of the freely available TLA$^+$ VSCode extension's nightly build for more than a year. During this time, the debugger has been used by the author when teaching TLA$^+$. In this setting, the engineers gain a better understanding of the meaning of complex formulae by stepping through their evaluation. Diagnosing evaluation errors has also become easier with the TLA$^+$ debugger. Additionally, debugging a state machine has been beneficial to explore the enabling conditions of actions. When working with real-world specifications, the debugger turned out to be useful to explore behaviors in the early stages of understanding an existing TLA$^+$ specification. Moreover, the debugger seems especially helpful to debug refinement mappings, which is notoriously difficult with TLC's existing

---

[5] https://github.com/eclipse/lsp4j.
[6] https://en.wikipedia.org/wiki/Time_travel_debugging.

functionality. In practice, the debugger's execution overhead has not been an issue.

A minor shortcoming of the TLA$^+$ debugger is its lack of expression-based breakpoints. Similarly, the difference of the AST and ASG causes unexpected behavior when stepping through formulae at the source level. However, the main limitation of the debugger is its missing support for liveness properties and fairness constraints. Since temporal logic is the major obstacle when learning TLA$^+$, support for debugging liveness and fairness is planned for the future. To support graphical debugging, the author has prototyped[7] combining the debugger with the existing TLA$^+$ animator [11].

The DAP is inspired by and designed for ordinary programming languages, not for logic and formal methods. Still, a large subset of DAP's functionality can be mapped to concepts of logic and formal methods. Because the specification of DAP is open source and constantly evolving. The formal methods community could propose and sponsor additions to DAP when needed.

Acknowledgment. The author thanks Andre Weinand, the creator of the Debug Adapter Protocol, for answering many questions during the development of the TLA$^+$ debugger. The author would also like to thank the anonymous reviewers whose suggestions helped improve and clarify this manuscript.

References

1. Chaudhuri, K.C., Doligez, D., Lamport, L., Merz, S.: A TLA+ proof system. arXiv:0811.1914 [cs] (2008)
2. Dijkstra, E.W.: Shmuel Safra's version of termination detection (1987)
3. Konnov, I., Kukovec, J., Tran, T.H.: APALACHE: abstraction-based parameterized TLA+ checker (2018)
4. Kuppe, M.A., Lamport, L., Ricketts, D.: The TLA+ toolbox. Electron. Proc. Theor. Comput. Sci. **310**, 50–62 (2019). https://doi.org/10.4204/EPTCS.310.6
5. Lamport, L.: The temporal logic of actions. ACM Trans. Program. Lang. Syst. **16**(3), 872–923 (1994). https://doi.org/10.1145/177492.177726
6. Lamport, L.: Specifying Systems: The TLA+ Language and Tools for Hardware and Software Engineers. Addison-Wesley, Boston (2003)
7. Merz, S.: On the logic of TLA+. Comput. Inf. **22**(3–4), 351–379 (2003)
8. Merz, S., Konnov, I., Kuppe, M.A.: Specification and Verification With the TLA+ Trifecta: TLC, Apalache, and TLAPS⋆. In: SpecifyThis. p. to appear (2022)
9. Newcombe, C.: Why Amazon Chose TLA+. In: Hutchison, D., et al. (eds.) Abstract State Machines, Alloy, B, TLA, VDM, and Z, vol. 8477, pp. 25–39. Springer, Heidelberg (2014). https://doi.org/10.1007/978-3-662-43652-3_3
10. Pnueli, A.: The temporal logic of programs, pp. 46–57. IEEE (1977). https://doi.org/10.1109/SFCS.1977.32
11. Schultz, W.: An animation module for TLA+ (2018)
12. Shukla, D.: TLA+ at Microsoft to build planetary-scale systems (2020)
13. Yu, Y., Manolios, P., Lamport, L.: Model checking TLA$^+$ specifications. In: Pierre, L., Kropf, T. (eds.) CHARME 1999. LNCS, vol. 1703, pp. 54–66. Springer, Heidelberg (1999). https://doi.org/10.1007/3-540-48153-2_6

---

[7] https://youtu.be/IO9ik850i0M.

Developing the UML-B Modelling Tools

Colin Snook[✉], Michael Butler, Thai Son Hoang,
Asieh Salehi Fathabadi, and Dana Dghaym

ECS, University of Southampton, Southampton, UK
{cfs,m.j.butler,t.s.hoang,A.Salehi-Fathabadi,D.Dghaym}@soton.ac.uk

Abstract. UML-B is a UML-like diagrammatic front end for the Event-B formal modelling language. We have been developing UML-B for over 20 years and it has gone through several iterations, each with significant changes of approach. The first version was an adaptation of a UML tool, the second generated a complete Event-B project, the third contributed parts of an Event-B model, and the fourth (currently under development) provides a human usable text persistence. Here we outline the reasons for these different developments and summarise the lessons learnt.

Keywords: UML-B · Event-B · Rodin platform

1 Introduction and Motivation

Towards the end of the last century it was widely recognised that formal modelling is beneficial in reducing specification errors, but despite various arguments regarding the cost benefits of early error detection, it was difficult to dispel the view that they were costly to achieve and required 'special' engineers or mathematicians. We investigated these beliefs through empirical experiments and interviews with industry experts. The experiments [23] established that formal specifications are no more difficult to understand than computer programs of equivalent complexity. However, when interviewed, industry exponents of formal methods warned that it is the choice of useful abstractions that is difficult and requires experience [22]. Abstraction is something of an art and often counter to the nature of engineers used to looking for solutions. Finding abstractions that are amenable to verification tools adds another complication which can only be mitigated by experience and expertise.

We postulated that a visual modelling tool would aid engineers in exploring and choosing different abstractions. This theory was grounded in 'The Cognitive Dimensions of Notations Framework' [5] which provides a "common vocabulary for discussing many factors in notation, UI or programming language design". (In the following, the terms from the framework are shown in italics). Using this framework, we postulated that, for systems modelling, we need *abstractions* for a *close mapping* to the problem domain, but this requires *premature commitment* (early decisions) which makes specification more difficult especially when compounded by *viscosity* (the effort needed to change the specification) which can be

P. Masci et al. (Eds.): SEFM 2022 Collocated Workshops, LNCS 13765, pp. 181–188, 2023.
https://doi.org/10.1007/978-3-031-26236-4_16

high in a large textual specification with many inter-dependencies. The UML-B diagrams help by increasing the *visibility* of chosen abstractions through visualisation and reducing viscosity. The reason the diagrams are efficient is because a single diagram entity represents many lines of formal specification text compared to a textual specification. A translation tool then converts the diagram into a textual form for formal verification and validation. This iterative *progressive evaluation* alleviates the difficulty of making premature commitments. A more detailed usability assessment of UML-B using cognitive dimensions is discussed in [17].

The B-method [1] is a method of software development using the formal modelling language, B which is based on set theory and first order predicate logic. It supports the concept of abstraction and incremental refinement with verification by proof. Event-B [2] is a formal modelling language for modelling discrete systems. Event-B was developed from the B-method and hence also supports abstraction and incremental refinement with verification by proof. We chose to use B, and later Event-B, as our underlying formal specification language because they provide a notion of formal refinement with strong tool support for verification using theorem provers as well as model checking and animation tools.

We chose to use the UML (Unified Modelling Language) [18] as the basis for our diagrammatic modelling because it was already fairly widespread and therefore familiar within industry. Event-B models are based on set theory which involves collections of instances and their relationships. This has a natural visualisation as an entity-relationship diagram which can be represented using UML class diagrams. Behaviour in Event-B is modelled as events that fire spontaneously when their guards are true and alter the variables using actions that are treated as a set of simultaneous parallel substitutions. Here there are some important differences between Event-B events and UML state-chart transitions. However, a state-machine representation, similar in structure to UML statecharts, is useful for representing the behaviour of Event-B models. Hence we developed the UML-B diagrammatic modelling tools [19,20] and have been supporting and developing them for over 20 years during which time we have enjoyed many collaborations with various industry sectors. Our current research work, industrial case studies and tool installations are shown on our UML-B website [12].

2   History of UML-B

Driven by experience gained through industrial collaboration, UML-B has been developed over the last 22 years, going through several distinct and fundamentally different versions. This section gives a history of the development of UML-B and the motivation for changing to a new approach in each case.

2.1   Version 1 - Extending Standard UML

The initial concept of UML-B (in 2000) was to translate from UML into the B formal notation. (This was before Event-B and Rodin existed). Hence the first version of UML-B [20] was based on the IBM Rational Rose UML tool. Rational Rose provided a visual basic scripting facility for the user to add tooling features to enhance the diagrams. UML-B was implemented as a script that traversed the UML diagrams and output a B model as a text file. The UML-B model was constructed as a standard UML class diagram but with some restrictions and additional properties added as UML stereotypes. Invariants, could be added to classes and guards and actions could be added to class methods, in order to fully specify the behaviour of the model. The notation used for these textual annotations was derived from the target notation, B, but with support for automatic quantification over instances of a class or parameterisation of the contextual class instance ('self'). Here we may have been able to use OCL for the constraint language and possibly, in a declarative style, for actions. However, this would have entailed more work to invent a translation and caused more separation between the specification and the verification languages. For this reason we took the easier route of basing our constrain/action language on Event-B rather than OCL.

The generated B file was then imported into the B-Core tool [4] for formal analysis. Unfortunately, the Rational Rose tool was a Windows-based application, whereas the B-Core tool was only available for Linux operating systems. Therefore the user had to switch to a different operating system in order to analyse the formal model.

2.2   Version 2 - UML-B: Like UML but Different

In 2004 the Rodin project [3,15] was started with the aim of developing a new extensible formal modelling platform to support the new Event-B notation for systems modelling. It includes Event-B editors, static checking tools and mathematical theorem provers for verification of the models. This gave an opportunity to greatly improve UML-B and a new version was developed with a different concept from the first version.

- We no longer tried to bend UML to our purpose but instead, developed our own diagrammatic modelling notation borrowing ideas from UML only when they fitted.
- We had an integrated extensible modelling platform based on Eclipse [7,8] which greatly improved the workflow from source model to verification results.
- The Event-B notation was aimed at systems level modelling and so UML-B followed suit. The concept of UML-B was always more aligned to systems level rather than software development, hence Event-B was a better fit for our purposes.

This version of UML-B [19] generated an entire Event-B project from a UML-B project. Hence all modelling had to be done in UML-B since anything the user did to the Event-B model would be overwritten the next time the UML-B was translated. More and more features were added to UML-B in order to support different modelling use cases. The action and constraint notation for invariants, guards and actions was continued in this version and developed further by adding new features. Class diagrams and state-machines were supported, but both deviated from their UML counterparts in order to provide a better correspondence with the target formalism. It should be noted that through our industrial collaborations we were gradually appreciating the significance of the very different semantics between UML statecharts and UML-B state-machines. An example of this was that users tended to attach the same event to two transitions of the same state-machine expecting one of them to fire depending on which state was active. However, in UML-B this creates two transitions that must fire together and hence never do so (since both sources can never be active at the same time). Therefore we referred to UML-B as being 'UML-like' from this point on and took care to prepare users for the differences.

The UML-B modelling language used the Eclipse Modelling Framework [24] (EMF) where a meta-model is constructed to define the abstract syntax of a modelling language and the EMF tools then generate Java code that can load model instances of that language and serialise (persist) them. The default format for model serialisation is XMI (an XML based notation for model interchange), but this can be overridden with any user-defined serialisation format. For this version of UML-B, the default XMI format was used for serialisation. EMF is a very useful basis for defining modelling notations and we have continued to use it for all our future version of UML-B as well as any other model tooling that we have developed. We used the Graphical Modelling Framework (GMF) [14] to develop the concrete diagram syntax, editors and tooling.

Although this version of UML-B was quite popular with industrial users that were relatively new to formal modelling, a significant portion of users were already familiar with Event-B and would prefer to have the full flexibility of working in Event-B and using the diagram notations more selectively.

2.3   Version 3 - iUML-B: Extending Event-B

In 2008, The 'Deploy' project [13] was started as a follow on from the Rodin project with the aim of promoting the use of the Rodin platform, and its associated plug-ins such as UML-B, in industry. During this project a new version of UML-B was developed that could work alongside Event-B, rather than overwrite the Event-B models all the time.

Since the new iUML-B needed to be an extension of Event-B rather than a separate language, a new EMF meta-model was needed. An Event-B text editor (Camille) was also developed by Heinrich Heine University in Dusseldorf and since both needed an EMF meta-model for Event-B, researchers at Dusseldorf and Southampton, as well as University of Newcastle, worked together to produce a common EMF based framework and meta-model for Event-B [21] which could be used as the basis for future tools. The iUML-B meta-model then extends the Event-B meta-model to support class diagrams and state-machines using a generic extension mechanism built into the meta-model. The iUML-B model was serialised (i.e. saved/persisted) within a single extension element within the Rodin Event-B model.

In this version of UML-B, the diagrams still generate Event-B elements but not the complete Event-B model. Some parts of the Event-B model are expected to already exist and the diagrams *elaborate* them by providing further details. For example a UML-B class no longer generates the data item (set, constant or variable) that models the set of instances, but it can generate invariants that constrain the set of instances. Similarly, attributes and associations, 'elaborate' existing data elements by generating invariants about their type (being a relation between the containing class instances and the attribute/association type). Class methods and state-machine transitions 'elaborate' events that already exist in the Event-B and contribute extra parameters, guards and actions. This strategy of elaboration allows the modeller to retain control over the Event-B model and choose which parts to model in Event-B and which parts to model diagrammatically in UML-B. (For expediency, the UML-B diagram editor provides an option to create the elaborated elements if they do not already exist in the Event-B).

However, a disadvantage of diagrammatic models is that it becomes more difficult to get a quick overview of all the details in the model. In a textual syntax all of the details of the model are visible in the same view, even if they are complicated to interpret, whereas in a diagram, it is cumbersome to show everything on the canvas. Hence in UML-B certain model details are given in the associated contextual properties view which only becomes visible when the appropriate model element is selected. This led to some users asking for a human readable text persistence for UML-B. Other advantages of a human readable text persistence are that it may be easier to compare different versions of models (provided order is maintained) and to copy and paste sections of models. (Note that the default persistence is XMI (a variant of XML) which is ASCII text, but designed for machine loading and therefore difficult to read).

2.4   Version 4 - xUML-B: A Human Usable Text Persistence

The Camille text editor for Event-B was very popular but still serialised models using the Rodin XML-based format. Another problem with Camille was that it is very difficult to extend a concrete syntax. Hence extensions to the Event-B modelling language (e.g. UML-B) were difficult to accommodate. To obtain an extensible and true human usable text serialisation for Event-B we developed a new 'front-end' for Event-B using XText [6,16] which we call 'CamilleX' [9]. Due to the difficulty of extending Rodin models, CamilleX models are written in a separate human readable text file. Hence the source models are separate from the Rodin models which are automatically re-generated for verification purposes when the CamilleX model is saved. Regeneration is efficient since the translations are very fast and the Rodin verification builders are designed to find and re-use existing proofs wherever possible. Further discussion on the development of CamilleX is given in [10].

However, this meant that the UML-B models can no longer be persisted inside the Rodin models. Hence we are now developing an alternative persistence scheme for iUML-B so that its models are stored separately from the elaborated

Rodin models. The new UML-B persistence is also based on XText so that we have a human readable persistence for UML-B. We call this version xUML-B.

3   Conclusions

The main lessons we have learnt from our experiences of developing UML-B are.

- Heavily featured semi-formal modelling languages such as UML are difficult to use for precise formally verifiable specification. While UML covers a wide range of users needs it doesn't support the precise mathematical semantics needed for proof. UML can be specialised through profiles and stereotypes, but users are confused if familiar features are not used or represent different semantics. Therefore, it is better not to try to translate UML but to invent a new notation that is better suited to the target formalism.
- A downside of making a new notation similar to a well-known existing one such as UML, is that users may be confused when the model does not behave as they are used to. An example of this is the difference between UML-B state-machines and UML statechart 'run to completion' semantics.
- Model edition, checking and verification needs to be highly integrated so that changes can be quickly assessed.
- While there are many users that are attracted to a self contained diagrammatic notation, experienced users want the flexibility to choose between diagrammatic and textual representations for different parts of a model.
- Even when diagrams are used, users express a strong desire for a human usable textual persistence which helps with maintenance activities such as version comparison and copy and paste as well as enabling a quick oversight of the content

A common reaction to UML-B is to question the decision not to translate standard UML. There is of course a desire not to proliferate new languages unnecessarily. As we have already discussed, the UML semantics is not easily used for representing Event-B semantics. For example, we have extensively researched ways to reconcile run to completion semantics (used in UML statecharts) with Event-B style refinement [11]. An alternative approach would be to develop a new formalised theory of refinement for UML and provide new theorem provers to support it. However, we believe this would be extremely difficult simply because great care was taken to achieve tractable refinement and proof in Event-B by keeping to a simple and appropriate semantics.

Acknowledgements. This work is supported by the HiClass project (113213), which is part of the ATI Programme, a joint Government and industry investment to maintain and grow the UK's competitive position in civil aerospace design and manufacture.

References

1. Abrial, J.-R.: The B Book - Assigning Programs to Meanings. Cambridge University Press, Cambridge (1996)
2. Abrial, J.-R.: Modeling in Event-B: System and Software Engineering. Cambridge University Press, Cambridge (2010)
3. Abrial, J.-R., Butler, M., Hallerstede, S., Hoang, T.S., Mehta, F., Voisin, L.: Rodin: an open toolset for modelling and reasoning in Event-B. Softw. Tools Technol. Transf. **12**(6), 447–466 (2010)
4. B-Core(UK). B-Toolkit User's Manual, Release 3.2. Oxford, UK (1996)
5. Blackwell, A., Green, T.: Chapter 5 - notational systems-the cognitive dimensions of notations framework. In: Carroll, J.M. (ed.) HCI Models. Theories, and Frameworks, Interactive Technologies, pp. 103–133. Morgan Kaufmann, San Francisco (2003)
6. Eysholdt, M., Behrens, H.: Xtext: implement your language faster than the quick and dirty way. In: OOPSLA, pp. 307–309. ACM (2010)
7. The Eclipse Foundation. The Eclipse Project Website (2009). http://www.eclipse.org. Accessed Sept 2022
8. Gamma, E., Beck, K.: Contributing to Eclipse: Principles, Patterns, and Plugins. Addison Wesley Longman Publishing Co., Inc, Redwood City (2003)
9. Hoang, T.S., Dghaym, D.: Event-B and Rodin Documentation Wiki: CamilleX (2018). http://wiki.event-b.org/index.php/CamilleX. Accessed Sept. 2022
10. Hoang, T.S., Snook, C., Dghaym, D., Salehi Fathabadi, A., Butler, M.: Building an extensible textual framework for the rodin platform. In: F-IDE 2022, Lecture Notes in Computer Science (to be published) (2022)
11. Morris, K., Snook, C., Hoang, T.S., Hulette, G., Armstrong, R., Butler, M.: Formal verification and validation of run-to-completion style state charts using event-b. In: Innovations in Systems and Software Engineering (2022)
12. The University of Southampton. The UML-B website (2021). https://uml-b.org/ Accessed Sept 2022
13. The Deploy Project. The deploy project website (2008). http://www.deploy-project.eu/. Accessed Sept. 2022
14. The Graphical Modelling Project. The GMP project website (2010). https://www.eclipse.org/modeling/gmp/. Accessed Sept 2022
15. The Rodin Project. Rigorous open development environment for complex systems (2004). http://rodin.cs.ncl.ac.uk/. Accessed Sept 2022
16. The XText Project. The XText project website (2020). https://www.eclipse.org/Xtext/. Accessed Sept 2022
17. Razali, R., Snook, C., Poppleton, M., Garratt, P.: Usability assessment of a UML-based formal modeling method using a cognitive dimensions framework. Hum. Technol. **4**(1), 26–46 (2008)
18. Rumbaugh, J., Jacobson, I., Booch, G.: The Unified Modeling Language Reference Manual. Addison-Wesley, Reading (1998)
19. Said, M.Y., Butler, M., Snook, C.: Language and tool support for class and state machine refinement in UML-B. In: Cavalcanti, A., Dams, D.R. (eds.) FM 2009. LNCS, vol. 5850, pp. 579–595. Springer, Heidelberg (2009). https://doi.org/10.1007/978-3-642-05089-3_37
20. Snook, C., Butler, M.: UML-B: formal modelling and design aided by UML. ACM Trans. Softw. Eng. Methodol. **15**(1), 92–122 (2006)

21. Snook, C., Fritz, F., Iliasov, A.: Event-B and Rodin Documentation Wiki: EMF Framework for Event-B (2009). http://wiki.event-b.org/index.php/EMF_framework_for_Event-B. Accessed Sept 2022
22. Snook, C., Harrison, R.: Practitioners' views on the use of formal methods: an industrial survey by structured interview. Inf. Softw. Technol. **43**(4), 275–283 (2001)
23. Snook, C., Harrison, R.: Experimental comparison of the comprehensibility of a z specification and its implementation in java. Inf. Softw. Technol. **46**(14), 955–971 (2004)
24. Steinberg, D., Budinsky, F., Paternostro, M., Merks, E.: Eclipse Modeling Framework: The Eclipse Series, 2 edn. Addison-Wesley Professional, Reading (2008)

CoSim-CPS 2022 - 6th Workshop on Formal Co-Simulation of Cyber-Physical Systems

CoSim-CPS 2022 Organizers' Message

CoSim-CPS is the premier workshop on the integrated application of formal methods and co-simulation technologies in the development of software for Cyber-Physical Systems. Co-simulation is an advanced simulation technique that allows developers to generate a global simulation of a complex system by orchestrating and composing the concurrent simulation of individual components. Formal methods link software specifications and program code to logic theories, providing means to exhaustively analyze program behaviors. The two technologies complement each other. Developers can create prototypes to validate hypotheses embedded in formal models, in order to ensure that the right system is being analyzed. Using formal methods, developers can generalize the results obtained with co-simulation, enabling early detection of latent design anomalies.

This year's workshop was held in Berlin, with live presentations and discussions started in the conference room and also held during the social dinner.

Our keynote speaker, Joachim Denil from the University of Antwerpen, talked about threats to and opportunities for validity in co-simulation. The keynote presented the co-simulation as an essential tool for the design of complex engineered systems combining models at different levels of abstraction and approximation to make decisions about the system under design. The keynote introduced the validity as creating a correct model to represent the actual system (under design) accurately and showed different related concepts such as, for example, the verification, which focuses on a correct implementation. As a final point the keynote discussed the different threats to the validity of a (co-)simulation and different opportunities that arise from explicit reasoning on the validity of (co-)simulation models.

The workshop was held in three sessions, the first one being focused on building FMUS for different purposes, the second one described different co-simulation frameworks, and the third showed the results of the application of co-simulation in robotic and maritime fields. We received a total of 8 submissions, 6 of which were accepted for presentation and publication. Each manuscript received 3 anonymous reviews, after a 5-day bidding period and before a final 3-day consensus discussions.

We are grateful to the Program Committee for the dedication to the critical task of reviewing the submissions. We are also grateful to members of the Organizing Committee of SEFM for making the necessary arrangements and helping to publicize the workshop and prepare the proceedings. Finally, we thank the authors for their efforts in writing their papers and for the excellent presentations.

November 2022

Cinzia Bernardeschi
Cláudio Gomes
Maurizio Palmieri
Paolo Masci

Organization

Program Committee Chairs

Cinzia Bernardeschi	University of Pisa, Italy
Cláudio Gomes	Aarhus University, Denmark
Maurizio Palmieri	University of Pisa, Italy
Paolo Masci	National Institute of Aerospace (NIA), USA

Program Committee

Julien A. Dit Sandretto	Ensta ParisTech, France
Jörg Brauer	Verified Systems International GmbH, Germany
Paul De Meulenaere	University of Antwerp, Belgium
Andrea Domenici	University of Pisa, Italy
Aaron Dutle	NASA Langley Research Center, USA
Adriano Fagiolini	University of Palermo, Italy
Francesco Flammini	Linnaeus University, Sweden
Ken Pierce	Newcastle University, UK
Rudolf Schlatte	University of Oslo, Norway
Neeraj Singh	INPT-ENSEEIHT/IRIT and University of Toulouse, France
Francisco J. González	University of A Coruña, Spain
Holger Pfeifer	Fortiss GmbH, Germany
Hugo Daniel Macedo	Aarhus University, Denmark
Stylianos Basagiannis	Collins Aerospace, Ireland

Validity in (Co-) Simulation

Joachim Denil[1,2]([✉])[iD]

[1] University of Antwerp, Antwerp, Belgium
Joachim.Denil@uantwerpen.be
[2] Flander Make, Lommel, Belgium

Abstract. Co-simulation is an essential tool for the design of complex engineered systems. From early on in the life cycle of a system, models at different levels of abstraction and approximation are combined to make decisions about the system under design. Validity is typically described as creating a correct model to represent the actual system (under design) accurately. This is different to verification, which focuses on the proper implementation. In this paper, we relate different concepts of validity. We look at the techniques that the community produces to check the validity of the system. Afterwards, we look at the different threats to the validity of a (co-)simulation and look at some opportunities that arise when we explicitly reason on the validity of (co-)simulation models. Finally, we look at some tools that offer point solutions to some of the threats presented.

Keywords: Validity · Co-simulation · Model-based systems engineering

1 Introduction

Co-simulation is an essential tool for the design of complex engineered systems. These complex engineered systems, commonly found in automotive, aerospace, transportation and logistics, etc., are typically engineered using a model-based systems engineering approach [8]. Model-based systems engineering advocates a top down design process where different trade-offs are evaluated at different stages of system design. To allow for this trade-off analysis from early on in the life cycle of a system, simulation models at different levels of abstraction and approximation are combined to make decisions about the system under design. Furthermore, with new developments in IoT and cloud computing, these simulations are now also used as physics-based digital shadows and twins.

However, it is important that the results from these simulation models are usable. As a model is created with particular assumptions in mind, it is easy to forget these assumptions and use the models in a context where the model

---

This invited contribution is based on the keynote presentation "Threats to and Opportunities for Validity in co-simulation" given by the author at the 2022 CoSim-CPS workshop, affiliated with SEFM'22, Berlin (DE).

P. Masci et al. (Eds.): SEFM 2022 Collocated Workshops, LNCS 13765, pp. 193–199, 2023.
https://doi.org/10.1007/978-3-031-26236-4_17

will produce wrong results. An example can be seen in [19], where they ask participants in a study to define the contextual influences of a simple model.

For this, the term validity has of a simulation model has been introduced. Validity is described as: *"A computerized model within its domain of applicability possesses a satisfactory range of accuracy consistent with the intended application of the model"* [16]. For a more philosophical discussion on validity, the reader is referred to [1].

In the rest of this paper, we first look at the notion of substitutability as a description for validity in Sect. 2. In Sect. 3, we look at the different techniques introduced by the simulation community and identify some threats and opportunities related to validity. Section 4, we look at some point solutions presented in research to mend some of the introduced threats.

2 The Notion of Substitutability

We define the notion of validity as substitutability. This means that we can replace the experiments we perform on the real system, using a measurement device, with computational experiments on the model. There has to be a commuting of the results (to a certain distance) of the real-world experiments and the computational experiments. As we are dealing with experiments, it is important to note that there are properties of interest (PoI) that are measured in both the computational and real-world experiments. Validity is thus always with respect to the property of interest.

Different approaches are used to check the validity of simulation models. More techniques can be found in [15].

The distance to the mental model of the expert: This distance is also known as face validity. An expert looks at the simulation and experimental data and draws a conclusion.

The distance between the structure of the model and the real world: Structural validity compares the structure of model with the structure of the real-world. As such, it verifies if the results are generated because of the right reasons. Sengel and Forester define a procedure to verify the structure of a systems dynamics model in [17].

The distance between the value(s) of the properties of interest: Different statistical techniques are available to check the distance between the values and traces of the properties of interest. Three main techniques can be found in the literature (a) Bayesian techniques, (b) hypothesis testing and, (c) area metrics. We refer the reader to [1,12] for more information.

Lots of related concepts exist in the literature. A very related term to validity is credibility. Credibility is a much broader term than validity and is assessed both qualitative and quantitative (e.g., statistical validity). In the qualitative assessment, the engineers also take into account operational aspects such as the workflow that was used that resulted in the model.

3   Threats and Opportunities to Validity

Figure 1 shows the commutative diagram between a real-world experiment and a computational experiment. The figure is annotated with the threats to the validity of our co-simulation.

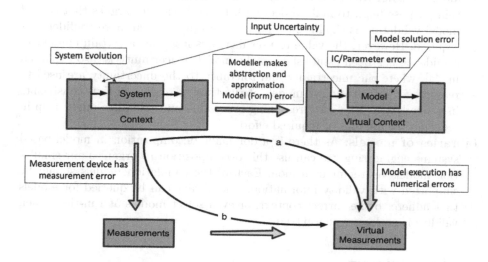

Fig. 1. Substitutability and uncertainty

Experiments: Design of both the computational and real-world experiments is needed to reduce the input uncertainty and parameter uncertainty.

Verification of sub-models: Each model and sub-model needs to be verified to avoid bugs. For co-simulation this also means that the master algorithm, responsible for the enactment of the simulation, is verified. We refer to [7] for an overview of methods and techniques for correct co-simulation.

Internal Validity: Each co-simulation unit should not exceed the boundaries of its own validity. For example, Hooke's law defines the relation the force of compression and extension to the distance ($F = kx$). However, this is a first-order approximation of the real-world behaviour of the spring. As such, it can only be used up to a certain distance (otherwise the spring is plastically deformed). If this component in the co-simulation exceeds that bound, the results can no longer be trusted, and a model (or combination of models) should be used with a broader validity range. Run-time monitoring tools can help here.

External Composition: It is not strictly defined that when composing a co-simulation with all valid models in a certain context, that the results of the co-simulation are valid. This is because the properties of interest are not necessarily the same as the properties of interest of the co-simulation units. For example, emergent behaviour from the composition is something which cannot be reasoned on for each individual co-simulation unit, it is only at the composed level that this property of interest exists. Nonetheless, sensitivity analysis presents itself as an opportunity here to see which co-simulation units have the most impact on the property of interest. Validity experiments should be setup to check these properties of interest.

Value and Tolerance: Uncertainty is not necessarily bad. A model has a certain purpose (e.g., to make a decision). In [15], Sargent argues that cost of model validation is significant, and increases more when more confidence is required. However, the value to user increases less once a certain amount of confidence has been established in the model. Uncertainty is also exploited in [4], where the uncertainty and tolerance to the uncertainty are used to reason over substitution of models at run-time to reach real-time constraints in a simulation. Explicitly reasoning over value and tolerance might help in reducing the amount of required effort.

Libraries of models: As there is a dominant decomposition in model-based systems engineering, we can use this decomposition to organise our simulation models in a similar fashion. Each of the simulation models should be supported with validity information. The library can be queried for models that adhere to the correct context, or even select models at run-time when validity is no longer guaranteed.

4   Tool Support

Different authors have worked on the concepts of defining validity for simulation models. We give a brief but not exhaustive overview of research tools that (might) help in mending some of the issues related to the validity of (co-) simulation.

Experimental Frames: Experimental frames were introduced by Zeigler in the Theory of Modelling and Simulation [22,23]. Zeigler defines the experimental frame as *"The conditions under which the system is observed and experimented with"*. The experimental frame has a dual purpose. As such, the idea is to make the contextual information about the simulation model explicit. For this purpose, it is both implemented as meta-data that is needed for validity, and it defines an operational view of the experiment using a generator, transducer and acceptor. In [5], the authors look at the uses of such an experimental frame: checking for a new context, calibration, searching for a model in a library of simulation models, reproducibility, etc. They conclude that the experimental frame might not be defined well enough for these different purposes.

System Structure and Parameterisation (SSP): An existing standard of use is the SSP standard defined by the Modelica Association [9]. SSP defined a complete system combining multiple FMUs and their parameters. As such, it works on the dimensional consistency of the co-simulation. The SSP could be extended to allow for structure verification, parameter verification and boundary adequacy testing.

Contracts and Model Signatures: Bender et al. define model signatures in [2]. The signature is used for both documentation and interfaces. Having such interface definitions propertly available allows to check for dimensional consistency and internal structure verification. Similarly, [24] introduces interfaces for simulation models parameters and initial conditions to allow for validation activities. The signatures include for example, admissible ranges to allow for better internal analysis of validity. Finally, contract theory helps in checking the internal validity of models by checking assumptions and guarantees on the interfaces of components (in this case co-simulation units) [3].

Model Identification Card: The authors in [18] propose the "Model Identity Card" (MIC) as a way to specify meta-data on the simulation models. The meta-data contains information on identification of the model, the methods to execute the model (e.g. solvers), model usage (e.g. tool versions), and model quality (e.g., validation and verification). MIC allows to create consistent architectures mixing existing, reworked or newly created models each connected through the port properties defined in their own MIC. As such, the MIC model does contain an indication of the model's validity scope in terms of variable ranges but it does not contain an indication on its accuracy.

Modelica Credibility Library: [13] proposes to annotate the parameters of a Modelica model with traceability, uncertainty and calibration information to improve model quality, thus increasing correct use of models. They weave machine-readable metadata within the models, instead of relying on external data formats.

Computational Experimental Modelling: In [10], the authors propose a domain-specific language to model the computational experiments needed in a simulation study for validation. Furthermore, validation metrics are automatically calculated using the area metrics defined in [12]. Similarly, [6], focuses on a domain-specific language to allow reproducability of computational experiments.

Workflow tracking and Provenance: The more broader term of credibility also requires a qualitative assessment. Therefore a recording the followed workflow is needed, e.g., [14] models a workflow and records a trace of the workflow followed. Other simulation experts record the provenance of their model, and detect patterns in these provenance models [21].

Validity Frames: Validity frames [5,11,20] are an evolution of the concepts defined in the experimental frame of Zeigler. It has the meta-data needed to reason over the model and run simulations (such as initial conditions, parameter ranges, model architecture and rationale, etc.), and the operational view where signal monitors are generated to check at run-time the bounds of the model. Validity frames extend this with a workflow for different necessary activities within the modelling and simulation process, such as calibration and validation workflows (to extend with experiments the valid context of a model).

References

1. Beisbart, C., Saam, N.J.: Computer Simulation Validation. Springer, Heidelberg (2019). https://doi.org/10.1007/978-3-319-70766-2
2. Bender, M., et al.: Signature required: making simulink data flow and interfaces explicit. Sci. Comput. Program. **113**, 29–50 (2015)
3. Benveniste, A., et al.: Contracts for system design. Found. Trends® Electron. Design Autom. **12**(2–3), 124–400 (2018)
4. Biglari, R., Denil, J.: Model validity and tolerance quantification for real-time adaptive approximation. In: Proceedings of the 25th International Conference on Model Driven Engineering Languages and Systems: Companion Proceedings, pp. 668–676 (2022)
5. Denil, J., Klikovits, S., Mosterman, P.J., Vallecillo, A., Vangheluwe, H.: The experiment model and validity frame in m&s. In: Proceedings of the Symposium on Theory of Modeling & Simulation, pp. 1–12 (2017)
6. Ewald, R., Uhrmacher, A.M.: Sessl: a domain-specific language for simulation experiments. ACM Trans. Model. Comput. Simul. **24**(2) (2014). https://doi.org/10.1145/2567895
7. Gomes, C., Thule, C., Broman, D., Larsen, P.G., Vangheluwe, H.: Co-simulation: a survey. ACM Comput. Surv. (CSUR) **51**(3), 1–33 (2018)
8. Haskins, C., Forsberg, K., Krueger, M., Walden, D., Hamelin, D.: Systems engineering handbook. In: INCOSE. International Council on Systems Engineering Seattle (2006)
9. Köhler, J., Heinkel, H.M., Mai, P., Krasser, J., Deppe, M., Nagasawa, M.: Modelica-association-project "system structure and parameterization"-early insights. In: The First Japanese Modelica Conferences, Tokyo, Japan, 23–24 May 2016, No. 124, pp. 35–42. Linköping University Electronic Press (2016)
10. Mertens, J., Denil, J.: Ess: Emf-based simulation specification, a domain-specific language for model validation experiments. In: 2022 Annual Modeling and Simulation Conference (ANNSIM), pp. 416–427. IEEE (2022)
11. Van Mierlo, S., Oakes, B.J., Van Acker, B., Eslampanah, R., Denil, J., Vangheluwe, H.: Exploring validity frames in practice. In: Babur, Ö., Denil, J., Vogel-Heuser, B. (eds.) ICSMM 2020. CCIS, vol. 1262, pp. 131–148. Springer, Cham (2020). https://doi.org/10.1007/978-3-030-58167-1_10
12. Oberkampf, W.L., Roy, C.J.: Verification and Validation in Scientific Computing. Cambridge University Press, Cambridge (2010)
13. Otter, M., Reiner, M., Tobolář, J., Gall, L., Schäfer, M.: Towards modelica models with credibility information. Electronics **11**(17), 2728 (2022)
14. Paredis, R., Exelmans, J., Vangheluwe, H.: Multi-paradigm modelling for model based systems engineering: Extending the ftg+ pm. In: 2022 Annual Modeling and Simulation Conference (ANNSIM), pp. 461–474. IEEE (2022)
15. Sargent, R.G.: Verification and validation of simulation models. In: Proceedings of the 2010 Winter Simulation Conference, pp. 166–183. IEEE (2010)
16. Schlesinger, S., et al.: Terminology for model credibility. Simulation **32**(3), 103–104 (1979)
17. Senge, P.M., Forrester, J.W.: Tests for building confidence in system dynamics models. Syst. Dyn. TIMS Stud. Manag. Sci. **14**, 209–228 (1980)
18. Sirin, G., Paredis, C.J., Yannou, B., Coatanéa, E., Landel, E.: A model identity card to support simulation model development process in a collaborative multidisciplinary design environment. IEEE Syst. J. **9**(4), 1151–1162 (2015)

19. Spiegel, M., Reynolds, P.F., Brogan, D.C.: A case study of model context for simulation composability and reusability. In: Proceedings of the Winter Simulation Conference, 2005, p. 8. IEEE (2005)
20. Van Acker, B., De Meulenaere, P., Denil, J., Durodie, Y., Van Bellinghen, A., Vanstechelman, K.: Valid (re-) use of models-of-the-physics in cyber-physical systems using validity frames. In: 2019 Spring Simulation Conference (SpringSim), pp. 1–12. IEEE (2019)
21. Wilsdorf, P., Wolpers, A., Hilton, J., Haack, F., Uhrmacher, A.M.: Automatic reuse, adaption, and execution of simulation experiments via provenance patterns. arXiv preprint arXiv:2109.06776 (2021)
22. Zeigler, B.P., Kim, T.G., Praehofer, H.: Theory of Modeling and Simulation. Academic press, Cambridge (2000)
23. Zeigler, B.P., Muzy, A., Kofman, E.: Theory of Modeling and Simulation: Discrete Event & Iterative System Computational Foundations. Academic press, Cambridge (2018)
24. Zerwas, T., et al.: Model signatures for the integration of simulation models into system models. Systems **10**(6) (2022). https://doi.org/10.3390/systems10060199, https://www.mdpi.com/2079-8954/10/6/199

Using INTO-CPS Tools in the Development of a Digital Twin for the F1TENTH Race Car

Malthe Faurschou Tøttrup$^{(\boxtimes)}$, Emil Chao Hu, Bastian Aron Kramer,
Hugo Daniel Macedo, and Lukas Esterle

DIGIT and Department of Electrical and Computer Engineering, Aarhus University,
Aarhus, Denmark
{201907882,201907692,201908709}@post.au.dk,
{hdm,lukas.esterle}@ece.au.dk

Abstract. This paper reports on the usage of the INTO-CPS tools
to build a digital twin for the F1TENTH race car which includes an
autonomous driving solution for the car and modelling of vehicle dynamics and motor control. The simulation implementation is based on pack-
aging existing simulator as Functional Mock-Up units which are run as
a co-simulation using the INTO-CPS application. The digital twin has
been tested on the actual F1TENTH car as well as the F1TENTH simulator acting as a physical asset substitute for the car.

Keywords: Digital twin · F1TENTH · INTO-CPS · Co-simulation ·
Autonomous driving

1 Introduction

The concept of digital twins has in recent years gone from being an idea to
getting adopted in many different industries. A digital twin (DT) is a virtual
replica of a physical system, referred to as a physical twin (PT), and can be
defined as *"a computerized model of a physical device or system that represents
all functional features and links with the working elements."* [2]. A DT has three
core functionalities:

- It can receive and process data from the PT,
- it can simulate the physical system in parallel in real time, and
- it can send instructions to the PT.

This interchange of data between the physical and digital systems helps optimize
the performance and thus maximize the potential of its physical counterpart.
However, creating a model replicating the behavior of a system and its environment can quickly become a demanding task due to the many factors that need
to be considered simultaneously. A practical way of handling this complexity is
through the Functional Mock-Up Interface (FMI), which allows to orchestrate

P. Masci et al. (Eds.): SEFM 2022 Collocated Workshops, LNCS 13765, pp. 200–209, 2023.
https://doi.org/10.1007/978-3-031-26236-4_18

simulators for different subsystems to obtain behaviours of the entire system as a co-simulation, therefore allowing individual components to be modelled separately but later simulated as a single system.

This paper provides a brief overview of how the INTO-CPS tool-chain, which provides the necessary boilerplate to follow FMI standard, has been used to develop a digital twin for a physical twin, namely a F1TENTH race car capable of autonomous driving. We present an implementation of a DT, which fulfills the above-mentioned criteria and utilizes an adapted Pure Pursuit algorithm to enable the PT to drive autonomously through the INTO-CPS platform[1]. Compared to related papers, our work follows the same approach reported in [7], but in our case we apply the INTO-CPS tools to model an off-the-shelf physical twin compared to a custom made hardware platform. One of the advantages of an off-the-shelf physical twin is the possibility to use the available simulators and assets from its ecosystem, but the effort of reverse engineering is bigger when compared to a hardware platform designed from scratch.

Thus, Sect. 2 of this paper will first present the key concepts used in this project. Then, Sect. 3 will outline the implementation of the digital twin. This includes a presentation of the digital model and the co-simulation setup. Section 4 will present the autonomous driving solution for the digital twin and Sect. 5 showcases the experiments performed in the project. Finally, Sect. 6 will provide concluding remarks on the obtained results.

2   Background Technologies

The implementation of the digital twin for the F1TENTH race car is based on a co-simulation utilizing the FMI standard. The FMI standard defines a container and an interface to exchange dynamic models, referred to as a Functional Mock-Up Unit (FMU), using a combination of XML files, binaries and code zipped into a single C file [10]. Thus, each FMU represents a part of the system and the multiple of FMUs of the system can be connected in a multi-model and run as a co-simulation. The co-simulation is driven by a collaborative simulation orchestration engine (COE), which handles the passage of time as well as how the data is shared between the models in the joint simulation [4]. In this project, the INTO-CPS application [8] has been used to run the co-simulation as well as configure the system setup. This includes specifying the inputs and outputs of the FMUs and setting the system parameters such as step size and initial parameter values. The creation of the FMUs has been done using the command line tool Universal Functional Mock-Up Unit (UniFMU), which creates a default Python FMU and thereby avoids creating the FMUs from scratch [6]. To achieve communication between the two twins, the RabbitMQ FMU (RMQFMU) has been used, which presents a convenient way of sending and receiving data from external processes and using it in the co-simulation [5]. Lastly, the F1TENTH race car is a four-wheeled ground robot that is roughly 1/10 the size of a regular Formula 1 race car [3].

---

[1] Project GitHub: https://github.com/LukasEsterle/AUF1Tenth.

3   Towards a INTO-CPS Based F1TENTH Digital Twin

This section presents the achieved multi-model for the F1TENTH DT, as well as details of the FMUs it consists of. The multi-model is used to conduct co-simulations and parallel operations with the PT or RViz simulation. The multi-model has been setup and configured using the INTO-CPS application.

3.1   Multi-model

Figure 1 presents the multi-model for the first prototype of a DT for the F1TENTH. It consists of four FMUs, each with different purposes and functionality:

- The `F1TENTH.FMU` is responsible for simulating the movement of the F1TENTH when inputs are provided to its motors.
- The `Controller.FMU` is a simulation of the control software, which produces adequate input signals to the motors to control the *velocity* and *steering angle* of the F1TENTH.
- The `RMQ-LiDAR.FMU` interfaces with the LiDAR in the robot.
- The `RMQ-PT.FMU` interfaces with the controllers on board the PT.

There are two instances of the RMQFMU, which has the unique property that it can communicate with processes that reside outside of the co-simulation. This means that the RMQFMUs send their input values out of the co-simulation, and receive their outputs values from messages from nodes that reside outside of the co-simulation. In this case the `RMQ-LiDAR.FMU` receives pre-processed *distance* and *angle* values, which are the results of processing the LiDAR data. Nnotice that connections from the external robot in the FMU are hidden, and the readings are forwarded as output ports of the FMU. The reason why the LiDAR data processing is not done in the co-simulation itself is due to the fact that it is difficult to deal with large arrays of data in the FMI. The `RMQ-PT.FMU` is responsible for the majority of the communication with the PT. It receives the states of the F1TENTH as measured by its sensors, i.e. x_s, y_s, ψ_s, *velocity_s*, and *steer_angle_s*, and compares them against the simulated states of the `F1TENTH.FMU`. Finally, the `RMQ-PT.FMU` sends driving instructions in the form of *desired_velocity* and *desired_steer_angle* to the controllers on board the PT. The *desired_velocity* and *desired_steer_angle* are calculated from the *distance* and *angle* inputs in the `Controller.FMU`. More details of the FMUs implementations and how they have been created and configured using the tool-chain will be elaborated on in the following sections.

3.2   Model of the F1TENTH

The first step towards building a DT for the F1TENTH is to make a model of the vehicle dynamics that can simulate the movement of the car when some inputs are provided to its motors. The modelling of the vehicle dynamics is based on

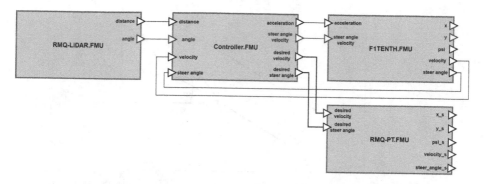

Fig. 1. Multi-model diagram for the F1TENTH DT. Lines between inputs and outputs show how they are connected. Some outputs have no connections. These has been defined such that they can be plotted via INTO-CPS live plotting feature.

Table 1. State variables for the bicycle model

Variable	Description
s_x, s_y	Coordinates describing the robot position
δ	Steering angle
ν	Velocity
Ψ	Yaw angle in relation to the world frame
$\dot{\Psi}$	Angular velocity of the yaw angle
β	Slip angle at the center of gravity

the bicycle model, which describes the motion of the car using state equations [1]. Table 1 presents the state variables for the model.

The bicycle model combines the rear and front of a 4-wheeled vehicle. This forms a two-wheeled model, which allows for easier calculations since it is only necessary to keep track of one steering angle. Additionally, the center of gravity is selected as a reference point as it forms a slip angle during turning. This principle is illustrated in Fig. 2. The F1TENTH is equipped with two different motors whom actuates states δ and ν. In this case the outputs of the motors have been modelled as the first derivative of the states, i.e. *steering angle velocity* and *acceleration* ($\dot{\delta}$ and $\dot{\nu}$) respectively.

The calculation of the states for the F1TENTH has been wrapped in the F1TENTH.FMU from the Fig. 1. To create this model of the F1TENTH as an FMU, a template Python FMU was generated using the UniFMU command line tool[2]. Afterwards, the outputs and inputs of this FMU was defined in the modelDescription.xml, which consists of the states as described in Table 1 and the $\dot{\delta}$ and $\dot{\nu}$ inputs. Finally, the state equations was implemented in the model.py file, and calculated every time the fmi2DoStep function is called.

---

[2] UniFMU GitHub: https://github.com/INTO-CPS-Association/unifmu.

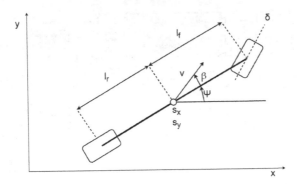

Fig. 2. The bicycle model used to model the motion of the F1TENTH robot. The model combines a *virtual* front and rear wheel, residing between the *real* front and rear wheels. Center of gravity is the reference point.

3.3   Control

We want to drive the state variables ν and δ to some desired values ν_d and δ_d via the motors of the F1TENTH. For this purpose, a simple proportional control scheme is chosen to drive ν and δ to their desired values as shown in Fig. 3.

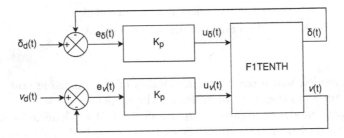

Fig. 3. Block diagram of the F1TENTH control system. The control inputs u_ν and u_δ corresponds to the first derivatives of the states, i.e. $\dot{\nu}$ and $\dot{\delta}$, respectively. It is assumed that these can be given directly as inputs to the F1TENTHs motors. Furthermore, it is assumed that the current values of ν and δ can be read directly by the sensors of the system without any noise or delay.

Similar to the model of the F1TENTH, the control logic has been wrapped in a single `Controller.FMU`. The same workflow has been applied, using UniFMU to generate a template FMU, switching out the inputs and outputs in the `modelDescription.xml` and changing the implementation in the `model.py`. Furthermore, the desired states ν_d and δ_d and the two different K_P values have been defined as parameters in the `modelDescription.xml`, allowing for easy manual configuration and tuning when co-simulating the FMU in the INTO-CPS application.

3.4   External Communication

It is a requirement that the DT can exchange data with its physical counterpart and vice versa. To achieve this, the RMQFMU[3] has been used, which is an FMU that can communicate with a RabbitMQ message broker that resides outside of the co-simulation environment [5]. Like other FMUs the RMQFMU specifies its inputs and outputs in the `modelDescription.xml` file, however, in this case, the inputs are exported out of the co-simulation and sent to the broker and the outputs are received from the broker. This way the RMQFMU can exchange data with external processes through the broker. Furthermore, important networking information can easily be specified and configured in the `modelDescription.xml` file of the RMQFMU. Using the RMQFMU allows the DT to communicate and exchange data with e.g. a RViz simulation or the physical robot itself. In the multi-model, there are two instances of the RMQFMU, i.e. `RMQ-LiDAR.FMU` and `RMQ-DT.FMU`. Preferably, we wanted to have only one RMQFMU in the multi-model, responsible for all communication between the co-simulation and the external processes. However, it was found that if two or more nodes were trying to send messages to the same RMQFMU, this would cause a delay in the data flow. To circumvent this issue we decided to make two instances of the RMQFMU, each receiving messages from only one external node.

The nodes that communicate with the RMQFMUs via the RabbitMQ broker are implemented as ROS nodes that convert messages to/from ROS and JSON formats. A high abstraction level diagram of the developed nodes and the data flowing between them and the co-simulation is illustrated in Fig. 4. Note that the full ROS architecture is not included in this figure, only the ROS nodes that perform format conversions and thereby acts as a sort of bridge between the co-simulation environment and ROS system. It has been the intention to give names to the nodes that indicates what processes/components they communicate with behind the scenes.

To ensure that timing is handled correctly it is required that the messages sent to the RMQFMU is time stamped. The RMQFMU blocks the stepping of the co-simulation until a message that satisfies the guard `messageTime StampInSimulationTime >=currentSimulationTime+simulationStepSize`, where `messageTimeStampInSimulationTime` is the time stamp of the received message, is received for all outputs of the RMQFMU(s). To accommodate this feature of the RMQFMU we decided to synchronise the message publishing frequency for the nodes and the step size of the co-simulation. Thus, the nodes are publishing messages at a rate of 100 Hz and the simulation step size is 0.01 s. Although, this might not have been necessary, we found this to work well in the for the experiments conducted during the project.

---

[3] RMQFMU GitHub: https://github.com/INTO-CPS-Association/fmu-rabbitmq/ releases/tag/v2.1.4.

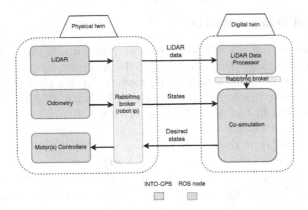

Fig. 4. Overview of nodes communicating with the co-simulation via RabbitMQ brokers.

4 Autonomous Driving

As briefly mentioned, the LiDAR data is used to determine the desired states for the velocity and steering angle for the car to drive As briefly mentioned, the LiDAR data is used to determine the desired states for the velocity and steering angle for the car to drive autonomously. The overall idea is that the robot should drive towards the way-point furthest away and in front of the robot, as measured by the LiDAR. Furthermore, the velocity should be proportional to the measured distance, i.e. when the distance is long the velocity is high, and when the distance is short the velocity is low.

However, simply driving toward the way-point that is furthest away is problematic, because it will often lead to the robot hitting the corner and crashing. As illustrated in the left Fig. 5, because the radius to the largest distance (the path of the robot) often intersects or touches corner points. In the case of a left curve, it is the case that the neighbours to the left of the largest distance are the points of the inner corner. Therefore, we opted driving toward the way-point that is furthest away, while keeping a safe distance to the corners. To achieve this, we offset the way-point by taking an average of its neighbours. To enforce this behaviour in the navigation strategy, we defined as a goal to drive to the largest average distance way-point.

Largest Average Distance Way-point. The largest average distance point is a point in the LiDAR point cloud field of view in the semicircle obtained in front of the vehicle, that is computed by selecting the maximal after averaging each point with its N neighbours in the point cloud. Mathematically, given the sequence of points in the semicircle: $x_1, \ldots, x_f$, we define the sequence $a_1, \ldots, a_f$, which is computed as $a_i = \frac{1}{2N+1} \sum_{j=i-N}^{i+N} x_i$, obtaining the way-point point as the result of $max(a_i)$. The resulting largest average distance and corresponding angle are the parameters being sent to the RMQ-LiDAR.FMU.

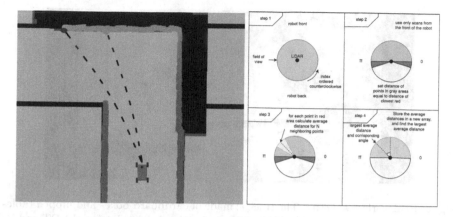

Fig. 5. The image on the left side illustrates a scenario where the F1TENTH has to drive around a corner. In the images the point cloud data from the LiDAR is represented by the red and orange dots. The blue point is the way-point furthest away in front of the vehicle. The green point is the largest average way-point, calculated following the procedure in the image to the right. The dotted lines gives a rough indication of the trajectory of the F1TENTH. These lines show that if the F1TENTH drives towards the blue point it will get dangerously close to the wall, while the green will guide it safely around the wall. Keep in mind that the way-points are continuously updated while the F1TENTH is driving. (Color figure online)

5 Experiments

The DT system has been tested in both real world and simulation using the F1TENTH simulator[4]. The main purpose of the experiments was to test whether the DT is able to assist the PT with autonomous navigation and simulate the motion of the PT at the same time by co-simulating the FMUs in the multi-model. In the tests the PT and simulation part of the DT are set to drive towards the point furthest away as described in 4. Figure 6 shows the setup for the real world tests. Both in real world and simulation it was found that the DT was able to assist with the navigation task. However, in the real world tests we did not have any positional reference for the robot to compare against the DT simulated position. Hence, it is difficult to verify whether the co-simulation is able to effectively approximate the behaviour of the system, or if some components needs to be modified. Although, from Fig. 7 we see that the simulated trajectory fits reasonably well with the constructed test-track shown in Fig. 6, however, more tests are in order, as well as comparison data from e.g. a GPS system such as Marvelmind [9].

---

[4] F1TENTH simulator GitHub: https://github.com/f1tenth/f1tenth_simulator.

Fig. 6. Real world test setup. The track is made of cardboard boxes and flipped tables. At the bottom of the image the INTO-CPS application is live-plotting the DT and PT *velocity* and *steering angle* over time.

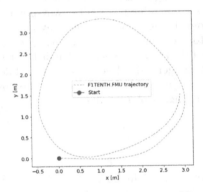

Fig. 7. Trajectory of the F1TENTH as calculated by the co-simulation of FMUs during real world testing.

6   Conclusion

In this demo paper, we develop a DT prototype for the F1TENTH using the INTO-CPS tool-chain. Modelling the system as multiple FMUs and co-simulating them is a convenient way of breaking down the system into multiple connectable parts, which ultimately makes it easier to understand and model the workings of the system. The INTO-CPS tools have allowed us to easily generate FMUs, connect them in a multi-model, and co-simulate them. The RMQFMU provides a simple mechanism for communicating with processes outside of the co-simulation, which is an essential step for making a DT application. Furthermore, using the RMQFMU to test the autonomous driving capabilities of the DT with the F1TENTH simulator has been essential for the project during the development phase. Using the RMQFMU also helped circumvent some of the limitations of the INTO-CPS tools we found during the project. Based on their experience of using the INTO-CPS tools, they are primarily concerned with modelling the system itself. This is acceptable when there is a moderate decoupling between the system and the surrounding environment, for instance, a temperature regulator or a water tank. However, in the case of the F1TENTH, the environment plays a crucial role in how the system should be operated. In this case, it is necessary to model the environment the F1TENTH is navigating in, using third-party simulation software such as RViz. Furthermore, the robot is equipped with a LiDAR which generates large arrays of data that are inconvenient to deal with in the FMI. Therefore, the LiDAR has been modelled as a ROS node instead of an FMU. While the INTO-CPS tools are great for modelling certain parts of the system, it is heavily dependent on communicating with external systems in this particular case, and the RMQFMU has allowed us to do exactly that.

Acknowledgements. The work presented here is partially supported by the Poul Due Jensen Foundation for funding the project Digital Twins for Cyber-Physical Systems (DiT4CPS).

References

1. Althoff, M., Koschi, M., Manzinger, S.: CommonRoad: composable benchmarks for motion planning on roads. In: IEEE Intelligent Vehicles Symposium, pp. 719–726 (2017). https://gitlab.lrz.de/tum-cps/commonroad-vehicle-models/blob/master/vehicleModels_commonRoad.pdf
2. Chen, Y.: Integrated and intelligent manufacturing: perspectives and enablers. Engineering **3**(5), 588–595 (2017)
3. F1Tenth Development Team: F1TENTH - Build Documentation. https://f1tenth.org/build.html
4. Fitzgerald, J., Larsen, P.G., Pierce, K.: Multi-modelling and co-simulation in the engineering of cyber-physical systems: towards the digital twin. In: ter Beek, M.H., Fantechi, A., Semini, L. (eds.) From Software Engineering to Formal Methods and Tools, and Back. LNCS, vol. 11865, pp. 40–55. Springer, Cham (2019). https://doi.org/10.1007/978-3-030-30985-5_4
5. Frasheri, M., Ejersbo, H., Thule, C., Esterle, L.: RMQFMU: bridging the real world with co-simulation Technical Report (2021). https://doi.org/10.48550/ARXIV.2107.01010
6. Legaard, C.M., Tola, D., Schranz, T., Macedo, H.D., Larsen, P.G.: A universal mechanism for implementing functional mock-up units. In: 11th International Conference on Simulation and Modeling Methodologies, Technologies and Applications. p. to appear, SIMULTECH 2021. Virtual Event (2021)
7. Lumer-Klabbers, G., Hausted, J.O., Kvistgaard, J.L., Macedo, H.D., Frasheri, M., Larsen, P.G.: Towards a digital twin framework for autonomous robots. In: SESS: The 5th IEEE International Workshop on Software Engineering for Smart Systems, COMPSAC 2021. IEEE, July 2021
8. Macedo, H.D., Rasmussen, M.B., Thule, C., Larsen, P.G.: Migrating the INTO-CPS application to the cloud. In: Sekerinski, E., et al. (eds.) FM 2019. LNCS, vol. 12233, pp. 254–271. Springer, Cham (2020). https://doi.org/10.1007/978-3-030-54997-8_17
9. Marvelmind Robotics: Marvelmind. https://marvelmind.com/product/starter-set-super-mp-3d/
10. Modelica Association: Functional Mock-Up Interface (2008). https://fmi-standard.org/. Accessed 04 Mar 2022

Do-it-Yourself FMU Generation

Cinzia Bernardeschi[ID], Pierpaolo Dini[ID], Andrea Domenici[ID],
Maurizio Palmieri[✉][ID], and Sergio Saponara[ID]

Department of Information Engineering, University of Pisa, Pisa, Italy
`maurizio.palmieri@ing.unipi.it`

Abstract. While many modeling and simulation environments provide tools for the generation of FMI-compliant FMUs, developers often have to design an FMU from scratch in order to co-simulate their own code or code from a third-party framework. This paper reports on the authors' experience in FMU development and presents some simple guidelines based on that experience. In particular, FMU generation is discussed in the context of a model predictive control framework using a robot arm as running example.

Keywords: Co-simulation · Model predictive control · FMI standard · Design space exploration · Cyber-physical system

1 Introduction

Due to the increasing complexity of cyber-physical systems (CPS), model-based design (MBD) is one of the techniques commonly used in industry to design and develop such systems. MBD provides a conceptual framework where the behavior of the system can be modeled and simulated at different levels of abstraction, before its prototype is built. In particular, the design of a CPS requires collaboration of teams from multiple domains, such as mechanical, electronic and software engineers. In this case, simulation may take the form of multi-model simulation, known as co-simulation [15], where dynamic models built with different formalisms and tools can be executed under an orchestration engine.

The Functional Mock-up Interface (FMI) [6] is an open standard for co-simulation that defines a common interface for the simulation units, and it is supported by several modeling and simulation tools that provide automatic generation of FMUs, such as Simulink [9] and OpenModelica [13] to name a few.

However, it is often the case that a co-simulation must include submodels either developed on frameworks lacking FMU generation tools, or coded anew.

This paper discusses the authors' experience in dealing with such situations, reporting a case study as an example, and proposes some guidelines that may hopefully be useful to other developers.

This work has been partially supported by the Italian Ministry of Education and Research (MIUR) in the framework of the CrossLab project (Department of Excellence) and by the HiEFFICIENT (Highly EFFICIENT and reliable electric drivetrains based on modular, intelligent and highly integrated wide bandgap power electronics modules) project, ECSEL Joint Undertaking (JU), under grant agreement no. 101007281.

P. Masci et al. (Eds.): SEFM 2022 Collocated Workshops, LNCS 13765, pp. 210–227, 2023.
https://doi.org/10.1007/978-3-031-26236-4_19

The FMU generation process is applied to code developed on the GRAMPC (Gradient-Based MPC) [18] framework for model predictive control (MPC), using a robot arm as a case study [7]. An FMU for the robot arm controller has been generated with the procedure exposed below, and co-simulated with an FMU containing a physical model of the robot, exported automatically in an OpenModelica environment. The master available in the INTO-CPS tool chain [19] has been used as the co-simulation orchestration engine.

In addition to simulations and visualization of results, the Design Space Exploration (DSE) available in the tool chain has been used to analyze the results for different time windows of the MPC and to choose the values for parameters that minimize the average error in the execution of the task of the arm.

The paper is organized as follows. Section 2 reports a representative set of related work; Sect. 3 briefly describes the FMI standard and the model predictive control framework object of this study; Sect. 4 reports how to design an FMU, using a GRAMPC-based application as an example; Sect. 5 analyses results from the co-simulation and the design space exploration applied to the robotic arm; finally, Sect. 6 reports a discussion and possible further work.

2 Related Work

Co-simulation is the technique of coupling different simulation tools to produce the behavior of the global system. Many works exist that use Simulink S-functions to connect different simulators, for example, in [27] a powertrain model was coupled to an MPC controller; while in [4], a human heart model was co-simulated with a model of a pacemaker. An ad-hoc infrastructure is used in [20] instead, to connect a physical plant simulator to a Simulink MPC-controller.

The Functional Mockup Interface (FMI) [5] is a widely used standard for co-simulation based on a master-slave approach, where a master algorithm coordinates many simulation units, called Functional Mockup Units (FMUs), possibly generated from different simulation tools. In [21], a universal mechanism for implementing FMUs is shown; in [25], a method to generate an FMU from a state machine (or MISRA C code) is shown; in [24] a procedure to export Prototype Verification System (PVS) theories as FMU is described; [26] proposes an extension to export VDM-RT models as FMUs from the Overture tool; [14] proposes a tool to check the correctness of the static information within an FMU. FMI Co-simulation was also used by the authors to verify control systems of various kinds [2,3], including robot vehicles [10,23].

Literature on model predictive control offers many fundamental texts, such as [16]. In particular, the application of MPC in the automotive field is discussed in [28]; The GRAMPC optimization algorithm implements an augmented Lagrangian method based on the gradient-descent paradigm. Examples of GRAMPC based adaptive and learning control techniques for modern mechatronic systems are [8] and [17].

A preliminary version of a hand-made FMU for GRAMPC is in [1], where the authors of the present paper applied co-simulation to the autonomous vehicle obstacle avoidance problem.

3   Background

This section reports background information for FMI co-simulation and GRAMPC framework.

3.1   The FMI Standard for Co-simulation

The FMI standard for co-simulation [12] covers the API that a co-simulation master can use to communicate with the FMUs, the information that each FMU must statically provide in a configuration file, and the contents of the artifact (a zip archive) where the FMU is deployed.

The API comprises many C functions (a) to instantiate, initialize, and terminate an FMU, (b) to write and read FMU variables, (c) to perform several other (possibly optional) tasks, and (d) to execute one communication step. A communication step is the interval between two communication points at which the FMUs exchange information through the master. In this interval, each FMU updates its variables in one or more steps of its own simulation algorithm.

The configuration file is an XML description of the FMU, including the lists of its variables and parameters. For example, the following fragment shows the entry for a variable x:

```
<ScalarVariable
    name="x" valueReference="1" causality="input"
    variability="continuous" > <Real start="0.0" />
</ScalarVariable>
```

This entry declares that x is an input variable to the FMU, it takes continuous real values with a zero initial value, and its *value reference* is 1. This value is an index into a table kept by the master to store the values of each FMU's variable.

The archive's contents include the FMI API implementation, the submodel, and possibly its simulation engine. These main components may be in the form of source or binary code, or both. Further artifacts may be present, too.

The connection between the master and an FMU can have a *self-contained* structure, where the FMU contains both the submodel and its simulation code, running in the same process, or a *tool coupling* structure, where the FMU is a wrapper that implements the FMI API by interacting with a separate simulation tool, which runs in its own process.

In general, the process of building an FMU consists in:

1. Creating a model of the subsystem to co-simulate. This model can be written in a textual programming or modeling language such as C or Matlab, or with a graphical environment such as Simulink or 20-sim.

2. Implementing the FMI API in term of the simulation algorithm's interface.
3. If necessary, producing the binary code, such as a loadable library, for the model, the API implementation, and possibly the simulation algorithm.
4. Writing the configuration file.
5. Building the archive.

These steps are often carried out automatically by a modeling or simulation environment that provides FMU generation. In the rest of the paper we discuss how to perform these steps without automatic support.

Interaction Between Master and FMU. A co-simulation environment provides a way to specify the connections among FMUs and the data they exchange. Each FMU declares, in the configuration file, its input and output variables and its parameters. The co-simulation designers then provide the environment with the required topological information. For example, if FMU F_1 declares x and y as outputs and z as an input, then x of F_1 could be connected to input variable u of FMU F_2, and y of F_1 could be connected to input x of FMU F_3.

The master writes into an FMU's input variable and reads from an output variable using functions with names of the form, respectively, *fmi2SetXXX* and *fmi2GetXXX*, where the string *XXX* stands for the name of the type declared for the variable. In order to access the variables independently of their names, the master uses their value reference declared in the FMU configuration files. It is up the FMU designer to associate that reference with the local variable in the implementation of the FMI API, as discussed in Sect. 4.3 below.

At each co-simulation step (Fig. 1), the master sends the FMU one or more *fmi2SetXXX* calls to pass input values from other FMUs, then it calls fmi2DoStep to have the FMU execute the step, and finally calls *fmi2GetXXX* to collect results to be forwarded to other FMUs.

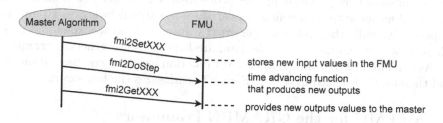

Fig. 1. Interaction Master-FMU

3.2   The GRAMPC Framework

The GRAMPC (Gradient-Based MPC) framework uses an optimization algorithm to control a system. Let us assume that the system is sampled at instants t_k and it is defined by a state vector $\mathbf{x}$, a command vector $\mathbf{u}$, and dynamics

$$M\dot{\mathbf{x}} = f(\mathbf{x}, \mathbf{u}, t_k + t) \,, \tag{1}$$

where M (the mass matrix) expresses the system's inertia and t is the time coordinate relative to the sampling time t_k. In the following, function f will be written in the form $f_k(\mathbf{x}, \mathbf{u}, t)$. The MPC algorithm minimizes the cost functional

$$J(\mathbf{u}, \mathbf{x}_k) = V(\mathbf{x}(T)) + \int_0^T l(\mathbf{x}, \mathbf{u}, t)dt \tag{2}$$

over the prediction horizon T, under some system constraints (not shown). In control applications, the cost functional is typically a function of the error between the current or final state (or output) values and the control setpoints.

During each control period $[t_k, t_{k+1})$, the control vector that minimizes the cost functional is applied to the system.

The GRAMPC framework implements a highly configurable optimization algorithm. The framework defines the signatures of a set of user-supplied functions called by the optimization algorithm. Among these functions, function ffct defines the system function f in (1), functions lfct and Vfct define the l and V functions in (2), and other functions define the gradients and Jacobians of the above functions with respect to state and control variables. A further set of functions express constraints.

Users also supply a main program that initializes system variables and algorithm parameters, then it enters a loop calling at each iteration the grampc_run() function, defined in the GRAMPC API, that executes one simulation step, computing the optimal control outputs. A GRAMPC-based simulation is executed by a self-standing application obtained by compiling and linking the framework files with user-supplied files containing the main program and the problem-specific functions required by the optimization algorithm.

The exchange of information between the GRAMPC framework and the problem-specific code relies on storing model variables and parameters in arrays whose dimension is provided by the problem-specific code. For example, the initial values for state and command variables are stored in arrays x0 and u0, respectively, while their reference (*desired*) values are in arrays xdes and udes. These arrays, with other accessible data, are kept in the C structure grampc.

As explained above, the grampc_run() function performs one simulation step and therefore it is called in a loop. Figure 2 synthesizes the framework.

4   An FMU for the GRAMPC Framework

This section introduces a co-simulation approach for GRAMPC applications, the running example of a robotic arm, the design of an FMU for GRAMPC, and the templates for a generalized and partially automated FMU generation.

4.1   Co-simulation with GRAMPC

As discussed above, The GRAMPC framework is used to build a self-standing, monolithic simulation for a model of a given system to be controlled by an

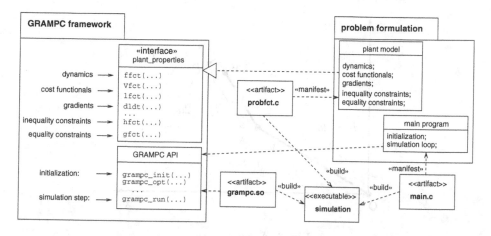

Fig. 2. Schematic view of the GRAMPC framework.

MPC algorithm. The framework provides the MPC algorithm and a choice of simulation engines with a large number of configurable parameters, while the developers provide the system model in the form of a set of C functions. They also provide the simulation's main program, whose main tasks are configuring the MPC and simulator algorithms, iterating over simulation steps, and storing or displaying simulation results.

It may be observed that, in the GRAMPC framework, it is not possible to simulate the plant and the controller separately, since the plant model coincides with the model embedded in the controller.

In order to integrate an MPC-controlled system model in the co-simulation of a larger system, the three tasks of the developer-supplied main program must be allocated to different elements. Parameter configuration is done by the FMU implementation of the FMI initialization functions, such as fmi2ExitInitializationMode(). Iteration over simulation steps is delegated to the co-simulation master, which cyclically calls fmi2DoStep, implemented in the FMU by calling grampc_run. Storing and displaying results can be done in the FMU itself, or by other FMUs, or by the co-simulation environment.

4.2 Example: A Robotic Arm

Let us consider as an example the design of a model predictive control (MPC) for a two-joint planar robot arm [7]. In Fig. 3, the rotational joint O anchors the first link of the arm to the fixed frame, C_1 and C_2 are the centers of mass of the two links, a_1 and a_2 their half lengths, q_1 and q_2 are, respectively, the angular position of the first link relative to the x axis, and the angular position of the second link relative to the first one. The absolute angular displacement of the two links from the x axis is represented by θ_1 and θ_2. The links rotate around the respective joints O and A under the torques τ_1 and τ_2, computed by the controller, applied by synchronous motors.

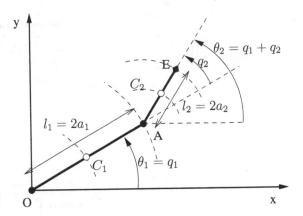

Fig. 3. A robotic arm.

As shown in [7], the system dynamics can be expressed as

$$M(\theta_1, \theta_2) \begin{bmatrix} \ddot{\theta}_1 \\ \ddot{\theta}_2 \end{bmatrix} + C(\theta_1, \theta_2, \dot{\theta}_1, \dot{\theta}_2) \begin{bmatrix} \dot{\theta}_1 \\ \dot{\theta}_2 \end{bmatrix} + G(\theta_1, \theta_2) = \begin{bmatrix} \tau_1 \\ \tau_2 \end{bmatrix}, \qquad (3)$$

where matrices M and C and vector G describe, respectively, the effects of inertia, of centrifugal and Coriolis forces, and of gravity. The latter are null for a planar arm working on a horizontal surface, as assumed in this work.

In order to apply MPC, the system dynamics must be recast in the form of (1). We then define the state $\mathbf{x}$ of the system by the relative angular positions (q_1, q_2) and velocities $(\dot{q}_1, \dot{q}_2)$ of the links, and the system command vector $\mathbf{u}$ by the pair of torques (τ_1, τ_2). Neglecting the moments of inertia of the robot links with respect to those of the actuating motors and solving (3) with respect to the variables just introduced, function f in (1) can be expressed as

$$f_{k1}(\mathbf{x}, \mathbf{u}, t) = \dot{q}_1$$
$$f_{k2}(\mathbf{x}, \mathbf{u}, t) = \dot{q}_2$$
$$f_{k3}(\mathbf{x}, \mathbf{u}, t) = \frac{(m_2 a_1 l_2 \cos(q_2)) A(\mathbf{x}, \mathbf{u}, t)}{B(\mathbf{x}, \mathbf{u}, t)} + \frac{(J_2 + m_2 l_2^2) C(\mathbf{x}, \mathbf{u}, t)}{D(\mathbf{x}, \mathbf{u}, t)}$$
$$f_{k4}(\mathbf{x}, \mathbf{u}, t) = -\left(\frac{A(\mathbf{x}, \mathbf{u}, t) F(\mathbf{x}, \mathbf{u}, t)}{2 a_2 a_1^2 m_2 + D(\mathbf{x}, \mathbf{u}, t)} + \frac{E(\mathbf{x}, \mathbf{u}, t)}{B(\mathbf{x}, \mathbf{u}, t)} \right),$$

where the auxiliary functions A, B, C, D, and E are shown in Fig. 4.

The controller must minimize the two cost terms in (2), computed by squaring the difference between each variable and its reference value (e.g., x_1 and $x_{1,r}$), multiplying by a weight (e.g., $\mathrm{w}_{\tau,1}$), and adding:

$$A(\mathbf{x}, \mathbf{u}, t) = m_2 l_2^2 + m_2 a_1 l_2 \cos(q_2) + \mathrm{J}_2$$

$$B(\mathbf{x}, \mathbf{u}, t) = m_1 l_1^2 m_2 l_2^2 + m_2^2 a_1^2 l_2^2 + \mathrm{J}_1 m_2 l_2^2 + \mathrm{J}_2 m_1 l_1^2 + \mathrm{J}_2 m_2 a_1^2 + \mathrm{J}_1 \mathrm{J}_2$$
$$- m_2^2 a_1^2 l_2^2 cos^2(q_2)$$

$$C(\mathbf{x}, \mathbf{u}, t) = (\tau_1 + \dot{q}_2(m_2 a_1 l_2 \dot{q}_1 \sin(q_2) + m_2 a_1 l_2 \dot{q}_2 \sin(q_2)) + m_2 a_1 l_2 \dot{q}_1 \dot{q}_2 sin(q_2)$$

$$D(\mathbf{x}, \mathbf{u}, t) = m_1 l_1^2 m_2 l_2^2 + m_2^2 a_1^2 4 a_2^2 + \mathrm{J}_1 m_2 l_2^2 + \mathrm{J}_2 m_1 l_1^2 + \mathrm{J}_1 m_2 a_2^2 + \mathrm{J}_1 \mathrm{J}_2$$
$$- m_2^2 a_1^2 l_2^2 \cos^2(q_2)$$

$$E(\mathbf{x}, \mathbf{u}, t) = m_1 l_1^2 + m_2 l_2^2 + m_2 a_1^2 + 2 m_2 a_1 l_2 \cos(q_2) + \mathrm{J}_1 + \mathrm{J}_2$$

Fig. 4. Auxiliary functions.

$$l(\mathbf{x}, \mathbf{u}) = \mathrm{w}_{\tau,1} \|\tau_1 - \tau_{1,\mathrm{r}}\|^2 + \mathrm{w}_{\tau,2} \|\tau_2 - \tau_{2,\mathrm{r}}\|^2 + \mathrm{w}_{\mathrm{q},1} \|q_1 - q_{1,\mathrm{r}}\|^2$$
$$+ \mathrm{w}_{\mathrm{q},2} \|q_2 - q_{2,\mathrm{r}}\|^2 + \mathrm{w}_{\dot{\mathrm{q}},1} \|\dot{q}_1 - \dot{q}_{1,\mathrm{r}}\|^2 + \mathrm{w}_{\dot{\mathrm{q}},2} \|\dot{q}_2 - \dot{q}_{2,\mathrm{r}}\|^2 \qquad (4)$$

$$V(\mathbf{x}) = \mathrm{w}_{\tau,1} \|\tau_1 - \tau_{1,\mathrm{r}}\|^2 + \mathrm{w}_{\tau,2} \|\tau_2 - \tau_{2,\mathrm{r}}\|^2 + \mathrm{w}_{\mathrm{q},1} \|q_1 - q_{1,\mathrm{r}}\|^2$$
$$+ \mathrm{w}_{\mathrm{q},2} \|q_2 - q_{2,\mathrm{r}}\|^2 + \mathrm{w}_{\dot{\mathrm{q}},1} \|\dot{q}_1 - \dot{q}_{1,\mathrm{r}}\|^2 + \mathrm{w}_{\dot{\mathrm{q}},2} \|\dot{q}_2 - \dot{q}_{2,\mathrm{r}}\|^2 . \qquad (5)$$

At the same time, the controller must satisfy a geometrical constraint on the second angle, forcing the values of q_2 between 0.17 and 2.97 rad (roughly 10° and 170°).

4.3 Designing an FMU

The controller FMU was developed with the self-contained connection schema. The code consists in two blocks: the FMI API implementation and the GRAMPC application. To achieve better modularity, the FMI implementation block is made of two modules, one to translate the FMI API into a generic *driver* interface, and one to provide a GRAMPC-specific implementation to the driver interface.

The Fmiapi Module. The *Fmiapi* module (`fmiapi.c`) currently contains the full implementations of a few fundamental FMI functions, namely `fmi2Instantiate`, `fmi2DoStep`, `fmi2FreeInstance`, `fmi2GetReal`, `fmi2SetReal`, `fmi2GetInteger`, and `fmi2SetInteger`. Other functions, whose full implementations are left for further work, only return void or an `fmi2OK` status, either because they are not expected to be called by the master, or they are actually no-operations in the application at hand.

The Driver Module. The *Driver* module (`driver.c`) provides functions for initialization (`init()`) and termination (`finish()`) of the GRAMPC application, for the execution of one co-simulation step (`tick()`), and for the value-passing functions (`getreal()` etc.), using the GRAMPC API. This module also contains the definitions and initializations of a few global data structures.

The Problem Module. The *Problem* module (`probfct.c`) provides the problem definition functions needed by the GRAMPC MPC algorithm.

Mapping Value References. The main issue in designing the Driver module is the mapping between the value references used by the co-simulation master and the variables used in the FMU. The master exchanges data with the FMU using one set-get pair of value-passing functions (e.g., `fmi2GetReal()` and `fmi2SetReal()`) for each type in the FMI standard, i.e., *Real, Integer, Boolean, String,* and *Enumeration* (the functions for Integers are used also for Enumerations). For example, the signature of `fmi2GetReal()` is

```
fmi2GetReal(fmi2Component c, const fmi2ValueReference vr[],
            size_t nvr, fmi2Real value[]);
```

The master uses this function to retrieve the values of `nvr` FMU real variables identified by their references passed through `vr`.

In the Driver module, these functions are implemented by functions with the same signatures, such as `getreal()` and `setreal()`.

The implementation of each get-set pair uses an array of the corresponding type as a buffer holding the values to be read or written by the master. The problem of associating variable references and application variables in the FMU reduces then to translating value references into indices for the buffers.

The translation mechanism adopted in this work relies on imposing a well-defined order in the list of variables contained in the model description file. In the list, the variables shall be grouped according to their type, and the groups shall follow a fixed order, e.g., first Reals, then Integers and Enumerations, then Booleans, and finally Strings. In our example we have twenty-seven variables, of which twenty-six Reals and one Integer:

```
<ScalarVariable name="q1" valueReference="1" ...>
    <Real start="0.17"/>  </ScalarVariable>
    ...
<ScalarVariable name="Thor" valueReference="26" ...>
    <Real start="3.0"/>  </ScalarVariable>
<ScalarVariable name="Nhor" valueReference="27" ...>
    <Integer start="300"/>  </ScalarVariable>
```

In file *driver.c*, two buffers are defined whose size accommodates all the variables of the respective type, plus one unused element to align the value reference (starting from one) with the array index (starting from zero):

```
fmi2Real realBuffer[R_COUNT + 1];
fmi2Integer intBuffer[I_COUNT + 1];
```

where R_COUNT and I_COUNT are defined as twenty-six and one in file *driver.h*. The indices into the buffers are computed in the value-passing functions, given the number of variables in each type. Function `getreal()` is coded, e.g., as:

```
getreal(fmi2Component c, const fmi2ValueReference vr[],
        size_t nvr, fmi2Real value[])
{   for (size_t i = 0; i < nvr; i++) {
        fmi2ValueReference vRef = vr[i];
        value[i] = realBuffer[vRef]; }
}
```

In the functions for Integer values we must take into account the offset between the value reference of the first Integer variable and the one of the first Real variable:

```
getint(fmi2Component c, const fmi2ValueReference vr[],
       size_t nvr, fmi2Integer value[])
{   for (size_t i = 0; i < nvr; i++) {
        fmi2ValueReference vRef = vr[i];
        value[i] = intBuffer[vRef - (R_COUNT + 1)]; }
}
```

The total number of variables of each FMI type and the ordering of the variables' declarations in the model description file is enough for the value-passing functions that read from or write to the FMU buffers. The next step is associating locations in the buffers with variables referred to in the GRAMPC-based application. For this, it is necessary to identify the different roles of each variable.

A first distinction is between model (or plant) variables, model parameters, and simulation parameters. The model variables may be *state* or *command* ones, while model parameters express properties or constraints of the model. The model parameters include the initial and desired values of the state and command vectors, the physical parameters of the plant, and parameters of the MPC algorithm, such as constraints and error weights. Simulation parameters configure various aspects both of the MPC algorithm and of the simulator proper.

Since the initialization and configuration of the GRAMPC runtime requires accessing a few arrays, the problem of copying data between arrays of different sizes shows up again, this time between GRAMPC arrays and FMU buffers. Again, we resort to grouping together variables of the same role so that their value references are consecutive, and ordering the groups according to a fixed pattern so that the offset of each group within the buffer can be computed. For example, the grouping of real-valued variables is shown in Table 1.

Table 1. Grouping of real variables and parameters

Value reference	Group
1–4	Current state variables
5–8	Desired state variables
9–10	Current command variables
11–25	Model parameters
26	Simulation parameters

The header file *driver.h* contains the macro definitions for the parameters obtained by the above procedure. For example, parameter RCS is the number *current* real state variables, and RDS is the number *desired* variables. These parameters are used to compute the offsets of each group in the buffer and the total number of real-valued variables:

```
#define R_MOFFS (RCS + RDS + RCU + RDU + RL)        // model parms
#define R_SOFFS (RCS + RDS + RCU + RDU + RL + RM) // simuln parms
#define R_COUNT (RCS + RDS + RCU + RDU + RL + RM + RS)
```

These macros are then used as in this code fragment, which copies the model parameters into the corresponding GRAMPC array:

```
for (fmi2Integer i = 0; i < RM; i++)
    ((typeRNum*)userparam)[i] = realBuffer[R_MOFFS + i + 1];
grampc_init(&grampc, userparam);
```

In file *driver.c*, a few GRAMPC structures are initialized as global variables, others in the init() function.

The execution of one simulation step is performed by function tick(). This function has one argument, communicationStepSize, that is the duration of the interval between two communication occurrences between master and FMU. This duration may be changed by the master as its duration is passed to the FMU in the call to fmi2DoStep(). The tick() function assigns this value to the GRAMPC simulation parameter dt:

```
grampc_setparam_real(grampc, "dt", communicationStepSize);
```

Then, the values passed by the master with *Set* operations are copied into the grampc structure:

```
for (fmi2Integer i = 0; i < RCS; i++)
    grampc->sol->xnext[i] = realBuffer[i + 1];
grampc_setparam_real_vector(grampc, "x0", grampc->sol->xnext);
for (fmi2Integer i = 0; i < RDS; i++)
    xdes[i] = realBuffer[RCS + i + 1];
grampc_setparam_real_vector(grampc, "xdes", xdes);
```

A GRAMPC simulation step can then be executed by calling grampc_run(grampc). At the end of the simulation step, arrays grampc->sol->xnext and grampc->sol->unext contain the updated values of the state and output variables, respectively.

Function tick() copies the output variables to the realBuffer array, where the co-simulation master retrieves them with a call to fmi2GetReal:

```
for (fmi2Integer i = 0; i < RCU + RDU; i++)
    realBuffer[RCS + RDS + 1 + i] = grampc->sol->unext[i];
```

4.4 Templates for GRAMPC-Based Co-simulation

The regular structure of GRAMPC-based applications makes it possible to define templates to adapt the Driver module to different projects. The Handlebars templating language [22] was used to define templates for files *driver.c* and *driver.h*. A Handlebars template is a text containing *expressions* delimited by Handlebars brackets '{{' and '}}'. The simplest expressions are identifiers that a Handlebars tool will replace with text supplied as an input in JSON format. For example, the text "#define NX {{NX}}" with the substitution ""NX": "4"" produces the code "#define NX 4".

As discussed in the previous sections, the application-specific parts of the Driver module depend on a number of constant values, such as array sizes and number of variables included in various groups. Hence, the template for *driver.h* contains macro definitions for those constants.

4.5 Guidelines for FMU Generation

This section summarizes the procedure used for the robotic arm case study, expressing it in more general terms to make it applicable to different situations.

First of all, it is necessary to identify the functions $\mathcal{F}_i$ that must be executed at each co-simulation step, and the functions f_{ij} on which they depend. In our example, only one function, grampc_run(), is called at each simulation step, and it depends on the various model-specific functions, such as ffct() or lfct(). Functions $\mathcal{F}_i$ are then called in the implementation of fmi2DoStep().

Then, the model variables and parameters that must be accessed by the co-simulation master must be identified and grouped according to their FMI type. The type groups are listed in the model description file according to the method exposed in the example to access variables by their value references. The cardinality of each group is used to determine the size of the FMI buffers in the implementation of value-passing FMI API functions. Subgrouping may be used to further classify variables and parameters according to their usage in the application, in particular in loop statements.

A next step consists in separating initialization code from "steady state" execution and termination code. These three sets of operations will be collected in the implementations of the FMI API functions for initialization, simulation, and finalization, respectively. In our example, the code for these implementations constitutes the functions init(), tick(), and finish(), respectively.

The FMU structure is then composed of:

- an *API wrapper* module implementing the FMI API. This module may be made of two submodules, an application-independent *façade* module implementing the FMI in terms of a lower-level generic interface, like Fmiapi in our example, and an *implementation* module like the Driver module, implementing the generic interface both with application-dependent operations, like init() and tick(), and application-independent ones, like getreal();

– an *application* module containing the core of the application code, unchanged
with respect to the code produced for monolithic simulation, such as the
problem module in the example, consisting in the `probfct.c` file.

5   Robotic Arm Co-simulation

This section shows how the FMU generation technique proposed in this work
can be applied to the robotic arm example.

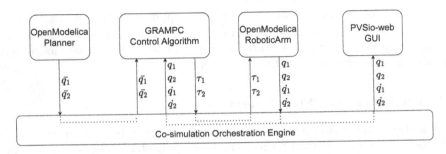

Fig. 5. Co-simulation architecture of the FMUs.

Figure 5 shows the architecture of the FMUs involved in the co-simulation:

– the `Planner` FMU generates the desired angles $q_{1,r}, q_{2,r}$ to drive the robotic
arm towards a predefined circle;
– the `Control Algorithm` FMU takes as input the desired angles $(q_{1,r}, q_{2,r})$
and the actual state of the robotic arm $(q_1, q_2, \dot{q}_1, \dot{q}_2)$ and produces as output
the torques (τ_1, τ_2) required to drive the robotic arm;
– the `RoboticArm` FMU takes the two torques (τ_1, τ_2) as input and evolves
accordingly the state of the robotic arm $(q_1, q_2, \dot{q}_1, \dot{q}_2)$;
– the `Graphical User Interface (GUI)` FMU takes the state of the robotic
arm $(q_1, q_2, \dot{q}_1, \dot{q}_2)$ as input and updates a graphic interface.

`Planner` and `RoboticArm` have been modeled with OpenModelica, which
provides a native FMU export feature. `GUI` has been modeled with PVSio-web,
whose FMU export feature has been implemented by the authors and discussed
in [24]. Finally, `Control Algorithm` has been modeled with GRAMPC and its
FMU export feature is the main contribution of this work.

All co-simulations in this work use the fixed-step co-simulation algorithm,
with a stepsize of 0.01 s, and last 100 simulated seconds. Figure 6 shows three
snapshots from a co-simulation run. In particular, Fig. 6a shows the initial position of the hand distant from the desired shape. Figure 6b shows the position at
the time the hand reaches the circle and Fig. 6c shows one position during the
operation following the path in counter-clockwise direction. The desired circle
has radius 5 cm, and is centered at coordinates $(-5, 10)$ cm. The first joint is
fixed at $(0, 0)$. The links are 10 cm long.

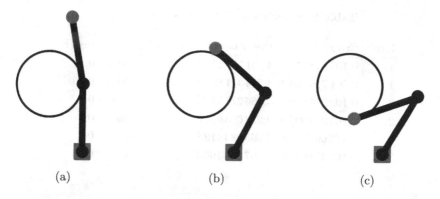

(a)   (b)   (c)

Fig. 6. GUI representation during a co-simulation.

Table 2. Part of results of DSE for the first analysis.

Rank	MET (ms)	AET (ms)	Thor (s)	Initial q_1 (rad)
1	5	2.2239	1	3.14
1	6	2.216	1	0
2	5	2.294	1	1.57
3	6	2.3565	1	−1.57
4	10	5.1558	2	1.57
4	11	5.0934	2	0
5	10	5.1706	2	3.14
6	14	5.1934	2	−1.57
7	14	8.0477	3	0
8	14	8.1245	3	1.57
8	22	8.0898	3	−1.57
9	15	8.1864	3	3.14

5.1   DSE Results

The Design Space Exploration feature of the INTO-CPS application has been applied to the analysis of the robotic arm.

A first set of experiments identifies the combinations of parameters that satisfy a safety constraint of the system: the control algorithm must provide the commands within 10 ms, which is the sampling rate used by the controller to read the actual state of the system. A set of twenty experiments have been designed with five values of the GRAMPC algorithm parameter Thor ($\{1, 2, 3, 4, 5\}$ s), which represents the size of the prediction window, and four values for the initial position q_1 of the robotic arm ($\{0, \pi/2, \pi, -\pi/2\}$ rad).

For each experiment, Maximum Execution Time (MET) and Average Execution Time (AET) are computed. The results show that (i) the initial position q_1 of the fixed joint does not affect the execution time; (ii) with a value

Table 3. Results of DSE for the second analysis.

Rank	Error	Power consumption (J)	x_c (m)	m_2 (Kg)
1	0.105 344 958	4.261 776 112 1	−0.05	0.2
1	0.101 716 064 2	4.264 371 893 8	−0.05	0.05
2	0.102 244 699 8	4.266 271 048 1	−0.05	0.1
2	0.165 053 937 3	4.263 693 928 6	0.05	0.2
2	0.163 665 917 8	4.265 083 412 8	0.05	0.1
3	0.163 454 011 6	4.267 103 760 4	0.05	0.05

of Thor less than or equal to 3 s, AET satisfies the GRAMPC control algorithm constraint; and (iii) MET satisfies the constraint only with a value equal to 1 s. As a consequence, for safety critical applications it is mandatory to have a value of 1 s for Thor. Table 2 reports the results for the first three values of Thor.

A second set of experiments identifies the combinations of parameters that provide the best trade-off between error and power consumption. The error is computed by averaging the instant error, calculated as $(q_1 - q_{1,r})^2 + (q_2 - q_{2,r})^2$, over the total simulation time. The power consumption is computed by summing up the instant total kinetic energy K, see Eq. 6.

$$K = \frac{1}{2}J_1\dot{q}_1{}^2 + \frac{1}{2}J_2(\dot{q}_1 + \dot{q}_2)^2 + \frac{1}{2}m_1\dot{q}_1{}^2a_1^2 + \frac{1}{2}m_2a_2^2(\dot{q}_1 + \dot{q}_2)^2 + \tag{6}$$
$$m_2\dot{q}_1(\dot{q}_1 + \dot{q}_2)a_1a_2\cos(q_2)$$

A further objective is to evaluate the response of GRAMPC when the model used by GRAMPC is slightly different from the physical process. In this analysis, the value of the mass of the second link (m_2) used in the OpenModelica model has been modified to values $\{0.1, 0.2, 0.05\}$ Kg, without changing the GRAMPC model (0.1 Kg). Moreover, the analysis has been performed for different x-coordinates of the center of the desired circle (x_c), from −0.05 to 0.05 m.

The results are shown in Table 3 where we may notice that when the x-coordinate of the center of the circle is 0.05 the error is higher; this is consistent with the constraints embedded in the GRAMPC model that limit q_2 between 0.17 (10°) and 2.97 (170°). With these constraints the bottom right part of the circle centered in (5, 10) is not reachable. On the other side, changes to m_2 have a low impact on error and power consumption, thus suggesting that the GRAMPC algorithm is resilient to small variations of this parameter.

6   Conclusions

This work shows a general process for the generation of FMUs. The process has been applied to the GRAMPC framework on a robotic arm as a running example and the generated FMU has been co-simulated together with an Open-Modelica model with a simple task of drawing a circle. Through the design space exploration feature, safe values for the prediction window of the MPC have been derived. Moreover, it has been shown that the DSE tool can be used to compute the impact on error and power consumption, varying the circle position on the Cartesian plane and one link mass of the robotic arm. The generalization of the results obtained on the robotic arm requires the specification of a campaign of extensive simulations to cover more environmental operational conditions.

As future work, the implementation of other FMI APIs, as `fmi2GetFMUstate` and `fmi2SetFMUstate`, could be useful to support complex master algorithms that involve step negotiation and algebraic loops.

Further, FMU generation will have to be updated in order to comply with the recently released FMI 3.0 specification [11]. The innovations most closely related to the issues addressed in this paper are a different type system and multi-dimensional variables.

The numeric types in FMI 3.0 are *Float32*, *Float64*, *Int8*, *UInt8*, *Int16*, *UInt16*, *Int32*, *UInt32*, *Int64*, and *UInt64*, so that two sizes of machine representations can be specified for floating-point variables, and four sizes for signed and unsigned integers (or, more precisely, for integers and naturals). This change, in addition to array variables, has led to a different syntax for variable declarations in the configuration file. In particular, the declarations of array variables contain *Dimension* clauses that specify the number of sub-arrays (e.g., rows or columns) indexed by each dimension. For example, an array A of 64-bit floating-point elements, with three rows and two columns, could be declared [11] as

```
<Float64 name="A" valueReference="2" causality="parameter"
variability="tunable"
  start="0.0 0.1 1.0 1.1 2.0 2.1">
  <Dimension start="3"/>
  <Dimension start="2"/>
</Float64>
```

The simple procedure, introduced in this paper, to map the value references used by the co-simulation master to the indices for the local buffers in the FMU will have to be adapted to the above changes, and serialization and deserialization algorithms will be needed to convert between one-dimensional indices in the buffers and multi-dimensional indices in the data structures used in the application-specific code.

References

1. Bernardeschi, C., et al.: Co-simulation of a model predictive control system for automotive applications. In: Bernardeschi, C., et al. (eds.) Software Engineering and Formal Methods. Lecture Notes in Computer Science, pp. 204–220. Springer, Cham (2022). https://doi.org/10.1007/978-3-031-12429-7_15
2. Bernardeschi, C., et al.: Cross-level co-simulation and verification of an automatic transmission control on embedded processor. In: Cleophas, L., Massink, M. (eds.) SEFM 2020. LNCS, vol. 12524, pp. 263–279. Springer, Cham (2021). https://doi.org/10.1007/978-3-030-67220-1_20

3. Bernardeschi, C., Dini, P., Domenici, A., Palmieri, M., Saponara, S.: Formal verification and co-simulation in the design of a synchronous motor control algorithm. Energies **13**(16), 4057 (2020). https://doi.org/10.3390/en13164057
4. Bernardeschi, C., Domenici, A., Masci, P.: A PVS-simulink integrated environment for model-based analysis of cyber-physical systems. IEEE Trans. Software Eng. **44**(6), 512–533 (2018). https://doi.org/10.1109/TSE.2017.2694423
5. Blochwitz, T., et al.: Functional mockup interface 2.0: the standard for tool independent exchange of simulation models. In: Proceedings of the 9th International MODELICA Conference, Munich, Germany, 3–5 September 2012, pp. 173–184. no. 76 in Linköping Electronic Conference Proceedings, Linköping University Electronic Press (2012). https://doi.org/10.3384/ecp12076173
6. Charif, A., Busnot, G., Mameesh, R.H., Sassolas, T., Ventroux, N.: Fast virtual prototyping for embedded computing systems design and exploration. In: Chillet, D. (ed.) Proceedings of the Rapid Simulation and Performance Evaluation: Methods and Tools, RAPIDO 2019, Valencia, Spain, 21-23 January 2019, pp. 3:1–3:8. ACM (2019). https://doi.org/10.1145/3300189.3300192
7. Dini, P., Saponara, S.: Model-based design of an improved electric drive controller for high-precision applications based on feedback linearization technique. Electronics **10**(23) (2021). https://doi.org/10.3390/electronics10232954, https://www.mdpi.com/2079-9292/10/23/2954
8. Dini, P., Saponara, S.: Processor-in-the-loop validation of a gradient descent-based model predictive control for assisted driving and obstacles avoidance applications. IEEE Access **10**, 67958–67975 (2022). https://doi.org/10.1109/ACCESS.2022.3186020
9. Documentation, S.: Simulation and model-based design (2020). https://www.mathworks.com/products/simulink.html
10. Domenici, A., Fagiolini, A., Palmieri, M.: Integrated simulation and formal verification of a simple autonomous vehicle. In: Cerone, A., Roveri, M. (eds.) SEFM 2017. LNCS, vol. 10729, pp. 300–314. Springer, Cham (2018). https://doi.org/10.1007/978-3-319-74781-1_21
11. Functional Mock-up Interface Specification, version 3.0, 2022-05-10 . https://fmi-standard.org/docs/3.0/ (2022)
12. Functional Mock-up Interface for Model Exchange and Co-Simulation. Technical report, Modelica Association (2020). http://fmi-standard.org/
13. Fritzson, P., et al.: The openmodelica modeling, simulation, and development environment. In: 46th Conference on Simulation and Modelling of the Scandinavian Simulation Society (SIMS2005) (2005)
14. Gomes, C., et al.: Application of model-based testing to dynamic evaluation of functional mockup units. In: Proceedings of the American Modelica Conference 2020, no. 16, pp. 149–158 (2020). https://doi.org/10.3384/ecp20169149
15. Gomes, C., Thule, C., Broman, D., Larsen, P.G., Vangheluwe, H.: Co-simulation: a survey. ACM Comput. Surv. (CSUR) **51**(3), 1–33 (2018)
16. Grüne, L., Pannek, J.: Nonlinear Model Predictive Control. CCE, Springer, Cham (2017). https://doi.org/10.1007/978-3-319-46024-6
17. He, W., Gao, H., Zhou, C., Yang, C., Li, Z.: Reinforcement learning control of a flexible two-link manipulator: an experimental investigation. IEEE Trans. Syst. Man Cybernet. Syst. **51**, 7326–7336 (2020). https://doi.org/10.1109/TSMC.2020.2975232
18. Käpernick, B., Graichen, K.: The gradient based nonlinear model predictive control software grampc. In: Proceedings 2014 European Control Conference (ECC), pp. 1170–1175 (2014). https://doi.org/10.1109/ECC.2014.6862353

19. Larsen, P.G., et al.: Integrated tool chain for model-based design of cyber-physical systems: the INTO-CPS project. In: 2016 2nd International Workshop on Modelling, Analysis, and Control of Complex CPS (CPS Data), pp. 1–6, April 2016. https://doi.org/10.1109/CPSData.2016.7496424

20. Lee, D., Lim, M.C., Negash, L., Choi, H.L.: EPPY based building co-simulation for model predictive control of HVAC optimization. In: 2018 18th International Conference on Control, Automation and Systems (ICCAS), pp. 1051–1055 (2018)

21. Legaard, C., Tola, D., Schranz, T., Macedo, H., Larsen, P.: A universal mechanism for implementing functional mock-up units. In: SIMULTECH, pp. 121–129 (2021). https://doi.org/10.5220/0010577601210129

22. Mardan, A.: Template engines: pug and handlebars. In: Practical Node.js, pp. 113–163. Apress, Berkeley, CA (2018). https://doi.org/10.1007/978-1-4842-3039-8_4

23. Palmieri, M., Bernardeschi, C., Masci, P.: Co-simulation of semi-autonomous systems: the line follower robot case study. In: Cerone, A., Roveri, M. (eds.) SEFM 2017. LNCS, vol. 10729, pp. 423–437. Springer, Cham (2018). https://doi.org/10.1007/978-3-319-74781-1_29

24. Palmieri, M., Bernardeschi, C., Masci, P.: A framework for FMI-based co-simulation of human–machine interfaces. Softw. Syst. Model. 19(3), 601–623 (2019). https://doi.org/10.1007/s10270-019-00754-9

25. Palmieri, M., Macedo, H.D.: Automatic generation of functional mock-up units from formal specifications. In: Camara, J., Steffen, M. (eds.) SEFM 2019. LNCS, vol. 12226, pp. 27–33. Springer, Cham (2020). https://doi.org/10.1007/978-3-030-57506-9_3

26. Thule, C., Lausdahl, K., Larsen, P.G.: Overture FMU: export VDM-RT models as tool-wrapper FMUs. In: Proceedings of the 16th overture workshop, School of Computing Science Technical report Series, vol. 1524, pp. 23–38 (2018)

27. Von Wissel, D., Talon, V., Thomas, V., Grangier, B., Lansky, L., Uchanski, M.: Linking model predictive control (MPC) and system simulation tools to support automotive system architecture choices. In: 8th European Congress on Embedded Real Time Software and Systems (ERTS 2016). TOULOUSE, France, Jan 2016. https://hal.archives-ouvertes.fr/hal-01289503

28. Yakub, F., Mori, Y.: Model predictive control for car vehicle dynamics system - comparative study. In: 2013 IEEE Third International Conference on Information Science and Technology (ICIST), pp. 172–177 (2013). https://doi.org/10.1109/ICIST.2013.6747530

A Co-simulation-Based System Using Vico for Marine Operation

Zizheng Liu[1] , Yingguang Chu[2] , Guoyuan Li[1] , and Houxiang Zhang[1]( )

[1] The Department of Ocean Operations and Civil Engineering, Norwegian University of
Science and Technology, Larsgårdsvegen 2, 6009 Ålesund, Norway
{zizheng.liu,guoyuan.li,hozh}@ntnu.no
[2] Department of Mechanical and Electrical Engineering, University of Southern Denmark,
Alsion 2, 6400 Sønderborg, Denmark
ychu@sdu.dk

Abstract. Marine operations are becoming more and more demanding. Efficient modeling and analysis of marine operations under environmental effects, especially in high sea states, will provide a means to improve operational safety. Traditional modeling and analysis are often carried out based on establishing the combined equations of the multi-body system. However, modeling, simulation and analysis of sub-systems may be performed in different software tools or require extensive derivation. It is inconvenient to vary the system configuration regardless of manufacturing design or behavior analysis perspectives. Co-simulation as an emerging technology enables the reusing and sharing of models so that different sub-systems can be modeled independently but simulated together. In this study, a system based on a co-simulation platform - Vico is proposed, which enables the digitalization of marine operations from modeling, configuration to simulation. The system consists of multiple sub-models of the ship, the marine crane and their coupling component, which are all converted and exported as functional mock-up units (FMUs). Various scenario settings such as environmental effect, ship maneuver and crane payload can be configured for the simulation of specific marine operations. Taking the research vessel Gunnerus as the testbed, two case studies about the impacts from the environment and a shipboard crane on marine operations are conducted. The simulation results verify the effectiveness of the marine operation system. The system could also be a foundation for further research on onboard support of marine operations.

Keywords: Co-simulation · Marine crane · Marine operation · FMI/FMU

1 Introduction

Marine cranes are indispensable for the modern maritime industry. They are configured on a wide range of vessels and platforms, which conduct a variety of operational

The author would like to thank China Scholarship Council for funding his research at Norwegian University of Science and Technology.

P. Masci et al. (Eds.): SEFM 2022 Collocated Workshops, LNCS 13765, pp. 228–241, 2023.
https://doi.org/10.1007/978-3-031-26236-4_20

tasks such as lifting, towing, and transferring loads between shores and decks. Generally, marine crane systems are large and work in a more unstable environment than land-based cranes. In spite of the positive effect from the dynamic positioning system (DP) on the ship's behaviors, the marine crane operation is still a challenging task involving load sway, positioning accuracy, suppression, collision avoidance, maneuvering safety and many other issues due to the tight coupling between the vessel and the crane on board, with the non-negligible impact of waves, currents and wind as external disturbances. These complex operating conditions make it harder to guarantee safety and achieve efficiency at the same time which is a core demand for maximizing the benefits. Therefore, it is becoming increasingly important and necessary for the maritime industry to work on how to increase the safety of marine crane operations.

Over recent years, there has been a growing interest in developing and employing digital twins, big data and cloud computing for maritime industry systems design, ship intelligence and operational services. Digitization has stepped up as a critical aspect into enabling the maritime industry to be more innovative, efficient and future-proof in operating [1]. Growing access to advanced technologies for designing and evaluating system performance, safety, and structural integrity is generating a range of digital models of both vessels and their sub-systems. NTNU Aalesund has been conducting digital twins of maritime systems and operations research for years [2]. For example, digital twins for vessel life cycle service were developed as an open virtual simulator of next-generation marine industrial infrastructure for overall system design, system configuration and operational performance verification, while enabling full life-cycle service support and system behavior prediction [3]. Such digitalized and intelligent systems are now also being increasingly focused on and realized by many maritime equipment suppliers, companies as well as research institutes such as Palfinger and SINTEF.

The digitalization for marine cranes has also largely advanced the support of its offshore operations, whether it involves stages of design, testing and analysis for optimization, as well as control-related areas [4]. The last few decades have seen more and more modeling and simulation approaches being studied. However, the marine crane system is an interdisciplinary integral involving such as mechanical, hydraulic and dynamic fields. It is challenging to develop models of complex multi-domain systems and to handle the simulations of dynamic models. Generally speaking, it is difficult to describe a complex system model with a single tool or in an individual environment. Co-simulation enables us to assemble and integrate different components by defining their interfaces and communication ways. As a result, different sub-systems can be modeled by different tools, especially for those that require specialized tools provided by the manufacturer to achieve. In this manner, a large complex system can be disassembled.

The development of model exchange and co-simulation provides the feasibility of developing tool-independent interface standards for complex information-physical systems. In such a co-simulation environment, the digital crane can be built as virtual prototyping by different units such as the dynamics unit and the kinematics unit, which can provide a platform for system analysis, crane operation evaluation and some other related research or testing [5].

In this paper, a co-simulation-based system is presented for simulation, testing, analysis of ship-crane operations and other advanced support. The vessel and crane Functional

Mock-up Units (FMU) are exported using the standard Functional Mock-up Interface (FMI) and constructed under the co-simulation platform VICO. Some system structure and parameterization details towards realizing the construction of the vessel and the crane are implemented. The ship R/V Gunnerus is employed as the testbed to verify the effectiveness of the presented system, based on which case studies are given discussion with result analysis.

The contributions of the present study are summarized as follows:

- The components of the crane are developed and the communications among the sub-models are built.
- The marine operation system is constructed by integrating the ship and the crane components as well as the motion and force transfer.
- Two case studies are implemented based on the marine operation system to simulate the environmental configuration and crane operations. The results verify the effectiveness of the marine operation system.

The rest of the paper is organized as follows. Section 2 introduces some related work from the viewpoint of modeling and co-simulation. An implementation description of the co-simulation-based system is given in Sect. 3. In Sect. 4, case studies are implemented with results discussed using the testbed Gunnerus which is operated by the Norwegian University of Science and Technology (NTNU) and serves as the test ship. Finally, conclusions and some future works are drawn in Sect. 5.

2 Related Work

2.1 Modeling

The modeling of cranes is challenging due to the excessive number of degrees of freedom in the system and the underactuated characteristic of the crane control [6]. Establishing an accurate dynamics model is the basis for studying system characteristics, designing control strategies, new components testing and even operator training purposes. There are many methods used to derive dynamic equations for mechanical systems, all of which result in equivalent sets of equations. As one of the more classic methods, Newton-Euler method is based on the interpretation of Newton's Second Law of Motion describing dynamic systems in terms of force and momentum. But the recursion of Newton-Euler method requires much formula derivation and calculation [7]. Different from Newton-Euler method, Lagrange method computes the motion equations from the viewpoint of energy, which can avoid derivative causality problems. In recent years, many researchers have employed Lagrange equations to implement dynamics modeling of cranes [8, 9], since it can provide an elegant clean form that supports better for the following system control.

The modeling of offshore operating systems is not limited to the mechanical dynamics of the crane, but also includes many other fields, such as the hydraulic system of the crane [10], the hydraulic system of the winch [11] and the hydrodynamics between the vessel and the waves [12], etc. There are also many different software tools to support the modeling of different systems. Software such as MATLAB/Simulink, SimulationX and

20-sim enable modeling and simulation to be carried out in a homogeneous environment [4, 13], which encourages the development of the toolboxes and packages. However, for modeling and simulation of complex multi-disciplinary systems like marine cranes, a homogeneous environment is no longer sufficient in some cases. At this level, one other trend comes up, that is, to distribute the modeling of subsystems after decomposing a complex system into several subsystems, which enables different systems modeling to be implemented in their corresponding specialized software tools or provided by the manufacturers. Nonetheless, there are still challenges regarding the interaction between different sub-models and the communication between different simulation tools.

2.2 Co-simulation

The development of modern engineering has led to the emergence of numerous complex systems, which are composed of physical, electronic, mechanical, software, network and other multi-disciplinary construction, which is why currently many systems must be built and optimized to be multi-threaded. In most cases, participants or suppliers develop the tools in their fields, which is a partial solution, not a holistic one, from which the idea of the co-simulation technology comes. There used to be no single simulation tool that is applicable for all purposes, and complex heterogeneous models with components from a couple of diverse fields may need to be developed in separate, domain-specific tools. A co-simulation enables model reusing, sharing and also the fusion of simulation domains compared to traditional monolithic simulations.

There are two standards for co-simulation, referred to as the High Level Architecture (HLA) [14] and the Functional Mock-up Interface (FMI) [15]. They are separately used for discrete event co-simulation and continuous time co-simulation. According to the survey from Schweiger [16], the FMI standard is considered the most promising standard for continuous time, discrete event and hybrid co-simulation. Based on the FMI standard, some open-source co-simulation frameworks have been developed with supporting the System Structure and Parameterization (SSP) [17] standard which is a tool-independent standard describing a complete system consisting of one or more components (e.g. FMUs), including their parameterization. For example, Libcosim is a cross-platform C/C++ library that supports co-simulation design and execution. It is developed based on the Open Simulation Platform (OSP) [18], which builds an ecosystem that enables the maritime industry can perform co-simulations and share simulation models with high efficiency and safety.

In recent years, FMI-based co-simulation has been applied to various research in the maritime domain. Hassani et al. [19] present four relevant cases of applications to demonstrate the use of co-simulation technology in the maritime industry in their paper. All the case studies are simulated using the Functional Mock-up Interface (FMI) standard based on the framework of Coral which is an open-source co-simulation software developed in the project. Chu et al. [20] present an object-oriented modeling (OOM) approach to model marine operation systems. A virtual prototyping (VP) framework is developed with the functional mock-up interface (FMI) standard. Based on the VP framework, an active heave compensated winch with a hybrid drive system and secondary control strategy are proposed where the simulation configuration and the customer interface are achieved by web technology through the WebSocket protocol.

The application of co-simulation makes it innovative progress in many research fields. The development makes it possible to carry out the study of coupling issues by disassembling complex systems into subsystems avoiding numerous calculations. However, almost all of the co-simulations are being carried out at the cost of losing much accuracy, especially in the cases where algorithms need to be incorporated to optimize the simulation efficiency. This is one of the currently foreseeable challenges in co-simulation. It is also important that benchmarks for model simplification and simulation performance should be established according to different simulation objectives since the simulation accuracy and stability are critical for FMI-based co-simulation.

3 Marine Operation System

3.1 System Structure

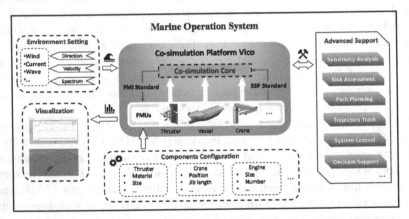

Fig. 1. The co-simulation-based system developed for marine operations

The present system in Fig. 1 is based on the co-simulation platform Vico. Vico is an advanced co-simulation framework that is developed based on the Entity-Component-System software architecture [3]. As one of the co-simulation platforms, Vico not only supports the FMI standard but also supports the SSP standard, which makes it possible that any type of vessel and crane even other onboard machinery can be simulated based on the system as long as the components can be modeled with defining the communication interfaces.

The most notable advantage of the present system is that in such a way all the FMUs exported by the FMI standard can be configured as desired using the SSP standard. For example, in the thruster model, the type, material and size of the thrusters can be modified; similarly, in the crane model, the position of the crane on the deck, the postures of the crane arms, the parameters of the cable and the payload can also be modified. This will be particularly beneficial for manufacturers to perform crane design, as well as test the performance of the system with various configurations. Since the system model is modularized by means of the co-simulation standard, the integrated model is more like a black box for the co-simulation platform and its inside construction or programming will not be exposed, which can protect the intellectual property of its owner.

One of the important factors affecting the safety of marine cranes is the sea state conditions during offshore operations. Regarding this issue, the system is also able to configure the environment setting where wind, waves, and currents can be manipulated to simulate the real sea state according to the offshore conditions, such as the velocity and the direction of the wind, the spectrum and the time of the wave, etc. What is more, it even provides the possibility, that is, to use the collected real sea state data as one of the inputs to the system, which makes the simulation with more fidelity different from the modeling of waves. In addition, diverse virtual scenarios can be generated to simulate the onboard operation of the crane, which makes it possible to analyze the behavior and interaction between the crane and the vessel. With further support, the system can contribute to advanced applications in various aspects like risk modeling, system automation and control.

3.2 Key Components

The present system in this research is conducted for performing the co-simulation of the marine crane offshore operations. Therefore, the following part introduces the key components including ship maneuvering, crane operation as well as motion and force transfer.

Ship Maneuvering. The engaged ship components for the maneuvering simulation are several detailed sub-models, such as the dynamic positioning controller, the thrusters, etc. As shown in Fig. 2, each block represents a single independent FMU, and the connections for the ship maneuvering are presented. There are too many interfaces inside the components, the details are not presented here.

In particular, the vessel is modeled in six degrees of freedom (6-DoF) with waves, implemented according to the unified non-linear model subjected to waves, wind and currents from Fossen [21]. The *VesselModel* was developed by SINTEF Ocean in the SimVal project [22]. It is mainly to solve the equations of motion containing the vessel's restoring force, mass, resistance and some other hydrodynamics information. The *Observer* is to compute the movement direction and the speed to get the position difference with time, and also it can filter short frequency waves for the DP system. The *DPController* can make sure the ship can stop at a relatively ideal fixed location in the world frame. The *Allocator* will get the direction and speed information from the *Observer*, and then allocate the forces to the thrusters. There are three thrusters with their own actuators, separately a port-side azimuth thruster, a starboard-side azimuth thruster, and a tunnel thruster, where a 3DOF force can be produced in heave, surge and sway directions. In the *PowerPlant*, a marine power plant system is provided with two equally large gensets.

Crane Operation. There are two strategies for crane operation: the active manipulation of the crane to control the tip and the feedback control with the compensation controller. Inside the model of the crane, there are defined input interfaces of all the joints for all kinds of operations depending on the type of the crane. For example, the users can set

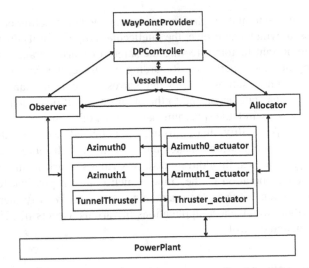

Fig. 2. Relationship of sub-model components for ship maneuvering

three interfaces for the mechanism with 3 DOF like RRP or RPR serial chain, or more interfaces for structures with more DOFs. The other strategy is to operate the crane with the controller with algorithms as the users desired. Normally heave compensation controllers and tip compensation controllers are applied in most of the research.

Figure 3 presents the components connection of a specific example for crane operations. In the *Crane*, the defined input interface contains four typical degrees of freedom of a Palfinger crane, where craneSetPoint1 [1] is the interface for slewing reference speed of the crane base, and craneSetPoint1 [2]- craneSetPoint1 [4] separately are the interfaces for the hydraulic actuator reference speed. In this way, by inputting the desired value of the above parameters, the crane can perform lifting, lowering and transferring operations in a certain operating space. The other four FMUs around the crane model are to perform control strategies. The *VesselModel* here provides information about the ship's motion, i.e., the speed in DOF of heave and rolling. *TipSetPoint* provides the desired velocity of the tip for the crane as a reference value for its control. There are two modes of compensation control. *TipController* is the developed controller under crane compensation mode, and *AHCController* is the developed controller under winch compensation mode. These two different strategies enable data analysis of the system response by comparing the cases with and without controllers; moreover, it is an indispensable basis for advanced controller development and onboard support.

Motion and Force Transfer. During crane operations, there is a coupling relationship between the ship and the crane that interacts. The center of gravity of the crane system will change due to the change in the posture of the crane joints and cylinders as well as the different positions of the payload at different times, which results in a change in the inertia matrix of the vessel. Therefore, we consider the conservative forces such as gravity generated by the crane and payload as external forces and apply them to different points of the vessel hull. The transfer relations of force and motion containing interfaces are shown in Fig. 4. In detail, the diagram specifics the relative position of the

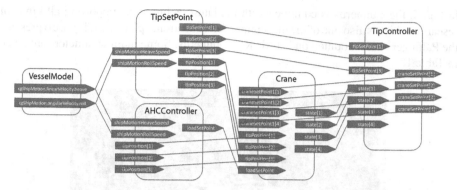

Fig. 3. Interfaces connections among sub-model components of a Palfinger crane

ship's center of gravity and the crane's center of gravity. The displacements and angular displacements of the ship in three different directions caused by the waves are also the movements of the crane base. The forces generated by the crane and the payload as well as their points of attack are reflected in the forces applied to the hull in different directions.

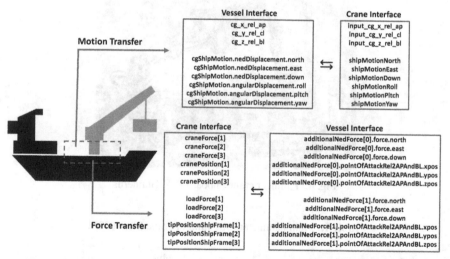

Fig. 4. Relationship of motion and force transfer between the vessel and the crane

4   Case Study

In this section, we introduce the configuration of R/V Gunnerus where the purpose is to employ the vessel as the testbed to test the present system with two cases. As shown in Fig. 5, the Gunnerus is equipped with the latest technology supporting all kinds of research, which is also one of the most important educational platforms. Figure 6 presents the Palfinger crane mounted on NTNU R/V Gunnerus. Some main parameters are given in Table 1.

Fig. 5. NTNU research vessel R/V Gunnerus [23]

Fig. 6. Palfinger crane onboard R/V Gunnerus

Table 1. Main parameters of Palfinger crane PK65002M

Parameter	Value
Max. lifting moment	62.0 mt
Max. lifting capacity	22000 kg
Max. hydraulic outreach	20.4 m
Slewing torque with 1 gear	4.5 mt
Stabilizer spread (std)	8.6 m

(continued)

Table 1. (*continued*)

Parameter	Value
Max. operating pressure	365 bar
Dead weight (std)	5040 kg

4.1 Case 1: Crane with Payload in Different Environment Conditions

In the first case, different environmental conditions are set as input to analyze the rolling motion of the ship, where we consider the direction of the environmental loads including wave, current and wind are varied from six different angles of three different sea state levels. The crane keeps in a fixed posture without any operation but with a 700 kg payload. The DP controller is activated at the 50s from the start of the simulation.

Table 2. Parameters of three sea states in co-simulation environment setting

Sea state	Wave			Current	Wind
	Height	Peak period	Spectrum	Velocity	Velocity
Slight	0.5 m	10 s	2 m²/Hz	0.1 m/s	1 m/s
Moderate	1.25 m	10 s	2 m²/Hz	0.2 m/s	3 m/s
Tough	2.5 m	10 s	2 m²/Hz	0.3 m/s	5 m/s

Figure 7 shows the eight different cases of environmental loads direction angles. Table 2 shows the parameters of three sea states in the co-simulation environment setting. The ship roll angle responses of the ship are processed to box-plot in Fig. 8, where it can be seen that the roll angle domains vary from the different directions of environmental loads. The balanced roll angle is not 0 but a positive angle, which indicates the center

Fig. 7. Eight different environmental conditions of wave and current direction

of gravity changes due to the installation of the crane. However, the amplitudes of the roll angles increase apparently with the increase of the sea state. The ship gets the most violent roll motion when the direction of environmental loads is 45° or 315°, while the mildest roll motion appears at the time the foreside of the ship has the same or opposite direction as the environmental loads.

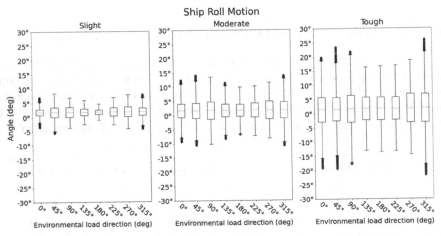

Fig. 8. Roll angles of the ship motion in different environmental conditions

4.2 Case 2: Crane Operations in Waves

In Case 2, we aim to simulate the crane operations in waves. Two Palfinger crane operations are defined in the scenario. The first operation is the slewing action of the crane base, and the second operation is the extension of the telescope cylinder. The animations of the operations are shown in Fig. 9. The environment parameters are set as the values of the slight state in Table 2. The direction of the environmental loads is 45°. The DP controller is also activated at the 50 s from the start of the simulation.

Fig. 9. Animations of the crane operation

As shown in Fig. 10., there are two operation commands for the crane actuators. At the 220 s from the start of the simulation, the slewing joint is given an operating signal to the positive direction lasting 60 s to the 280 s, with the result of the crane base slewing around 30°. The displacement of the crane tip relative to the hull coordinate frame in the north and east changes. Instead of remaining relatively stationary with the ship body, it is subjected to the environmental loads at sea and shows a simple harmonic motion. During this operation, the angle response of the ship roll motion decreases. After 40 s, the telescope cylinder starts to extend from its initial length of 1.2 m to around 5.5 m. The displacement of the crane tip in the north and east directions changes again. Instead of simple harmonic motion, it shows a linear change and finally stabilizes at the desired position. During the two operations, the displacement of the crane tip in the down direction keeps stable because it has the same motion frequency as the ship hull. In overall, the ship roll motion is subjected to the operations to some degree, which can be seen in the frequency of the roll angle response. The crane tip position response reflects the actions of the crane actuators from another perspective. The crane operation without controllers in waves is affected by the ship roll motion subjected to the sea

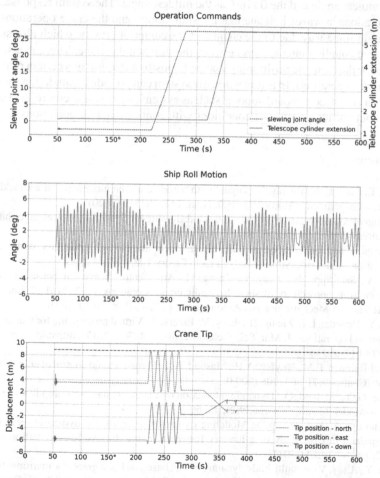

Fig. 10. Operation commands and system response of the ship and crane

state; meanwhile, it also has an impact on the ship motion in waves, which is a coupling interaction between each other.

5 Conclusion

In this paper, we presented a system based on the platform Vico, which is developed based on co-simulation technology. A marine operation system is constructed by functional mock-up units (FMUs) exported from sub-models. Two case studies are conducted from the perspective of testing the co-simulation system regarding the configuration of the components and scenarios. The results of the case studies show that the system can perform the simulation of marine operations including the environment configuration and marine crane operations, which verify the effectiveness of the system. The ship motion roll is subjected to the direction of the environmental loads with the 45°/135° as the most violent angle and the 0°/180° as the mildest angle. The system responses of the crane operations in waves indicate that the ship motion and the crane operations affect each other in some way due to the change of the center of gravity, which also supports that there are coupling interactions between the ship and the crane. This can also give a reference for the dynamic positioning system to position the ship in a certain orientation during marine operations. In future work, the system can provide a foundation for further research on advanced onboard support such as system decision and control by sensitive analysis under different offshore conditions with complex marine operations.

References

1. Moi, T., Cibicik, A., Rølvåg, T.: Digital twin based condition monitoring of a knuckle boom crane: an experimental study. Eng. Fail. Anal. **112**, 104517 (2020)
2. Intelligent Systems Lab @ NTNU Aalesund: Intelligent Systems Lab webpage. http://org.ntnu.no/intelligentsystemslab/
3. Hatledal, L.I., Chu, Y., Styve, A., Zhang, H.: Vico: an entity-component-system based co-simulation framework. Simul. Model. Pract. Theory **108**, 102243 (2021)
4. Chu, Y., Sanfilippo, F., Æsøy, V., Zhang, H.: An effective heave compensation and anti-sway control approach for offshore hydraulic crane operations. In: 2014 IEEE International Conference on Mechatronics and Automation, pp. 1282–1287. IEEE (2014)
5. Chu, Y., Hatledal, L.I., Zhang, H., Æsøy, V., Ehlers, S.: Virtual prototyping for maritime crane design and operations. J. Mar. Sci. Technol. **23**(4), 754–766 (2017). https://doi.org/10.1007/s00773-017-0509-z
6. Abdel-Rahman, E.M., Nayfeh, A.H., Masoud, Z.N.: Dynamics and control of cranes: a review. J. Vib. Control **9**(7), 863–908 (2003)
7. Tysse, G.O., Egeland, O.: Dynamic interaction of a heavy crane and a ship in wave motion. MIC—Model. Identif. Control **39**(2), 45–60 (2018)
8. La Hera, P.M., Morales, D.O.: Modeling dynamics of an electro-hydraulic servo actuated manipulator: a case study of a forestry forwarder crane. In: World Automation Congress 2012, pp. 1–6. IEEE (2012)
9. Chu, Y., Æsøy, V.: A multi-body dynamic model based on bond graph for maritime hydraulic crane operations. In: International Conference on Offshore Mechanics and Arctic Engineering, Vol. 56475. American Society of Mechanical Engineers (2015)

10. Chu, Y., Æsøy, V., Zhang, H., Bunes, O.: Modelling and simulation of an offshore hydraulic crane. In: ECMS, pp. 87–93 (2014)
11. Skjong, S., Pedersen, E.: Model-based control designs for offshore hydraulic winch systems. Ocean Eng. **121**, 224–238 (2016)
12. Weymouth, G.D., Yue, D.K.: Physics-based learning models for ship hydrodynamics. J. Ship Res. **57**(01), 1–12 (2013)
13. Almutairi, N.B., Zribi, M.: Sliding mode control of a three-dimensional overhead crane. J. Vib. Control **15**(11), 1679–1730 (2009)
14. Dahmann, J.S., Fujimoto, R.M., Weatherly, R.M.: The department of defense high level architecture. In: Proceedings of the 29th Conference on Winter Simulation, pp. 142–149 (1997)
15. Blockwitz, T., et al.: Functional mockup interface 2.0: the standard for tool independent exchange of simulation models. In: Proceedings (2012)
16. Schweiger, G., et al.: An empirical survey on co-simulation: promising standards, challenges and research needs. Simul. Model. Pract. Theory **95**, 148–163 (2019)
17. Köhler, J., Heinkel, H.M., Mai, P., Krasser, J., Deppe, M., Nagasawa, M.: Modelica-association-project system structure and parameterization–early insights. In: The First Japanese Modelica Conferences, no. 124, pp. 35–42. Linköping University Electronic Press (2016)
18. Open simulation platform. Open simulation platform joint industry project for the maritime industry (2020). https://opensimulationplatform.com/
19. Hassani, V., et al.: Virtual prototyping of maritime systems and operations. In: International Conference on Offshore Mechanics and Arctic Engineering, vol. 49989, p. V007T06A018. American Society of Mechanical Engineers (2016)
20. Chu, Y., Hatledal, L.I., Æsøy, V., Ehlers, S., Zhang, H.: An object-oriented modeling approach to virtual prototyping of marine operation systems based on functional mock-up interface co-simulation. J. Offshore Mech. Arct. Eng. **140**(2) (2018)
21. Fossen, T.I.: A nonlinear unified state-space model for ship maneuvering and control in a seaway. Int. J. Bifurcat. Chaos **15**(09), 2717–2746 (2005)
22. Hassani, V., Ross, A., Selvik, Ø., Fathi, D., Sprenger, F., Berg, T.E.: Time domain simulation model for research vessel Gunnerus. In: International Conference on Offshore Mechanics and Arctic Engineering, vol. 56550, p. V007T06A013. American Society of Mechanical Engineers (2015)
23. Norges teknisk-naturvitenskapelige universitet: Research vessel: R/V Gunnerus. https://www.ntnu.edu/oceans/gunnerus

Paving the Way for Reinforcement Learning in Smart Grid Co-simulations

Dominik Vereno$^{(\boxtimes)}$ ⓘ, Jonas Harb ⓘ, and Christian Neureiter ⓘ

Josef Ressel Centre for Dependable System-of-Systems Engineering,
5412 Puch, Salzburg, Austria
{dominik.vereno,jonas.harb,christian.neureiter}@fh-salzburg.ac.at

Abstract. This paper identifies and addresses a gap in research on using reinforcement learning (RL) in co-simulation. Co-simulation is an effective simulation paradigm for systems of systems such as smart grids. It relies on combining heterogeneous simulators into a coupled simulation. RL is a promising machine-learning tool for complex grid applications—for instance, demand-side management. However, existing literature does not specifically address challenges of integrating RL with a co-simulation environment. Therefore, we focus on two challenges: how an RL agent is best integrated into a co-simulation architecturally, and to what extent typical RL frameworks are interoperable with orchestrated co-simulation tools. First, we introduce, categorize, and evaluate four approaches of architecturally integrating RL into co-simulation. Additionally, we provide guidance on selecting an appropriate approach. Second, we conduct a case study where we use and incorporate a framework-based RL agent into a co-simulation framework for a simple demand-side management scenario; we identify the need to change the control flow traditionally used in RL frameworks to achieve interoperability. In conclusion, our work is a basis for future academic or industrial applications of RL in co-simulation. Our architectural and framework-specific advice facilitates the implementation of RL in smart-grid co-simulations.

Keywords: Model-based systems engineering · Power-grid simulation · Demand-side management · Software architecture · Artificial intelligence

1 Introduction

Recently, traditional power grids are evolving into so-called smart grids. They combine electrical infrastructure with information and communications technology to enable intelligent monitoring and control [10]. Contemporary power-systems engineering faces many challenges: The increasing share of hard-to-predict and volatile renewable-energy generation forces grids to become more

The financial support by the Austrian Federal Ministry for Digital and Economic Affairs and the National Foundation for Research, Technology and Development and the Christian Doppler Research Association as well as the Federal State of Salzburg is gratefully acknowledged.

P. Masci et al. (Eds.): SEFM 2022 Collocated Workshops, LNCS 13765, pp. 242–257, 2023.
https://doi.org/10.1007/978-3-031-26236-4_21

flexible. In addition, the rising number of electric vehicles (EVs) is straining electrical infrastructure with high peaks in consumption [7]. This stress may be alleviated by intelligently controlling the charging process as part of demand-side–management strategies [6]. Demand-side management includes measures for improving the power-grid operation from consumer side [24].

Data-based methods—such as machine learning—have proven to be an effective tool for such tasks [2]. A promising branch of machine learning that has been gaining traction recently is reinforcement learning (RL) where an agent learns optimal behavior by trial and error. RL has the potential of finding new state-of-the-art algorithms that surpass expert knowledge [23]. The machine-learning paradigm shows great application potential for many smart-grid tasks [37]. Training an RL agent is usually done in a simulation. For RL training in smart grids, we need a realistic simulation that is both extensive and detailed. However, comprehensive simulations of smart grids, which constitute *systems of systems* according to the criteria defined by DeLaurentis [8], present particular challenges. This is because systems of systems span across multiple domains and have heterogeneous and independent subsystems. Co-simulation is capable of addressing these challenges by coordinating multiple heterogeneous simulators [22]. It is the coordinated execution of models with different representations and runtime environments [28]. To obtain a realistic co-simulation environment for RL, models that contain domain knowledge are required. Dealing with the heterogeneity of modeling paradigms and notations of cyber-physical systems of systems—such as modern power grids—is challenging [12]. Model-based systems engineering (MBSE) is an established discipline that deals with the modeling of such systems [20].

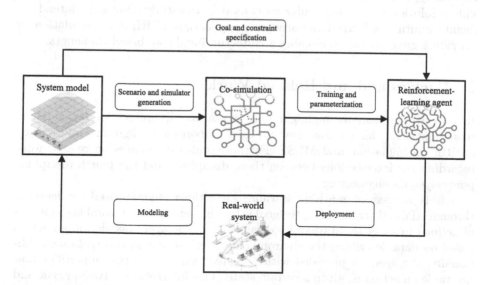

Fig. 1. Overview of discipline artifacts and their interactions

It follows, that to exploit the potential of RL for smart-grid tasks such as demand-side management, four research disciplines must be considered. Figure 1 illustrates the four disciplines' central artifacts as well as their interactions. *Power-systems engineering*, represented by the real-world system, is needed to gain domain knowledge. This knowledge must be captured in system models using methods of *model-based systems engineering*. The models then facilitate the creation of a *co-simulation* and implementation of *reinforcement learning* algorithms. The co-simulation serves as the environment for developing and training the RL agent. This agent may then be deployed to the real-world system. To the best of our knowledge, existing research does not address how RL agents can be trained and validated in co-simulations. In particular, no research discusses architectural integration and framework-specific interoperability concerns between the respective tools.

This paper contributes to the state of the art by addressing the challenges and obstacles of integrating an RL agent into a smart-grid co-simulation. The fundamental requirements for RL when it comes to interfacing with a simulation are quite basic and should be unproblematic in principle. However, we have identified two areas in need of research: First, we identify a lack of research about how to integrate an RL agent into a co-simulation architecturally. Thus, we identify architectural approaches, classify them, and give guidance for applying them. Second, there is no literature demonstrating the practical challenges of using RL in a co-simulation regarding their respective software tools. Consequently, we conduct case study–based experiments using a co-simulation and an RL framework to uncover integration obstacles and issues. We describe one such issue concerning the incompatibility of the typical control flow of RL frameworks and the typical control flow of orchestrated co-simulation. Consequently, we provide a solution for the particular tools used in the study. Our work intends to facilitate future industrial and academic applications of RL in co-simulation by providing guidance on overcoming architectural and tool-based challenges.

2   Background and Related Work

In the introduction, we highlight four important disciplines for using RL in co-simulations. This sections now provides important background information on RL, co-simulation, and MBSE. Furthermore, it elaborates on related work regarding the intersections between these disciplines and the fourth discipline: power-systems engineering.

RL is a class of machine learning algorithms characterized by learning through trial and error. In RL, the goal is for an *agent* to take favorable sequences of *actions* to affect the state of its *environment*. The agent decides on an action based on data describing the environment's state, so-called *observations*. Additionally, the agent is provided with a real-valued *reward* that quantifies how favorable an action is, given a certain state. This interaction between agent and environment is depicted in Fig. 2. We refer interested readers to Sutton and Barto [32], who provide a comprehensive overview of RL.

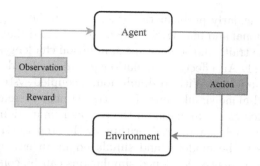

Fig. 2. Interaction between an RL agent and its environment

Since smart-grid systems are critical infrastructure, they require a high degree of dependability. Therefore, real-world exploration of an untrained RL agent via trial and error is too risky to be feasible. Consequently, we need a simulated environment to train the agent.

Table 1. System-of-systems traits, their simulation challenges, and advantages of co-simulation for addressing the challenges

System-of-systems trait	Simulation challenge	Advantage of co-simulation
Heterogeneity	Subsystems are modeled with different tools that support their respective algorithmic and computational needs	Coupling is done on solver level, removing the need for model consolidation
Operational and managerial independence	Simulators of various organizations are combined. Some underlying models may be confidential.	Co-simulation facilitates black-box integration of simulators
Trans-domain	Experts of specific domains do not have in-depth knowledge of the entire trans-domain system of systems	Domain experts can work on an appropriate simulation of the subsystem without regard for the entire coupled simulation

Simulation is well-established in the grid domain; in fact, Palensky et al. [25] describe it as "fundamental in power engineering". Simulating smart grids is a demanding task; in addition to being complex systems, smart grids can be classified as systems of systems [18]. Thus, they exhibit all their defining traits introduced by Sage and Cuppan [27] and expanded by DeLaurentis [8]. We deem three of them to be particularly problematic for simulation: heterogeneity of subsystems, their operational and managerial independence, and that they span multiple domains. These traits and some of the simulation challenges they exacerbate are listed in Table 1. An effective simulation paradigm for dealing with theses challenges is *co-simulation*. With co-simulation, a coupled system is simulated by coordinating stand-alone simulations of the constituent systems [13]. A simulation can be regarded as *co*-simulation if the coupled simulations differ regarding the used simulation tool, the solver algorithm, or the step size [15]. Co-simulation allows subsystems to be modeled and simulated in an environment native to them [21, 25]. Independently-developed simulations can be combined into large-scale scenarios [26]. Therefore, "modeling can be done on the subsystem level without having the coupled problem in mind" [28]. In Table 1, we explain how co-simulation can alleviate smart-grid simulation problems. Furthermore, simulators can either be coupled with bilateral interfaces or by using an orchestrating framework that handles data exchange between simulators and synchronizes their execution [31]. With bilateral interfaces, the data exchange and synchronization becomes increasingly complex. According to Nguyen et al. [21] framework-based, *orchestrated* co-simulation simplifies the simulation architecture. For more information on co-simulation in general, Schweiger et al. [30] give an empirical insight into the usage and prevalence of co-simulation while Gomes et al. [13] and Hafner and Popper [15] have each surveyed the field extensively.

A comprehensive co-simulation requires specifying the behavior of the subsystems and the simulated scenario, i.e. the entities and their connections to each other [30]. Such specifications can be supplied by models used in power-grid engineering—for example, the mathematical description of power flow, a model containing electric lines, buses, and transformers, or the architecture description of control software. However, MBSE provides a comprehensive methodology for managing these models "beginning in the conceptual design phase and continuing throughout development and later life cycle phases" [36]. It is inherently well suited to dealing with the complexity of smart grids [20]. In the context of this paper, we use the term *model* as an artifact containing a purposeful abstraction of a system. Creating detailed models that are a suitable basis for co-simulation requires modeling know-how as well as smart-grid domain expertise.

For this researcher endeavor, we must examine how the discussed disciplines—co-simulation, RL, and MBSE—interface with each other and with the power-systems domain. For RL, various research projects have demonstrated the efficacy of the paradigm for smart-grid applications. According to Zhang et al. [37], RL was used in numerous grid-related areas, such as cyber-security defense, load forecasting, anomaly detection, and demand-side management; Vázquez-Canteli and Nagy [35] survey the available literature on RL in demand-side management specifically. Cabot et al. [5] state that system models could also be used to support AI methods, although they identify a lack of research on that topic. Binder et al. [3] show that system models can be used as a basis for (semi-)automatic generation of co-simulation simulators. Regarding the simulation of smart grids, Palensky et al. [25] and Steinbrink et al. [31] outline the open challenges of smart-grid co-simulation while highlighting its necessity. Even though the co-simulation paradigm is beneficial for many smart-grid simulations [25], to the best of our knowledge, its use with RL is very sparsely discussed in literature. Some examples that make use of co-simulation to train RL agents are Fischer et al. [11] and Veith et al. [33]. They present a specialized form of RL called Adversarial Resilience Learning and train it using co-simulation. Their work serves as an implicit demonstration that RL can be used in a co-simulation context. Although Veith et al. [33] go into more detail about their specific implementation, neither discuss the general architectural and tool-interoperability considerations explicitly.

3 Research Approach and Methodology

The overarching goal of this study is to explore and examine the challenges of integrating an RL agent into a smart-grid co-simulation. Achieving this goal facilitates future academic and industrial applications of RL training in co-simulation environments—for example, to develop an intelligent charging algorithm for demand-side management by training an RL agent. This goal includes an in-depth analysis of the approaches for inserting the agent into an orchestrated co-simulation architecture. Furthermore, a closer look at the compatibility and interoperability of RL and co-simulation tools is necessary.

Concerning architectural integration, we started with a descriptive approach of identifying architecture candidates and devising a classification scheme. First, we determined components and the required information flows for developing viable architecture candidates. Following that, we clustered the candidates and removed redundant ones. Thus, we arrived at a set of four candidates. Then, an extensive analysis of the candidates was conducted, which led to a categorization scheme that may be used as an aid for architectural decision making. In Sect. 4, a detailed discussion of the architectural integration can be found.

To address the goal of integrating RL and co-simulation tools (see Sect. 5) we first established an overview of widely used tools in both disciplines. Then, we selected one co-simulation and one RL framework that we have deemed to be representative. Our further examinations strongly hinge on a simple fictitious case-study scenario: conducting demand-side management for a smart EV-charging scenario using RL. Crozier et al. [6] describe smart charging as the "coordinated scheduling of the charging time and power of EVs". We implement a simple distribution-grid co-simulation in which we integrate an RL agent which controls the charging process. The agent's task is to avoid peaks in demand while keeping average charge rates as high as possible. The case study serves two purposes in the context of our research: On the one hand, we want to uncover framework integration issues and obstacles. Ideally, the findings should identify issues that do not just occur with the specific pair of frameworks, but issues that relate to how co-simulation tools and RL tools are generally structured. On the other hand, we use the case study to evaluate our architecture candidates. This evaluation allows us to better assess the characteristics of each candidate to give more comprehensive and accurate guidance on using them.

4   Architectural Integration of Reinforcement Learning Agents with Co-simulation

In this section, we discuss architectural considerations and options for integrating RL agents in a co-simulation context. We identify and classify four flexible candidates for architectural integration and contrast them with a more naïve alternative. Finally, we provide guidance on choosing an appropriate candidate depending on different requirements and situations.

4.1   Introducing Terms and Notation

To facilitate discussion about the architecture candidates and their classification, we define their constituent components:

- The **RL agent** is the component that encapsulates the RL algorithm as well as any pre- and postprocessing of input and output data respectively. The reward may be passed together with the observation or is alternatively calculated internally. It should be noted that the literature is not clear on what exactly the boundaries of the agent are; there is no unanimous opinion whether aspects like pre- and postprocessing are part of the RL agent.
- In this context, a **simulation model** is a formal description of the simulated system's approximate behavior. It can be agnostic to its use in a co-simulation framework and does not have to adhere to a particular modeling paradigm or language. To emphasize that the model in question is the one controlled by the RL agent, we use the term *controlled (simulation) model.*
- The **(co-simulation) framework interface** enables data exchange between a simulation model and the orchestrating framework and allows the framework to control the simulation model (e.g. via a step function).
- A **simulator** contains one or more simulation models as well as a framework interface. It further comprises a simulation kernel on which the model is run [9] to make it an "independently executable piece of software that implements a simulation model" [31]. In a *co*-simulation, multiple simulators are coupled and coordinated.

4.2   Naïve Architecture Candidate

The most basic way of implementing an architecture for RL in co-simulation is direct integration of all RL logic into the simulation-model component. The RL agent receives observation data directly from the simulation model and passes the calculated action right back to it. This does not require any explicitly defined interface. Figure 3 depicts this architecture candidate.

This approach is intuitive; putting the system and its controlling algorithm into the same component makes sense, because they represent aspects of the same entity. This also does not require a lot of overhead and may be an attractive starting point for initial exploration. However, the tight coupling between the two components may lead to several issues. It may be difficult for different teams

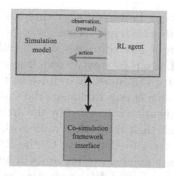

Fig. 3. Naïve approach for architectural integration

to work on the simulation model and RL agent independently. Furthermore, an existing simulation model may have to be changed significantly. Also, the simulation model is not reusable for other simulation scenarios without RL.

4.3   Alternative Architecture Candidates

To address the issues with the naïve approach, we introduce four architecture candidates for RL integration into co-simulation. We classify them based on two independent categories, and give suggestions on when to use each approach.

Classification Matrix and Architecture Candidates. We consider two independent binary categories. One the one hand, we differentiate if the RL agent receives its own framework interface. This creates an independent RL simulator in the co-simulation that can be individually coupled to other simulators. On the other hand, the agent may either be limited to receiving observation and reward only from the simulation model or, alternatively, be open to receiving this information from other sources. If not limited, the RL agent can be supplied with data not available through the controlled simulation model. With these distinctions, we can create a classification matrix, as depicted in Fig. 4. Each square in the matrix contains one architecture candidate:

- **Candidate A:** The interface component only exchanges data with the simulation model, while the RL agent only communicates with the simulation model. Comparing it to the naïve approach, the simulation-model component is loosely coupled with the RL agent. There must be a clearly defined interface for exchanging observation and action. This candidate does not require the framework interface to be altered due to the addition of RL.
- **Candidate B:** In contrast to Candidate A, the RL agent does not receive observation data from the simulation model. Instead, it receives the data directly from the framework interface. In this case, the interface must be changed to accommodate this data flow. However, the data flows to the agent can be defined and adapted more freely. For example, the simulation model

might only receive voltage data from other simulators whereas the RL agent is additionally supplied with temperature data; in this case the simulation model does not need to be altered to support the additional data flow.

- **Candidate C:** The RL agent receives its own framework interface, making it an independent simulator that must be coupled to the co-simulation. Similar to Candidate A, the RL agent only exchanges data with the simulation model. However, their communication is handled by the orchestrating framework and therefore passes through their respective framework interfaces.
- **Candidate D:** In contrast to Candidate C, the RL-agent simulator is now connected to an arbitrary number of simulators in addition to the simulation-model simulator. Optionally, the RL agent may receive data from the controlled system. However, the gathering of observation data can be largely independent of the simulation-model simulator.

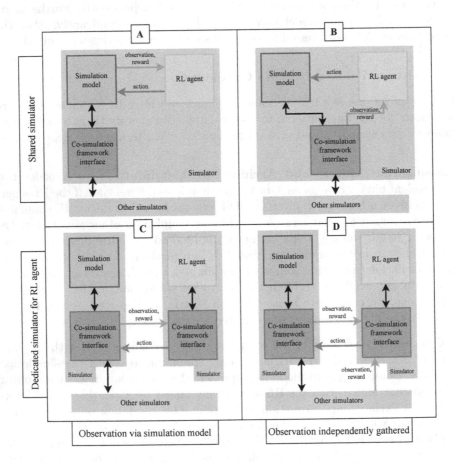

Fig. 4. Classification matrix for architecture candidates

Guidance on Candidate Selection. When deciding on how to integrate an RL agent into a co-simulation architecturally, one is faced with multiple considerations that are specific to the project at hand. We deem the presented classification scheme to be a helpful support for such a decision-making process. The two distinct binary categories shown in Fig. 4 represent two independent binary decisions:

1. Should the observation (and the reward) for the RL agent be gathered independently from its simulation model?
2. Should the RL agent receive a dedicated co-simulation framework interface?

Regarding the first decision: An advantage of having independent data flow is that it allows for flexibility. This is especially useful for exploratory and experimental projects where the input data for the agent is not yet carved in stone. For example, a project may try to find which data can improve the RL agent's performance. Another project may attempt to evaluate the benefit of supplying the RL agent with an additional piece of information. Furthermore, the existing simulation components need less modification and are instead mostly extended, adhering to the open-close principle [19]. Also, the RL agent may be substituted for any other form of decision-making component that is not based on observation data. However, if the flexibility is not needed—in case of having unalterable and clearly defined data flow—the additional complexity of both information flow as well as dependencies, and implementation effort may be unnecessary. In the architecture candidates B and D shown in Fig. 4, the agent gathers observation data independently. A summary of these considerations is presented in Fig. 5a.

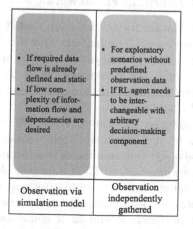

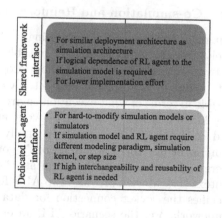

(a) Independence of data gathering   (b) Simulator dedicated to RL agent

Fig. 5. Considerations for selecting architecture candidates

To decide whether to use a dedicated simulator, the primary consideration is the mutability of the simulator containing the controlled simulation model. If the simulator is provided as a black-box executable, the only option is to create a dedicated simulator for the agent. This may be the case if an organization refuses to share implementation details of its simulation model. A further critical consideration is to what degree the simulation model is modifiable. Having a dedicated simulator alleviates the need for editing the simulation model since the communication runs across a predefined connection. Similarly, one must judge the heterogeneity of the simulation model and the RL agent. If the simulation model is of a different modeling language or paradigm, or requires a different runtime environment or simulation step size, it is advantagous to create an individual simulator for each. Moreover, having a dedicated simulator for RL leads to looser coupling and thus easier exchangeability as well as reusability of individual components. However, it separates components that are fundamentally conceptually linked and will likely be part of the same system in deployment. Architecture candidates C and D both use independent simulators, as shown in Fig. 4. Figure 5b compactly presents the discussed trade-offs.

5   Identifying Framework Integration Problems

This section describes the implementation of an RL agent based on the case study. First, the co-simulation and RL framework we used are discussed and our reasons for choosing them are delineated. Next, we uncover an issue with control flow when using RL and co-simulation frameworks together. We also provide a possible solution that works with the tools we use.

5.1   Co-simulation and Reinforcement Learning Frameworks

Our main requirements for choosing a co-simulation framework were that it be freely available as open-source, suitable to power-grid simulation, and flexible in two ways: First, it should allow programmatical scenario definition that is not bound to a graphical user interface. Second, the framework ought to be flexible in terms of what execution environment the simulators are run in. Among the 26 frameworks presented by Vogt et al. [34], we chose Mosaik[1], a smart-grid co-simulation framework originally introduced by Schutte et al. [29] and Rohjans et al. [26]. The framework's goal is to run coordinated simulations of energy-system scenarios that facilitate the use of existing simulators in a common context [17]. Mosaik provides two APIs for user interaction: The component API specifies the socket connection for data exchange between simulators and the framework. Via the scenario API, an executable co-simulation scenario can be created in which the entity instances, their parameters, and their connections are defined [31].

Regarding reinforcement learning, OpenAI Gym [4] presents a general structure for modeling environments as single classes with specified interfaces. The

---

[1] https://mosaik.offis.de.

agent then exchanges action, observation, and reward with the environment (cf. Fig. 2). Many RL frameworks support OpenAI Gym environments, such as TensorForce[2], Stable Baselines 3[3], and TF-Agents[4]. We have chosen to use the latter for this case study due to its flexibility. TF-Agents is described by Guadarrama et al. [14] and is based on the TensorFlow machine-learning library presented by Abadi et al. [1]. The framework implements several state-of-the-art RL algorithms and supports user-created environments. It uses modular components that are made to be extensible, and allows both high- and low-level access to many of its features.

5.2 Carrying Out and Implementing the Case Study

We conduct our case-study experiments based on the fictitious scenario outlined in Sect. 3. A small distribution grid was simulated including simulators for the power grid, the EV charging stations, a charging-station management system, as well as households. We implemented a Deep Q-Learning [16] agent to control the charging-station management system which is responsible for limiting the available charging power for all stations. The agent's learning goal was to determine an appropriate charging strategy that maximizes the available charging power while avoiding demand peaks. We tested the naïve architecture candidate (see Sect. 3) and the four candidates described in Sect. 4.3 while leaving the specifics of the RL agent unchanged. The experiments uncovered an issue: The intended control flow of TF-Agents must be changed for agents to be integrated into an orchestrated Mosaik co-simulation. This issue, its implications, and a possible solution are discussed in the following section.

5.3 Need for Changed Control Flow

RL frameworks generally implement a control paradigm based on the information flow seen in Fig. 6a; these frameworks put the agent in control of stepping the environment through simulated time. The environment realizes the action and then returns an observation and usually a reward. In other words, the environment remains idle until it is prompted by the agent. In contrast, orchestrated co-simulation requires both the agent and the environment be part of the co-simulation; the orchestrator is responsible for stepping the simulators and exchanging data between them (see Fig. 6b). Therefore, the RL frameworks' typical practice of modeling the environment as a single class and placing the agent in control of stepping the environment is incompatible with the paradigm of orchestrated co-simulation. This makes it necessary to consider how a given RL framework can be adapted to work with co-simulation, or—alternatively—to use a framework-independent RL implementation.

---

[2] https://github.com/tensorforce/tensorforce.
[3] https://github.com/DLR-RM/stable-baselines3.
[4] https://www.tensorflow.org/agents.

When integrating an RL framework into an orchestrated co-simulation, several modifications are necessary. For example, when using TF-Agents, the agent class may stay intact; however, we suggest removing the environment class altogether. Instead, the orchestrator gathers observation and reward from other simulators and passes it to the simulator with the RL agent. As discussed in Sect. 4, that could be a simulator exclusively housing the agent or the agent together with other simulation models. The agent generates the action, which is collected by the orchestrator the next time it can be processed. Furthermore, it is necessary to implement some functionality from the environment class in the agent's simulator. This includes translating observations into a format that is compatible with the agent and generating a reward for each state-action pair. With these changes, TF-Agents was successfully integrated with Mosaik.

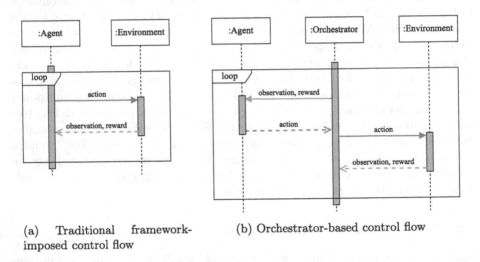

(a) Traditional framework-imposed control flow

(b) Orchestrator-based control flow

Fig. 6. Control flow and information exchange between RL agent and environment

6   Conclusion and Outlook

RL shows great potential for smart-grid applications such as demand-side management. However, RL hinges on the quality of simulation, and smart grids, as systems of systems, are inherently difficult to simulate. Co-simulation is a promising tool to address this issue and enable RL in complex systems of systems by providing a suitable environment for training and testing. However, research on RL in co-simulation is lacking. With this paper we take a first step towards closing that gap in literature. The paper establishes a preliminary overview of the disciplines required for using RL in a smart-grid co-simulation and analyzes co-simulation-specific challenges for RL. First, we examined architectural integration. Second, we conducted a case study to reveal framework-specific interoperability challenges.

To address the first research goal, we identify and assess a set of four architecture candidates. We further categorize them in a 2-by-2 matrix using two independent binary categories: the independence of the data flow to the integrated RL agent, and whether the agent receives a dedicated co-simulation framework interface. We then test the architecture candidates to evaluate them. Next, we discuss the application scenarios of each candidate according to their categorization and give guidance on when which candidate is appropriate. Furthermore, we tackle the second research goal-identifying framework integration issues-using a case study–based approach. The co-simulation framework Mosaik was used in tandem with the RL framework TF-Agents to implement a simple, fictitious scenario where smart EV charging is used for demand-side management. The experiments uncovered an issue: While RL frameworks typically assume a specific control flow, using RL in an orchestrated co-simulation requires changing that control flow. For the frameworks used in the case study, this issue could be resolved, showing that TF-Agents can be trained in Mosaik co-simulation scenarios.

Future research should be conducted in several areas. First, we assume that the framework-integration issue is not just limited to TF-Agents and Mosaik but instead we postulate that it hints at a general incompatibility of the control flow typically found in RL frameworks and the concept of orchestrated co-simulation. However, further research is required to verify that claim. To this end, it would be beneficial to analyze various combinations of tools to check for compatibility. Moreover, our architectural guidance should be applicable to multi-agent RL as well as the single-agent RL paradigm discussed here. This could be validated by applying our findings to multi-agent RL in smart-grid co-simulations, ideally in a more realistic and comprehensive case-study experiment.

Acknowledgements. We thank Katharina Polanec for insightful discussions, valuable critique, and thorough proofreading.

References

1. Abadi, M., et al.: TensorFlow: large-scale machine learning on heterogeneous systems (2015). https://www.tensorflow.org/. Software available from tensorflow.org
2. Antonopoulos, I., et al.: Artificial intelligence and machine learning approaches to energy demand-side response: a systematic review. Renew. Sustain. Energy Rev. **130**, 109899 (2020). https://doi.org/10.1016/j.rser.2020.109899
3. Binder, C., Fischinger, M., Altenhuber, L., Draxler, D., Lastro, G., Neureiter, C.: Enabling architecture based co-simulation of complex smart grid applications. Energy Inform. **2**(1), 1–19 (2019). https://doi.org/10.1186/s42162-019-0084-0
4. Brockman, G., et al.: OpenAI gym. arXiv preprint arXiv:1606.01540 (2016)
5. Cabot, J., Clarisó, R., Brambilla, M., Gérard, S.: Cognifying model-driven software engineering. In: Seidl, M., Zschaler, S. (eds.) STAF 2017. LNCS, vol. 10748, pp. 154–160. Springer, Cham (2018). https://doi.org/10.1007/978-3-319-74730-9_13
6. Crozier, C., Morstyn, T., McCulloch, M.: The opportunity for smart charging to mitigate the impact of electric vehicles on transmission and distribution systems. Appl. Energy **268**, 114973 (2020). https://doi.org/10.1016/j.apenergy.2020.114973

7. Das, H., Rahman, M., Li, S., Tan, C.: Electric vehicles standards, charging infrastructure, and impact on grid integration: a technological review. Renew. Sustain. Energy Rev. **120**, 109618 (2020). https://doi.org/10.1016/j.rser.2019.109618

8. DeLaurentis, D.: Understanding transportation as a system-of-systems design problem. In: 43rd AIAA Aerospace Sciences Meeting and Exhibit, Reno, Nevada, pp. 123–136. American Institute of Aeronautics and Astronautics (2005). https://doi.org/10.2514/6.2005-123

9. Denil, J., Meyers, B., De Meulenaere, P., Vangheluwe, H.: Explicit semantic adaptation of hybrid formalisms for FMI co-simulation. In: Proceedings of the Symposium on Theory of Modeling & Simulation: DEVS Integrative & Symposium, DEVS 2015, San Diego, CA, USA, pp. 99–106. Society for Computer Simulation International (2015)

10. Farhangi, H.: The path of the smart grid. IEEE Power Energ. Mag. **8**(1), 18–28 (2010). https://doi.org/10.1109/MPE.2009.934876

11. Fischer, L., Memmen, J.M., Veith, E.M., Tröschel, M.: Adversarial resilience learning - towards systemic vulnerability analysis for large and complex systems (2018). https://arxiv.org/abs/1811.06447

12. Fitzgerald, J., Pierce, K., Larsen, P.G.: Co-modelling and co-simulation in the engineering of systems of cyber-physical systems. In: 2014 9th International Conference on System of Systems Engineering (SOSE), pp. 67–72 (2014). https://doi.org/10.1109/SYSOSE.2014.6892465

13. Gomes, C., Thule, C., Broman, D., Larsen, P.G., Vangheluwe, H.: Co-simulation: a survey. ACM Comput. Surv. **51**(3) (2018). https://doi.org/10.1145/3179993

14. Guadarrama, S., et al.: TF-agents: a library for reinforcement learning in tensorflow (2018). https://github.com/tensorflow/agents. Accessed 25 June 2019

15. Hafner, I., Popper, N.: An overview of the state of the art in co-simulation and related methods. SNE Simul. Notes Europe **31**(4), 185–200 (2021). https://doi.org/10.11128/sne.31.on.10582

16. van Hasselt, H., Guez, A., Silver, D.: Deep reinforcement learning with double q-learning. In: Proceedings of the Thirtieth AAAI Conference on Artificial Intelligence, AAAI 2016, pp. 2094–2100. AAAI Press (2016). https://doi.org/10.1609/aaai.v30i1.10295

17. Lehnhoff, S., et al.: Exchangeability of power flow simulators in smart grid co-simulations with mosaik. In: 2015 Workshop on Modeling and Simulation of Cyber-Physical Energy Systems (MSCPES), pp. 1–6 (2015). https://doi.org/10.1109/MSCPES.2015.7115410

18. Lopes, A., Lezama, R., Pineda, R.: Model based systems engineering for smart grids as systems of systems. Procedia Comput. Sci. **6**, 441–450 (2011). https://doi.org/10.1016/j.procs.2011.08.083

19. Meyer, B., Milner, R., Bertrand, M.: Object-Oriented Software Construction. Prentice-Hall International Series in Computer Science. Prentice-Hall, Hoboken (1988)

20. Neureiter, C., Binder, C., Lastro, G.: Review on domain specific systems engineering. In: 2020 IEEE International Symposium on Systems Engineering (ISSE), pp. 1–8 (2020). https://doi.org/10.1109/ISSE49799.2020.9272214

21. Nguyen, V.H., et al.: Using power-hardware-in-the-loop experiments together with co-simulation for the holistic validation of cyber-physical energy systems. In: 2017 IEEE PES Innovative Smart Grid Technologies Conference Europe (ISGT-Europe), Turin, Italy, pp. 1–6. IEEE (2017). https://doi.org/10.1109/ISGTEurope.2017.8260122

22. Nguyen, V.H., Besanger, Y., Tran, Q.T., Nguyen, T.L.: On conceptual structuration and coupling methods of co-simulation frameworks in cyber-physical energy system validation. Energies **10**(12) (2017). https://doi.org/10.3390/en10121977

23. Nian, R., Liu, J., Huang, B.: A review on reinforcement learning: introduction and applications in industrial process control. Comput. Chem. Eng. **139**, 106886 (2020). https://doi.org/10.1016/j.compchemeng.2020.106886

24. Palensky, P., Dietrich, D.: Demand side management: demand response, intelligent energy systems, and smart loads. IEEE Trans. Ind. Inf. **7**(3), 381–388 (2011). https://doi.org/10.1109/TII.2011.2158841

25. Palensky, P., Meer, A.A.V.D., Lopez, C.D., Joseph, A., Pan, K.: Cosimulation of intelligent power systems: fundamentals, software architecture, numerics, and coupling. IEEE Ind. Electron. Mag. **11**(1), 34–50 (2017). https://doi.org/10.1109/MIE.2016.2639825

26. Rohjans, S., Lehnhoff, S., Schütte, S., Scherfke, S., Hussain, S.: Mosaik - a modular platform for the evaluation of agent-based smart grid control. In: IEEE PES ISGT Europe 2013, pp. 1–5 (2013). https://doi.org/10.1109/ISGTEurope.2013.6695486

27. Sage, A.P., Cuppan, C.D.: On the systems engineering and management of systems of systems and federations of systems. Inf.-Knowl.-Syst. Manag. **2**, 325–345 (2001)

28. Schloegl, F., Rohjans, S., Lehnhoff, S., Velasquez, J., Steinbrink, C., Palensky, P.: Towards a classification scheme for co-simulation approaches in energy systems. In: 2015 International Symposium on Smart Electric Distribution Systems and Technologies (EDST), pp. 516–521. IEEE (2015). https://doi.org/10.1109/SEDST.2015.7315262

29. Schutte, S., Scherfke, S., Troschel, M.: Mosaik: a framework for modular simulation of active components in smart grids. In: 2011 IEEE First International Workshop on Smart Grid Modeling and Simulation (SGMS), Brussels, Belgium, pp. 55–60. IEEE (2011). https://doi.org/10.1109/SGMS.2011.6089027

30. Schweiger, G., et al.: An empirical survey on co-simulation: promising standards, challenges and research needs. Simul. Model. Pract. Theory **95**, 148–163 (2019). https://doi.org/10.1016/j.simpat.2019.05.001

31. Steinbrink, C., et al.: CPES testing with mosaik: co-simulation planning, execution and analysis. Appl. Sci. **9**(5), 923 (2019). https://doi.org/10.3390/app9050923

32. Sutton, R.S., Barto, A.G.: Reinforcement Learning. Adaptive Computation and Machine Learning Series, 2nd edn. Bradford Books, Cambridge (2018)

33. Veith, E.M., Wenninghoff, N., Frost, E.: The adversarial resilience learning architecture for AI-based modelling, exploration, and operation of complex cyber-physical systems (2020). https://arxiv.org/abs/2005.13601

34. Vogt, M., Marten, F., Braun, M.: A survey and statistical analysis of smart grid co-simulations. Appl. Energy **222**, 67–78 (2018). https://doi.org/10.1016/j.apenergy.2018.03.123

35. Vázquez-Canteli, J.R., Nagy, Z.: Reinforcement learning for demand response: a review of algorithms and modeling techniques. Appl. Energy **235**, 1072–1089 (2019). https://doi.org/10.1016/j.apenergy.2018.11.002

36. Walden, D., Roedler, G., Forsberg, K., Damelin, D., Shortell, T.: INCOSE Systems Engineering Handbook: A Guide for System Life Cycle Processes and Activities, 4th edn. Wiley, Hoboken (2015)

37. Zhang, D., Han, X., Deng, C.: Review on the research and practice of deep learning and reinforcement learning in smart grids. CSEE J. Power Energy Syst. **4**(3), 362–370 (2018). https://doi.org/10.17775/CSEEJPES.2018.00520

CoCoSim: A Tool for Co-simulation of Mobile Cooperative Robots

Matías Richart[✉][ID], Felipe Velázquez, Federico Ciuffardi, Jorge Visca[ID], and Javier Baliosian[ID]

University of the Republic, Montevideo, Uruguay
{mrichart,fvelazquez,fciuffardi,jvisca,javierba}@fing.edu.uy

Abstract. High-quality and efficient simulation is a critical component of robotics development and research. Currently, simulations for multi-robot systems are split across several independent tools, such as *Gazebo* for physics and mobility, *ROS2* for software development, and *ns-3* for communications and networking infrastructure. Those are mature, well-tested tools worth reusing that implement different modeling techniques, interfaces, and, more importantly, time-passing representation strategies; Gazebo uses fixed time steps and ns-3 discrete events. This article presents CoCoSim, a framework that integrates both simulators to allow multi-robot co-simulation, capable of running experiments that combine all the involved robotic systems. We show how the time synchronization and data exchange between the simulators that keeps a consistent state across them is achieved with minimal modifications to their original code.

Keywords: Co-simulation · Cooperative robots · Digital twins · ROS · ns-3

1 Introduction

A team of multiple robots with common goals is often called a multi-robot system (MRS). Researchers have a broad consensus on the desirability of using *MRS* versus single-robot systems [14]. The most frequent motivations for their use arise precisely from the nature of the problems one wishes to tackle [2,14]. For example, when the problem is inherently distributed, or when the tasks to be performed can be decomposed, the inherent parallelism of the hardware can be exploited to solve them more efficiently (e.g., distributed sensing, mapping, or robotic distribution systems). Often, systems are faced with tasks that would not be solvable by a single robot. In these cases, a team acts as a task enabler making it possible to address them adaptively (e.g., transportation or logistics problems involving objects of varying dimensions or weights). The natural redundancy of a team of robots (individual fault tolerance) coupled with the potential simplification of its members' unique design often increases the system's robustness and reliability. Finally, it is often cheaper and simpler to build many simple units than to build one complex unit with all the capabilities required by the problem.

P. Masci et al. (Eds.): SEFM 2022 Collocated Workshops, LNCS 13765, pp. 258–268, 2023.
https://doi.org/10.1007/978-3-031-26236-4_22

The most common reasons for using *MRS* are efficiency, cost, robustness, reliability, and adaptability. However, the design or conception of a *MRS* requires that a set of additional aspects be carefully considered [2,10]. From the highest level of abstraction, the different approaches to organizing the control software of a *MRS* can be classified into two broad categories known as *collective swarm systems* and *intentionally cooperative systems* [14]. On the one hand, robotic swarms are systems of multiple homogeneous robots where each individual executes tasks with minimal knowledge about teammates and little or no communication. Meanwhile, intentionally cooperative systems require their members to recognize each other to act together in the coordinated solving of the same problem [14]. Therefore, explicit communication is needed to support the coordination of actions. This last aspect, only sometimes adequately weighted, involves additional hardware, computation, and power requirements in addition to negatively affecting system reliability in the presence of noisy channels, interference, or rogue agents [2].

Coordination strategies between agents must be designed to implement cooperative solutions effectively to benefit from using a multi-robot system. In this regard, network communication is a crucial factor. For a team of mobile robots, the wireless network through which they communicate is not only a constraint of the problem to be solved but also an object that the team can manipulate and use as a tool. According to their needs, robots can modify the network by altering various transmission parameters as it is usually done but, above all, modifying the network topology as the robots move.

Experimenting with robots is a very costly endeavor. Robots are complex and expensive systems, and the deployment scenarios of interest can be too long-running to be reproduced in real-time. At the same time, the place of deployment can be non-accessible beforehand or even unknown. These difficulties strongly motivate using simulators to evaluate and develop robotic architectures and solutions.

Thus, a simulation environment, such as the one in Fig. 1, that can accurately model both robot movements and control and communication behavior is essential in this discipline's research and development process. Moreover, in the context of *digital twins*, this accuracy is critical since simulations are used to test, validate or learn aspects of the system that will later be used in the physical environment. In addition to the accuracy and reliability of models and simulations, time constraints are added in the context of *digital twins*. Simulation tools must allow processes to run faster than in a real environment. Herefore, co-simulation is a possible solution to address this problem in a feasible and scalable way, albeit with a significant list of challenges.

Therefore, in this paper, we present CoCoSim[1], a tool for simulating cooperative robots which also allows us to simulate the wireless communications among them precisely. The primary motivation for embracing the development of a new platform resides in the fact that existing tools do not allow us to run faster than real-time or do not adequately model our cooperative robots scenario.

---

[1] https://cocosim.pages.fing.edu.uy/homepage/en/.

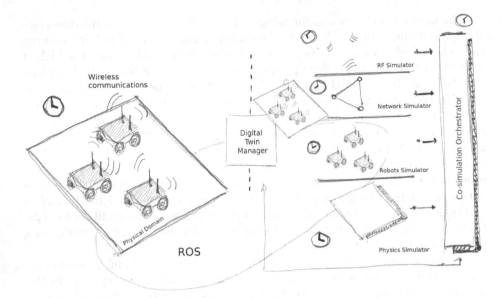

Fig. 1. A cooperative robotics scenario co-simulated by four different simulators, each with its notion of time step and its data models and semantics, coordinated by an orchestrator. In the case of an interaction with the physical world, the digital twin makes use of co-simulation to evaluate multiple solutions to a real-world situation.

With CoCoSim, we can co-simulate the physics, movements, and behaviors of the robots jointly with the wireless medium used for communications. CoCoSim can model the wireless channel with great detail for communications, considering low-level aspects such as interference, collisions, propagation, path-loss, and high-level elements such as routing.

The design of CoCoSim is based on existing simulation tools, namely ROS2, Gazebo, and ns-3, which allow running the same code in the co-simulation and on a real robot with minimal or no changes. The main CoCoSim characteristics are:

- Can simulate multiple robots with wireless communications.
- Can run simulations faster than in a real environment.
- Can obtain feedback from the environment (work as a Digital Twin).
- Can execute the same logic as in the real environment.

The rest of the paper is organized as follows. In Sect. 2, we briefly present some of the most relevant related work. In Sect. 3, we present the design and architecture of CoCoSim and provide some details about the implementation. In Sect. 4, we discuss some open challenges and current work in progress. Finally, we conclude the article in Sect. 5.

2   Related Work

Some works have attempted to integrate existing simulation tools to co-simulate multi-robot systems. A relevant work in this regard is RoboNetSim [8], which proposes the integration of a network simulator (ns-2 or ns-3) with the *ARGoS* robotics simulator [11]. This work proposes solutions for the two fundamental problems of tool integration, time synchronization between simulators and information exchange. However, it does not follow any theoretical guidelines; it is a specific solution for the mentioned simulators. For example, it does not propose a straightforward interface between the simulators but modifies them internally to perform the integration. Nevertheless, some of the proposed ideas will be useful for our solution.

Another work integrating a network simulator with a robotics simulator is FlyNetSim [3]. In this case, the work is oriented to non-cooperative aerial robots as the goal is to simulate communication between the control base and the robot, not between robots. This co-simulator consists of a *middleware* that works as an intermediary between the robotics and the network simulator. For communication between the simulators, it uses the ZMQ queuing communication standard. For synchronization between the simulators to be integrated, both simulators (ns-3 and ArduPilot SITL in this case) run in real-time. Although this facilitates synchronization, the main disadvantage is that the simulation cannot be accelerated.

In CORNET [1], the FlyNetSim proposal is modified to improve synchronization between simulators. For this, it proposes a variable stepping method where the robotics discrete-time simulator drives the time step. Between two consecutive steps, the events of the network simulator are executed, and, if necessary, the robotics simulator is updated. In this sense, the synchronization is based on two key points: at each step, the robotics simulator reports the robot positions to the network simulator, and the network simulator executes the corresponding network events in the interval between two steps and reports to the robotics simulator the results. Although it presents interesting improvements over Fly-NetSim, the system implementation is not available for use and evaluation.

A more general approach is developed in ROS-NetSim [4]. This work proposes a framework for integrating robotics and network simulators and shares some characteristics with our proposal. It is based on the ROS robot platform [12] and, in theory, allows the connection of any network and physics simulator. One of its main characteristics is the usage of TUN interfaces to capture ROS robots' communications to pass them through the network simulator. It also proposes a window-based synchronization approach between simulators. However, as it is based on ROS rather than on the more recent ROS2, it does not capture the particular characteristics of the ROS2 communication system.

In summary, co-simulation research is an active and growing discipline. There are several approaches to co-simulation, each with particular characteristics and different levels of usability and popularity. However, it can be observed that several challenges still need to be solved. In particular, most previous approaches run in real-time, not allowing them to execute faster than in a real deployment.

This is a hard limitation in implementing a digital-twin platform. In the case of ROS-NetSim, although it does not have this restriction, it does not use a packet-level network simulator but a system-level one which reduces the complexity but also accuracy. Even more, most existing solutions are specific to a particular use case and hardly generalizable for the cooperative mobile robot simulation presented in this work.

3   CoCoSim Design and Architecture

As previously mentioned, CoCoSim integrates three different tools to implement an integrated co-simulation platform of robots and networks. For the simulation of the robots, we use ROS2 [12,15] and Gazebo [7], and for networking, we integrate the ns-3 Network Simulator [13].

ROS (Robot Operating System) is a flexible open-source framework for developing robot software. It consists of a collection of tools, libraries, and conventions that ease the robot's control system software development. It allows abstracting the software from the specific hardware platform and simplifies the re-utilization of software modules across platforms. ROS2 is the evolution of ROS, which, in particular, changes the communication paradigm to address neglected use cases such as multi-robot systems. The communication between ROS nodes follows a publish/subscribe strategy, where topics are defined, and the nodes can publish data topics and simultaneously have subscriptions to topics.

Gazebo is a free, open-source 3D multi-robot simulator with a physics engine that models the dynamics and kinematics associated with articulated rigid bodies. It works as a Discrete-Time simulator with configurable step sizes and can simulate complex indoor and outdoor environments. ROS and Gazebo are already well integrated through a set of Gazebo plugins and ROS packages that support many existing robots and devices (sensors and actuators). In this scenario, Gazebo works as several ROS nodes; therefore, it uses the ROS communication paradigm for synchronization and data communication. Specifically, Gazebo manages the time by publishing a particular topic to which all nodes are subscribed.

ns-3 is a free, open-source discrete event network simulator primarily intended for research and educational use. It provides models for all the network stack layers, from the physical layer up to the transport and application layer. In particular, there are models for wireless technologies such as WiFi, Bluetooth, and LTE.

CoCoSim design is based on a distributed architecture where all these tools run independently but exchange information and stay synchronized to achieve the co-simulation (see Fig. 2). For the integration of these simulation tools into a co-simulation platform, two main challenges must be addressed: (i) synchronization between a discrete-time simulator (Gazebo and ROS) and a discrete-event simulator (ns-3) and (ii) data and status sharing between the simulators.

All the communication between the different components is implemented through inter-process communication using sockets. We follow a client-server

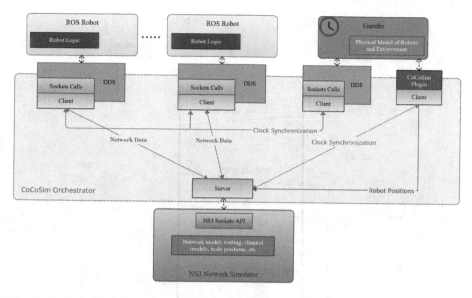

Fig. 2. CoCoSim distributed architecture diagram. Each platform component runs as a separate process, and all the information exchange is implemented through sockets.

architecture where ns-3 act as a server that receives network data from the robots and synchronization and status signals from Gazebo. Regarding data and status sharing, in the context of CoCoSim, Gazebo, ROS and ns-3 need to share the robots' positions, and the messages exchanged between robots. The first task is solved by making Gazebo periodically communicate the positions to ns-3. CoCoSim makes the communication between ROS robots (coordination messages) be passed through the network simulator for the second task. To achieve this, CoCoSim extends ns-3 to provide an interface where external applications can send and receive messages following the socket's API paradigm. We call this *ns-3 as a Service* (NS3aaS). For the synchronization, CoCoSim implements a signaling mechanism between Gazebo and ns-3, where Gazebo governs the simulation clock. In the following sections, we provide more details about this implementation.

3.1   Synchronization and Status Sharing

Under CoCoSim, Gazebo's discrete-time scheduler controls the time and progress of the co-simulation. As the network simulator runs independently in parallel, tight synchronization between both simulators must be performed. CoCoSim implements a simple synchronization strategy based on fixed time steps and inter-process signaling between both simulators.

At ns-3, a time step of fixed sized is set (t), and after all events in the interval [t−1, t] are executed, it sends a signal to Gazebo informing it has already reached time t. In Gazebo, the time step t is executed, and when finished, it sends a

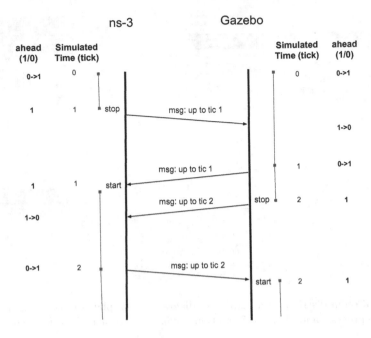

Fig. 3. A time-based synchronization approach through inter-process signaling.

signal to ns-3. At both simulators, a Boolean state (*ahead*) is also maintained, which indicates if the simulator is ahead of the other simulator. When receiving a signal, this state changes from 1 to 0, indicating that the other simulator has already reached time **t**. At each time step **t**, the simulators check the *ahead* state and only continue the execution if it is set to 0, setting it again to 1; otherwise, the execution is stopped waiting for the appropriate signal.

An execution example of the strategy using a time step size of 1 is depicted in Fig. 3. In the beginning, both simulators start at time 0 and with the *ahead* variable in 0. Both start executing at the same time, and both change the ahead variable to 1. At time-step 1, ns-3 has already executed all the events between 0 and 1 but has not received a signal from Gazebo; therefore, it pauses the execution and sends a message to Gazebo informing it that it has reached time step 1. When Gazebo receives this message from ns-3, it sets the *ahead* variable to 0. When Gazebo finishes the execution of time step 0 and is ready to execute time step 1, it sends a message to ns-3 informing it that it has reached time step 1 and checks the *ahead* variable, which allows executing time step 1 without pausing. When ns-3 receives the signal that Gazebo has already reached time step 1, it resumes the execution of all events between time steps 1 and 2. The example shown in Fig. 3 continues by depicting the same behavior but in the opposite direction; Gazebo is paused, waiting for ns-3 to finish the execution of all the events between time steps 1 and 2.

The proposed synchronization strategy guarantees that the difference between the simulated time of both simulators is always less than or equal to one time-step. The time step duration is configurable and can be set accordingly to the simulated scenario. Among others, the central aspect to consider for this setting is the speed at which the robots move. A time discrepancy between the simulators would translate into different visions of the robots' positions in the scenario.

The other interaction between Gazebo and ns-3 implemented by CoCoSim is sharing robots' positions. In Gazebo, each robot position is modeled with 3D coordinates, which ns-3 also needs for placing the network nodes in the simulated environment. Therefore, at each time step, the robots' positions are sent through a message to ns-3.

These two interactions between Gazebo and ns-3 are implemented through a Gazebo plugin. A Gazebo plugin consists of a piece of code that is compiled as a shared library and added into the simulation, thus not requiring any modification to the source code of the simulator. Given that the plugin has access to all of Gazebo's functionalities, it permits us to implement the synchronization mechanism by controlling the pausing and resuming of the simulation.

In the following sub-section, we explain how all this data is received and processed by ns-3.

3.2 NS3aaS: ns-3 as a Service

The approach followed to integrate ns-3 into CoCoSim consists of avoiding any internal modifications to the simulator. This is achieved through a simulation script that receives simulation, configuration, and execution commands through a public interface. This simulation script can be seen as the main component of the CoCoSim network simulation, which uses ns-3 as a library.

Via the public interface (implemented with sockets), ns-3 receives the synchronization signals and the robots' positions from Gazebo. These messages are transformed into specific events scheduled and executed by ns-3 to perform the necessary tasks. For example, events are periodically scheduled (at each time step) for sending synchronization messages to Gazebo.

The same socket-based interface can also receive commands that mimic socket calls; this allows the robots simulated on Gazebo and ROS to communicate through the ns-3 simulation of the network. This way, when the robot software uses the sockets API to send or receive a message, this call is deviated to the interface and appropriately simulated by ns-3. This is achieved by translating the POSIX socket call generated by the ROS robot into a call for the ns-3 socket API.

As can be seen, this would require modifications to the source code of the robot software so that instead of using the operating system's socket calls, it uses NS3aaS socket calls. In the case of CoCoSim, since ROS is being used, these calls are only present in ROS2 communication middleware. In the following, we explain how CoCoSim extended ROS to be able to use NS3aaS.

3.3 ROS Integration with NS3aaS

ROS2 communication is implemented with Data Distribution Service (DDS) [5] as its middleware. DDS provides a publish/subscribe transport and contains attributes such as distributed discovery. ROS2 allows using DDS implementations from different vendors by implementing a *ROS Middleware interface*. Therefore, the complexity of DDS specification and the details of its different implementations are hidden from the ROS2 user.

Leveraging this characteristic of ROS2, CoCoSim provides a modified DDS implementation based on *Cyclone DDS* [6], where the socket calls are replaced with calls to NS3aaS. This modification is transparent to ROS nodes, not requiring additional code changes.

The CoCoSim-DDS implementation transparently translates networking calls to their equivalent inside the network simulator. ROS2 offered the ability to transparently integrate a simulation for the robot dynamics and motion control using Gazebo; CoCoSim extends this to the robot's communication tasks and radio environment using ns-3.

4 Discussion and Future Work

CoCoSim can co-simulate multiple robots where the physical aspects are modeled and run by Gazebo, and ns-3 simulates wireless communications. Moreover, each robot can run ROS code without any modification compared to the code running in a traditional robot simulation or in a real robot. Therefore, we can model more realistic scenarios where multiple robots interact through wireless communications.

Although the previous description, CoCoSim is currently a work in progress, and some essential features are still being developed. Specifically, we are developing three lines of work: speed, scalability, and feedback from the environment.

Regarding the co-simulation speed, we are improving the synchronization strategy to avoid unnecessary delays while maintaining a good simulation fidelity level. There are situations where it is possible to allow one simulator to go ahead of the other and only synchronize at relevant points in time. For example, one crucial event where both simulators must synchronize is when sending or receiving a message. There could be scenarios where this event is sporadic, and the signaling overhead to keep the simulators synchronized is unnecessary. That is an exciting research challenge for which some existing works on the subject may be helpful [9].

The current CoCoSim prototype has only been evaluated in small scenarios, with few robots and no obstacles. We will soon test our implementation with more realistic scenarios, including tens of robots in an indoor scenario with various obstacles like walls and furniture. These obstacles not only have an impact on the robot's mobility but also on the wireless signal propagation. In this sense, the distributed architecture of CoCoSim permits allocating dedicated resources to each simulator if necessary.

Finally, one of the main objectives of CoCoSim is to be used as a Digital Twin for a fleet of cooperative robots in different scenarios. To achieve this, CoCoSim needs to receive feedback from the real system, such as robots' positions, the quality of the wireless transmissions to adapt to the network capabilities and characteristics, and possible changes in the physical environment. Therefore, a *Digital Twin Manager* is being developed, which will communicate with the different modules of CoCoSim using the existing interfaces and the software running in the real robots.

5   Conclusions

We have presented our ongoing work and initial prototype for CoCoSim, a tool for co-simulating cooperative robots that integrates a physical engine simulator, a network simulator, and a robotics platform. It integrates different simulators into a common platform, each with its paradigm, data models, and interfaces. In this regard, one of the main advantages of CoCoSim is that it does not require any modifications to the internals of each simulator but provides *wrappers* to orchestrate the communication and synchronization among them. Furthermore, this is achieved while maintaining the ROS capability to use the same code base for the real robots and the simulated environment.

We have also highlighted some open research challenges and our current work. The development of this prototype has allowed us to validate our initial ideas and has demonstrated that it is possible to integrate existing tools to develop a co-simulation platform. Moreover, as part of CoCoSim, we have developed NS3aaS, and a modified DDS implementation which we are very confident can also be applied in other scenarios.

Acknowledgments. This work is partially supported by the project *Co-simulación en Sistemas Ciber-Físicos* funded by CSIC-UdelaR.

References

1. Acharya, S., Bharadwaj, A., Simmhan, Y., Gopalan, A., Parag, P., Tyagi, H.: CORNET: a co-simulation middleware for robot networks. In: 2020 International Conference on COMmunication Systems and NETworkS, COMSNETS 2020, pp. 245–251 (2020). https://doi.org/10.1109/COMSNETS48256.2020.9027459
2. Arkin, R.C., Arkin, R.C., et al.: Behavior-Based Robotics. MIT Press, Cambridge (1998)
3. Baidya, S., Shaikh, Z., Levorato, M.: FlyNetSim. In: Proceedings of the 21st ACM International Conference on Modeling, Analysis and Simulation of Wireless and Mobile Systems, pp. 37–45. ACM, New York (2018). https://doi.org/10.1145/3242102.3242118. https://dl.acm.org/doi/10.1145/3242102.3242118
4. Calvo-Fullana, M., Mox, D., Pyattaev, A., Fink, J., Kumar, V., Ribeiro, A.: ROS-NetSim: a framework for the integration of robotic and network simulators. IEEE Robot. Autom. Lett. **6**(2), 1120–1127 (2021). https://doi.org/10.1109/LRA.2021.3056347

5. DDS Foundation: OMG Data Distribution Service (DDS^{TM}). https://www.dds-foundation.org/what-is-dds-3/. Accessed 30 July 2022
6. Eclipse Foundation: Eclipse Cyclone DDS^{TM}. https://projects.eclipse.org/projects/iot.cyclonedds. Accessed 31 July 2022
7. Koenig, N., Howard, A.: Design and use paradigms for gazebo, an open-source multi-robot simulator. In: 2004 IEEE/RSJ International Conference on Intelligent Robots and Systems (IROS) (IEEE Cat. No. 04CH37566), vol. 3, pp. 2149–2154. IEEE (2004)
8. Kudelski, M., Gambardella, L.M., Di Caro, G.A.: RoboNetSim: a integrated framework for multi-robot and network simulation. Robot. Auton. Syst. **61**(5), 483–496 (2013). https://doi.org/10.1016/j.robot.2013.01.003
9. Liboni, G., Deantoni, J., Portaluri, A., Quaglia, D., De Simone, R.: Beyond time-triggered co-simulation of cyber-physical systems for performance and accuracy improvements. In: Proceedings of the Rapido 2018 Workshop on Rapid Simulation and Performance Evaluation: Methods and Tools, pp. 1–8 (2018)
10. Murphy, R.: Introduction to AI Robotics, 1st edn. MIT Press, Cambridge (2000)
11. Pinciroli, C., et al.: ARGoS: a modular, multi-engine simulator for heterogeneous swarm robotics. In: 2011 IEEE/RSJ International Conference on Intelligent Robots and Systems, pp. 5027–5034 (2011)
12. Quigley, M., et al.: ROS: an open-source robot operating system. In: ICRA Workshop on Open Source Software, Kobe, Japan, vol. 3, p. 5 (2009)
13. Riley, G., Henderson, T.: The ns-3 network simulator. In: Wehrle, K., Güneş, M., Gross, J. (eds.) Modeling and Tools for Network Simulation, pp. 15–34. Springer, Heidelberg (2010). https://doi.org/10.1007/978-3-642-12331-3_2
14. Siciliano, B., Khatib, O. (eds.): Springer Handbook of Robotics. Springer, Cham (2016). https://doi.org/10.1007/978-3-319-32552-1
15. Thomas, D., Woodall, W., Fernandez, E.: Next-generation ROS: building on DDS. In: ROSCon Chicago 2014, Mountain View, CA. Open Robotics (2014). https://doi.org/10.36288/ROSCon2014-900183. https://vimeo.com/106992622

High-Fidelity Modeling & Co-simulation with πHyFlow

Fernando J. Barros[(⊠)]

Department of Informatics Engineering, University of Coimbra, Coimbra, Portugal
barros@dei.uc.pt

Abstract. Developing high-fidelity representations of cyber-physical systems (CPSs) requires an accurate description of continuous signals, a problem that remains a challenge for many modeling approaches. This paper presents πHyFlow, a modeling and simulation formalism that provides both dense outputs and sampling constructs to support an accurate representation of continuous systems. πHyFlow can describe hierarchical and modular models that facilitate the representation of complex systems. πHyFlow extends the original HyFlow formalism by introducing supporting for the process interaction worldview. For demonstrating formalism's ability to represent high-fidelity hybrid systems, the paper describes a πHyFlow model of the exponential time differential (ETD) integrator, a numerical method able to produce very accurate/exact solutions for some types of systems. As an application, paper describes the model of a simplified microwave oven (MWO) grill element driven by an on-off digital controller. πHyFlow++, a C++ implementation of πHyFlow, is also presented.

Keywords: Cyber-physical systems · Modeling & simulation · Co-simulation · High-fidelity models

1 Introduction

The development of high-fidelity representations of cyber-physical systems (CPSs) requires an accurate description of continuous signals and it remains a challenge for many modeling frameworks. A common description based on piecewise constant signals, used for example by the Functional Mockup Interface [7], make it difficult to achieve the high-fidelity models required for representing CPSs. High-accuracy numerical integrators like the Exponential Time Differencing (EDT) have an exponential function solution [8] that cannot be faithfully represented by piecewise constant signals nor by integrators based on polynomials [1]. Moreover, conventional integrators like BDF (Backward Differentiation Formulae) [1], cannot be used to simulate long periods of 2nd-order energy preserving systems that impose the use of geometric integrators [15]. High-fidelity representations require advances in continuous signal representation and in model interoperability.

P. Masci et al. (Eds.): SEFM 2022 Collocated Workshops, LNCS 13765, pp. 269–285, 2023.
https://doi.org/10.1007/978-3-031-26236-4_23

The Hybrid Flow System Specification (HYFLOW) formalism was developed to represent hierarchical and modular hybrid systems [3]. HYFLOW defines sampling and dense outputs as first-order constructs, enabling a simple specification of pull-communication as a complement to push-communication, typical of discrete event systems. HYFLOW models also exhibit a dynamic topology, making it possible to make arbitrary changes in model composition and coupling at simulation runtime [5].

This paper introduces πHYFLOW, an extension of HYFLOW formalism, for describing hybrid models using the *Process Interaction Worldview* (PI). This worldview was introduced by the SIMULA language [10] and it enables to describe a system by the flow of its entities that are represented by processes. PI makes it easier to model complex systems [28] when compared to other worldviews, like the event scheduling [29]. PI was later supported by GPSS [17] and Simscript [28]. More recently, the PI has also been supported in Java [16], Python [24], and C++ [25]. However, most of the PI frameworks are non-modular making it difficult to represent complex systems. On the other hand modular M&S formalisms impose severe restrictions on what can be represented within a base model, being common that a base model can only represent one event [3,23]. PI greatly simplifies the specification of simple systems, that would impose otherwise a more complex network representation [26]. πHYFLOW supports PI while keeping model modularity, giving the modeler a larger flexibility on what can be represented in a base model.

For demonstrating πHYFLOW ability to accurately represent hybrid systems, the papers provides a description of the ETD integrator. As an application the paper presents the model of a simplified microwave oven (MWO) grill element that demonstrates πHYFLOW capability to combine ETDs integrators with other components like an on-off controller used to drive the grill. πHYFLOW ability to dynamically adapt model topology is used to represent the switching semantics of Hybrid Automata [18].

The paper is organized as follows. Section 2 gives an overview of the microwave oven (MWO) grill element. Section 3 introduces the πHYFLOW formalism base and network models. Section 4 describes the Exponential Time Differencing (ETD) integrator. Section 5 presents ETD description in the πHYFLOW^{++} M&S environment, a C++ implementation of πHYFLOW. Section 6 describes the grill network component and presents simulation results. Section 7 compares πHYFLOW with other M&S approaches.

2   MWO Grill Overview

For illustrating the modeling abilities of πHYFLOW a simplified version of a MWO grill component is used in this paper. The grill helps to highlight some difficulties exhibited by current modeling approaches in providing high-fidelity models of physical devices. The hybrid automaton describing grill temperature (T) is depicted in Fig. 1. The grill is modeled by three ODEs for the different modes of operation. Mode A represents the MWO with the door closed and with the grill power turned on. The external temperature is represented by T_{ext}, P_{grill} is the grill power when turned on, and k_{cld} is the temperature coefficient corresponding to the closed door. Mode B models the temperature when the grill power is turned off, and the door is closed. Mode C represents the oven with the door open. In this mode, the grill must be turned off by the oven control logic. In mode C the temperature coefficient is given by k_{opn}. A more detailed model requires additional variables, including, for example, the cooking time and the presence of food in the MWO [14]. The hybrid automaton implicitly assumes an underlying analog computer and the use of a continuous controller. It does not consider that the model may be implemented on a digital computer, and the heater can be driven by a digital controller. Although this automaton can be used for verification purposes it does not reflect the constraints that a model needs to obey for its implementation on a digital computer, where, for example, the numerical methods employed to solve the ODEs have an impact on solution accuracy. A digital on-off controller is a simple device for driving grill power. This controller samples the temperature at fixed time intervals and establishes a control signal of zero (off) when the temperature is above a reference value. When the value is below the reference it turns the power to level P_{grill} (on). A more advance strategy could involve, for example, the use of a continuous slide mode controller (CSMC). However, CSMCs tend to be more complex [8], and, in some cases, an on-off controller may be effective.

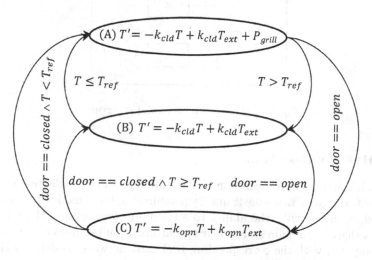

Fig. 1. Grill temperature hybrid automaton.

Although the hybrid automaton provides a good starting point to specify MWO grill temperature, is does not capture all the details that enable a high-fidelity model that runs on a digital computer/micro-controller. In particular, the diagram misses the exact time and temperature when the door is open/closed. Section 4 describes a representation for achieving an accurate solution of the ODEs of Fig. 1 on a digital computer.

272 F. J. Barros

3   The πHyFlow Formalism

A πHyFlow base model defines a modular entity that encloses a set of processes
$\{\pi_1, ..., \pi_n\}$ communicating through a shared p-state p, as represented in Fig. 2.
Each process keeps its own (private) p-state, and it can perform read/write operations on the shared p-state. Processes have suspend/resume semantics but are
non-preemptive making them implementable by coroutines, avoiding the synchronization problems associated with (preemptive) threads [21]. Base models
communicate through modular input (X) and output (Y) interfaces. Processes
do not have an input, since after their creation they are suspended at some
point on their flows waiting for being reactivated. Process communication with
the external entities can only thus be achieved, indirectly, through the shared
p-state p, that can be modified by all processes and by the model input function
ζ. Processes, however, have a modular output interface. Base model output is
computed by function $\Lambda = \{\Lambda_p\}$ that uses the outputs from all processes. Since
πHyFlow base models have a modular interface, they can be composed to form
networks as described in Sect. 3.3. A formal definition of the πHyFlow base
model is provided in the next section.

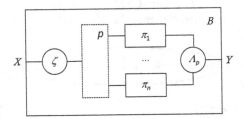

Fig. 2. πHyFlow base model structure.

3.1   πHyFlow Base Model

In the original HyFlow formalism a base model can only schedule one event.
πHyFlow removes this constraint by enabling a base model to run several
processes, each one with the ability to schedule its own event. Moreover, since
processes share a common state, their synchronization becomes easier to achieve
when compared with the corresponding HyFlow network model. A πHyFlow
base model associated with name B is defined by:

$$M_B = (X, Y, P, P_0, \zeta, \Pi, \pi, \sigma, \{\Lambda_p\}),$$

where:

$X = X^{\mathrm{c}} \times X^{\mathrm{d}}$ is the set of input flow values, with
  X^{c} is the set of continuous input flow values,
  X^{d} is the set of discrete input flow values,

$Y = Y^c \times Y^d$ is the set of output flow values, with
    Y^c is the set of continuous output flow values,
    Y^d is the set of discrete output flow values,
P is the set of partial shared states (p-states),
P_0 is the set of (valid) initial p-states,
$\zeta : P \times X^\varnothing \longrightarrow P$ is the input function,
    with $X^\varnothing = X^c \times (X^d + \varnothing)$,
Π is a set of processes,
$\pi : P \longrightarrow \mathcal{P}(\Pi)$ is the current-processes function, where $\mathcal{P}$ is the power set,
$\sigma : \mathcal{P}(\Pi) \longrightarrow P^*$ is the ranking function, where P^* is the set of all sequences
    based on set P, constrained to: $\sigma(A) = (a_1, \ldots, a_n) \Rightarrow \{a_1, \ldots, a_n\} ==$
    $A \wedge |\sigma(A)| == |A|$,
for all $p \in P$:
    $\Lambda_p \colon \underset{i \in A}{\times} Y_i^\varnothing \longrightarrow Y^\varnothing$ is the output function associated with p-state p,
    with $A = \sigma(\pi(p))$, and $Y^\varnothing = Y^c \times (Y^d + \varnothing)$.

The base model receives and produces both continuous, and discrete flows (events) thought the modular interfaces X and Y. The input function ζ is responsible for updating the current p-state when the model receives a value either through sampling or event communication. The set of processes is dynamic, being the current set given by function π. Given processes can access the shared p-state only one can be active at any time. The ranking function σ decides process resume order. The output function $\Lambda = \{\Lambda_p\}$ maps the outputs of all processes into the output associated with the base model. The formal description of a πHYFLOW process is provided in the next section.

3.2 πHYFLOW Process Model

A process is a sequence of actions that usually take some amount of time to be executed. Processes are coordinated by the base model that acts as a scheduler. When scheduled, the base model chooses a process that is enabled to execute and resumes it. After execution, the process suspends itself and gives the control back to the base model that selects the next process to run. A process becomes enabled when a given time interval has elapsed, or when the current guard condition is fulfilled. Given a base model B with a set of processes Π_B, the model of a process $\varpi \in \Pi_B$ is defined by:

$$M_\varpi^B = (Y, I, P, P_0, \kappa, \{\rho_i\}, \{\omega_i\}, \{\varkappa_i\}, \{\delta_i\}, \{\Lambda_i^c\}, \{\lambda_i^d\}),$$

where:

Y is the set of output flow values,
    Y^c is the set of continuous output flows,
    Y^d is the set of discrete output flows,
I is the set of indexes,
P is the set of p-states,

P_0 is the set of (valid) initial p-states,

$\kappa\colon P \longrightarrow I$ is the index function,

for all $i \in I$:

$\rho_i\colon P \longrightarrow \mathbb{H}_0^{+\infty}$ is the time-to-input function,

$\omega_i\colon P \longrightarrow \mathbb{H}_0^{+\infty}$ is the time-to-output function,

$\varkappa_i\colon P \times P_B \longrightarrow \{\top, \bot\}$ is the condition function,

$\delta_i\colon S \times P_B \longrightarrow P \times P_B$ is the transition function,

$\Lambda_i^c\colon S \times P_B \longrightarrow Y^c$ is the continuous output function,

$\lambda_i^d\colon P \times P_B \longrightarrow Y^d$ is the partial discrete output function,

$\Lambda_i^d\colon S \times P_B \longrightarrow Y^d \cup \{\varnothing\}$ is the discrete output function defined by:

$$\Lambda_i^d((p,e),p_B) = \begin{cases} \lambda_i^d(p,p_B) & \text{if } e == \omega_i(p) \\ \varnothing & \text{otherwise} \end{cases}$$

with $S = \{(p,e)\mid p \in P,\ 0 \le e \le \nu_{\kappa(p)}(p)\}$, the state set,

and $\nu_i(p) = \min\{\rho_i(p), \omega_i(p)\}$, $i = \kappa(p)$, is the time-to-transition function.

For time specification, πHyFlow uses the set of hyperreal numbers $\mathbb{H}$, that enables causality to be expressed, by assuming that a transition occurring at time t, changes process p-state at time $t + \varepsilon$, where $\varepsilon \in \mathbb{H}$ is an infinitesimal [3]. Time functions ρ and ω are constrained to the positive hyperreal values $\mathbb{H}_0^{+\infty}$.

A process defines only its output Y, while the *input* is *inferred* from base model p-state. A process defines its own p-state P, for reducing inter process dependency. A process dynamic behavior is ruled by six structured/segmented functions, being the segments currently active determined by the index function κ.

The active segments associated with p-state $p \in P$ are $(\rho_i, \omega_i, \varkappa_i, \delta_i, \Lambda_i^c, \lambda_i^d)|_{i=\kappa(p)}$.

The time-to-input-function $\{\rho_i\}$ specifies the interval for sampling (reading) a value. Since each process specifies its own reading interval, sampling is made asynchronously, and it can be made independently by any process. The time-to-output-function $\{\omega_i\}$ specifies the interval to produce a discrete flow. The condition/guard function $\{\varkappa_i\}$, checks whether the process has conditions to run given base model and process current p-states. Functions $\{\rho_i\}$ and $\{\omega_i\}$ specify a time interval for process re-activation, while $\{\varkappa_i\}$ checks if the process can be re-activated at the *current time*. Function $\{\delta_i\}$ specifies process and base model p-states after process re-activation. Function $\{\Lambda_i^c\}$ specifies process continuous output flow, and $\{\Lambda_i^d\}$ specifies process discrete output flow. The former can be non-null at every time instant, while the latter can only be non-null at a finite number of time instants during a finite time interval. $\{\Lambda_i^c\}$ can provide an exact description for an arbitrary continuous signal based on a discrete formalism. This feature is used in Sect. 4 to describe the continuous output flow of the ETD integrator.

3.3 πHYFLOW Network Model

A πHYFLOW network is composed by base or other network models. Additionally, each network has a special component, named as executive, that is responsible for defining network topology (composition and coupling). A πHYFLOW network model associated with name N is defined by:

$$M_N = (X, Y, \eta),$$

where:

N is the network name,
$X = X^c \times X^d$ is the set of network input flows,
$Y = Y^c \times Y^d$ is the set of network output flows,
η is the name of the network executive.

The executive is a πHYFLOW base model extended with topology related operators. The executive model is defined by:

$$M_\eta = (X, Y, P, P_0, \zeta, \Pi, \pi, \{\Lambda_p\}, \Sigma^*, \gamma),$$

where:
    Σ^* is the set of network topologies,
    $\gamma \colon P \longrightarrow \Sigma^*$ is the topology function.

The network topology $\gamma(p_\alpha) \in \Sigma$, corresponding to the p-state $p_\alpha \in P$, is given by:

$$\gamma(p_\alpha) = (C_\alpha, \{I_{i,\alpha}\} \cup \{I_{\eta,\alpha}, I_{N,\alpha}\}, \{F_{i,\alpha}\} \cup \{F_{\eta,\alpha}, F_{N,\alpha}\}),$$

where:

C_α is the set of names associated with the executive p-state p_α,
for all $i \in C_\alpha + \eta$:
    $I_{i,\alpha}$ is the sequence of influencers of i,
    $F_{i,\alpha}$ is the input function of i,
$I_{N,\alpha}$ is the sequence of network influencers,
$F_{N,\alpha}$ is the network output function,

for all $i \in C_\alpha$
    $M_i = (X, Y, P, P_0, \zeta, \Pi, \pi, \sigma, \{\Lambda_p\})$, for base models
    $M_i = (X, Y, \eta)$, for network models

Network topology is defined by executive function γ that maps executive p-state into network composition and coupling. Coupling information includes, for each model, a set of influencers and an input function. Changes in executive p-state can be mapped into changes in network topology, enabling the definition of dynamic structure models [5]. Since HYFLOW models have a continuous output flow, the sampling operation reads atomically all current outputs form the influencers models, and applies the input function, providing the influenced model with a single input value. This operation provides thus support for interface matching. The network has an output function for mapping the output values of its influencers into the network output Y. Likewise the base HYFLOW formalism [3] networks and base models are kept during simulation, enabling the co-simulation of πHYFLOW models. The MWO grill of Sect. 6 is described as a network model.

4   Exponential Time Differencing (ETD)

πHYFLOW ability to describe hybrid models is demonstrated by considering the exponential time differencing (ETD) integrator for solving ordinary differential equations (ODEs). Common numerical integrators, like BDF and Adams types, are based on polynomial interpolation. A different approach has been taken by ETD that uses the exact solution for the linear part of the ODE [9]. ETD has several advantages over conventional integrators including the possibility of using large stepsizes, even when solving so-called stiff ODEs. ETD considers ODEs in the form of:

$$y' = ky + F(x(t), y(t)), y(0) = y_0, \tag{1}$$

where k is a constant coefficient and F represents the non-linear part. The *exact* solution for $t \in [0, T]$ is given by [9]:

$$y(t) = y_0 e^{kt} + e^{kt} \int_0^t e^{-k\tau} F(x(\tau), y(\tau)) d\tau. \tag{2}$$

Considering the 0th-order approximation for F:

$$F(x(t), y(t)) \approx F(x(0), y(0)), \tag{3}$$

the corresponding approximation for the solution $y(t), t \in [0, T]$ is given by:

$$y(t) \approx -\frac{F(x_t, y_t)}{k} + \left(y_0 + \frac{F(x_t, y_t)}{k} \right) e^{kt}, \tag{4}$$

yielding the numerical integrator with a fixed sampling interval T described by:

$$y_{n+1} = -\frac{F(x_n, y_n)}{k} + \left(y_n + \frac{F(x_n, y_n)}{k} \right) e^{kT}. \tag{5}$$

While Eq. (5) can be used for numerical integration, Eq. (4) provides the dense output between steps that can be sampled, without the need for interpolation, by other components. If we constraint the input signal F to be piecewise constant, Eq. (4) becomes *exact*, and the ETD can be driven by input discontinuities, obviating the use of sampling (stepsize $= \infty$). This case is typical of some controllers, like on-off digital controllers that produce piecewise constant output values.

An ETD for integrating piecewise constant signals is described by:

$$M_R = (X, Y, P, P_0, \zeta, \Pi, \pi, \sigma, \{\Lambda_p\}),$$

where:

2   $X = \{\} \times \mathbb{R},$
   $Y = \{\} \times \mathbb{R},$
4   $P = \mathbb{R} \times \{\top, \bot\},$
   $P_0 = \{F, event = \bot\},$
6   $\zeta((F, event), (F', event)) = (F', \top),$
   $\Pi = \{\eta\},$
8   $\pi(F, event) = \eta,$
   $\sigma(F, event) = (\eta),$
10   $\Lambda_{(F, event)}(F, event) =$
     $(\Lambda^c_{\kappa_\eta(p_\eta), \eta}((p_\eta, e_\eta), (F, event, k)), \Lambda^d_{\kappa_\eta(p_\eta), \eta}((p_\eta, e_\eta), (F, event))).$

The partial state includes the last input value F, and the flag *event* to signal a change in the input value (lines 4–5). Each time the input signal changes, the ETD receives an update, that is processed by the input function ζ (line 6). When this happens, the *event* flag is set to $\top$, informing the integration process η (line 7) that a discontinuity has occurred. ETD output is computed from process η (lines 10–11). Process η is defined by:

$$M_\eta^{ETD} = (Y, I, P, P_0, \kappa, \{\rho_i\}, \{\omega_i\}, \{\varkappa_i\}, \{\delta_i\}, \{\Lambda_i^c\}, \{\lambda_i^d\})$$

where:

2   $Y = \mathbb{R} \times \mathbb{R},$
   $I = \{0, 1\},$
4   $P = I \times \mathbb{R}^3,$
   $P_0 = \{id = 0, y \in \mathbb{R}, F \in \mathbb{R}, k \in \mathbb{R}\},$
6   $\kappa(id, y, F, k) = id,$
   $\rho_{0,1}(id, y, F, k) = \infty,$
8   $\omega_0(id, y, F, k) = \infty,$
   $\omega_1(id, y, F, k) = 0,$
10   $\varkappa_0((id, y, F, k), (F', event)) = event,$
   $\varkappa_1((id, y, F, k), (F', event)) = \bot,$
12   $\delta_0(((id, y, F, k), dt), (F', event)) =$
     $((1, -\frac{F}{k} + (y + \frac{F}{k})e^{k \cdot dt}, F', k'), (F', \bot)),$
14   $\delta_1(((id, y, f, k, sTime), dt), (F', event)) =$
     $((0, y, f, k), (F', event)),$
16   $\Lambda^c_{0,1}(((id, y, f, k), dt), (F', event)) = -\frac{F}{k} + (y + \frac{F}{k})e^{k \cdot dt},$
   $\lambda^d_0((id, y, f, k), (F', event)) = \varnothing,$

18 $\lambda_1^d((id, y, f, k), (F', event)) = y.$

The process produces $Y = \mathbb{R} \times \mathbb{R}$ (line 1), a continuous flow with the ODE solution, and a discrete flow with the current output value, available at discontinuities instants. The process cycles between indexes 0 and 1 (line 3). At index 0 the process performs ODE integration. Index 1 is used to produce a discrete flow. Process p-state variables include the current index id, the last computed output flow y, the input value F, and the constant k to describe Eq. (4) (lines 4–5). The model never samples its input, as set by $\rho_{0,1}(id, y, f, k) = \infty$ (line 7), since it is designed for integrating piecewise constant signals. The model is passive at index 0, waiting for an event (a discontinuity in the input value) that will re-activates it (line 10). At index 0, when an event arrives, the model performs function δ_0 (lines 12–13) that updates the current value y according to Eq. (4). The model changes then to index 1, and it immediately produces a discrete flow, as set by $\omega_1(id, y, f, k) = 0$ (line 9), and goes back to index 0 (lines 14–15). The discrete output is given by line 18 and it corresponds to ETD current value y that was previously updated in line 13. The continuous output flow is defined by $\Lambda_{0,1}^c$ (line 16) that implements Eq. (4). The next section provides an implementation of the ETD in the πHyFlow^{++} framework.

5 πHyFlow^{++} ETD

πHyFlow^{++} is an implementation of πHyFlow in MSVC++ 20. πHyFlow^{++} uses C++ support for modules, variants, lambdas, and coroutines. It uses the concept of port to segment continuous and discrete flows. For each discrete flow input πHyFlow^{++} assigns an input buffer that collects all values directed to that port. Each continuous output port is assigned to a process that defines a function parameterized by the elapsed time since process last transition. For modeling the ODEs in Fig. 1, instead of switching the ETD component, the same ETD is kept but the ETD described in the previous section is extended with the possibility to adjust the ODE coefficient k. Listing 1 provides πHyFlow^{++} implementation of the ETD component that represents the modified ETD integrator. The ETD has discrete input ports "event" and "k" (line 4) to receive information about changes in input function value, and in ODE coefficient, respectively. The continuous input port "value" (line 3) enables ETD to sample the current value of the input function. ETD output is available at the continuous port "value" (line 5), while events are produced at discrete port "event" (line 6).

```
class ETD: public sim::component {                                        1
public:                                                                   2
    std::vector<sim::port> in_ports_c() {return {"value"};}               3
    std::vector<sim::port> in_ports_d() {return {"event", "k"};}          4
    std::vector<sim::port> out_ports_c() {return {"value"};}              5
    std::vector<sim::port> out_ports_d() {return {"event"};}              6
public:                                                                   7
    ETD(std::string_view const name, double k, double y): sim::component(name) {   8
        init();                                                           9
        integrator("ETD", k, y);                                         10
    }                                                                    11
```

```
sim_void integrator(std::string_view const name, double k, double y) {    12
    sim_start(name);                                                      13
    double F = 0.;                                                        14
    output_c("value", [&] (const double& dt) {                            15
        return −F / k + (y + F / k) * exp(k * dt);                        16
    });                                                                   17
    sim_wait sample("value", F);                                          18
    auto& events = buffers_d["event"];                                    19
    auto& k_buf = buffers_d["k"];                                         20
    while (true) {                                                        21
        sim_wait until([&] {return events.any() || k_buf.any();});        22
        events.clear();                                                   23
        y = sample_out<double>("value");                                  24
        sim_wait out("event", y);                                         25
        if (k_buf.any())                                                  26
            k = std::get<double>(k_buf.remove());                         27
        sim_wait sample("value", F);                                      28
    }                                                                     29
}                                                                         30
};                                                                        31
```

Listing 1. πHYFLOW^{++} definition of the ETD component.

The EDT defines process "integrator" that performs the numerical integration. ETD output is defined in lines 15–17 and it implements Eq. 4 providing the continuous output in port "value". The model samples the current input value "F" in line 18, enabling EDT to be inserted in simulation at any time, avoiding the creation of an initialization by the component that produces by the input function. The ETD performs a loop (line 21) where it waits for a discrete flow in port "event" or in port "k" (line 22). When a discontinuity is signaled, the ETD reads the current output value available at port "value" (line 24). This value is sent as a discrete flow through port "event" (line 25). If the ETD integration coefficient is modified the new value is read in line 27. The current value of the input is read in line 28. Since the coefficient "k" can also affect EDT input function, this sampling operation guarantees the value is updated. This situation occurs in the grill component, as described in Fig. 1. The next section presents the grill network model that generates its temperature using the ETD integrator.

6 πHYFLOW^{++} Grill Component

For simulation is focused on MWO grill temperature as described by the automaton of Fig. 1. The grill is modeled by the network model depicted in Fig. 3. It is composed by the executive and the ETD component named "Temp". As mentioned in Sect. 3.3 the executive is responsible to keep network topology (composition and coupling). Although composition remains constant, coupling needs to be modified for reflecting the ODEs associated with modes A, B and C of Fig. 1. The executive receives information from an external door sensor through the continuous and discrete ports named "door". When mode is changed the executive uses discrete output port "k" to update the ETD with a new ODE coefficient. Grill continuous input port "on-off" receives a value from an on-off digital controller: a piecewise constant signal with values 0 (off) and P_{grill} (on).

The discrete input port "event" receives the events generated by the controller indicating a discontinuity in the control signal. The executive runs process "door" described in Listing 2 to manage grill mode switching. Initialization parameters include "k_opn" and "k_cld", representing the ODEs coefficients of Fig. 1 k_{opn} and k_{cld}, respectively. The constant external temperature t_{ext} is represented by parameter "t_ext".

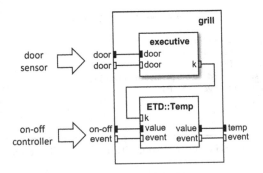

Fig. 3. Grill network model.

```
sim_void door(std::string_view const name, double k_opn, double k_cld, double t_ext) {      1
    sim_start(name);                                                                          2
    int door;                                                                                 3
    sim_wait sample("door", door);                                                            4
                                                                                              5
    if (door) {                                                                               6
        merger_c("Temp", "value", [k_cld, t_ext] (const sim::vector<sim::cvalue>& v) {        7
            double on_off = std::get<double>(v[0]);                                           8
            return -k_cld * t_ext + on_off;                                                   9
        });                                                                                  10
        sim_wait out("k", k_cld);                                                            11
    }                                                                                         12
    auto& door_buf = buffers_d["door"];                                                      13
    while (true) {                                                                           14
        sim_wait until([&] {return door_buf.any();});                                        15
        int door = door_buf.remove<int>();                                                  16
        double k = (door == 0)? k_opn: k_cld;                                                17
        merger_c("Temp", "value", [k, t_ext] (const sim::vector<sim::cvalue>& v) {          18
            double on_off = std::get<double>(v[0]);                                          19
            return -k * t_ext + on_off;                                                      20
        });                                                                                  21
        sim_wait out("k", k);                                                                22
    }                                                                                         23
    sim_end;                                                                                 24
}
```

Listing 2. πHYFLOW^{++} oven grill 'door' process.

Initial network topology assumes the door oven is open being the current ODE associated with parameter "k_opn" $\equiv k_{opn}$. The process starts by sampling the continuous input port "door" (line 4), to check whether the assumption holds. If the door is actually closed the input function associated with "ETD::Temp" continuous input port "value" is adjusted with parameter "k_cld" (lines 6–9). Additionally, the updated coefficient is also sent to "ETD::Temp" through discrete output port "k" (line 10). The continuous output value from the on-off controller is read in line 7. The process follows a loop (line 13) where it waits for a change in door state (line 14). Each time the door status is modified the executive adapts the merger function (lines 17–20) and updates ETD temperature coefficient (line 21). The ability to define the grill as a network greatly simplifies topology adaptation that are kept local within the grill. This representation hides grill internal details from other components.

Simulation Results

Grill simulation uses a simple scenario with a sequence of steps described in Listing 3. This testing driver is part of larger MWO oven model that emulates oven door, grill knob, clock, and oven scale. Line 3 establishes a cooking time of 200 s. The door is initially open (line 4), and the grill knob is turned "on" (line 5). The oven is loaded with 0.5 kg (line 6). The door is closed at time 10 (line 7), opened at time 60, and closed again at time 70. The grill knob is turned off at time 170, and the door is finally opened at time 230. The grill on-off controller is switched on from time 10 (door closed) to time 60 (door open). It is off from time 60 to time 70 (door closes), and on from time 70 to time 170 (grill knob off.)

```
sim_void test(std::string_view const name) {                                         1
    sim_start(name);                                                                 2
    cooking_time = hhmmss(0, 3, 20);          //cooking time = 3m20s                  3
    sim_wait out("door_emul", 0);             //open door                            4
    sim_wait out("grill_emul", 1);            //grill knob on                        5
    sim_wait out("scale_emul", weight = .5);  //add 0.5 kg food into oven            6
    sim_wait out(10., "door_emul", 1);        //10 s                                 7
    sim_wait out(50., "door_emul", 0);        //60 s                                 8
    sim_wait out(10., "door_emul", 1);        //70 s                                 9
    sim_wait out(100., "grill_emul", 0);      //170 s                                10
    sim_wait out(60., "door_emul", 0);        //230 s                                11
    sim_end;                                                                         12
}                                                                                    13
```

Listing 3. Testing the grill.

The process in Listing 3 shows the simplicity of PI for describing the flow of a simulation entity. Although not detailed here, the corresponding HYFLOW implementation would be more complex as can be seen in other HYFLOW models [2]. Simulation was performed with the parameters listed in Table 1, where "stime" is the sampling interval used by the on-off controller.

When turned on, the controller commands the grill, producing a piecewise constant signal of 0, when the temperature is above the reference value T_{ref}, and P_{grill} when the grill temperature is below T_{ref}. The effect of the controller in grill temperature is shown in Fig. 4. In the interval [0, 10] the temperature corresponds to the external temperature (20 °C). The grill is turned on at time 10 and the temperature rises until it crosses the reference value. The temperature

Table 1. Simulation parameters.

T_{ext}	20.00 °C
T_{ref}	140.00 °C
k_{opn}	−0.10
k_{cld}	−0.02
P_{grill}	7.00
s_{time}	2.00 s

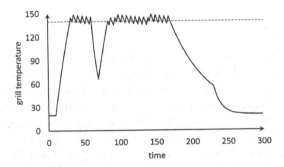

Fig. 4. Grill temperature.

oscillates around $T_{ref} = 140$ °C until time 60. The amplitude of the oscillations is related to controller sampling interval since the grill runs without control between sampling instants. Larger sampling intervals will produce larger oscillations, except in cases when the reference temperature is too high, and the grill has not enough power to reach that value. When the door is opened the controller is turned off and the temperature starts to drop until time 70 where the door is closed again, and the controller starts driving the grill. The grill knob is turned off at time 170, and the temperature stats to drop with the closed door. When the door is opened at time 230, the temperature continues to drop but at a different rate, asymptotically decreasing to the external temperature. Given simulation parameters, the grill temperature is computed without error by the ETD. Except for the few samples taken at initialization and at discontinuous, the ETD takes no additional samples for performing the integration, making the simulation very efficient. The representation of hybrid systems provided by πHYFLOW^{++} makes it possible to compose the ETD integrator with the digital controller.

7   Related Work

Traditionally, the representation of continuous/hybrid systems involves the composition of models using a facade modular GUI, being the set of resulting ODEs flattened for numerical integration [12]. Although a model can have a modular appearance its simulation may not be modular. Models are usually translated into a set of ODE/DAE that are solved with a common type of numerical integrator. The combination of heterogeneous integrators like ETD or geometric solvers is not possible, affecting the fidelity of models. Model flattening poses also problems for supporting changes in model topology.

More recently, techniques of co-simulation have been developed, guaranteeing that both models and their simulation are modular. A major problem with these solutions is the low accuracy in the representation of continuous signals, that are commonly described by piecewise constant functions [7,22]. This kind of approach make it difficult to produce high-fidelity models. Q-DEVS [23], also uses piecewise constant signals making it not suitable to represent the ETD integrator. GDEVS [13] support for dense outputs is limited to polynomials, being unable to provide an exact description of the ETD integrator, for example. Additionally, models need to export their polynomial coefficients so its dense output can be computed by other models. Models require thus to know their set of influencers in order to compute their current outputs and their combined effect, compromising modularity and reuse. πHyFlow, on the contrary, relies on the sampling operation that hides composition details, ensuring that models are independent of the network they belong to. The lack of dense outputs can be mitigated if all models sample synchronously. However, in systems involving, for example, several digital controllers the absence of synchronicity can easily occur requiring the support for dense outputs. When using digital twins (DTs), dense outputs may also be necessary for enabling the seamlessly swap between the real system and the DT.

The Continuous Flow System Specification formalism (CFSS) has introduced the concepts of generalized sampling and continuous flows (dense outputs) [4]. These two constructs enable the exact representation of continuous signals in a digital computer, making it possible to sample continuous flows that can be made both time and component varying. CFSS supports co-simulation since it guarantees modularity of both models and the corresponding simulation. πHyFlow uses CFSS operators to enable co-simulation and the accurate description of continuous signals. The support for multiple clocks was introduced in Esterel [6] and Modelica [11] languages, but continuous flows are limited to piecewise constant segments. These limitations do not enable the representation of continuous flows required, for example, to model the ETD integrator described in Sect. 4. Other representations, like Communication sequential processes (CSPs) [19], and Khan networks [20], can only provide support for piecewise constant signals.

A set of modeling formalisms and their interconnections to achieve a representation of hybrid systems has been presented by [27]. HyFlow concepts of sampling and dense output provide a unifying framework where existing formalism like, for example, discrete time and memory-less functions are just particular cases of HyFlow models, requiring no additional operators for enabling their composition. Contrarily to Modelica [11] and formalisms like DESS&DEVS [27], πHyFlow does not provide a direct representation of ODEs. πHyFlow, however, was designed to provide an open framework where new numerical methods can be represented.

Conclusion

The πHYFLOW is a modeling and simulation formalism for describing hybrid models based on continuous flows, generalized sampling, and discrete events. These operators enable the representation of high-fidelity models on digital computers based on non-conventional integrators like ETD. The process interaction worldview (PI) greatly simplifies model development enabling modeler to choose the granularity level of the base model. πHYFLOW support for PI ensures the hierarchical and modular representation required to model complex systems. πHYFLOW dynamic network topologies simplify the representation of Hybrid Automata. πHYFLOW^{++} is a C++20 implementation of the πHYFLOW formalisms that uses coroutines to provide an efficient implementation of simulation processes. Future work will address the integration of πHYFLOW^{++} with a standard co-simulation framework.

References

1. Ascher, U., Petzold, L.: Computer Methods for Differential Equations and Differential-Algebraic Equations. SIAM (1988)
2. Barros, F.: A modular representation of fluid stochastic Petri nets. In: Theory of Modeling and Simulation Symposium (2016)
3. Barros, F.: On the representation of time in modeling & simulation. In: Winter Simulation Conference (2016)
4. Barros, F.: A framework for representing numerical multirate integration methods. In: AI, Simulation, and Planning in High Autonomy Systems, pp. 149–154 (2000)
5. Barros, F.: Dynamic structure multiparadigm modeling and simulation. ACM Trans. Model. Comput. Simul. **13**(3), 259–275 (2003)
6. Berry, G., Sentovich, E.: Multiclock esterel. In: Margaria, T., Melham, T. (eds.) CHARME 2001. LNCS, vol. 2144, pp. 110–125. Springer, Heidelberg (2001). https://doi.org/10.1007/3-540-44798-9_10
7. Blochwitz, T., et al.: Functional mockup interface 2.0: the standard for tool independent exchange of simulation models. In: 9th International Modelica Conference (2012)
8. Cho, H., Wanichanon, T., Udwadia, F.E.: Continuous sliding mode controllers for multi-input multi-output systems. Nonlinear Dyn. **94**(4), 2727–2747 (2018). https://doi.org/10.1007/s11071-018-4521-6
9. Cox, S., Matthews, P.: Exponential time differencing for stiff systems. J. Comput. Phys. **176**, 430–455 (2002)
10. Dahl, O.J., Myhrhaug, B., Nygaard, K.: SIMULA - an ALGOL-based simulation language. Commun. ACM **9**(9), 671–678 (1966)
11. Elmqvist, H., Mattsson, S.E., Otter, M.: Object-oriented and hybrid modeling in modelica. J. Européen des Systèmes Automatisés **35**(1) (2001)
12. Fritzson, P.: Principles of Object-Oriented Modeling and Simulation with Modelica 2.1. Wiley (2003)

13. Giambiasi, N., Escude, B., Ghosh, S.: GDEVS: a generalized discrete event specification for accurate modelling of dynamic systems. SIMULATION: Trans. the SCS **17**(3), 120–134 (2000)
14. Gomaa, H.: Designing Software Product Lines with UML
15. Hairer, E., Lubich, C., Wanner, G.: Geometrical Numerical Integration: Structure-Preserving Algorithms for Ordinary Differential Equations. SSCM, vol. 31, 2nd edn. Springer, Berlin (2005)
16. Healy, K., Kilgore, R.: Silk: a Java-based process simulation language. In: Winter Simulation Conference, pp. 475–482 (1997)
17. Henriksen, J.: GPSS - finding the appropriate world-view. In: Winter Simulation Conference, pp. 505–516 (1981)
18. Henzinger, T.: The theory of hybrid automata. In: 11th Annual IEEE Symposium on Logic in Computer Science, pp. 278–292 (1996)
19. Hoare, C.: Communicating sequential processes. Commun. ACM **21**(8), 666–677 (1978)
20. Khan, G.: The semantics of a simple language for parallel programming. In: IFIP Congress (1974)
21. Lee, E.: The problem with threads. Computer **39**(5), 33–42 (2006)
22. Lee, E.A., Zheng, H.: Operational semantics of hybrid systems. In: Morari, M., Thiele, L. (eds.) HSCC 2005. LNCS, vol. 3414, pp. 25–53. Springer, Heidelberg (2005). https://doi.org/10.1007/978-3-540-31954-2_2
23. Lee, J., Zeigler, B.: Theory of quantized systems: formal basis for DEVS/HLA distributed simulation environment. In: SPIE Proceedings, pp. 49–58 (1998)
24. Liu, J.: Simulus: easy breezy simulation in Python. In: Winter Simulation Conference, pp. 2329–2340 (2020)
25. Marzolla, M.: libcppsim: a SIMULA-like, portable process-oriented simulation library in C++. In: 18th European Simulation Multiconference, pp. 222–227 (2004)
26. Paredis, R., Mierlo, S., Vangheluwe, H.: Translating process interaction world view models to DEVS: GPSS to (Python(P))DEVS. In: Winter Simulation Conference, pp. 2221–2232 (2020)
27. Praehofer, H.: Systems theoretic formalisms for combined discrete-continuous system simulation. Int. J. Gen. Syst. **19**(3), 219–240 (1991)
28. Russel, E.: Building Simulation Models with Simscript II.5. CACI, La Jolla (1999)
29. Schruben, L.: Simulation modeling with event graphs. Commun. ACM **26**(11), 957–963 (1983)

CIFMA 2022 - 4th International Workshop on Cognition: Interdisciplinary Foundations, Models and Applications

CIFMA 2022 Organizer's Message

The workshop on Cognition: Interdisciplinary Foundations, Models and Applications (CIFMA) aims first and foremost to bring together practitioners and researchers from academia, industry and research institutions who are interested in the foundations and applications of cognition from the perspective of their areas of expertise and aim at a synergistic effort in integrating approaches from different areas. It also aims to nurture cooperation among researchers from different areas and establish concrete collaborations; and to present formal methods to cognitive scientists as a general modelling and analysis approach, whose effectiveness goes well beyond its application to computer science and software engineering.

The fourth edition of this workshop (CIFMA 2022), held on September 27, 2022, included presentations by 12 speakers. The edition received 14 submissions, out of which five papers were accepted for both presentation and publication, four papers were accepted only for presentation with a conditional acceptance for publication, two papers were accepted only for presentation, two papers were rejected, and one was withdrawn by the author. All papers initially underwent a single-blind peer review process in which three reviewers were assigned to each paper. Conditionally accepted papers received a further round of review (double-blind) after presentation at the workshop: only three of them were accepted for publication and one was rejected. The workshop program also featured a keynote talk titled "Information flow in proofs by contradiction and effective learnability" by Ulrich Kohlenbach (Technische Universität Darmstadt).

I would like to thank the Program Committee members and the external reviewers for their enthusiasm and effort in actively participating in the review process. I am also grateful to the Workshop Chair, Paolo Masci, for his management commitment. Finally, I would like to thank all workshop attendees for their active participation in discussions and for the feedback they provided to the authors.

December 2022   Pierluigi Graziani

Organization

Program Committee Chair

Pierluigi Graziani   University of Urbino, Italy

Steering Committee

Antonio Cerone   Nazarbayev University, Kazakhstan
Pierluigi Graziani   University of Urbino, Italy
Paolo Masci   National Institute of Aerospace (NIA),
                                         USA

Program Committee

Samuel Alexander   U.S. Securities and Exchange Commission,
                                         New York, USA
Oana Andrei   University of Glasgow, UK
John A. Barnden   University of Birmingham, UK
Francesco Bianchini   University of Bologna, Italy
Stefano Bonzio   University of Cagliari, Italy
José Creissac   University of Minho, Portugal
Antonio Cerone   Nazarbayev University, Kazakhstan
Gustavo Cevolani   IMT School for Advanced Studies, Lucca,
                                         Italy
Peter Chapman   Edinburgh Napier University, UK
Gianluca Curzi   University of Birmingham, UK
Luisa Damiano   IULM University, Italy
Edoardo Datteri   University of Milano-Bicocca, Italy
Anke Dittmar   Rostock University, Germany
Alan Dix   Swansea University, UK
Pierluigi Graziani   University of Urbino, Italy
Yannis Haralambous   IMT Atlantique, France
Bipin Indurkhya   Jagiellonian University, Poland
Reinhard Kahle   NOVA University Lisbon, Portugal
Karl Lermer   ZHAW, Switzerland
Antonio Lieto   University of Turin, Italy
Kathy L. Malone   Nazarbayev University, Kazakhstan
Paolo Masci   National Institute of Aerospace (NIA),
                                         USA

Mieke Massink	Institute of Information Science and Technologies (CNRISTI), Italy
Paolo Milazzo	University of Pisa, Italy
Stefano Nicoletti	University of Twente, Netherlands
Eugenio Omodeo	University of Trieste, Italy
Antti Oulasvirta	Aalto University, Finland
Graham Pluck	Nazarbayev University, Kazakhstan
Giuseppe Primiero	University of Milan, Italy
Ka I Pun	Western Norway University of Applied Sciences, Norway
Pedro Quaresma	University of Coimbra, Portugal
Viola Schiaffonati	Politecnico di Milano, Italy
Giuseppe Sergioli	University of Cagliari, Italy
Sandro Sozzo	University of Leicester, UK
Mirko Tagliaferri	University of Urbino, Italy
Gentiane Venture	Tokyo University of Agriculture and Technology, Japan

Additional Reviewers

Alessandro Aldini	University of Urbino, Italy
Ekaterina Kubyshkina	University of Milan, Italy
Marcel Ertel	Eberhard Karls Universität Tübingen, Germany

Robot Nudgers. What About Transparency?

Stefano Calboli[✉]

Centre for Ethics, Politics and Society, University of Minho, Braga, Portugal
calbolistefano@gmail.com

Abstract. Robot nudgers – i.e. robots who employ nudges to steer users toward targeted behaviours – are a concrete reality nowadays. Although robot nudgers look like a promising technology for making individuals and society better off, some ethically relevant questions in programming them have been so far under-examined. The paper aims to contribute to filling this gap, identifying two ethical issues concerning nudges' transparency relevant when robots step into the shoes of nudgers. I proceed as follows. The paper begins by outlining what policy tools can be considered nudges (Sect. 1) and why scholars advocate for making their implementation transparent in order to shield persons' decision-making autonomy (Sect. 2). Therefore, I focus on the still unripe literature on robot-nudging and, in light of it, I properly frame ethical issues concerning nudges' transparency in human-robot interactions (Sect. 3). In Sect. 4, I discuss two ethically relevant points concerning transparency in robot-nudging so far overlooked. First, Robot nudgers - in contrast with human-nudgers - are potentially able to customize the kind of transparency granted to a specific user. Second, robot nudgers are able to monitor the impact of any feasible mixes of nudges and transparency on the effectiveness of the nudges in steering decision-makers. In both cases, ethically relevant questions emerge. I conclude by advocating for the involvement of ethicists in robot nudgers' programming at an early stage, in line with an integrative approach to social robotics (Sect. 5).

Keywords: Nudge · Ethics of nudging · Robot-nudging · Nudge transparency

1 Introduction

At least since the publication of the book *"Nudge: Improving Decisions About Health, Wealth and Happiness"* by Thaler and Sunstein in 2008 [39] (last edition: [40]), nudges should, and in fact often are [27], valuable parts of policymakers' toolbox. To understand what nudges are and why they are considered no-conventional policy tools, we should briefly delve into the theoretical background that has made possible their conception. The research carried out by Herbert

This work has been supported by Fundação para a Ciência e a Tecnologia, prot. UI/BD/152568/2022.

Simon on human bounded rationality has provided fertile ground for the coming of what has been called the "behavioural revolution" and the development of approaches aimed at modeling decision-making truest to *human cognition*, as it is. Such approaches contrast with the one adopted in neoclassical economics in which *homo oeconomicus* (HO henceforth) is the model, which is based on deliberately highly idealized assumptions (see [24]). Relevant to the purpose of the present paper, HO is featured by the following three traits. First, HO is *perfectly rational and has infallible cognitive* abilities. For instance, she is able to evaluate the expected utility of lotteries with no chance of failure. Second, HO has *perfect willpower and practical abilities*. Let us say that the agent decides to participate in a lottery; if so, afterthoughts, procrastination and akrasia will not hamper her decision. Last, a critical trait featuring HO is to be *perfectly informed* on, first, the options available and, second, the consequences associated with each option relevant for the utility. For instance, let us imagine that a communication for which the lottery prize is paid in annuities rather than in a lump-sum payment is released. If such information is relevant in terms of the utility enjoyed, the model assumes that she is certainly aware of it. In sum, if the information is available and relevant in terms of utility, the agent knows it. The "behavioural revolution" consisted in the endeavour of enriching and eventually revising the HO model in the belief that empirically and psychologically informed assumptions lead to better predictions of human behaviours. The seminal work by Amos Tversky and Daniel Kahneman showed the value of such an approach first, followed by the research carried out, among others, by Richard Thaler, one of the fathers of behavioral economics [38]. The "heuristic and bias" program sprang from the behavioural revolution and casts light on several systematic, and consequently predictable, deviations of humans' behaviours from HO [21]. Thaler and Sunstein have brilliantly considered such deviations as opportunities rather than impediments. Since flesh-and-blood humans are hopelessly driven by cognitive biases, why not take advantage of this and *nudge* decision-makers toward desirable behaviors? Indeed, Sunstein and Thaler consider a nudge to be "any aspect of the choice architecture that alters people's behavior in a predictable way without forbidding any options or significantly changing their economic incentives. To count as a mere nudge, the intervention must be easy and cheap to avoid. Nudges are not mandates" [39, p. 6]. In other words, nudges are kind of interventions that would be irrelevant if the world were populated by *homines oeconomici*, namely agents whose decisions are affected exclusively by bans, coercion, economic incentives, both positive and negative, and information necessarily unavailable up to that time. In other words, nudges can be conceived as interventions leverage on what Thaler calls *supposedly irrelevant factors*, namely factors that it would be correct to suppose to be irrelevant if humans behaved as *homines oeconomici*. Such definition of nudges has been deemed too vague, resulting in the difficulty of discerning between a policy that should be considered a nudge and more conventional policies [2,15]. In the remaining part of the paper, I adopt the term 'nudge' slightly more narrowly than as Thaler and Sunstein do, following the influential considerations made by Hausman and Welch [17]. Given the original definition, even reiterating already available information relevant to the options' utilities should be considered a nudge. Indeed, as seen, HO is assumed to be perfectly informed, so reiterating certain information is a supposedly irrelevant factor. However, to make salient information seems to be a traditional and well-established policymaking strategy, surely not as unconventional as nudges are described. Borrowing the words by Hausman and Welch, albeit partially decontextualized: "Thaler and Sunstein's characterization of paternalism mistakenly counts giving advice and rational persuasion that aims at the good of the advisee as paternalistic" [17, p. 127]. In order to formulate a definition of nudges that account for their disruptive originality, hereinafter I refer to nudges as policy tools leveraging on factors retained to be irrelevant (for HO), *except for reiterating information.*[1] Now that we have a definition of nudges that pays tribute to their originality, in the next section I will discuss the main ethical issue in nudging decision-makers, namely the lack of transparency.

2   Transparency in Nudging

The definition just outlined is narrow enough to exclude iterating information as nudges but, appreciably, large enough to include *all* kinds of interventions conceived to leverage human cognitive biases. The meaning of taking into account human cognitive biases in policymaking is twofold. First, it means exploiting cognitive biases, for instance, the default effect. Briefly, the default effect affects our propensity to choose a particular option within a defined set. Basically, the default effect captures the fact that agents will choose a certain option with more probability if it is the option they end up with if they do nothing. For instance, let us consider a topical subject: vaccine choice. Policymakers can arrange the choice environment relevant to the vaccine choice in at least two ways. On the one hand, policymakers can ask citizens to make an appointment proactively (opt-in option). On the other hand, vaccine appointments could be set by default; hence citizens who are not interested in vaccinating are asked to opt-out actively and cancel the vaccine appointment. This last condition turned out to promote a higher number of appointments and, in turn, a higher vaccination rate than the alternative condition [10,23]. However, *exploiting* cognitive biases is only one of the two feasible paths. Indeed, policymakers can also shape the choice environment to refrain, or at least mitigate, the effect of cognitive biases, encouraging more careful considerations. An instance of such kind of intervention is providing cooling-off periods when decision-makers face choices that have formerly involved a great deal of regret among peers. These different typologies of nudges are usually framed referring to the dual-system theory of mind developed by Kahneman and Tversky. Briefly, such theory brings into play two fictional characters, System 1 and System 2, that work in parallel to evaluate the option available and lead to a certain behaviour. System 1 includes

---

[1] This does not amount to saying that informing cannot be a form of nudging; instead, informing should be considered a form of nudging when cognitive biases are exploited (see [26]).

the intuitive, effortless and automatic cognitive processes. Cognitive biases are precisely due to the misuse of system 1, that is, either cases in which we rely on system 1, the automatic pilot, when system 2 should be called into play instead, or cases in which system 1-processes mislead our ongoing deliberations, as in the case of miscalculation of probabilities. Instead, system 2 includes all the deliberative, high-level and conscious cognitive processes. In light of Kahneman and Tversky's theory of mind, we could distinguish between system-1-nudges, namely nudges that leverage cognitive biases, and system-2-nudges, that is nudges that encourage the deliberative process to resist cognitive biases' influences. Such categorization is not just helpful in acknowledging the heterogeneity of the nudge theory; rather, it guides us in identifying the exact cases of ethically controversial nudging in liberal democracies. When nudgees find themselves in a choice environment featured by a system-2-nudge, they can easily recognize the attempt to influence their decisions made by the nudger. In the case of cooling-off periods, for instance, nudgees can easily detect the presence of the policy intervention and arguably become aware of its behavioral aim. Such kind of transparency on the policymakers' influence attempt is pivotal in liberal democracies where decisional autonomy is an essential value [36, 42]. Evidently, decisions made by agents who live in liberal democracies can, under certain circumstances, be influenced and directed by policymakers, as in the case of bans, coercion and economic incentives. However, what is instead impermissible to policymakers is imposing an influence without citizens being able to detect it, its behavioral aim and, eventually, being able to resist it [16, 33]. Unfortunately, system-1-nudges could easily involve this kind of concealed influence. As seen, system-1-nudges leverage human cognitive biases, which are deeply wired into our brains, making their influences typically go unnoticed. Let us consider nudges based on the default effect, specifically, the case concerning vaccine appointments just considered. Here, even if nudgees, in fact, could in some way be able to detect the intervention implemented (i.e. the setting of vaccine appointments as default) and eventually its behavioral aim, they would hardly be able to fully recognize the influence exerted by the intervention on their decisions, making it virtually impossible to resist it. This does not amount to saying that concealed influence attempts *feature all system-1-nudges*. For instance, it is not the case with the fake flies in the urinals adopted in airports worldwide. Here, although automatic processes are harnessed to reduce men's "spillage", nudgees can detect the intervention, the behavioral aim pursued through it, the influence exerted (take the shot!) and, eventually, be able to stupidly resist the influence. Nevertheless, many system-1-nudges other than nudges based on the default effect seems to easily impose a concealed influence; among them are nudges that rest on the framing effect [41] and the decoy effect [19]. For this reason, many scholars argue for providing some kind of transparency when such kinds of system-1-nudges are introduced. That is, scholars argued for additional interventions to make it easier for citizens to recognize the influence attempts made by nudgers. We could say that such kinds of intervention are meant to turn some system-1-nudges from tools of covert influence into *tools of transparent influence*. It is immaterial for the purpose of the paper to exhaustively overview the several proposals advanced to bring concealed influences into the light to make ethically justified the employing of challenging system-1-nudges in liberal democracies [20]. Here, it shall be sufficient to discuss the two lines along which such proposals have been developed. First, proposals differ from each other in the partition between nudgee and nudgers of the burden required to make nudges' influences actually transparent. If on the one hand, the empirical research on the impact of transparency on nudges' effectiveness provides for cases in which nudgers are asked to disclose information meant to avoid concealed influence [7,9,25], on the other hand, Bovens [6] and Ivankovic and Engelen, [20], albeit through different modalities, ask for greater accountability of nudgees, requiring them to be watchful. Secondly, the debate on what, in fact, should be made transparent to factually defuse the exploitation of hidden influences is not settled. Empirical works on nudges' transparency consider a wide range of information meant to make evident several aspects of nudges, beginning with information concerning the mere existence of an intervention and its behavioral aim. Other than that, information on the effect exploited, the cognitive mechanisms underlying the effect (on which we often know little, see [12]), the nudge's political aim, and the side effects involved (that is, make salient the fact that nudges could steer some nudgeers toward a behaviour undesirable for them) have been considered. This section made evident that "transparency" is at the heart of the discussion on the ethics of nudges, other than establishing that the available strategies to practically make transparent nudges are manifold. This makes it somewhat surprising that, to my best knowledge, nudges' transparency did not duly enter the debate around the ethics of robot-nudging yet, that is, cases in which robots step into the shoes of nudgers. In the next section, I will briefly overview the current debate on robot-nudging' ethics and set the stage for delving into the debate on transparency in robot-nudging, which, as we will see in Sect. 4, raises questions specific to robot-human interactions.

3   The Ethics of Robot-Nudging (So Far)

The technology to build robots able to influence users' behaviour through nudges (henceforth RN, which stands for robot nudgers) is already available. Factually, RN have already been conceived. For instance, Ali Mehenni and colleagues [1] experimented the use of nudger dialogue systems as Pepper, a social robot, among children from five to ten years old. Hang and colleagues [14] investigated if the positive effect on altruism that nudges showed in human-human interaction characterises also cases in which social robots are nudgers. In addition, it is not that hard to imagine reprogramming robots already built and eventually placed on the market, to make them able to nudge. For example, let us consider the robot trainer developed by Rea and colleagues [30] to assess the strength of polite and impolite verbal encouragement in steering users to exercise better. This robot could be reprogrammed to convey, other than im(polite) encouragements, sentences designed to prompt peer pressure, so sentences meant to make salient that the members of the relevant social network, let us say elderly people, train harder than the user. Notwithstanding RN are an already available computing technology and a widespread one in the near future, the debate on the ethics of robot-nudging is scarce, though not absent. In 2017, the IEEE Standards Association established the *Ethically Driven Nudging for Robotic, Intelligent and Autonomous Systems* committee, and, in 2020, the team "Affective and social dimensions in the spoken interactions" led by Laurence Devillers, along with other colleagues, launched the "Bad Nudge - Bad Robot?" program. The program aims to delve into the risk posed by nudges to vulnerable people. The current literature on the ethics of RN stresses how when robots are considered as nudgers, new ethical questions emerge compared to those relevant when human-human interactions are in place. Investigation around robot-nudging's ethics can be roughly divided into two macro areas. The first macro area is devoted to ethical concerns linked to the *behavioral goals* RN should help to achieve. The second macro area instead addresses the ethical questions raised when the *nudging processes* are considered. Research investigation carried out by Borenstein and Arkin on nudging social justice [4], by Klincewicz [22] on stoic ethics, and by Howard and Sparrow [18] on nudging sexual behaviours belong to the first research area. Borenstein and Arkin [4] should be mentioned as well as research belonging to the second macro area. Their paper indeed discussed as well the level and the kind of control on nudges' behavioral aims that should be granted to nudgees. Rodogno [31] points out how social robots, as opposed to human nudgers, could promote behavioral changes influencing users' overall cognitive and affective states. Finally, Calboli and colleagues [8] discussed the impact of robots' design traits on their strength in nudging. Within the research investigation on nudging processes in robot-nudging, the debate on transparency completely lacks albeit transparency on the influence attempt made by human nudgers is at the heart of the literature on the ethics of nudging. In the light of the foregoing, it looks fundamental to investigate transparency as an ethical condition for robot-nudging, especially due to the peculiarity of human-robot interactions. It is worth stressing that here transparency has as its object the influence imposed on behaviours; hence it is dissimilar to the transparency relevant in the debate on AI explainability. in explainable AI, the focus is instead on users' chance to scrutinize the decisions performed by AI systems. It is even more earnest to focus on transparency if we consider the fact that, being robots embodied and physically present, they are able to nudge humans both directly and indirectly. Nudging directly means exploiting the physical presence, as in the case of the robot trainer above-mentioned. On the other hand, robots can also nudge indirectly, that is intervene in the choice environment inhabited by the would-be nudgees, as in the case in which a robot rearrange the pantry following behavioral sciences' insights. This last case marks a sharp difference with virtual AI agents. The following section is meant to pave the way to carry out research to fill this gap and, in turn, begin to see whether the request for transparency in robot-nudging implies ethical issues that do not emerge when human-human interactions are on focus.

4 Transparency in Robot-Nudging

This section aims to provide starting points to integrate issues related to transparency within the debate on the ethics of robot-nudging. In order to do so, I present two broad, ethically relevant points. First, when human-human interactions are in place, nudgers typically implement nudges to modify *univocally* the choice environment. That is, nudgers do not tailor the nudge's influence to the specific nudgee. Considering the case of vaccine appointments by default, the nudge applies to *all* citizens, regardless of personal tendencies, for instance, in terms of vaccine hesitancy [32]. In truth, it is worth noticing that customized nudging is available and, in fact, increasingly implemented even when human-human interactions are in place. However, when humans are nudgers, nudges are typically tailored to sub-groups rather than individuals, as in the work by Page and colleagues on reminder text messages to apply for receiving federal student aid. These reminders were customized in that they varied according to the stage in which students were: application not yet started, halfway through, or finished but follow-up requirements were coming [28]. With RN is another matter. For instance, thanks to facial recognition technologies, robots are tools able to customize their actions in accordance with the specific user. Let us recall the case of the robot-trainer developed by Rea and colleagues (cf. Sect. 3). Being fundamental to mentioning the actual reference network to successfully nudge (see [3]), the robot should convey peer-pressure-triggering information referred to older adults when an older adult uses the robot, and teenagers when a teenager trains (a classical example of peer-pressure is [11]). The degree of detailing in identifying the exact reference network can be virtually customized to an individual level. RN can for instance be programmed in a way in which facial recognition technologies are employed to nudge a specific user exclusively among many users or nudge several nudgees differently according to the specific users. Moreover, this very same strength opens the possibility to customize not only the nudging but also the kind and degree of transparency granted to the nudgee. That is, considering robots customized transparency is available. Hence, the following questions arise: *should it be done? If so, how? Are some customizations improper?* In other words, the nudgee who knows the robot's ability to nudge can be asked to choose the kind and level of transparency she wants to be in place, should it be deliberately done? Should RN be programmed in such a way? If so, the nudgee might opt for a different kind of transparency compared to the one considered to be the more suitable by the nudger. For instance, the nudgee could prefer a version of transparency for which the burden to detect and comprehend nudge are totally on her and, contrariwise, the nudger could retain more suitable to take charge of that burden, at least partially. Should nudgees be enabled to customize transparency? If so, a second ethically relevant question, strictly connected with this one, emerges: *are there options that should be forbidden from being deemed ethically improper?* Let us consider a case in which an obese person relies upon the help of a robot-nudger to lose weight and virtually save her life. Let us consider a case in which that person is persuaded, rightly or wrongly, that any form of transparency would impede her from reaching the aim and consequently opt for a complete and irrevocable opacity of nudges. Should this - namely, a choice that reminds the Millian case of self-enslavement - be permitted? On the opposite side of the spectrum, there could be cases where nudgees prefer instead, for whatever reason, that the burden required to detect nudges' influence is totally on the nudger's shoulders and that a full range of information should be released by the robot. It could be well the case, although it should be empirically investigated, that such kind of maximum transparency would impair the relationship between nudgees and RN, turning it into a series of annoying exchanges, breaking the harmony of the interaction and as a result hampering nudging processes[2]. The second ethically relevant question that emerges specifically when human-robot interactions are at hand concerns robots' potential to enhance their ability to nudge. RN can indeed be programmed to collect data in order to *profile* the nudgee, and so being able to identify the best mix between nudges and transparency in terms of nudges' efficacy. For instance, RN could identify the best timing to both nudge and make transparent the exerted influence in light of a developed model of users' circadian rhythms ([29], this case has been considered by Borenstein and Arkin [5] albeit in a different context). Hence, a second question emerges: *should RN be programmed to collect data to fulfil such an aim?* At first sight, once assumed that privacy issues can be overcome, collecting such data seems an unmissable opportunity. Indeed, these data would be able to help nudgees to independently achieve their behavioral goals by identifying the choice environments helpful to do so. Secondly, the data collected would make able RN suggest nudgees on how to proactively shape the choice environments they are responsible for to make them more likely to achieve the behavioral goals they yearned for. Nevertheless, a thorough analysis reveals the possibility that letting RN collect data on the best mix between transparency and nudge processes could result in severe side effects. The feeling to be observed, and monitored could indeed easily result in psychological reactance, namely the "unpleasant motivational arousal that emerges when people experience a threat to or loss of their free behaviors [...; this] results in behavioral and cognitive efforts to reestablish one's freedom" ([37, p. 205]). Unfortunately, psychological reactance is the primary concern among scholars regarding nudges' transparency. If this happens, it would jeopardize the harmony of the interactions between human nudgees and RN, compromise their social interaction, lead nudgees to avoid RN and ultimately curb the chance that users are factually nudged. The points I just made should be reasonably expected to be just two of the many instances of the ethically relevant questions that transparency in robot-nudging would raise. Even though these ethical issues should be high on the agenda of roboticists and ethicists, factually, they are not. Hopefully, the present work will encourage taking steps in this direction and inspire scholars to explore systematically transparency in robot-nudging. In the next section, I will summarize the paper's major points and clarify the methodological approach so far implicitly assumed.

---

[2] It is reasonable to believe that the same could result from boosting strategies, in which decisionmakers are put in the condition to exercise their agency [13].

5   Conclusion

In this paper, I discussed the conceptual background of the nudge theory and proposed a working definition of nudges capables of accounting for their originality and status as unconventional policy tools. Then, I engaged in the debate on the ethics of nudges and analyzed the request for transparency. Afterwards, I reviewed the current literature on the ethics of RN, and I stressed how the issues linked to nudges' transparency are overlooked and surprisingly so. In the last section, I discussed two ethically relevant points concerning transparency in robot-nudging in the hope of encouraging further research on the topic. I conclude the paper by making explicit the methodological assumption underlying the research investigations on transparency in robot-nudging I sketched. The research line described here would be fruitfully developed following the method paradigm called "integrative social robotics" (see [34]). Integrative social robotics advocates for an interdisciplinary approach, claiming that investigations on what social robots *can* do should advance hand in hand with investigations on what social robots *should* do [29]. This method paradigm aims at the setting of a complex investigation where value-theoretic research is involved since the early stages of social robots' development, being *interactions* what roboticists actually design and so products that inherently imply ethical norms (see the integrative social robotics' quality principles in [35]). The need to investigate the role that transparency plays in interactions among human nudgeers and RN can be successfully fulfilled following integrative social robotics. This approach enables us to identify and investigate the ethical significance of particular interactions, and doing so concerning transparency in robot-nudging is of paramount importance.

References

1. Ali Mehenni, H., Kobylyanskaya, S., Vasilescu, I., Devillers, L.: Nudges with conversational agents and social robots: a first experiment with children at a primary school. In: D'Haro, L.F., Callejas, Z., Nakamura, S. (eds.) Conversational Dialogue Systems for the Next Decade. LNEE, vol. 704, pp. 257–270. Springer, Singapore (2021). https://doi.org/10.1007/978-981-15-8395-7_19
2. Barton, A., Grüne-Yanoff, T.: From libertarian paternalism to nudging—and beyond. Rev. Philos. Psychol. **6**(3), 341–359 (2015). https://doi.org/10.1007/s13164-015-0268-x
3. Bicchieri, C.: Norms in the Wild: How to Diagnose, Measure and Change Social Norms. Cambridge University Press, Cambridge (2014)
4. Borenstein, J., Arkin, R.: Robotic nudges: the ethics of engineering a more socially just human being. Sci. Eng. Ethics **22**(1), 31–46 (2015). https://doi.org/10.1007/s11948-015-9636-2
5. Borenstein, J., Arkin, R.C.: Nudging for good: robots and the ethical appropriateness of nurturing empathy and charitable behavior. AI Soc. **32**(4), 499–507 (2016). https://doi.org/10.1007/s00146-016-0684-1
6. Bovens, L.: The ethics of nudge. In: Grüne Yanoff, T., Hansson, S.O. (eds.) Preference Change: Approaches from Philosophy, Economics and Psychology, pp. 207–219. Springer, New York (2009). https://doi.org/10.1007/978-90-481-2593-7_10

7. Bruns, H., Kantorowicz Reznichenko, E., Jonsson, M.L., Rahali, B.: Can nudges be transparent and yet effective? J. Econ. Psychol. **65**, 41–59 (2018)
8. Calboli, S., Graziani, P., Even, J.: The ethics of robot-nudgers' design. In: Proceedings of Robophilosophy. IOS Press (forthcoming)
9. Casal, S., Guala, F., Mittone, L.: On the transparency of nudges: an experiment. CEEL Working Papers no. 1902 (2019)
10. Chapman, G.B., Li, M., Colby, H., Yoon, H.: Opting in vs opting out of influenza vaccination. JAMA **304**, 43–44 (2010). https://doi.org/10.1001/jama.2010.892
11. Goldstein, N.J., Cialdini, R.B., Griskevicius, V.: A room with a viewpoint: using social norms to motivate environmental conservation in hotels. J. Consum. Res. **35**(3), 472–482 (2008). https://doi.org/10.1086/586910
12. Grüne-Yanoff, T.: Why behavioural policy needs mechanistic evidence. Econ. Philos. **32**(3), 463–483 (2016). https://doi.org/10.1017/s0266267115000425c
13. Grüne-Yanoff, T., Hertwig, R.: Nudge versus boost: how coherent are policy and theory? Mind. Mach. **26**, 149–183 (2016)
14. Hang, C., Ono, T., Yamada, S.: Designing nudge agents that promote human altruism. In: Li, H., et al. (eds.) ICSR 2021. LNCS (LNAI), vol. 13086, pp. 375–385. Springer, Cham (2021). https://doi.org/10.1007/978-3-030-90525-5_32
15. Hansen, P.G.: The definition of nudge and libertarian paternalism: does the hand fit the glove? Eur. J. Risk Regul. **7**(1), 155–174 (2016). https://doi.org/10.1017/s1867299x00005468
16. Hansen, P.G., Jespersen, A.M.: Nudge and the manipulation of choice: a framework for the responsible use of the nudge approach to behaviour change in public policy. Eur. J. Risk Regul. **41**, 3–28 (2013)
17. Hausman, D.M., Welch, B.: Debate: to nudge or not to nudge. J. Polit. Philos. **18**(1), 123–136 (2010)
18. Howard, M., Sparrow, R.: Nudge nudge, wink wink: sex robots as social influencers. In: Fan, R., Cherry, M.J. (eds.) Sex Robots. PSCC, vol. 28, pp. 57–74. Springer, Cham (2021). https://doi.org/10.1007/978-3-030-82280-4_4
19. Huber, J., Payne, J.W., Puto, C.: Adding asymmetrically dominated alternatives: violations of regularity and the similarity hypothesis. J. Consum. Res. **9**(1), 90–98 (1982)
20. Ivanković, V., Engelen, B.: Nudging, transparency, and watchfulness. Soc. Theory Pract. **45**, 43–73 (2019). https://doi.org/10.5840/soctheorpract20191751
21. Kahneman, D.: Thinking, Fast and Slow. Macmillan, New York (2011)
22. Klincewicz, M.: Robotic nudges for moral improvement through stoic practice. Techné: Res. Philos. Technol. **23**(3), 425–455 (2019). https://doi.org/10.5840/techne2019122109
23. Lehmann, B.A., Chapman, G.B., Franssen, F.M., Kok, G., Ruiter, R.A.: Changing the default to promote influenza vaccination among health care workers. Vaccine **34**, 1389–1392 (2016). https://doi.org/10.1016/j.vaccine.2016.01.046
24. Levine, D.K.: Is Behavioral Economics Doomed?: The Ordinary versus the Extraordinary. Open Book Publishers, Cambridge (2020)
25. Loewenstein, G., Bryce, C., Hagmann, D., Rajpal, S.: Warning: you are about to be nudged. Behav. Sci. Policy **1**, 35–42 (2015)
26. Loewenstein, G., Charter, N.: Putting nudges in perspective. Behav. Public Policy **1**(1), 26–53 (2017). https://doi.org/10.1017/bpp.2016.7
27. OECD: Behavioural Insights and Public Policy: Lessons from Around the World. OECD Publishing, Paris (2017)

28. Page, L.C., Castleman, B.L., Meyer, K.: Customized nudging to improve FAFSA completion and income verification. Educ. Eval. Policy Anal. **42**(1), 3–21 (2020). https://doi.org/10.3102/0162373719876916
29. Park, S., Moshkina, L., Arkin, R.C.: Mood as an affective component for robotic behavior with continuous adaptation via learning momentum. In: Proceedings of 10th IEEE-RAS International Conference on Humanoid Robots (2010)
30. Rea, S., Schneider, S., Kanda, T.: "Is this all you can do? Harder!": the effects of (im)polite robot encouragement on exercise effort. In: Proceedings of the 2021 ACM/IEEE International Conference on Human-Robot Interaction, pp. 225–233 (2021). https://doi.org/10.1145/3434073.3444660
31. Rodogno, R.: Nudging by social robots. In: Nørskov, M., Seibt, J., Quick, O.S. (eds.) Culturally Sustainable Social Robotics: Proceedings of Robophilosophy, pp. 337–345. IOS Press, Amsterdam (2020)
32. SAGE: Strategic Advisory Group of Experts on Immunization. Report of the SAGE Working Group on Vaccine Hesitancy (2014)
33. Schmidt, A.: The power to nudge. Am. Polit. Sci. Rev. **111**(2), 404–417 (2017)
34. Seibt, J.: Integrative social robotics–a new method paradigm to solve the description problem and the regulation problem? In: Seibt, J., Nørskov, M., Andersen, S.S. (eds.) What Social Robots Can and Should Do: 104–114. Springer, New York (2016)
35. Seibt, J., Damholdt, M., Vestergaard, C.: Five principles of integrative social robotics. In: Seibt, J., Nørskov, M., Coeckelbergh, M., Loh, J., Funk, M. (eds.) Envisioning Robots in Society – Power, Politics, and Public Space Proceedings of Robophilosophy 2018, pp. 28–42. IOS Press, Amsterdam (2018)
36. Smith, C., Goldstein, D., Johnson, E.: Choice without awareness: ethical and policy implications of defaults. J. Public Policy Mark. **32**, 159–172 (2013)
37. Steindl, C., Jonas, E., Sittenthaler, S., Traut-Mattausch, E., Greenberg, J.: Understanding psychological reactance. Zeitschrift Für Psychologie **223**(4), 205–214 (2015). https://doi.org/10.1027/2151-2604/a000222
38. Thaler, R.H.: Misbehaving: The Making of Behavioral Economics. W. W. Norton & Company (2016)
39. Thaler, R.H., Sunstein, C.R.: Nudge: Improving Decisions About Health, Wealth, and Happiness. Yale University Press, New Haven (2008)
40. Thaler, R.H., Sunstein, C.R.: Nudge: The Final Edition (Revised edn.). Penguin Books (2021)
41. Tversky, A., Kahneman, D.: Framing of decisions and the psychology of choice. Science **211**(4481), 453–458 (1981)
42. Wilkinson, T.M.: Nudging and manipulation. Polit. Stud. **61**(2), 341–355 (2012). https://doi.org/10.1111/j.1467-9248.2012.00974.x

Robot as Embodied Agent?
A Phenomenological Critique

Laura Corti[✉][iD]

University Campus Bio-Medico of Rome, Rome, Italy
l.corti@unicampus.it

Abstract. The problem of embodiment recurs several times in the contemporary debate in diverse disciplines, such as philosophy, neuroscience, and robotics. In particular, it is possible to define robots as (physical) embodied AI (Artificial Intelligence). From a philosophical point of view, this description opens a series of problems, such as: is the robotics embodiment comparable to the human one? In this paper, I will dig into this question by analyzing the robotics body compared with Embodied Cognition and the phenomenological tradition. Specifically, I will use the distinction between Körper and Leib as an epistemological pathway to dig into robotics. This essay wants to prove that the composite nature of the notion of the body, highlighted by phenomenology, is able to interpret the potentialities and limitations of robotics systems.

Keywords: Embodied robotics · Phenomenology · Body

1 Introduction

"Cognitive scientists have much to learn from Merleau-Ponty". This sentence introduces the essay titled *The challenge of Merleau-Ponty Phenomenology of embodiment for cognitive science* [1]. It is intriguing that the warning of 'guided' cognitive science by Merleau-Ponty implies that we face new challenges ahead. Dreyfus and Dreyfus faced the problem of a practical way of integration analyzing the concept of intentional arc and maximum grip; nevertheless, the idea of a "phenomenological-informed" cognitive science implies the need to re-interpret the history of cognitive science highlighting new perspectives. Specifically, this idea is very interesting in relation to Embodied Cognition, a flourishing research program in the last decade of the XX century. Embodied Cognition [2] is a research field in cognitive science that rediscovers the importance of the body for cognition; in this perspective, it has a direct (genetic, perhaps) link to Merleau-Ponty and phenomenology. For example, Merleau-Ponty argues that "Insofar as, when I reflect on the essence of subjectivity, I find it bound up with that of the body and that of the world, this is because my existence as subjectivity [= consciousness] is merely one with my existence as a body and with the existence of the world, and because the subject that I am, when taken concretely, is inseparable from this

P. Masci et al. (Eds.): SEFM 2022 Collocated Workshops, LNCS 13765, pp. 302–312, 2023.
https://doi.org/10.1007/978-3-031-26236-4_25

body and this world" [3]. Identifying an in-depth relationship between conscious-ness, body, and the world will prove to be a keyword for the development of the research program; for this reason, the french phenomenologist is recognized, de facto, as one of the significant inspiring and influencing philosophers for Embod-ied Cognition. So, on the one hand, it seems evident that at least a part of cogni-tive scientists refers directly to Merleau-Ponty; nevertheless, on the other hand, it is questionable in which ways the "phenomenological-inclined" cognitive sci-ence hinges upon the notion of bodiliness in phenomenology. This issue is partic-ularly relevant when we examine the application of Embodied Cognition to con-texts of use, such as robotics. In this perspective, the contribution wants to argue that "also roboticists have much to learn from Merleau-Ponty and phenomenol-ogy" deepening how it is possible and why this perspective is relevant. To achieve this goal, I assume the enactive paradigm [4] as a form of Embodied Cognition that defines cognition as body-environment dynamics involving the living body, sensorimotor capacities, and actions. It is particularly relevant for robotics since several studies develop enactive models for robots; this paradigm has been repeat-edly applied to developing solutions for human-like cognition in robotics [5,6]. But why is it necessary to discuss phenomenology in relation to robotics? The main reason is that, in literature, it is possible to identify a deep link between the enac-tive approach and phenomenology. For example, Thompson writes, "once science turns its attention to subjectivity and consciousness, to experience as it is lived, then it cannot do without phenomenology, which thus needs to be recognized and cultivated as an indispensable partner to the experimental sciences of mind and life. "[7]. In the above quote, Thompson recognizes three essential passages: 1) The role of phenomenology as an essential component in research on subjectivity and consciousness, 2) based on this, an inter-disciplinary interest in phenomenol-ogy, and 3) The application of phenomenology to different contexts. For this rea-son, a more in-depth investigation of the phenomenological and robotics body is (at least) appropriate, as current systems aim to incorporate cognitive systems that simulate the structures of the human being. In particular, this essay wants to deepen the topic of the body, aiming at analyzing how and why we need to re-consider the phenomenological approach in the field of robotics. In order to achieve this goal, the paper is structured as follows. Section 2 provides a brief overview of the meaning of the body in robotics. Then, in Sect. 3, I examine the distinction between the phenomenological and functional approach to the body, defining it as a key concept to deepen an inquiry into robotics. Finally, I address the benefits and the limits of a phenomenological-inclined approach to robotics (Sect. 4).

2 The Body in Robotics

If we accept that robotics has a lot to learn from Merleau-Ponty and that this means, primarily, addressing the question of the embodiment, then we need to start from the question, "what is a robot?". Specifically, it is necessary to inves-tigate the importance of a broader definition of robots instead of the common engineering perspective, which is focused on a functional-based description in which functionality and technical equipment are underlined. The urgency to adopt a more comprehensive description of robots is also related to epistemological and ethical needs. In the contemporary debate, robotics is often described as the technology of the future as [8] affirms[1]. From a technical point of view, a robot is a physical entity capable of acting in the real world through sensors (S), which are the basic units to receive information from the environment, and actuator/effectors (A) that are able to respond to sensory inputs and achieve goals. The two phases, detection, and action, are controlled by an overall system called controller (C) [9]. These three components are also listed as essential in the two main definitions of robotics, such as [10][2] and [11][3]. Comparing the two definitions proposed, it is possible to highlight three common ideas: 1) the idea that a robot is a physical entity capable of acting in the real world, 2) the fact that this machine is designed to do a particular job, 3) the idea that the purpose of this machine that is fulfilled autonomously or in coordination with humans.

In sum, the physical body and its ability to move and act in a natural environment are considered critical features of identifying the robot properly, contrasting with AI systems. In this sense, it is possible to broadly speak about the body in the context of robotics because it seems obvious to talk about robots as embodied agents. So, naively and somehow, there is a connection between robotics and the body. From the above, the body, defined as a physical element, is necessary to realize the goals of robotics, even though this idea does not necessarily imply an influence of the body on cognition.

Nevertheless, the definition of the robot as an embodied agent is consistent with the European perspective; in a previous version of the document titled A definition of Artificial Intelligence: main capabilities and scientific disciplines[4] robotics is defined as a "embodied AI" because it is a form of Artificial Intelligence that acts in the physical world.

Following this pathway, even those who, such as Andrea Bertolini, criticize the lack of a clear definition of robotics because every attempt is described as a "pointless exercise", identify the idea of bodiliness as a critical idea for

---

[1] the growing trend is also confirmed by the International Federation of Robotics (https://ifr.org/free-downloads).

[2] Robot is defined as "(1)a machine equipped with sensing instruments for detecting input signals or environmental conditions, but with reacting or guidance mechanisms that can perform sensing, calculations, and so on, and with stored programs for resultant actions; for example, a machine running itself; (2) a mechanical unit that can be programmed to perform some task of manipulation or locomotion under automatic control" [10].

[3] He defines the robots as "a smart machine that does routine, repetitive, hazardous mechanical tasks, or performs other operations either under direct human command and control or on its own, using a computer with embedded software (which contains previously loaded commands and instructions) or with an advanced level of machine (artificial) intelligence (which bases decisions and actions on data gathered by the robot about its current environment)" [11].

[4] https://digital-strategy.ec.europa.eu/en/library/definition-artificial-intelligence-ma in-capabilities-and-scientific-disciplines.

a description of robotics. He proposed a classification for robots considering various criteria, such as 1) Embodiment, 2) Level of autonomy, 3) Function, 4) Environment, and 5) Human-robot interaction. Thus, he affirms that a robot is "a machine which

(i) may either have a tangible physical body, allowing it to interact with the external world, or rather have an intangible nature-such as software or program,

(ii) which in its functioning is alternatively directly controlled or simply supervised by a human being, or may even act autonomously in order to

(iii) perform tasks, which present different degrees of complexity (repetitive or not) and may entail the adoption of non-predetermined choices among possible alternatives, yet aimed at attaining a result or providing information for further judgment, as so determined by its user, creator or programmer,

(iv) including but not limited to the modification of the external environment, and which in so doing may

(v) interact and cooperate with humans in various forms and degrees." [12].

So, for epistemological and ethical reasons, the body can serve as a valuable ally in defining robotics. The robotics body understood as a physical instance could be considered as a descriptive element because the robot's output always implies actions in the natural/physical world. Thus, in line with Ziemke[5] [20], the idea of the physical embodiment can be applied to robotics, meaning that the robotic system must necessarily have a physical instance capable of realizing output. In a general sense, starting from this consideration, it seems possible to conclude that the term embodiment, in the case of robotics, refers to the possession of a body[6] which is capable of moving and acting (physical embodiment). From a philosophical point of view, this consideration implies the necessity to deepen the topic of embodiment.

3   From Functional to Phenomenological Perspective on Body

The problem of embodiment recurs several times in the contemporary debate in diverse disciplines as it is recurrent in many fields of research, such as cognitive science [4], psychology [14], neuroscience [15], and robotics [16]. In the last research field, in parallel with the "naive" idea that the notion of body is relevant to robotics (Sect. 2), has been affirmed the idea that the body is not only the physical correlation necessary for the performativity of robotics but that the body determines (and not only is determined by) cognition. Indeed, since the

---

[5] Ziemke identifies six notions of embodiment, 1. structural coupling, 2. historical embodiment, 3. physical embodiment, 4. organismoid embodiment, 5. organismic embodiment, and 6. social embodiment [20].

[6] In this sense, it is possible to recognize the importance of"having a body" for robotics [13].

90s, in robotics, it is emerging the "Embodied Turn", which revalues the body dimension for artificial intelligence systems as cognition is considered embodied.

The Embodied Turn completely disrupts the "Cartesian inheritance" [17] that builds upon a clear dualism between mind and body in order to emphasize the integration of the two dimensions and a revaluation of the role of the body. So, embodiment holds that cognition occurs through the body, which thus assumes a role of primary importance. In the field of AI, this assumption is declined in the form "intelligence always requires a body" [17][7]. Pfeifer argues that, since the mid-1980s, the concept of embodied intelligence has been introduced in AI to indicate a clear contrast with the classic symbol processing method. The change of approach is mainly motivated by the inability to process symbols to "deepen our understanding of many intelligent processes" [17] as this perspective lacked in enhancing the interaction between the system and the environment. A central representational modeling error was found in the classic method, which limits its ability to manage systems synergistically. In direct contradiction, Rodney Brooks [16] proposes a parallel architecture that does not require a central computer to perform actions. From a theoretical point of view, intelligence is released from the concept of representation and is firmly anchored to a structural coupling between the body and the environment [19–21]. Based on this consideration, it is possible to argue that robotics, specifically after the Embodied Turn, can be described according to the framework of Embodied Cognition because it emphasizes the positive and direct role of the body for artificial agents. For example, Kerstin Dautenhahn clarifies that the robotics body is "adapted to the environment in which the agent is living." [18]. So, cognition is situated in the world, and the environment is more than just an input. From this statement, the researcher derives the fact that it is necessary to study intelligence as a phenomenon of a complex system, "embedded and coupled to its environment" [18]. In this perspective, the emphasis on bodiliness highlights the thesis of Embodied Cognition, which argues that mental states depend on the body and its properties. Specifically, as Shapiro notes, the central idea of robotics embodiment is the Replacement. "Proponents of Replacement deny that cognition lends itself to any useful sort of computational description; they similarly question the utility of a concept that is central both to connectionist and computational theories of mind: representation." [2]. Thus, the replacement hypothesis denies a computational-inspired approach, which is grounded in symbols, internal representation, and computation. In other words, the idea is to build open systems that interact with the environment in a productive way. As summarised in [21], this perspective could be framed in terms of the weak (embodied cognition) thesis, which emphasizes the positive role played by the body in cognition, but does not imply a phenomenological example based on the body. In conclusion, in robotics, embodiment means human activities in the body tending towards the need to discuss the boundary between mind and body again. It does so by "incorporating" the mind into a body that becomes

---

[7] In 1998, Kerstin Dautenhahn affirms "Life and intelligence only develops inside a body" [18].

the engine of action and cognition in the world. If, on the one hand, it is a substantial revolution against the classical paradigm, it is also doubtful the phenomenological background of this idea. In conclusion, the perspective of the AI introduces the concept of embodiment and expresses the need for possession of the body (physical embodiment) in order to have an open exchange relationship with the environment.

Despite the theoretical and practical urgency of this shift in robotics, the embodied perspective for robotics misses something[8]; specifically, I agree with [24] arguing that "the "complete agents" built by embodied AI are cognitive agents that lack a biological-like bodily organization and, thus, a body in the proper sense. Despite its focus on living organisms, embodied AI still misses a deep understanding of the role played by the biological bodily organization in generating a form of cognition that, far from performing extrinsic problem-solving, continuously addresses the problem of maintaining the system's coherence in an ever-changing environment, by charging external perturbing events with internally generated operational meanings that support effective self-regulation". Specifically, declining this critique following a phenomenological approach, there remains an underlying ambiguity between two opposing views of the concept of body, namely the phenomenological character of Leib, "what we are" and the functional anatomical character of the Körper, "which belongs to us" [13]. Despite this, the embodied breakthrough in robotics does not call into question the deterministic principle of a body as a machine but argues that cognitive states have a bodily component (physical embodiment).

4   A Phenomenological-Inclined Approach to Robotics

The reference of robotics to the notion of body is tangible, understanding it as a physical structure that binds the action and determines the goals of the system in the surrounding environment. This idea has primary consequences from the epistemological point of view because, taking up Damiano's criticism, the interpenetration of the robot-environment system takes place at a functional and goal-oriented level but does not imply any biological-like organization. Expanding the argument, we can say that not only does robotics functionally address the surrounding environment, but it also fails to grasp the phenomenological value of the body.

Embodiment has a deep root in the phenomenological movement since it was the first philosophical movement to develop a paradigm that revalued the bodily role of experience, for example, in the reflection of Husserl and Merleau-Ponty. For this reason, it is mandatory to deepen the idea of a living body, which is rediscovered, in the contemporary debate, by phenomenology [25]. As Zipoli Caiani argues, in phenomenology, "the notion of embodiment overlaps with the rebuttal of what is usually considered the Cartesian dualistic conception of the mind" [26]. In opposition to Descartes' dualism, phenomenology reconsiders the significance of the body as a living structure necessary for the experience. In the

---

[8] see also [19–21, 23].

perspective proposed in this essay, phenomenology is useful for talking about robotic systems since

1. phenomenology does not deny the physical dimension of the body (relevant for robotics), which has its own peculiar aim;
2. phenomenology highlights a human-world systemic approach that characterizes cognition, showing a clear break with the cognitive models of current robots.

In particular, there will be two specific issues that will be addressed: 1) How compatible is the phenomenological notion of the body with the use in robotics? 2) After it has been established that there are differences between the phenomenological meaning of the body and the robotics one, what are the consequences for the development of systems that are able to mimic the human body?

4.1 Body Between Humans and Robots

There is no doubt that the notion of the body is central and relevant to both Edmund Husserl, the founder of phenomenology, and Maurice Merleau-Ponty, who have already been mentioned in this paper. There are two types of bodily forms that Husserl distinguishes between, namely Körper and Leib. The first form (Körper) represents the body as a physical entity described from a mechanistic point of view; on the contrary, the Leib represents the animated and living body. Husserl describes the relationship between the lived and the physical body as an intimate fusion. Thus, in Husserl, experience is given through a material thing (Ding); nevertheless, the experience is also characterized by a living body, which has peculiar characteristics [27], defined as a first-person approach. In line with the articulation of the body expressed by Husserl, Merleau-Ponty also recognizes a twofold perspective on the body. Notwithstanding that, the peculiarity of the French phenomenologist lies in making the body intended as flesh, the focal point for phenomenological analysis. In an (ideal) line of continuity with the dichotomy of Körper and Leib, Merleau-Ponty delineates a distinction between an objective and a subjective meaning of the body. He traces the first form of objectivity of the body in mechanical physiology. As an object or pars extra parte, the body is analyzed from a mechanical and functional perspective. In this approach, a "linear dependence of the receptor on the stimulus" is established to explain behaviors. A 1:1 structure is created in which each stimulus element, coming from outside or local parts of the body, corresponds to one and only one element of the general body receptor.

Based on this first perspective on the body and the robotics use of the concept (Sect. 2), we can tentatively conclude that robotics intends the body as a machine with linear dependence. Even if we consider the Embodied Turn, which redefines the relationship with the environment, an objective perspective on bodies persists. As stated earlier, the Embodied Turn in robotics aims at the ultimate abandonment of a centralized computational strategy in favor of a distributed system embedded in the environment; nevertheless, in order to achieve this goal, it is not necessary to abandon a functional perspective on the body, which could be conceived as a (neurophysiological) machine. Thus, it is possible to claim that the Embodied Turn abandons a paradigm centered on the brain as a commanding organ, reevaluating the nervous system, but does not contradict the concept of the body as a machine. For instance, Brooks modifies the work setting and the internal organization of the robot, but this does not change his view on the biological-like body organization [16]. This approach collides with a serious problem in the implementation of phenomenological dimensions, such as feeling or sensation, in robotics [30].

4.2   A Phenomenological Structure for Artificial Systems?

Having ascertained that the difference between the phenomenological meaning of the body and the robotics meaning is significant, it is now necessary to investigate the consequences for cognition. Preliminary, I assume that it is possible to describe, for robotics, every new interaction with the environment as a heuristic trial-and-error process. On the contrary, the notion of Leib or own's body refers to the phenomenological understanding of cognition that necessarily relates the embodied subject to the world. For Merleau-Ponty-Ponty, the phenomenologically own's body is not a physical or physiological structure but a living incarnate res; "One's own body is in the world just as the heart is in the organism: it continuously breathes life into the visible spectacle, animates it and nourishes it from within, and forms a system with it." [3]. This means conceiving experience not as a collection and analysis of data but as an (ego-eco)system that develops vitally in the continuous interaction of the human being with the environment. This node brings out a first and crucial question that takes us back to robotics, what is cognition made if it is not conceivable as data collection? We can take, for example, the case of a service robot that changes the context of use, for example, the house in which it works; every new environment implies a specific training phase through a trial and error process. Can we argue that the same mechanism represents the way in which we interact in a new environment? Following Merleau-Ponty, we can respond negatively because human action in the world is determined by a phenomenological meaning of bodiliness, called body schema. The body schema is not a "mere result of associations", a mechanism that, in turn, we can say characterizes robotics, but rather" global awareness of my posture in the inter-sensory world, a "form" in Gestalt psychology's sense of the word." [3]. This refers not only to the spatiality of the body but also to knowledge as that, inevitably, is located as phenomenological. To comprehend the phenomenological embodied approach to cognition, the example of Merleau-Ponty of the organist is emblematic. "The example of instrumentalists demonstrates even more clearly how habit resides neither in thought nor in the objective body, but rather in the body as the mediator of a world. It is said that an experienced organist is capable of playing an organ with which he is unfamiliar, and that has additional or fewer keyboards, and whose stops are differently arranged than the stops on his customary instrument. He needs but an hour of practice to be ready to execute his program. Such a brief apprenticeship prohibits the assumption that new conditioned reflexes are simply substituted for the already established collection, unless, that is, they together form a system and if the change is global, but this would be to go beyond the mechanistic theory since in that case the reactions would be mediated by a total hold on the instrument." [3]. If we compare the example of the organist with the heuristic process of the robot in a new environment, we immediately realize the points of difference between the cognition of the human being and the robot. In summary, I trace the difference back to the meaning of the body involved. Based on these two approaches, we can trace the epistemological difference between the principle of "testing", proper to robotics, compared to the "feeling", which regards human beings. Assuming that the phenomenological ideas of Leib and body schema can apply to robotics, the question remains: why is the difference between the two meanings of bodiliness relevant to robotics? In line with Metzinger, [28] from an engineering point of view, it seems possible to conclude that there are no scientific/ontological limits to the reproduction of the salient aspects in artificial agents[9]. Current robotic developments seem to blur the distance between human beings and artificial things through the development of bio-inspired systems; this way of developing robots is based on two principles that phenomenology call into doubts [30]: 1) The absence of formal constraints to build sentient robots, and 2) the idea that human being must be fully explainable according to a functional and computational approach. In conclusion, the points mentioned above are helpful in defining a "phenomenological inclined" approach to robotics dealing with the limits of robotics and the unseen resources of phenomenology for robotics systems. Thus, the point of distance and detachment between human beings and robots is clear; it opens new questions about the direction that programming for robotic cognitive systems should take in order to develop more and more human-like structures.

5   Conclusion

Starting from the fact that the concept of the body is relevant to defining robotics, the essay affirms that robots could be described as embodied agents according to a non-phenomenological meaning of the term, which highlights the positive role of a body embedded in an environment for cognition. This idea is called physical embodiment. Nevertheless, a question remains open: is this meaning consistent with the phenomenological approach? Based on the distinction between Leib and Körper, I deny the consistency because embodiment robotics, which we can summarize as having a body, does not entail the living body and the body schema, which are the main ideas of the phenomenological approach. In conclusion, the essay attempts to prove that the difference between Leib and Körper defines two diverse realms from an ontological and epistemological point of view. Even if we can talk about robotics as embodied AI, the robotics bodiliness concerns a functional perspective and an objective meaning of the body;

---

[9] Other researchers argue that "There is no known law of nature that forbids the existence of subjective feelings in artifacts designed or evolved by humans" [29].

on the other hand, phenomenology shows an innovative resource to reflect on diverse ways to develop robotics systems.

References

1. Dreyfus, H.L., Dreyfus, S.E.: The challenge of Merleau-Ponty's phenomenology of embodiment for cognitive science. The intersections of nature and culture, Perspectives on embodiment, pp. 103–120 (1999)
2. Shapiro, L.: Embodied Cognition. Routledge, Milton Park (2010)
3. Merleau-Ponty, M.: Phenomenology of Perception. Routledge, Milton Park (2013)
4. Varela, F.J., Thompson, E., Rosch, E.: The embodied mind, revised edition: cognitive science and human experience. MIT Press, Cambridge (2017)
5. Sandini, G., Metta, G., Vernon, D.: The *iCub* cognitive humanoid robot: an open-system research platform for enactive cognition. In: Lungarella, M., Iida, F., Bongard, J., Pfeifer, R. (eds.) 50 Years of Artificial Intelligence. LNCS (LNAI), vol. 4850, pp. 358–369. Springer, Heidelberg (2007). https://doi.org/10.1007/978-3-540-77296-5_32
6. Vernon, D., Metta, G., Sandini, G.: The icub cognitive architecture: interactive development in a humanoid robot. In: 2007 IEEE 6th International Conference on Development and Learning. IEEE (2007)
7. Thompson, E.: Mind in Life: Biology, Phenomenology, and the Sciences of Mind. Harvard University Press, Cambridge (2010)
8. Gates, B.: A robot in every home. Sci. Am. **296**(1), 58–65 (2007)
9. Mataric, M.J.: The Robotics Primer. MIT Press, Cambridge (2007)
10. Rosenberg, J.M.: Dictionary of Artificial Intelligence and Robotics. John Wiley and Sons Inc., New York (1986)
11. Angelo, J.A.: Robotics: A Reference Guide to the New Technology. Greenwood Press, Westport (2007)
12. Bertolini, A.: Robots as products: the case for a realistic analysis of robotic applications and liability rules. Law Innov. Technol. **5**(2), 214–247 (2013)
13. De Vignemont, F.: Habeas corpus: the sense of ownership of one's own body. Mind Lang. **22**(4), 427–449 (2007)
14. Thelen, E., Smith, L.B.: A dynamic systems approach to the development of cognition and action. MIT press, Cambridge (1994)
15. Damasio, A.R.: Descartes' Error. Random House, New York (2006)
16. Brooks, R.A.: Intelligence without representation. Artif. Intell. **47**(1–3), 139–159 (1991)
17. Pfeifer, R., Bongard, J.: How the Body Shapes the Way We Think: A New View of Intelligence. MIT press, Cambridge (2006)
18. Dautenhahn, K.: Embodiment and interaction in socially intelligent life-like agents. In: Nehaniv, C.L. (ed.) CMAA 1998. LNCS (LNAI), vol. 1562, pp. 102–141. Springer, Heidelberg (1999). https://doi.org/10.1007/3-540-48834-0_7
19. Ziemke, T.: What's Life Got to Do with It. Artificial Consciousness, pp. 48–66 (2007)
20. Ziemke, T.: What's that thing called embodiment?. In: Proceedings of the Annual Meeting of the Cognitive Science Society, vol. 25, no. 25 (2003)
21. Ziemke, T.: The body of knowledge: on the role of the living body in grounding embodied cognition. Biosystems **148**, 4–11 (2016)

22. Giannotta, A.P.: Corpo funzionale e corpo senziente. La tesi forte del carattere incarnato della mente in fenomenologia. Riv. Internazionale di Filosofia e Psicologia **13**(1), 41–56 (2022)

23. Di Paolo, E.A.: Organismically-inspired robotics: homeostatic adaptation and teleology beyond the closed sensorimotor loop. Dyn. Syst. Approach Embodiment Soc. 19–42 (2003)

24. Damiano, L., Stano, P.: Synthetic biology and artificial intelligence. grounding a cross-disciplinary approach to the synthetic exploration of (embodied) cognition. Complex Syst. **27**, 199–228 (2018)

25. Lanfredini, R.: The mind–body problem in husserl and merleau-ponty. In: Reboul, A. (ed.) Mind, Values, and Metaphysics, pp. 471–482. Springer, Cham (2014). https://doi.org/10.1007/978-3-319-04199-5_31

26. Zipoli Caiani, S.: Mindsets. Conceiving Cognition in Nature. Mimesis International (2014)

27. Husserl, E.: Ideas pertaining to a pure phenomenology and to a phenomenological philosophy: Second book studies in the phenomenology of constitution, vol. 3. Springer Science & Business Media, Berlin (1989)

28. Metzinger, T.: The Ego Tunnel: The Science of the Mind and the Myth of the Self. Basic Books (AZ) (2009)

29. Chella, A., Manzotti, R.: Artificial Consciousness. Andrews UK Limited, Luton (2013)

30. Corti, L.: Towards a quanto-qualitative biological engineering: the case of the neuroprosthetic hand. In: The Quantification of Bodies in Health: Multidisciplinary Perspectives. Emerald Publishing Limited (2021)

Markov Blankets for Sustainability

Maria Raffa[✉] [iD]

IULM University, Milan, Italy
`maria.raffa@studenti.iulm.it`

Abstract. This paper's aim is twofold: on the one hand, to provide an overview of the state of the art of some kind of Bayesian networks, i.e. Markov blankets (MB), focusing on their relationship with the cognitive theories of the free energy principle (FEP) and active inference. On the other hand, to sketch how these concepts can be practically applied to artificial intelligence (AI), with special regard to their use in the field of sustainable development. The proposal of this work, indeed, is that understanding exactly to what extent MBs may be framed in the context of FEP and active inference, could be useful to implement tools to support decision-making processes for addressing sustainability. Conversely, looking at these tools considering how they could be related to those theoretical frameworks, may help to shed some light on the debate about FEP, active inference and its linkages with MBs, which still seems to be clarified. For the above purposes, the paper is organized as follows: after a general introduction, Sect. 2 explains what a MB is, and how it is related to the concepts of FEP and active inference. Thus, Sect. 3 focuses on how MBs, joint with FEP and active inference, are employed in the field of AI. On these grounds, Sect. 4 explores whether MBs, FEP, and active inference can be useful to face the issues related to sustainability.

Keywords: Markov blankets · Free energy principle · Active inference · Artificial intelligence · Sustainability

1 Introduction

One of the most discussed topics in the debate around cognition, lately, has been the Free Energy Principle (FEP), advocated by philosophers and neuroscientists as a more or less mysterious unificatory principle, which can be applied to almost every field of knowledge, from thermodynamics, to biology, to the study of the mind. FEP shares its formal foundations with probability theory, and with some specific statistical structures, i.e. Markov blankets (MBs). MBs are a kind of Bayesian networks, which are generally used to model algorithms capable of performing decision-making tasks. Traditionally, FEP has been used to describe the behavior of biological organisms and of dynamics systems, but since it offers a very general framework for resource optimization, it could be also suitable to address issues related to sustainability. Indeed, since it is in the public eye that our planet is running out of resources and climate change is having disastrous

P. Masci et al. (Eds.): SEFM 2022 Collocated Workshops, LNCS 13765, pp. 313–323, 2023.
https://doi.org/10.1007/978-3-031-26236-4_26

consequences on people and lands, the urge of dealing with these issues with all the means at our disposal is increasingly pressing. Artificial intelligence (AI) too, is demanded to give its contribution in this sense, especially after the publication of the 17 Sustainable Development Goals (SDGs) defined by the United Nations General Assembly in 2015 [1]. For instance, many efforts are being done to address SDG 1, i.e. reducing poverty, with machine learning classification models to help track and monitor wealth indices [2], and SDG 6, i.e. ensure access to water and sanitation for all, with models to predict water pressure in some areas of the planet, in order to optimize water pumping and avoid waste [3].

All that considered, my attempt in this paper is trying to make a good marriage among the topics mentioned above, which are very present in the contemporary debate about sustainability, AI and philosophy of cognition. Specifically, it seems that the literature still lacks an overall discourse including both the theoretical description of MBs, within FEP and active inference, and their several different employments for AI, in order to tackle the question of sustainable development.

In order to succeed in the aforementioned purposes, this paper is structured as follows: firstly, Sect. 2 sketches briefly what a MB is, and how it is linked to the concepts of FEP and active inference. It shapes the original notion of MB within statistics, and further, it stresses how the concept has been integrated with Karl Friston's cognitive theories of FEP and active inference. Secondly, Sect. 3 provides an overview of AI applications of MBs, joint with FEP and active inference. Thirdly, Sect. 4 discusses if all this can be useful to address the issue of sustainability.

2   MB, FEP and Active Inference

The concept of MB was first introduced by Judea Pearl [4] in the following terms: «the Markov blanket of a variable X is the set consisting of the parents of X, the children of X, and the variables sharing a child with X» [5]. Specifically, a MB is a kind of Bayesian network, i.e. a statistical multivariate model where its graphical structure allows us to represent and reason about an uncertain domain [11]: each node is associated with one variable of the domain, and the direct links between the nodes represent informational or cause-effect relationships. These dependencies are quantified by conditional probability distributions, meaning the extent to which one node is likely to be affected by the others. The nodes forming the MB of X simplify a lot the computation of the value of a variable: «so, for instance, if X is embedded in a graph, with a hundred variables but its MB consists only of five variables, one can safely ignore ninety-five variables in the computation» [7]. Hence, the MB of a random variable is the only knowledge one may need to predict the behavior of that variable.

Therefore, the concept of MB has been developed in the context of statistics, and later it has been adopted in different fields, such as philosophy of mind and cognitive science, thanks to Karl Friston's FEP and active inference [8–13]. FEP has been employed in different contexts and with various purposes.

First, it has been proposed to explain how the sensory cortex infers the causes of its inputs and learns causal regularities, and then, it has been applied to explain the function of action, perception and attention, and to account for an organism's evolution and development. Eventually, it has been presented as a tool to characterize and predict the adaptive behavior of living organisms, or as an objective feature of target systems [14].

FEP is essentially a mathematical formulation of how adaptive organisms (i.e. biological agents, like animals or brains) resist a natural tendency to disorder. It claims that agents that exist do so because they can persist, maintaining their equilibrium through free energy minimization. Free energy is «an upper bound on surprise and [...] a function of two things which the agents have access: its sensory states and a recognition density that is encoded by its internal states. The recognition density is a probabilistic representation of what caused a particular sensation» [10]. The sets of physiological and sensory states in which an organism can be are of course limited, and this means that the probability of these sensory states must have low entropy. Entropy is a measure of uncertainty, which is "surprise", and on minimizing surprise depends the survival of an organism. Mathematically, this means minimizing the sum of the negative log-probability of the expected outcomes. An organism performs the minimization of free energy - and surprise - through active inference, that is the sampling of the expected sensory inputs to increase the accuracy of predictions. That is, leading to self-generated changes in status and to the suppression of prediction errors through the information derived from the history of previous interactions with the environment [16,17]. Active inference could be intuitively explained as: «feeling our way in darkness: we anticipate what we might touch next and then try to confirm those expectations» [10].

In this paper, we will not delve into the mathematical details of free energy. Nonetheless, to understand how FEP can be applied not only to organisms but in a wider sense to describe the optimal usage of resources in social or collective systems, it's worth mentioning the basic formula

$$F = E - TS \tag{1}$$

where E is the total amount of energy, T is the temperature and S is the entropy. This formula has been used to describe also human society [15], where E can represent the amount of resources available for human consumption, and changes in entropy ensemble changes in randomness. Moreover, an increase in randomness represents an increase in freedom in a system. Considering that entropy is the tendency to spread out, it can be said that spreading out is also a wish of the human being, and therefore, entropy can be understood as a measure of freedom in human society. In a physical system – which is, also, a biological organism – the free energy will move spontaneously to its minimum, and when E is fixed, T and S will tend to increase until TS reaches its maximum. In a social system, this may be intended as the idea that people will seek the highest possible level of spending and freedom.

In the framework of FEP and active inference as previously sketched, Friston has introduced the statistical concept of MB that we have described at the beginning of this section. MBs are advocated by Friston as a tool to draw a specific form of conditional independence between a dynamical system and its environment and are addressed as *real* boundaries of living systems [16,17]. Indeed, they are associated with the physical boundaries surrounding cells (i.e. their membrane), through which all influences between the intracellular and extracellular spaces are mediated. Furthermore, MBs have been used to explain neural networks, such that the superficial and deep pyramidal cells of the cerebral cortex play the role of a MB, through mediating interactions between different cortical columns. This can be applied also at a larger scale in the biological systems, considering muscles and sensory receptors acting as an organism's MB, and specific organisms acting as blankets to separate groups of other organisms. What these different cases have in common is that they represent a separation of the world into two different sets of states, which interact only via MB [18]. Hence, although living systems need to interact with the environment, since they are open systems, they also need to distinguish themselves from the external environment. In this context, we speak of conditional independence: if the state of the organism/environment boundary, i.e. the MB, is fixed, what happens on one side of the boundary has no influence on what happens on the other side. This means that all the necessary information to explain the behavior of the internal system is given by the state of the blanket [19,20].

Considering all that said above, concerns may raise about the exact nature of MBs, from the evidence that the literature looks to be filled with confusion about the two different souls of MB, since they are addressed in some cases as statistical models, and in others as real objects. Specifically, MBs seen as real boundaries, such as they are described in Friston's work, have been criticized, among others, by Jelle Bruineberg and colleagues, as this view forms «an example of reification fallacy: treating something abstract as something concrete» [21]. Bruineberg stresses the difference between the so-called Pearl blankets and the Friston blankets. The former (Pearl blankets) describe a property of statistical models, since they capture relations of conditional independence between variables in the model. This means that the probability that the independencies associated with an entire causal structure are true is computed, and later, a particular hypothesis of interest, such as "Does X cause Y?", can be made about all possible causal structures based on these probabilities [23]. The latter (Friston blankets) are a particular interpretation of that property for studying agent-environment systems. This is, Pearl blankets are formal tools that are used to make inferences about some system, using a model of that system, while Friston blankets embrace a sensorimotor interpretation of the model and assume that the system of interest is itself performing inferences [21]. Bruineberg's argument has been challenged by Maxwell Ramstead [22], who seems to find no significant mathematical difference between Friston blankets and Pearl blankets. Nonetheless, the core idea of the ontological ambiguity of the concept is still crucial.

Hence, when establishing research on MBs, one should be very careful about the basic assumptions to be made: this is, on the one hand, MB can be used instrumentally in their original statistical form, i.e. as a formal mathematical construct for inference on a generative model, e.g. a Bayesian network. On the other hand, this usage cannot come from the strong assumptions on which FEP as a unificatory principle is based: indeed, MBs as an ontological construct defining actual boundaries in the world cannot be justified only with the "traditional" mathematics drawn by Pearl, and need additional techniques which the literature still seems to lack [21].

Awareness of these critical aspects of MBs, the definition of which is still in progress, is essential if its use is to be extended to different fields than the traditional areas of statistics and cognitive sciences. Indeed, it's remarkable that FEP, MB and active inference offer a very general and overcompassing framework to address the issue of long-term survivals and optimal usage of resources for any entity at any time scale. To assess whether they may be applied beyond the cases considered so far, two areas will be examined in the next two sections: first, the existing application of MBs to AI tools for different purposes, and then how the needs expressed by the various agencies about sustainability are linked to AI, FEP and active inference.

3   MB, FEP, Active Inference and AI

In the field of AI, and specifically, machine learning, many of the current applications are based on neural models built on feedforward architectures trained by backpropagation, which learn to map a fixed-size input, e.g. an image, to a fixed-size output, e.g. a probability for each of several categories [24]. This kind of model is very powerful in terms of generating quick outputs, but it often results in hard-to-explain black box situations, since the inputs are known, but the path to the outputs is less clear. Hence, to address the problem of algorithms' explainability, generative models are more reliable [25]. Generative models are MB-based, since they are Bayesian networks. They trace the propagation of events across multiple ambiguous points, where the event diverges probabilistically between pathways, and at any given point in the network, the probability of that node being visited is dependent on the joint probability of the preceding nodes. This means that all processes can be traced and understood, because Bayesian networks, unlike neural networks, track explicit reasoning, even though they are probabilistic. The idea behind MB-based generative models is the same as for predictive perception based on Bayesian inference, namely minimization by error. Indeed, these algorithms can produce sensory signals that match predicted causes, as they learn from small quantities of data and generalize to new situations [26]. Nevertheless, it may be risky to consider Bayesian networks as models of cognition on which to build AI design [27]. As a matter of fact, this kind of model relies on a basic decision theory assuming an optimal decision maker able to calculate and choose, in each phase of problem-solving, the move that maximizes the utility function. However, these theories of expected utility maximization, and specifically Bayesian models of cognition, that can be considered "optimality-seeking" models, have been criticized as being computationally intractable, since they assume perfect knowledge and lack empirical evidence about the existence of stable utility functions over time [28,29].

Besides, due to their advantages in terms of explainability, generative models are becoming increasingly popular for various tasks: image generation, text prediction, video modeling, and prediction of system dynamics, e.g. environment, so they have been studied for control, exploration and anomaly detection [30].

Referring to the concrete employments of generative models based on MBs, joint with active inference, their implications in robotics are remarkable. Indeed, recent studies have shown how active vision can emerge from active inference [31,32], and this is useful to address the problem of finding and reaching a certain object in a robotic space [33]. More in detail, Toon Van de Maele and his team implemented a generative model using deep neural networks that can fuse multiple views into an abstract representation, trained from data by minimizing variational free energy. The model has been tested in a simulation environment, where the robotic agent has been designed as separated from the world state through a MB, meaning that the agent can only update its knowledge about the surrounding space by interacting with the world through its chosen actions and its observed sensory information [34,35]. The actions the agent can perform consist of moving toward a new viewpoint to observe the environment. So, the action space has been defined as a set of potential viewpoints the agent can move to. In this case, the generative model has been depicted considering an environment where things do not change appearance or position, but other studies have considered also dynamic situations [36]. Van de Maele proved that a robotic agent, which starts moving without any knowledge about the workspace, at each step chooses the next view pose by evaluating the expected free energy, and this means that it is possible to use the active inference paradigm as a «natural solution for active vision on complex tasks in which the distribution over the environment is not defined upfront» [34]. Furthermore, with the appropriate amount of GPU memory, a more complex generative model could be trained to compute the expected free energy for all potential viewpoints of an agent, rather than just a limited set of considered viewpoints: this would allow to qextend the use of the neural network for real-time control of physical robot manipulators [34].

Regarding other uses of MBs for AI, it's worth mentioning also their application to models for music generation. A special case of MB, i.e. Markov chain, is a model describing a sequence of possible events, where the probability of the next state depends on a previous state and not on *all* previous states [17]. This kind of network has the right features for the task of music generation, as the idea is to consider, e.g. in a corpus of chords, which is the probability for a chord to follow another particular chord. However, for this specific task, Jeffrey Cruz [37] has proven that using deep neural networks works better than MB-based models.

Given the above examples, the take-away message of this section is that MB-based models - or, more generally, Bayesian networks - are suitable for the development of AI tools. The next section, as already anticipated, will discuss whether such techniques are applicable to sustainable development issues.

4   MB, FEP, Active Inference, AI and Sustainability

So far, we have dealt with the concept of MB, its connections to the theoretical framework of FEP and active inference, and its applications in the field of AI. This final section focuses on the possible use of MB-based AI to address the urgent problem of sustainability, since environmental exploitation and the lack of energy resources are everyday more dramatic.

Admittedly, it seems difficult in the literature to find a bridge between the theoretical frameworks outlined by Friston and AI applications in sustainability. The hypothesis put forward by this work is that understanding the connection among FEP and active inference on the one hand, and Bayesian network-based AI for sustainability through MB structures, on the other, may be useful in both enriching the awareness about the use of AI for these concrete purposes, and clarifying the discourse about FEP. This suggestion firstly comes from the trivial fascination that a sustainable organism – or society – should be, as a matter of fact, independent, and manage to keep itself in equilibrium, perhaps minimizing surprise in predicting its next states, such as FEP and active inference claim. Moreover, as we saw in Sect. 2, FEP has been applied not only in the context of a single organism, but also to explain complex and hierarchical systems of different natures [15,38,39]. This is closely related to the dynamics of Bayesian networks, which, as emphasized earlier, allow knowledge of the effects given causes and causes due to the effects, which means that they are useful to calculate the probability of a given hypothesis and, thus, support decision-making. Indeed, because nodes in Bayesian networks are modeled using probability distributions, uncertainty can be estimated more accurately than in models that typically consider only mean values. In addition, Bayesian networks are useful for incorporating data from different sources and domains.

Thanks to these characteristics, Bayesian network-based algorithms have already been used to address sustainability issues. This may be intended in two different ways: on the one hand, MB-based models have been used to measure how effectively an AI is sustainable, in terms of production, maintenance and disposal costs, and on the other, MB models are useful to address issues related, for instance, to the SDGs. In the former case, it is worth mentioning the work of Juhwan Kim [40] and his team, who developed a statistical method that combines social network analysis and Bayesian modeling, to provide a technological hierarchical structure that can be applied to understand and measure the sustainability of AI technology. In this case, Kim and his team used as a benchmark the International Patent Classification codes of patent documents related to sustainable AI technology, and the final evaluation of the results was assigned to the domain experts.

In the latter case, i.e. considering Bayesian networks to directly address environmental issues, they have already been used for decision-making tasks in the field of water resource management [41,42]. On this path, David Requejo-Castro [43] has proposed a data-driven Bayesian network approach, taking into reference the SDG 6 of the 2030 Agenda, i.e. ensuring access to water and sanitation for all. Requejo-Castro's work combines expert opinion and quantitative data to support informed decision-making. Specifically, he uses Bayesian networks-based structure learning algorithms to replicate composite indicators-based conceptual frameworks, which represent experts' knowledge, and identifies interlinkages associated with a complex context, coupled with bootstrapping, to reduce results uncertainty, and with a comprehensive result robustness analysis. His results, validated on SDG 6, shows that this combined approach improves model inference capacity, identifies the interlinkages among the variables considered, and can be useful for analysis of the complexities also in different contexts.

All the sources mentioned above show the reliability of Bayesian networks to support decision-making processes, and their efficacy if used in the context of the concrete issue of nowadays lack of environmental resources. Following up, the final proposal of this paper is that understanding exactly to what extent Bayesian networks, especially in the reduced form of MBs, are framed in the context of FEP and active inference, could be useful to implement concrete tools to support decision-making processes for research addressed to sustainable development. Conversely, looking at these tools considering how they could be related to those theoretical frameworks, may help to shed some light on the debate about FEP, active inference and its linkages with the statistical structures of MBs.

5   Conclusion

So far, this paper has sketched the notion of MBs inside the contexts of FEP and active inference. It has outlined their problematic epistemic status, and how these concepts have been used to implement AI models. Moreover, it has shown how Bayesian networks have already been used for tasks related to sustainable development.

I am aware that this paper only suggests one possible direction of work and does not answer many questions that come to mind when talking about MB, FEP and AI: for example, whether MBs are actually better from a technical point of view than other neural models in evaluating sustainability issues. Nonetheless, the core idea behind this work is just to suggest that MB, FEP and active inference may have a wider use than the traditional one. Indeed, these concepts have been used to explain the behavior of biological organisms or complex systems in nature, and, as argued in the previous sections, I propose that their properties may also make them suitable for AI for sustainability. Hence, this paper aims to be the very starting point for research that delves into tentative applications of MBs, framed into the contexts of FEP and active inference, to assess sustainable development. As a matter of fact, on the one hand, it is worth following up on the promising stream of research that aims to implement MB-inspired AI tools to support decision-making processes to accomplish the Agenda 2030 SDGs. On the other hand, the theoretical frameworks of FEP and active inference still need to be clarified and further explored.

Acknowledgements. I would like to thank the three anonymous reviewers for their comments and very useful feedback on the first version of this paper.

References

1. United Nations General Assembly: Transforming our World: The Sustainable Development Agenda to 2030 (2015)
2. Pedemonte, V.: AI for Sustainability: an overview of AI and the SGDS to contribute to the European policy making (2020)
3. Alsharkawi, A., Al-Fetyani, M., Dawas, M.: Poverty classification using machine learning: the case of Jordan. Sustainability **13**, 1412 (2021). https://doi.org/10.3390/su13031412
4. Pearl, J.: Probabilistic Reasoning in Intelligent Systems: Networks of Plausible Inference. Morgan Kauffman, Burlington (1988)
5. Koski, T., Noble, J.M.: Bayesian Networks: An Introduction. Wiley and Sons, Chichester (2009)
6. Korb, K., Nicholson, A.: Bayesian Artificial Intelligence. Chapman and Hall/CRC, Florida (2004)
7. Facchin, M.: Extended predictive minds: do Markov blankets matter? Rev. Philos. Psychol. (2021). https://doi.org/10.1007/S13164-021-00607-9
8. Friston, K.: Learning and inference in the brain. Neural Netw. **16**, 1325–1352 (2003)
9. Friston, K.: The free-energy principle: a rough guide to the brain? Trends Cogn. Sci. **13**, 293–301 (2009)
10. Friston, K.: The free-energy principle: a unified brain theory? Nat. Rev. Neurosci. **11**(2), 127–38 (2010)
11. Friston, K.: Life as we know it. J. Roy. Soc. Interface **10**, 20130475 (2013). https://doi.org/10.1098/rsif.2013.0475
12. Friston, K., Stephan, K.: Free-energy and the brain. Synthese **159**, 417–458 (2007). https://doi.org/10.1007/s11229-007-9237-y
13. Friston, K., FitzGerald, T., Rigoli, F.: A free energy principle for the brain. J. Physiol. Paris **100**, 70–87 (2006)
14. Colombo, M., Wright, C.: First principles in the life sciences: the free-energy principle, organicism, and mechanism. Synthese **198**(14), 3463–3488 (2018). https://doi.org/10.1007/s11229-018-01932-w
15. Chen, J.: Understanding social systems: a free energy perspective. J. Hum. Thermodyn. **5** (2009). https://doi.org/10.2139/ssrn.1269035
16. Friston, K., Mattout, J., Kilner, J.: Action understanding and active inference. Biol. Cybern. **104**, 137–160 (2011)
17. Kirchhoff, M., Parr, T., Palacios, E.: The Markov blankets of life: autonomy, active inference and the free energy principle. J. Roy. Soc. Interface **15**(138), 20170792 (2018). https://doi.org/10.1098/rsif.2017.0792
18. Rubin, S., Parr, T., Da Costa, L.: Future climates: Markov blankets and active inference in the biosphere. J. Roy. Soc. Interface **17**, 20200503 (2020). https://doi.org/10.1098/rsif.2020.0503

19. Hohwy, J.: Quick'n'Lean or slow and rich? Andy Clark on predictive processing and embodied cognition. In: Colombo, M., Irvine, E., Stapleton, M. (Eds.): Andy Clark and His Critics, pp. 191–205. Oxford University Press, New York (2019)

20. Palacios, E.R., Razi, A., Parr, T.: On Markov blanket and hierarchical self-organization. J. Theor. Biol. **486**, 110089 (2020)

21. Bruineberg, J., Dolega, K., Dewhurst, J.: The emperor's new Markov blankets. Behav. Brain Sci. 1–63 (2021). https://doi.org/10.1017/S0140525X21002351

22. Ramstead, M.: The empire strikes back: Some responses to Bruineberg and colleagues. Behav. Brain Sci. **45** (2022). https://doi.org/10.1017/s0140525x22000139

23. Spirtes, P., Glymour, C., Scheines, R.: Causation, Prediction, and Search. MIT Press, Cambridge (2000)

24. LeCun, Y., Bengio, Y., Hinton, G.: Deep Learning. Nature **52**(7553), 436–444 (2015)

25. Derks, I.P., de Waal, A.: A taxonomy of explainable Bayesian networks. In: Gerber, A. (ed.) Artificial Intelligence Research. CCIS, Springer, Cham (2020). https://doi.org/10.48550/arXiv.2101.11844

26. Seth, A.: The brain as a prediction machine. In: Mendonça, D., Curado, M., Gouveia, S. S. (Eds.). The Philosophy and Science of Predictive Processing, pp. XIV-XVII. Bloomsbury, London (2020)

27. Lieto, A.: Cognitive Design for Artificial Minds. Routledge, New York (2021)

28. Friedman, D., Isaac, R.M., James, D.: Risky Curves: On the Empirical Failure of Expected Utility. Routledge, New York (2014)

29. Gigerenzer, G.: How to explain behavior? Top. Cogn. Sci. **12**(4), 1363–1381 (2019)

30. Mazzaglia, P., Verbelen, T., Çatal, O.: The free energy principle for perception and action: a deep learning perspective. Entropy **24**(2), 301 (2022)

31. Mirza, M.B., Adams, R.A., Mathys, C.D.: Scene construction, visual foraging, and active inference. Front. Comput. Neurosci. **10**, 56 (2016). https://doi.org/10.3389/fncom.2016.00056

32. Daucé, E.: Active fovea-based vision through computationally-effective model-based prediction. Front. Neurorobotics **12**, 76 (2018). https://doi.org/10.3389/fnbot.2018.00076

33. Lanillos, P., Meo, C., Pezzato, C.: Active inference in robotics and artificial agents: survey and challenges. ArXiv (2021). arXiv:2112.01871

34. Van De Maele, T., Verbelen, T.: Çatal, O: Active vision for robot manipulators using the free energy principle. Front. Neurorobotics **15**, 642780 (2021). https://doi.org/10.3389/fnbot.2021.642780

35. Friston, K., FitzGerald, T., Rigoli, F.: Active inference and learning. Neurosci. Biobehav. Rev. **68**, 862–879 (2016). https://doi.org/10.1016/j.neubiorev.2016.06.022

36. Çatal, O., Wauthier, S., De Boom, C.: Learning generative state space models for active inference. Front. Comput. Neurosci. **14**(103), 574372 (2020). https://doi.org/10.3389/fncom.2020.574372

37. Cruz, J.: Deep Learning vs Markov Model in Music Generation. Honors College Theses [graduate thesis] (2019)

38. Ramstead, M.J.D., Badcock, P.B., Friston, K.: Answering schrödinger's question: a free-energy formulation. Phys. Life Rev. **24**, 1–16 (2018)

39. Veissière, S.P.L., Constant, A., Ramstead, M.J.D.: Thinking through other minds: a variational approach to cognition and culture. Behav. Brain Sci. **43**, e90 (2020)

40. Kim, J., Jun, S., Jang, D.: Sustainable technology analysis of artificial intelligence using bayesian and social network models. Sustainability **10**(1), 115 (2018)

41. Bromley, J.: Guidelines for the use of Bayesian Networks as a Participatory Tool for Water Resource. Wallingford, United Kingdom (2005)
42. Phan, T.D., Smart, J.C., Capon, S.J.: Applications of Bayesian belief networks in water resource management: a systematic review. Environ. Model. Softw. **85**, 98–111 (2016). https://doi.org/10.1016/j.envsoft.2016.08.006
43. Requejo Castro, D.: Data driven Bayesian networks modelling to support decision-making: application to the context of sustainable development goal 6 on water and sanitation. Universitat Politècnica de Catalunya. Ph.D. thesis (2021)

Executive Function and Intelligent Goal-Directed Behavior: Perspectives from Psychology, Neurology, and Computer Science

Graham Pluck[1]([✉])[ID], Antonio Cerone[2][ID], and David Villagomez-Pacheco[3][ID]

[1] Faculty of Psychology, Chulalongkorn University, Bangkok, Thailand
graham.ch@chula.ac.th
[2] Department of Computer Science, School of Engineering and Digital Sciences,
Nazarbayev University, Astana, Kazakhstan
antonio.cerone@nu.edu.kz
[3] Universidad Nacional de Educación, Azogues, Ecuador
david.villagomez@unae.edu.ec

Abstract. The concept of executive function, as top-down control of processes, originated in computer science in the 1950s. However, it has since become an important concept in a range of human sciences, particularly for its explanatory power in psychology, education, and clinical neurosciences. Nevertheless, its use has been limited by vague definitions and confusion between the related conceptualizations of executive process and intelligence. Here we explore the concept of executive control in detail, drawing on psychology, neurology, and computer science/human-machine interaction. We explore both computationalist and embodied cognition approaches. We describe the core goal-directed and resource-limited features of executive control, its fractionation into components, and partial overlap with psychometric conceptions of intelligence. We also examine its associations with neurological systems beyond those usually linked to executive function (i.e., the frontal lobes). We propose that executive functions are 'intelligent', and can be defined by their goal-directedness. Furthermore, executive function tasks can be classified by their task goals into one of three types: Those that involve i) convergent, or ii) divergent thinking, or iii) not responding, such as in psychomotor response inhibition. Conventional intelligence tests measure only convergent thinking. The recognition of non-convergent executive functions allows the identification of executively controlled intelligent goal-directed behavior beyond that controlled by domain-general cognitive processes. This reconceptualization may benefit research in education, clinical and cognitive sciences, as well as the quest for artificial general intelligence.

Work partly funded by Project SEDS2020004 "Analysis of cognitive properties of interactive systems using model checking", Nazarbayev University, Kazakhstan (Award number: 240919FD3916), and a Chulalongkorn University, Faculty of Psychology Research Grant.

P. Masci et al. (Eds.): SEFM 2022 Collocated Workshops, LNCS 13765, pp. 324–350, 2023.
https://doi.org/10.1007/978-3-031-26236-4_27

Keywords: Executive function · Cognitive control · Divergent thinking · Intelligence · Neuroscience · Frontal lobes · Human-computer interaction · Artificial intelligence

1 The Origins of Executive Function as a Concept

Although now a well-known expression in psychology and neuroscience, the original conception of executive processes came from the need to coordinate aspects of programs running on computers. In 1956, an early attempt at control of programs, essentially batch processing, was referred to as 'Automatic Supervisor' for the IBM 702 computer [82]. This approach was developed into what may be one of the first ever operating systems, designed by General Motors for the IBM 704, the GM-NAA Monitor [19], also known as the General Motors Executive System. Subsequent operating systems had more explicit executive control, particularly FACT in the late 1950s (designed to run on the Honeywell 800 computer). This included a system described as an Executive Schedule and Monitor, which was an operating system that coordinated the running of programs: locating them on tape reals, checking they could run simultaneously, allocating memory resources, starting, restarting (if necessary) and stopping programs, and adjusting program run schedules [29]. Through the early 1960s s many other operating systems were developed which used similar principles, and had names such as University of Michigan Executive System, Exec 1, Master Control Program, Executive, and Supervisory Control Program [19]. This technology, invoking top-down control of computers, coincided exactly with the 'birth' of cognitive science in 1956, a field which explicitly drew on computer science in order to understand the mind [80].

A consequence of this technological origin has been that executive function has historically been conceived of in computational terms [34,86,114,116]. A leading model of executive function, for example, proposes multiple processing units and stages, with information transmitted between the various stores for computation [115]. Nevertheless, there are approaches to executive function from an embodied cognition perspective. These place less emphasis on computation, instead focusing on the needs and limitations that come from possession of a physical body. Many of these approaches link 'executive control' with the primal need for organisms to act within their environments. For example, people likely possess basic approach and avoidance modes of action, which are evolutionary ancient, and in simple organisms can enhance survival without the need for any computational representations [28]. Such basic principles may continue to influence human cognitive systems: executive control by people is particularly employed when avoidance cues are present [70] indicating the importance of survival and links between perception and action systems. A further aspect of embodied executive function draws on how reinforcement learning can influence motor learning to produce adaptive action [15,72]. A separate corpus of research has examined how the body's glucose levels influence top-down behavioral control and decision making [83,121,123,124].

Whether from computationalist or embodied perspectives, executive function is now an intensely studied topic, spanning psychology, neuroscience, and linguistics. It has been adopted by many applied fields to explain aspects of behavior, such as education, neurology, psychiatry, and human-computer interaction.

1.1 The Utility of Executive Functions as a Concept in Human Sciences

Within human sciences, executive functions are generally defined, from a computational perspective, as being cognitive processes that guide behavior when deliberate, attentional selection of responses is necessary, such as inhibiting behavior, switching between tasks, or dealing with novel situations [45,79,81]. More embodied perspectives define executive control as behavior that is adaptive and promotes survival of the organism [15,72]. As such, executive functions are related to behavior regulation and producing 'intelligent' outcomes. For this reason, the concept of executive function has become very popular within behavioral and clinical sciences, particularly education.

Although intelligence test scores are a good predictor of performance in education in general [91,97] researchers have highlighted the specific contribution of domain-specific cognitive abilities which associate with achievement in specific subjects [119,122]. These include the commonly identified executive functions of working memory, inhibition, and flexibility [42,81,129]. Flexibility is the ability to switch from one activity to another, or to go back and forth between activities, redirecting our attention and planning actions that allow us to achieve a goal. It allows people to experience and learn from different perspectives, being aware of their own mistakes, and to take advantage of unexpected events [42]. It may be the most important executive function relating to school performance, particularly for reading and mathematical achievement [129]. Working memory is a supposed system for processing and temporary storage of information which will be used to perform cognitive tasks of varying complexity [12]. It is linked to success in language learning and mathematics [119] and science [122], as well as good classroom behavior [98]. Inhibition is the ability to voluntarily restrict a dominant or instinctive response triggered by a stimulus. It has been found to be a good predictor achievement in school [98], including in higher education [97]. Furthermore, executive functions allow students to process material, to focus and maintain attention, and, importantly, adapt a socially accepted behavior according to the cultural context [129]. These cognitive abilities are essential for success in school because they 'make possible mentally playing with ideas' [42, p. 135]. Consequently, executive function ability is seen as more important for success in school, and later in life, including physical and mental health, than intelligence or socioeconomic background [43].

One reason for the strong links between executive function and ability to learn is that the neurodevelopmental condition- attention deficit/hyperactivity disorder is defined by difficulties with cognitive control. In fact, executive function symptoms are observed in almost all neuropsychiatric disorders, including neurodevelopmental, neurological and psychiatric disorders [118]. They may be risk-factors for clinical problems such as substance dependence [94] and deliberate self-harm [96]. Beyond education and clinical applications, executive functions have proven to be important correlates or life-challenges, being sensitive to poor sleep quality, loneliness, sadness, being physically unfit etc. [42]. They also predict workplace performance better than intelligence [93] and help to explain failures of human-machine interaction [22]. Consequently, this once obscure concept originating in the rarefied world of computer architecture is now of interest across a range of academic, applied, and clinical human sciences.

1.2   The Psychological Background to Executive Functions

The term 'executive function' was first used within psychology in 1967, by the psychologist J.P. Guilford [58]. In his attempts to classify the range of human cognitive processes, he noted a 'set of executive abilities, concerned with putting ideas into action through implied intention' [62, p. 35]. And with the 'organization and control of motor output' [56, p. 99]. The concept of executive function has since developed within psychology, particularly from a cognitive perspective. There have been multiple cognitive models provided, but two approaches have dominated theory in this field, the Supervisory Attentional System of Tim Shallice and colleagues [34,86,114,116,117], and the Working Memory model of Alan Baddeley and colleagues [7,9–12,41].

The Supervisory Attentional System. In 1980 Norman and Shallice proposed a model of the control of human behavior that involved two systems. Firstly, the Supervisory Attentional System is active in situations that are novel, dangerous, or require planning, or complex procedures that have not yet been learnt [86]. That attentional mechanism acts to bias selection of action schemas that already exist. However, appropriate behavior can usually be achieved when it is triggered by perceptions and controlled by those schemas based in memory, which interact through excitation and inhibition to select the most appropriate response. This schema-based system of activation is known as Contention Scheduling and instigates well-learned, procedural, and habitual actions. This model has developed, but is still widely accepted and applied to the executive control of action and thought [34,115,117]. In this model, executive processes are carried out by the 'general purpose, limited-capacity mechanism', that is, the Supervisory Attentional System, while the Contention Scheduling System does not have central processing limitations [86, p. 12]. Shallice drew on early AI research on problem solving that used tasks with clear goals, that would require decomposition into sub-goals, extending his theory into human planning ability and executive functions [114].

Working Memory. The dominant model of human memory, proposing separate long-term and short-term stores, originally invoked a number of control process within the short-term store [5]. However, this was unable to explain experimental observations, and in 1974 Alan Baddeley proposed a limited capacity Central Executive, separate from short-term memory [12]. Nevertheless, in early versions, the Central Executive component was only vaguely described. When the Supervisory Attentional System was proposed by Shallice at al., this was adopted as the theoretical basis for the Central Executive of Working Memory [7,9]. A main difference between the models is simply the emphasis on what is controlled by the executive component. In Working Memory it is temporary memory systems, in particular, a phonological store and a visuospatial store [7,9–12], and an episodic buffer [6,11]. The Central Executive is proposed as an attentional mechanism, lacking storage capacity, that is responsible for coordination of processing between different tasks [7,41], focusing processing on information from different sources, and manipulating and modifying information [6].

1.3   The Neurological Background to Executive Functions

It has long been observed that brain damage can produce disorganized behavior. A famous case being Phineas Gage, who, in 1848, suffered a brain injury in an industrial accident. Although he survived, his behavior became erratic, with difficulties in planning, decision making, and disinhibition. Although his cognitive ability was sufficiently intact for him to work, he changed occupations frequently. His doctor said that 'his mind was radically changed' [59, p. 227]. It is now known that the brain damage was limited to the prefrontal cortex, mainly of the left hemisphere [35]. A modern case, who survived a similar injury to the left prefrontal cortex, was able to pass many cognitive tests and had an IQ well above average. But like Phineas Gage, he suffered a disorganization of behavior, including chronic unemployment and relationship instability [21]. Many other patients have been reported with damage to the frontal lobes resulting in disorganization of behavior manifest in occupational and educational instability, despite normal or above average IQ [18,49,60,116].

This disorganization of behavior, following damage to the frontal lobes, appears to reflect impairment of top-down cognitive control, the processes associated with executive functions. In 1973, drawing on computer science, and the need for programs to coordinate information-processing demands with a central processor, Karl H. Pribram proposed that the frontal lobes may function in that way. Thus, 'executive programs' were proposed as a means for the brain to handle competing processing demands, and damage to the frontal lobes disturbs that control [99]. Such behavioral syndromes in neurology have been increasingly interpreted as reflecting an impairment of executive control, and are now often known as the dysexecutive syndrome [8].

This association between the frontal lobes and executive control has become widely accepted, due to multiple reports of dysexecutive syndrome following frontal lobe damage [8,18,21,27,34,35,48,55,59,60,64,107,114,116,117]. Although such an association exists, it provides a seductive but overly simplistic and pseudoscientific reduction of process to physiology that has been referred to as 'frontal lobology' [36]. Additionally, the frontal lobe cortical systems which control behavior operate through other brain regions, particularly circuits involving subcortical structures which include input from other cortical regions, particularly the parietal lobes [3]. These circuits operate as loops, with the initiation of a simple goal-directed action, such as a finger movement, likely involving at least 20 passes through the frontal-subcortical loop [112].

Accordingly, brain imaging has identified a system involving areas on the frontal lobes, as well as the parietal lobes, and subcortical structures, which appears to have a domain-general function (i.e., it responds to tasks regardless of type -visuospatial, language, auditory etc.) [47,50,84]. This system is said to allow the representation of goals from diverse tasks, and to be the physiological substrate of both general intelligence and some aspects executive function. A popular functional description of this brain network is as a multiple demand system [47,50]. However, there may be several domain-general processes that overlap in performance on any given task, and it is these domain-general processes that are described as executive [71].

In addition, the brain's default mode network is functionally linked to executive functions. That network comprises frontal, parietal and temporal lobe regions that are active during rest but deactivate when performing executive-demanding tasks [100,101]. The default mode network likely plays some role in cognitive executive control [76] and may also coordinate action-schema maintenance [13,127]. Semantic control is also a theme that has emerged recently. Neuroscience research using multiple methods has suggested that in addition to semantic representations in the brain, there is a system for executive control of semantic information. This semantic control network in the prefrontal and parietal regions, but also regions of the temporal lobe, is involved with goal-directed control of the processing of lexical information [102].

1.4   Computer Science and Human Executive Functions

We have previously computationally modeled human executive functions for both the Supervisory Attentional System and Working Memory models [22,24]. We have implemented these models with Behavior and Reasoning Description Language, based on Real-time Maude, a language developed to model human reasoning within the context of intentional (executive) and automatic action [23]. In this approach, deliberate attentional action is modelled by task goals (equivalent to the role of the Supervisory Attentional System) and based on declarative semantic knowledge. In contrast, automatic behavior is based on knowledge in procedural memory stores [25].

Part of the motivation behind these in silico models is to understand intentional and automatic aspects of human-computer interaction. Executive functions play an important role in the way users interact with computer interfaces as well as with any machine interface, and especially when they carry out articulated tasks which involve interactions with multiple interfaces of embedded computer systems. This can be the case of both routine activities occurring in ordinary daily life, such as driving, and work-related activities of operators of control systems, such as air traffic control, industrial machine, medical device, and control room operators. Tasks such as these have safety-critical aspects but are normally carried out under automatic control. Moreover, they may involve multitasking (an operator often has to monitor a number of distinct readouts simultaneously) or, being performed under automatic control, may actually encourage multitasking (drivers often listen to music or talk, or even unsafely use mobile phones, while driving). In such contexts the role of an executive controller is fundamental in changing the behavior control from automatic to intentional when required by sudden changes in the environment and, if such changes determine hazards, in preventing dangerous situations or the violation of safety requirements. We have considered typical situations that activate the Supervisory Attentional System [22]:

required decision which may be needed in the normal operation of the system;
expectation failure when the user/operator's expectations are not met;
emotions determined by something perceived through implicit attention.

Expectation failures requires conscious assessment, normally in terms of novelty or hazard, to drive the intentional behavior that must be carried out to cope with them. Typical emotions are curiosity, temptation, and anger. They not only trigger emotional reactions, but they normally necessitate the establishment of new goals, hence intentional behavior. For example, while driving under automatic control, we may need to resort to intentional behavior in each of the above situations. When we are at a crossing on an unfamiliar route, we must consciously evaluate the directions given by the road signs and make the appropriate decisions. An expectation failure could be a strange sound from the engine, to which we may consciously react by slowing down and possibly stopping the car, or a deviation signal on a familiar route, which make us consciously planning how to best reroute. Finally, several emotions may be triggered by events we encounter while driving. Curiosity may be triggered by the presence of police and emergency vehicles on the road. A temptation may be represented by the sight of a stall selling some food we are craving for, which may urge us to consciously stop to purchase it. Anger which may be caused by another driver honking to ask for space to overtake and may result in several possible reactions, usually inappropriate and, sometimes, even associated with conscious revenge.

Our previous work [22] also considers Contention Scheduling. For example, in the case of driving, the driver's behavior while approaching an amber light. In this situation, the driver has two possible responses: (1) stop at the traffic light; (2) speed up. The driver's behavior is determined by the activation of the schema-based Contention Scheduling System. Depending on the behavior learned through practice, which resulted in the creation of a procedural, habitual schema that consistently instigates the driver to either stop or speed up, without a proper evaluation of which of the two responses is safer. Although the two schemas may both be present in the driver Contention Scheduling System, the actual choice that leads to the contention resolution is not determined by a proper evaluation of the situation, but by a mental state. For example, a driver who is in a hurry is more likely to choose to speed through the crossing.

2 Current Issues and Controversies Regarding Executive Function

2.1 Is There a Unitary Central Executive?

Both of the models presented here, the Supervisory Attentional System [34,86, 114,116,117] and Working Memory model [6,7,9–12,41], are usually represented with a single, central, executive process. However, it is reasonable to think that the 'executive' may fractionate into different components. Alan Baddeley has suggested this about his Working Memory model [6,7,9], as has Tim Shallice about his Supervisory Attentional System [114,115], in fact, he has recently presented evidence that different forms of brain damage produce qualitatively different impairments of the Supervisory Attentional System [117]. Similarly, it has been argued that executive processes, such as task setting, energization, and behavior monitoring may be independently impaired by damage to the frontal lobes. The authors conclude that there can be no 'central executive', nor a unitary neurological 'dysexecutive syndrome' [120]. Similarly, analysis of brain regions indicated in functional imaging studies, radiological studies of neurological patients, and split-brain patients that lack corpora callosa (the main connections between the brain's hemispheres) have provided no evidence for a single central executive [89].

From an embodied cognition perspective, it has been argued that executive control may be better described as the functioning of several different modules. This has been argued from both neurophysiological [72] and in silico/robotics perspectives [15]. Furthermore, from cognitive psychology, research comparing test scores from healthy participants has shown that many executive function test scores barely correlate, suggesting they are measuring independent processes [77]. From a psychometric perspective, clusters of task-performance scores have been analyzed, with one important study suggesting both 'unity and diversity of executive functions' [81]. As there is a lack of clarity of what are executive functions, there is a need to more clearly define them.

2.2 What is, and What is Not, Executive Function?

The concept of executive function has developed mainly within psychology, albeit with substantial influence from AI. Within neuroscience, a similar concept is cognitive control. However, these are used interchangeably, and both can be defined as 'the ability to coordinate thought and action and direct it toward obtaining goals' [79, p. 99]. A classic definition has been that 'Executive functions are high-level cognitive processes, often associated with the frontal lobes, that control lower level processes in the service of goal-directed behavior' [81, p. 186]. From an embodied cognition perspective, executive control has been defined as 'the functions an organism employs to act independently in its own best interest as a whole', and that 'action (or movement) and goal-directed behavior are inherent in the concepts and definitions of cognition and EF (executive function)'

[72, p. 506]. Although vague, these definitions share one important feature- the importance of goal-directedness.

There are various classes of behavior that are not goal-directed, and consequently not usually under executive control, including innate motor reflexes such as eye-blinks to stimulation of the eyeball, defensive fixed reaction patterns, such as freezing, and conditioned fear responses [74]. Many types of cognitive response are not goal-directed, such as attending to our own name heard in background speech- the cocktail party phenomenon [32]. A particularly important class of non-goal-directed behaviors are instrumental actions that are habitual [16, 37, 38, 44, 46, 128].

Expanding on this important distinction, it is known that instrumental conditioning proceeds from goal-directed control to automatic habitual responses [37]. A rat trained to press a lever for reinforcement will, during early trials, press the lever to achieve the reinforcer. This is known because devaluation of the reinforcer produces rapid extinction of responses. After multiple learning trials, even if the reinforcer is devalued, the subject continues to respond [2]. This procedure distinguishes goal-directed from habitual responding [44]. The distinction is also known as model-based and model-free in computational reinforcement learning [38, 46], and as declarative and procedural memory in cognitive psychology [38]. The role of declarative memory is associated with representing the goal while also involving executive processes in action directed toward that goal [16]. Indeed, goal-directed instrumental learning (model-based learning) and executive cognitive control are thought to have common neural substrates [88].

Therefore, on approaching a situation that requires a response, people may use either goal-directed actions, that are controlled by the consequences, or habits, that are controlled by their antecedents. The neurological bases of these systems have been explored in humans and other species, and as would be expected, goal-directed action is cortically driven by the prefrontal and parietal regions and their subcortical loops [128]. When that brain system is damaged, a common clinical consequence is a reduction in goal-directed behavior [95], and such patients display 'goal neglect' [48].

Instrumental actions to achieve a goal, such as pressing a button to receive something, seems rather simple. Nevertheless, they represent the basics of the top-down cognitive control which constitutes executive function. Analysis of single-cell recordings in the monkey brain, and imaging studies of the human brain, have revealed how complex tasks are broken down and processed as subgoals, leading to the highly complex, intelligent goal-directed behavior that is usually described as executive function [47]. Parallel support for this approach comes from classical approaches to formal AI, such as the General Problem Solver [85] and ACT [4], in which emphasis is placed on breaking down tasks into subgoals. This supports the implementation of means-end analysis, a classical approach to human and machine problem solving. The establishment of subgoals drives the performance of actions that shorten the distance to the final goal within the state space, although such actions do not directly seem to contribute to the achievement of the final goal. For example, if we need to move a heavy box, we may establish the subgoal of emptying it before moving it. But, obviously, emptying a box does not directly contribute to moving it. This breaking down of goals into subgoals was demonstrated eloquently in a classic AI study that showed that it produced much more efficient solutions [110].

Tim Shallice has expressly argued that the goal-directed instrumental behavior system is equivalent to his Supervisory Attentional System and the habit-based system equivalent to his schema-based Contention Scheduling System [34]. Goal-directed (executive) action is performed with a conscious component, but habitual, schema-based actions, driven by stimuli, are performed without awareness [64, 86, 113, 128]. Furthermore, in dealing with novel situations, actions are at first conscious, executive, and goal-directed, but become stimuli-driven habits if repeated several times [37, 128]. It is likely that the goal-directed action system is the more advanced, which has developed to allow more flexible behavior. From an evolutionary perspective, the development of goal-directed action represents 'a quantum jump in general intelligence above that exhibited by simple stimulus-response systems' [44, p. 68]. The evolution of goal-directed action, as the basis of intelligence, has been described in humans and other vertebrates, and suggested as a principle that could be applied in robotics to allow flexible, intelligent behavior [52]. Accordingly, the concepts discussed here, of goal-directed behavior, underlying what is commonly known as executive function, can be readily applied to AI. Baldassarre and Granato suggest that goal-directness is consistent with many classical definitions of artificial general intelligence and is necessary for cognitive flexibility [14]. Executive functions are goal-directed by definition. But is it correct to equate them with intelligence?

2.3   Are Executive Functions 'Intelligent'?

Some researchers have expressly linked goal-directed executive functions with intelligent behavior [14, 47, 48, 93]. Furthermore, as described above, executive function ability appears to predict a range of educational and occupational outcomes, perhaps even better than intelligence does. Executive function as a concept developed in cognitive science and neuropsychology, while cognitive control developed in neuroscience, and intelligence is a core topic of differential psychology. One of the reasons for this historical separation is that opinion in neuropsychology and behavioral neurology was that patients with damage to the frontal lobes showed a dysexecutive syndrome, but often without any impairment of intelligence [18, 49, 59, 60, 116]. This dissociation seemed to confirm that executive function and intelligence relied on separate processes.

It is now known that the connection is in fact much closer than originally thought. The problem was that psychometric intelligence tests, as used in neuropsychology and neurology, tend to contain assessments that are insensitive to impairment [87]. However, the concept of general intelligence, often known as the g factor, is a somewhat different idea, and refers to some general feature shared by all cognitive processes [66]. It is revealed by the positive manifold of correlations- the observation that all cognitive test scores positively correlated with each other [92]. When patients with dysexecutive syndromes were tested for general intelligence, impairments were apparent [48,107].

Similarly, research in differential psychology uses factor analysis and related methods to study human cognitive architecture. Such methods show that variation in one aspect of executive functioning, working memory, is almost completely explained by variation in general intelligence [31] and when executive function is considered as a singular trait, it may be fully explained by general intelligence [109]. Furthermore, when this factor analytic approach is extended to patients with brain lesions, the patterns of damage causing reduced general intelligence are almost identical to those producing reduced single-trait executive function ability- the fronto-parietal system [17]. Accordingly, imaging studies of brain activation in healthy participants suggest a singular fronto-parietal system that is involved with general problem-solving activities associated with either general intelligence or executive functions [47,50]. In summary, this body of research suggests that there may be no such thing as specific executive functions, independent of a domain-general intelligence.

Nevertheless, the direct measurement of general intelligence requires analysis of multiple cognitive tests to derive the g factor. It may be that what is being measured is the overlap of many different processes, including a domain-general process, such as working memory, as well as other more domain-specific executive processes [71]. Furthermore, measures of general intelligence based on single tests (as opposed to latent variables from factor analysis) are usually used in research outside of differential psychology. The most common of these tests are versions of Raven's Progressive Matrices [103,104]. When such tests have been used with neurological patients, they have confirmed that many tests of 'executive function' do not reveal any impaired performance beyond that explained by general intelligence [107]. However, that is not true of all executive function tests. There are some that appear to reveal impairments independently of loss of general intelligence. These tests appear to measure abilities such as motor response cancelation, verbal response suppression, multi-tasking, and verbal abstraction [107], as well as Stroop task performance [27], and cognitive estimation [26], amongst others. Therefore, these neuropsychological studies indicate some executive processes cannot be equivalent to general intelligence.

2.4   Is Executive Function Resource Limited?

An important aspect of executive function is that it may have limited capacity. Baddeley described the Central Executive as a 'limited capacity attentional system' [9, p. 8], and Shallice described the Supervisory Attentional System as 'a general purpose limited capacity mechanism' [86, p. 12]. It might see obvious that all brain processes are limited by available processing resources. But executive processing does appear to be special in this respect. At least from a phenomenological perspective, processes involving interoception (such as monitoring one's own body temperature) or exteroception (such as vision) do not involve any experience of effort, or suffer performance declines over time, in contrast, executive cognitive processes do [73]. These observations suggest that whatever processes underlie executive functions, they may be limited by available resources. However, we can think of these limitations in various ways, including from biological, psychological, and human-machine interaction perspectives.

The Biological Aspect of Resource Limits. One aspect of resource limitation of cognitive ability is fundamentally embodied. Brains, whether human or not, are subject to evolutionary pressure. One of these pressures is to be only as proficient in the control of behavior as is necessary. Brains are 'expensive' organs which consume large amounts of the body's oxygen: approximately 20%, despite being only about 2% of body mass [108]. Therefore, it could be that executive control is limited as a resource by the need to maintain a brain that is only as physiologically active as necessary. Costs of neural activity can be measured by blood oxygen consumption. When people engage in task performance, as compared to being at rest, the absolute increase in blood oxygen use can be calculated through magnetic resonance brain imaging. Within brain areas linked to executive functioning, the increases in oxygen consumption are indeed quite large, up to 26% [67]. However, with increased cognitive load, the increase in oxygen use over the whole brain is only about 4% [130]. This increase is probably important, but would constitute less than 1% increase in overall body oxygen consumption, and so other reasons may limit our use of executive resources.

One of these may be that engagement of brain regions involved in executive control is typically associated with simultaneous deactivation of the default mode network [51]. This system of interconnected brain regions, separate from the executive control regions, appears to become active whenever a person is at rest but awake [100,101]. The fact that engagement of executive-related neural processes involves the disengagement of the default mode network, suggests that a cost of executive control may be to processing in that latter system. The default mode network is dynamically involved in 'sense making' that integrates incoming social information with existing schemas to produce models of situations over time [127]. It has been directly implicated [13] in the processing of a type of schema proposed in a well-known AI and human cognition theory of procedural knowledge- script theory [111].

Related to this, the default mode network may be responsible for pre-planned, reflexive behaviors, as such it may produce impulsive behavior [100]. This would suggest that not only do the executive-linked brain regions and default mode network function antagonistically, but they also represent the distinction between executive function and routine or stimuli-driven actions, such as the Contention Scheduling aspect of the Supervisory Attentional System [34,86,114,116,117]. Goal-directed executive function may be resource limited because the default mode network requires interruption of goal-directed behavior so that it can continually develop and maintain procedural action schemas.

The approach described above has focused on the real-time capacity limitation of executive processing. However, research in social psychology has examined a related, and embodied concept, over time. This is the notion of ego depletion. This theory suggests that mental effort is a limited resource, and doing tasks that require executive control, particularly response inhibition, weaken the performance of later tasks [83]. The original developers of ego depletion theory likened self-control to being like a muscle, which becomes less effective with continued use. Several researchers have attempted to link ego depletion to reduced blood glucose levels. This approach has been extended to suggest that body glucose levels may be used to forecast resource needs and regulate adaptive behavior, ultimately driving decision making [124]. However, empirical studies have tended to find only weak associations between mental effort and glucose levels [121]. Furthermore, a recent multi-site study with meta-analysis failed to support the concept of ego depletion at all [123].

The Psychological Aspect of Resource Limits. The evidence for the Central Executive being limited came particularly from dual-task procedures in which research participants would perform memory tasks simultaneously with some other tasks. From the outset of the Working Memory model, dual-task performance that hindered reasoning ability, beyond that explicable by the cognitive load in the phonological store, was used to hypothesize a flexible 'limited capacity workspace' [12, p. 57]. Chess playing, a highly executive skill, and production of random numbers are both impaired by a secondary task that use executive processes, suggesting that the executive control mechanism is resource limited [9].

Likewise, the Supervisory Attentional System, the other canonical model of executive functioning, was based partly on arguments from dual-task performance, particularly in the distinction between (executive) attentional control and routine action generation [86]. Indeed, its development was based on analysis of hierarchies of control, drawing on computer science and cybernetics, to argue that only one action plan can be fully active at any one time. Accordingly, when multiple goals are pursued, the full activation of one plan will ultimately inhibit performance of other goal-directed systems [113]. Persisting with individual goal-directed processes therefore has costs as they prevent other processes from achieving their goals [73]. This approach has also been applied from an embodied perspective. Drawing on biology and robotics, it has been suggested that only a small number of processing modules can be active at any one time, for practical reasons. This consequently produces a need to activate modules to control behavior judiciously, providing the raison d'être of executive control [15].

Human-Machine Interaction and Resource Limits. Limitations to memory capacity and processing are often responsible for the errors by machine/system operators. The so-called human error is incorrectly perceived as caused by an erroneous behavior of the operator. However, in reality, the error emerges from a mismatch between the computer interface with which the operator interacts and the physiological, hence normal, limitations of human processing capabilities. Using operators as scapegoats obscures the real responsibilities in industrial and transportation disasters. In most cases, poor system design is the actual source of the error.

Post-completion error is a subtle executive error, which has been noted and extensively investigated during the last thirty years. This kind of error occurs when a subsidiary task is not carried out because its execution is preceded by achievement of the goal. In fact, once a goal is achieved, working memory stores may be cleared, with a consequent loss of the information associated with the completed task. This is an essential memory process, called short-term memory closure, which makes the capacity-limited short-term memory stores ready to work on a new task. However, some of the lost information may be needed for the performance of the subsidiary task. A typical example of post-completion error occurs where we forget our bank card after withdrawing cash from an ATM. Our goal is achieved when we collect the cash and, if the ATM is programmed to deliver cash before returning the card, then the card may be forgotten [22].

This post-completion kind of error has been recently identified as the cause of several aviation accidents. A typical situation is engine maintenance. In fact, engine doors may be left unlocked after maintenance, because the goal is the completion maintenance, whereas locking the door is a subsidiary task. Unfortunately, such a subsidiary task cannot be easily anticipated. Thus, this instance of post-completion error cannot be prevented, but may be reduced by establishing strict executive protocols.

2.5   Current Challenges to Understand Executive Functions

The identification of a domain-general multiple demand system in the brain, that underlies general intelligence and top-down cognitive control [47,50], has been a useful development. This system appears to be resource limited, in that greater task difficulty is associated with greater engagement within that neural system [50]. This seems to be a core part of executive function. However, several established clinical tests of executive function appear to be sensitive to cognitive impairment independently of changes in general intelligence [26,27,107] and many cognitive processes appear to involve top-down cognitive control, beyond those currently conceived as being the core executive processes of working memory, inhibition and switching (e.g., semantic control). A current challenge in cognitive sciences is the identification of processes, and cognitive tests, which define specific executive functions that are not simply measures of domain-general intelligence. If executive function assessment merely measure intelligence, the concept of executive function is effectively redundant.

One point which may be relevant is that intelligence tests measure convergent thinking. This concept refers to cognitive processes that focus in on a single unique solution, the task working to channel processing in the direction of the answer. This is contrasted with divergent thinking in which processing may search many different possible solutions, with usually no unique response considered correct [57]. Finding alternative uses for objects is an example of divergent thinking, while deductive reasoning is an example of convergent thinking. Common intelligence tests, such as the Weschler tests of intelligence, or Raven's Progressive Matrices, invariably define what are correct responses. This is supported by validity studies which indicate that IQ predicts convergent thinking ability, but not divergent thinking ability [75]. However, this is not necessarily true of common tests that are used to measure executive functions.

3   A Proposal

A separation between convergent thinking and divergent thinking has been used in psychology since the 1950s [57]. The concept has been particularly applied to educational outcomes [63]. Convergent thinking ability has been associated with achievement in science and engineering [91], and divergent thinking with humanities and arts, as an example, when compared to demographically-matched controls, skilled musicians have been found to have better divergent thinking ability, which is associated with greater activation levels in the frontal lobes [53]. Interestingly, a large meta-analysis of divergent thinking ability has shown that it appears to have only a weak relationship with intelligence test performance [68], suggesting assessments of divergent thinking primarily measure something other than general intelligence.

A classic test of divergent thinking is the Alternative Uses Test, which requires participants to produce as many different uses for common objects as possible during a time limit [58]. Performance for identifying new uses for objects is often compared with production of multiple, but not varied, uses. The ability to produce many uses is considered to indicate creativity. Furthermore, the production of ideas for new uses appears to be closely related to executive function, as shown by relatively high correlations with performance on phonemic fluency, a common measure of executive function [54]. On the other hand, production of multiple non-creative uses is said to indicate fluent responding, but measure memory access rather than executive processes.

Although intelligence testing is closely linked to convergent, but not divergent thinking [68,75], it is not simply the case that executive function assessments show the opposite pattern. In fact, most widely used assessments of executive functioning require convergent thinking too. We argue here that this may be one of the reasons why statistically, intelligence is closely related executive function [31,109].

3.1   Divergent Processes and Limited-Resource Executive Control

Divergent executive processes appear to be sensitive to dual-tasking, which likely indicates the role of a resource-limited processor, such as the Central Executive. The performance of a secondary task impairs the identification of new uses of objects, but does not impair the production of multiple, non-creative uses [69]. As previously indicated, sensitivity to dual-tasking is consistent with the use of a resource-limited attention mechanism such as the Supervisory Attentional System [86] or the Central Executive [9,11]. It is also consistent with embodied approaches to cognition which propose limits on the number of processing modules that can be active at any point, producing difficulties with dual-task performance [15].

Divergent tasks produce greater brain activations than non-divergent control tasks, particularly in prefrontal regions [126] and the frontal lobes in general are more active during divergent tasks in highly creative people compared to normal control participants [53]. The regions indicated are thought to be the core aspect of the systems underlying executive functions, in particular the resource-limited multiple-demand system [47], which becomes more active with increasing cognitive load [50]. Level of activation in these frontal lobe regions may be considered as a physiological marker of resource usage, as they typically increase their blood oxygenation substantially during increased load [67]. The resource limitation is often linked to working memory, which may be the core executive function, underlying resource-limited domain-general processing [31]. However, even when tasks are matched for cognitive load, divergent executive processes appear to produce more widespread activations of the frontal lobes than working memory task performance [1]. Divergent tasks not only challenge domain-specific aspects of executive processes, such as a 'central executive', but also domain-specific executive processes. One candidate for this is semantic control, identified as being executive mechanisms that interact with semantic representations [106].

3.2 Divergent Executive Processes and Neural Systems

If divergent thinking involves executive functions, it would be expected to activate the same brain networks as standard executive tasks do. This has been found using functional magnetic imaging, and it has also been shown that the interaction with the default mode network is important, suggesting both executive and controlled activity of heuristic processing, such as schema or habitual modes of responding [61]. Although the default mode network is often considered to be a brain system that is anticorrelated with executive control, the deactivations are likely important features of cognitive processing and predict behavioral performance on executive tasks [39,125] and some parts appear to be actively involved in executive-attentional control [76].

A meta-analysis of brain imaging studies of divergent thinking confirmed the involvement of executive and default mode brain networks, but also the semantic control network [30]. Thus, the neural basis of divergent thinking appears to involve wider networks linked to goal-directed, top-down cognitive control than those implicated in domain-general intelligence [47,50,84], specifically the cognitive control system and the default mode network. Executive tasks that incorporate divergent goals may involve a wider range of top-down cognitive control mechanisms than convergent tasks.

3.3 A Taxonomy of Executive Functions Based on Task Goals

From a practical perspective there is a need to recognize executive control mechanisms that do not substantially overlap with intelligence or the core domain-general process that supports it. That is, processes that fractionate from the domain-general process. An obvious place to look would be at executive functions which involve divergent process. Here we propose a taxonomy of executive functions based on the convergent-divergent distinction. For most cognitive tasks, the method by which cognitive performance is measured can be classified based on the goal that is given to the participant. For example, a participant may be told to recall a set of numbers or words, or to reorganize them and then recall them. In such cases there is a right answer, and any other response is incorrect. Examples of such tests are various short-term memory and complex span tasks [33]. Some tests require recognition of the correct meaning of words or phrases, such as in the Proverb Test, or logical deduction as in the Twenty Questions Test, or overcoming distraction, such in the Stroop Test [40]. Assessments such as those clearly invoke convergent processes- responses are either correct or incorrect.

In contrast, in some cognitive tests, participants are given open-ended goals. They may be told to produce as many exemplars as possible from large sets. Multiple such fluency tasks exist and are commonly used in neuropsychology, including phonemic, semantic, ideational, design and gesture [105]. The goal given to the research participant or patient is to produce as many different examples as possible, a divergent processing instruction. As examples, design fluency tasks involve production of unique designs, albeit limited by rules such as joining dots. Similarly, phonemic fluency tasks involve production of as many different words beginning with a particular letter.

Some tests require participants to avoid any predictable patterns, such as random number generation [65]. A participant in such a procedure is tasked with saying random numbers at a set rate, e.g., one per second. Another example of an executive task that involves avoiding patterns is the Hayling test, in which participants are asked to rapidly complete sentences with words that make no sense [20,98]. Such task goals are not at all convergent, and appear to be better classified as divergent. Thus, many assessments of executive function can be classified based on the instructed goal requirement- as either divergent or convergent. This classification is shown in Fig. 1.

There is a third commonly used goal requirement of executive function tests. This is to not respond. This occurs in psychomotor tasks such as the Go/No-go task in which participants are required to rapidly response to some stimuli, for example with a button press, but to not respond to other stimuli. Performance may be recorded as errors (omissions or commissions), response times, or estimates of processing times related to response cancelation, such as in the Stop-signal task [78]. Related to this, though not explored as an executive control mechanism, is the deliberate delaying of simple response times. This is a task goal that severely slows performance [66], suggesting that it invokes attentional top-down control at the cost of automatic, habitual responding.

The benefit to focusing on cognitive tasks that are not convergent, is that this approach fits more closely with the concept of top-down, goal-directed control, that is, executive functions that deal with novel processing requirements. Tasks that have convergent goals, tend to have procedures which can achieve them.

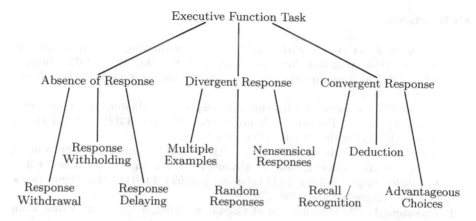

Fig. 1. An incomplete taxonomy of executive function tasks based on the goal of the task.

Or at the least, tend to become proceduralized, and thus reduce their executive demands. As evidence of this, classic (convergent) 'executive function' tasks, such as the Towers of Hanoi, show substantial practice effects- performance improves on each administration [90].

Finally, convergent and divergent process, as defined here, can be independently impaired by brain damage [27]. In neuropsychological terms, they doubly dissociate, indicating their functional independence. Furthermore, executive function measures that are non-convergent may be better than convergent measures at predicting real-life intelligent performance, such as in the arts [53], academic achievement in high school [98] or university [97,98], or predicting work-place performance such as in sales [93]. They therefore represent a relatively independent facet of intelligent behavior.

4   Conclusions

Executive functions, though originating in computer science, can be understood in terms of goal-directed behavior, a concept originating in psychology and neuroscience. Goal-directedness is a necessary component for both natural [44] and artificial intelligence [14]. Executive functions can also be considered as producing intelligent behavior. However, to provide some separation from the concept of psychometric intelligence, as it is customarily used, we also emphasize psychomotor inhibition and divergent cognition in the overall concept of executive processes. This point harks back to the first use of the term 'executive function' within psychology by J.P. Guildford, who also proposed the concept of divergent thinking [58]. Although speculative, the division of task types by goals, as shown in Fig. 1, could be applied in other areas to explore, and perhaps advance the understanding of top-down executive control of intelligent goal-directed action in the human sciences. Such an approach could also be applied in computer science to better understand the production of artificial general intelligence.

References

1. Abraham, A., et al.: Creativity and the brain: uncovering the neural signature of conceptual expansion. Neuropsychologia **50**(8), 1906–1917 (2012). https://doi.org/10.1016/j.neuropsychologia.2012.04.015, https://www.ncbi.nlm.nih.gov/pubmed/22564480
2. Adams, C., Dickinson, A.: Instrumental responding following reinforcer devaluation. Q. J. Exp. Psychol. B Comp. Physiol. Psychol. **33**(2), 109–121 (1981). https://doi.org/10.1080/14640748108400816
3. Alexander, G.E., DeLong, M.R., Strick, P.L.: Parallel organization of functionally segregated circuits linking basal ganglia and cortex. Annu. Rev. Neurosci. **9**, 357–81 (1986). https://doi.org/10.1146/annurev.ne.09.030186.002041, https://www.ncbi.nlm.nih.gov/pubmed/3085570
4. Anderson, J.: The Architecture of Cognition. Harvard University Press, Cambridge, MA (1983)
5. Atkinson, R.C., Shiffrin, R.M.: The control of short-term memory. Sci. Am. **225**(2), 82–91 (1971)
6. Baddeley, A.: The episodic buffer: a new component of working memory?. Trends Cogn. Sci. **4**(11), 417–423 (2000). https://doi.org/10.1016/s1364-6613(00)01538-2, https://www.ncbi.nlm.nih.gov/pubmed/11058819
7. Baddeley, A., Della Sala, S.: Working memory and executive control. Philos. Trans. R. Soc. B Biol. Sci. **351**(1346), 1397–403 (1996). https://doi.org/10.1098/rstb.1996.0123, https://www.ncbi.nlm.nih.gov/pubmed/8941951
8. Baddeley, A., Wilson, B.: Frontal amnesia and the dysexecutive syndrome. Brain Cogn. **7**(2), 212–230 (1988). https://doi.org/10.1016/0278-2626(88)90031-0, https://www.ncbi.nlm.nih.gov/pubmed/3377900
9. Baddeley, A.D.: Is working memory working? the fifteenth Bartlett lecture. Q. J. Exp. Psychol. A Hum. Exp. Psychol. **44**(1), 1–31 (1992). https://doi.org/10.1080/14640749208401281
10. Baddeley, A.D., Bressi, S., Della Sala, S., Logie, R., Spinnler, H.: The decline of working memory in Alzheimer's disease: a longitudinal study. Brain **114**(6), 2521–2542 (1991). https://doi.org/10.1093/brain/114.6.2521, https://www.ncbi.nlm.nih.gov/pubmed/1782529
11. Baddeley, A.D., Hitch, G.J.: The phonological loop as a buffer store: an update. Cortex **112**, 91–106 (2019). https://doi.org/10.1016/j.cortex.2018.05.015, https://www.ncbi.nlm.nih.gov/pubmed/29941299
12. Baddeley, A., Hitch, G.: Working memory. In: Bower, G.H. (ed.) Psychology of Learning and Motivation: Advances in Research and Theory. Academic Press, New York (1974)
13. Baldassano, C., Hasson, U., Norman, K.A.: Representation of real-world event schemas during narrative perception. J. Neurosci. **38**(45), 9689–9699 (2018). https://doi.org/10.1523/JNEUROSCI.0251-18.2018, https://www.ncbi.nlm.nih.gov/pubmed/30249790
14. Baldassarre, G., Granato, G.: Goal-directed manipulation of internal representations is the core of general-domain intelligence. J. Artif. Gen. Intell. **11**(2), 19–23 (2020). https://doi.org/10.2478/jagi-2020-0003
15. Ballard, D.H., Kit, D., Rothkopf, C.A., Sullivan, B.: A hierarchical modular architecture for embodied cognition. Multisensory Res. **26**(1–2), 177–204 (2013). https://doi.org/10.1163/22134808-00002414

16. Balleine, B.W., Liljeholm, M., Ostlund, S.B.: The integrative function of the basal ganglia in instrumental conditioning. Behav. Brain Res. **199**(1), 43–52 (2009). https://doi.org/10.1016/j.bbr.2008.10.034, https://www.ncbi.nlm.nih.gov/pubmed/19027797

17. Barbey, A.K., Colom, R., Solomon, J., Krueger, F., Forbes, C., Grafman, J.: An integrative architecture for general intelligence and executive function revealed by lesion mapping. Brain **135**(4), 1154–1164 (2012). https://doi.org/10.1093/brain/aws021, http://www.ncbi.nlm.nih.gov/pubmed/22396393

18. Blair, R.J., Cipolotti, L.: Impaired social response reversal: a case of 'acquired sociopathy'. Brain **123**(6), 1122–1141 (2000). https://doi.org/10.1093/brain/123.6.1122, https://www.ncbi.nlm.nih.gov/pubmed/10825352

19. Bullynck, M.: What Is an Operating System? A Historical Investigation (1954–1964). In: De Mol, L., Primiero, G. (eds.) Reflections on Programming Systems. PSS, vol. 133, pp. 49–79. Springer, Cham (2018). https://doi.org/10.1007/978-3-319-97226-8_3

20. Burgess, P.W., Shallice, T.: Response suppression, initiation and strategy use following frontal lobe lesions. Neuropsychologia **34**(4), 263–272 (1996). https://doi.org/10.1016/0028-3932(95)00104-2, http://www.ncbi.nlm.nih.gov/pubmed/8657357

21. Cato, M.A., Delis, D.C., Abildskov, T.J., Bigler, E.: Assessing the elusive cognitive deficits associated with ventromedial prefrontal damage: a case of a modern-day Phineas gage. J. Int. Neuropsychol. Soc. **10**(3), 453–65 (2004). https://doi.org/10.1017/S1355617704103123, https://www.ncbi.nlm.nih.gov/pubmed/15147602

22. Cerone, A.: Closure and attention activation in human automatic behaviour: a framework for the formal analysis of interactive systems. Electron. Commun. EASST **45**, 1–18 (2011)

23. Cerone, A.: Behaviour and reasoning description language (BRDL). In: Camara, J., Steffen, M. (eds.) SEFM 2019. LNCS, vol. 12226, pp. 137–153. Springer, Cham (2020). https://doi.org/10.1007/978-3-030-57506-9_11

24. Cerone, A., Murzagaliyeva, D., Nabiyeva, N., Tyler, B., Pluck, G.: In silico simulations and analysis of human phonological working memory maintenance and learning mechanisms with behavior and reasoning description language (BRDL). In: SEFM 2021 Collocated Workshops. Lecture Notes in Computer Science, vol. 13230, pp. 37–52. Springer, Cham (2022). https://doi.org/10.1007/978-3-031-12429-7_3

25. Cerone, A., Pluck, G.: A formal model for emulating the generation of human knowledge in semantic memory. In: Bowles, J., Broccia, G., Nanni, M. (eds.) DataMod 2020. LNCS, vol. 12611, pp. 104–122. Springer, Cham (2021). https://doi.org/10.1007/978-3-030-70650-0_7

26. Cipolotti, L., et al.: Cognitive estimation: performance of patients with focal frontal and posterior lesions. Neuropsychologia **115**, 70–77 (2018). https://doi.org/10.1016/j.neuropsychologia.2017.08.017, https://www.ncbi.nlm.nih.gov/pubmed/28811256

27. Cipolotti, L., et al.: Inhibition processes are dissociable and lateralized in human prefrontal cortex. Neuropsychologia **93**(Pt A), 1–12 (2016). https://doi.org/10.1016/j.neuropsychologia.2016.09.018, https://www.ncbi.nlm.nih.gov/pubmed/27671485

28. Cisek, P.: Resynthesizing behavior through phylogenetic refinement. Atten. Percept. Psychophys. **81**(7), 2265–2287 (2019). https://doi.org/10.3758/s13414-019-01760-1. https://www.ncbi.nlm.nih.gov/pubmed/31161495

29. Clippinger, R.F.: Fact - a business compiler: description and comparison with Cobol and commercial translator. Int. Tra. Comput. Sci. Technol. Appl. **2**, 231–292 (1961). https://doi.org/10.1016/B978-1-4831-9779-1.50014-8

30. Cogdell-Brooke, L.S., Sowden, P.T., Violante, I.R., Thompson, H.E.: A meta-analysis of functional magnetic resonance imaging studies of divergent thinking using activation likelihood estimation. Hum. Brain Mapp. **41**(17), 5057–5077 (2020). https://doi.org/10.1002/hbm.25170, https://www.ncbi.nlm.nih.gov/pubmed/32845058

31. Colom, R., Rebollo, I., Palacios, A., Juan-Espinosa, M., Kyllonen, P.C.: Working memory is (almost) perfectly predicted by g. Intelligence **32**(3), 277–296 (2004)

32. Conway, A.R., Cowan, N., Bunting, M.F.: The cocktail party phenomenon revisited: the importance of working memory capacity. Psychon. Bull. Rev. **8**(2), 331–335 (2001). https://doi.org/10.3758/bf03196169, https://www.ncbi.nlm.nih.gov/pubmed/11495122

33. Conway, A.R., Kane, M.J., Bunting, M.F., Hambrick, D.Z., Wilhelm, O., Engle, R.W.: Working memory span tasks: A methodological review and user's guide. Psychon. Bull. Rev. **12**(5), 769–786 (2005). https://doi.org/10.3758/BF03196772, http://www.ncbi.nlm.nih.gov/pubmed/16523997

34. Cooper, R.P., Shallice, T.: Hierarchical schemas and goals in the control of sequential behavior. Psychol. Rev. **113**(4), 887–916 (2006). https://doi.org/10.1037/0033-295X.113.4.887, https://www.ncbi.nlm.nih.gov/pubmed/17014307

35. Damasio, H., Grabowski, T., Frank, R., Galaburda, A.M., Damasio, A.R.: The return of Phineas gage: clues about the brain from the skull of a famous patient. Science **264**(5162), 1102–5 (1994). https://doi.org/10.1126/science.8178168, https://www.ncbi.nlm.nih.gov/pubmed/8178168

36. David, A.: Frontal lobology- psychiatry's new pseudoscience. Br. J. Psychiatry **161**(2), 244–248 (1992). https://doi.org/10.1192/bjp.161.2.244

37. Daw, N., O'Doherty, J.P.: Multiple systems for value learning. In: Glimcher, P., Fehr, E. (eds.) Neuroeconomics: Decision Making and the Brain, pp. 393–410. 2nd edn. Academic Press, London (2013)

38. Dayan, P.: Goal-directed control and its antipodes. Neural Netw. **22**(3), 213–219 (2009). https://doi.org/10.1016/j.neunet.2009.03.004, https://www.ncbi.nlm.nih.gov/pubmed/19362448

39. De Pisapia, N., Turatto, M., Lin, P., Jovicich, J., Caramazza, A.: Unconscious priming instructions modulate activity in default and executive networks of the human brain. Cereb. Cortex **22**(3), 639–49 (2012). https://doi.org/10.1093/cercor/bhr146, https://www.ncbi.nlm.nih.gov/pubmed/21690258

40. Delis, D., Kaplan, E., Kramer, J.: Delis-Kaplan Executive Function System: Technical Manual. Psychological Corporation, San Antonio, TX (2001)

41. Della Sala, S., Baddeley, A., Papagno, C., Spinnler, H.: Dual-task paradigm: a means to examine the central executive. Ann. N. Y. Acad. Sci. **769**, 161–171 (1995). https://doi.org/10.1111/j.1749-6632.1995.tb38137.x, https://www.ncbi.nlm.nih.gov/pubmed/8595023

42. Diamond, A.: Executive functions. Annu. Rev. Psychol. **64**, 135–168 (2013). https://doi.org/10.1146/annurev-psych-113011-143750, https://www.ncbi.nlm.nih.gov/pubmed/23020641

43. Diamond, A.: Want to optimize executive functions and academic outcomes?: simple, just nourish the human spirit. In: Minnesota Symposia on Child Psychology Series, vol. 37, pp. 205–232 (2014), https://www.ncbi.nlm.nih.gov/pubmed/25360055

44. Dickinson, A.: Actions and habits: the development of behavioural autonomy. Philos. Trans. R. Soc. B Biol. Sci. **308**(1135), 67–78 (1985). https://doi.org/10.1098/rstb.1985.0010

45. Doebel, S.: Rethinking executive function and its development. Perspect. Psychol. Sci. **15**(4), 942–956 (2020). https://doi.org/10.1177/1745691620904771, https://www.ncbi.nlm.nih.gov/pubmed/32348707

46. Dolan, R.J., Dayan, P.: Goals and habits in the brain. Neuron **80**(2), 312–325 (2013). https://doi.org/10.1016/j.neuron.2013.09.007, https://www.ncbi.nlm.nih.gov/pubmed/24139036

47. Duncan, J.: The multiple-demand (md) system of the primate brain: mental programs for intelligent behaviour. Trends Cogn. Sci. **14**(4), 172–179 (2010). https://doi.org/10.1016/j.tics.2010.01.004, https://www.ncbi.nlm.nih.gov/pubmed/20171926

48. Duncan, J., Emslie, H., Williams, P., Johnson, R., Freer, C.: Intelligence and the frontal lobe: the organization of goal-directed behavior. Cogn. Psychol. **30**(3), 257–303 (1996). https://doi.org/10.1006/cogp.1996.0008, https://www.ncbi.nlm.nih.gov/pubmed/8660786

49. Eslinger, P.J., Damasio, A.R.: Severe disturbance of higher cognition after bilateral frontal lobe ablation: patient EVR. Neurology **35**(12), 1731–1741 (1985). https://doi.org/10.1212/WNL.35.12.1731, https://www.ncbi.nlm.nih.gov/pubmed/4069365

50. Fedorenko, E., Duncan, J., Kanwisher, N.: Broad domain generality in focal regions of frontal and parietal cortex. Proc. Natl. Acad. Sci. USA **110**(41), 16616–16621 (2013). https://doi.org/10.1073/pnas.1315235110, https://www.ncbi.nlm.nih.gov/pubmed/24062451

51. Fox, M.D., Snyder, A.Z., Vincent, J.L., Corbetta, M., Van Essen, D.C., Raichle, M.E.: The human brain is intrinsically organized into dynamic, anti-correlated functional networks. Proc. Natl. Acad. Sci. USA **102**(27), 9673–9678 (2005). https://doi.org/10.1073/pnas.0504136102, https://www.ncbi.nlm.nih.gov/pubmed/15976020

52. Freeman, W.: The limbic action-perception cycle controlling goal-directed animal behavior. In: Proceedings of the 2002 International Joint Conference on Neural Networks. IJCNN 2002 (Cat. No. 02CH37290), vol. 3, pp. 2249–2254. IEEE (2002)

53. Gibson, C., Folley, B.S., Park, S.: Enhanced divergent thinking and creativity in musicians: a behavioral and near-infrared spectroscopy study. Brain Cogn. **69**(1), 162–169 (2009). https://doi.org/10.1016/j.bandc.2008.07.009, https://www.ncbi.nlm.nih.gov/pubmed/18723261

54. Gilhooly, K.J., Fioratou, E., Anthony, S.H., Wynn, V.: Divergent thinking: strategies and executive involvement in generating novel uses for familiar objects. Br. J. Psychol. **98**(4), 611–25 (2007). https://doi.org/10.1348/096317907X173421

55. Godefroy, O., et al.: Dysexecutive disorders and their diagnosis: a position paper. Cortex **109**, 322–335 (2018). https://doi.org/10.1016/j.cortex.2018.09.026, https://www.ncbi.nlm.nih.gov/pubmed/30415091

56. Guilford, J.P.: A psychology with act, content, and form. J. Gen. Psychol. **90**(1), 87–100 (1974). https://doi.org/10.1080/00221309.1974.9920746

57. Guilford, J.: The structure of intellect. Psychol. Bull. **53**(4), 267–293 (1956). https://doi.org/10.1037/h0040755

58. Guilford, J.: The Nature of Human Intelligence. McGraw-Hill, New York (1967)

59. Harlow, J.M.: Recovery from the passage of an iron bar through the head. Hist. Psychiatry **4**(14), 274–281 (1993). https://doi.org/10.1177/0957154X9300401407

60. Heck, E.T., Bryer, J.B.: Superior sorting and categorizing ability in a case of bilateral frontal atrophy: an exception to the rule. J. Clin. Exp. Neuropsychol. 8(3), 313–316 (1986). https://doi.org/10.1080/01688638608401321, https://www.ncbi.nlm.nih.gov/pubmed/3722354

61. Heinonen, J., Numminen, J., Hlushchuk, Y., Antell, H., Taatila, V., Suomala, J.: Default mode and executive networks areas: association with the serial order in divergent thinking. PLoS One 11(9), e0162234 (2016). https://doi.org/10.1371/journal.pone.0162234, https://www.ncbi.nlm.nih.gov/pubmed/27627760

62. Hendricks, M., Guilford, J.P., Hoepfner, R.: Measuring creative social intelligence (report no. 42 from the psychological laboratory). Report, The University of Southern California. (1969), https://eric.ed.gov/?id=ED040476

63. Hudson, L.: Contrary Imaginations: A Psychological Study of the English Schoolboy. Schocken Books, New York (1966)

64. Jahanshahi, M.: Willed action and its impairments. Cogn. Neuropsychol. 15(6–8), 483–533 (1998). https://doi.org/10.1080/026432998381005, https://www.ncbi.nlm.nih.gov/pubmed/22448836

65. Jahanshahi, M., Saleem, T., Ho, A.K., Dirnberger, G., Fuller, R.: Random number generation as an index of controlled processing. Neuropsychology 20(4), 391–399 (2006). https://doi.org/10.1037/0894-4105.20.4.391, https://www.ncbi.nlm.nih.gov/pubmed/16846257

66. Jensen, A.: g: outmoded theory or unconquered frontier? Creative Sci. Technol. 2, 16–29 (1979)

67. Kim, J., Whyte, J., Wang, J., Rao, H., Tang, K.Z., Detre, J.A.: Continuous ASL perfusion FMRI investigation of higher cognition: quantification of tonic CBF changes during sustained attention and working memory tasks. Neuroimage 31(1), 376–385 (2006). https://doi.org/10.1016/j.neuroimage.2005.11.035, https://www.ncbi.nlm.nih.gov/pubmed/16427324

68. Kim, K.H.: Can only intelligent people be creative? a meta-analysis. J. Second. Gift. Educ. 16(2/3), 57–66 (2005). https://doi.org/10.4219/jsge-2005-473

69. Kleinkorres, R., Forthmann, B., Holling, H.: An experimental approach to investigate the involvement of cognitive load in divergent thinking. J. Intell. 9(1) (2021). https://doi.org/10.3390/jintelligence9010003, https://www.ncbi.nlm.nih.gov/pubmed/33430304

70. Koch, S., Holland, R.W., van Knippenberg, A.: Regulating cognitive control through approach-avoidance motor actions. Cognition 109(1), 133–142 (2008). https://doi.org/10.1016/j.cognition.2008.07.014, https://www.ncbi.nlm.nih.gov/pubmed/18835601

71. Kovacs, K., Conway, A.R.: Process overlap theory: a unified account of the general factor of intelligence. Psychol. Inq. 27(3), 151–177 (2016)

72. Koziol, L.F., Budding, D.E., Chidekel, D.: From movement to thought: executive function, embodied cognition, and the cerebellum. Cerebellum 11(2), 505–525 (2012). https://doi.org/10.1007/s12311-011-0321-y, https://www.ncbi.nlm.nih.gov/pubmed/22068584

73. Kurzban, R., Duckworth, A., Kable, J.W., Myers, J.: An opportunity cost model of subjective effort and task performance. Behav. Brain Sci. 36(6), 661–679 (2013). https://doi.org/10.1017/S0140525X12003196, https://www.ncbi.nlm.nih.gov/pubmed/24304775

74. LeDoux, J., Daw, N.D.: Surviving threats: neural circuit and computational implications of a new taxonomy of defensive behaviour. Nat. Rev. Neurosci. 19(5), 269–282 (2018). https://doi.org/10.1038/nrn.2018.22, https://www.ncbi.nlm.nih.gov/pubmed/29593300

75. Lee, C.S., Therriault, D.J.: The cognitive underpinnings of creative thought: a latent variable analysis exploring the roles of intelligence and working memory in three creative thinking processes. Intelligence **41**(5), 306–320 (2013). https://doi.org/10.1016/j.intell.2013.04.008

76. Leech, R., Kamourieh, S., Beckmann, C.F., Sharp, D.J.: Fractionating the default mode network: distinct contributions of the ventral and dorsal posterior cingulate cortex to cognitive control. J. Neurosci. **31**(9), 3217–3224 (2011). https://doi.org/10.1523/JNEUROSCI.5626-10.2011, https://www.ncbi.nlm.nih.gov/pubmed/21368033

77. Lehto, J.: Are executive function tests dependent on working memory capacity? Q. J. Exp. Psychol. A Hum. Exp. Psychol. **49**(1), 29–50 (1996). https://doi.org/10.1080/713755616

78. Littman, R., Takacs, A.: Do all inhibitions act alike? a study of go/no-go and stop-signal paradigms. PLoS One **12**(10), e0186774 (2017). https://doi.org/10.1371/journal.pone.0186774, https://www.ncbi.nlm.nih.gov/pubmed/29065184

79. Miller, E., Wallis, J.: Executive function and higher-order cognition: definition and neural substrates. In: Squire, L.R. (ed.) Encyclopedia of Neuroscience, vol. 4. Academic Press, Oxford (2009)

80. Miller, G.A.: The cognitive revolution: a historical perspective. Trends Cogn. Sci. **7**(3), 141–144 (2003). https://doi.org/10.1016/s1364-6613(03)00029-9, https://www.ncbi.nlm.nih.gov/pubmed/12639696

81. Miyake, A., Friedman, N.P., Emerson, M.J., Witzki, A.H., Howerter, A., Wager, T.D.: The unity and diversity of executive functions and their contributions to complex "frontal lobe" tasks: a latent variable analysis. Cogn. Psychol. **41**(1), 49–100 (2000). https://doi.org/10.1006/cogp.1999.0734, https://www.ncbi.nlm.nih.gov/pubmed/10945922

82. Moncreiff, B.: An automatic supervisor for the IBM 702. In: AIEE-IRE 1956 Joint ACM-AIEE-IRE Western Computer Conference, pp. 21–25 (1956)

83. Muraven, M., Baumeister, R.F.: Self-regulation and depletion of limited resources: does self-control resemble a muscle?. Psychol. Bull. **126**(2), 247–259 (2000). https://doi.org/10.1037/0033-2909.126.2.247, https://www.ncbi.nlm.nih.gov/pubmed/10748642

84. Ness, V., Beste, C.: The role of the striatum in goal activation of cascaded actions. Neuropsychologia **51**(13), 2562–2571 (2013). https://doi.org/10.1016/j.neuropsychologia.2013.09.032, https://www.ncbi.nlm.nih.gov/pubmed/24080261

85. Newell, A., Shaw, J.C., Simon, H.A.: The processes of creative thinking. In: Gruber, H., Terrell, G., Wertheimer, M. (eds.) Contemporary Approaches to Creative Thinking, pp. 63–109. Atherton Press, New York (1962)

86. Norman, D.A., Shallice, T.: Attention to action: willed and automatic control of behavior. Report, Human Information Processing Technical Report no. 99 (1980)

87. de Oliveira, M.O., Nitrini, R., Yassuda, M.S., Brucki, S.M.: Vocabulary is an appropriate measure of premorbid intelligence in a sample with heterogeneous educational level in brazil. Behav. Neurol. **2014**, 875960 (2014). https://doi.org/10.1155/2014/875960, https://www.ncbi.nlm.nih.gov/pubmed/24803737

88. Otto, A.R., Skatova, A., Madlon-Kay, S., Daw, N.D.: Cognitive control predicts use of model-based reinforcement learning. J. Cogn. Neurosci. **27**(2), 319–333 (2015). https://doi.org/10.1162/jocn_a_00709, https://www.ncbi.nlm.nih.gov/pubmed/25170791

89. Parkin, A.J.: The central executive does not exist. J. Int. Neuropsychol. Soc. **4**(5), 518–522 (1998). https://doi.org/10.1017/s1355617798005128, https://www.ncbi.nlm.nih.gov/pubmed/9745241

90. Pluck, G., Amraoui, D., Fornell-Villalobos, I.: Brief communication: reliability of the D-KEFS tower test in samples of children and adolescents in Ecuador. Appl. Neuropsychol. Child **10**(2), 158–164 (2021). https://doi.org/10.1080/21622965. 2019.1629922, https://www.ncbi.nlm.nih.gov/pubmed/31339376

91. Pluck, G., Bravo Mancero, P., Ortiz Encalada, P.A., Urquizo Alcivar, A.M., Maldonado Gavilanez, C.E., Chacon, P.: Differential associations of neurobehavioral traits and cognitive ability to academic achievement in higher education. Trends Neurosci. Educ. **18**, 100124 (2020). https://doi.org/10.1016/j.tine.2019.100124, https://www.ncbi.nlm.nih.gov/pubmed/32085910

92. Pluck, G., Cerone, A.: A demonstration of the positive manifold of cognitive test inter-correlations, and how it relates to general intelligence, modularity, and lexical knowledge. In: Fitch, T., Lamm, C., Leder, H., Teßmar-Raible, K. (eds.) Proceedings of the 43rd Annual Conference of the Cognitive Science Society, pp. 3082–3088 (2021)

93. Pluck, G., Crespo-Andrade, C., Parreño, P., Haro, K.I., Martínez, M.A., Pontón, S.C.: Executive functions and intelligent goal-directed behavior: a neuropsychological approach to understanding success using professional sales as a real-life measure. Psychol. Neurosci. **13**, 158–175 (2020). https://doi.org/10.1037/pne0000195

94. Pluck, G., et al.: Premorbid and current neuropsychological function in opiate abusers receiving treatment. Drug Alcohol Depend. **124**(1–2), 181–184 (2012). https://doi.org/10.1016/j.drugalcdep.2012.01.001, https://www.ncbi.nlm.nih.gov/pubmed/22284835

95. Pluck, G., Lee, K.: Negative symptoms and related disorders of diminished goal directed behavior. Minerva Psichiatr. **54**(1), 15–29 (2013), http://www.minervamedica.it/en/journals/minerva-psichiatrica/article.php?cod=R17Y2013N01A0015

96. Pluck, G., et al.: Clinical and neuropsychological aspects of non-fatal self-harm in schizophrenia. Eur. Psychiatry **28**(6), 344–348 (2013). https://doi.org/10.1016/j.eurpsy.2012.08.003, https://www.ncbi.nlm.nih.gov/pubmed/23062836

97. Pluck, G., Ruales-Chieruzzi, C.B., Paucar-Guerra, E.J., Andrade-Guimaraes, M.V., Trueba, A.F.: Separate contributions of general intelligence and right prefrontal neurocognitive functions to academic achievement at university level. Trends Neurosci. Educ. **5**(4), 178–185 (2016). https://doi.org/10.1016/j.tine.2016.07.002

98. Pluck, G., Villagomez-Pacheco, D., Karolys, M.I., Montano-Cordova, M.E., Almeida-Meza, P.: Response suppression, strategy application, and working memory in the prediction of academic performance and classroom misbehavior: a neuropsychological approach. Trends Neurosci. Educ. **17**, 100121 (2019). https://doi.org/10.1016/j.tine.2019.100121, https://www.ncbi.nlm.nih.gov/pubmed/31685128

99. Pribram, K.: The primate frontal cortex-executive of the brain. In: Pribram, K., Luria, A. (eds.) Psychophysiology of the Frontal Lobes, pp. 293–314. Academic Press, New York (1973). https://doi.org/10.1016/B978-0-12-564340-5.50019-6

100. Raichle, M.E.: The brain's default mode network. Annu. Rev. Neurosci. **38**, 433–447 (2015). https://doi.org/10.1146/annurev-neuro-071013-014030, https://www.ncbi.nlm.nih.gov/pubmed/25938726

101. Raichle, M.E., MacLeod, A.M., Snyder, A.Z., Powers, W.J., Gusnard, D.A., Shulman, G.L.: A default mode of brain function. Proc. Natl. Acad. Sci. USA **98**(2), 676–682 (2001). https://doi.org/10.1073/pnas.98.2.676, https://www.ncbi.nlm.nih.gov/pubmed/11209064

102. Ralph, M.A., Jefferies, E., Patterson, K., Rogers, T.T.: The neural and computational bases of semantic cognition. Nat. Rev. Neurosci. **18**(1), 42–55 (2017). https://doi.org/10.1038/nrn.2016.150, https://www.ncbi.nlm.nih.gov/pubmed/27881854

103. Raven, J., Raven, J., Court, J.: Raven Manual Section 4: Advanced Progressive Matrices. Oxford University Press, Oxford, UK (1998)

104. Raven, J.: Mental tests used in genetic studies: The performance of related individuals on tests mainly educative and mainly reproductive. Thesis (1936)

105. Robinson, G., Shallice, T., Bozzali, M., Cipolotti, L.: The differing roles of the frontal cortex in fluency tests. Brain **135**(7), 2202–2214 (2012). https://doi.org/10.1093/brain/aws142, https://www.ncbi.nlm.nih.gov/pubmed/22669082

106. Robson, H., Sage, K., Ralph, M.A.: Wernicke's aphasia reflects a combination of acoustic-phonological and semantic control deficits: a case-series comparison of Wernicke's aphasia, semantic dementia and semantic aphasia. Neuropsychologia **50**(2), 266–275 (2012). https://doi.org/10.1016/j.neuropsychologia.2011.11.021, https://www.ncbi.nlm.nih.gov/pubmed/22178742

107. Roca, M., et al.: Executive function and fluid intelligence after frontal lobe lesions. Brain **133**(Pt 1), 234–247 (2010). https://doi.org/10.1093/brain/awp269, https://www.ncbi.nlm.nih.gov/pubmed/19903732

108. Rolfe, D.F., Brown, G.C.: Cellular energy utilization and molecular origin of standard metabolic rate in mammals. Physiol. Rev. **77**(3), 731–758 (1997). https://doi.org/10.1152/physrev.1997.77.3.731, https://www.ncbi.nlm.nih.gov/pubmed/9234964

109. Royall, D.R., Palmer, R.F.: "Executive functions" cannot be distinguished from general intelligence: two variations on a single theme within a symphony of latent variance. Front. Behav. Neurosci. **8**, 369 (2014). https://doi.org/10.3389/fnbeh.2014.00369, https://www.ncbi.nlm.nih.gov/pubmed/25386125

110. Sacerdoti, E.: Planning in a hierarchy of abstraction spaces. Artif. Intell. **5**, 115–135 (1974). https://doi.org/10.1016/0004-3702(74)90026-5

111. Schank, R., Abelson, R.: Scripts, Plans, Goals, and Understanding: An Inquiry into Human Knowledge Structures. Erlbaum, Hillsdale, NJ (1977)

112. Schultz, W.: The primate basal ganglia and the voluntary control of behaviour. J. Conscious. Stud. **6**(8–9), 31–45 (1999)

113. Shallice, T.: Dual functions of consciousness. Psychol. Rev. **79**(5), 383–393 (1972). https://doi.org/10.1037/h0033135

114. Shallice, T.: Specific impairments of planning. Philos. Trans. R. Soc. B Biol. Sci. **298**(1089), 199–209 (1982). https://doi.org/10.1098/rstb.1982.0082, https://www.ncbi.nlm.nih.gov/pubmed/6125971

115. Shallice, T., Burgess, P.: The domain of supervisory processes and temporal organization of behaviour. Philos. Trans. R. Soc. B Biol. Sci. **351**(1346), 1405–1411 (1996). https://doi.org/10.1098/rstb.1996.0124, https://www.ncbi.nlm.nih.gov/pubmed/8941952

116. Shallice, T., Burgess, P.W.: Deficits in strategy application following frontal lobe damage in man. Brain **114**(2), 727–741 (1991). https://doi.org/10.1093/brain/114.2.727, http://www.ncbi.nlm.nih.gov/pubmed/2043945

117. Shallice, T., Cipolotti, L.: The prefrontal cortex and neurological impairments of active thought. Annu. Rev. Psychol. **69**, 157–180 (2018). https://doi.org/10.1146/annurev-psych-010416-044123, https://www.ncbi.nlm.nih.gov/pubmed/28813204

118. Snyder, H.R., Miyake, A., Hankin, B.L.: Advancing understanding of executive function impairments and psychopathology: bridging the gap between clinical and cognitive approaches. Front. Psychol. **6**, 328 (2015). https://doi.org/10.3389/fpsyg.2015.00328, https://www.ncbi.nlm.nih.gov/pubmed/25859234

119. St Clair-Thompson, H.L., Gathercole, S.E.: Executive functions and achievements in school: shifting, updating, inhibition, and working memory. Q. J. Exp. Psychol. **59**(4), 745–759 (2006). https://doi.org/10.1080/17470210500162854, http://www.ncbi.nlm.nih.gov/pubmed/16707360

120. Stuss, D.T., Alexander, M.P.: Is there a dysexecutive syndrome?. Philos. Trans. R. Soc. B Biol. Sci. **362**(1481), 901–915 (2007). https://doi.org/10.1098/rstb.2007.2096, https://www.ncbi.nlm.nih.gov/pubmed/17412679

121. Vadillo, M.A., Gold, N., Osman, M.: The bitter truth about sugar and willpower: the limited evidential value of the glucose model of ego depletion. Psychol. Sci. **27**(9), 1207–1214 (2016). https://doi.org/10.1177/0956797616654911, https://www.ncbi.nlm.nih.gov/pubmed/27485134

122. Villagómez, D., Pluck, G., Almeida, P.: Relación entre la memoria de trabajo, inhibición de respuesta, y habilidad verbal con el éxito académico y el comportamiento en adolescente. Maskana 8(Actos del Simposio Internacional de Neurociencias: Interacción Humana con la Inteligencia Artificial, la Realidad Virtual y el Medio Ambiente, 2017), pp. 87–100 (2017)

123. Vohs, K.D., et al.: A multisite preregistered paradigmatic test of the ego-depletion effect. Psychol. Sci. **32**(10), 1566–1581 (2021). https://doi.org/10.1177/0956797621989733, https://www.ncbi.nlm.nih.gov/pubmed/34520296

124. Wang, X.T.: Resource signaling via blood glucose in embodied decision making. Front Psychol 9, 1965 (2018). https://doi.org/10.3389/fpsyg.2018.01965, https://www.ncbi.nlm.nih.gov/pubmed/30374322

125. Weissman, D.H., Roberts, K.C., Visscher, K.M., Woldorff, M.G.: The neural bases of momentary lapses in attention. Nat. Neurosci. **9**(7), 971–978 (2006). https://doi.org/10.1038/nn1727, https://www.ncbi.nlm.nih.gov/pubmed/16767087

126. Wu, X., et al.: A meta-analysis of neuroimaging studies on divergent thinking using activation likelihood estimation. Hum. Brain. Mapp. **36**(7), 2703–2718 (2015). https://doi.org/10.1002/hbm.22801, https://www.ncbi.nlm.nih.gov/pubmed/25891081

127. Yeshurun, Y., Nguyen, M., Hasson, U.: The default mode network: where the idiosyncratic self meets the shared social world. Nat. Rev. Neurosci. **22**(3), 181–192 (2021). https://doi.org/10.1038/s41583-020-00420-w, https://www.ncbi.nlm.nih.gov/pubmed/33483717

128. Yin, H.H., Knowlton, B.J.: The role of the basal ganglia in habit formation. Nat. Rev. Neurosci. **7**(6), 464–476 (2006). https://doi.org/10.1038/nrn1919, https://www.ncbi.nlm.nih.gov/pubmed/16715055

129. Zelazo, P.D., Blair, C.B., Willoughby, M.T.: Executive function: implications for education. Report (2016)

130. Zou, Q., Gu, H., Wang, D.J., Gao, J.H., Yang, Y.: Quantification of load dependent brain activity in parametric n-back working memory tasks using pseudo-continuous arterial spin labeling (PCASL) perfusion imaging. J. Cogn. Sci. (Seoul) **12**(2), 127–210 (2011), https://www.ncbi.nlm.nih.gov/pubmed/24222759

A BRDL-Based Framework
for Motivators and Emotions

Antonio Cerone(⊠) (iD)

Department of Computer Science, School of Engineering and Digital Sciences,
Nazarbayev University, Astana, Kazakhstan
`antonio.cerone@nu.edu.kz`

Abstract. Motivation and emotion are essential for finalising human reasoning and behaviour toward the accomplishment of life objectives. In this paper we extend our modelling and analysis framework, based on the Behaviour and Reasoning Description Language (BRDL), to include motivation and emotion. We use labelled transition systems to model both external environment and internal human physiology. Their composition with the BRDL model of human cognition supports the description of the way motivation drives need satisfaction and generates emotional responses. When the external environment is a computer/physical system, our approach provides a realistic model of human-computer interaction.

Keywords: Behaviour and Reasoning Description Language (BRDL) · Labelled Transition Systems (LTSs) · Theory of motivation · Theory of emotion · Human-computer interaction

1 Introduction

The old view that emotions are in opposition to reasoning and prevent humans from behaving in an effective way has been recently challenged by a number of studies in psychology and neuroscience. After all, if emotions have developed throughout human evolution, they must be important and useful. And this should apply to both positive and negative emotions. In fact, emotions play two important roles: they motivate human behaviour and drive it toward directions that are beneficial to the individual as well as the human species as a whole, and they support the decision-making process by finalising human reasoning and other rational processes toward a single practical outcome.

Positive emotions, such as joy, are essential to motivate individuals to meet physiological needs. For example, our joy in eating food contributes to motivate us to regularly feed ourselves, thus guaranteeing the survival of both individuals and the human species. Fear is an essential negative emotion that allows individuals to avoid dangers, thus also contributing to survival. Positive emotions

Work partly funded by Project SEDS2020004 "Analysis of cognitive properties of interactive systems using model checking", Nazarbayev University, Kazakhstan (Award number: 240919FD3916).

related to sentimental relationships, such as joy and acceptance, make up the feeling of love, which is essential for reproduction and, hence, for the survival of the human species.

In his book "Descartes' error — Emotion, reason and the human brain" neuroscientist Antonio Damasio [12] describes the change of behaviour that occurred in one of his patients, whom he called Elliot, after a surgery for removing a brain tumor. The damage to Elliot's prefrontal cortex, expecially the right one, did not affect his reasoning ability but made him unable to feel emotion and, as a consequence, unable to make decisions.

In our previous work [6], we defined a high-level notation, the Behaviour and Reasoning Description Language (BRDL) that allows psychologists and cognitive scientists to model and analyse human tasks in terms of their required attentional, reasoning and action components. BRDL has also been implemented using the Maude rewrite language and toolset [18], thus providing a framework for the in silico simulation of human reasoning [10], some aspects of human learning [8,11] and the human behaviour in interacting with an external environment consisting of heterogenous physical components [3,5].

In this work, we incorporate motivation and emotion in our framework. In our previous work [3], we used labelled transition systems to describe human interaction with the external environment. Now we also use them to describe the interaction between human cognition and human physiology.

The rest of the paper is organised as follows. Section 2 provides the necessary psychological background on theories of motivation and emotion. Section 3 starts with an overview of BRDL and then presents our approach for using labelled transition systems to model external environment and internal human physiology and for combining them with the BRDL model in order to describe how motivation drives need satisfaction and generates emotional responses. Finally, Sect. 4 draws conclusions and discusses possible future work.

2   Motivation and Emotion

Motivation is an impulse or desire, often determined by a need, that causes human beings to act. Emotion is a psychological feeling, usually accompanied by a physiological reaction. Motivation and emotion are very closely related, which makes sometimes difficult to distinguish them. In fact, they both are perceived as feelings that drive human behaviour, they both seem to originate within us and they both involve some physiological sensations. However,

- the prompting stimulus is generally observable for emotions, but not for motivations;
- motivations (e.g., hunger) seem to be cyclical and tend to directly sustain human activities, whereas emotions (e.g. fear), tend to interfere with or change human activities;
- motivational responses are normally directed toward the external environment whereas emotional responses are normally directed toward internal physiological and cognitive activities.

The first explanation of human motivation was given by William James [13] in terms of two kinds of instincts: *physical instincts*, such as sucking and loco-motion, and *mental instincts*, such as curiosity and fearfulness. Other theories of motivation tried to look for the influence of human physiology: *homeostatic-regulation theory* [2] explains motivation as the tendency of the body to maintain a state of equilibrium (e.g., hunger is balanced by eating), *opponent-process theory* [20] links motivation to emotion by explaining the acquisition of motivation as the result of a pattern of emotional experience (e.g., the motivation to use psychoactive drugs) and *arousal theory* [1,21], according to which the activity of the central nervous system determines the appropriate level of arousal for a given task in relation to the individual's personality (e.g., in general a low level of arousal would help in a complex task to prevent anxiety, but this is not the case for anxious personalities).

In Sect. 2.1, we briefly recall two approaches that emphasise on the fact that physiological and psychological needs influence motivation. In Sect. 2.2, we introduce basic emotions and we briefly discuss their relations to motivation.

2.1 Needs and Motivation

Henry Murray [17] defined a set of 20 needs that are based in human physiology and determine the core of human personality. For example, the need for food has 'hunger' as its *motivator*. Murray believed that the environment creates forces to which humans have to respond in order to adapt. In this sense, motivation can be understood in terms of the interaction between the individual's internal need and the stimuli from the environment.

Abraham Maslow [14,15] organised needs in a hierarchy, from physiological needs at the lowest level, to safety and security needs, belongness and love needs, esteem needs, up to self-actualisation needs at the highest level. Only when we have satisfied a specific level of needs, we move to the higher level. Thus, according to Maslow, we consider our safety and security only after having satisfied our physiological needs, such as food, water, sleep. Maslow's need hierarchy is illustrated in Fig. 1.

2.2 Basic Kinds of Human Emotions

A number of basic emotions have been commonly recognised as being fundamental to all humans: joy, fear, anger, sadness and disgust. Some other emotions have been added, such as surprise, which appear fundamental across cultures. Plutchik [19] suggested that emotion can be organised in a circle, as shown in Fig. 2. Emotions that are close to each other in the circle are closely related. Relatedness between emotions decreases with the distance along the circumference. Emotion that are opposite to each other in the circle are semantically opposite and represent a pair consisting of a positive emotion and a negative emotion.

Motivation is strongly related to emotion. Positive emotions, such as joy, may occur as the result of need satisfaction. For example, we feel joy after eating

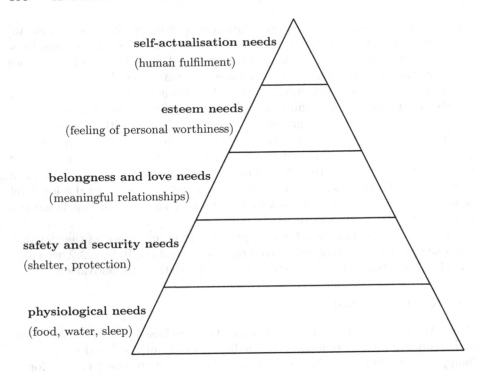

Fig. 1. Maslow's need hierarchy

food to satisfy our hunger. Furthermore the expectation of feeling joy acts as a psychological motivation in combination with physiological motivators such as hunger. Negative emotions, instead, may occur as the result of failing to satisfy our needs. For example, if we are hungry and do not have food availability, we are likely to become sad and possibly angry.

3   BRDL-Based Model

3.1   An Overview of BRDL

BRDL models the content of *long-term memory (LTM)* in terms of *cognitive rules* (also called *LTM rules*) that either drive selective attention or represent *factual knowledge* or *procedural knowledge*. In this paper we focus on the rules for attention and procedural knowledge, which determine human behaviour. Cognitive rules drive the processing of information that has been transferred to *short-term memory (STM)* and may consists of

– facts retrieved from LTM;
– perceptions from the environment;
– action to be carried out on the environment;
– goals defining the will of carrying out tasks.

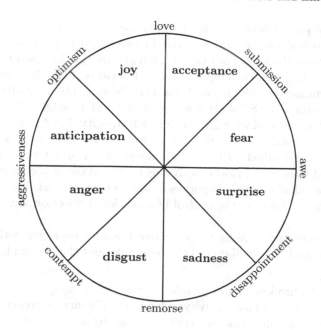

Fig. 2. Plutchik's emotion wheel

Thus STM acts as temporary store and is often called *working memory* (WM) when it is considered together with all its information processing functionalities.

Each cognitive rule has a general structure

$$g : info_1 \uparrow perc \Longrightarrow act \downarrow info_2$$

where

- g is a goal;
- $perc$ is a perception from the environment;
- act is an action performed on the environment;
- $info_1$ is the information to be removed from STM;
- $info_2$ is the information or goal to be stored in STM.

Symbol $\uparrow$ suggests removal from STM whereas symbol $\downarrow$ suggests storage in STM. We call *enabling* the part of the rule on the left of $\Longrightarrow$ and *performing* the part of the rule on the right of $\Longrightarrow$. Thus the execution of a cognitive rule is enabled by information $info_1$ from STM and/or perception $perc$ from the environment and results in the human performance of action act on the environment and/or the storage of new information $info_2$ in STM.

The information consists of a set of basic items, syntactically represented as a sequence whose elements are separated by commas (the order is irrelevant). Each basic item may be a perception, an action or a cognitive state. Depending on which components are present, a cognitive rule models distinct cognitive activities.

When the goal g is present in the rule, the control of attentional selection and behaviour is *deliberate* and is finalised to accomplish the information that is the arguments of the goal. For example goal $goal(eat)$ is finalised to the accomplishment of eating, which is represented by the eat action. The goal is achieved when its argument is accomplished, because its elements are either performed as action or stored in STM. When a goal in STM is achieved, it is removed from STM. Moreover, since STM has limited capacity, 7 ± 2 items according to Miller's experimental results [16], it needs to be freed once the goal is achieved. A memory process called *STM closure* aims at removing information that is no longer needed from STM. How exactly this is carried out is not fully understood and a number of alternative hypotheses have been proposed. When the goal g is not present in the rule, the control of attentional selection and behaviour is *automatic.*

In this paper, we consider two cognitive rules for cognitive activities under deliberate control: the deliberate behaviour rule and the the explicit attention rule.

Deliberate Behaviour rule: $g : info_1 \uparrow \implies act \downarrow info_2$

This rule models a basic activity of human deliberate behaviour, that is, the performance of an action act that is driven by a goal g stored in STM as a response to the presence of some information $info_1$ (which is not a goal) in STM and may result in further information $info_2$, which may be a goal, stored in STM. Only g and act are necessary, the other rule elements are optional.

For example, a person who wants to eat (the goal $goal(eat)$ is stored in STM) and is aware that there is *food available* (i.e., information *food available* is stored in STM) will perform action *eat*:

$$goal(eat) : \; food \; available \uparrow \implies eat \downarrow \qquad (1)$$

In rule 1, $info_1 = food \; available$ is present whereas $info_2$ is not present. If we suppose that there is only one burger available, a person who eats it also becomes aware of the fact that there is no more burger available. This can be expressed as:

$$goal(eat) : one \; burger \; available \uparrow \implies eat \; burger \downarrow no \; burger \; available$$

where both $info_1 = one \; burger \; available$ and $info_2 = no \; burger \; available$ are present.

Moreover, we may suppose that the food is in a cupboard in the kitchen and we do not know if there is food available at the moment. Then, if we want to eat, we open the cupboard and discover that there is no food available:

$$goal(eat) : \uparrow \implies open \; cupboard \downarrow no \; food \; available$$

where $info_1$ is not present whereas $info_2 = no \; food \; available$ is present.

Finally, if in the morning we open the window to allow some fresh air in the room, then neither $info_1$ nor $info_2$ is present:

$$goal(open \; window) : \uparrow \implies open \; window \downarrow$$

Explicit Attention rule: $g : info_1 \uparrow perc \Longrightarrow \downarrow info_2$

This rule models a basic activity of human explicit attention, that is, the explicit selection, driven by goal g and possibly by the presence of some information $info_1$ (which is not a goal) in STM, of focusing on a specific perception $perc$ from the environment and transfer such a perception to STM by representing it as information $info_2$. Such information may be a direct representation of the perception (e.g., $perc = info_2$) or include some form of processing. Only $perc$ and $info_2$ are necessary, whereas $info_1$ is optional.

For example, a person who wants to eat will focus on the perception of food available and will internalise such a perception as information in STM:

$$goal(eat) : \uparrow food\ available \Longrightarrow \downarrow food\ available \qquad (2)$$

In rule 2, $info_2 = food\ available$ is present whereas $info_1$ is not present. We may suppose that the person's explicit attention is triggered not only by the will of eating (expressed by $goal(eat)$) but also by the information, previously stored in STM, that the food, if available, must be on the table. This can be expressed as:

$$goal(eat) : on\ the\ table \uparrow food\ available \Longrightarrow \downarrow food\ available$$

where both $info_1 = on\ the\ table$ and $info_2 = food\ available$ are present.

Therefore, if we start from an STM containing $goal(eat)$ and an environment containing $food\ available$, only cognitive rule 2 is enabled. The execution of rule 2 results in the storage of $food\ available$ in STM. Now STM contains both $goal(eat)$ and $food\ available$, thus enabling rule 1, whose execution results in the removal of $food\ available$ from STM and in the performance of action eat. Moreover, the accomplishment of performing action eat determines the goal achievement. Thus also $goal(eat)$ is removed from STM, which is finally empty, thus completing the eating task.

BRDL is a flexible notation, which can be used at different levels, with various degree of formality. It may be used informally, at an intuitive level, to provide a conceptual model of human behaviour. For example, cognitive rules 1 and 2 provide a conceptual model of the eating human behaviour.

Formality may be added to this conceptual model by defining how information and goals are stored in and retrieved from STM, according to alternative cognitive psychology theories. For example, there are several questions on how STM closure is carried out: how much information is removed? under which circumstances? which information is removed first? Different answers to these questions lead to different hypotheses, whose implementations can provide distinct formal semantics for BRDL. Quantitative aspects may also be introduced at the semantic level, such has STM capacity as well as persistence, storage and retrieval times. These semantics variants have been used to compare alternative cognitive psychology theories [9,11].

Finally, each component of a cognitive rule may also have different levels of formality: from an informal phrase in natural language to a complex data structure. For example, the information to be retrieved from STM is described in rule 1 by phrase *food available*, whereas the goal is structured as the operator *goal* and its accomplishment action *eat* as an argument. In our previous work we used a linguistic approach to formally define such components as linguistic structures [7].

3.2   Modelling External Environment and Internal Physiology

BRDL describes human reasoning through the manipulation of information in STM and human behaviour through the generation of a sequence of performed actions. How these actions model the interaction with the environment is not described by BRDL. It requires instead another notation.

This is another aspect of BRDL flexibility. When describing human interaction with a computer system, the system component may be modelled using any formal approach. In our previous work we have used labelled transition systems [3], process algebras [4] and rewrite systems [3,5]. In this work, we consider labelled transition systems, not only to describe human interaction with a computer system (*external interaction*), but also the interaction between human cognition and human physiology (*internal interaction*).

Labelled Transition Systems (LTSS). We define an LTS by

- a set of perceptions;
- a set of invisible atomic states;
- a initial state consisting of a set of perception and a set of invisible atomic states;
- a set of transition rules having the form

   $visible_1\ [invisible_1] \xrightarrow{act} visible_2\ [invisible_2]$

   where sets of perceptions $visible_1$ and $visible_2$ and set of invisible atomic states $invisible_1$ and $invisible_2$ are represented by element separated by commas.

The system evolves starting from the initial state. Each transition rule models the transition from a source state consisting of a visible components $visible_1$ and an invisible component $invisible_1$ to a target state consisting of a visible components $visible_2$ and and invisible component $invisible_2$. The transition is triggered by action act.

External Interaction. It is the action performed by the user on the environment (interface, device, human/animal, etc.). The interaction between the human and the system is given through the synchronisation between a cognitive rule

$$g : info_1 \uparrow perc \Longrightarrow act \downarrow info_2$$

and a transition rule

$$perc, visible_1\ [invisible_1] \xrightarrow{act} visible_2\ [invisible_2]$$

which share the same action act. The transition is enabled if the current state of the LTS includes $perc, visible_1$ as a subset of its visible component and $invisible_1$ as a subset of its invisible component. The transition changes the state of the LTS by replacing $perc, visible_1$ by $visible_2$ in its visible component and $invisible_1$ by $invisible_2$ in its invisible component. Note that $visible_2$ may or may not contain $perc$.

For example, a vending machine selling both food and drink has a display showing the words $burger$ and $drinks$ and contains m burgers and n drinks. The machine action of selling a lunch consisting of one burger and one drink is formalised by transition rule

$$burgers, \; drinks \; [b(m), d(n)] \xrightarrow{buy \; lunch} burgers, \; drinks \; [b(m-1), d(n-1)]$$
$$(3)$$

where $m > 0$, $n > 0$ and the machine action of selling is actually formalised by the human action of buying ($buy \; lunch$). The application of the transition rule makes invisible atomic states $b(m)$ and $d(n)$, describing that the machine contains m burgers and n drinks respectively, change to $b(m-1)$ and $d(n-1)$, since a lunch (one burger and one drink) has been purchased.

After the user has perceived, through explicit attention, the availability of burgers and drinks and internalised this information in STM, transition rule 3 may interact with cognitive rule

$$goal(buy \; lunch) : \uparrow burgers, drinks \implies buy \; lunch \downarrow \qquad (4)$$

Note that the user only sees the writings $burgers$ and $drinks$ on the display (visible state of the vending machine), which show the availability of at least one burger and one drink, respectively, but does not know how many items are available (invisible state of the vending machine).

Finally, we point out that the environment may evolve independently of human actions. This is expressed by a transition rule of the form

$$visible_1 \; [invisible_1] \longrightarrow visible_2 \; [invisible_2]$$

which is not labelled by any actions.

Internal Interaction. It is the interaction occurring between cognition and physiology of the the same human. Such an interaction is modelled through the direct effect of a transition rule on STM or through the transition being triggered by the content of STM. There are three kinds of transition rules that directly effect STM. Given information $info$, which may include goals,

- $visible_1 \; [invisible_1] \xrightarrow{\downarrow info} visible_2 \; [invisible_2]$
  stores $info$ in STM;
- $visible_1 \; [invisible_1] \xrightarrow{info \uparrow} visible_2 \; [invisible_2]$
  removes $info$ from STM;

– $visible_1$ $[invisible_1]$ $\overset{\downarrow info \uparrow}{\longrightarrow}$ $visible_2$ $[invisible_2]$

is triggered by the presence of *info* in STM but does not change the content of STM.

The use of these transition rules is illustrate in Sects. 3.3 and 3.5.

3.3   Motivator Activation and Need Saturation

In this section we show how to model motivators and emotion at a physical level. We consider basic needs, the ones that occur at the physiological level, the lowest in Maslow's need hierarchy.

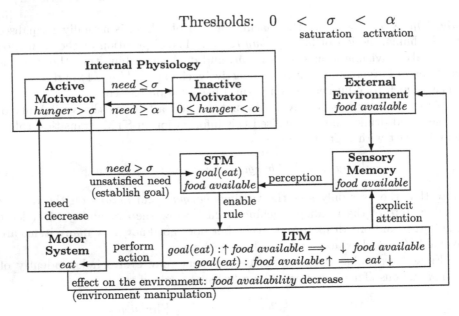

Fig. 3. Model of motivator activation and need saturation

As an example, Fig. 3 refers to the feeling of hunger, which is the motivator determined by the need of food. We can identify the need with the feeling/motivator (the need of food is identified with its motivator 'hunger') and associate a numerical value with the need. We consider two threshold for the need, an activation threshold α and a saturation threshold σ such that $0 < \sigma < \alpha$.

We can suppose that initially the value of the need, which in our example is *hunger*, is below the α threshold. In this situation the motivator is inactive. The passing of time makes the need increase as a function of the human activity. When the need reaches the α threshold, the motivator becomes active. This means that we must carry out the appropriate activity, driven by a goal, to satisfy the need and, as a result, decrease its numerical value. Therefore, an iterative activity is carried out until the need has dropped down to the saturation threshold σ. Each step of the iterative cycle is driven by the goal, which is the eat action ($goal(eat)$) in our example, and continues while the need is greater than the saturation threshold σ. Such a goal is established in STM and drives the deliberate behaviour of eating, first by directing the explicit attention toward food availability

$$goal(eat) : \uparrow food\ available \implies \ \downarrow food\ available \tag{5}$$

and then by eating the food

$$goal(eat) : \ food\ available \uparrow \implies eat \downarrow. \tag{6}$$

Once the need is as low as the saturation threshold σ, the motivator goes back to the inactive state.

LTM rules 5 and 6 model the cognitive aspects of hunger, that is our deliberate eating activity. However, there are several physiological aspects that control the feeling of hunger and motivate us to eat and to stop eating. We use LTSs to model such physiological aspects.

With reference to our example, the *physiological motivation process* can be modelled using three transition rules:

activation $[hunger > \alpha,\ inactive] \longrightarrow [active]$
This transition rule is enabled when condition $hunger > \alpha$ holds and the motivator state is *inactive*. The transition changes the state from *inactive* to *active*.

iteration $[hunger > \sigma,\ active] \xrightarrow{goal(eat)\downarrow} [active]$
While condition $hunger > \sigma$, the motivator state is *active* and there is no goal $goal(eat)$ in STM, goal $goal(eat)$ keeps being stored in STM.

saturation $[0 \leq hunger \leq \sigma,\ active] \longrightarrow [inactive]$
This transition rule is enabled when condition $0 \leq hunger \leq \sigma$ holds and the motivator state is *active*. The transition changes the state from *active* to *inactive*.

At the end of each iteration step of the physiological motivating process, the STM closure process driven by cognitive rule 6 causes the removal of the $goal(eat)$ goal from STM. In this way a physiological process modelled by an LTS and a cognitive process modelled by STM work in synergy.

The *physiological satisfaction process* is determined by the feedback of the eating activity, which decreases the feeling of hunger. By denoting such a decrease by δ, we can model the satisfaction process as follows:

$$[hunger > \sigma] \xrightarrow{eat} [hunger\ -=\ \delta] \tag{7}$$

This transition rule is enabled when condition $hunger > \sigma$ holds and the transition occurrence decreases $hunger$ by a quantity δ.

We note that physiological states, such as needs, are modelled as invisible states since they are not directly visible from outside the LTS that models them. What is visible is the resultant behaviour, for example the fact that we eat.

3.4 Environment Manipulation

In Sect. 3.3, we have used LTSs to model physiological processes. Now we use LTSs to model the environment.

The actions included in cognitive rules should be considered as directives to the motor system and synchronise with physical actions carried out by the motor system. Thus the environment manipulation should occur through the synchronisation on the action label shared by the LTS that models the motor system and the LTS that models the environment. However, since our focus is on modelling cognition and its interaction with some neurophysiological aspects, for sake of simplicity we do not model the motor system and we assume that actions established at cognitive level directly act on the environment.

In our example, we can quantify the *food available* as discrete quantity $food(q)$, with $q > 0$. We can thus also model *food unavailable* as $food(0)$. We can assume that the food is eaten as a discrete unit at a time, which corresponds to each iteration step of the feedback provided to the physiological satisfaction process described in Sect. 3.3.

Therefore, the environment manipulation in the form of eating food can be modelled by the following transition:

$$food(q) \xrightarrow{eat} food(q - 1)$$
$$\text{if } q > 0 \tag{8}$$

Differently from transition rule 3 in Sect. 3.2, in which the precise quantity of burgers and drinks available is not visible, because it is stored in the vending machine, here the human can see the actual quantity of food, for example because it is visible on a plate.

3.5 Modelling Emotions

In Sect. 3.3, we have modelled the effect of the eating activity on the feeling of hunger by transition rule 7. However, on the one hand, eating also determines a positive emotion, which can be classified as joy. On the other hand, unsatisfied hunger determines a negative emotion, which can start in terms of sadness, but may also escalate to anger. In order to capture the development of such emotions, we need to modify transition rule 7 depending on the current emotional state. If *joy* is already a current emotion, the rule is:

$$[hunger > \sigma, joy] \xrightarrow{eat} [hunger -\!\!= \delta, joy] \tag{9}$$

If *joy* is not already a current emotion and neither *sadness* nor *anger* is also a current emotion, *joy* is added to the emotions:

$$[hunger > \sigma, emotions] \xrightarrow{eat} [hunger -\!\!= \delta, emotions, joy]$$
$$\text{if } joy, sadness, anger \notin emotions \tag{10}$$

However, if either *sadness* or *anger* is a current emotion, such a negative emotion is replaced by the positive emotions:

$$[hunger > \sigma, negative] \xrightarrow{eat} [hunger -- = \delta, joy]$$

$$\text{if } negative = sadness \text{ or } negative = anger \qquad (11)$$

Note that emotions are modelled as invisible states. In fact, we do not see emotions directly, but as the interpretation of the visible behaviour they yield.

Negative emotions are caused by the failure in satisfying a need. In our example, the need of food is not satisfied when food is not available. The acquisition of awareness of food unavailability occurs at the level of explicit attention and can be modelled by the following cognitive rule:

$$goal(eat) : \uparrow food(0) \implies \downarrow food \ unavailable. \qquad (12)$$

Such awareness causes *sadness*, which is modelled by transition

$$[hunger > \sigma, emotions] \xrightarrow{\uparrow food \ unavailable \downarrow} [hunger, emotions, sadness]$$

$$\text{if } joy, sadness, anger \notin emotions \qquad (13)$$

when neither *joy* nor *sadness* nor *anger* is a current emotion, and by transition

$$[hunger > \sigma, joy] \xrightarrow{\uparrow food \ unavailable \downarrow} [hunger, sadness] \qquad (14)$$

when *joy* is a current emotion.

Finally *sadness* may escalate to *anger*

$$[hunger > \sigma, sadness] \xrightarrow{\uparrow food \ unavailable \downarrow} [hunger, anger] \qquad (15)$$

and *anger* is preserved by food unavailability

$$[hunger > \sigma, anger] \xrightarrow{\uparrow food \ unavailable \downarrow} [hunger, anger] \qquad (16)$$

In our model emotions are not quantified, they are either present or absent. Although a quantitative model could be defined, we believe it would be just arbitrary. In fact, we cannot really measure emotions but we can identify them based on observable physiological responses. For this reason we have chosen the approach to quantify physiological aspects and just consider emotions as present or absent.

4   Conclusion and Future Work

We have extended our framework for modelling and analysing human reasoning and behaviour [6] by including motivators and emotions. The extended framework is based on BRDL and LTSs, which cooperate by identifying human perceptions expressed in BRDL with the visible states of the LTS and through two kinds of syncronisation:

external syncronisation between the actions carried out by the cognitive human component (BRDL model) and the transition labels of the external system component (LTS model);

internal synchronisation between goals stored or to be stored in the STM of the cognitive human component (BRDL model) and the transition labels of the internal physiological human component (LTS model).

The mechanism for defining internal synchronisation and the distinction between visible and invisible LTS states are novel in this work.

Psychologists and cognitive scientists may use the framework for formalising theories of motivation and emotion and compare alternative theories. Computer scientists and usability analysts may use it as a general tool to explore human-computer interaction and verify physical/computer systems taking into account not only cognitive aspects but also motivational and emotional aspects of the human component.

Our extended framework is based on the same notations, BRDL and LTSs, and the same cooperation mechanisms, identification of perceptions with visible states, and synchronisation on the transition labels, as in our previous work [6]. Therefore, as part of our future work, we plan to extend the Maude-based implementation of BRDL [3,5,8–11] by modifying the rewrite rules for external interaction to distinguish between visible and invisible states and to add the new operators for defining the LTS information-based labels ($\downarrow$ *info*, *info* $\uparrow$ and $\downarrow$ *info* $\uparrow$) and new rewrite rules for internal interaction. This extended implementation will then be incorporated in our web-based tool [7].

Finally, we plan to test our extended framework and its Maude-based implementation by revisiting our previous case studies and applying it to new case studies. Our previous work analysed the possible emergence of post-completion error in the interaction with an automatic teller machine (ATM) [3,5]. However, this possibility may become reality only under certain motivational and emotional conditions. For example, if we have a specific motivation to withdraw cash, the emotional state determined by this motivation is likely to make us more vulnerable to post-condition error. Moreover, if we unexpectedly see our card returned to us before the cash is delivered, a strong motivation to withdraw cash may make us more persistent in reattempting the transaction, whereas the fear to have the card confiscated will inhibit us from trying again.

References

1. Anderson, K.L.: Arousal and the inverted-u hypothesis: a critique of neiss's "reconceptualizing arousal". Psychol. Bull. **17**, 96–100 (1990)
2. Cannon, W.B.: The wisdom of the body. Norton (1932)
3. Cerone, A.: A cognitive framework based on rewriting logic for the analysis of interactive systems. In: De Nicola, R., Kühn, E. (eds.) SEFM 2016. LNCS, vol. 9763, pp. 287–303. Springer, Cham (2016). https://doi.org/10.1007/978-3-319-41591-8_20
4. Cerone, A.: Closure and attention activation in human automatic behaviour: a framework for the formal analysis of interactive systems. In: Proceedings of the FMIS 2011 Electronic Communications of the EASST, vol. 45 (2011)

5. Cerone, A.: Towards a cognitive architecture for the formal analysis of human behaviour and learning. In: Mazzara, M., Ober, I., Salaün, G. (eds.) STAF 2018. LNCS, vol. 11176, pp. 216–232. Springer, Cham (2018). https://doi.org/10.1007/978-3-030-04771-9_17

6. Cerone, A.: Behaviour and reasoning description language (BRDL). In: Camara, J., Steffen, M. (eds.) SEFM 2019. LNCS, vol. 12226, pp. 137–153. Springer, Cham (2020). https://doi.org/10.1007/978-3-030-57506-9_11

7. Cerone, A., Mengdigali, A., Nabiyeva, N., Nurbay, T.: A web-based tool for collaborative modelling and analysis in human-computer interaction and cognitive science. In: Bowles, J., Broccia, G., Pellungrini, R. (eds.) DataMod 2021. Lecture Notes in Computer Science, vol. 13268, pp. 175–192. Springer, Cham (2022). https://doi.org/10.1007/978-3-031-16011-0_12

8. Cerone, A., Murzagaliyeva, D.: Information retrieval from semantic memory: BRDL-based knowledge representation and Maude-based computer emulation. In: Cleophas, L., Massink, M. (eds.) SEFM 2020. LNCS, vol. 12524, pp. 159–175. Springer, Cham (2021). https://doi.org/10.1007/978-3-030-67220-1_13

9. Cerone, A., Murzagaliyeva, D., Tyler, B., Pluck, G.: In silico simulations and analysis of human phonological working memory maintenance and learning mechanisms with behavior and reasoning description language (BRDL). In: SEFM 2021. Lecture Notes in Computer Science, vol. 13230, pp. 37–52. Springer, Cham (2022). https://doi.org/10.1007/978-3-031-12429-7_3

10. Cerone, A., Ölveczky, P.C.: Modelling human reasoning in practical behavioural contexts using real-time Maude. In: Sekerinski, E., et al. (eds.) FM 2019. LNCS, vol. 12232, pp. 424–442. Springer, Cham (2020). https://doi.org/10.1007/978-3-030-54994-7_32

11. Cerone, A., Pluck, G.: A formal model for emulating the generation of human knowledge in semantic memory. In: Bowles, J., Broccia, G., Nanni, M. (eds.) DataMod 2020. LNCS, vol. 12611, pp. 104–122. Springer, Cham (2021). https://doi.org/10.1007/978-3-030-70650-0_7

12. Damasio, A.: Descartes' Error–Emotion, Reason and the Human Brain. Avon Books, New York City (1994)

13. James, W.: Psychology. Holt (1890)

14. Maslow, A.H.: A theory of human motivation. Psychol. Rev. **50**, 370–396 (1943)

15. Maslow, A.H.: Motivation and Personality, 2nd edn. Harper, New York (1970)

16. Miller, G.A.: The magical number seven, plus or minus two: some limits on our capacity to process information. Psychol. Rev. **63**(2), 81–97 (1956)

17. Murray, H.A.: Exploration in Personality. Oxford University Press, Oxford (1938)

18. Ölveczky, P.C.: Designing Reliable Distributed Systems. UTCS, Springer, London (2017). https://doi.org/10.1007/978-1-4471-6687-0

19. Plutchik, R.: Emotion: A Psychoevolutionary Analysis. Harper and Row, New Yark (1980)

20. Solomon, R.L.: The opponent-process theory of motivation: the costs of pleasure and the benefits of pain. Am. Psychol. **35**, 681–712 (1980)

21. Yerkes, R.M., Dodson, J.B.: The relation of strength of stimulus to rapidity of habit formation. J. Comp. Neurol. Psychol. **18**, 459–482 (1908)

A Depth-Bounded Semantics
for Becoming Informed

Marco Larotonda[1] and Giuseppe Primiero[2(✉)]

[1] Kube Partners, Monza, Italy
marcolarotonda@kubepartners.com
[2] Logic, Uncertainty, Computation and Information Group Department
of Philosophy, University of Milan, Milan, Italy
giuseppe.primiero@unimi.it

Abstract. We present the three-valued modal logic DBBL-BI$_n$ to formally express information transmission among ordered agents bounded by limited access to repositories and where secrecy is admissible, viz. agents are not forced to transmit every data they possess to everyone else. The language, along with standard formulae for information holding at reachable states, includes formulae for agent and group information transmission, as well as assertion of trustworthy information. The description of information accessibility and transmission among agents is represented by formulae that hold in virtue of two distinct kinds of relations. We illustrate the application of the formal system with some intuitive examples.

Keywords: Logic of information · Bounded resources ·
Trustworthiness

1 Introduction

Among the debates currently open in AI research, some have a notoriously long tradition, and a variety of methodological approaches and solutions. First, resource-bounded rationality aims to account for agents who may have limited inferential abilities or informational resources, like humans in their interactions with computational agents. Second, modeling dynamic rationality considers aids to knowledge and computational processes by externally received information. Third, a large number of models for trustworthy communication is emerging, in which information may be considered reliable if consensus among a sufficiently large or relevant set of sources is reached. While logics that address these aspects individually abound in the literature, a model to formalize trustworthy communications within a resource-bounded context is yet to be offered, and would be highly desirable. A logic to model coordinated reasoning in a multi-agent systems in which agents may suffer from limited abilities but can rely on reputable

This research has been partially funded by the Project PRIN2020 BRIO (2020SSKZ7R) awarded by the Italian Ministry of University and Research (MUR).

P. Masci et al. (Eds.): SEFM 2022 Collocated Workshops, LNCS 13765, pp. 366–382, 2023.
https://doi.org/10.1007/978-3-031-26236-4_29

external source to receive information would represent a useful tool in both knowledge representation, planning and learning in complex environments. The present work aims at offering a semantics with these features.

Regarding resource-bounded rationality, Depth-Bounded Boolean Logic (DBBL) [13] is a logic for single-agent reasoning characterized by an informational semantics that allows to distinguish between actual and virtual information. The former is information actually held by the agent; when an agent limits herself to actual information, she is said to reason at 0-depth. The latter is best explained proof-theoretically as the information that an agent might assume and then discharge for the derivation of new knowledge through an application of the rule of bivalence (RB):

$$\text{Rule of Bivalence } \dfrac{[\phi]^1 \quad [\neg\phi]^1}{\psi} \, 1$$

When an agent employs k nested instances of RB, she is said to reason at depth k. At each k-depth a tractable inference relation is obtained, and the limit of this sequence is the classical entailment relation. We start from DBBL as our basis to model agents with limited inferential capabilities.

As for dynamic rationality, Multi-Agent Depth-Bounded Boolean Logic (MA-DBBL) [12] is an extension of DBBL modelling a multi-agent setting by shifting the interpretation of bound from the cognitive abilities of the agents to their ability to acquire information through the use of external resources. Under this interpretation, the depth k at which an agent is able to infer measures the number of distinct external sources that offer information necessary for the inference. Accordingly, MA-DBBL accounts for dynamic contexts where agents share information, via a modal operator of "becoming informed" inspired by [20,21], simulating the epistemic action of a private announcement. The interepretation of bound offered by MA-DBBL seems to be a good fit for complex networks of agents exchanging information when the modeler wants to keep track of the reliability of information received in terms of intermediate transmissions between source and receiver.

Finally for trustworthy communications: the notion of trust has received great attention in order to reason about the security of a system [3,22,23]. MA-DBBL contains itself a policy of trust: an additional operator for "being informed" inspired by [6,15] holds when an agent receives the same message by every other agent more informed than herself, thus expressing truthful information as content on which consensus between agents holds [26]. Hence an agent is truthfully informed only in case of trustworthy information. Such distinction seems crucial in contexts of information exchange where possible biases or disinformation campaigns are in place, also through artificial agents.

In this light, MA-DBBL seems well-placed to model systems where the above mentioned requirements are needed. But it suffers from a major limitation, since it allows no secrecy: every agent transmits every information she possesses. This might be a welcomed feature when the aim is to model communication in highly collaborative settings, but it is not realistic in many ordinary contexts. Moreover, MA-DBBL is developed only proof-theoretically. In this paper we present DBBL-BI$_n$, a variant logic equipped with a relational semantics that accounts for a multi-agent system where agents are ordered hierarchically and have access to increasingly extensive information states. In the tradition of role based access control theory [24], we intend such a hierarchy as defined among agents with shared competencies but with different degrees of access to sensitive or relevant information. Agents whose epistemic states do not allow to infer the truth value of given contents can obtain information externally and are free to share it or keep it private. Truthful and trustworthy information for an agent is characterised by content shared by all agents higher in the hierarchy. Given the condition imposed on the hierarchy, trustworthiness does not reduce to a form of democratic consensus. Indeed, when an agent evaluates whether she can trust some information, she considers only the most reputable sources, i.e. those agents that are higher than herself with respect to the aforementioned hierarchy. In this sense, it is neither unanimity (which might be considered condition too strong for trustworthiness) nor majority: it is fairly possible that an agent might trust information that is justified only by a minority of agents, but these represent reputable sources as far as the agent is concerned. Hence we believe that it is appropriate in this context to qualify this information as trustworthy.

The paper is structured as follows. In Sect. 2 we draw some comparisons with some related works, in Sect. 3 we consider some scenarios that our logic models, in Sect. 4 we introduce the syntax and in Sect. 5 the semantics. In Sect. 6 we come back to the examples to show their formalization. Finally, in Sect. 7 we suggest some possible extensions of the logic.

2   Related Works

Resource-bounded reasoning is a long-standing and crucial problem in knowledge representation and reasoning, with extensive research especially in variations of temporal logics like RBTL [4,5,8]. More specifically for our model, the kind of bound that agents may suffer can be due to cognitive or computational capabilities, like the inability of iterated applications of a specific inferential rule described above and motivating the static, single-agent setting of DBBL. Overcoming such limitation in a multi-agent, dynamic setting may be possible through dynamic setting, which is what we set to do in the present paper with DBBL-BI$_n$. Notice that this type of resolution is not a core task in RBTL and as such our work answer not just a modelling task for resource-bounded agents, but one where such agents are able to overcome their limitations through communication.

When considering aids to reasoning in the form of dynamic information modeling, Dynamic Epistemic Logic (DEL) is one of the main frameworks that deal with information update. Within DEL, standard epistemic models are updated with action models in order to represent how knowledge changes when a certain action takes place [7]. Notwithstanding the success of DEL, our choice for a different framework is motivated by three reasons.

First, DBBL-BI$_n$ interprets states differently from DEL. In the latter case, states represent possible ways the world could be according to someone's knowledge. For the former, states are distinct repositories containing pieces of information. Therefore, we are able to represent within our logic the authorizations that each agent possess for reading the content of a particular source. The representation of distinct partition of an agent's memory space is a way to embed without much technicalities a notion of secrecy, as an agent becomes able to share only parts of her memory space, while preserving other parts. This makes the relational semantics of DBBL-BI$_n$ able to account for important phenomena (e.g. in security protocols and cryptography) that so far has been modelled in terms of e.g. typed logic calculi or untyped logic programs for authentication [1], semantics for security [18] and most recently session types for information flow control type systems [14].

The second reason regards how actions are described. Even though DEL is able to account for highly complex and structured actions via appropriate action models, they lack a relevant feature that we are interested in. Indeed, an action model is underspecified with respect to the agent (or group of agents) that is responsible for the occurrence of an action. On the contrary, we include formulae which make explicit the agent involved in the information-changing action. This is particularly relevant when trust assessments enter the picture: it does make a difference whether information is sent by a trusted or an untrusted source.

The third point regards depth-boundedness. In the present work, differently from DBBL [13], virtual information is interpreted as information received by a distinct agent, and the depth of the reasoning is the distance between the receiver of a content and its original source. Therefore, depth measures how much a content has been shared among the agents. This is another parameter missing in DEL that could be important for trust assessment.

Trust is a central notion for the analysis of secure computational systems. In particular, the cognitive theory of Castelfranchi and Falcone [9], which analyses the notion of trust in terms of goals, beliefs, capabilities, and intentions, has received great attention from logicians. For example, [17] builds BDI-like [19] logical models of trust based on [9]. A distinct approach on trust is encompassed by [2, 16]. Those works are characterized by a "speaks for" modality which expresses delegation among agents. Moreover, [16] formalizes a "says" modality, and in this logic a content is trusted if it is said by an agent who is delegated via the "speaks for" modality. Finally, in [22] trust is conceived as a consistency checking function: an agent trusts an incoming message if it is consistent with her own profile; when this is not the case, two distinct policies may occur. On the one hand, if the message was issued by a less reputable agent, then that content is distrusted, i.e. rejected. On the other hand, if the message was issued by a more reputable agent, then an operation of mistrust follows, leading to accepting the message and to a contraction of the reader's initial profile. In the present work, we conceive trust as agreement between a relevant set of agents: an agent needs to check if everyone more informed than herself agrees on a content in order to trust it.

3   Examples

We start by providing an example to illustrate the type of situations which our logic aims at modelling. Anne, Bob, and Charles have distinct authorizations to access three servers: s_1, s_2, and s_3. Charles is authorized to read from all of them, Bob from all but s_3, and Anne only from s_1. This is reflected by an order $c \prec b \prec a$. Each of them is at liberty to share information with the others. In this context the transmission of information is represented by acquiring new authorizations to access more servers.

Example 1. Bob knows that $\neg(p \wedge u)$, since p and u cannot both be true at the same time but he does not know whether $\neg p$ or $\neg u$ is the case. This gap is filled by Charles, who decides to share information p and r stored on s_3 with Bob who can read these contents from its access to s_2. As no one in the hierarchy above Bob disagrees on those formulae, he decides to write them on s_2, and now Bob is in a position to determine a previously unnoticed fact, i.e. that $\neg u$ is true. Bob chooses to write p and r on different parts of s_2 based on whether he wants to share or not those contents as each partition is allowed different accessibility rights to other agents.

Example 2. Bob decides to share p with Anne who can now read this content from its access to s_1. But as long as she gets it only from Bob, she might be in doubt whether to trust it. But if Charles shares himself p from s_3 in a way that Anne can read it from s_1, then every agent above Anne will have shared p with her directly, and now she trusts p, and writes that content on s_1.

Example 3. Bob shares $\neg q$ from s_2 in a way that Anne can read it from s_1. But Anne does not trust $\neg q$, because she does not receive it by every agent more informed than herself. Finally, Charles shares also r from s_3 in a way that Bob can read it from s_2. Bob trusts r. He is therefore allowed to share r on its own, but he chooses to not transmit r to Anne, possibly because r is reserved information. Indeed, Bob gave to Anne only the authorization to access the part of s_2 containing $\neg q$, and not that with r.

Few remarks are worth making about the above scenarios. The ability to save data on separate partitions of an agent's available memory is a crucial way to model selective access granted to other agents: this is what happens for Bob in Example 1, where he wants to make p accessible to others, but r private. Another important aspects in communication between resource-bounded agents is that they might receive redundant information, and use it as a confirmation proxy: this is what happens to Anne in Example 2, who receives p from Bob and then separately from Charles, both agents who she knows have access to more information than herself, thereby getting the kind of trustworthiness she is seeking to accept p. Finally, the combination of the above characteristics makes it clear that although sometimes information *is* trustworthy (in the sense of all agents being potentially able to transmit it to others), secrecy can reduce the amount of information available to the group as a whole, as it happens to Anne in Example 3.

4 Syntax

In the present section we specify the elements of the syntax. Firstly, we declare what are the symbols employed within the language, then we explain how formulae are built from those sets of symbols.

For the language of DBBL-BI$_n$ we need the following objects: a finite set $\mathcal{A}$ of variables for agents; a finite set $\mathcal{S}^0$ of variables for atomic informational states; a symbol for a composition function $+$ which takes as arguments a pair of states, and returns as output a state which is the composition of the two. The latter is a composition function which allows us to distinguish between the separate partitions of an agent's memory to preserve separate access granted to other agents, as above in Example 2. $\mathcal{R}$ is a set of relation symbols for accessibility relations: R_i is for single agent i accessibility among states and $R_{i,j}$ for information transmission from agent i to agent j. R_G and $R_{G,j}$ are the relations for accessibility and for transmissions from group of agents $G \subseteq \mathcal{A}$. $\mathcal{P}$ is a finite set of propositional variables. Formation of complex formulae is closed under the set $\mathcal{C}$ of classical connectives, and under the set $\mathcal{K}$ of epistemic operators.

Definition 1 (Syntax of DBBL-BI$_n$). *The following sets constitutes the elements of the syntax.*

$$\mathcal{A} = \{i, j, \ldots, l\}$$
$$\mathcal{S}^0 = \{s, s', s'', \ldots, s^n\}$$
$$\mathcal{F} = \{+\}$$
$$\mathcal{R} = \{R_i, R_{i,j}, R_G, R_{G,j}\}$$
$$\mathcal{P} = \{p, q, \ldots, r\}$$
$$\mathcal{C} = \{\wedge, \vee, \rightarrow, \neg\}$$
$$\mathcal{K} = \{\lozenge, BI_i, DBI_i, I_i\}$$

Definition 2 (Language of DBBL-BI$_n$). *Formulae of the language of DBBL-BI$_n$ are inductively defined by the following grammar in BNF:*

$$s : \phi_j ::= s : p_j \mid s : (\neg\phi)_j \mid s : (\phi \wedge \phi)_j \mid s : (\phi \vee \phi)_j \mid s : (\phi \rightarrow \phi)_j \mid$$
$$s : \lozenge\phi_j \mid s : BI(\phi_i)_j \mid s : DBI(\phi_G)_j \mid s : I(\phi_i)_j$$
$$\mathfrak{r} \quad ::= R_j(s, s') \mid R_{i,j}(s, s')$$

Note that as it is standard in labelled logics [27], also relational formulae are introduced within the syntax. Labelled formulae of the form $s : \phi_j$ are read as "agent j has access to information ϕ at state s". Moreover, since labelled formulae could be indexed by groups of agents as well, $s : \phi_G$ is read as "group G distributively holds information ϕ at state s". In the following, to aid readability we rewrite respectively $s : BI(\phi_i)_j$ as $s : BI_j\phi_i$, $s : DBI(\phi_G)_j$ as $s : DBI_j\phi_G$ and $s : I(\phi_i)_j$ as $s : I_j\phi_i$.

Relational formulae express accessibility between states:

- we read $R_j(s, s')$ as "state s' is accessible from state s for agent j";
- we read $R_{i,j}(s', s)$ as "agent i gives the authorization to agent j to access state s' from state s".

Modal formulae allow to reason about processes of information access and transmission:

- we read $s : \Diamond\phi_j$ as "agent j can access from state s a state that contains information ϕ";
- we read $s : BI_j\phi_i$ as "agent j becomes informed at state s of information ϕ by agent i";
- we read $s : DBI_j\phi_G$ as "agent j becomes distributively informed at state s of information ϕ by group G";
- we read $s : I_j\phi_i$ as "agent j is informed at state s of information ϕ".

The meanings of the last three sentences have substantial differences. If $s : BI_j\phi_i$ holds, then there is a channel across which agent i makes available to agent j information ϕ. The DBI operator is analogous to the notion of distributed knowledge in standard epistemic logic: in this case a channel is established by possibly many agents in the group G for a single agent j to access information available to them. Note that in the case of DBI is the group G who possesses distributed information about ϕ. The difference between becoming informed and being informed lies in the degree of warranty that an agent has towards some information. If $s : BI_j\phi_i$ holds, then agent j has just received access to a piece of information ϕ from i at state s. If $s : I_j\phi_i$, additionally the agent possesses a sufficient amount of warranty that the information ϕ she received access to at state s is trustworthy in terms of the same information becoming accessible from all agents that stand in a certain relation with her, namely those higher in a shared hierarchy. For this reason, if agent j is informed of ϕ, then she might make that content available to other agents. This does not happen if $s : BI_j\phi_i$ but not $s : I_j\phi_i$.

5   Semantics

In the semantics the elements of the syntax are interpreted as agents, states, functions, and accessibility relations. We don't use another notation to distinguish the symbols of the syntax from their interpretation in the semantics in order to avoid unnecessary burden on the reader. The choice of model will determine which set of states are selected and accordingly which formulae are valid at those states.

Definition 3 (Model). *A model for DBBL-BI$_n$ is a tuple:*

$$\mathcal{M} = ((\mathcal{S}^0, +), \mathcal{A}, \{R_i\}_{i\in\mathcal{A}}, \{R_{i,j}\}_{\{i,j\}\subseteq\mathcal{A}}, \preceq, \mathcal{P}, v)$$

where:

- $+$ *is a commutative, associative, and idempotent dyadic function such that:*

$$\mathcal{S}^{n+1} = \mathcal{S}^n \cup \{s' + s'' \mid s', s'' \in \mathcal{S}^n\};$$

$$\mathcal{S} = \bigcup_{n \in \mathbb{N}} \mathcal{S}^n;$$

i.e. $\mathcal{S}^0$ is the set of atomic states; $\mathcal{S}^{n+1}$ is the union of $\mathcal{S}^n$ and of the set of all states composed from elements of $\mathcal{S}^n$; $\mathcal{S}$ is the union of all $\mathcal{S}^n$;
- $\mathcal{A}$ *is a finite set of agents;*
- $R_i \subseteq \mathcal{S} \times \mathcal{S}$ *is a preorder such that:*

$$\text{if } (s, s' + s'') \in R_i, \text{ then } (s' + s'', s') \in R_i \text{ and } (s' + s'', s'') \in R_i;$$
$$\text{if } (s, s') \in R_i \text{ and } (s, s'') \in R_i, \text{ then } (s, s' + s'') \in R_i;$$

i.e. if an agent is able to access a composite state $s' + s''$, then she can access also to its parts s' and s''. Moreover, if an agent is able to access to two distinct states s' and s'', then she can access also to their composition $s' + s''$.
- $R_{i,j} \subseteq \{(s', s) \mid (s', s') \in R_i, (s, s) \in R_j\}$ *such that:*

$$\text{if } (s, s) \in R_i, \text{ then } (s, s) \in R_{i,i};$$

i.e. $R_{i,j}$ satisfies a trivial condition for self-information: if an agent is authorized to access s, then she receives by herself all information stored at s.
- $\preceq \subseteq \mathcal{A} \times \mathcal{A}$ *is a preorder;*
- $\mathcal{P} = \{p, q, \ldots, r\};$
- $v : \mathcal{S} \mapsto (\mathcal{P} \rightharpoonup \{1, 0\})$ *is the valuation function (with $\rightharpoonup$ denoting a partial function) s.t. for all $s, s', s'' \in \mathcal{S}$:*
  - *if $(p, 1) \in v(s)$, then $(p, 0) \notin v(s')$;*
  - *if $(p, 0) \in v(s)$, then $(p, 1) \notin v(s')$;*
  - *if $s' + s'' = s$, then $v(s') \subseteq v(s)$ and $v(s'') \subseteq v(s)$.*

The function v associates to each state a partial valuation over $\mathcal{P}$. The valuation function satisfies three constraints. The first two impose monotonicity: if a proposition is true (resp. false) at some state, then it cannot be false (resp. true) elsewhere. Accordingly, the present work does not consider the transmission of contradictory information. The third condition is needed in order to correctly represent the fact that some states are part of other states.

Via these elements of the semantics, we are now in a position to define new objects: the hierarchy $\preceq \subseteq \mathcal{A} \times \mathcal{A}$, and the accessibility relations for groups of agents. We start with the former.

Definition 4. *Agent i is informed at least as much as agent j if and only if i has access to every state at which j has access: $i \preceq j$ iff $S_j \subseteq S_i$, where $S_i = \{s \in \mathcal{S} \mid R_i(s, s)\}$.*

Both R_i and $R_{i,j}$ could be extended for groups of agents. $(s, s') \in R_G$ means that group G is authorized to access state s' from s; $(s, s') \in R_{G,j}$ means that the group G gives the authorization to j to access the composite set s from s'. As standard, we denote with $\prec$ the non-reflexive counterpart of $\preceq$. The extension to groups of agents is obtained as follows.

Definition 5 (Accessibility relations for groups of agents).

$(s, s') \in R_G$ iff $(s, s') \in R_i$ is an element of the transitive closure of $\bigcup_{i \in G} R_i$;

$(s_1 + \cdots + s_n, s) \in R_{G,j}$ iff for every $1 \leq m \leq n$ there is $i \in G$ s.t. $(s_m, s) \in R_{i,j}$.

These definitions say that a group G can access a state if and only if at least one agent $i \in G$ can. Moreover, a group G gives the authorization to access a composite state if and only if every component of that state is made accessible to j by some agent $i \in G$. Note that when a group is formed by a single agent we treat $R_{\{i\},j}$ and $R_{i,j}$ as equivalent.

Below we use A as a meta-variable for both labelled and relational formulae.

5.1   Satisfiability Relations

In this subsection we introduce the satisfiability relations. $\mathcal{M} \Vdash^k$ A means that model $\mathcal{M}$ makes A true at depth k. Falsity is standard by negation. A model makes a labelled formula undetermined ($*$) just in case it makes it neither true nor false, i.e. $\mathcal{M} \Vdash^k_* s : \phi_i$ iff $\mathcal{M} \not\Vdash^k s : \phi_i$ and $\mathcal{M} \not\Vdash^k s : \neg\phi_i$, where $s : \phi_i$ means that i holds ϕ true at s, and $s : \neg\phi_i$ means that i holds $\neg\phi$ true at s, i.e. ϕ is false at s. When a model $\mathcal{M}$ does not satisfy at a depth k either of these two formulae, agent i lacks any information about the truth-value of ϕ at s, remaining undetermined for her.

Recall that informally the depth at which a formula is validated is a parameter that measures the distance between the agent who evaluates a formula and the original source. Hence, for example, $\mathcal{M} \Vdash^k s : \phi_i$ means that ϕ is true at state s for agent i after that formula went through at most k many informational channels. We consider this depth as a meta-information not available to the agents, but known to the modeller. Nonetheless, agents are conscious of the lowest k-bound by counting the nested operators in formulae in which their index occurs as the outermost one for a BI operator. For example, if an agent h holds at some state that $BI_h BI_j BI_l p_i$, she knows that the distance between herself and the agent who issued p, i.e. agent i, is at least 3. Satisfaction of relational formulae is not qualified by a depth, since they do not express epistemic states of the agents but properties of the model.

In the following we employ two special function symbols, $\mathcal{F}^v_\neg$ and $\mathcal{F}^v_\bullet$, with
• ranging over $\{\wedge, \vee, \rightarrow\}$. $\mathcal{F}^v_\neg$ is the deterministic function that computes the truth-value of the negation of formulae given valuation v, and $\mathcal{F}^v_\bullet$ is the non-deterministic function that computes the truth-value of formulae whose main connective is one of $\{\wedge, \vee, \rightarrow\}$ given valuation v. Those functions agree with the truth-tables of Table 1. Note that in the following clauses, s and s' ranges over the full set of states $\mathcal{S}$.

Table 1. Informational truth-tables.

$\wedge$	1	0	$*$
1	1	0	$*$
0	0	0	0
$*$	$*$	0	$*,0$

$\vee$	1	0	$*$
1	1	1	1
0	1	0	$*$
$*$	1	$*$	$*,1$

$\rightarrow$	1	0	$*$
1	1	0	$*$
0	1	1	1
$*$	1	$*$	$*,1$

$\neg$	
1	0
0	1
$*$	$*$

Definition 6 (Satisfaction of formulae).

1. $\mathcal{M} \Vdash R_i(s, s')$ iff $(s, s') \in R_i$
2. $\mathcal{M} \Vdash R_{i,j}(s, s')$ iff $(s, s') \in R_{i,j}$
3. $\mathcal{M} \Vdash^0 s : p_i$ iff $(p, 1) \in v(s)$ and $\mathcal{M} \Vdash R_i(s, s)$
4. $\mathcal{M} \Vdash^k s : \neg\phi_i$ iff $\mathcal{F}_\neg^v(s : \phi_i) = 1$
5. $\mathcal{M} \Vdash^k s : (s : \phi_i \bullet s : \psi_i)$ iff $\mathcal{F}_\bullet^v(s : \phi_i, s : \psi_i) = 1$ with $\bullet \in \{\wedge, \vee, \rightarrow\}$
6. $\mathcal{M} \Vdash^k s : \Diamond\phi_j$ iff $\mathcal{M} \Vdash^k s' : \phi_j$ for some s' s.t. $\mathcal{M} \Vdash R_j(s, s')$
7. $\mathcal{M} \Vdash^{k+1} s : BI_j\phi_i$ iff $\mathcal{M} \Vdash^k s' : \phi_i$ for some s' s.t. $\mathcal{M} \Vdash R_{i,j}(s', s)$
8. $\mathcal{M} \Vdash^{k+1} s : DBI_j\phi_G$ iff $\mathcal{M} \Vdash^k s' : \phi_G$ for some s' s.t. $\mathcal{M} \Vdash R_{G,j}(s', s)$
9. $\mathcal{M} \Vdash^{k+1} s : I_j\phi_i$ iff $\mathcal{M} \Vdash^{k'+1} s : BI_j\phi_i$ for all (at least one) $i \prec j$, and $k' \leq k$

The formula $R_i(s, s')$ is true in a model $\mathcal{M}$ if an access relation for agent i holds in $\mathcal{M}$ from state s to state s' in $\mathcal{S}$. The semantic clause for $R_{i,j}$ is similar.

The formula $s : p_i$ is true at depth 0 in $\mathcal{M}$ iff $(p, 1)$ is in the valuations at s and the agent i has access to s. The negation and other connectives are as by the Table 1.

Clause 6 is for the standard modal operator $\Diamond$. Informally, if $\Diamond\phi_i$ holds at s, then agent i has access to a state reachable from s where ϕ_i holds.

Clause 7 introduces the BI operator. Agent j becomes informed at depth $k + 1$ and at state s of ϕ from agent i iff: at the lower depth k agent i gives the authorization to j to access a state s' where ϕ_i is true. By this definition and clause 4, the interpretation of $\mathcal{M} \Vdash^{k+1} s : \neg BI_j\phi_i$ is that $\mathcal{F}_\neg^v(s : BI_j\phi_i) = 1$ and this holds iff for all s' s.t. $\mathcal{M} \Vdash R_{i,j}(s', s)$, then $\mathcal{M} \Vdash^k s' : \neg\phi_i$ holds. The same reasoning holds for the other modal operators. Note that redundant and trivial information transmissions are allowed: an agent might become informed of a formula she already holds, and since $R_i(s, s)$ implies $R_{i,i}(s, s)$ (see Definition 3), then every agent becomes informed by herself of every formula she holds. Moreover, this clause accounts also for satisfaction of formulae with nested BI operators: for example $\mathcal{M} \Vdash^{k+2} s : BI_h BI_j p_i$ is satisfied when h becomes informed at s by j that j becomes informed by i that p. As before, an analogous reasoning holds for the other modal operators.

Clause 8 introduces the DBI operator for distributed becoming informed. This operator works as a closure under connectives for BI formulae. Suppose $s : BI_h\phi_i$ and $s : BI_h\psi_j$. It seems reasonable to hold also $s : BI_h(\phi \wedge \psi)_{i,j}$. However, the semantics of BI forbids this inference, because BI represents the transmission of information as a one-to-one relation between agents: exactly one agent is the access provider and exactly one other agent is the access recipient.

On the contrary, DBI represents a many-to-one transmission of information between agents: there is exactly one agent who is the recipient of access authorization, but there are possibly many providers in $\mathcal{A}$. In other words, an agent j is distributively informed of ϕ by a group G when G is distributively informed that ϕ is true, and ϕ is sent by G to j.

Finally, clause 9 says that an agent is informed that ϕ at s and at depth $k + 1$ iff she becomes informed at s and at a maximum depth $k + 1$ that ϕ by every other agent (at least one) higher than herself in the hierarchy imposed by $\prec$. For conceptual clarity, note that we assume that each agent is aware of this hierarchy.

Definition 7 (Structural conditions).

10. $\mathcal{M} \Vdash^k s : \phi_i$ implies $\mathcal{M} \Vdash^k s + s' : \phi_i$ (Composition)
11. $\mathcal{M} \Vdash^k s : \phi_i$ implies $\mathcal{M} \Vdash^k s : \phi_{i,j}$ (Grouping)
12. $\mathcal{M} \Vdash^k s : \phi_i$ implies $\mathcal{M} \Vdash^{k+1} s : \phi_i$ (Depth-Monotonicity)
13. $\mathcal{M} \Vdash^{k+1} s : I_j\phi_i$ implies $\mathcal{M} \Vdash^{k+1} s : \phi_j$ (Trust)
14. If $\mathcal{M} \Vdash^{k+1} s : I_j\phi_i$ for all ϕ_i s.t. there is s' $\mathcal{M} \Vdash^{k'} s' : \phi_i$ with $k' \leq k$, and if $\mathcal{M} \Vdash R_{i,j}(s', s)$, and $\mathcal{M} \Vdash R_{j,h}(s, s'')$,
    then $\mathcal{M} \Vdash R_{i,h}(s', s'')$ (New Channel)

The clause of state composition says that if an arbitrary ϕ_i is true at state s, then it is also true also at $s + s'$.

The grouping clause says that if agent i holds that ϕ, then also any group $\{i, j\}$ including i distributively holds that ϕ.

It is worth highlighting the importance of depth-monotonicity: if a formula is determined after at most k steps of information transmission, it remains determined even after $k + 1$ processes. What this conditions says is that the transmission of information is conservative (no information is lost), and that it is cumulative (the indeterminacy may be eventually reduced). Moreover, it produces a desirable side-effect: it permits to manipulate formulae that hold at different depths. For example, suppose $\mathcal{M} \Vdash^0 s : p_i$ and $\mathcal{M} \Vdash^1 s : q_i$. By Depth-Monotonicity, $\mathcal{M} \Vdash^1 s : p_i$, and finally $\mathcal{M} \Vdash^1 s : (p \wedge q)_i$. Without the help of Depth-Monotonicity, this kind of inference would require a more complex reasoning.

The I operator yields a policy of trust: when an agent is informed that ϕ then she can write within her state that ϕ.

Finally, clause 14 produces a kind of restricted transitivity for $R_{i,j}$ relations. It says that when an agent j is informed at s of every formula ϕ_i satisfied at a state s'', then $R_{i,j}(s'', s)$ and $R_{j,h}(s, s')$ entail $R_{i,h}(s'', s')$. Informally, if there is a channel from agent i to j and one from j to h, and if j checked that every content from the former channel is trustworthy, then there is also an indirect channel from i to h. We give a simple example in order to make the idea clear.

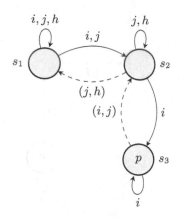

Fig. 1. Model $\mathcal{M}_1$

In model $\mathcal{M}_1$ (see Fig. 1) there are two channels represented by the following statements: $\mathcal{M}_1 \Vdash R_{i,j}(s_3, s_2)$ and $\mathcal{M}_1 \Vdash R_{j,h}(s_2, s_1)$ (these relations are represented by dashed lines in the model). Therefore, at s_2 agent j receives p from i, and at s_1 agent h receives $BI_j p_i$ from j. Hence, $\mathcal{M}_1 \Vdash^1 s_2 : BI_j p_i$ and $\mathcal{M}_1 \Vdash^2 s_1 : BI_h BI_j p_i$. Suppose that we are interested in the satisfaction of the formula $s_1 : I_h BI_j p_i$. By clause 9, $\mathcal{M}_1 \Vdash^2 s_1 : I_h BI_x p_i$ iff $\mathcal{M}_1 \Vdash^2 s_1 : BI_h BI_x p_i$ for all $x \prec h$, i.e. iff $\mathcal{M}_1 \Vdash^2 s_1 : BI_h BI_j p_i$ and $\mathcal{M}_1 \Vdash^2 s_1 : BI_h BI_i p_i$. $\mathcal{M}_1 \Vdash^2 s_1 : BI_h BI_j p_i$ holds just by clause 7. But clause 14 is needed for the satisfaction of $\mathcal{M}_1 \Vdash^2 s_1 : BI_h BI_i p_i$. Indeed, in this case h must receive $BI_i p_i$ from i, and by clause 7 this means that model $\mathcal{M}_1$ should satisfy $R_{i,h}(s_3, s_1)$. We know that agent j considers s_3 a trusted source, i.e. $\mathcal{M}_1 \Vdash^1 s_2 : I_j \phi_i$ for every ϕ_i that holds at s_3, and that s_2 is accessed by h via the authorization granted by j ($\mathcal{M}_1 \Vdash R_{j,h}(s_2, s_1)$). These conditions are sufficient to establish a new indirect informational channel from i to h through the mediation of j. Therefore, clause 14 entails $\mathcal{M}_1 \Vdash R_{i,h}(s_3, s_1)$. Now, both $\mathcal{M}_1 \Vdash^2 s_1 : BI_h BI_j p_i$ and $\mathcal{M}_1 \Vdash^2 s_1 : BI_h BI_i p_i$ hold. Then it is also the case that $\mathcal{M} \Vdash^2 s_1 : I_h BI_j p_i$, and by *Trust* (clause 13) $\mathcal{M} \Vdash^2 s_1 : BI_h p_i$. This conclusion is perfectly consistent with the semantic clause for BI, since clause 14 entails $\mathcal{M}_1 \Vdash R_{i,h}(s_3, s_1)$.

Note that when two agents are unrelated, e.g. $j \not\preceq i$ and $i \not\preceq j$ there is no propagation of trust. Indeed, according to clause 14 this may occur only when a hierarchy can be established. Consider for example the variant model $\mathcal{M}_{1b}$ (see Fig. 2). In this example i and j are unrelated by $\preceq$. It is easy to check that in this case there is no propagation of trust from i to j to h as it occurs in $\mathcal{M}_1$ because there is no trust at all between j and i. In order to trust a formula issued by i, agent j needs to be lower than i in the hierarchy imposed by $\prec$, i.e. it is required that $i \prec j$. Since they are unrelated, j is not able to trust any information coming from agent i, i.e. she is not able to infer any formula $s_2 : I_j \phi_i$, for any $\mathcal{M}_{1b} \Vdash^k s_3 : \phi_i$.

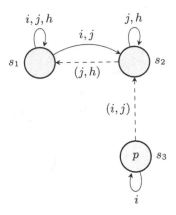

Fig. 2. Model $\mathcal{M}_{1b}$

6 Back to the Example

We now provide a detailed analysis of model $\mathcal{M}_2$ which represents the transmission of information between Anne, Bob, and Charles as for the Examples in Sect. 3, see Fig. 3. Dotted lines in the model represent state composition, e.g. $s_{2.1}$ and $s_{2.2}$ jointly compose s_2.

Consider Example 1. Bob knows that $\neg(p \wedge u)$, but he does not know whether $\neg p$ or $\neg u$ is the case (this fact is legitimate since propositional connectives have a non-deterministic semantics). Charles gives the authorization to Bob to access s_3 from his access to s_2, thus receiving both p and r. However, Bob has distinct plans for those two pieces of information: he is prepared to share p, but not r. Therefore, he decides to store incoming information on different parts of s_2. This is reflected by the satisfaction of the following relational formulae:

- $\mathcal{M}_2 \Vdash R_{c,b}(s_{3.2}, s_{2.2})$, says that information stored at $s_{3.2}$ i.e. r is made available for access at $s_{2.2}$;
- $\mathcal{M}_2 \Vdash R_{c,b}(s_{3.1}, s_{2.1})$, says that information stored at $s_{3.1}$ i.e. p is made available for access at $s_{2.1}$.

Since p is information that Charles owns on its own, then it holds at depth 0 for him, i.e. $\mathcal{M}_2 \Vdash^0 s_{3.1} : p_c$. Bob receives that formula at depth 1: $\mathcal{M}_2 \Vdash^1 s_{2.1} : BI_b p_c$. As Bob receives p from Charles, and there is no one else in the hierarchy above Bob who disagrees with p, then Bob is informed of p at depth 1: $\mathcal{M}_2 \Vdash^1 s_{2.1} : I_b p$. Now Bob satisfies the constraint to trust p, therefore he writes that content on s_2. Hence, $\mathcal{M}_2 \Vdash^1 s_{2.1} : p_b$. An analogous analysis holds with respect to r. Before receiving information from Charles, Bob knew that $\neg(p \wedge u)$ but he lacked any information about the truth-value of $\neg p$ and $\neg u$, i.e. $\mathcal{M}_2 \Vdash^0 s_2 : \neg(p \wedge u)_b$, $\mathcal{M}_2 \Vdash^0_* s_2 : \neg p_b$, and $\mathcal{M}_2 \Vdash^0_* s_2 : \neg u_b$. But having trusted p, at depth 1 Bob is able to fill these truth-value gaps concluding that $\neg u$ is the case: $\mathcal{M}_2 \Vdash^1 s_2 : \neg u_b$.

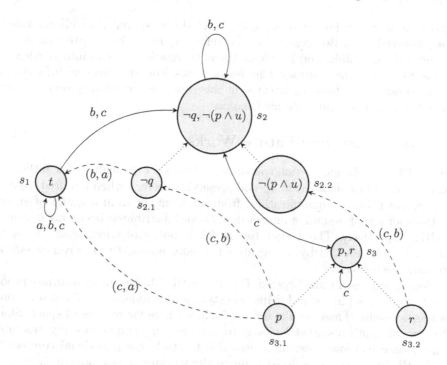

Fig. 3. Model $\mathcal{M}_2$

Consider now Example 2. After having written p on $s_{2.1}$, Bob shares that content with Anne. Therefore, $\mathcal{M}_2 \Vdash R_{b,a}(s_{2.1}, s_1)$. Since the original source of p is Charles, it means that Anne receives p after it went through 2 channels (the first is from Charles to Bob, and the second from Bob to Anne). Therefore: $\mathcal{M}_2 \Vdash^2 s_1 : BI_a p_b$. Additionally, Anne receives p at depth 1 from Charles, i.e. $\mathcal{M}_2 \Vdash R_{c,a}(s_{3.1}, s_1)$. Then, every agent above Anne has shared p with her. We can conclude that Anne is informed that p at depth 2 and that she trusts p at the same depth: i.e. $\mathcal{M}_2 \Vdash^2 s_1 : I_a p$ and $\mathcal{M}_2 \Vdash^2 s_1 : p_a$.

Example 3 is now straightforward. Anne receives $\neg q$ from Bob, but not from Charles. This is reflected in the relational formulae satisfied by the model: $\mathcal{M}_2 \Vdash R_{b,a}(s_{2.1}, s_1)$ and $\mathcal{M}_2 \nVdash R_{c,a}(s_{2.1}, s_1)$. For this reason, $\mathcal{M}_2 \nVdash^1 s_1 : BI_a p_c$, and therefore Anne is not able to trust p.

Finally, we highlight two more facts. The first is about DBI. At s_1, Anne receives $\neg q$ from Bob, and p by Charles. So, $\mathcal{M}_2 \Vdash^1 s_1 : BI_a \neg q_b$ and $\mathcal{M}_2 \Vdash^1 s_1 : BI_a p_c$. Thanks to the structural rules and by the definition of transmission by a group (Definition 5), we infer that the group formed by Bob and Charles has distributed information that $(p \wedge \neg q)$, and they transmit that information from the composite state $s_{2.1} + s_{3.1}$ to Anne, who can read that information at s_1: $\mathcal{M}_2 \Vdash R_{\{b,c\},a}(s_{2.1} + s_{3.1}, s_1)$. Hence, Anne receives distributed information at s_1 that $(p \wedge \neg q)$ by Bob and Charles: $\mathcal{M}_2 \Vdash^1 s_1 : DBI_a(p \wedge \neg q)_{b,c}$. As for the second fact, note that information might or might not be preserved at reachable states. For example, Bob can read t at s_1, but that information is not preserved when Bob reaches s_2. Therefore, s_1 might be a state that is only temporarily accessible, and Bob loses the authorization to read into s_1 when he access to s_2. On the contrary, Charles does not lose any piece of information when he reaches s_3 from s_2, because in this case the accessibility relation from these two states is symmetric for Charles.

7   Conclusions and Future Works

DBBL-BI$_n$ models information transmission by agents through access authorization to parts of available memory and preserving secrecy when required. Agents can receive private communications from an agent, or from a group of agents by the operator of becoming informed (BI), and distributed becoming informed (DBI) respectively. The I operator models a policy of trust: when the same information is received by all agents with more access, the receiver is safe in trusting the message.

Several extensions are foreseen. Firstly, DBBL-BI$_n$ has an appropriate proof-theory formulated in natural deduction style, and standard soundness and completeness results. These results are not included here for reasons of space. Since the aim of depth-bounded logics is to account for computationally tractable consequence relations, then it is desirable to study computational complexity for DBBL-BI$_n$, devising a decision procedure working in polynomial time.

Secondly, DBBL-BI$_n$ can be extended with an additional parameter expressing different degrees of inferential ability as standardly understood in DBBL [13], to complement the measure of the distance between source and receiver presented here.

Finally, we aim at enriching DBBL-BI$_n$ with a suitable way to compute trustworthiness by means of a threshold function and of degrees of beliefs as in [3,10,11,25]. Moreover, it would be desirable to model updates with contradictory information, and have a method to eliminate inconsistencies by means of operations of negative trust as in [22].

References

1. Abadi, M., Blanchet, B.: Analyzing security protocols with secrecy types and logic programs. J. ACM **52**(1), 102–146 (2005). https://doi.org/10.1145/1044731.1044735
2. Abadi, M., Burrows, M., Lampson, B., Plotkin, G.: A calculus for access control in distributed systems. ACM Trans. Program. Lang. Syst. (TOPLAS) **15**(4), 706–734 (1993)
3. Aldini, A., Tagliaferri, M.: Logics to reason formally about trust computation and manipulation. In: Saracino, A., Mori, P. (eds.) ETAA 2019. LNCS, vol. 11967, pp. 1–15. Springer, Cham (2020). https://doi.org/10.1007/978-3-030-39749-4_1
4. Alechina, N., Bulling, N., Demri, S., Logan, B.: On the complexity of resource-bounded logics. Theor. Comput. Sci. **750**, 69–100 (2018). https://doi.org/10.1016/j.tcs.2018.01.019, https://www.sciencedirect.com/science/article/pii/S0304397518300665. reachability Problems: Special Issue

5. Alechina, N., Bulling, N., Logan, B., Nguyen, H.N.: On the boundary of (un) decidability: decidable model-checking for a fragment of resource agent logic. In: Twenty-Fourth International Joint Conference on Artificial Intelligence (2015)
6. Allo, P.: The logic of 'being informed' revisited and revised. Philos. Stud. **153**(3), 417–434 (2011)
7. Baltag, A., Moss, L.S., Solecki, S.: The logic of public announcements, common knowledge, and private suspicions. In: Arló-Costa, H., Hendricks, V.F., van Benthem, J. (eds.) Readings in Formal Epistemology. SGTP, vol. 1, pp. 773–812. Springer, Cham (2016). https://doi.org/10.1007/978-3-319-20451-2_38
8. Bulling, N., Farwer, B.: Expressing properties of resource-bounded systems: the logics RTL* and RTL. In: Dix, J., Fisher, M., Novák, P. (eds.) CLIMA 2009. LNCS (LNAI), vol. 6214, pp. 22–45. Springer, Heidelberg (2010). https://doi.org/10.1007/978-3-642-16867-3_2
9. Castelfranchi, C., Falcone, R.: Trust Theory: A Socio-cognitive and Computational Model. Wiley, Hoboken (2010)
10. Ceolin, D., Primiero, G.: A granular approach to source trustworthiness for negative trust assessment. In: Meng, W., Cofta, P., Jensen, C.D., Grandison, T. (eds.) IFIPTM 2019. IAICT, vol. 563, pp. 108–121. Springer, Cham (2019). https://doi.org/10.1007/978-3-030-33716-2_9
11. Chen, T., Primiero, G., Raimondi, F., Rungta, N.: A computationally grounded, weighted doxastic logic. Stud. Logica. **104**(4), 679–703 (2015). https://doi.org/10.1007/s11225-015-9621-4
12. Cignarale, G., Primiero, G.: A multi-agent depth bounded Boolean logic. In: Cleophas, L., Massink, M. (eds.) SEFM 2020. LNCS, vol. 12524, pp. 176–191. Springer, Cham (2021). https://doi.org/10.1007/978-3-030-67220-1_14
13. D'Agostino, M.: An informational view of classical logic. Theoret. Comput. Sci. **606**, 79–97 (2015)
14. Derakhshan, F., Balzer, S., Jia, L.: Session logical relations for noninterference. In: 2021 36th Annual ACM/IEEE Symposium on Logic in Computer Science (LICS), pp. 1–14 (2021). https://doi.org/10.1109/LICS52264.2021.9470654
15. Floridi, L.: The logic of being informed. Logique Anal. **196**, 433–460 (2006)
16. Genovese, V., Rispoli, D., Gabbay, D.M., Van Der Torre, L.: Modal access control logic-axiomatization, semantics and FOL theorem proving. In: STAIRS 2010, pp. 114–126. IOS Press (2010)
17. Herzig, A., Lorini, E., Hübner, J.F., Vercouter, L.: A logic of trust and reputation. Logic J. IGPL **18**(1), 214–244 (2010)
18. Jacobs, B., Hasuo, I.: Semantics and logic for security protocols. J. Comput. Secur. **17**(6), 909–944 (2009). https://doi.org/10.3233/JCS-2009-0348
19. Meyer, J.J., Broersen, J., Herzig, A.: BDI logics. In: van Ditmarsch, H., Halpern, J., van der Hoek, W., Kooi, B., et al. (eds.) Handbook of Epistemic Logic. College Publications (2015)
20. Primiero, G.: An epistemic constructive definition of information. Logique Anal. **200**, 391–416 (2007)
21. Primiero, G.: An epistemic logic for becoming informed. Synthese **167**(2), 363–389 (2009)
22. Primiero, G.: A logic of negative trust. J. Appl. Non Class. Logics **30**(3), 193–222 (2020). https://doi.org/10.1080/11663081.2020.1789404
23. Primiero, G., Raimondi, F.: A typed natural deduction calculus to reason about secure trust. In: 2014 Twelfth Annual International Conference on Privacy, Security and Trust, pp. 379–382. IEEE (2014)

24. Sandhu, R.S., Ferraiolo, D.F., Kuhn, D.R.: The NIST model for role-based access control: towards a unified standard. In: Rebensburg, K., Youman, C.E., Atluri, V. (eds.) Fifth ACM Workshop on Role-Based Access Control, RBAC 2000, Berlin, Germany, 26–27 July 2000, pp. 47–63. ACM (2000). https://doi.org/10.1145/344287.344301

25. Termine, A., Primiero, G., D'Asaro, F.A.: Modelling accuracy and trustworthiness of explaining agents. In: Ghosh, S., Icard, T. (eds.) LORI 2021. LNCS, vol. 13039, pp. 232–245. Springer, Cham (2021). https://doi.org/10.1007/978-3-030-88708-7_19

26. Van Ditmarsch, H., van Der Hoek, W., Kooi, B.: Dynamic Epistemic Logic, vol. 337. Springer, Cham (2007)

27. Viganò, L.: Labelled Non-Classical Logics. Springer, Boston (2000)

Knowledge-of-Own-Factivity, the Definition of Surprise, and a Solution to the Surprise Examination Paradox

Alessandro Aldini[1]([✉])[ID], Samuel Allen Alexander[2][ID], and Pierluigi Graziani[1][ID]

[1] University of Urbino, Urbino, Italy
{alessandro.aldini,pierluigi.graziani}@uniurb.it
[2] The U.S. Securities and Exchange Commission, Washington, D.C., USA
samuelallenalexander@gmail.com

Abstract. Fitch's Paradox and the Paradox of the Knower both make use of the *Factivity Principle*. The latter also makes use of a second principle, namely *the Knowledge-of-Factivity Principle*. Both the principle of factivity and the knowledge thereof have been the subject of various discussions, often in conjunction with a third principle known as *Closure*. In this paper, we examine the well-known *Surprise Examination paradox* considering both the principles on which this paradox rests and some formal characterisations of the surprise notion, crucial in this paradox. Standard formalizations of the Surprise Examination paradox in modal logic do not seem, at first glance, to depend on either factivity or knowledge-of-factivity, but we will argue that both factivity and knowledge-of-factivity play a key implicit role in the paradox. Namely, they are implicitly, perhaps unintentionally, used in order to simplify the definition of surprise. We analyze modal logical formalizations of three versions of the paradox concluding that the Surprise Examination paradox is the result of two flaws: the assumption of knowledge-of-factivity, and the over-simplification of the definition of "surprise" accordingly. By fixing these two flaws, the Surprise Examination paradox vanishes.

1 Introduction

Many epistemic paradoxes are based on the *Factivity Principle*, which says that if p is knoswn, then p is true. For example, Fitch's Paradox and the Paradox of the Knower both make use of this principle. The latter also makes use of a second principle, namely: it is known that if p is known then p is true. We call this second principle *Knowledge-of-factivity*. Both the principle of factivity and the knowledge thereof have been the subject of various discussions [21], often in conjunction with a third principle known as *Closure*, i.e., if C is provable from a set of premises, and those premises are known, then C is known [15]. In this paper, we examine the well-known *Surprise Examination paradox* (see for example [6,8,10,13,16,20] for thorough surveys of the literature on this paradox). Standard formalizations of this paradox in modal logic do not seem,

P. Masci et al. (Eds.): SEFM 2022 Collocated Workshops, LNCS 13765, pp. 383–399, 2023.
https://doi.org/10.1007/978-3-031-26236-4_30

at first glance, to depend on either factivity or knowledge-of-factivity, however both principles play a key implicit role in the paradox.[1] Namely, they are implicitly, perhaps unintentionally, used in order to simplify the definition of the core notion of surprise. In standard modal logical formalizations of the paradox, students are said to be "surprised" if and only if, just prior to the occurrence of the weekly surprise exam, the students do not know that the exam will occur that day. Certainly this is a sufficient condition for the students to be surprised, but we argue it should not (at least by the students) be considered a necessary condition. We argue the students' definition of surprise should also include another disjunct: if the surprise exam occurs on day n and, just prior to its occurrence, the students know that the surprise exam will occur on day m (where $m > n$), this also should count as an instance of surprise. Such a situation is impossible assuming factivity, and thus, if we (consciously or unconsciously) assume the students know their own factivity, then the students know the additional disjunct is false; this seemingly justifies the simpler definition of surprise. We will analyze modal logical formalizations of three versions of the paradox. The first (standard) version uses the simplified definition of surprise, and a contradiction is achieved even without assuming factivity or knowledge-of-factivity. The second version uses the modified definition of surprise, and a contradiction is achieved assuming both factivity and knowledge-of-factivity. The third version uses the modified definition of surprise, and it assumes factivity, but it only assumes a weaker form of knowledge-of-factivity, namely, that on each day, the students know that they were factive on all earlier days. By constructing a model, we prove that (if the school week has at least 3 days) this third formalization does not lead to a contradiction. Thus in our opinion the Surprise Examination paradox is the result of two flaws: the assumption of knowledge-of-factivity, and the over-simplification of the definition of "surprise" accordingly. By fixing these two flaws, the Surprise Examination paradox vanishes.

The rest of the paper is organized as follows: in Sect. 2 we introduce the Surprise Examination paradox. In Sect. 3 we describe a standard modal logic formalization of the paradox in which a contradiction is achieved. In Sect. 4 we introduce a version of the paradox with surprise re-defined, in which case a contradiction is achieved as well if we assume factivity and knowledge of factivity. In Sect. 5, we discuss a new resolution to the paradox. We show that by redefining surprise as in the previous section and weakening knowledge-of-factivity (while still requiring factivity), the Surprise Examination paradox disappears. In Sect. 6, we address whether knowledge-of-factivity should be assumed. We conclude with remarks on the obtained results and possible future work.

2   Surprise Examination Paradox

The paradox discussed in this article has many names and many variants, namely the unexpected hanging, the unexpected tiger, the prediction paradox, etc., and although it has often been underestimated as a topic, many scholars have devoted

---

[1] See also [13, 21].

attention to it by exploring its possible solutions and/or criticality. So correctly Michael Scriven [19] wrote "a new and powerful paradox has come to light". The paradox was first circulated by word of mouth in the early 1940's and today *PhilPapers* has more than 1000 articles on this topic. The more common version of the surprise examination paradox goes as follows:

A teacher announces that there will be a surprise exam next week. The students reason that the exam cannot occur on Friday (the final day of the school week), because if it did, they would already know by then (by process of elimination) that it must be Friday, and thus it would not be surprising. Having ruled out Friday, Thursday is then the last day on which the exam can possibly occur. By the exact same reasoning, then, the exam cannot be on Thursday, because if it were, they would already know by then (by process of elimination) that it must be Thursday (since they have ruled out Friday already). In similar manner, the examination cannot occur on Wednesday, Tuesday, or Monday. The students conclude that the exam cannot occur at all. They are therefore quite surprised when the teacher gives them the exam anyway.

As John Earman remarked [8] there are three mutually reinforcing reasons for the longevity of the surprise exam paradox:

One is that the paradox resonates with a number of other paradoxes including the liar, sorities, Moore's paradox, the lottery paradox. Second, the surprise exam is a kind of Rorschach test for philosophy. Logicians see it is an opportunity to display their wares—including Gödel's incompleteness theorems (e.g. Ardeshir and Ramezanian 2012, Chow 1998, Fitch 1964, Halpern and Moses 1968, and Kritchman and Raz 2010). Epistemologists see it as an opportunity to explore the concepts of knowledge and justified belief (e.g. Sorensen 1982, 1984, 1988, and 2017). Still others see it as a hybrid of logical and epistemological issues (e.g. Kaplan and Montague 1960). Third, the variety of reactions to this Rorschach test is fueled by the fact that the surprise exam announcement is a misnomer: there are multiple ways of reading the announcement, and the resulting paradoxes, if any, call for resolutions that may differ from reading to reading.

In the following, we will analyze three epistemic modal logic formalizations of the paradox and consider the role that the assumptions of factivity and knowledge of factivity play in these reformulations.

3   The Surprise Examination Paradox in Modal Logic

In this paper we consider a simple propositional epistemic logic to formalize the Surprise Examination paradox, because its schematic characterization of knowledge and its logical machinery allow us to tackle clearly the issues raised by the paradox and, in particular, those related to the properties of (ideal) knowers. The paradox is set out in such a formal setting in several works, see for example

[5,11,17,18]. In particular, we introduce propositional variables $D_1, \ldots, D_n$ for the n days of the school week, each D_i being thought of as *the exam takes place on day i*. Moreover, in order to take into proper consideration the dynamic nature of the paradox, we use a notion of knowledge related explicitly to time and occurences of subsequent events.

Generalized and more expressive forms of knowledge are obtained by enriching the classical modal operator K with parameters expressing, e.g., the agent or the instant of time under consideration when evaluating knowledge of a given formula [4]. In our setting, it is particularly convenient to reason about the knowledge of students at specific days. Thus, we consider a formalization of knowledge in which the epistemic operator K is indexed. While in the tradition of epistemic logic K_i refers to what agent i knows, in this paper we let the modal operator K_i denote the knowledge of the subjects at the time of event e_i. In particular, in our setting $K_i(\phi)$ is going to be read as: "ϕ is known by the students at midnight just before day i". Such an interpretation is adopted similarly in [17,18]. Thus, for example, the formula $D_2 \rightarrow K_2(\neg D_1)$ might be read: *On midnight just before day 2, if the exam is on such a day, the students know that the exam was not on day 1.*

When dealing with agents and time it is worth setting some assumptions that justify the properties of our family of epistemic operators (we refer to [9] for an overview of the following considerations).

The propositions (and formulas) that we use to describe our problem are *stable*, so that their truth values do not change over time.

Moreover, our formal system is not explicitly multi-agent. This means that we will not model the teacher and each student as separate entities. On one hand, the truth values of the propositions D_i will express the teacher's decision. To this aim, we assume that the teacher is not a liar when announcing that there will be a (unique) surprise exam next week. On the other hand, the classroom of students is considered as the unique entity to which the knowledge operators refer. In other words, $K_i(\phi)$ expresses that the whole classroom of students know ϕ at the time of event e_i. By the way, such an assumption implies that our system is synchronous: time (and hence the passage of time) is common knowledge, i.e., all the students have somehow access to a shared clock and their knowledge is aligned.

As another assumption, the students are *perfect recall* agents. Their knowledge might grow over time to reflect that new knowledge can be acquired, while still keeping track of old knowledge. To clarify, it is reasonable to assume that the students do not forget what happened in the previous days of the week.

Based on such assumptions, we are now ready to discuss intuitively the most important properties that we consider when formalizing the Surprise Examination paradox. This is typically done by stating a list of axioms, all of which seem quite plausible based on the scenario of a teacher announcing a surprise examination.

We start with the formalization of "surprise". The fact that the exam will be a surprise will be modeled by the disjunction $\bigvee_i (D_i \wedge \neg K_i(D_i))$. Therefore, for some i the following is true: the exam occurs on day i but the students do not know (at midnight before the exam) that the exam occurs on that day. Certainly, if this is true, then we should consider the students to be surprised. For example, if $D_3 \wedge \neg K_3(D_3)$ holds, then that means the exam is on day 3, but at midnight before day 3, the students do not know the exam is on day 3.

The fact that there will be an exam can be captured by the axiom $\bigvee_i D_i$, while the fact that the exam will only fall on one unique day is captured by $\bigwedge_{i<j} \neg(D_i \wedge D_j)$. These two axioms, together, express that the teacher is not a liar.

The stability and perfect recall assumptions allow us to state two more properties concerning knowledge. On the one hand, the fact that as days go without the exam taking place the students refine their knowledge, is captured by $\bigwedge_i((\neg D_i) \rightarrow K_{i+1}(\neg D_i))$. On the other hand, the fact that the acquired knowledge is not forgotten is captured by $K_i(\phi) \rightarrow K_j(\phi)$ for $j > i$ (this is also called the *retention principle* [17,18]).

In addition to these properties, which are specific to the given problem, we will also assume a minimum set of standard properties of knowledge that will be used in the proofs, like, e.g., the fact that knowledge is closed under implication. However, we will exclude a property that has always been controversial in the history of the paradox, that is the KK principle, stating that if the students know ϕ, then they know that they know ϕ. We will show that the paradox arises even in the absence of such a general condition of positive introspection, contrary to [17,22] and other authors who argued that KK was the cause of the paradox (see also [18]).

But before introducing the formal system, let us consider the definition of surprise more closely. We argued that $\bigvee_i(D_i \wedge \neg K_i(D_i))$ seems to imply surprise. What about the converse? Are there any other ways the students could be surprised, not included in this disjunction? It seems to us that there is another way the students could be surprised. If the students know the exam will be on Friday, they will be very surprised indeed if the exam is on Thursday. Thus, a more inclusive definition for surprise would be as follows. The students are surprised if the disjunction

$$\bigvee_i (D_i \wedge \neg K_i(D_i)) \vee \bigvee_{i<j} (D_i \wedge K_i(D_j))$$

holds. But is the second disjunct above even possible? Knowledge is supposed to be factive, in other words, truthful. If the students know the exam is on Friday, then the exam cannot be on Thursday—that would violate the truthfulness of the students' knowledge. Since knowledge is factive, the two definitions of surprise are equivalent. However, there remains a much deeper question. We ourselves, as outside observers, know that knowledge is factive and therefore that the two definitions of surprise are equivalent. But do the students themselves know that? We should neither assume the students know the two definitions are equivalent, nor that they know themselves to be factive. We discuss this more in Sect. 6, but in short: the students cannot predict the teacher won't announce contradictions in future, thus *to them*, K_i should be thought of as a "provable-from-teacher" (not a "knowledge") operator. If *we* know the teacher is truthful, then *we* know that said provability is in fact knowledge (hence our choice of the letter K), but that doesn't imply the students know that.

We will show that by redefining surprise in the above way, and weakening knowledge-of-factivity (while still requiring factivity), the Surprise Examination paradox disappears.

In the next section we will specify the details of the semantics we use in this paper, but in short, we use propositional semantics, treating purely-modal formulas $K_i(\phi)$ like propositional atoms.

3.1   Formalizing the Paradox

Based on the motivations and intuitions surveyed above, we will state a theory containing formalized versions of the assumptions of the Surprise Examination paradox. But first, we will define the logic we are using.

Definition 1. *We work in the language $\mathscr{L}$ consisting of propositional atoms $D_1, D_2, \ldots$ and modal operators $K_1, K_2, \ldots$, whose syntax and semantics are as follows.*

- *Formulas of $\mathscr{L}$ are defined by induction as follows:*
  1. *Every D_i ($i = 1, 2, \ldots$) is a formula.*
  2. *For every formula ϕ and every $i = 1, 2, \ldots$, $K_i(\phi)$ is a formula.*
  3. *Whenever ϕ and ψ are formulas, so are $\neg\phi$, $\phi \wedge \psi$, $\phi \vee \psi$, and $\phi \rightarrow \psi$.*
- *By the* basic formulas *of $\mathscr{L}$ we mean formulas of the form D_i or $K_i(\phi)$.*
- *By a* model *we mean an assignment of truth-values to the basic formulas of $\mathscr{L}$.*
- *If $\mathscr{M}$ is a model and ϕ is a formula, we define the truth-value of ϕ in $\mathscr{M}$, writing $\mathscr{M} \models \phi$ if that truth-value is True or $\mathscr{M} \not\models \phi$ if that truth-value is False, as follows:*
  1. *If ϕ is a basic formula of $\mathscr{L}$ then $\mathscr{M} \models \phi$ iff $\mathscr{M}$ assigns truth value True to ϕ.*
  2. *$\mathscr{M} \models \neg\phi$ iff $\mathscr{M} \not\models \phi$.*
  3. *$\mathscr{M} \models \phi \wedge \psi$ iff $\mathscr{M} \models \phi$ and $\mathscr{M} \models \psi$.*
  4. *$\mathscr{M} \models \phi \vee \psi$ iff $\mathscr{M} \models \phi$ or $\mathscr{M} \models \psi$.*
  5. *$\mathscr{M} \models \phi \rightarrow \psi$ iff $\mathscr{M} \not\models \phi$ or $\mathscr{M} \models \psi$.*
- *A* theory *is a set of formulas.*
- *For any model $\mathscr{M}$ and theory T, $\mathscr{M} \models T$ means $\mathscr{M} \models \phi$ for all $\phi \in T$.*
- *A theory T is* consistent *if there is some model $\mathscr{M}$ such that $\mathscr{M} \models T$; otherwise T is* inconsistent.
- *For any theory T and formula ϕ, $T \models \phi$ means that for every model $\mathscr{M}$, if $\mathscr{M} \models T$ then $\mathscr{M} \models \phi$.*
- *For any theories T_1, T_2, $T_1 \models T_2$ means $T_1 \models \phi$ for all $\phi \in T_2$.*
- *A* tautology *is a formula ϕ such that $\emptyset \models \phi$.*

Thus, e.g., $K_1(D_1) \to K_1(D_1)$ is a tautology, but $K_1(D_1 \to D_1)$ is not.

Since our semantics are propositional, we have the usual completeness result for propositional logic, namely:

Lemma 1. *(Completeness) For any theory T and any formula ϕ, $T \models \phi$ if and only if there exist finitely many $\phi_1, \dots, \phi_n \in T$ such that $\phi_1 \to \cdots \to \phi_n \to \phi$ is a tautology.*

We also make use of shorthands such as $\bigwedge_{i=1}^{n} D_i$ for $D_1 \wedge \cdots \wedge D_n$, $\bigvee_{i=1}^{n} \phi_i$ for $\phi_1 \vee \cdots \vee \phi_n$, and so on. These are not new symbols in $\mathscr{L}$, they are simply meta-symbols. In every case, it will be clear what the actual $\mathscr{L}$-formulas denoted by them are.

The following theory is intended to capture the standard assumptions in the Surprise Examination paradox (for a week with n school-days).

Definition 2. *For each $n \geq 1$, let T_n be the theory consisting of:*

- (A_1^n) $\bigvee_{i=1}^{n} D_i$.
- (A_2^n) $\bigwedge_{1 \leq i < j \leq n} \neg(D_i \wedge D_j)$.
- (A_3^n) $\bigvee_{i=1}^{n}(D_i \wedge \neg K_i(D_i))$.
- (A_4^n) $\bigwedge_{i=1}^{n-1}((\neg D_i) \to K_{i+1}(\neg D_i))$.
- (A_5^n) $K_i(\phi)$ *for all $1 \leq i \leq n$ and tautologies ϕ.*
- (A_6^n) $K_i(\phi \to \psi) \to K_i(\phi) \to K_i(\psi)$ *for all $1 \leq i \leq n$ and all ϕ, ψ.*
- (A_7^n) $K_i(\phi) \to K_j(\phi)$ *for all $1 \leq i < j \leq n$.*
- (A_∞^n) $K_i(\phi)$ *for all $1 \leq i \leq n$ and all ϕ such that $T_n \models \phi$.*

As previously stated informally, A_1^n and A_2^n express the truthfulness of the announcement made by the teacher, A_3^n formalizes the idea of surprise, A_4^n and A_7^n express properties of knowledge that hold by virtue of the stability and perfect recall assumptions. Moreover, we have three more axioms expressing standard properties of knowledge: A_5^n formalizes the necessitation principle (all tautologies are known), A_6^n states that knowledge is closed under logical consequence, and A_∞^n is the classical closure axiom expressing that what can be derived is also known [7,15]. In the following, after a preliminary Lemma, we prove the contradiction underlying the paradox.

Lemma 2. *(Closure Lemma) Let $n \geq 1$, $1 \leq i \leq n$. Suppose T is any $\mathscr{L}$-theory such that:*

- *T includes A_5^n and A_6^n.*
- *T includes $K_i(\phi)$ whenever T includes ϕ.*

Then:

(1) For any ϕ, if $T \models \phi$, then $T \models K_i(\phi)$.
(2) For any $\phi_1, \dots, \phi_\ell$ and ϕ, if $\phi_1 \to \cdots \to \phi_\ell \to \phi$ is a tautology, and if $T_n \models \phi_j$ for all $1 \leq j \leq \ell$, then $T_n \models K_i(\phi)$.

Proof.(1) Assume $T \models \phi$. Then there are finitely many $\phi_1, \ldots, \phi_\ell \in T$ such that $\phi_1 \to \cdots \to \phi_\ell \to \phi$ is a tautology. By A_5^n,

$$T \models K_i(\phi_1 \to \cdots \to \phi_\ell \to \phi).$$

By repeated application of A_6^n,

$$T \models K_i(\phi_1) \to \cdots \to K_i(\phi_\ell) \to K_i(\phi).$$

By assumption, since T contains $\phi_1, \ldots, \phi_\ell$, T contains $K_i(\phi_1), \ldots, K_i(\phi_\ell)$. Thus $T \models K_i(\phi)$.

(2) Since $T_n \models \phi_j$ for all $1 \leq j \leq \ell$, by (1) we see $T_n \models K_i(\phi_j)$ for all $1 \leq j \leq \ell$. The rest of the proof is similar to the proof of (1). $\qquad \square$

Theorem 1. *(The Surprise Examination paradox) For any $n \geq 1$, T_n is inconsistent.*

Proof. By induction on n. The base case $n = 1$ is trivial because $A_1^1 \equiv D_1$, thus A_∞^1 includes $K_1(D_1)$, and $A_3^1 \equiv D_1 \to \neg K_1(D_1)$.

Assume $n > 1$.

Preliminary claim: $T_n \models \neg D_n$. To see this, we reason within T_n as follows:

- Assume D_n.
- From A_2^n it follows that $(\neg D_1) \wedge \cdots \wedge (\neg D_{n-1})$.
- From A_4^n it follows that $K_2(\neg D_1) \wedge \cdots \wedge K_n(\neg D_{n-1})$.
- From A_7^n it follows that $K_n(\neg D_1) \wedge \cdots \wedge K_n(\neg D_{n-1})$.
- By A_5^n, $K_n((\bigvee_{i=1}^n D_i)) \to \neg D_1 \to \cdots \to \neg D_{n-1} \to D_n)$.
- By repeated usages of A_6^n, it follows from the previous bullet that $K_n(\bigvee_{i=1}^n D_i) \to K_n(\neg D_1) \to \cdots \to K_n(\neg D_{n-1}) \to K_n(D_n)$.
- By A_∞^n and A_1^n, it follows that $K_n(\bigvee_{i=1}^n D_i)$.
- From the previous four bullets it follows that $K_n(D_n)$.
- By A_3^n, $\bigvee_{i=1}^n (D_i \wedge \neg K_i(D_i))$.
- Since $(\neg D_1) \wedge \cdots \wedge (\neg D_{n-1})$, the previous bullet implies $\neg K_n(D_n)$.
- Contradiction. Discharge assumption and conclude $\neg D_n$.

This proves the preliminary claim.

To finish the proof, it will suffice to show $T_n \models T_{n-1}$, since T_{n-1} is inconsistent by induction. For this, it suffices to prove that whenever $T_{n-1} \models \phi$, then $T_n \models \phi$. We prove this by induction on the number of applications of A_∞^{n-1} needed to prove $T_{n-1} \models \phi$.

Case A_1^{n-1}: ϕ is $\bigvee_{i=1}^{n-1} D_i$. Then $T_n \models \phi$ by A_1^n plus the preliminary claim.

Case A_2^{n-1}: ϕ is $\bigwedge_{1 \leq i < j \leq n-1} \neg(D_i \wedge D_j)$. Then $T_n \models \phi$ by A_2^n.

Case A_3^{n-1}: ϕ is $\bigvee_{i=1}^{n-1}(D_i \wedge \neg K_i(D_i))$. By A_3^n, $T_n \models \bigvee_{i=1}^n (D_i \wedge \neg K_i(D_i))$. By the preliminary claim, $T_n \models \neg D_n$. It follows that $T_n \models \phi$.

Case A_4^{n-1}: ϕ is $\bigwedge_{i=1}^{n-2}(\neg D_i) \to K_{i+1}(\neg D_i)$. Then $T_n \models \phi$ by A_4^n.

Cases A_5^{n-1}, A_6^{n-1}, A_7^{n-1}: similar to the previous cases, the results follow by A_5^n, A_6^n, and A_7^n, respectively.

Case A_∞^{n-1}: ϕ is $K_i(\psi)$ for some $1 \leq i \leq n-1$ and some ψ such that $T_{n-1} \models \psi$. Since $T_{n-1} \models \psi$, there are $\psi_1, \ldots, \psi_\ell \in T_{n-1}$ such that $\psi_1 \to \cdots \to \psi_\ell \to \psi$ is a tautology and such that for all $1 \leq j \leq \ell$, $T_{n-1} \models \psi_j$ can be proven using fewer applications of A_∞^{n-1} than are needed to prove $T_{n-1} \models \phi$. Thus by induction, $T_n \models \psi_j$ for each $1 \leq j \leq \ell$. By Lemma 2 (part 2), $T_n \models K_i(\psi)$. □

4   Redefining the Surprise Axiom

As suggested in Sect. 2, we now consider a variant of our formal system in which the axiom modeling surprise is re-defined by adding a disjunct. The following definition states such a variant.

Definition 3. *For each $n \geq 1$, by U_n we mean the theory consisting of the following axioms:*

- A_1^n, A_2^n, A_4^n, A_5^n, A_6^n, A_7^n.
- $(A_3^{n\prime})$ $\bigvee_{i=1}^n (D_i \wedge \neg K_i(D_i)) \vee \bigvee_{1 \leq i < j \leq n}(D_i \wedge K_i(D_j))$.
- (A_T^n) $K_i(\phi) \to \phi$ for all $1 \leq i \leq n$ and all ϕ.
- $(A_\infty^{n\prime})$ $K_i(\phi)$ for all $1 \leq i \leq n$ and all ϕ such that $U_n \models \phi$.

Note that A_3^n is replaced by the more inclusive property we discussed above, called $A_3^{n\prime}$. As we mentioned, such an extension is actually equivalent to the original axiom if we assume truthfulness of knowledge and knowledge of such a factivity principle. Hence, under this hypothesis, the paradox is not actually solved. To state this result formally, the system we consider combines the new version of surprise $A_3^{n\prime}$, the factivity axiom (see A_T^n, which states the truthfulness of knowledge), and, by virtue of $A_\infty^{n\prime}$, also the knowledge of such a factivity.

Theorem 2. *(A modified Surprise Examination paradox) For any $n \geq 1$, U_n is inconsistent.*

Proof. Since Theorem 1 says T_n is inconsistent, it will suffice to show $U_n \models T_n$. For this, it suffices to prove that whenever $T_n \models \phi$, then $U_n \models \phi$. We prove this by induction on the number of applications of T_∞^n needed to prove $T_n \models \phi$.

Trivial case: ϕ is an instance of A_1^n, A_2^n, A_4^n, A_5^n, A_6^n, or A_7^n. Then $U_n \models \phi$ since U_n includes these axioms too.

Case A_3^n: ϕ is $\bigvee_{i=1}^n (D_i \wedge \neg K_i(D_i))$. By $A_3^{n\prime}$, $U_n \models \bigvee_{i=1}^n(D_i \wedge \neg K_i(D_i)) \vee \bigvee_{1 \leq i < j \leq n}(D_i \wedge K_i(D_j))$. To show $U_n \models \phi$, it suffices to show that for all $1 \leq i < j \leq n$, $U_n \models \neg(D_i \wedge K_i(D_j))$. Fix $1 \leq i < j \leq n$. We reason within U_n as follows:

- Assume $D_i \wedge K_i(D_j)$.
- By A_2^n, it follows that $\neg D_j$.
- By A_T^n, $K_i(D_j) \to D_j$.
- Contradiction. Discharge assumption and conclude $\neg(D_i \wedge K_i(D_j))$.

Case A_∞^n: ϕ is $K_i(\psi)$ for some $1 \leq i \leq n$ and some ψ such that $T_n \models \psi$. Since $T_n \models \psi$, there are $\psi_1, \ldots, \psi_\ell \in T_n$ such that $\psi_1 \to \cdots \to \psi_\ell \to \psi$ is a tautology and such that for all $1 \leq j \leq \ell$, $T_n \models \psi_j$ can be proved using fewer applications of A_∞^n than are needed to prove $T_n \models \phi$. By induction, $U_n \models K_i(\psi_j)$ for all $1 \leq j \leq \ell$. By Lemma 2 (part 2), $U_n \models K_i(\psi)$. □

5   A Resolution to the Paradox

Apparently, extending the notion of surprise alone does not bring benefits. This is true if a general notion of knowledge of factivity is assumed. For instance, in the system of the previous section we can derive forms like, e.g., $K_1(K_2(\phi) \to \phi)$. Generally speaking, at any time the factivity of any knowledge – past, present, or future – is known. However, we argue that if we limit the knowledge of factivity, then we obtain a system in which the paradox disappears.

Formally, in order to limit the knowledge of factivity, we restrict axiom A_T^n by assuming that only the factivity of the knowledge of past events is known, thus obtaining a new axiom $A_T^{n\prime}$.

Definition 4. *For each $n \geq 1$, by $(V_n)_0$ we mean the theory containing the following axioms:*

- *A_1^n, A_2^n, $A_3^{n\prime}$, A_4^n, A_5^n, A_6^n, A_7^n.*
- *$(A_T^{n\prime})$ $K_j(K_i(\phi) \to \phi)$ for all $1 \leq i < j \leq n$ and all ϕ.*
- *$(A_\infty^n{}'')$ $K_i(\phi)$ for all $1 \leq i \leq n$ and all ϕ such that $(V_n)_0 \models \phi$.*

For each $1 \leq i \leq n$, by $(V_n)_0^i$ we mean the theory containing the following axioms:

- *$(V_n)_0$.*
- *$(A_{T,i}^n)$ $K_j(\phi) \to \phi$ for all $1 \leq j < i$ and all ϕ.*
- *$(A_{i,\infty}^n)$ $K_j(\phi)$ for any $1 \leq j \leq i$ and all ϕ such that $(V_n)_0^j \models \phi$.*

For each n, by V_n we mean the theory containing:

- *$(V_n)_0^1$, ..., $(V_n)_0^n$.*
- *(A_T^n) $K_i(\phi) \to \phi$ for all $1 \leq i \leq n$ and all ϕ.*

The inductive definition of the theory V_n preserves the condition stating that $K_j(K_i(\phi) \to \phi)$ holds for all $j > i$, i.e., simply put, the students become aware tomorrow of the factivity of what they know today. Such an inductive definition will allow us to prove by induction that V_n is consistent (if $n > 2$), thus making the paradox disappear. We will show V_n is consistent by constructing a model, i.e., an assignment of truth values to the basic formulas of $\mathscr{L}$ (see Definition 1), and showing that that model satisfies V_n.

Lemma 3. *For any n, for any $1 \leq i < j \leq n$, $(V_n)_0^i \subseteq (V_n)_0^j$.*

Proof. By inspection.   □

Theorem 3. *For every $n > 2$, V_n is consistent.*

Proof. The intuitive idea is that we will construct a model in which on each day, the students' knowledge consists of the bare minimum required to satisfy V_n, namely, exactly those facts which V_n requires them to know on that day, and nothing else. We will then verify that the resulting model satisfies all the required axioms, and this will be mostly straightforward, with the exception of $A_3^{n\prime}$, for which we will have to construct another model (see below).

Since $n > 2$, we may fix some $1 \leq m < n - 1$. For each $1 \leq i \leq n$, let W_i be the theory containing the following axioms:

- $(V_n)_0^i$.
- $\bigwedge_{1 \leq j < i, j \neq m} \neg D_j$.

By Lemma 3 it follows that whenever $1 \leq i < j \leq n$, $W_j \models W_i$.
   We define a model $\mathcal{M}$ as follows:

- $\mathcal{M} \models D_m$.
- For all $i \neq m$, $\mathcal{M} \not\models D_i$.
- For all $1 \leq i \leq n$, for all ϕ, $\mathcal{M} \models K_i(\phi)$ iff $W_i \models \phi$.

To show V_n is consistent, it suffices to show that $\mathcal{M} \models V_n$.
   Claim 1: For each $1 \leq p \leq n$, $\mathcal{M} \models W_p$. We prove this by induction on p.
We will show $\mathcal{M} \models \phi$ for all $\phi \in W_p$. Fix any such ϕ.
   Case A_1^n: ϕ is $\bigvee_{i=1}^n D_i$. Then clearly $\mathcal{M} \models \phi$.
   Case A_2^n: ϕ is $\bigwedge_{1 \leq i < j \leq n} \neg(D_i \wedge D_j)$. Then clearly $\mathcal{M} \models \phi$.
   Case $A_3^{n'}$: ϕ is $\bigvee_{i=1}^n (D_i \wedge \neg K_i(D_i)) \vee \bigvee_{1 \leq i < j \leq n}(D_i \wedge K_i(D_j))$. To show
$\mathcal{M} \models \phi$, it suffices to show $\mathcal{M}$ satisfies any one of the disjuncts. We will
show $\mathcal{M} \models D_m \wedge \neg K_m(D_m)$. By construction $\mathcal{M} \models D_m$. It remains to show
$\mathcal{M} \models \neg K_m(D_m)$. In other words, we must show $W_m \not\models D_m$. We will construct
a model $\mathcal{N}$ such that $\mathcal{N} \models W_m$ and $\mathcal{N} \not\models D_m$.
   The intuitive idea is that in $\mathcal{N}$, the exam will occur on day $n-1$, the students
will initially (before day m) know the bare minimum that W_m requires them to
know, but, starting on day m, the students' knowledge will become inconsistent:
from that day on, they will know everything (including incorrectly knowing that
the exam will occur on day m). The fact that the students are not factive in $\mathcal{N}$
(on days $\geq m$) is not problematic: the purpose of $\mathcal{N}$ is not to, itself, directly
satisfy V_n (which requires factivity), but only to show that $W_m \not\models D_m$.
   Let $\mathcal{N}$ be the model defined by:

- $\mathcal{N} \models D_{n-1}$.
- For all $i \neq n - 1$, $\mathcal{N} \not\models D_i$.
- For all $1 \leq j < m$ and all ϕ, $\mathcal{N} \models K_j(\phi)$ iff $W_j \models \phi$.
- For all $m \leq j \leq n$ and all ϕ, $\mathcal{N} \models K_j(\phi)$.

Since $m < n - 1$, $\mathcal{N} \not\models D_m$. We claim $\mathcal{N} \models W_m$. We will prove more, for the
sake of a stronger induction hypothesis: we will prove by induction on q that
$\mathcal{N} \models W_q$ for all $q \leq m$. Let $\psi \in W_q$.
   Subcase $A_1^n(W_q)$: ψ is $\bigvee_{i=1}^n D_i$. Then clearly $\mathcal{N} \models \psi$.
   Subcase $A_2^n(W_q)$: ψ is $\bigwedge_{1 \leq i < j \leq n} \neg(D_i \wedge D_j)$. Then clearly $\mathcal{N} \models \psi$.
   Subcase $A_3^{n'}(W_q)$: ψ is $\bigvee_{i=1}^n (D_i \wedge \neg K_i(D_i)) \vee \bigvee_{1 \leq i < j \leq n}(D_i \wedge K_i(D_j))$. To show
$\mathcal{N} \models \psi$, it suffices to show $\mathcal{N}$ satisfies any one of the disjuncts. We will show
$\mathcal{N} \models D_{n-1} \wedge K_{n-1}(D_n)$. By construction $\mathcal{N} \models D_{n-1}$. And $\mathcal{N} \models K_{n-1}(D_n)$
because $m \leq n - 1 \leq n$ (so K_{n-1} is defined in the 4th bullet of the definition of
$\mathcal{N}$).
   Subcase $A_4^n(W_q)$: ψ is $\bigwedge_{i=1}^{n-1}((\neg D_i) \rightarrow K_{i+1}(\neg D_i))$. Fix any $1 \leq i \leq n - 1$, we will show $\mathcal{N} \models (\neg D_i) \rightarrow K_{i+1}(\neg D_i)$. If $i + 1 < m$, then, since W_{i+1}
contains $\bigwedge_{1 \leq j < i+1, j \neq m} \neg D_j$, in particular (using $j = i$), $W_{i+1} \models \neg D_i$. Thus

$\mathcal{N} \models K_{i+1}(\neg D_i)$ by bullet 3 in the definition of $\mathcal{N}$. On the other hand, if $i + 1 \geq m$, then $\mathcal{N} \models K_{i+1}(\neg D_i)$ by bullet 4 in the definition of $\mathcal{N}$.

Subcase $A_5^n(W_q)$: ψ is $K_i(\rho)$ for some $1 \leq i \leq n$ and some tautology ρ. If $i < m$ then $W_i \models \rho$ (because ρ is a tautology) and thus $\mathcal{N} \models K_i(\rho)$ (by bullet 3 in the definition of $\mathcal{N}$). On the other hand, if $i \geq m$, then $\mathcal{N} \models K_i(\rho)$ by bullet 4 in the definition of $\mathcal{N}$.

Subcase $A_6^n(W_q)$: ψ is $K_i(\rho \rightarrow \tau) \rightarrow K_i(\rho) \rightarrow K_i(\tau)$ for some $1 \leq i \leq n$ and some ρ, τ. If $i \geq m$ then $\mathcal{N} \models K_i(\tau)$ by bullet 4 in the definition of $\mathcal{N}$. But assume $i < m$. Assume $\mathcal{N} \models K_i(\rho \rightarrow \tau)$ and $\mathcal{N} \models K_i(\rho)$. By bullet 3 in the definition of $\mathcal{N}$ this means $W_i \models \rho \rightarrow \tau$ and $W_i \models \rho$. Thus $W_i \models \tau$, so $\mathcal{N} \models K_i(\tau)$.

Subcase $A_7^n(W_q)$: ψ is $K_i(\rho) \rightarrow K_j(\rho)$ for some $1 \leq i < j \leq n$. If $j \geq m$ then $\mathcal{N} \models K_j(\rho)$ by bullet 4 in the definition of $\mathcal{N}$. But assume $j < m$. Assume $\mathcal{N} \models K_i(\rho)$. By bullet 3 in the definition of $\mathcal{N}$, $W_i \models \rho$. Since $i < j$, we have $W_j \models W_i$, thus $W_j \models \rho$, so $\mathcal{N} \models K_j(\rho)$.

Subcase $A_7^{n\,\prime}(W_q)$: ψ is $K_j(K_i(\rho) \rightarrow \rho)$ for some $1 \leq i < j \leq n$ and some ρ. If $j \geq m$ then $\mathcal{N} \models K_j(K_i(\rho) \rightarrow \rho)$ by bullet 4 in the definition of $\mathcal{N}$. But assume $j < m$. By $A_{T,j}^n$, $(V_n)_0^j \models K_i(\rho) \rightarrow \rho$, thus $W_j \models K_i(\rho) \rightarrow \rho$ since W_j includes $(V_n)_0^j$. Thus $\mathcal{N} \models K_j(K_i(\rho) \rightarrow \rho)$ by bullet 3 in the definition of $\mathcal{N}$.

Subcase $A_\infty^{n\,\prime\prime}(W_q)$: ψ is $K_i(\rho)$ for some $1 \leq i \leq n$ and some ρ such that $(V_n)_0 \models \rho$. If $i \geq m$ then $\mathcal{N} \models K_i(\rho)$ by bullet 4 in the definition of $\mathcal{N}$. But assume $i < m$. Since $(V_n)_0 \subseteq (V_n)_0^i \subseteq W_i$, we have $W_i \models \rho$ and thus $\mathcal{N} \models K_i(\rho)$ by bullet 3 in the definition of $\mathcal{N}$.

Subcase $A_{T,q}^n(W_q)$: ψ is $K_j(\rho) \rightarrow \rho$ for some $1 \leq j < q$. Assume $\mathcal{N} \models K_j(\rho)$. Since $j < q \leq m$, bullet 3 in the definition of $\mathcal{N}$ says $W_j \models \rho$. Since $j < q$, we can finally use our strong q-induction hypothesis: by induction, $\mathcal{N} \models W_j$. Thus $\mathcal{N} \models \rho$.

Subcase $A_{q,\infty}^n(W_q)$: ψ is $K_j(\rho)$ for some $1 \leq j \leq q$ and some ρ such that $(V_n)_0^j \models \rho$. If $j \geq m$ then $\mathcal{N} \models K_j(\rho)$ by bullet 4 in the definition of $\mathcal{N}$. But assume $j < m$. Since $(V_n)_0^j \models \rho$ and $(V_n)_0^j \subseteq W_j$, we see $W_j \models \rho$ and thus $\mathcal{N} \models K_j(\rho)$ by bullet 3 in the definition of $\mathcal{N}$.

Subcase $\bigwedge_{1 \leq j < q, j \neq m} \neg D_j$ (W_q): ψ is $\bigwedge_{1 \leq j < q, j \neq m} \neg D_j$. If $q = 1$ then the conjunction is empty, so $\mathcal{N} \models \psi$ vacuously. Assume $q > 1$. Let $1 \leq j < q$, $j \neq m$. Since $q \leq m < n - 1$, it follows that $j < n - 1$, so $\mathcal{N} \models \neg D_j$ by bullet 2 in the definition of $\mathcal{N}$.

This concludes the proof that $\mathcal{N} \models W_q$ for all $q \leq m$. In particular, $\mathcal{N} \models W_m$. Since $\mathcal{N} \not\models D_m$, this concludes the proof that $W_m \not\models D_m$. This concludes the proof that $\mathcal{M} \models \neg K_m(D_m)$. Since $\mathcal{M} \models D_m$, this concludes the proof that $\mathcal{M} \models D_m \wedge \neg K_m(D_m)$. This concludes Case $A_3^{n\,\prime}$.

Case A_4^n: ϕ is $\bigwedge_{i=1}^{n-1}((\neg D_i) \rightarrow K_{i+1}(\neg D_i))$. Fix $1 \leq i \leq n - 1$ and assume $\mathcal{M} \models \neg D_i$. Since $\mathcal{M} \models D_m$, this implies $i \neq m$. Thus, since W_{i+1} includes $\bigwedge_{1 \leq j < i+1, j \neq m} \neg D_j$, we see $W_{i+1} \models \neg D_i$. Thus $\mathcal{M} \models K_{i+1}(\neg D_i)$.

Case A_5^n: ϕ is $K_i(\psi)$ for some $1 \leq i \leq n$ and some tautology ψ. Since ψ is a tautology, $W_i \models \psi$, thus $\mathcal{M} \models K_i(\psi)$.

Case A_6^n: ϕ is $K_i(\psi \to \rho) \to K_i(\psi) \to K_i(\rho)$ for some $1 \le i \le n$ and some ψ, ρ. Assume $\mathcal{M} \models K_i(\psi \to \rho)$ and $\mathcal{M} \models K_i(\psi)$. Then $W_i \models \psi \to \rho$ and $W_i \models \psi$, thus $W_i \models \rho$, thus $\mathcal{M} \models K_i(\rho)$.

Case A_7^n: ϕ is $K_i(\psi) \to K_j(\psi)$ for some $1 \le i < j \le n$. Assume $\mathcal{M} \models K_i(\psi)$, so $W_i \models \psi$. Since $W_j \models W_i$, we see $W_j \models \psi$. Thus $\mathcal{M} \models K_j(\psi)$.

Case $A_T^{n\prime}$: ϕ is $K_j(K_i(\psi) \to \psi)$ for some $1 \le i < j \le n$ and some ψ. By $A_{T,j}^n$, $(V_n)_0^j \models K_i(\psi) \to \psi$. Since $(V_n)_0^j \subseteq W_j$, we see $W_j \models K_i(\psi) \to \psi$, thus $\mathcal{M} \models K_j(K_i(\psi) \to \psi)$.

Case $A_\infty^{n\prime\prime}$: ϕ is $K_i(\psi)$ for some $1 \le i \le n$ and some ψ such that $(V_n)_0 \models \psi$. Since $(V_n)_0 \subseteq (V_n)_0^i \subseteq W_i$, we see $W_i \models \psi$, thus $\mathcal{M} \models K_i(\psi)$.

Case $A_{T,p}^n$: ϕ is $K_r(\psi) \to \psi$ for some $1 \le r < p$. Assume $\mathcal{M} \models K_r(\psi)$, so $W_r \models \psi$. By our p-induction hypothesis, $\mathcal{M} \models W_r$. Thus $\mathcal{M} \models \psi$.

Case $A_{p,\infty}^n$: ϕ is $K_j(\psi)$ for some $1 \le j \le p$ and some ψ such that $(V_n)_0^j \models \psi$. Since $(V_n)_0^j \subseteq W_j$, we see $W_j \models \psi$. Thus $\mathcal{M} \models K_j(\psi)$.

Case $\bigwedge_{1 \le j < i, j \ne m} \neg D_j$: ϕ is $\bigwedge_{1 \le j < i, j \ne m} \neg D_j$. Then clearly $\mathcal{M} \models \phi$. This concludes the proof of Claim 1.

Claim 2: $\mathcal{M} \models K_i(\phi) \to \phi$ for all $1 \le i \le n$ and all ϕ. Fix any such i and assume $\mathcal{M} \models K_i(\phi)$, which means $W_i \models \phi$. By Claim 1, $\mathcal{M} \models W_i$. Thus $\mathcal{M} \models \phi$. Since each W_i includes $(V_n)_0^i$, Claims 1–2 together show $\mathcal{M} \models V_n$. □

It is a straightforward exercise to show that $(V_2)_0 \models \neg D_2$ (by similar reasoning as in the preliminary claim in the proof of Theorem 1), so by Lemma 2, $(V_2)_0 \models K_1(\neg D_2)$. From this it is an easy exercise to show $(V_2)_0 \models K_1(D_1)$. Together this rules out the first two disjuncts of

$$A_3^{2\prime} \equiv (D_1 \wedge \neg K_1(D_1)) \vee (D_2 \wedge \neg K_2(D_2)) \vee (D_1 \wedge K_1(D_2)),$$

so $(V_2)_0 \models D_1 \wedge K_1(D_2)$. By $A_T^{2\prime\prime}$, $V_2 \models D_2$. But $V_2 \models \neg D_2$. So V_2 is inconsistent. And V_1 is clearly inconsistent. Thus the requirement $n > 2$ in Theorem 3 is sharp.

6   Whether Knowledge-of-Factivity Should be Assumed?

We will argue that knowledge-of-factivity should not be assumed. Due to anticipated controversy, we will address the question in the style of a metaphysical disputation, giving the top priority not to ourselves but to our opponents, as in Thomas Aquinas's *Summa Theologica*. For in philosophy, anyone can argue anything, thus the real test is not how one argues one's own position, as much as how one replies to objections. Thus we present, in order:

- Anticipated objections to our answer.
- Our answer.
- Replies to objections.

Objection 1: Factivity is part of the definition of knowledge, which definition knowers should know. Therefore, knowledge-of-factivity should be assumed.

Objection 2: Knowledge should conform to Kripke's possible-worlds semantics. And factivity itself should certainly be assumed, thus factivity should hold in all possible worlds. But in Kripke's semantics, anything that holds in all possible worlds is known.

Objection 3: The teacher's implicit trustworthiness is essential to the surprise examination paradox. Presumably the students are aware that they trust the teacher. And presumably they would have known their own factivity, had the teacher stayed silent. But an announcement from a trusted source should not cause the students to suddenly doubt their own factivity.

Objection 4: For any statement $S(X)$, for any A and B, if $A = B$, then $S(B)$ implies $S(A)$. Let $S(X)$ be "The students know the factivity of X". Let A be the consequences of the teacher's announcements, and let B be the true consequences of the teacher's announcements. Clearly we should assume $S(B)$. But the teacher is truthful, thus $A = B$, so $S(B)$ implies $S(A)$.

Objection 5: If the paradox is allegedly resolved by weakening knowledge-of-factivity, it re-emerges if the teacher announces "there will be a surprise exam next week, and you are factive". Thus, as far as paradoxes go, we gain little or nothing by refusing knowledge-of-factivity.

We answer that: There are different types of students. On one extreme, there are students who merely take the teacher's sayings as a guide to more quickly discover what they could have discovered on their own. Thus, the boy in Plato's *Meno* (82b-85d) could have discovered geometry on his own, without Socrates. For this type of student, knowledge-of-factivity might be a very reasonable assumption. On the opposite extreme, some students accept whatever the teacher says. For example, a robot might be programmed to accept everything its owner tells it. Students of the former extreme can never be taught contingent facts, just as Russell could not teach Wittgenstein that there is no rhinocerus in the room. Examinations are contingent, thus the surprise examination paradox only makes sense for students who accept what the teacher tells them. So we should here treat students as if they're bound to accept whatever their teacher says. Now, the students can remember things the teacher said in the past, but they cannot predict what the teacher will say in the future. On Monday, they cannot predict that "tomorrow (or even later today) the teacher will not declare anything contradictory," and so they cannot predict that what they can deduce from the teacher will, on Tuesday, be factive. Indeed, the students themselves might not even call their knowledge "knowledge", but rather "belief" or "teacher-provability". But if we outside observers do know that the teacher is truthful, then *we* can call the students' belief "knowledge" even if they themselves don't. So our answer is, we should not assume knowledge-of-factivity, because students cannot predict the teacher won't say something false.

Finally, we can reply to the previous objections.

Reply to Objection 1: When the students reason about what they can or cannot deduce from their teacher, they do not know that they are reasoning about their own knowledge. To them, the K_i operators of Definition 1 are provability operators, some of which might be un-factive if, in future, the teacher says something contradictory. If we outside observers know the teacher will never contradict herself, then we can think of K_i as knowledge, but that doesn't imply the students must. "For it is possible for us to think we do not know what in fact we do know" (Descartes).

Reply to Objection 2: Kripke semantics are only appropriate when the knower knows that the modalities in question conform to Kripke semantics. See also [3].

Reply to Objection 3: Prior to the teacher's saying anything, the students may have known the factivity of their past knowledge. But they could not then have known the factivity of what we call their future knowledge (and what they might call "things we will be able to deduce from the teacher in future"), because they cannot predict the future.

Reply to Objection 4: This fallacy is known as the morning star paradox [12]. For, let $S(X)$ be "Everyone knows the morning star is X", let A be the evening star, and let B be the morning star. Then $S(B)$ seems plausible, and $A = B$ (A and B equal planet Venus), yet $S(A)$ seems implausible. This shows replacement does not work this way in modal logic in general.

Reply to Objection 5: If the teacher announces factivity, then the set of all things the teacher has announced becomes a theory that proves its own consistency. If the resulting inconsistency is a "paradox", then by the same logic, so is Gödel's 2nd incompleteness theorem. But said theorem is not generally considered a paradox.

7   Conclusion

We have argued that factivity, and knowledge-of-factivity, play an implicit role in the surprise examination paradox, even though at first glance the paradox might not seem to assume them at all. If students know the surprise exam will take place on Friday, then it would be surprising to them if the surprise exam takes place on Thursday. That such situations are not included in the definition of surprise in standard formalizations of the paradox is apparently because such situations are impossible: the students *cannot* know the exam will take place on Friday if in fact the exam takes place on Thursday, because knowledge is factive. But for the students themselves to simplify the definition of surprise in this way, they themselves would need to know their own factivity. So, even though at first glance the paradox does not seem to hinge on factivity or the knowledge thereof, it seems that factivity and knowledge-of-factivity play an implicit role in the definition of surprise.

One might hope that the surprise examination paradox would vanish if we merely redefined surprise to include such impossible situations as the students knowing the exam will be Friday even though the exam is in fact Thursday. But we showed in Theorem 2 that the paradox evades this attempted resolution, provided that factivity and knowledge-of-factivity are assumed.

However, in Theorem 3, we showed that if surprise is thus redefined, and if the assumption of knowledge-of-factivity is dropped (even while still assuming factivity itself), then the paradox vanishes. In fact, we showed even more. We showed the paradox still vanishes even if knowledge-of-factivity is not totally dropped: if knowledge-of-factivity is weakened to the statement that, on each day, the students know the factivity of their own knowledge from prior days, then that weakening is already sufficient to remove the paradox.

Thus, in our opinion, the surprise examination paradox results from two flaws: the assumption of knowledge-of-factivity (that, in addition to the students' knowledge being factive, that the students themselves *know* as much), and the over-simplification of the definition of surprise accordingly. This is an important step forward with respect to conjectures proposed in the literature (as those, e.g., by McLelland and Chihara [17]) and focusing on the role of different forms of positive introspection (based on the KK rule) as the causal factors triggering the paradox. Along this line of reasoning, in [18] the authors show that the KK principle is unrelated to the causes of the paradox, and in fact even in our formalization this rule is not assumed to derive a contradiction[2]. The same authors of [18] focus instead on the retention principle, by showing that invalidating it suffices to restore consistency. In other cases, the paradox is resolved by assuming that the teacher's announcement is actually never known, or that the students do not trust it for the whole week, which is similar to stating that the students do not retain knowledge in general. With respect to these proposals, our work contributes with a new perspective allowing us to resolve the paradox by giving up a very specific form of knowledge.

We also point out that our solution relies purely on arguments about knowledge, thus differing from other approaches that deal with the paradox by replacing the notion of knowledge by the notion of provability [6], as done, e.g., in [14], where Gödel's second Incompleteness Theorem is used to offer a way out of the antinomy.

In future work, we would like to investigate the possibility of simultaneously resolving multiple epistemic paradoxes at once by the construction of a single model. For example, imagine that to the formulas of $\mathscr{L}$ (Definition 1) we added an additional clause saying that for every $i = 1, 2, \ldots$, there is a non-atomic formula L_i; and imagine that for semantics, we declare that for every model $\mathscr{M}$, $\mathscr{M} \models L_i$ iff $\mathscr{M} \models K_i(\neg L_i)$. Thus L_i is a variation of the liar sentence for the students' knowledge on midnight just before day i: intuitively, L_i could be thought of as the sentence: "On midnight just before day i, we know this sentence is false". In this expanded logic, it can be shown that, e.g., S4 (or even weaker systems including knowledge-of-factivity) are inconsistent—this is a temporal variation of the Paradox of the Knower. We conjecture that by modifying the construction in Sect. 5, it would be possible to construct a single model which simultaneously resolves the surprise examination paradox and this temporal version of the Paradox of the Knower. We conjecture it would even be possible to construct the model in such a way as to satisfy $K_j(\neg L_i)$ whenever $i < j$, i.e., so that the students know (on any day) the falsehood of earlier days' liar sentences. Resolving multiple paradoxes at once, with the same model, and by weakening the same assumption, would be, in our opinion, strong evidence in favor of

---

[2] It can be shown that a temporal version of the KK axiom can be added to V_n, without disrupting its consistency, thus emphasizing once more that KK is *not* the cause of the paradox.

the correctness of said resolution. Moreover, it would confirm the central role of own factivity and its knowledge/ignorance, as already emphasized, e.g., in computational contexts, see, e.g., [1, 2].

References

1. Aldini, A., Fano, V., Graziani, P.: Theory of knowing machines: revisiting gödel and the mechanistic thesis. In: Gadducci, F., Tavosanis, M. (eds.) HaPoC 2015. IAICT, vol. 487, pp. 57–70. Springer, Cham (2016). https://doi.org/10.1007/978-3-319-47286-7_4

2. Alexander, S.A.: A machine that knows its own code. Studia Logica **102**, 567–576 (2014)

3. Artemov, S.: Knowing the model (2016). https://doi.org/10.48550/arXiv.1610.04955

4. Ben-Zvi, I., Moses, Y.: Agent-time epistemics and coordination. In: Lodaya, K. (ed.) ICLA 2013. LNCS, vol. 7750, pp. 97–108. Springer, Heidelberg (2013). https://doi.org/10.1007/978-3-642-36039-8_9

5. Binkley, R.: The surprise examination in modal logic. J. Phil. **65**(5), 127–136 (1968)

6. Chow, T.Y.: The surprise examination or unexpected hanging paradox. Am. Math. Monthly **105**(1), 41–51 (1998)

7. Collins, J.M.: Epistemic closure principles. The Internet Encyclopedia of Philosophy (2006)

8. Earman, J.: A user's guide to the surprise exam paradoxes. PhilSci Archive (2021)

9. Fagin, R., Halpern, J.Y., Moses, Y., Vardi, M.Y.: Reasoning About Knowledge. MIT Press, Cambridge (2003)

10. Gardner, M.: The paradox of the unexpected hanging. In: The Unexpected Hanging and Other Mathematical Diversions, pp. 11–23. The University of Chicago Press (1991)

11. Gerbrandy, J.: The surprise examination in dynamic epistemic logic. Synthese **155**(1), 21–33 (2007)

12. Kanger, S.: The morning star paradox. Theoria **23**(1), 1–11 (1957)

13. Kaplan, D., Montague, R.: A paradox regained. Notre Dame J. Formal Logic **1**(3), 79–90 (1960)

14. Kritchman, S., Raz, R.: The surprise examination paradox and the second incompleteness theorem. Not. AMS **57**(11), 1454–1458 (2010)

15. Luper, S.: Epistemic closure. The Stanford Encyclopedia of Philosophy (2020)

16. Margalit, A., Bar-Hillel, M.: Expecting the unexpected. Philosophia **13**, 263–288 (1984)

17. McLelland, J., Chihara, C.: The surprise examination paradox. J. Phil. Logic **4**(1), 71–89 (1975)

18. Murzi, J., Eichhorn, L., Mayr, P.: Surprise, surprise: KK is innocent. Thought J. Phil. **10**(1), 4–18 (2021)

19. Scriven, M.: Paradoxical announcements. Mind **60**, 403–407 (1951)

20. Sorensen, R.: Epistemic paradoxes. The Stanford Encyclopedia of Philosophy (2022)

21. Stjernberg, F.: Restricting factiveness. Phil. Stud. **146**(1), 29–48 (2009)

22. Williamson, T.: Knowledge and its Limits. Oxford University Press, Oxford (2000)

Using Justified True Beliefs to Explore Formal Ignorance

Mirko Tagliaferri$^{(\boxtimes)}$ (iD)

Università degli Studi di Urbino "Carlo Bo", Urbino, Italy
`mirko.tagliaferri@uniurb.it`

Abstract. The possibility of better understanding belief and knowledge modalities through justifications is not a novel one, however, the machinery of justifications has never been employed to explore the nature of ignorance from a formal perspective. By including justification terms into a modal logic for belief a major project (among others) can be pursued: different cognitive attitudes can be formalized that imply ignorance, therefore highlighting even better the possible culprits of the emergence of the phenomenon of being ignorant. This would allow the possibility of developing strategies that could be employed in different scenarios to tackle ignorance, thus adapting interventions to the specific situations in which ignorance arises.

Keywords: Doxastic justification logic · Formal ignorance · Radical ignorance

1 Introduction and Motivations

In recent years, there has been a renaissance of interest in the formal treatment of ignorance [1,7,8,10,14]. This renewed interest is partly dependant on the necessity of understanding how ignorance can influence different reasoning dynamics. This is especially important when it is noticed that ignorance is a wide phenomenon that influences many different fields. Both human beings and artificial intelligent (AI) systems will often have to reason with incomplete sets of data, which means that they will be ignorant about various facts[1] that might influence their decision making capabilities. Therefore, a good grasp of the characteristics and formal properties of ignorance could help to devise strategies that can be useful both in educating people and in programming AI systems. Moreover, as shown by Kit Fine [9], it is also important to better understand the dynamics that bridge simple and radical forms of ignorance. This is due to the fact that once an agent becomes second-order ignorant about a specific fact

---

[1] Throughout the paper, I will take propositions and facts as synonyms. In particular, a proposition will indicate a fact, i.e., that the world is in a particular way. At the same time, each fact could be represented with a proposition, i.e., the fact specifies a way in which the world is and the proposition describes such world.

P. Masci et al. (Eds.): SEFM 2022 Collocated Workshops, LNCS 13765, pp. 400–417, 2023.
https://doi.org/10.1007/978-3-031-26236-4_31

(s/he is ignorant that s/he is ignorant that the fact is true), s/he will spiral into a black hole of ignorance, unable to escape from it by him/herself.

A common practice is to define ignorance in terms of (lack of) knowledge, which can then, in turn, be interpreted in various possible ways depending on the underlying logical languages that are employed.[2] This kind of approach has the advantage of being extremely simple and allows a first basic understanding of various characteristics of ignorance. However, this simplicity comes at a cost. The causes of ignorance are left obscure and connections between the phenomenon of being ignorant and other cognitive phenomena are left unexplained.

A first step in the direction of exploring the connection between different cognitive phenomena and ignorance can be found in [1]. In the paper, the authors propose three formal representations of doxastic attitudes[3] and show how those attitudes can lead to ignorance, thus partially explaining the potential causes of ignorance. However, while their approach is successful in highlighting some of the connections between beliefs and ignorance, some of the cognitive phenomena they describe seem confusing[4] and thus fail to provide the whole picture.

In this paper, I propose to augment their formal machinery with evidence formulas, thus obtaining the language of evidence-based beliefs as presented in [4,5], although with a slightly different interpretation of the operators. The idea is that such additional evidence could be interpreted as standing for justifications for specific facts. The inclusion of a justification element would then allow a definition of knowledge inside the language as justified true belief, bringing it closer to a standard definition of knowledge employed in philosophical debates. Furthermore, having the extra element of evidence could clarify better some of the cognitive attitude already analysed, while also allowing novel formal definitions for other attitudes relevant for ignorance that agents might have. Those added cognitive attitudes and the finer-grained level of description allowed by this formal language would then allow relevant stakeholders to develop strategies that could be employed in different scenarios to tackle ignorance, thus adapting interventions to the specific situations in which ignorance arises.

This possibility of better understanding belief and knowledge modalities through justifications is not a novel one (see, e.g., [2,3] for a good introduction), however, to my knowledge, the machinery of justifications has never been employed to explore the nature of ignorance from a formal perspective. By including justification terms into a modal logic for belief a major project (among others) can be pursued: different cognitive attitudes can be formalized that imply ignorance, therefore highlighting even better the possible culprits of the emergence of the phenomenon of being ignorant.

---

[2] Obviously, other approaches are also possible, e.g., interpreting ignorance as a primitive notion [6]. Moreover, even following this simple approach of reducing ignorance to the lack of knowledge can produce different formalizations depending on how the authors interpret the phrase "lack of knowledge", e.g., as *not knowing that* or *not knowing whether*.

[3] Being agnostic: $\neg B(\phi) \wedge \neg B(\neg \phi)$, misbelieving: $B(\phi) \wedge \neg \phi$, and doubting: $B(\phi) \wedge \phi \wedge \neg K(\phi)$. Where $B(\phi)$ should be interpreted as ϕ is believed and $K(\phi)$ as ϕ is known.

[4] The phenomenon of doubting seems particularly obscure, since it is left unexplained why ϕ is not known even though it is believed and it is true.

In order to achieve this goal, the paper will do three things: first (Sect. 2), I will introduce the syntax and semantics of the language of evidence-based beliefs. I will also explain in which way my interpretation of the operators on formulas varies from the one proposed by the original authors of the language in [4,5]. Even though practically identical from the formal point-of-view, I'll call this language in a different way, i.e., *JTB* (Justified True Belief). This is done to make clear the aim of this specific paper and to highlight the difference in interpretation of the operators. Then (Sect. 3), the phenomenon of basic ignorance (i.e., ignoring a fact) will be analysed by providing formal definitions of attitudes that imply ignorance. Intuitive examples of the presence of each attitude will be provided. Finally (Sect. 4), some concluding remarks will follow, and potential future direction of this work will be presented.

2   Justified True Belief Logic

In this section, the logical language for justified true beliefs will be introduced through its syntax and semantics. Due to the exploratory nature of this work, no axiomatization has been created and thus will not be included. The novelty of the language is in the interpretation of the two evidence operators (Definition 4). Semantically, the language combines a relational semantics for the belief operators and neighbourhood semantics for the evidence operators. While each semantic approach is common in modal logic (especially in epistemic logic), often the two are employed in isolation and not together. The idea to employ them together is to highlight the distinctive nature of beliefs and of evidence. Moreover, differently from most approaches that put together beliefs and evidence, in this paper the two notions will be independent. This means that an agent could have evidence for a fact, without believing it and, at the same time, s/he could believe it without evidence. While the latter possibility seems unproblematic, the former is indeed at the core of this paper, and is a controversial position. The idea of defending this position is derived by the analysis of scenarios of belief perseverance, where it is noted that individuals who are exposed to conclusive evidence about a fact do not form appropriate beliefs due to emotional and/or cultural considerations. This seems to suggest that for some agents, having evidence and forming beliefs should be kept independent.

2.1   Syntax

Definition 1 (*JTB*). *Given a set Φ of atomic propositions, the language JTB of formulas $\varphi \in JTB$ is defined recursively as follows:*

$$\varphi := p \in \Phi \mid \neg\varphi \mid \varphi \wedge \varphi \mid B(\varphi) \mid E_l(\varphi) \mid E_c(\varphi)$$

The other logical connectives are defined as usual from negation and conjunction. Intuitively, the modal formulas should be read in the following way: $B(\varphi)$ means that φ is believed; $E_l(\varphi)$ means that there is limited evidence for φ; finally, $E_c(\varphi)$ means that there is conclusive evidence for φ. The difference between limited and conclusive evidence is the following: someone has limited evidence for a fact whenever part of the evidence s/he possesses is consistent with the truth of the fact, but other pieces of evidence might defeat such truth (i.e., it might indicate that the fact is indeed false). On the other hand, conclusive evidence completely supports the truth of the fact, eliminating any potential doubt on such truth from an evidential standpoint. Obviously, someone possessing conclusive evidence implies that s/he also possesses limited evidence, but not vice versa.

Given the language JTB, it is possible to define a knowledge operator as justified true belief. Then, from this knowledge operator, it is possible to define an ignorance operator as (lack of) knowledge whether. Formally:

- $K(\varphi) := B(\varphi) \land \varphi \land E_c(\varphi)$[5];
- $I(\varphi) := \neg K(\varphi) \land \neg K(\neg\varphi)$.

Those two definitions will constitute the main elements of the analysis carried out in the later sections of this paper.

2.2 Semantics

In order to interpret the formulas of the language JTB, the following structure will be employed.

Definition 2 (Models). *A model* $\mathfrak{M} = (W, \pi, R_B, \mathcal{E})$ *is a structure consisting of a nonempty set* W *of possible worlds, a valuation function* $\pi : \Phi \to \mathcal{P}(W)$, *a binary relation* $R_B \subseteq W \times W$, *and an evidence function* $\mathcal{E} : W \to \mathcal{P}(\mathcal{P}(W))$ *(abusing notation, throughout the text* $\mathcal{E}$ *will sometimes be interpreted as a set indicating the value of the function* $\mathcal{E}$ *for a generic win* W, *instead of the function itself). Some assumptions included in this paper are the following:*

- R_B *is serial;*
- *the value of the function* $\mathcal{E}$ *is finite;*
- *the empty set is not contained in* $\mathcal{E}$;
- *the universe set is always contained in it.*

Formally:

- $\forall w \in W, \exists v \in W \ s.t. \ wR_Bv;$
- $\forall w \in W, \emptyset \notin \mathcal{E}(w);$
- $\forall w \in W, W \in \mathcal{E}(w).$

A pair $(\mathfrak{M}, w)$ *is called a pointed model.*

The set W is treated as in standard modal logic and contains elements (the possible worlds) that are maximally consistent descriptions of how the world could be. Those descriptions are maximal because all possible details

---

[5] It might be useful to keep track of the fact that $\neg K(\varphi) := \neg B(\varphi) \lor \neg\varphi \lor \neg E_c(\varphi)$.

are described, and they are consistent because no contradictory information is allowed in the same possible world.

The valuation function π determines the truth of all of the atomic propositions inside the structure.

The binary relation R_B is a doxastic accessibility relation and determines which worlds are doxastically accessible, i.e., which worlds are taken into consideration to determine the beliefs of a given agent. The seriality of R_B ensures that beliefs are always consistent. It is possible to add properties to the binary relation R_B to obtain beliefs with various characteristics[6]; however, since only consistency will be important in the formalization of the cognitive attitudes introduced in Sect. 3 and the derivations from those attitudes to basic ignorance, only the property of seriality will be assumed.

The last element of the structure is the evidence function $\mathcal{E}$ that indicates at each possible state of the model which pieces of evidence are available. In JTB, pieces of evidence are interpreted as set of possible worlds. This is a common practice in the formalization of uncertainty [11] and follows from the intuitive idea that a piece of evidence indicates to an agent a set of possibilities (possible worlds) from which the world s/he thinks s/he is in has to be chosen. The first assumption made about $\mathcal{E}$ is that the value of such function is finite. This assumption could be easily relaxed in the semantics. The idea behind the assumption is that agents only have access to finite numbers of pieces of evidence. The second assumption assures that individual pieces of evidence are consistent, i.e., there is no direct piece of evidence supporting a contradiction. Even though contradictions may not be supported directly by evidence, it is still possible that two pieces of evidence contradict each other, i.e., the intersection of all the evidence possessed by an agent might still be the empty set. It would be possible to require that all the pieces of evidence possessed by an agent must be consistent with each other. This assumption, however, might be too strong given that evidence is often gathered in different contexts and from different sources, thus allowing for the possibility of receiving conflicting evidence. The second assumption made, simply assures that the whole space of possibilities is supported, i.e., an agent has always access to trivial evidence.

As said above, the set of evidence might contain elements that are conflicting, indicating that a fact is both true and false. This means that it might not always be possible to combine this evidence in order to obtain answers. Nonetheless, it is still possible to take consistent subsets of the evidence and combine it in order to obtain partial indications over the potential truth of the fact. Those subsets of evidence will be called *maximal consistent evidence sets* and will be employed to interpret the evidence operators of JTB. In the following definition I will use X_i to indicate subsets of W, i.e., $X_i \in \mathcal{P}(W)$, and use $\mathcal{X}_i$ to indicate sets of subsets of W, i.e., $\mathcal{X}_i \in \mathcal{P}(\mathcal{P}(W))$.

Definition 3 (Maximal consistent evidence sets). *Given an evidence set* $\mathcal{E}(w)$, *a subset* $\mathcal{X}_i \subseteq \mathcal{E}(w)$ *is a maximal consistent evidence set iff*

---

[6] See [16] for some examples.

1. *It has the finite intersection property (f.i.p.), i.e., $\bigcap_{X \in \mathcal{X}_i} X \neq \emptyset$;*
2. *It is a maximal set with such property, i.e., there is no set $\mathcal{X}_j \subseteq \mathcal{E}(w)$ such that $\mathcal{X}_i \subset \mathcal{X}_j$ and $\mathcal{X}_j$ has the finite intersection property.*

The formal structure provides an interpretation for the language *JTB*.

Definition 4 (Truth). *Given a model $\mathfrak{M}$, a possible world w and a formula φ of the language JTB, the satisfaction of a formula φ at a pointed model $(\mathfrak{M}, w)$, formally $(\mathfrak{M}, w) \models \varphi$, is defined recursively as follows:*

1. *$(\mathfrak{M}, w) \models p$ for $p \in \Phi$ iff $w \in \pi(p)$;*
2. *$(\mathfrak{M}, w) \models \neg\varphi$ iff $(\mathfrak{M}, w) \not\models \varphi$;*
3. *$(\mathfrak{M}, w) \models \varphi \wedge \psi$ iff $(\mathfrak{M}, w) \models \varphi$ and $(\mathfrak{M}, w) \models \psi$;*
4. *$(\mathfrak{M}, w) \models B(\varphi)$ iff $\forall v, w R_B v, (\mathfrak{M}, v) \models \varphi$;*
5. *$(\mathfrak{M}, w) \models E_l(\varphi)$ iff $\exists \mathcal{X}_i \subseteq \mathcal{E}(w)$, s.t., $\mathcal{X}_i$ is a maximal consistent evidence set and $\forall v \in \bigcap_{X \in \mathcal{X}_i} X, (\mathfrak{M}, v) \models \varphi$;*
6. *$(\mathfrak{M}, w) \models E_c(\varphi)$ iff $\forall \mathcal{X}_i \subseteq \mathcal{E}(w)$, s.t., $\mathcal{X}_i$ are maximal consistent evidence sets, it follows that $\forall v \in \bigcap_{X \in \mathcal{X}_i} X, (\mathfrak{M}, v) \models \varphi$.*

I will indicate with $\|\varphi\|_{\mathfrak{M}}$ the truth set of φ, i.e., $\|\varphi\|_{\mathfrak{M}} = \{w \mid (\mathfrak{M}, w) \models \varphi\}$. The first three conditions of Definition 4 are the classical satisfaction relations of propositional logic. The fourth says that something is believed whenever it is true in all doxastically accessible worlds and it is a common definition in modal logic. The fifth and sixth conditions is where I diverge a little from the approach taken in [4,5]. In those papers, the authors took the evidence operator as being true whenever there exists a single piece of evidence completely supporting the fact, i.e., if $\exists X \in \mathcal{E}$, s.t., $X \subseteq \|\varphi\|_{\mathfrak{M}}$. While I understand the benefits of doing so and do realize that sometimes this might indeed be the case, I think their approach could be improved. In particular, their approach has the following downsides: agents rarely just employ one piece of evidence in order to assess whether they indeed have evidence for a specific fact. They combine all the (consistent) evidence they possess and form a general opinion based on this whole set of evidences. The approach followed in this paper is to allow this combination of evidence to happen right away, highlighting what facts the agents can have evidence for through the interconnections of all the pieces of evidence s/he possesses. In fact, in [4,5], the authors themselves seem to agree that taking all the consistent evidence and combine it is indeed a useful practice, but they then use this intuition to define the belief operator, instead of a stronger evidence operator, which does not seem to capture the intuition. While this aligns with their aims of bridging the gap between the formation of beliefs and availability of evidence, I have some reserves about the fact that the former should collapse on the latter. Having evidence (even consistent and conclusive evidence) does not always lead to the formation of an associated belief. For those reasons I have chosen to follow a different route.

I claim that there is limited evidence about a fact being true whenever there is at least a consistent set of pieces of evidence that indicate the truth of the given fact. Note that this condition is open to the possibility that the set of pieces of evidence is indeed a singleton set (containing only one piece of evidence). In this case, my condition would collapse onto that given in [4,5]. It is easy to see that someone could have limited evidence for contradictory facts, i.e., it is possible to satisfy both $E_l(\varphi)$ and $E_l(\neg\varphi)$ in a model (see the example 6 about credulity later in the paper to see how this could happen).

On the other hand, there is conclusive evidence about a fact being true only when all pieces of evidence are taken into consideration with respect to their maximal consistent sets and the fact is true in all worlds that are compatible with such evidence. Note that the way conclusive evidence is evaluated is different from taking the intersection of all the available evidence and then checking the truth of the fact. A simple example should help to clarify the difference in the two procedures. I'll present first the procedure using the simple intersection of evidence. Suppose you have two pieces of evidence, one indicating that φ is true and one indicating that it is false. Now, if the intersection is taken between the two pieces of evidence, then the empty set would obtain (the two pieces of evidence are disjoint). This would result in having conclusive evidence for both φ and its negation, which is absurd. Using the other procedure: being the two pieces of evidence disjoint, it would mean that there are two maximal consistent sets of evidence that should be taken into consideration, one constituted by the single piece of evidence supporting φ and one constituted by the single piece of evidence supporting $\neg\varphi$. At this point, in order to establish whether there is conclusive evidence for either φ or its negation, it would be necessary to check their truth in all worlds that are members of both the maximal consistent sets of evidence. Obviously, neither of the two would hold in all of those states, meaning that there is no conclusive evidence for one or the other, as intuitively expected. It is important to notice that the assumption $\emptyset \notin \mathcal{E}$ guarantees that there will always be at least a maximal consistent set of evidence pieces in $\mathcal{E}$ and, moreover, by the definition of maximal consistent set (Definition 3), there will always be a possible world to check. This guarantees that there is no vacuous conclusive evidence for anything. Moreover, being tautologies true in all possible worlds, it is easy to see that there will always be conclusive evidence for those, no matter the evidence function.

Finally, it is also easy to see that the implication from conclusive evidence to limited evidence that was discussed in Subsect. 2.1 holds. This is due to the fact that if a fact is true in all worlds that are indicated by all maximal consistent evidence sets, then this fact must be true also in all worlds that are indicated by one of the maximal consistent evidence sets.

3   The Origins of Basic Ignorance

In this section, various attitudes will be explored and it will be shown that they all imply basic ignorance (ignorance of a fact φ). The starting point of the reflections of this section are the results obtained in [1]. In the paper, the authors managed to show that three doxastic attitudes were sufficient and jointly

Table 1. Cognitive attitudes that imply ignorance.

Disbelief	$\neg B(\varphi) \wedge \neg B(\neg\varphi) \wedge (E_c(\varphi) \vee E_c(\neg\varphi))$
Skepticism	$\neg B(\varphi) \wedge \neg B(\neg\varphi) \wedge (E_l(\varphi) \vee E_l(\neg\varphi)) \wedge (\neg E_c(\varphi) \vee \neg E_c(\neg\varphi))$
Unawareness	$\neg B(\varphi) \wedge \neg B(\neg\varphi) \wedge \neg E_l(\varphi) \wedge \neg E_l(\neg\varphi)$
Mislead	$B(\varphi) \wedge \neg\varphi \wedge E_c(\varphi)$
Negative belief perseverance	$B(\varphi) \wedge \neg\varphi \wedge E_c(\neg\varphi)$
Credulity	$B(\varphi) \wedge \neg\varphi \wedge E_l(\varphi) \wedge \neg E_c(\varphi)$
Misbelief	$B(\varphi) \wedge \neg\varphi \wedge \neg E_l(\varphi)$
Positive belief perseverance	$B(\varphi) \wedge \varphi \wedge E_c(\neg\varphi)$
Doubt	$B(\varphi) \wedge \varphi \wedge E_l(\varphi) \wedge \neg E_c(\varphi)$
Intuition	$B(\varphi) \wedge \varphi \wedge \neg E_l(\varphi)$

necessary conditions for *ignoring whether*[7]. While their results did help to shed some lights on the origins of ignorance, some aspects where unclear. In this section, those aspects will be clarified and a more fine-grained analysis of the origins of basic ignorance will be pursued. Specifically, employing the evidence component of *JTB*, all doxastic attitudes (agnosticism, misbelieving, and doubting) will be further analysed and novel more interesting attitudes will be presented. Table 1 contains a summary of all the attitudes with their formalization[8].

Disbelief. *Disbelief* is a attitude of mental rejection of a fact even in the face of conclusive evidence in its favour. An example of this attitude could be a parent that refuses to believe that her son committed a crime, even when she is presented with conclusive evidence that he did commit the crime. Another possibility of this attitude is when the evidence, even though conclusive, is considered forged by the agent, i.e., when the agent thinks that $E_c(\varphi) \wedge \neg\varphi$ holds.

Example 1 (Formal model example). Take the following model $\mathfrak{M} = (W, \pi, R_B, \mathcal{E})$ where $W = \{w_1, w_2, w_3\}$, $\pi(p) = \{w_1, w_2\}$, $R_B = \{(w_1, w_2), (w_1, w_3), (w_2, w_3), (w_3, w_2)\}$, and $\mathcal{E}(w_1) = \{\{w_1, w_2\}, \{w_1, w_2, w_3\}\}$. It is easy to check that:

- $(\mathfrak{M}, w_1) \models \neg B(p)$
- $(\mathfrak{M}, w_1) \models \neg B(\neg p)$
- $(\mathfrak{M}, w_1) \models E_c(p)$

---

[7] The origin of the notion of ignoring whether could be traced back to Hintikka [12], who, however, only discusses it briefly. In short, ignoring whether describes ignorance as a lack of knowledge both about a proposition ϕ and its negation $\neg\phi$. On the other side, ignorance could also be interpreted as lack of knowledge that, where only one of the two propositions is taken into consideration.

[8] In order to define the attitudes that are indicated in this paper, I employed the Oxford Languages online dictionary [13]. Note that different interpretations of the attitudes might modify the way that they are formalized.

From the above satisfiability relations, it follows that in the pointed model $(\mathfrak{M}, w_1)$, the formula $\neg B(p) \wedge \neg B(\neg p) \wedge (E_c(p) \vee E_c(\neg p))$ holds, showing that a *disbelief attitude* is present.

I will now show that a disbelief attitude leads to basic ignorance.

Theorem 1 (From Disbelief to Ignorance). *A disbelief attitude implies basic ignorance. Formally:*

$$(\neg B(\varphi) \wedge \neg B(\neg \varphi) \wedge (E_c(\varphi) \vee E_c(\neg \varphi))) \rightarrow I(\varphi) \tag{1}$$

Before giving the proof, some procedures that will be employed during all the proofs can be set, in order to avoid repetitions of procedures along all proofs. First, it should be noted that $I(\varphi)$ can always be unpacked through its definition to $\neg K(\varphi) \wedge \neg K(\neg \varphi)$. Moreover, in order to show that $\neg K(\varphi) \wedge \neg K(\neg \varphi)$ holds in a pointed model, it must be shown that $(\mathfrak{M}, w) \models \neg K(\varphi)$ and $(\mathfrak{M}, w) \models \neg K(\neg \varphi)$. This procedure will be referenced at as procedure α. In addition, the following procedure will also be employed: unpack the definition of $\neg K(\varphi)$ into $\neg B(\varphi) \vee \neg \varphi \vee \neg E_c(\varphi)$. In order to show that $\neg B(\varphi) \vee \neg \varphi \vee \neg E_c(\varphi)$ holds in a pointed model, it must be shown that either $(\mathfrak{M}, w) \models \neg B(\varphi)$, $(\mathfrak{M}, w) \models \neg \varphi)$, or $(\mathfrak{M}, w) \models \neg E_c(\varphi)$. This procedure will be referenced at as procedure β. Finally, the following procedure will also be employed: unpack the definition of $\neg K(\neg \varphi)$ into $\neg B(\neg \varphi) \vee \varphi \vee \neg E_c(\neg \varphi)$. In order to show that $\neg B(\neg \varphi) \vee \varphi \vee \neg E_c(\neg \varphi)$ holds in a pointed model, it must be shown that either $(\mathfrak{M}, w) \models \neg B(\neg \varphi)$, $(\mathfrak{M}, w) \models \varphi)$, or $(\mathfrak{M}, w) \models \neg E_c(\neg \varphi)$. This procedure will be referenced at as procedure γ.

Proof. Take an arbitrary pointed model $(\mathfrak{M}, w)$. Assume that $(\mathfrak{M}, w) \models \neg B(\varphi) \wedge \neg B(\neg \varphi) \wedge (E_c(\varphi) \vee E_c(\neg \varphi))$. Show that $(\mathfrak{M}, w) \models I(\varphi)$. Apply procedure α. Apply procedure β. The first element of the disjunction obtained through procedure β follows directly from the initial assumption, i.e., $(\mathfrak{M}, w) \models \neg B(\varphi)$. Apply procedure γ. The first element of the disjunction obtained through procedure γ follows directly from the initial assumption, i.e., $(\mathfrak{M}, w) \models \neg B(\neg \varphi)$. Given the fact that the pointed model chosen was arbitrary, the result holds for all pointed models and the theorem follows. $\square$

Skepticism. *Skepticism* is the attitude that is closest to the agnosticism effect given in [1]. Someone who is in a skeptic attitude might have some evidence in favour of a specific fact, but still decides to suspend his/her judgement waiting for further evidence in favour or against the truth of the fact.

Example 2 (Formal model example). Take the following model $\mathfrak{M} = (W, \pi, R_B, \mathcal{E})$ where $W = \{w_1, w_2, w_3\}$, $\pi(p) = \{w_2\}$, $R_B = \{(w_1, w_2), (w_1, w_3), (w_2, w_3), (w_3, w_2)\}$, and $\mathcal{E}(w_1) = \{\{w_1, w_2\}, \{w_1, w_3\}, \{w_2, w_3\}, \{w_1, w_2, w_3\}\}$. It is easy to check that:

- $(\mathfrak{M}, w_1) \models \neg B(p)$
- $(\mathfrak{M}, w_1) \models \neg B(\neg p)$

- $(\mathfrak{M}, w_1) \models E_l(p)$
- $(\mathfrak{M}, w_1) \models \neg E_c(p)$

From the above satisfiability relations, it follows that in the pointed model $(\mathfrak{M}, w_1)$, the formula $\neg B(p) \wedge \neg B(\neg p) \wedge (E_l(p) \vee E_l(\neg p)) \wedge (\neg E_c(p) \vee \neg E_c(\neg p))$ holds, showing that a *skeptic attitude* is present.

Theorem 2 (From Skepticism to Ignorance). *A skeptic attitude implies basic ignorance. Formally:*

$$(\neg B(\varphi) \wedge \neg B(\neg\varphi) \wedge (E_l(\varphi) \vee E_l(\neg\varphi)) \wedge (\neg E_c(\varphi) \vee \neg E_c(\neg\varphi))) \rightarrow I(\varphi) \quad (2)$$

Proof. The proof of Theorem 2 is similar to that of Theorem 1. ☐

Unawareness. *Unawareness* is the attitude that describes an agent who does not have any information regarding a specific fact. This could happen for two reasons: either i) the agent never had the chance to gather evidence for or against the fact, thus is completely unaware of whether it might be true or false; or ii) the agent simply did not even consider to gather the evidence because s/he have never even entertained the idea of the fact.

Example 3 (Formal model example). Take the following model $\mathfrak{M} = (W, \pi, R_B, \mathcal{E})$ where $W = \{w_1, w_2, w_3, w_4\}$, $\pi(p) = \{w_1, w_2\}$, $R_B = \{(w_1, w_2), (w_1, w_3), (w_1, w_4), (w_2, w_3), (w_3, w_4), (w_4, w_2)\}$, and $\mathcal{E}(w_1) = \{\{w_1, w_2, w_3\}, \{w_1, w_3\}, \{w_1, w_2, w_3 w_4\}\}$. It is easy to check that:

- $(\mathfrak{M}, w_1) \models \neg B(p)$
- $(\mathfrak{M}, w_1) \models \neg B(\neg p)$
- $(\mathfrak{M}, w_1) \models \neg E_l(p)$
- $(\mathfrak{M}, w_1) \models \neg E_l(\neg p)$

The third and fourth points follow because the only maximal consistent set available, given $\mathcal{E}(w_1)$, is indeed the whole $\mathcal{E}(w_1)$. At that point, taken the intersection of all the sets contained in $\mathcal{E}(w_1)$, the set $\{w_1, w_3\}$ is obtained. Given the valuation $\pi(p) = \{w_1, w_2\}$, and the valuation $\pi(\neg p) = \{w_3, w_4\}$, it follows that neither are true in all the worlds in the set $\{w_1, w_3\}$, thus the agent has no (limited) evidence for either of them. From the above satisfiability relations, it follows that in the pointed model $(\mathfrak{M}, w_1)$, the formula $\neg B(p) \wedge \neg B(\neg p) \wedge \neg E_l(p) \wedge \neg E_l(\neg p)$ holds, showing that an *unawareness attitude* is present.

Theorem 3 (From Unawareness to Ignorance). *An unawareness attitude implies basic ignorance. Formally:*

$$(\neg B(\varphi) \wedge \neg B(\neg\varphi) \wedge (E_l(\varphi) \vee E_l(\neg\varphi)) \wedge (\neg E_c(\varphi) \vee \neg E_c(\neg\varphi))) \rightarrow I(\varphi) \quad (3)$$

Proof. The proof of Theorem 3 is similar to that of Theorem 1. ☐

Note that the proofs of Theorems 1, 2, and 3 are almost equivalent. This is because the negative beliefs components of the respective attitudes is what implies ignorance, i.e., it is the fact that the agent does not believe either φ or $\neg\varphi$ that implies his/her ignorance of the fact. This class of attitudes represent a failure of the first component of the tripartite definition of knowledge.

The reader might think that the evidence component is useless in those cases, and s/he would not be completely wrong. In the cases in which beliefs are withheld, this attitude alone is sufficient to imply ignorance. However, the added component of evidence could highlight potential strategies to avoid ignorance. For example, if it is known that an agent is in an unawareness attitude, then it might be possible to eliminate his/her ignorance by providing him/her with evidence in favour or against the fact that is ignored. Differently, if it is known that the agent is in a disbelief attitude, the strategy would be almost useless and more drastic measurements might be required. Obviously, those considerations apply only partially in the context of this paper, since the language introduced is static in nature (i.e., it does not contain elements that allow for a change of evidence and/or beliefs). Nonetheless, having an initial understanding of those phenomena could help in the future to design strategies inside potential extensions of JTB that allow updates to happen.

The next two classes of attitudes[9] that will follow have an important feature, i.e., they are equivalent *modulo* the truth of the fact that is evaluated. Assuming that agents do not have direct access to such truth, for them it is practically impossible to subjectively understand whether they are in the first class of attitudes (those in which what they believe is false) or the second (those in which what they believe is actually true). In the real world, there might be pragmatic considerations that could help an agent to distinguish the two classes of attitudes. Those considerations involve the way in which evidence is gathered and the expertise of the agent in the specific matter on which s/he is forming his/her beliefs. Since in JTB no reference is made to how the evidence is gathered, the language is not in a position to formalize those considerations. Again, the aim of this paper is to understand the potential origins of ignorance and not of solving the problem right away (e.g., by indicating which considerations should be made to enter attitudes that are less troublesome from the point-of-view of ignorance).

Mislead. *Mislead*[10] is the attitude that describes an agent who has a false belief supported by conclusive evidence. Given that the fact is indeed false, it follows that the conclusive evidence possessed by the agent is misleading, possibly convincing the agent to believe the fact over false premises. This attitude is the most worrisome among all the ones presented in this paper because the only difference between a mislead attitude and knowledge is the truth of the fact itself. Given the assumption that the agent does not have direct access to such

---

[9] First class: Mislead, negative belief perseverance, credulity, misbelief; second class: positive belief perseverance, doubt, and intuition.

[10] From now on, the attitudes are presented employing only $B(\varphi)$. Obviously, the same considerations would be true employing, *mutando mutandis*, $B(\neg\varphi)$.

truth, it is subjectively impossible to distinguish between the two. This implies that mislead individuals might end up having troublesome higher-order beliefs about their cognitive state, i.e., they might believe that they know something even when they are actually ignorant. Therefore, whenever a mislead attitude is recognized, particular attention must be paid in the treatment of the agent's ignorance.

Example 4 (Formal model example). Take the following model $\mathfrak{M} = (W, \pi, R_B, \mathcal{E})$ where $W = \{w_1, w_2, w_3\}$, $\pi(p) = \{w_2, w_3\}$, $R_B = \{(w_1, w_2), (w_1, w_3), (w_2, w_3), (w_3, w_2)\}$, and $\mathcal{E}(w_1) = \{\{w_2, w_3\}, \{w_1, w_2, w_3\}\}$. It is easy to check that:

- $(\mathfrak{M}, w_1) \models \neg p$
- $(\mathfrak{M}, w_1) \models B(p)$
- $(\mathfrak{M}, w_1) \models E_c(p)$

From the above satisfiability relations, it follows that in the pointed model $(\mathfrak{M}, w_1)$, the formula $B(p) \wedge \neg p \wedge E_c(p)$ holds, showing that a *mislead attitude* is present.

Theorem 4 (From Mislead to Ignorance). *A mislead attitude implies basic ignorance. Formally:*

$$(B(\varphi) \wedge \neg\varphi \wedge E_c(\varphi)) \to I(\varphi) \tag{4}$$

Proof. Take an arbitrary pointed model $(\mathfrak{M}, w)$. Assume that $(\mathfrak{M}, w) \models B(\varphi) \wedge \neg\varphi \wedge E_c(\varphi)$. Show that $(\mathfrak{M}, w) \models I(\varphi)$. Apply procedure α. Apply procedure β. The second element of the disjunction obtained through procedure β follows directly from the initial assumption, i.e., $(\mathfrak{M}, w) \models \neg\varphi$. Apply procedure γ. I will prove $(\mathfrak{M}, w) \models \neg B(\neg\varphi)$ of the disjunction obtained through the application of procedure γ. By Definition 4, this means that $(\mathfrak{M}, w) \not\models B(\neg\varphi)$. Again, by definition 4, this means that $\exists v, w R_B v$ s.t., $(\mathfrak{M}, v) \models \varphi$. By seriality (definition 2), it is guaranteed that at least one $v, w R_B v$ exists. It must now be shown that for such v, $(\mathfrak{M}, v) \models \varphi$. Using the initial assumption of the proof, it is known that $(\mathfrak{M}, w) \models B(\varphi)$, which means, by definition 4, that $\forall s, w R_B s, (\mathfrak{M}, s) \models \varphi)$. Since, by construction, $w R_B v$, such property must hold also for v, which means that $(\mathfrak{M}, v) \models \varphi$. This proves $(\mathfrak{M}, w) \models \neg B(\neg\varphi)$. Given the fact that the pointed model chosen was arbitrary, the result holds for all pointed models and the theorem follows. □

Negative Belief Perseverance. *Negative belief perseverance* is the attitude that describes an agent whose false belief holds even in the light of evidence contradicting their beliefs. This attitude is in place when there are phenomena such as the backfire effect [17], where agents persevere on their beliefs (or even strengthen them) even after being exposed to evidence that point to their beliefs being false.

Example 5 (Formal model example). Take the following model $\mathfrak{M} = (W, \pi, R_B, \mathcal{E})$ where $W = \{w_1, w_2, w_3\}$, $\pi(p) = \{w_2, w_3\}$, $R_B = \{(w_1, w_2), (w_1, w_3), (w_2, w_3), (w_3, w_2)\}$, and $\mathcal{E}(w_1) = \{\{w_1\}, \{w_1, w_2, w_3\}\}$. It is easy to check that:

- $(\mathfrak{M}, w_1) \models \neg p$
- $(\mathfrak{M}, w_1) \models B(p)$
- $(\mathfrak{M}, w_1) \models E_c(\neg p)$

From the above satisfiability relations, it follows that in the pointed model $(\mathfrak{M}, w_1)$, the formula $B(p) \wedge \neg p \wedge E_c(\neg p)$ holds, showing that a *negative belief perseverance attitude* is present.

Theorem 5 (From negative belief perseverance to Ignorance). *A negative perseverance attitude implies basic ignorance. Formally:*

$$(B(\varphi) \wedge \neg \varphi \wedge E_c(\neg \varphi)) \to I(\varphi) \tag{5}$$

Proof. The proof of Theorem 5 is similar to that of Theorem 4.   □

Credulity. *Credulity* is the attitude that describes an agent who holds a belief even though s/he only has limited evidence for the fact that s/he believes and this belief is indeed false. This happens in situations in which an agent forms beliefs even on grounds of limited evidence pieces. Note that this might be warranted in some situations, especially those where gaining conclusive evidence is hard and only the limited version of evidence is available.

Example 6 (Formal model example). Take the following model $\mathfrak{M} = (W, \pi, R_B, \mathcal{E})$ where $W = \{w_1, w_2, w_3\}$, $\pi(p) = \{w_2, w_3\}$, $R_B = \{(w_1, w_2), (w_1, w_3), (w_2, w_3), (w_3, w_2)\}$, and $\mathcal{E}(w_1) = \{\{w_1\}, \{w_2, w_3\}, \{w_1, w_2, w_3\}\}$. It is easy to check that:

- $(\mathfrak{M}, w_1) \models \neg p$
- $(\mathfrak{M}, w_1) \models B(p)$
- $(\mathfrak{M}, w_1) \models \neg E_c(p)$
- $(\mathfrak{M}, w_1) \models E_l(p)$
- $(\mathfrak{M}, w_1) \models E_l(\neg p)$

From the above satisfiability relations, it follows that in the pointed model $(\mathfrak{M}, w_1)$, the formula $B(p) \wedge \neg p \wedge E_l(p) \wedge \neg E_c(p)$ holds, showing that a *credulity attitude* is present.

Theorem 6 (From Credulity to Ignorance). *A credulity attitude implies basic ignorance. Formally:*

$$(B(\varphi) \wedge \neg \varphi \wedge E_l(\varphi) \wedge \neg E_c(\varphi)) \to I(\varphi) \tag{6}$$

Proof. The proof of Theorem 6 is similar to that of Theorem 4.   □

Misbelief. *Misbelief* is the attitude that is closest to the misbelieving effect given in [1]. Someone is in a misbelieving attitude if s/he holds a false beliefs which is based on no evidence whatsoever. This is typical of situations in which agents believe unjustified myths, either in the form of prejudices or simply due to irrational thinking. In those situations, agents often hold false beliefs based on various forms of biases. This is also common in situations in which unconscious beliefs are held unknowingly from the agents.

Example 7 (Formal model example). Take the following model $\mathfrak{M} = (W, \pi, R_B, \mathcal{E})$ where $W = \{w_1, w_2, w_3, w_4\}$, $\pi(p) = \{w_2, w_3\}$, $R_B = \{(w_1, w_2), (w_1, w_3), (w_2, w_3), (w_3, w_4), (w_4, w_2)\}$, and $\mathcal{E}(w_1) = \{\{w_1, w_2\}, \{w_3, w_4\}, \{w_1, w_2, w_3, w_4\}\}$. It is easy to check that:

- $(\mathfrak{M}, w_1) \models \neg p$
- $(\mathfrak{M}, w_1) \models B(p)$
- $(\mathfrak{M}, w_1) \models \neg E_l(p)$

From the above satisfiability relations, it follows that in the pointed model $(\mathfrak{M}, w_1)$, the formula $B(p) \wedge \neg p \wedge \neg E_l(p)$ holds, showing that a *misbelief attitude* is present.

Theorem 7 (From Misbelief to Ignorance). *A misbelief attitude implies basic ignorance. Formally:*

$$(B(\varphi) \wedge \neg \varphi \wedge \neg E_l(\varphi)) \to I(\varphi) \tag{7}$$

Proof. The proof of Theorem 7 is similar to that of Theorem 4. □

Note that the proofs of Theorems 4, 5, 6 and 7 are almost equivalent. This is because it is the fact that something false is believed that implies ignorance. Therefore, this class of attitudes represent a failure of the conjunction of the first two components of the tripartite definition of knowledge. As with the previous class, also in this case the evidence component is useful only as far as it explains the cognitive attitude of the agent who is subject to the false belief and could therefore provide insights into how to treat his/her ignorance properly.

The last class of attitudes that will follow is what constitutes the major advancement from the work in [1]. In this work, the doubting effect what formalized as having a true belief of a fact that was not known. With the addition of evidence in the language, this lack of knowledge can be explained rather than being assumed. I would like to stress again that all the attitudes that will follow might apply, *mutando mutandis*, to the same scenarios that were just introduced. Again, the difference in those scenarios is just the truth of the fact examined, which is often not a directly accessible feature in the real world. However, the examples proposed will show exemplary cases in which it is likely that those attitudes are present instead of the ones just introduced. True, in practical terms it would be difficult to prove that one attitude is present instead of the other, but it is hoped that, in the future, further studies on how evidence is gathered could help in discerning the attitudes.

Positive Belief Perseverance. *Positive belief perseverance* is the attitude that obtains when someone holds on to his/her beliefs even when presented with false conclusive evidence. While this attitude is desirable when observed from the outside, i.e., the agent is able to resist the false conclusive evidence and is indeed correct in doing so (because what s/he believes is indeed true), from a subjective perspective, it is as troublesome as the negative belief perseverance attitude. For instance, if a scientist has a firm belief in his theory (which turns out to be true), s/he might reject the conclusive evidence s/he is presented against it, even though good scientific practices would require him/her to at least consider it while forming his/her beliefs. Now, even though in the future it might turn out that s/he was correct in resisting such conclusive evidence (because it was false), this would still not justify his/her behaviour when the evidence was received.

Example 8 (Formal model example). Take the following model $\mathfrak{M} = (W, \pi, R_B, \mathcal{E})$ where $W = \{w_1, w_2, w_3\}$, $\pi(p) = \{w_1, w_2\}$, $R_B = \{(w_1, w_1), (w_1, w_2), (w_2, w_3), (w_3, w_2)\}$, and $\mathcal{E}(w_1) = \{\{w_3\}, \{w_1, w_2, w_3\}\}$. It is easy to check that:

- $(\mathfrak{M}, w_1) \models p$
- $(\mathfrak{M}, w_1) \models B(p)$
- $(\mathfrak{M}, w_1) \models E_c(\neg p)$

From the above satisfiability relations, it follows that in the pointed model $(\mathfrak{M}, w_1)$, the formula $B(p) \wedge p \wedge E_c(\neg p)$ holds, showing that a *positive belief perseverance attitude* is present.

Theorem 8 (From positive belief perseverance to Ignorance). *A positive belief perseverance attitude implies basic ignorance. Formally:*

$$(B(\varphi) \wedge \varphi \wedge E_c(\neg\varphi)) \rightarrow I(\varphi) \tag{8}$$

Proof. Take an arbitrary pointed model $(\mathfrak{M}, w)$ and the corresponding evidence set $\mathcal{E}(w)$. Assume that $(\mathfrak{M}, w) \models B(\varphi) \wedge \varphi \wedge E_c(\neg\varphi)$. Show that $(\mathfrak{M}, w) \models I(\varphi)$. Apply procedure α. Apply procedure β. I will prove $(\mathfrak{M}, w) \models \neg E_c(\varphi)$ of the disjunction obtained through the application of procedure β. By Definition 4, this holds whenever $(\mathfrak{M}, w) \not\models E_c(\varphi)$, which, in turn, means that $\exists \mathcal{X}_i \subseteq \mathcal{E}(w)$, s.t., $\mathcal{X}_i$ is a maximal consistent evidence sets, and $\forall v \in \bigcap_{X \in \mathcal{X}_i} X, (\mathfrak{M}, v) \models \neg\varphi$. By the initial assumption $(\mathfrak{M}, w) \models E_c(\neg\varphi)$, it follows that $\forall \mathcal{X}_i \subseteq \mathcal{E}(w)$, s.t., $\mathcal{X}_i$ are maximal consistent evidence sets, it follows that $\forall v \in \bigcap_{X \in \mathcal{X}_i} X, (\mathfrak{M}, v) \models \varphi$. Moreover, by the assumption made in definition 2 that $\mathcal{E}(w)$ contains the universal set, we have the guarantee that at least one maximal consistent set exists in $\mathcal{E}(w)$. Whatever the set is, it implies that $\exists \mathcal{X}_i \subseteq \mathcal{E}(w)$, s.t., $\mathcal{X}_i$ is a maximal consistent evidence sets, and $\forall v \in \bigcap_{X \in \mathcal{X}_i} X, (\mathfrak{M}, v) \models \neg\varphi$, which provides the required proof. Apply procedure γ. The second disjunct obtained through procedure γ follows directly from the initial assumption. Given the fact that the pointed model chosen was arbitrary, the result holds for all pointed models and the theorem follows. $\square$

Doubt. *Doubt* is possibly the attitude that is closest to the doubting effect presented in [1]. A doubt attitude is present when an agent believes something which is true but only on the ground of limited evidence. Obviously, this limited evidence is not sufficient for knowledge to be present, but could constitute a good starting point for the agent to indeed form this knowledge. This is common of many scientific practices where conclusive evidence is sought, but it is still lacking. In fact, it could be claimed that science in itself is the practice of looking for conclusive evidence for hypothesis that are currently based only on limited forms of evidence. Thus, it could be fairly safe to assume that a doubting attitude is present in each scientist that is performing his/her work properly.

Example 9 (Formal model example). Take the following model $\mathfrak{M} = (W, \pi, R_B, \mathcal{E})$ where $W = \{w_1, w_2, w_3\}$, $\pi(p) = \{w_1, w_2\}$, $R_B = \{(w_1, w_1), (w_1, w_2), (w_2, w_3), (w_3, w_2)\}$, and $\mathcal{E}(w_1) = \{\{w_1, w_2\}, \{w_3\}, \{w_1, w_2, w_3\}\}$. It is easy to check that:

- $(\mathfrak{M}, w_1) \models p$
- $(\mathfrak{M}, w_1) \models B(p)$
- $(\mathfrak{M}, w_1) \models E_l(p)$
- $(\mathfrak{M}, w_1) \models \neg E_c(p)$

From the above satisfiability relations, it follows that in the pointed model $(\mathfrak{M}, w_1)$, the formula $B(p) \wedge p \wedge E_l(p) \wedge \neg E_c(p)$ holds, showing that a *doubt attitude* is present.

Theorem 9 (From Doubt to Ignorance). *A doubt attitude implies basic ignorance. Formally:*

$$(B(\varphi) \wedge \varphi \wedge E_l(\varphi) \wedge \neg E_c(\varphi)) \rightarrow I(\varphi) \tag{9}$$

Proof. Take an arbitrary pointed model $(\mathfrak{M}, w)$. Assume that $(\mathfrak{M}, w) \models B(\varphi) \wedge \varphi \wedge E_l(\varphi) \wedge \neg E_c(\varphi)$. Show that $(\mathfrak{M}, w) \models I(\varphi)$. Apply procedure α. Apply procedure β. The last element of the disjunction obtained through procedure β follows directly from the initial assumption. Apply procedure γ. The second disjunct obtained through procedure γ follows directly from the initial assumption. Given the fact that the pointed model chosen was arbitrary, the result holds for all pointed models and the theorem follows. □

Intuition. *Intuition* is a attitude that is present whenever an agent holds a belief that is true without any form of evidence whatsoever. This kind of attitude is typical of early stages of research in which a scientist might form a belief in the truth of a fact (which is indeed true) based on intuition alone and then proceeds to seek evidence to corroborate or falsify this belief.

Example 10 (Formal model example). Take the following model $\mathfrak{M} = (W, \pi, R_B, \mathcal{E})$ where $W = \{w_1, w_2, w_3, w_4\}$, $\pi(p) = \{w_1, w_2\}$, $R_B = \{(w_1, w_1), (w_1, w_2), (w_2, w_3), (w_3, w_4), (w_4, w_2)\}$, and $\mathcal{E}(w_1) = \{\{w_1, w_3\}, \{w_2, w_4\}, \{w_1, w_2, w_3, w_4\}\}$. It is easy to check that:

- $(\mathfrak{M}, w_1) \models p$
- $(\mathfrak{M}, w_1) \models B(p)$
- $(\mathfrak{M}, w_1) \models \neg E_l(p)$

From the above satisfiability relations, it follows that in the pointed model $(\mathfrak{M}, w_1)$, the formula $B(p) \wedge p \wedge \neg E_l(p)$ holds, showing that an *intuition attitude* is present.

Theorem 10 (From Intuition to Ignorance). *An intuition attitude implies basic ignorance. Formally:*

$$(B(\varphi) \wedge \varphi \wedge \neg E_l(\varphi)) \rightarrow I(\varphi) \tag{10}$$

Proof. Take an arbitrary pointed model $(\mathfrak{M}, w)$ and the corresponding evidence set $\mathcal{E}(w)$. Assume that $(\mathfrak{M}, w) \models B(\varphi) \wedge \varphi \wedge \neg E_l(\varphi)$. Show that $(\mathfrak{M}, w) \models I(\varphi)$. Apply procedure α. Apply procedure β. I will prove $(\mathfrak{M}, w) \models \neg E_c(\varphi)$. To show this, it must be shown that $\exists \mathcal{X}_i \subseteq \mathcal{E}(w)$, s.t., $\mathcal{X}_i$ is a maximal consistent evidence set and $\exists v \in \bigcap_{X \in \mathcal{X}_i} X, (\mathfrak{M}, v) \models \neg \varphi$. Now note that the initial assumption $(\mathfrak{M}, w) \models \neg E_l(\varphi)$, implies that $\forall \mathcal{X}_i \subseteq \mathcal{E}(w)$, s.t., $\mathcal{X}_i$ are maximal consistent evidence sets, $\exists v \in \bigcap_{X \in \mathcal{X}_i} X, (\mathfrak{M}, v) \models \neg \varphi$. Moreover, by the assumption made in definition 2 that $\mathcal{E}(w)$ contains the universal set, we have the guarantee that at least one maximal consistent set exists. Those two fact, taken together, imply that $\exists \mathcal{X}_i \subseteq \mathcal{E}(w)$, s.t., $\mathcal{X}_i$ is a maximal consistent evidence set and $\exists v \in \bigcap_{X \in \mathcal{X}_i} X, (\mathfrak{M}, v) \models \neg \varphi$. Apply procedure γ. The second disjunction obtained through the application of procedure γ. Given the fact that the pointed model chosen was arbitrary, the result holds for all pointed models and the theorem follows directly from the initial assumption. □

4   Conclusion and Future Works

In this paper, a new interpretation of an existing language for evidence-based beliefs [4,5] has been presented. This new interpretation has then been employed to define knowledge as justified true belief. This formal language has then been employed to describe various cognitive attitudes that lead to ignorance. Those attitudes are believed to improve the understanding already given in [1] about the relationship between doxastic cognitive attitudes and ignorance. Each attitude has been described and examples have been given from potential scenarios in the real world where the attitude might be present. Then, it has been shown how each of the attitudes imply ignorance. In the future, two main venues of research might be pursued: i) the language of *JTB* could be used to explore cognitive attitudes that inhibit or produce higher-order levels of ignorance (e.g., ignoring to ignore); moreover, ii) the language could be augmented with dynamic operators (in the spirit of [5]) to analyse the effects of different actions on the ignorance of the agents described by the language. Finally, it would be interesting to provide an axiomatic system for the language, exploring potential properties relating evidence and beliefs.

References

1. Aldini, A., Graziani, P., Tagliaferri, M.: Reasoning about ignorance and beliefs. In: Cleophas, L., Massink, M. (eds.) SEFM 2020. LNCS, vol. 12524, pp. 214–230. Springer, Cham (2021). https://doi.org/10.1007/978-3-030-67220-1_17
2. Artemov, S., Fitting, M.: "Justification Logic", The Stanford Encyclopedia of Philosophy, Edward N. Zalta (ed.) (Spring 2021 Edition). https://plato.stanford.edu/archives/spr2021/entries/logic-justification/
3. Artemov, S., Fitting, M.: Justification Logic: Reasoning with Reason. Cambridge University Press, Cambridge (2019)
4. Van Benthem, J., Duque, D.F., Pacuit, E.: Evidence logic: a new look at neighborhood structures. In: Kracht, M., de Rijke, M., Wansing, H., Zakharyaschev, M. (eds.) Advances in Modal Logic, pp. 97–118 (2012)
5. van Benthem, J., Pacuit, E.: Dynamic logics of evidence-based beliefs. Stud. Logica. **99**, 61–92 (2011)
6. Bonzio, S., Fano, V., Graziani, P.: Logical modeling of severe ignorance. J. Philos. Logic (2022). to appear
7. Fan, J.: A logic for disjunctive ignorance. J. Philos. Log. **50**(6), 1293–1312 (2021). https://doi.org/10.1007/s10992-021-09599-4
8. Fano, V., Graziani, P.: A working hypothesis for the logic of radical ignorance. Synthese **199**, 601–616 (2020)
9. Fine, K.: Ignorance of ignorance. Synthese **195**(9), 4031–4045 (2018)
10. Goranko, V.: On relative ignorance. Filosofiska Notiser **8**(1), 119–140 (2021)
11. Halpern, J.Y.: Reasoning About Uncertainty. The MIT Press, Cambridge (2005)
12. Hintikka, J.: Knowledge and Beliefs: An Introduction to the Logic of the Two Notions. Cornell University Press, Ithaca (1962)
13. Oxford Languages Online Dictionary. https://languages.oup.com/google-dictionary-en/
14. Kubyshkina, E., Petrolo, M.: A logic for factive ignorance. Synthese **198**, 5917–5928 (2021)
15. Plato, Theaetetus, L. Campbell (transl.), Clarendon Press (1883)
16. Rasmus, R., Symons, J.: Epistemic Logic, The Stanford Encyclopedia of Philosophy, Edward, N., Zalta (ed.). (Summer 2021 Edition). https://plato.stanford.edu/archives/sum2021/entries/logic-epistemic
17. Swire-Thompson, B., DeGutis, J., Lazer, D.: Searching for the backfire effect: measurement and design considerations. J. Appl. Res. Mem. Cogn. **9**(3), 286–299 (2020)

Author Index

P. Masci et al. (Eds.): SEFM 2022 Collocated Workshops, LNCS 13765, pp. 419–420, 2023.
https://doi.org/10.1007/978-3-031-26236-4

Printed in the United States
by Baker & Taylor Publisher Services

Printed in the United States
by Baker & Taylor Publisher Services